AN INTRODUCTION TO THE AMERICAN LEGAL SYSTEM

The West Legal Studies Series

Your options keep growing with West Legal Studies
Each year our list continues to offer you more options for every area of the law to meet your course or on-the-job reference requirements. We now have over 140 titles from which to choose in the following areas:

Administrative Law	Family Law
Alternative Dispute Resolution	Federal Taxation
Bankruptcy	Intellectual Property
Business Organizations/Corporations	Introduction to Law
Civil Litigation and Procedure	Introduction to Paralegalism
CLA Exam Preparation	Law Office Management
Client Accounting	Law Office Procedures
Computer in the Law Office	Legal Research, Writing, and Analysis
Constitutional Law	Legal Terminology
Contract Law	Paralegal Employment
Criminal Law and Procedure	Real Estate Law
Document Preparation	Reference Materials
Environmental Law	Torts and Personal Injury Law
Ethics	Will, Trusts, and Estate Administration

You will find unparalleled, practical support
Each book is augmented by instructor and student supplements to ensure the best learning experience possible. We also offer custom publishing and other benefits such as West's Student Achievement Award. In addition, our sales representatives are ready to provide you with dependable service.

We want to hear from you
Our best contributions for improving the quality of our books and instructional materials is feedback from the people who use them. If you have a question, concern, or observation about any of our materials, or you have a product proposal or manuscript, we want to hear from you. Please contact your local representative or write us at the following address:

West Legal Studies, 3 Columbia Circle, P.O. Box 15015, Albany, NY 12212-5015

For additional information point your browser at
www.westlegalstudies.com

WEST
™
THOMSON LEARNING

An Introduction to the American Legal System

John M. Scheb

Judge, Florida Court of Appeal, Second District (Ret.) Distinguished Professorial Lecturer, Stetson University, College of Law

John M. Scheb II

Professor of Political Science, University of Tennessee

WEST

THOMSON LEARNING

Australia Canada Mexico Singapore Spain United Kingdom United States

WEST
★
THOMSON LEARNING

WEST LEGAL STUDIES

An Introduction to the American Legal System
John M. Scheb and John M. Scheb, II

Business Unit Director:
Susan L. Simpfenderfer

Executive Editor:
Marlene McHugh Pratt

Senior Acquisitions Editor:
Joan M. Gill

Developmental Editor:
Rhonda Dearborn

Editorial Assistant:
Lisa Flatley

Executive Production Manager:
Wendy A. Troeger

Production Manager:
Carolyn Miller

Production Editor:
Betty L. Dickson

Technology Project Manager:
James Considine

Executive Marketing Manager:
Donna J. Lewis

Channel Manager:
Nigar Hale

Cover Designer:
Dutton and Sherman

For permission to use material from this text or product, contact us
by   Tel (800) 730-2214
            Fax (800) 730-2215
            www.thomsonrights.com

Library of Congress Cataloging-in-Publication Data
Scheb, John M. (John Malcolm), 1926–
    An introduction to the American legal system / John M. Scheb,
    John M. Scheb II.
        p. cm.
    "West Legal Studies Series."
    Includes index.
    ISBN 0-7668-2759-3
        1. Law-United States. I. Scheb, John M., 1955– II. Title

KF385 S34 2001
349.73--dc21   2001026179

NOTICE TO THE READER

This book is dedicated, with love, to
Ryan Patrick Scheb
and John M. Scheb III

BRIEF CONTENTS

CONTENTS

PART IV   LEGISLATIVE AND ADMINISTRATIVE DEVELOPMENTS IN THE LAW   355

PREFACE

This book is designed as an introductory text on American law and the legal system; its undergraduate students in political science, sociology, criminal justice, and legal studies, as well as students in paralegal programs. Our goal is to introduce students to basic legal concepts principles, and procedures. Of necessity, we have painted with a broad brush, as American law and legal procedures are extremely complex, highly dynamic, and vary considerably across jurisdiction.

ORGANIZATION

The book is organized in four parts. Part I sets forth the fundamental concepts and concerns of the law, while examining the historical development of the American legal system from its English common-law roots, and surveys the structures of the American legal system as well as the legal profession. Part II provides an overview of the substantive law, including constitutional law, criminal law, torts, property, contracts, and business law and family law. Part III surveys the procedural law, covering civil and criminal procedure, the rules of evidence, and the appellate process. Finally, Part IV looks at two very important areas of modern law: legislation and administrative law and procedure. Because this book will be many students' first encounter with legal studies, we have included an extensive glossary of legal terms (Appendix B).

SPECIAL FEATURES

To the beginning student, an introduction to the law can be somewhat overwhelming. To make the book more accessible and useful to the student, every chapter contains a list of learning objectives, a chapter outline, a chapter summary, and a set of boldfaced key terms, all of which are defined in the glossary. To make the book more provocative, each chapter also contains a set of questions for thought and discussion. For the student who wishes to learn more about the topics addressed in the book, each chapter also contains a list of additional reference materials.

Because judicial decisions are central to the development of the law, we have incorporated two features into the text designed to alert students to especially important cases. One of these features, entitled "Case in Point," is a short summary of a significant court decision. There are multiple Case in Point features in each chapter. A related feature, "Opinion of the Court," appears in each chapter and provides substantial excerpts from landmark opinions of the U.S. Supreme Court. These opinions range from classic, such as *Marbury v. Madison* (1803), which is excerpted in Chapter 1, to the very recent, such as *United States v. Morrison* (2000), an excerpt reprinted in Chapter 11.

Another special feature, entitled "The Law in Action," focuses on practical applications of the law and real-world controversies involving legal issues. Topics addressed in this feature range from "Civil Disobedience and the Struggle for Civil Rights" (Chapter 1) to "Buying a House (Chapter 6) to "The Case against Microsoft" (Chapter 11). Students will also find a set of "Sidebar" features throughout the book. These features provide miscellaneous information relevant to chapter topics. For example, see the Sidebar in Chapter 5, "The Infamous McDonald's Coffee Case," which is of interest to every student of tort law. Other Sidebar features focus on such topics as canons of judicial conduct (Chapter 2), warranty deeds (Chapter 6), and the law regarding employment discrimination (Chapter 11). We hope that all these features will make the text more informative and more interesting.

ABOUT THE AUTHORS

John M. Scheb

was born in Orlando, Florida, in 1926. He practiced law in Sarasota, Florida, from 1950 until 1974, serving as associate municipal judge from 1957 to 1959 and as city attorney from 1959 to 1970. In 1975, he was appointed to the Second District Court of Appeal where he served until 1992. Judge Scheb also served in the United States Air Force Reserve, retiring in 1980 with the rank of colonel in the Judge Advocate General's Department. Judge Scheb is a member of the American Bar Association, American Judicature Society, the Florida Bar, and the Sarasota County Bar Association. He holds a B.A. from Florida Southern College, a J.D. from the University of Florida, and a LL.M. from the University of Virginia. Judge Scheb is currently a distinguished professorial lecturer at Stetson University College of Law. He has published articles in *Judicature, Stetson Law Review,* and *Tennessee Law Review.* He is coauthor of the *Criminal Law & Procedure* (3d ed., West/Wadsworth 1999).

John M. Scheb II

was born in Sarasota, Florida, in 1955. He attended the University of Florida from 1974 to 1982, receiving a B.A., M.A., and Ph.D. in political science. He is now professor of political science at the University of Tennessee, Knoxville, where he specializes in public law and the judicial process. Professor Scheb has authored numerous articles in professional journals, including *Social Science Quarterly, Political Behavior, American Politics Quarterly, Judicature, Journal of Politics, Law and Policy,* and *Tennessee Law Review.* He is the coauthor of several other textbooks, including *American Constitutional Law* (2d ed., West/Wadsworth 1999); *Criminal Law & Procedure* (3d ed., West/Wadsworth 1999); and *American Government: Politics and Political Culture* (West 1995).

ACKNOWLEDGMENTS

In preparing this book, we have relied on the excellent assistance of a number of able persons, whose efforts we gratefully acknowledge:

- Peter F. Lake, a professor at Stetson University College of Law in St. Petersburg, Florida, and member of the New York Bar.
- Richard R. Garland, Esq., an attorney in Sarasota, Florida, who is certified in appellate practice.
- Donna-Lee M. Roden, Esq., an attorney in Venice, Florida, who is certified in wills, trusts, and estates.
- Marjorie Anne Schmoyer, an attorney in Sarasota, Florida, who is certified in marital and family law.
- Sarah E. Warren, Esq., a practicing attorney and former assistant county attorney in Sarasota, Florida.
- John Barbrey, Keith Clement, and Daniel Hull, graduate students in political science at the University of Tennessee.

We extend our thanks to the reviews of this text:

Kenneth Agram, University of California, Irvine
Bernadette Agresti, Gannon University, PA
Holly Enterline, State Technical Institute of Memphis, TN
Michael Haridopolis, Brevard Community College, FL
Janet Holt, Georgetown University, Washington D.C.
Ted Maloney, Skagit Valley College, WA
Tim Ostroot, Minnesota School of Business, MN
Charles Perkins, Fisher College, MA
Barbara Ricker, Andover College, ME

We also wish to thank Hon. Nancy Donnellan, a circuit court judge in Sarasota, Florida, for allowing us to stage and photograph a scene in her courtroom (see Chapter 8).

Finally, we extend our appreciation to the West Legal Studies staff, Joan Gill, Senior Acquisitions Editor, Rhonda Dearborn, Developmental Editor, and Betty Dickson, Production Editor, for their help and encouragement throughout this project.

Of course, we assume full responsibility for any errors of commission or omission contained in these pages.

John M. Scheb
John M. Scheb II
February 7, 2001

TEACHING AIDS AND SUPPLEMENTS

- **Instructor's Manual with Testbank** Written by the authors of the text, the *Instructor's Manual* consists of sample test questions (including true–false, multiple choice, completion, and essay questions) as well as teaching tips and classroom exercises geared to each chapter.
- **Transparency Masters** are available online at www.westlegalstudies.com.
- **Web page** Come visit our website at *www.westlegalstudies.com,* where you will find valuable information specific to this book such as hot links and sample materials to download, as well as other West Legal Studies products.

- **Computerized Test Bank** The Test Bank found in the *Instructor's Manual* is also available in a computerized format on CD-ROM. The platforms supported include Windows™ 3.1 and 95, Windows™ NT, and Macintosh. Features include:
  - Multiple methods of question selection
  - Multiple outputs, that is, print, ASCII, and RTF
  - Graphic support (black and white)
  - Random questioning output
  - Special character support
- **WESTLAW®** West's online computerized legal research system offers students hands-on experience with a system commonly used in law offices. Qualified adopters can receive 10 free hours of WESTLAW®. WESTLAW® can be accessed with Macintosh and IBM PC and compatibles. A modem is required.
- **Court TV Videos** West Legal Studies is pleased to offer the following videos from Court TV available for a minimal fee:
  - *Fentress v. Eli Lilly & Co., et al.*—Prozac on Trial
    ISBN 0-7668-1095-X
  - *Flynn v. Goldman Sachs*—Fired on Wall Street: A Case of Sex Discrimination?
    ISBN 0-7668-1096-8
  - *Dodd v. Dodd*—Religion and Child Custody in Conflict
    ISBN 0-7668-1094-1
  - *In Re Custody of Baby Girl Clausen*—Child of Mine: The Fight for Baby Jessica
    ISBN 0-7668-1097-6
  - *New York v. Ferguson*—Murder on the 5:33: The Trial of Colin Ferguson
    ISBN 0-7668-1098-4
  - *Ohio v. Alfieri*—Road Rage
    ISBN 0-7668-1099-2
- **West's Paralegal Video Library** includes:
  - The Making of a Case Video
    ISBN 0-314-07300-0
  - Mock Trial Video—Anatomy of a Trial: A Contracts Case–Business Litigation
    ISBN 0-314-07343-4
  - Mock Trial Video—Trial Techniques: A Products Liability Case
    ISBN 0-314-07342-6
  - Arguments to the United States Supreme Court Video
    ISBN 0-314-07070-2

These videos are available at no charge to qualified adopters.

Please note the Internet resources are of a time-sensitive nature and URL addresses may often change or be deleted.

Contact us at westlegalstudies@delmar.com

PART I

FOUNDATIONS OF THE LEGAL SYSTEM

CHAPTER 1
FOUNDATIONS OF AMERICAN LAW

CHAPTER 2
STRUCTURES OF AMERICAN LAW

1

FOUNDATIONS OF AMERICAN LAW

Courtesy of West Group.

LEARNING OBJECTIVES

This chapter should enable the student to understand:

- the functions of law in society
- the forms and sources of law
- how the English common law influenced the development of the American legal system
- the ideas and experiences that led to formation of the U.S. Constitution
- the supremacy of the U.S. Constitution and the Bill of Rights
- the role of statutory law and judicial decision making
- why courts, legislatures, and administrative agencies are important

CHAPTER OUTLINE

Introduction

The Functions of Law in Society

The Development of Law

The Common Law Tradition

The American Constitution

Modern Statutes and Codification

Administrative Regulation

The Decisional Law

Conclusion

Summary of Key Concepts

Questions for Thought and Discussion

Key Terms

For Further Reading

INTRODUCTION

American society is very much preoccupied with law. We have an elaborate system to make and enforce the law. A large professional class is engaged in the practice of law. Numerous academic institutions are devoted to teaching the law. There are thousands of publications dedicated to legal education, research, and advocacy. Our mass media and popular culture reflect the social preoccupation with law, in that we are exposed to a steady barrage of books, films, newspaper articles, television shows, and even radio programs dealing with the law.

Despite this cultural preoccupation with the law, an essential question remains: What precisely is *law*? Numerous definitions have been proposed, reflecting the variety of philosophical and theoretical orientations to the concept. Bearing in mind that any definition is imperfect, we begin with the following simple formulation: *Law is a set of rules promulgated and enforced by government.*[1] This formulation is often referred to as **positive law,** which the nineteenth-century English legal theorist John Austin defined simply as "the command of the sovereign." Positive law is indeed the command of the sovereign, in that it is enunciated by government and backed by the coercive power of the state. But there is more to law than this. To be law, the command of the sovereign must take the form of a rule, a principle, or a directive that applies with equal force to everyone.[2] Moreover, to be accepted as legitimate, the law must be perceived as rational, fair, and just. Some would argue that for positive law to be legitimate, it must conform to a higher law.

Higher Law

Natural law is law that is presumed to flow from man's *natural* condition, that is, the social condition existing prior to the emergence of government. Natural law is sometimes used to refer to universal principles of morality and justice; however, precisely what those principles are is subject to conflicting interpretations. In *De Republica,* the ancient Roman orator Cicero (106–43 B.C.) defined natural law as "right reason in agreement with nature." In *Summa Theologica,* the medieval philosopher Thomas Aquinas (1224–1274) viewed natural law as the "participation in the Eternal Law by rational creatures." In a less theological approach, the seventeenth-century Dutch jurist Hugo Grotius defined natural law as rules of human conduct that can be discovered solely by the use of reason. In his influential *Commentaries on the Laws of England* (1769), William Blackstone asserted the primacy of natural law. Blackstone's *Commentaries* would become something of a legal bible in America, which helped to perpetuate natural law theory in this country.

Even today, legal theorists, lawyers, lawmakers, and judges sometimes invoke natural law, but in itself, it is not an enforceable body of rules. It is more of a philosophical concept—the idea that there is a set of principles of morality and justice that transcends the positive law.

Divine law is the law of God, the best example of which is the Ten Commandments that Exodus tells us were given to Moses on Mount Sinai. Regardless of one's religious beliefs, no one can dismiss the historical importance of divine law in shaping the moral foundations of our legal system. Our Declaration of Independence asserts that "all men are created equal, that they are endowed by their Creator with certain unalienable rights, that among these are Life, Liberty, and the pursuit of Happiness." Those who created the basic framework of our legal system and system of government believed that rights ultimately are not of secular origin. Rather, they flow from divine ordinance.

Natural law and divine law continue to be important because they provide a basis upon which to judge the positive law. Quite often, opponents of the death penalty will cite the biblical injunction, "Thou shalt not kill." Similar arguments are often made regarding abortion and euthanasia. Obviously, people can and will disagree on the requirements of natural law, Scripture, and divine ordinance. Because we have a secular government committed to the ideas of separation of church and state and religious toleration, divine law as such is not enforceable through our legal institutions. But the concept of divine law, like that of natural law, remains an important historical and philosophical underpinning of our legal system. Moreover, it provides citizens with a philosophical anchor, a sense that there is a higher law by which positive law can be judged.[3]

The Problem of Civil Disobedience

If we assume that there is no higher law than the law promulgated by the state, how do we ever justify disobedience to the positive law? By the same token, how do we punish those who have perpetrated wrongs but have done so within the confines of the law? This problem confronted the prosecutors at the Nuremberg war crimes trials after World War II. What the Nazis did was atrocious, yet much of it was authorized by German law at the time. Those in the civil rights movement faced a somewhat similar problem in the United States during the 1950s and 1960s. Much of the segregation and discrimination suffered by African-Americans at that time was authorized by law. What gave them the right to break these laws, to engage in **civil disobedience?** Some would argue that without belief in some form of higher law, there is no way to justify a breach of the positive law. Belief in a higher law or some higher standard of justice permits us to evaluate the operations and policies of our legal system, to object when a particular legal rule is established or a particular legal decision is rendered, and to argue for the need for legal change. In extreme circumstances, belief in a higher law may provide a justification for violating the positive law, as long as the violator is willing to accept the consequences of disobedience.

The nineteenth-century American writer Henry David Thoreau is best known for his advocacy of civil disobedience when the demands of conscience conflict with the dictates of law. Thoreau argued that the conscience of the individual is superior to the law of the state and that individuals have the right, indeed the duty, to violate the law when the law contravenes conscience.

Like all philosophical positions, Thoreau's views on civil disobedience are not universally accepted. There are two principal criticisms. One is that citizens have an obligation to obey laws that are adopted by legitimate democratic procedures. Another objection is that individual conscience is an insufficient basis for disobedience—that an individual cannot be permitted to become a law unto oneself. Despite these objections, Thoreau's view of civil disobedience has been extremely influential in the United States and throughout the world.

THE LAW IN ACTION

CIVIL DISOBEDIENCE AND THE STRUGGLE FOR CIVIL RIGHTS

In 1963, Dr. Martin Luther King Jr. was arrested in Birmingham, Alabama, after leading a civil rights demonstration in the city. The specific charge against him was "parading without a permit." Dr. King had led the demonstration to protest segregation and had applied for a permit, but had been denied. In his famous "Letter from the Birmingham Jail," King defended his disobedience of an "unjust" law. Echoing St. Thomas Aquinas, Dr. King wrote, "An unjust law is a human law that is not rooted in eternal and natural law." In a more modern vein, he also argued that an unjust law is one "that a majority inflicts on a minority that is not binding on itself." King was referring to the entire regime of laws that maintained racial segregation. King argued that "an individual who breaks a law that conscience tells him is unjust, and willingly accepts the penalty . . . is in reality expressing the very highest respect for the law." Not everyone at the time agreed with Dr. King's goals or tactics. But today, he is widely hailed as an American hero.

Legitimacy of Law in a Democratic Society

The legitimacy of law does not depend solely on its content or its perceived relationship to some higher authority. In a democratic society, the legitimacy of law depends greatly on how the law is made. In a representative democracy, law is made by elected representatives serving in a **legislature.** All members of the legislature have the right to introduce legislation; a majority is required to enact a law. In a democracy, legislators are elected through free and fair elections in which all adult citizens have the right to participate.

The United States relies on representative democracy, but our system of government is much more complex than that. We are not a simple representative democracy, but a constitutional republic in which majority rule is tempered by minority rights protected by law. Moreover, lawmaking power is not only vested in legislators but also in executive officials, regulatory agencies, and courts of law. However, the way in which these bodies make law remains vital, and is key to whether their legal pronouncements are regarded as legitimate. Thus, in thinking about the legitimacy of law, we need to think both about **substantive legitimacy** and **procedural legitimacy.** Substantive legitimacy refers to the content of law; procedural legitimacy refers to how the law is enacted and applied.[4] The law is substantively legitimate if people believe that it is based on fair, just, and reasonable principles. It is procedurally legitimate if it is enacted, applied, and enforced according to procedures that people regard as fair, just, and reasonable.

Forms and Sources of Positive Law

As we have suggested, law emanates from several sources. It also takes on different forms. In the American legal system, the major forms of law are as follows:

- **constitution** A fundamental law that sets forth the structure and powers of government as well as the rights of citizens vis-à-vis that government.
- **statute** Enacted by a legislature, a law that is generally applicable within the jurisdiction of that legislature.

- **ordinance** A law enacted by a local governing body such as a city council or a county commission. Ordinances deal with minor matters of local concern.
- **executive order** An order issued by a president, governor, county executive, or mayor relating to matters over which the executive official has authority.
- **treaty** A legally binding agreement between countries.
- **regulation** A rule promulgated by a regulatory agency.
- **judicial decision** A decision by a court of law enunciating a principle of law.

When we speak of the "law," we are really talking about the sum total of all these elements as they coexist at any point in time. As such, the law is extremely complex, somewhat uncertain, always dynamic, and sometimes self-contradictory.

THE FUNCTIONS OF LAW IN SOCIETY

Law performs many different functions in society. Law promotes social order and stability, but it can also be a force for change.[5] Law seeks to establish justice, but law is no guarantee thereof. Law determines to a great extent how government operates, although law cannot ensure good government.

Fundamentally, law protects people and their property. To the social contract thinkers of the seventeenth and eighteenth centuries, protection was the primary purpose of law. Without law backed by the coercive power of the state, people must protect themselves, their families, their land, and their possessions by force. Law, at least ideally, protects the rights of both the weak and the strong.

Law, Liberty, and Morality

Classical liberals like Thomas Jefferson viewed law not only as a means of protecting life and property, but of liberty as well. To the classical liberals, freedom of speech and freedom of religion were as important as the right to own property and engage in private enterprise. In the classical liberal view, the purpose of law was to safeguard these basic human rights. In the nineteenth century, the English philosopher and economist John Stuart Mill argued that the law should be limited to protecting the security of the individual and should not enforce traditional notions of morality. Today, this **libertarian view of law** commands considerable support in the United States and other advanced democratic countries.

Conservatives, on the other hand, see law and morality as inextricably intertwined. They believe that the maintenance of societal morality is an essential function of law. One of the best statements of this perspective can be found in Lord Devlin's *The Enforcement of Morals*, published in 1959.[6] Devlin argued that law must preserve traditional morality to prevent disintegration of the society. In a response to Devlin, H.L.A. Hart suggested that a society willing to sacrifice freedom by imposing morality through law may not be a society worthy of maintaining.[7] Although the "debate" between Devlin and Hart took place in Great Britain in the late 1950s and early 1960s, the debate over law and morality continues today. It is a debate that must take place in any legal system that values individual freedom and social cohesion.

Law and Economic Life

A society's economic system affects its law, and vice versa. As the great social theorist Max Weber recognized, a capitalist economy requires a highly developed legal system.[8] The legal system must be capable of enforcing contracts and property claims and must generally provide a predictable climate in which business can take place. Uncertainty in the law regarding property, contracts, and commercial transactions impedes voluntary economic activity. Therefore, it is not surprising that one tends to find the most highly developed legal systems in the most advanced capitalist countries of Europe and North America. It should be pointed out, however, that while law facilitates economic development by regulating transactions and rationalizing risk, it can also serve as an impediment to economic innovation. When too many conflicting demands are placed on the law, it becomes excessively complex, bureaucratic, redundant, and inscrutable, which frustrates economic activity. Some commentators believe that we have such a situation in the contemporary United States!

Of course, not everyone takes a benign view of the relationship between law and capitalism. Marxists, anarchists, and radicals of various persuasions generally see law, at least in capitalist society, as a tool of oppression and a protector of inequality. In the Marxist view, law in capitalist society is little more than a cloak for the power of the ruling class. Today, the **critical legal studies** movement carries on this radical tradition in legal thought.

The Marxist view of law is based on the assumption that all conflict derives from material inequality. In contrast, most social theorists today regard economic inequality as only one of many sources of human conflict. And most regard law as an essential element of modern society—an expression of societal consensus as well as a means of conflict resolution.

Social Control

Law is a means of social control, but it is certainly not the only means. Informal, unwritten rules are transmitted and enforced by social groups, including families, peers, and colleagues. Moral principles are developed and enforced by the individual conscience. Religious precepts are developed, transmitted, and reinforced by religious institutions. Social norms, moral principles, and religious precepts constrain the behavior of most people, at least most of the time, yet they are inadequate. Social norms can be vague or weak, religious precepts vary somewhat across faiths and denominations, and moral principles can be totally lacking in some individuals. Law is necessary to pick up where informal means of social control leave off.

Resolution of Conflict

Law is a means of conflict resolution, but, again, there are numerous methods of conflict resolution at work every day. Individuals, groups, families, corporations, and governments usually can work out their differences informally through discussion, negotiation, and compromise. The law serves as a framework for such interactions. When informal means of conflict resolution are not fruitful, parties often seek recourse through formal legal means. Law provides a mechanism for the peaceful resolution of conflict, but it is by no means always successful at preventing violence.

Most theorists believe that modern society, which is increasingly conflictual, requires a formal system of law. As society becomes more diverse, impersonal, complex, and specialized, this requirement grows ever stronger. At the same time, however, the strains on the legal system become increasingly powerful. Law is the command of the sovereign, and therefore reflects the existing structure of power in society. But in a democratic society such as ours, law also depends on a reasonable degree of social consensus. With increasing social, economic, and political diversity, such a consensus is difficult to maintain.

Law and Societal Values

Law is an expression of a society's values. In our complex and diverse society, the law expresses many competing values, which often come into conflict. A few prominent examples of such conflict are:

- Private enterprise versus the public good
- Freedom versus equality
- Privacy versus crime control
- Private property versus environmental protection
- National security versus freedom of the press
- Public order versus the right of public assembly
- Freedom of expression versus decency and civility
- Majority rule versus minority rights

Although law expresses many competing values, it also provides mechanisms to resolve conflicts between competing values.

THE DEVELOPMENT OF LAW

Primitive, tribal societies had no formal systems of law. These societies were governed by rulers who relied on sheer power and charisma buttressed by claims of supernatural authority. Individual behavior and social and economic relationships were governed by custom, and often reinforced by religion, magic, and superstition. Offenses against the tribe, such as sacrilege or consorting with an enemy, were dealt with by sanctions such as shunning, banishment, or even death. Wrongs against individuals, such as murder, rape, and theft, were avenged by the victim's family, often in actions against the family of the wrongdoer that were grossly disproportionate to the offense that gave rise to the vengeance.

With the emergence of agriculture, isolated tribal societies evolved into territorial confederations. Systems of government emerged, and with them came the beginnings of law, as leaders (usually monarchs) began formalizing and enforcing customs that had evolved among their peoples. Eventually, informal norms and customs came to be formalized as written codes of law.

Ancient Legal Codes

The oldest known, written legal code is the Code of Hammurabi, which was produced in Babylonia some 2,000 years before Christ. Although the Emperor Hammurabi promulgated the code that bears his name, popular acceptance of the idea that law was of divine origin helped buttress its legitimacy. The Code of Hammurabi dealt with property rights, family relationships, personal injuries, and debt collection. It also covered legal procedure and imposed penalties for unjust accusations and false testimony. In terms of crimes and punishments, the code adopted the *lex talionis,* or law of retaliation, similar to the Hebrew law calling for "an eye for an eye." Perhaps the most striking feature of the Code of Hammurabi, however, is that it purported to protect people of both genders and all social classes, including slaves. Thus, in this most ancient legal code, we find the germ of the idea that is so fundamental to our law today—the ideal of equal protection of the law.

The ancient Greeks also contributed to the development of law. In the seventh century B.C., Draco, an Athenian legislator, developed a strict legal code for the Athenian city-state. Even today, one hears strict rules or penalties characterized as "draconian." A century later the Code of Draco would be replaced by the Code of Solon. Beyond its more liberal character, the distinctive feature of this code was that it permitted litigants to appeal the decisions of magistrates to public assemblies of Athenians, an innovation that foreshadowed the right of trial by a jury of one's peers.

Roman Law

By far the most significant of the ancient legal codes was the **Roman law,** which formally began with the introduction of the Twelve Tables in the mid-fifth century B.C. Prior to the Twelve Tables, disputes between Roman citizens were decided on the basis of unwritten customary rules. When these rules were in doubt, the College of Pontiffs, made up of patrician aristocrats, rendered authoritative interpretations. Plebeians (common citizens) often objected to the interpretations rendered by the College of Pontiffs, and eventually demanded that the Roman law be codified. The resulting Twelve Tables would serve as the basis of Roman law for 1,000 years. Over the centuries, however, Roman law was modified, expanded, and extended through a series of imperial edicts. In the early sixth century A.D., the Emperor Justinian commissioned the legal scholar Trebonian to produce a systematic codification of Roman law. The result was the *Corpus Juris Civilis,* or Body of Civil Law, also known as the **Code of Justinian.** When completed, it was supplemented by the *Novels* (new laws) placing in statutory form long-established Roman customs. After the decline of the Roman Empire, the feudal system relied largely on customs and later on royal decrees. A remnant of Roman law remained and during the twelfth century the study of Roman law was revived in Italy and later in France. Throughout the Middle Ages the **canon law** of the Roman Catholic Church exercised great control in personal relations such as marriage and inheritance. The Roman law eventually became the basis of law throughout the continent of Europe.

The Napoleonic Code

The **Napoleonic Code,** promulgated under Napoleon Bonaparte in 1804 as a codification of all the civil and criminal laws of France, was based in large part on the Code of Justinian. The Napoleonic Code became a model for a uniform system of law for the nations of Western Europe. This is why the legal systems of Western Europe are often said to be "Roman law" systems.[9] Roman law systems are based on the primacy of statutes enacted by the legislature. These statutes are integrated into a comprehensive code designed to be applied by the courts with a minimum of judicial interpretation.

THE COMMON LAW TRADITION

American law is derived largely from the **English common law,** which dates from the eleventh century. At the time of the Norman Conquest of 1066, English law was a patchwork of local laws and customs, often applied by feudal courts, and church law enforced by ecclesiastical courts. William the Conqueror, the first Norman king of England, strengthened the royal courts established by his Anglo-Saxon predecessors. His son, King Henry I, dispatched royal judges to preside in county courts. His successor, Henry II, greatly expanded the role of the royal judges by instructing them to travel throughout the kingdom, taking jurisdiction in cases formerly under the province of feudal and local courts.

The king's judges settled disputes based on the customs of the Anglo-Saxon people and the well-established principles of feudal society. These royal courts grew increasingly popular due to their reliance on trial by jury, which of course would become a bedrock principle of Anglo-American justice. Out of the decisions of these courts grew a law common to the entire kingdom, hence the term "common law."

Magna Carta

One of the greatest moments in the development of Anglo-American law occurred in 1215, when a reluctant King John placed his seal on the **Magna Carta.** Essentially, Magna Carta was a series of promises that the king would follow concerning the dictates of the law in dealing with his subjects and vassals. This document established the principle that government is subject to the rule of law, which is the essential idea upon which the U.S. Constitution is based. Magna Carta is also the source of another bedrock principle in our legal system today—the idea of **due process of law.** Magna Carta stipulated that, "No free man shall be taken or imprisoned or disseised or outlawed or exiled or in any way destroyed, nor will we go or send against him, except by the lawful judgment of his peers or by the law of the land." Later statutes and court decisions would use the term "due process of law" as synonymous with "the law of the land." The American Bill of Rights (1789) uses the term "due process of law" in protecting citizens' rights to life, liberty, and property. But the essential idea was expressed nearly 600 years earlier in the Magna Carta.

The Common-Law Courts

By the time Magna Carta was signed, there were three common-law courts: the King's Bench, the Court of Common Pleas, and the Court of Exchequer. The Court of King's Bench dealt primarily with "pleas of the Crown," which later came to be known as criminal cases. The Court of Common Pleas had jurisdiction over "common pleas," disputes between individuals that would later come to be termed "civil" cases. The Court of Exchequer originally dealt with matters involving the king's property and revenue. Later, through a procedural device called the writ of Quominus, the Court of Exchequer extended its jurisdiction to private controversies.[10]

The Doctrine of *Stare Decisis*

In 1292, court clerks began recording the rulings of the common-law courts and by the fourteenth century these decisions were serving as **precedents** to guide judges in similar cases. As the centuries passed, coherent principles of law emerged from the decisions of the judges. Thus, in contrast to Roman law systems, which are based on **legal codes**, the common law developed primarily through judicial decisions. The common-law doctrine of following precedent, known as *stare decisis,* really took hold with the development of the printing press in the fifteenth century. Today, it remains an important component of both the English and American legal systems. The doctrine holds that a court should follow the principle of law enunciated in previous decisions by the highest court within its jurisdiction, assuming that the principle is relevant to the current decision and makes sense in contemporary circumstances.

Civil and Criminal Law

As noted, early on the common law developed a distinction between **civil law** and **criminal law.** The criminal law sought to punish people for offenses against the Crown; the civil law provided remedies for essentially private wrongs. As defined by the common law, a **crime** was an intentional evil act that produced harm to the society. Thus, **criminal prosecutions** were brought by the Crown in cases styled, for example, *Rex v. Jones* or *Regina v. Smith* (in Latin, *Rex* means "king"; *Regina* means "queen"). In criminal cases the sovereign was always the **plaintiff,** that is, the party initiating the legal action. The accused offender was always the **defendant,** the party against whom legal action has been brought.

By 1600, the common law classified criminal offenses as **felonies,** which were punishable by death, or **misdemeanors,** which were punishable by less severe sanctions. Felonies included the crimes of murder, manslaughter, mayhem, robbery, burglary, arson, larceny, rape, suicide, and sodomy. Misdemeanors included various offenses against public order and the administration of justice.

Civil wrongs were not seen as offenses against the entire society, but only against private parties. In a **civil suit,** the plaintiff was the aggrieved party; the defendant was the party accused of the wrongful act. Much of the early common-law litigation involved disputes over land, giving rise to a complex body of property law. Other civil offenses came to be classified as breaches of contract or torts. A **breach of contract** occurred when a party to a contract violated the terms of the agreement. A **tort,** on the other hand, was a wrongful act that did not violate any enforceable agreement but nevertheless violated a legal right of the injured party.

The Writ System

The common law developed a complex series of writs. A **writ** is simply another term for a court order. To obtain justice at common law, a plaintiff had to petition a court for the appropriate writ. For example, a plaintiff who had been wrongfully dispossessed of personal property sought a writ of replevin. One seeking to collect money owed brought an action in debt. However, if the debt was based on a sealed contract, one brought an action of covenant. An action of trespass was filed to recover damages in cases of torts. Failure to seek the proper writ was fatal to a plaintiff's case. To the average plaintiff, the writ system was bewildering. This meant that plaintiffs had to rely on experts in litigation, which gave rise to the legal profession.

Without question, the most celebrated common law writ was **habeas corpus.** Literally meaning "you have the body," habeas corpus was a device by which a court of law would require a person to show just cause for holding another person in custody. The primary purpose of the writ was to protect people from unlawful confinement. The Framers of the U.S. Constitution believed the writ of habeas corpus to be so important that they provided that "the Privilege of the Writ of Habeas Corpus shall not be suspended unless when in Cases of Rebellion or Invasion the public Safety may require it."[11]

Juries

As noted, one key to the success of the common law was the emergence of the institution of the jury trial. Prior to the advent of the common law, trials took the form of combat, ordeal, or compurgation. In trial by combat, opposing parties would engage in combat or hire champions to do battle on their behalf. In the most ritualistic form of trial by combat, knights acting as champions would do battle by joust, charging one another on horseback and wielding lances. The assumption was that God would intervene on the side of justice and truth. Thus, the litigant whose champion prevailed in the joust prevailed in the legal dispute.

In a trial by ordeal, the defendant was tortured by fire or water. If a defendant survived the ordeal, God had intervened to prove the defendant's innocence before the law. In a trial by compurgation, a person accused of wrongdoing would recruit a body of men to attest to his honor. Custom required that the oath be repeated according to an exact form; any deviation undermined the value of the oath.

In the place of these irrational modes of trial, the common-law courts substituted a more rational process of fact-finding. Early on, common-law judges heard testimony from witnesses. Eventually, neighbors of the accused or of the litigants served as fact finders, basing their conclusions only on evidence introduced in court. By the fourteenth century, the jury system was well established. Indeed, by that time, the law recognized two types of juries: the grand jury, which would decide whether an individual should be indicted for a crime; and the petit jury, which would serve as fact finder in both civil and criminal cases.

The jury system developed at common law became an integral part of the American legal system. In most civil cases the defendant has the right to a jury trial. All individuals accused of serious crimes have a right to a trial by jury. Grand juries continue to be widely used to review criminal charges prior to trial.[12]

The Adversarial System

Early on, the English common law developed the concept of trial by jury as a means of resolving both civil and criminal cases. The jury would hear the evidence and decide the factual issues in the case; the judge would preside over the trial and decide questions of law.

Arguing the case would be *barristers,* lawyers permitted to cross the *bar* in the courtroom that separated the judge's bench from the spectators. Thus, in England, a barrister is a trial lawyer. The barristers received their training in the Inns of Court, institutions in London located close to Westminster Hall, where the higher courts sat. Experienced barristers, called benchers, gave lectures and presided over moot courts (practice courts). After several years of training, students became eligible to serve as barristers. Although we do not use the term *barrister* in the United States, we do refer to licensed attorneys as having been "admitted to the bar."

In contrast to the more inquisitorial style of trial developed under the Roman law tradition, the English common law developed an **adversarial system of justice.** This refers to a system of administering justice in which opposing parties contend with one another to achieve a favorable outcome. In this system, the role of the judge is one of neutral referee. In what is derisively called the "sporting theory of justice," barristers would do battle in the courtroom, much as knights on horseback charging one another with lances. Indeed, the adversarial legal system has its roots in the medieval joust. If the barristers can be seen as knights, their lances were their legal acumen and their rhetorical skills.

Today, we carry on the common-law adversarial tradition, although there is much in the everyday working of the law that is more cooperative than combative. When a legal "dream team" defending a celebrity accused of a crime does battle against the prosecution in a highly publicized trial, we see the adversarial system in its starkest form. Indeed, in such instances people often question whether the adversary system eclipses the search for truth. The assumption behind the medieval joust was that God was on the side of the victor. Similarly, the adversarial system of justice assumes that truth and justice are most likely to emerge from the clash of opposing factual and legal claims. In general this may be true, but there is no assurance that competition in the courtroom will always produce truth or justice.

Equity

In its formative period, the common law was characterized by considerable flexibility. By the fourteenth century, the common law had become highly technical and rigid. Moreover, litigation was expensive. Aggrieved parties who were unable to secure a remedy at common law would appeal to the king directly for justice. The king often delegated such matters to his chancellor, a cleric and a member of the king's court who was often referred to as the "keeper of the King's conscience." Eventually this practice of referring disputes to the chancellor evolved into a secular tribunal called the Court of Chancery, which developed its own jurisprudence called **equity**. The term *equity* comes from the Latin *aequitas*, which means "justice or equality." The idea of equity as a supplement to law can be traced to the Roman law and ultimately to Aristotle. The idea is that when existing legal rules and procedures are insufficient to remedy injustice, a court should rely on general principles of fairness in granting relief. The Court of Chancery did not follow the writ system nor did it utilize juries—chancellors made factual determinations in addition to fashioning equitable remedies. Although the Court of Chancery did not follow the common law or the doctrine of *stare decisis,* chancellors eventually came to rely on maxims derived from previous equitable decisions. Perhaps the chief distinction between the common law and equity was that common-law courts were limited to awarding damages to plaintiffs who prevailed in civil actions, whereas the Court of Chancery could issue an **injunction** to prevent or terminate injurious conduct and order **specific performance** in cases of breach of contract. Development of the law of trusts represented a principal achievement of the Chancery Courts. Eventually, common law and equity would be merged, both in England and the United States, at least in the sense that law and equity jurisdiction would be vested in the same courts.

The Emergence of Parliament

The English Parliament stems from a thirteenth-century dispute between King Henry III and the feudal lords. By the fourteenth century, Parliament heard petitions from aggrieved subjects and presided over abdications of kings.[13] Later in the century, Parliament was divided into two chambers: the House of Lords and the House of Commons. Parliament came to play a significant role in the formation of the law by adopting statutes that revised and supplemented the common law. For example, in 1540, Parliament enacted the Statute of Wills, which allowed people to will real estate to their heirs. Prior to that enactment, the common law recognized only the right to will personal property. Numerous other enactments followed, modifying, extending, or superceding the common law in many ways.

The most significant moment in the history of the English Parliament was the Glorious Revolution of 1688, which established the supremacy of Parliament over the Crown. With the popularization of democratic political ideas, the role of the English monarchy became increasingly a symbolic one. Today, executive power resides in the British prime minister and the cabinet ministers, all of whom are members of Parliament. Thus, **sovereignty** (the right to rule), which once resided solely in the Crown, is now vested in Parliament.

Reception of the Common Law in America

As England became a colonial power, the common-law tradition was exported throughout the empire. Thus the common law was extended not only throughout the United Kingdom, but to Australia, New Zealand, Canada (with the exception of Quebec), and to some extent India. The American colonies for the most part followed the common law, but there were significant variations. New York, Maryland, Virginia, Georgia, and the Carolinas followed the common law closely, but New Jersey and the New England colonies did not.

After independence was declared, some of the new American states adopted statutes or constitutional provisions that maintained the English common law to the extent that it did not conflict with the new state and federal constitutions.[14] Other states adopted the common law, in whole or in part, through judicial decision making. Of the 50 states in the Union, Louisiana is the only one whose legal system is not based essentially on the common law. Rather, it is based primarily on the Napoleonic Code.

In the decades prior to the American Revolution, American lawyers often traveled to London to receive formal legal education in the **Inns of Court.** After independence, the new American judges and lawyers were greatly aided by **Blackstone's** *Commentaries,* published in 1769, in which Sir William Blackstone, a professor at Oxford, codified the principles of the common law. Blackstone's seminal effort was a noble undertaking, but it had the effect of demystifying English law. Consequently, Blackstone's encyclopedic treatment of the law was less than popular among English barristers, who by this time had developed a close fraternity and took great pride in offering their services to "discover the law." In America, however, Blackstone's *Commentaries* became something of a legal bible.

THE AMERICAN CONSTITUTION

By the spring of 1776 it was apparent to most Americans that independence from England was both necessary and desirable. On July 4, the Continental Congress adopted the **Declaration of Independence.** Authored by Thomas Jefferson, the document outlined the colonies' grievances against the king and asserted the right of revolution. The ideas expressed in the writing were by no means original to Jefferson or to the American colonies. They were articulated a century earlier in John Locke's *Two Treatises of Government.* When the Declaration of Independence refers to "life, liberty and the pursuit of happiness" as being the "unalienable rights" of individuals, it echoes John Locke's formulation of the natural rights of "life, liberty and property." Although the document asserted American independence from the mother country, it did so by drawing on ideas that had already taken hold in England. Thus, in a sense, the Declaration of Independence was an affirmation of the linkage between English and American political cultures. Despite considerable cultural differences that led to the Revolution, the essential ideas of the Declaration of Independence came from England.

The Articles of Confederation

After the American Revolution, the United States was a confederation of sovereign states barely held together by an agreement called the **Articles of Confederation.** Congress had no power to tax and no power to regulate interstate commerce. There was no presidency to provide leadership and speak for the new nation with a unified voice. Nor was there a national court system to settle disputes between states or parties residing in different states. Finally, the Articles of Confederation could not be amended except by unanimous consent of the states. Any state could veto a proposed change in the agreement. This system was not working. In early 1787, Congress issued the call for a federal convention to meet in Philadelphia "for the sole and express purpose of revising the Articles of Confederation."

Adoption of the Constitution

The delegates to the Philadelphia Convention decided to scrap the Articles of Confederation and draft a new constitution. The Framers accepted the existence of the states as sovereign political entities. Indeed, they drew inspiration from the recent experience of the states in adopting their own constitutions after independence from England was declared in 1776. There was no question of doing away with the states and creating a unitary system of government. Yet most of the delegates knew that without a strong national government, economic growth and political stability would be seriously undermined by interstate rivalries. Thus, their central objective was to create a viable political system based on the principle of **federalism,** one in which sovereignty is exercised by the national government and the states, although it is vested ultimately in the people.

To create a viable federal system, the delegates had to confront a number of contentious issues. The two greatest sources of contention were (1) a disagreement between the small and large states over representation in Congress and (2) the conflict between northern and southern states over slavery. For a time it appeared that the Philadelphia Convention might fail altogether. Ultimately, through persuasion and compromise, members reached agreement. On September 17, 1787, 39 delegates representing 12 states placed their signatures on what would become the nation's new fundamental law. Although ratification of the Constitution was in some states a close question, by the end of 1790 all 13 of the original states had ratified the document.

The Constitution succeeded in correcting the major deficiencies of the Articles of Confederation. It strengthened the national government, gave Congress ample legislative powers, established an executive branch, and provided for a national court system. Above all, it provided a blueprint for a workable government, one that could adapt to dramatic social, economic, and technological change.

The Rule of Law and Constitutional Supremacy

The **United States Constitution** stands in sharp contrast to the English model. The English constitution is not a written document, but rather a collection of documents, statutes, judicial decisions, and customs dating back to Magna Carta. The English constitution can be altered at any time by an act of Parliament. The U.S. Constitution stands above ordinary legislation and is extremely difficult to amend, requiring a two-thirds vote of each house of Congress and ratification by at least three-fourths of the states.

The Constitution is the embodiment of the founders' belief in the **rule of law.** The idea is that government and society can be regulated by law, not subjected to the whims of powerful but potentially capricious rulers. The Constitution rests on the belief that no one in power should be above the law. Even the legislature, the people's elected representatives, should be bound to respect the principles and limitations contained in the "supreme law of the land." The subordination of government to law was seen by the Framers as a means of protecting individual rights to life, liberty, and property.

Separation of Powers

The Framers of the Constitution had no interest in creating a **parliamentary system,** because they believed that parliaments could be manipulated by monarchs or captured by impassioned but short-lived majorities. Accordingly, parliaments provided insufficient security for liberty and property. The delegates believed that only by allocating the three basic functions of government (legislative, executive, and judicial) into three separate, coordinate branches could power be appropriately dispersed. Thus the Constitution allocates the legislative, executive, and judicial powers of the national government across three separate, independent branches. The first three articles of the Constitution, known as the **distributive articles,** define the structure and powers of Congress (Article I), the executive (Article II), and the judiciary (Article III).

The Framers of the Constitution believed that a system of checks and balances would be necessary if separate, coordinate branches of government were to be maintained. Thus, the Constitution contains a number of what James Madison referred to as "auxiliary precautions." The president is authorized to veto bills passed by Congress, but Congress can override the president's veto by a two-thirds majority in both houses. The president is given the power to appoint judges, ambassadors, and other high government officials, but the Senate must consent to these appointments. The president is commander in chief, but Congress has the authority to declare war, raise and support an army and a navy, and make rules governing the armed forces. The president is empowered to call Congress into special session, but is duty-bound to appear "from time to time" to inform Congress as to the "state of the Union." These provisions were designed to create a perpetual competition between the Congress and the executive for control of the government, with the expectation that neither institution would permanently dominate the other. That is in fact how things have worked out.

The Framers said much less about the judiciary, which Alexander Hamilton described as the "least dangerous branch" of the new national government.[15] The president and the Senate are given the shared power to appoint federal judges, but these appointments are for life. Congress is authorized to establish lower federal courts and determine their jurisdiction; it may even regulate the appellate jurisdiction of the Supreme Court. But Congress is prohibited from reducing the salaries of sitting judges. The only means of removing members of the judiciary is through a cumbersome impeachment process, but this requires proof that the judge has committed "high crimes or misdemeanors." Clearly, the Framers wanted to create an independent federal judiciary that would be insulated from partisan political pressures.

Judicial Review

The text of the Constitution is silent on the means by which the judiciary can check and balance the other branches. In *Marbury v. Madison* (1803),[16] the single most important case

CASE IN POINT

ESTABLISHMENT OF THE POWER OF JUDICIAL REVIEW

Marbury v. Madison

United States Supreme Court
5 U.S. (1 Cranch) 137, 2 L.Ed. 60 (1803)

William Marbury's commission as justice of the peace for the District of Columbia had been signed by President John Adams following Senate confirmation on March 3, 1801, President Adam's last day in office. Everything was in order, but Marbury never received the commission. Thomas Jefferson was sworn in as the nation's third president on March 4, 1801. His secretary of state, James Madison, declined to deliver the commission to Marbury. Marbury filed suit in the Supreme Court, invoking the Court's original jurisdiction. Marbury asked the Court to issue a writ of mandamus, an order directing Madison to deliver the disputed judicial commission to him. The Supreme Court held that Marbury was entitled to the commission, but declined to issue the writ of mandamus. The Court held that the act of Congress giving the Supreme Court the power to issue the writ of mandamus in cases brought under its original jurisdiction was un-

constitutional. Although the Court denied to itself the power to issue writs of mandamus in cases of original jurisdiction, it claimed the much more important power to declare acts of Congress null and void. In support of this assumption of power, Chief Justice John Marshall reasoned that, since the Constitution is the "supreme law of the land," and it is the duty of the judiciary to interpret the law, judicial review is both necessary and inevitable. It was in this context that Marshall made his frequently quoted assertion that "[i]t is emphatically the province and duty of the judicial department, to say what the law is." In reaching this conclusion, Marshall stressed the fact that judges take an oath to support and defend the Constitution. Marshall ended his landmark opinion with the question: "Why does a judge swear to discharge the duties agreeable to the Constitution of the United States, if that constitution forms no rule for his government?"

in American constitutional history, the Supreme Court asserted the power to review acts of Congress and declare them null and void if they are found to be contrary to the Constitution. Later the Court extended this power to encompass the validity of state laws under the federal Constitution. Commonly referred to as **judicial review,** the power of the federal courts to rule on the constitutionality of legislation is nowhere explicitly provided for in the Constitution. However, many of the Framers of the Constitution supported the concept of judicial review, and most probably expected the courts to exercise this power. In any event, the power of judicial review is now well established. By assuming this power, the federal judiciary greatly enhanced its role in the system of checks and balances. Moreover, the courts took on primary responsibility for interpreting and enforcing the Constitution. Today, both state and federal courts exercise this authority.

Individual Rights under the Constitution

There is no question but that the protection of the liberty and property of the individual was one of the Framers' highest goals. Yet the original Constitution had little to say about individual rights, because the Framers assumed that the limited national government they were creating would not be a threat to individual liberty and property. Moreover, citizens were already protected against their respective state governments by provisions in their own state constitutions. Still, the Framers found it desirable to enumerate certain particular protections for individual liberty. As we have noted, Article I, Section 9 recognized the writ of habeas corpus; and Section 10 prohibited state legislatures from interfering with rights and obligations under contracts. Indeed, the desire to protect private contracts from governmental interference was one of the principal motivations of the delegates to the Constitutional Convention.

Circumscribing the Crime of Treason

At common law, the offense of high treason included plotting to kill or overthrow the king, making war against the king, or giving aid to the enemies of the Crown. In some instances, mere words were deemed sufficient wrongful acts to allow for conviction of high treason. Indeed, in one seventeenth-century case, a writer was convicted of treason for suggesting that the king should be accountable to his subjects. Prior to the American Revolution, the Crown accused some supporters of American independence of treason. The Framers of the Constitution believed that the crime of treason needed to be defined more narrowly. Thus they provided in Art. III, § 3 that:

> (1) Treason against the United States, shall consist only in levying War against them, or in adhering to their Enemies, giving them Aid and Comfort. No Person shall be convicted of Treason unless on the Testimony of two Witnesses to the same overt Act, or on Confession in open Court.
> (2) The Congress shall have Power to declare the Punishment of Treason, but no Attainder of Treason shall work Corruption of Blood, or Forfeiture except during the Life of the Person attainted.

Ex Post Facto Laws and Bills of Attainder

The Constitution also prohibited both Congress and the state legislatures from adopting **ex post facto laws** and **bills of attainder**.[17] Parliament had, often at the king's behest, passed ex post facto laws subjecting people to punishment for acts that were not illegal when performed. Parliament had also adopted bills of attainder imposing punishments on individuals without granting them the benefit of trial by jury. The common law did not prohibit ex post facto laws or bills of attainder, nor did the English Bill of Rights of 1689. The Framers of the American Constitution decided that Congress would not be permitted to foster such abuses.

Prohibition of Religious Tests

Article VI of the Constitution provides, among other things, that "no religious Test shall ever be required as a Qualification to any Office or Public Trust under the United States." This clause means, in effect, that personal views regarding religion may not officially qualify or disqualify one for public service. The prohibition against religious tests reflects the

Framers' commitment to the idea that government ought to be neutral with respect to matters of religion, a view that was strongly reinforced by adoption of the Establishment Clause of the First Amendment to the Constitution.

The Bill of Rights

Not everyone thought that the Constitution went far enough in protecting individual rights. Thomas Jefferson, who has been described as the "missing giant" of the Constitutional Convention, was disappointed that the Framers failed to include a more complete enumeration of rights in the document. Jefferson's concern was widely shared in his native state of Virginia, where ratification of the Constitution was a close question. Fortunately, a gentlemen's agreement was worked out whereby ratification was obtained in Virginia and other key states on the condition that Congress would immediately take up the matter of creating a bill of rights. The first 10 amendments to the Constitution, known collectively as the **Bill of Rights,** were adopted by the First Congress in 1789 and ratified by the requisite nine states in 1791. All provisions of the Bill of Rights were responses to abuses of official power and the perceived inadequacies of the common law in curtailing such abuses.

Freedom of Religion

The First Amendment prohibits Congress from making laws "respecting an establishment of religion or prohibiting the free exercise thereof." English history was to a great extent the history of religious warfare. Prior to the Protestant Reformation, the Roman Catholic Church was the established religious authority in England. After the Reformation, the Church of England assumed that role. Prior to the modern era, both the Catholic Church and the Church of England were intolerant of dissent and persecuted those who differed on matters of faith. The common law recognized the establishment of religion and offered no protection to dissenters. A principal motivation in the settlement of the American colonies had been the desire to escape religious persecution. The Framers of the Bill of Rights decided that there would be no official religion in the United States, at least none established by the national government. Moreover, the national government would not attempt to interfere with the practices of different religions. For further discussion of the religion clauses of the First Amendment, see Chapter 3.

The Freedoms of Speech, Press, Assembly, and Petition

The First Amendment also prohibited Congress from "abridging the freedom of speech, or of the press; or the right of the people peaceably to assemble, and to petition the Government for a redress of grievances." Although the common law recognized the right of the press to be free from "prior restraints," the common law did not go very far in protecting freedom of the press or freedom of speech. Indeed, the common-law offense of seditious libel permitted the

Crown to prosecute its critics, even if their statements were true. For example, in 1735 John Peter Zenger was tried for seditious libel by the colonial government of New York after Zenger published newspaper articles criticizing the governor. Although truth was not a defense to a charge of seditious libel under common law, the jury nevertheless acquitted Zenger. The celebrated case helped build support in the American colonies for freedom of the press, a value enshrined in the First Amendment to the Constitution. Historically, and especially in the modern era, the First Amendment protections of speech, press, assembly, and petition have been extremely important in facilitating free political activity and a "free marketplace of ideas" in the society. See Chapter 3 for more discussion of these First Amendment freedoms.

The Right to Keep and Bear Arms

The Framers of the Bill of Rights did not see the need for the United States to maintain a standing army. Rather, they believed that all adult male citizens should be prepared to serve in the militia when the need arose. Therefore, they provided in the Second Amendment that "A well-regulated Militia, being necessary to the security of a free state, the right of the people to keep and bear arms shall not be infringed." Today, with all of the concern about gun violence in our society, a lively debate is underway as to the meaning of the Second Amendment. For further discussion of this topic, see Chapter 3.

Subordination of the Military

The Third Amendment prohibits military authorities from quartering troops in citizens' homes without their consent. This was a matter of serious concern to the Framers, because English troops had been forcibly billeted in colonists' homes during the Revolutionary War. Today, the Third Amendment is little more than an historical curiosity, since it has not been the subject of any significant discussion. The Third Amendment, however, reflects an important principle of American government; that is, the military is subordinate to civilian authority.

Protection from Unreasonable Searches and Seizures

One of the colonists' principal grievances against the Crown was that the king's agents had unbridled powers of search and seizure. The Fourth Amendment addressed this concern by stating that: "The right of the people to be secure in their persons, houses, papers, and effects, against unreasonable searches and seizures, shall not be violated, and no Warrants shall issue, but upon probable cause, supported by Oath or affirmation, and particularly describing the place to be searched, and the persons or things to be seized." Today, the Fourth Amendment remains extremely important, as police officers rely heavily on search and seizure in their effort to ferret out crime. The courts must constantly interpret the Fourth Amendment in the context of criminal prosecutions when incriminating evidence has been obtained via search and seizure.

EARL WARREN—CHAMPION OF JUSTICE

SIDEBAR

Earl Warren, a former governor of California, was appointed chief justice of the United States Supreme Court by President Dwight Eisenhower in 1953. He served until his retirement in 1969. The Warren Court greatly expanded individual rights by reinterpreting provisions of the Bill of Rights and the Fourteenth Amendment. The Warren Court's most memorable achievement, however, was the 1954 decision in *Brown v. Board of Education,* which declared unconstitutional state laws requiring racially segregated public schools. Chief Justice Warren was known not for his technical command of the law, but for his abiding sense of fairness. His favorite question in reference to a law or ruling was "Is it fair?" Warren believed that a court decision or law should be "evaluated in terms of practical application. Everything we do must include the human equation, for what we do with our legal system will determine what American life will be. . . ."

Rights of Persons Accused of Crimes

The Framers of the Bill of Rights were acutely aware of the abuses of the criminal law that had characterized England and all of Europe for many centuries. They wanted to abolish barbaric methods of obtaining confessions and inflicting punishments. They also believed that the English common law provided inadequate protection of individual rights in this area. The authors of the Bill of Rights wanted to ensure that persons charged with crimes would be treated fairly—that they would have ample opportunity to defend themselves. Thus the Fifth, Sixth, and Eighth Amendments contain provisions protecting the right to a speedy and public trial by an impartial jury, the right to counsel, the right to confront prosecution witnesses, and the right to compel the testimony of witnesses for the defense. They also contain protections against compulsory self-incrimination, double jeopardy, excessive bail, excessive fines, and cruel and unusual punishments. All of these provisions remain extremely important in the day-to-day administration of justice in this country. In the 1960s, under the leadership of the U.S. Supreme Court, courts in this country greatly expanded the rights of the accused by reinterpreting many of the provisions of the Bill of Rights. Many commentators praised the courts for reforming criminal justice; others believed that the courts were coddling the criminals.

Protecting citizens against crime is a fundamental obligation of government. In the United States, however, government must perform this function while respecting the constitutional rights of individuals. Courts of law are constantly trying to balance the interest of society in crime control with the rights of individuals accused or convicted of crimes. Given the prevalent fear of crime in contemporary America, the balance can be difficult to maintain. For an extensive discussion of the rights of persons accused or convicted of crimes, see Chapter 10.

Protection against Eminent Domain

The power of government to take private property for public use is known as **eminent domain.** The Takings Clause of the Fifth Amendment specifically protects citizens against this power by requiring that property owners be justly compensated for such takings. Moreover, the Due Process Clause of the Fifth Amendment permits owners to challenge in court takings of their property. As noted, protection of private property was a major goal of the Framers of the Constitution. The Bill of Rights added additional protections in this area. Today, questions of governmental authority to take or even regulate private property continue to be important issues of law.

The Ninth Amendment

The Ninth Amendment states: "The enumeration in the Constitution, of certain rights, shall not be construed to deny or disparage others retained by the people." This language was included in the Bill of Rights as a solution to a problem raised by James Madison; namely, that the specification of particular liberties might suggest that individuals possessed only those specified. The Ninth Amendment makes it clear that individuals retain a reservoir of rights and liberties beyond those listed in the Constitution. This reflects the dominant thinking of late-eighteenth-century America: Individual rights precede and transcend the power of government; individuals possess all rights except those that have been surrendered to government for the protection of the public good. Although they have rarely relied solely on the Ninth Amendment, federal and state courts have over the years recognized a number of rights that Americans take for granted but which are not specifically enumerated in the Constitution. The right to marry, to determine how one's children are to be reared and educated, to choose one's occupation, to start a business, to travel freely across state lines, to sue in the courts, and to be presumed innocent of a crime until proven guilty are all examples of individual rights that have been recognized as constitutional, despite their absence from the text of the Constitution.

The Civil War Amendments

The Constitution has been amended 17 times since the ratification of the Bill of Rights. Undoubtedly the most important of these amendments are the Thirteenth, Fourteenth, and Fifteenth Amendments, ratified in 1865, 1868, and 1870, respectively. The Thirteenth Amendment abolished slavery, or "involuntary servitude." The Fourteenth Amendment was designed primarily to prohibit states from denying equal protection and due process of law to the newly freed former slaves. The Fifteenth Amendment forbade the denial of voting rights on the basis of race. These so-called Civil War Amendments attempted to eradicate the institution of slavery and the inferior legal status of black Americans. Although the abstract promises of the Civil War Amendments went unfulfilled for many years, they represented the beginning of a process of democratization that has fundamentally altered the character of the American political system. It is important to recognize that the Fourteenth Amendment in particular, with its broad requirements of equal protection and due process, has become a major source of legal protection for civil rights and liberties, extending far beyond issues of racial discrimination.

Beyond the Bill of Rights, the **Fourteenth Amendment** (1868) is the most important constitutional amendment in the field of civil rights and liberties. This amendment places broad restrictions on the power of states to infringe upon the rights and liberties of citizens.

The Equal Protection Clause of Section 1 of the Fourteenth Amendment serves as the primary basis for protecting the civil rights of minority groups against discriminatory state action. The Due Process Clause of Section 1 is the most far-reaching provision of the Fourteenth Amendment. This clause prohibits states from depriving persons of life, liberty, or property without due process of law.

Due Process of Law

In its most generic sense, due process refers to the exercise of governmental power under the rule of law with due regard for the rights and interests of individuals. Due process has both procedural and substantive aspects. The concept of **procedural due process** embraces government's obligation to provide **fair notice** and a **fair hearing** to individuals before depriving them of "life, liberty or property." Under **substantive due process,** government is barred from enforcing policies that are irrational, unfair, unreasonable, or unjust, even if such policies do not run counter to other specific constitutional prohibitions.

Incorporation of the Bill of Rights

The Bill of Rights was created as a set of limitations on the power of the national government.[18] Citizens of states had to look to the rights enshrined in their state constitutions for legal protection against the actions of their state or local governments. One of the most significant impacts of the Fourteenth Amendment has been to make the provisions of the Bill of Rights enforceable against the state and local governments as well as the national government. Under the **doctrine of incorporation,** the Supreme Court has held that most of the provisions of the Bill of Rights are embraced within the terms "liberty" or "due process" and are thus applicable to the states.[19] This is significant because it means that there are now national standards of liberty and due process by which governments at all levels must abide.

MODERN STATUTES AND CODIFICATION

Although the American legal system is based on English common law, Congress and the 50 state legislatures have become extremely active in adopting statutes to meet modern conditions. Once adopted, a statute supersedes the common law within that jurisdiction. Many modern statutes deal with subjects unknown to the common law, such as civil rights, public health, antitrust law, environmental protection, and social welfare (see Chapter 11). Although Congress was not vested with a general **police power** under the Constitution, it has relied upon its broad authority under the Commerce Clause (Art. I, § 8) to legislate in many areas that are only indirectly related to commerce.

Historically, many of the landmark statutes passed by Congress have resulted from great political struggles. For example, the Civil Rights Act of 1964 is one of the most significant pieces of federal legislation in the civil rights area. It was passed only after the civil rights movement of the late 1950s and early 1960s overcame staunch public resistance and after President Lyndon Johnson used all of his political skills to shepherd the legislation through Congress.

Statutory Construction

Although the adversarial system of justice and the basic common law concepts remain today defined essentially as they were by the common-law judges centuries ago, the law has now been codified by legislatures to a great extent. Thus, when attempting to answer questions of law, lawyers and judges now look first to the relevant statutes. Of course, statutory provisions do not always have plain or obvious meanings. One principal function of contemporary courts, therefore, is **statutory construction**, which is the task of assigning concrete meaning to statutory provisions that may allow for different interpretations. For example, the Civil Rights Act of 1964 contained provisions barring racial discrimination in employment. It remained for the courts to decide what constituted discrimination in particular instances and what policies could be utilized to combat discrimination in the workplace. In particular, courts have had to decide whether and under what circumstances employers could utilize affirmative action programs to remedy discrimination and promote diversity in the workplace.

Codification

One of the most important developments in the American legal system has been the **codification** of the common law. Through codification, a legislature transforms the common law in a given area into a clear, systematic code of laws. The first area of law in which this took place was civil procedure.

As noted previously, civil procedure under English common law was extremely complex, technical, and esoteric. In the mid-nineteenth century, a movement began to codify the rules of civil procedure. The leader of this movement was David Dudley Field, whose 1846 monograph, entitled *The Reorganization of the Judiciary,* was instrumental in persuading the state of New York to codify its laws. In 1848, the state legislature adopted a code of civil procedure drafted by Field. Subsequently, the code was adopted, at least in part, by more than half of the states. Even the British Parliament adopted the code in 1873. A code of criminal procedure drafted by Field also diffused widely among the states. In 1857, Field chaired a commission to codify the entire body of substantive law in New York. Other states followed suit, so that today every state has its laws codified. Thus, for example, one wishing to research a point of criminal law in Indiana would begin with the Title 35 of the Indiana Code, which is entitled "Criminal Law and Procedure." Similarly, the laws of the United States are codified in the United States Code. One interested in researching a question of federal criminal law would begin with Title 18, "Crimes and Criminal Procedure." Of course, statutory provisions often require interpretation, which is the function of the courts. Therefore, one must examine any court decisions interpreting the code provision in question.

The Diffusion of Uniform Codes

One way that the law has been standardized is through the diffusion of **uniform codes.**
Consider the case of commercial law, which covers sales, leases, negotiable instruments, insurance, brokerage, shipping, and other matters pertaining to business. The common law,
which had developed in a rural, agrarian, preindustrialized setting, was not very relevant to
modern commercial practices. States had enacted statutes in this area, but prior to the 1950s
there was little uniformity among states' commercial laws. In 1952, the Uniform
Commercial Code was developed by legal scholars and business practitioners. It spread
rapidly among the states, as state legislators saw the wisdom of adopting uniform business
laws. All 50 states have now adopted the code, in whole or in part, which has greatly facilitated interstate commerce.

Another area in which we have seen the influence of a uniform code is criminal law.
The American Law Institute, an organization of prominent lawyers, judges, and academics,
drafted the Model Penal Code (MPC) in 1962. Although the MPC is not itself law, many
of its provisions defining crimes have either been adopted by or led to reform of the criminal statutes in the majority of states.

ADMINISTRATIVE REGULATION

The role of government has changed dramatically in the two centuries since the American
nation was founded. In the early days of the republic, government essentially followed the
dictum, "that government is best which governs least." For the most part, the national government left such functions as social welfare and education to state and local governments
and concerned itself with the regulation of foreign trade, internal improvements such as
canals and post roads, and the protection of the national security. State and local governments, in turn, tended to leave matters of social welfare and education to neighborhoods,
churches, and families. Perhaps most fundamentally, individuals were regarded as responsible for their own problems as well as their own good fortune.

In the wake of post–Civil War industrialization and the emergence of an economy dominated by giant corporations, the limited role of government began to change. A new ethos
emerged, one in which government assumed primary responsibility for solving social problems. With the passage of the Interstate Commerce Act in 1887 and the concomitant establishment of the Interstate Commerce Commission, the relatively unobtrusive government
envisaged by the Founders began to evolve in the direction of ever more complex and intrusive regulation. The Progressive Era reform in the early twentieth century and the subsequent
New Deal fostered by President Franklin D. Roosevelt in the 1930s contributed mightily to
the growth of such regulation, as did the New Frontier and Great Society of the 1960s.

The expansive role now played by the national government renders the legislative task
of Congress considerably more difficult. Consequently, Congress has come to rely more and
more on so-called experts for the development as well as the implementation of regulations.
These experts are found in a host of government departments, commissions, agencies,
boards, and bureaus that comprise the modern administrative state. Through a series of broad

delegations of legislative power, Congress has transferred to the **federal bureaucracy** much of the responsibility for making and enforcing the rules and regulations deemed necessary for a technological society. The Food and Drug Administration (FDA), the Nuclear Regulatory Commission (NRC), the Federal Aviation Administration (FAA), the Occupational Safety and Health Administration (OSHA), the Environmental Protection Agency (EPA), and the Securities and Exchange Commission (SEC) are just a few of the myriad government agencies to which the Congress has delegated broad authority to make public policy.

Frequently, the enabling legislation creating these agencies provides little more than vague generalities to guide agency **rule making.** For example, in 1970, Congress gave OSHA the power to make rules that are "reasonably necessary or appropriate to provide safe and healthful employment and places of employment." The rules that OSHA promulgates as "necessary" or "appropriate" take on the force of law.

A good example of legislative delegation is seen in the Americans with Disabilities Act (ADA) of 1990. The ADA, which built upon the existing body of federal civil rights law, mandates the elimination of discrimination against individuals with disabilities. A number of federal agencies, including the Department of Justice, the Department of Transportation, the Equal Employment Opportunity Commission (EEOC), and the Federal Communications Commission (FCC), are given extensive regulatory and enforcement powers under the act.

Most observers agree that broad delegations of legislative power are necessary to enable agencies to develop the programs required to deal with targeted problems. These delegations of power may be to a great extent desirable or even inevitable, but they do raise serious questions about constitutional theory. As we shall see in Chapter 12, one of these questions stems from the fact that in many instances agencies exercise lawmaking, law enforcement, and quasi-judicial functions, which flies in the face of the constitutional principle of separation of powers.

THE DECISIONAL LAW

Although substantive and procedural law are often modified by the adoption of federal and state statutes, courts play an equally important role in the development of law. **Trial courts** exist primarily to make factual determinations, apply settled law to established facts, and impose sanctions. In reviewing the decisions of trial courts, **appellate courts** must interpret the federal and state constitutions and statutes. The federal and state constitutions are replete with majestic phrases such as "equal protection of the laws" and "privileges and immunities" which require interpretation. That is, courts must define exactly what these grand phrases mean within the context of particular legal disputes. Likewise, federal and state statutes often use vague language such as "affecting commerce" or "reasonable likelihood." Courts must assign meaning to these and a multitude of other terms. Although the majority of states have abolished all, or nearly all, common-law crimes, and replaced them with statutorily defined offenses, the common law remains a valuable source of statutory interpretation, because legislatures frequently use terms known to the common law without defining such terms. For example, in proscribing burglary, the legislature may use the term *curtilage* without defining it. In such an instance, a court would look to the common law, which defined the term to mean "an enclosed space surrounding a dwelling."

In rendering interpretations of the law, appellate courts generally follow precedent, in keeping with the common-law doctrine of *stare decisis.* However, in our rapidly changing society, courts often encounter situations to which precedent arguably does not or should not apply. In such situations courts will sometimes deviate from or even overturn precedent. Moreover, in certain situations there is no applicable precedent. When this occurs, the appellate courts will have the opportunity to make new law. Thus, appellate courts perform an important **lawmaking function** as well as an **error-correction function.** Today any serious student of law must follow developments in the **decisional law,** that is, law as developed by courts in deciding cases.

Constitutional Law

The U.S. Constitution and the constitutions of the 50 states are more than mere suggestions or exhortations. This is due primarily to the institution of judicial review, under which federal and state courts test government action and ordinary law against constitutional principles. Consequently, we have an elaborate body of constitutional law, which consists of the decisions of federal and state courts interpreting constitutional provisions (see Chapter 3).

Opinion of the Court . . .

MARBURY V. MADISON

1 Cranch (5 U.S.) 137; 2 L. Ed. 60 (1803)

Mr. Chief Justice Marshall delivered the opinion of the Court.

. . . The Constitution is either a superior paramount law, unchangeable by ordinary means, or it is on a level with ordinary legislative acts, and, like other acts, is alterable when the legislature shall please to alter it. If the former part of the alternative be true, then a legislative act, contrary to the Constitution, is not law; if the latter part be true, then written constitutions are absurd attempts, on the part of the people, to limit a power, in its own nature, illimitable.

Certainly, all those who have framed written constitutions contemplate them as forming the fundamental and paramount law of the nation, and consequently, the theory of every such government must be, that an act of the legislature, repugnant to the Constitution, is void. . . .

If an act of the legislature, repugnant to the Constitution, is void, does it notwithstanding its invalidity, bind the courts, and oblige them to give it effect? Or, in other words, though it be not law, does it constitute a rule as operative as if it was a law? This would be to overthrow, in fact, what was established in theory; and would seem, at first view, an absurdity too gross to be insisted on. . . .

So, if a law be in opposition to the Constitution; if both the law and the Constitution apply to a particular case, so that the court must either decide that case, conformable to the law, disregarding the Constitution; or conformable to the Constitution, disregarding the law; the court must determine which of these conflicting rules governs the case: this is of the very essence of judicial duty. . . .

CONCLUSION

As we have seen, the foundations of American law have a rich cultural and political history. The English common law, with its emphasis on precedent and requiring the sovereign to be subject to the law, and with its inflexibility eventually tempered by the concept of equity, became the basis for law and political institutions in America. The laws established by sovereign authority, referred to as the positive law, became the essence of American law—yet the natural law and its concept of right and wrong has tempered their application.

The law has many dimensions. Today American law is based on the supremacy of written federal and state constitutions and laws enacted pursuant to those constitutions by elected representatives. Yet in allocating power among the branches of the government the Framers of the U.S. Constitution and the Bill of Rights painted with a broad brush allowing an independent judiciary the prerogative of interpreting and applying the Constitution and laws enacted pursuant to it. Wisely, the states have followed the same pattern. Thus, in America, we have created a government ruled by the majority but protective of the rights of the minority.

The framework of our national and state constitutions is sufficiently flexible to allow implementation by laws and delegation to administrative agencies to enact regulations made necessary as the nation has advanced from an agrarian economy to an industrial and, more recently, to a technological society. But laws and regulations are words spread upon documents and, no matter how positive the law, it is the application of the law that affects society. Congress and the state legislatures have the primary role in enacting laws. No one, however, has succeeded in drafting a law that provides for every contingency. Consequently, it becomes the function of independent federal and state courts to interpret those laws with wisdom and often with compassion. There will always be *gaps* in the law and today every serious student of law and government must realize that the courts must at times *make law* to fill in those gaps.

In studying the remaining chapters it is important to recognize how the dynamic nature of our society is reflected in the laws that govern us. It is also essential to remember that the U.S. Constitution, as interpreted by the Supreme Court, is the law of the land. The Court has the power of judicial review of acts of Congress, administrative agencies, and the decisions of the highest tribunals of the states, which may contravene the Constitution. In succeeding chapters we will see how the Supreme Court's actions have effectively set national standards for administration of the criminal law, and to a lesser extent, has affected the ongoing development of the civil law.

SUMMARY OF KEY CONCEPTS

In describing the foundations of American law, we have identified the forms and sources of law and explained how law functions in the economic and social life of our nation and how it plays an increasingly significant role in conflict resolution and societal values in our public and private lives.

As we move through the remaining chapters it is important to realize how law developed and to grasp the concept of how the American legal system was influenced by earlier forms of law. The primary influence was the English common law and we will see frequent references to common-law principles in many of the remaining chapters.

To comprehend the American legal system one should be aware of the concepts and experience that led to its adoption. It is essential to understand the pivotal role of the U.S. Constitution and the Bill of Rights as well as succeeding constitutional amendments. The most significant of these later amendments has been the Fourteenth Amendment, which has become the bedrock of "due process of law" and "equal protection of the laws." Yet, the framework of our national and state constitutions is sufficiently flexible to allow Congress and state legislatures to enact statutory laws and to permit federal, state, and local executive agencies to promulgate administrative regulations. Finally, at this point the student should begin to understand how courts, legislatures, and administrative agencies function and the crucial role played by the judicial branch, particularly in judicial review.

QUESTIONS FOR THOUGHT AND DISCUSSION

1. What would society be like in the absence of positive law? Under what conditions could society function without law?
2. Under what conditions, if any, is civil disobedience justified?
3. Why has the English common law been important in the development of the American legal system?
4. What is the difference between the substantive and the procedural law?
5. Why did the Framers of the United States Constitution not include the Bill of Rights in the original document?
6. What is meant by the term "judicial review" from a constitutional perspective?

KEY TERMS

positive law

natural law

divine law

civil disobedience

legislature

substantive legitimacy

procedural legitimacy

constitution

statute

ordinance

executive order

treaty

regulation

judicial decision

libertarian view of law

critical legal studies

lex talionis

Roman law

Code of Justinian

canon law

Napoleonic Code

English common law

Magna Carta

due process of law

precedents

legal codes

stare decisis

civil law

criminal law

crime

criminal prosecutions

plaintiff

defendant

felonies

misdemeanors

civil suit

breach of contract

tort

writ

habeas corpus

adversarial system of justice

equity

injunction

specific performance

sovereignty

Inns of Court

Blackstone's *Commentaries*

Declaration of Independence

Articles of Confederation

federalism

United States Constitution

rule of law

parliamentary system

distributive articles

judicial review

ex post facto laws

bills of attainder

Bill of Rights

eminent domain

Fourteenth Amendment

procedural due process

fair notice

fair hearing

substantive due process

doctrine of incorporation

police power

statutory construction

codification

uniform codes

federal bureaucracy

rule making

trial courts

appellate courts

lawmaking function

error-correction function

decisional law

ENDNOTES

[1] By "rules," we mean authoritative directions as to what should be done or how it should be done. By "promulgated," we mean made known officially, publicly, and formally. By "enforced," we mean imposed by force or the threat of force. Finally, by "government," we mean the set of officials and institutions exercising a monopoly on the legitimate use of force in society.

[2] Of course, the law does not always achieve this rule-like quality, but most commentators believe that this remains an ideal to which the law must strive and by which it must be judged.

[3] Some would argue that utilitarianism, the doctrine that the goal of any policy should be to promote the greatest happiness of the greatest number of people, is an adequate basis upon which to evaluate law. Others would argue that utilitarianism fails to provide adequate protection for the rights of individuals and minority groups. If, in a hypothetical population of 100 people, 99 people are extremely happy that one troublesome individual has been put to death, is the sum total of their happiness enough to offset the *unhappiness* of the one who is killed? Of course, this assumes that one can quantify happiness in a way that would permit such a calculation. Assuming this could be done, can the morality of the execution be judged merely on the basis of comparative happiness?

[4] See Lon L. Fuller, *The Morality of Law* (Yale University Press 1964).

[5] See, for example, *Brown v. Board of Education,* 347 U.S. 483 (1954), in which the U.S. Supreme Court interpreted the Fourteenth Amendment to the U.S. Constitution to prohibit compulsory racial segregation in the public schools.

[6] See Lord Devlin, *The Enforcement of Morals* (Oxford University Press 1959).

[7] See H.L.A. Hart, *Law, Liberty and Morality* (Stanford University Press 1963).

[8] See Max Weber, *The Protestant Ethic and the Spirit of Capitalism* (Scribner's 1958).

[9] The term *civil law* is often used to denote the Roman law tradition. We prefer to use *civil law* in reference to the law-governing disputes between private parties, as distinguished from criminal matters.

[10] A private party wishing to collect an unpaid debt from another private party could claim that he was indebted to the king and was less able (quominus) to pay the King due to the unpaid debt. Even though the claim of indebtedness to the king was often fictitious, the Court of Exchequer would routinely issue the writ of Quominus to take jurisdiction of

the case. By this ingenious legal device, the Court was able to expand its jurisdiction to a category of private suits.

[11]U.S. Const. Art. I, § 9.

[12]In the United States, grand juries are used in criminal prosecutions in the federal courts and in many states. Great Britain abolished the institution of the grand jury in 1933. In Britain today, criminal indictments are prepared by clerks of the criminal courts.

[13]Parliament presided over the abdications of King Edward II in 1327 and King Richard II in 1399.

[14]For example, Article 25 of the Delaware Constitution of 1776 provided: "The common law of England, as well as so much of the statute law as has been heretofore adopted in practice in this state, shall remain in force unless they shall be altered by a future law of the Legislature, such parts only excepted as are repugnant to the rights and privileges contained in this Constitution and the declaration of rights, & agreed by this convention."

[15]Alexander Hamilton, *The Federalist,* No. 78.

[16]*Marbury v. Madison,* 5 U.S. 137, 2 L.Ed. 60 (1803).

[17]U.S. Const. Art. I, §§ 9–10.

[18]See *Barron v. Baltimore,* 32 U.S. 243, 8 L.Ed. 672 (1833).

[19]See, e.g., *Duncan v. Louisiana,* 391 U.S. 145, 88 S.Ct. 1444, 20 L.Ed.2d 491 (1968).

FOR FURTHER READING

Adams, David M., *Philosophical Problems in the Law* (2d ed., Wadsworth 1996).

Amar, Akhil Reed, *The Bill of Rights: Creation and Reconstruction* (Yale University Press 1998).

Bodenheimer, Edgar, John Bilyeu Oakley, and Jean C. Love, *An Introduction to the Anglo-American Legal System: Readings and Cases* (2d ed., West Publishing Co. 1988).

Devlin, Lord, *The Enforcement of Morals* (Oxford University Press 1959).

Friedman, Lawrence M., *A History of American Law* (2d ed., Simon and Schuster 1985).

Hall, Kermit L., *The Magic Mirror: Law in American History* (Oxford University Press 1989).

Hart, H. L. A., *Law, Liberty and Morality* (Stanford University Press 1963).

Horowitz, Morton, *The Transformation of American Law, 1780–1860* (Harvard University Press 1977).

Musson, Anthony, and W.M. Ormrod, *The Evolution of English Justice: Law, Politics and Society in the Fourteenth Century* (St. Martin's Press 1999).

Scheppele, Kim L., *Legal Secrets: Equality and Efficiency in the Common Law* (University of Chicago Press 1988).

2

STRUCTURES OF AMERICAN LAW

Courtesy of West Group.

LEARNING OBJECTIVES

This chapter should enable the student to understand:

- the role of the U.S. Congress and state legislatures and the processes they follow in exercise of their powers
- the organization, jurisdiction, and functions of federal and state trial and appellate courts
- the role of the federal and state executive officers and regulatory and administrative agencies
- how law enforcement and prosecutorial agencies operate
- the legal profession and the adversary and alternative dispute processes

CHAPTER OUTLINE

Introduction
Legislatures
Judicial Systems
The Role of the Chief Executive
Regulatory and Administrative Agencies
Law Enforcement Agencies
Prosecutorial Agencies
The Legal Profession
The Adversarial System of Justice
Alternative Dispute Resolution
Conclusion
Summary of Key Concepts
Questions for Thought and Discussion
Key Terms
For Further Reading

INTRODUCTION

Any explanation of the American legal system necessarily involves the principle of **federalism.** As noted in Chapter 1, federalism is one of the hallmarks of the American constitutional system: the fundamental division of authority between the national government in Washington, D.C., and the 50 state governments. Each of the states has its own machinery of government as well as its own constitution that empowers and limits that government. Of course, the provisions of the state constitutions, as well as the statutes adopted by the state legislatures, are subordinate to the provisions of the U.S. Constitution and the laws adopted by Congress.

There are significant legal differences between the national government and the states. Of course, the authority of the federal government extends throughout the United States and its territories, whereas state authority is confined within state borders. The national government has sole authority to make treaties with other nations, enact laws governing the high seas, coin money, regulate standards of weights and measures, regulate international trade, regulate immigration and naturalization, and provide for the national defense. The national government also has primary, although not exclusive, authority to regulate interstate commerce, which is a major source of federal legislative power.

The states, on the other hand, have exclusive authority over their own machinery of government. They have exclusive power to establish and control local governments (cities, counties, and townships). States have sole responsibility for conducting elections and apportioning electoral districts, although in exercising these functions they must comply with federal constitutional standards. States are the primary locus of the **police power**—the power to make laws in furtherance of the public health, safety, welfare, and morality. States also have primary (though no longer exclusive) authority over commerce within their borders.

The federal government and the states also possess a number of **concurrent powers,** that is, powers vested in both levels of government. These powers include the power to tax, to spend and borrow money, to enact legislation, to charter and regulate banks, to establish courts of law and administrative and regulatory agencies. The national government and the states also both possess the power of eminent domain, which is the power to take private property for public use, as long as property owners are compensated for the taking.

Fifty-One Legal Systems

Although this book is entitled *An Introduction to the American Legal System,* the national government and each of the states has its own legal system. Although there is significant variance among these systems, there are certain common features. Each system is based on a constitution, which represents the fundamental and supreme law within the system. Like the U.S. Constitution, each of the 50 state constitutions is based on the principle of separation of powers, which means that governmental power is distributed among coordinate legislative, executive, and judicial branches. Each system has a **legislature** empowered to enact statutes—laws that apply generally within the system. Each has a chief executive responsible for administering the government, and each has its own bureaucracy located within its executive branch. Each jurisdiction has its own set of **law enforcement agencies,** which are also located within the executive branch.

Each of the 51 legal systems in the United States has its own "governmental law office" in the form of a department of justice or attorney general's office. These government lawyers represent the interests of the people within their jurisdictions in both civil and criminal matters. Therefore, they prosecute crimes, defend against lawsuits, file suits on the public's behalf, and present legal arguments in court. Many state attorneys general also render opinions for public officials and agencies on questions of law.

Finally, each of the 51 legal systems has its own system of courts, the structures of which we will examine in some detail in the next chapter. Courts of law play the pivotal role in the legal system. They preside over the resolution of civil and criminal cases by conducting trials and hearing appeals. In so doing, courts interpret the constitutional provisions, statutes, ordinances, regulations, executive orders, treaties, and principles of common law that bear on the outcome of these cases. They also exercise the power of **judicial review**—the power to determine the constitutionality of all governmental enactments and actions.

LEGISLATURES

All governments make laws, or legislation. In a democracy, the governmental institution with primary responsibility for enacting legislation is the legislature. Legislatures in the United States and other democratic countries are comprised of the people's elected representatives chosen through free and fair elections. The members of these assemblies are known as **legislators.** In the lawmaking process, legislators follow either the preferences of their constituents or their own best judgment, depending on whether they consider themselves to be **delegates** or **trustees.** The delegate tries to discern what his or her constituents prefer the laws to be and votes accordingly. The trustee relies on a sense of what is best, irrespective of what his or her constituents prefer. In reality, legislators often alternate between these approaches, depending on the issue involved. And, because nearly all legislators are elected as Democrats or Republicans, and because legislatures are organized along party lines, the positions taken by their respective parties are usually quite important in determining how legislators will vote. Ultimately, what legislators do en masse is a function of constituent preferences, individual policy judgments, and partisan politics.

The U.S. Congress

In the United States, the national legislature is called the **Congress.** As noted in Chapter 1, the Framers of the Constitution wanted a strong legislature to be the central feature of the new national government. Thus, the Constitution gave Congress much broader powers than the legislature that existed under the Articles of Confederation. Legislative authority of Congress may be divided into two broad categories: **enumerated powers** and **implied powers.** The former category includes those powers that are mentioned specifically in the Constitution, such as the power to tax and the power to regulate interstate commerce. The latter category includes those powers that are deemed to be "necessary and proper for carrying into Execution the foregoing Powers, and all other Powers vested . . . in the Government of the United States, or in any Department or Officer thereof."[1] Under the doctrine of implied powers, scarcely any area exists over which Congress is absolutely barred from legislating, because most social and economic problems have a conceivable relationship to the broad powers and objectives contained in the Constitution. Of course, Congress may not enact laws that violate constitutional limitations such as those found in the Bill of Rights.

In addition to adopting laws governing the nation, Congress has the responsibility to see that the laws it passes are administered by the executive branch in the ways that Congress intended when it passed them. This function is known as **oversight,** and has become extremely important in the modern era as Congress has found it necessary to delegate a considerable degree of lawmaking power to agencies within the executive branch (see Chapter 12).

Congress is also occasionally required to act in a judicial fashion, such as when considering whether to impeach and remove the president, vice president, or a federal judge. After President Clinton was impeached by a majority vote of the House of Representatives in late 1998, the case went to the Senate for trial, as required by Article I, Section 3 of the U.S. Constitution; but the Senate failed to muster the necessary two-thirds majority to remove the president, so Clinton completed his second term in the White House.

How a Bill Becomes Law

Congress is made up of two chambers, the House of Representatives and the Senate. Laws enacted by Congress begin as bills introduced by members of either chamber. (The only exception is that bills to raise revenue must originate in the House of Representatives.) Once introduced, a bill is assigned to a committee for discussion and possible approval. Most bills never make it out of committee. Those that do are sent to the floor for a vote. For ordinary legislation, a simple majority is needed to pass a bill. To become law, both houses of Congress must pass a bill in the identical form. Once this happens, the bill is sent to the president, who has several options: (1) sign the bill into law, which is what usually occurs; (2) **veto** the bill, which can be overridden by a two-thirds majority of both houses of Congress; or (3) neither sign nor veto the bill, and thus allow it to become law automatically after 10 days.[2]

Publication of Federal Statutes

Once a bill has become law, it is published in *United States Statutes at Large,* an annual publication dating from 1789 in which federal statutes are arranged in order of their adoption. Statutes are not arranged by subject matter nor is there any indication of how they affect existing laws. Because the body of federal statutes is quite voluminous, and because new statutes often repeal or amend their predecessors, it is essential that new statutes be merged into legal codes that systematically arrange the statutes by subject. To find federal law as it currently stands, arranged by subject matter, one must consult the latest edition of the Official Code of the Laws of the United States, generally known as the **U.S. Code.** The U.S. Code is broken down into 50 subjects, or titles (see Figure 2-1). It is indexed by subject matter and by statutes' popular names, making it relatively easy to find what the U.S. Code currently has to say on a given matter.[3] One popular compilation of the federal law widely used

FIGURE 2-1 Overview of the U.S. Code

Title 1	General Provisions	Title 28	Judiciary and Judicial Procedure
Title 2	The Congress	Title 29	Labor
Title 3	The President	Title 30	Mineral Lands and Mining
Title 4	Flag and Seal, Seat of Government, and the States	Title 31	Money and Finance
		Title 32	National Guard
Title 5	Government Organization and Employees	Title 33	Navigation and Navigable Waters
Title 6	Surety Bonds (repealed)	Title 34	Navy (repealed)
Title 7	Agriculture	Title 35	Patents
Title 8	Aliens and Nationality	Title 36	Patriotic Societies and Observances
Title 9	Arbitration		
Title 10	Armed Forces	Title 37	Pay and Allowances of the Uniformed Services
Title 11	Bankruptcy		
Title 12	Banks and Banking	Title 38	Veterans' Benefits
Title 13	Census	Title 39	Postal Service
Title 14	Coast Guard	Title 40	Public Buildings, Property, and Works
Title 15	Commerce and Trade		
Title 16	Conservation	Title 41	Public Contracts
Title 17	Copyrights	Title 42	The Public Health and Welfare
Title 18	Crimes and Criminal Procedure	Title 43	Public Lands
Title 19	Customs Duties	Title 44	Public Printing and Documents
Title 20	Education	Title 45	Railroads
Title 21	Food and Drugs	Title 46	Shipping
Title 22	Foreign Relations and Intercourse	Title 47	Telegraphs, Telephones, and Radiotelegraphs
Title 23	Highways	Title 48	Territories and Insular Possessions
Title 24	Hospitals and Asylums		
Title 25	Indians	Title 49	Transportation
Title 26	Internal Revenue Code	Title 50	War and National Defense
Title 27	Intoxicating Liquors		

by lawyers, judges, and criminal justice professionals is the *United States Code Annotated* (U.S.C.A.). Published by West Group, the U.S.C.A. contains the entire current U.S. Code, but each section of statutory law in the U.S.C.A. is followed by a series of annotations consisting of court decisions interpreting the particular statute along with historical notes, cross-references, and other editorial features.

State Legislatures

Under the U.S. Constitution, each state must have a democratically elected legislature because that is the most fundamental element of a "republican form of government." State legislatures for the most part resemble the U.S. Congress. Each is composed of representatives chosen by the citizens of their respective states. All of them, except Nebraska, are bicameral (i.e., two-house) institutions. In adopting statutes, they all follow the same basic procedures.

When state legislatures adopt statutes, they are published in volumes known as **session laws.** Then statutes are integrated into state codes. Annotated versions of all 50 state codes are available to anyone who wishes to see how state statutes have been interpreted and applied by the state courts.

As noted in Chapter 1, after the American Revolution, states adopted the English common law as their own state law. (Congress, on the other hand, never did.) Eventually, however, state legislatures codified much of the common law by enacting statutes, which in turn have been developed into comprehensive state codes. Periodically, states revise portions of their codes to make sure they retain relevancy to a constantly changing society. For example, in 1989, the Tennessee General Assembly undertook a modernization of its criminal code. Old offenses that were no longer being enforced were repealed; other offenses were redefined; and sentencing laws were completely overhauled.

JUDICIAL SYSTEMS

Law evolves not only through the legislative process, but also through a process of judicial interpretation in the context of particular cases. These cases may arise in either federal or state courts. The federal government and each of the 50 state governments maintain their own system of courts. These systems include both **trial courts** and **appellate courts.** Trial courts conduct civil and criminal trials and various types of hearings. Trial courts make factual determinations and are the primary settlers of legal disputes. Appellate courts hear appeals from the trial courts. They are not fact-finding bodies; rather, their role is to review the proceedings of lower courts, correct errors, and settle unresolved legal issues.

The Federal Court System

Article III of the U.S. Constitution provides that "[t]he judicial Power of the United States, shall be vested in one supreme Court, and in such inferior Courts as the Congress may from time to time ordain and establish." Beginning with the landmark Judiciary Act of 1789,[4] Congress has used this authority to create, empower, and regulate the federal court system. The current Federal Court System is shown in figure 2-2. Congress determines the structure of the federal judiciary, sets the number of federal judges, determines the jurisdiction of the lower federal courts, and provides for the funding of the federal judiciary.

Federal Court Jurisdiction

The jurisdiction of the U.S. Supreme Court is provided for in Article III of the Constitution, although Congress may regulate to some extent the Supreme Court's authority to hear appeals.[5] The jurisdiction of the lower federal courts is determined solely by Congress. The jurisdiction of the federal courts, while broad, is not unlimited. There are two basic categories of federal jurisdiction. First, and most important for students of constitutional law, is **federal question jurisdiction.**[6] The essential requirement here is that a case must present a federal question, that is, a question arising under the U.S. Constitution, a

FIGURE 2-2 The Federal Court System

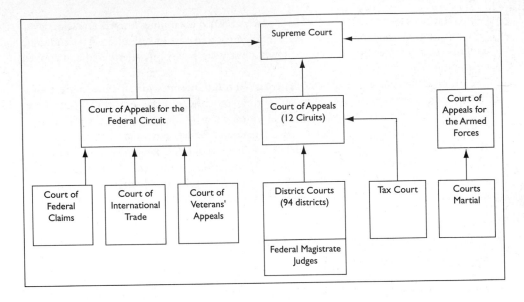

federal statute, regulation, executive order, or treaty. Of course, given its expansive modern role, the federal government has produced a myriad of statutes, regulations, and executive orders. Consequently, most important questions of public policy can be framed as issues of federal law, thus permitting the federal courts to play a tremendous role in the policymaking process.

The second broad category, **diversity of citizenship jurisdiction,** applies only to civil suits and is unrelated to the presence of a question of federal law. To qualify under federal diversity jurisdiction, a case must involve parties from different states and an amount in controversy that exceeds $75,000.[7]

Federal courts also have sole jurisdiction over bankruptcies, actions by which individuals and corporations seek protection from their creditors.

U.S. District Courts

The **U.S. District Courts** are the major trial courts in the federal system.[8] These courts are granted authority to conduct trials and hearings in civil and criminal cases meeting the previously discussed jurisdictional requirements. Each of the federal district courts also has its own bankruptcy court. Because the Constitution gives the federal government exclusive power over bankruptcies, all bankruptcy cases are filed in federal bankruptcy courts.[9]

There are currently 94 federal judicial districts, with each state being allocated at least one.[10] Some states have more districts, depending on population and geographical size. Tennessee, for example, has three federal judicial districts corresponding to the traditional eastern, middle and western "grand divisions" of the state.[11] California, New York, and Texas are the only states with 4 federal judicial districts.[12]

In 1999, there were 646 judgeships in the federal district courts. The number of judges assigned to a district depends primarily on caseload, which is in turn largely a function of population within the district. There are currently 12 judges assigned to the Northern District of Texas, which is based in Dallas, 18 judges assigned to the Southern District based in Houston, 10 judges assigned to the Western District based in San Antonio, and 7 judges assigned to the Eastern District based in Tyler. [13]

Although there are multiple judges assigned to each federal judicial district, normally only one judge presides at hearings and trials, although federal law permits certain exceptional cases to be decided by panels of three judges.

In 1999, 260,271 civil cases and 59,923 criminal cases were filed in the federal district courts. Another 1,354,376 cases were filed in the bankruptcy courts. [14] In 1982, 206,193 civil cases, 31,623 criminal cases, and 412,852 bankruptcy cases were filed. [15] Thus, over the 17-year period, civil filings increased 26 percent, while criminal cases increased by 89 percent. To a great extent, the dramatic increase in criminal caseload was the result of the national government's "war on drugs" launched during the 1980s. However, the growth in bankruptcy cases is much more startling, increasing by 228 percent over the same 17-year period. The overwhelming majority of these cases were personal bankruptcies. This massive increase in bankruptcy filings reflected Americans' growing levels of personal debt, which stemmed in part from the easy availability of credit to consumers in the 1980s and 1990s.

The U.S. Courts of Appeals

The intermediate appellate courts in the federal system are the **U.S. Courts of Appeals**. [16] These courts did not exist until passage of the Judiciary Act of 1891. [17] Prior to that time, appeals from the decisions of the district courts were heard by the Supreme Court or by the circuit courts, which no longer exist. Today, the courts of appeals are commonly referred to as circuit courts, because each one of them presides over a geographical area known as a circuit. The nation is divided into 12 circuits, with each circuit comprising one or more federal judicial districts. There is also a federal circuit, which is authorized to grant appeals from decisions of specialized federal courts (See figure 2-3.). The circuit courts hear appeals from the federal districts within their circuits. For example, the U.S. Court of Appeals for the Eleventh Circuit, based in Atlanta, hears appeals from the district courts located in Alabama, Georgia, and Florida. The Court of Appeals for the District of Columbia Circuit, based in Washington, has the very important additional function of hearing appeals from numerous quasi-judicial tribunals in the federal bureaucracy (see Chapter 12).

Appeals in the circuit courts are normally decided by rotating panels of three judges, although under exceptional circumstances these courts will decide cases *en banc,* meaning that all of the judges assigned to the court will participate in the decision. On average, 14 judges are assigned to each circuit, but the number varies from 6 judges in the First Circuit (Maine, Massachusetts, New Hampshire, Rhode Island, and Puerto Rico) to 28 judges in the Ninth Circuit (Alaska, Arizona, California, Hawaii, Idaho, Montana, Nevada, Oregon, Washington, Guam, and the Northern Mariana Islands).

In 1982, the caseload of the U.S. Courts of Appeals was 27,946 filings; in 1999 (excluding the federal circuit), it was 54,693 cases. Two-thirds of these cases were civil appeals; roughly 20 percent were criminal appeals; the remainder consisted of appeals from administrative agency actions, bankruptcy appeals, and original proceedings in the circuit courts. [18]

FIGURE 2-3 The
Federal Judicial Circuits

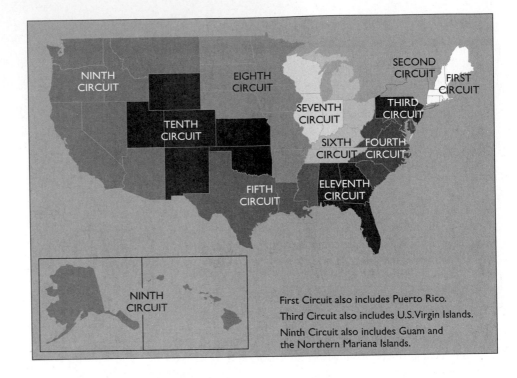

The U.S. Supreme Court

Although the **U.S. Supreme Court** is explicitly recognized in Article III of the Constitution, it was not formally established until passage of the Judiciary Act of 1789.[19] The Judiciary Act provided for a court composed of a chief justice and five associate justices. In 1807, the Court was expanded to include seven justices, and in 1837, Congress increased the number to nine. During the Civil War, the number of justices was briefly increased to ten. In 1869, Congress reestablished the number at nine where it has remained to this day. Although Congress theoretically could expand or contract the membership of the Court, powerful tradition militates against doing so. (Information on the nine current Justices of the Supreme Court is provided in figure 2-4.)

The Supreme Court's first sessionwas held in February 1790. It had no cases on the docket and adjourned after 10 days. During its first decade, 1790–1801, the Court met twice a year for brief terms beginning in February and August. Over the years, the Court's annual sessions have expanded along with its workload and its role in the political and legal system. As the nation has become more populous, complex, and more litigious, the Supreme Court's agenda has swelled. The Court now receives more than 7,000 petitions each year from parties seeking review, and there is no indication that the Court's caseload will soon decline.

Since 1917, the Court's annual term has begun on the first Monday of October. Until 1979, the Court adjourned its sessions for the summer, necessitating special sessions to handle urgent cases arising in July, August, or September. Since 1979, however, the Court has stayed in continuous session throughout the year, merely declaring a recess (typically near the end of June) for a summer vacation.

FIGURE 2-4 The Justices of the Supreme Court, 2001

Name	Born	State Appointed from	Year Appointed	Appointed by President	Political Party Affiliation
William H. Rehnquist (Chief Justice)	1924	Arizona	1971 (Elevated to Chief Justice in 1986)	Nixon (elevated to Chief Justice by President Reagan)	Republican
John Paul Stevens	1920	Illinois	1975	Ford	Republican
Sandra Day O'Connor	1930	Arizona	1981	Reagan	Republican
Antonin Scalia	1936	New Jersey	1985	Reagan	Republican
Anthony M. Kennedy	1936	California	1987	Reagan	Republican
David Souter	1939	New Hampshire	1990	Bush	Republican
Clarence Thomas	1948	Virginia	1991	Bush	Republican
Ruth Bader Ginsburg	1933	Washington, D.C.	1993	Clinton	Democrat
Stephen G. Breyer	1938	Massachusetts	1994	Clinton	Democrat

Article III of the Constitution declares that the Supreme Court shall have **original jurisdiction** "[i]n all Cases affecting Ambassadors, other public Ministers and Consuls, and those in which a state shall be a party . . ." (modified by the Eleventh Amendment). Congress has enacted legislation giving the district courts **concurrent jurisdiction** in cases dealing with "Ambassadors, other public Ministers and Consuls," as well as in cases between the U.S. government and one or more state governments. As a result, the Supreme Court exercises exclusive original jurisdiction only in suits between state governments, which often involve boundary disputes or disputes over water rights. These cases, although important in themselves, represent a minute proportion of the Court's caseload.

The Supreme Court's **appellate jurisdiction** extends to all federal cases "with such Exceptions, and under such Regulations as the Congress shall make."[20] Appellate cases coming to the Supreme Court from the lower federal courts usually come from the 13 courts of appeals, although they may come from the U.S. Court of Appeals for the Armed Forces, or, under special circumstances, directly from the district courts. Appellate cases may also come from the state courts of last resort, usually, but not always, designated as state supreme courts.[21]

In recent years Congress made the appellate jurisdiction of the Supreme Court almost entirely discretionary by greatly limiting the so-called **appeals of right.** Today, the Court's appellate jurisdiction is exercised almost exclusively through the **writ of certiorari,** which is issued at the Court's discretion. Federal law authorizes the Court to grant certiorari to review all cases, state or federal, which raise substantial federal questions. This broad discretion permits the Court to set its own agenda, facilitating its role as a policymaker, but allowing the Court to avoid certain issues that may carry undesirable institutional consequences. The Court may deflect, or at least postpone dealing with, issues that it considers

THE LAW IN ACTION

HOW THE SUPREME COURT GRANTS CERTIORARI

In most instances a litigant who has exhausted all available remedies in the lower federal courts may file a petition for certiorari in the Supreme Court. As long as a substantial federal question is involved, a party who has exhausted appellate remedies in the state courts may also seek certiorari in the nation's highest court. The chances of the Supreme Court granting review in a given case are slim. Of the more than 7,000 petitions for certiorari ("cert") coming to it each year, the Court will normally grant review in only about 100. The Court tends to favor those cases in which the federal government is a party, in which lower courts are in conflict, and those involving issues of great public importance. The process of case selection actually begins with the justices' **law clerks** (staff attorneys) reading the numerous petitions for certiorari and preparing summary memoranda. With the assistance of law clerks, the chief justice, who bears primary responsibility for Court administration, prepares a list of cases to be considered. The associate justices may add cases to the list. Unless at least one justice indicates that a petition should be discussed, review is automatically denied, which disposes of more than 70 percent of the petitions. The Court considers petitions on the discuss list in private conferences. Regular conferences are held throughout the term, both for the purpose of reviewing cert petitions and for discussing and deciding the cases in which the Court has granted review. At least four justices must vote to grant certiorari in order for the Court to accept a case for review. The denial of cert carries no weight as precedent. The fact that the Court has decided not to review a lower court decision does not mean that the Court necessarily approves of the way it was decided. Should the same issue be presented to the Court in a later case, the previous denial of certiorari would have no bearing on the Court's decision.

"too hot to handle." This flexible jurisdiction, then, can be used as a means to expand or limit the Court's policymaking role, depending on the issue at hand.

Although Congress is authorized to regulate the appellate jurisdiction of the Supreme Court, it has rarely used this power to curtail the Court's authority. Rather, Congress has facilitated the institutional development of the Court by minimizing its mandatory appellate jurisdiction and thus giving it control over its own agenda. Likewise, Congress has delegated to the Court the authority to promulgate **rules of procedure** for itself and the lower federal courts.[22] Consequently, the Supreme Court is nearly autonomous with respect to the determination of its decision-making process.

Specialized Federal Tribunals

All of the federal tribunals we have discussed thus far are considered "Article III courts," which means that they are part of the judicial branch. Congress has also created a set of specialized tribunals under its authority under Article I of the Constitution. The principal difference between Article III courts and Article I courts is that the judges of the former are appointed for life, whereas the judges of the latter serve for set terms of office (in most instances, 15 years). Otherwise, the distinction between these two types of tribunals is rather blurred. These Article I courts include:

- the **Tax Court,** established in 1924 to resolve disputes between taxpayers and the Internal Revenue Service;
- the **Court of Veterans' Appeals,** created in 1988 to review decisions of the Board of Veterans' Appeals regarding veterans' claims to benefits; and
- the **Court of Federal Claims** (first established in 1855 as the Court of Claims), which is responsible for adjudicating **tort claims** (civil suits for damages) against the federal government.

The **Court of International Trade** (first established in 1926 as the Customs Court) adjudicates controversies between the federal government and importers of foreign goods. This specialized tribunal located in New York City has been declared by Congress to be an Article III court and, therefore, its nine judges are appointed for life.[23]

Decisions of the Tax Court are appealable to the U.S. Court of Appeals for the D.C. Circuit. Appeals from the Court of Veterans' Appeals, the Court of Federal Claims, and the Court of International Trade are directed to the Court of Appeals for the Federal Circuit, which is the thirteenth federal circuit court (not to be confused with the D.C. Circuit).[24]

Under the **Uniform Code of Military Justice,**[25] crimes committed by persons in military service are prosecuted before **courts-martial.** Each branch of service has its own court of military review, the decisions of which are subject to review by an Article I court called the **U.S. Court of Appeals for the Armed Forces.** This court, composed of five judges, sits only in Washington, D.C. In most cases the court speaks with finality, although some of its decisions are reviewable by the Supreme Court on a writ of certiorari.

Selection, Tenure, and Removal of Federal Judges

As provided by the Constitution, the President, subject to the consent of the Senate, appoints all federal judges. With the exception of those serving on the Article I courts, the appointments are for life.[26] Normally, the Senate consents to presidential judicial appointments with a minimum of controversy. However, Senatorial approval is by no means pro forma, especially when it involves appointments to the Supreme Court. In fact, historically the Senate has rejected about 20 percent of presidential nominations to the Supreme Court.

Article III, Section 1 of the Constitution states that "judges, both of the supreme and inferior Courts, shall hold their Offices during good Behaviour . . ." This grant of life tenure to federal judges was intended to make the federal courts independent of partisan forces and transitory public passions so that they could dispense justice impartially, according to the law. But not everyone accepts the need for a life-tenured, appointed federal judiciary. In a democratic nation that extols the will of the people, such sentiments are apt to be viewed as elitist, even aristocratic. From time to time proposals have surfaced to impose limitations on the terms of federal judges, but no such effort has ever gained serious political momentum. Life tenure for federal judges, like most of the elements of our eighteenth-century Constitution, remains a firmly established principle of the political order.

The only means of removing a federal judge is through the **impeachment** process provided in the Constitution. First, the House of Representatives must approve one or more articles of impeachment by at least a majority vote.[27] Then, a trial is held in the Senate presided over by the chief justice of the Supreme Court. To be removed from office, a judge must be convicted by a vote of at least two-thirds of the Senate.[28]

Since 1789, the House of Representatives has initiated impeachment proceedings against 13 federal judges, and only 7 of these have been convicted in the Senate. The first federal judge to be impeached was John Pickering, a district judge from New Hampshire, who was impeached and removed from office in 1803 for reasons of mental instability and intoxication. The most recent impeachment was that of Judge Walter L. Nixon from the Southern District of Mississippi, who was impeached and removed from office in 1989 for committing perjury before a federal grand jury.

CANONS OF CONDUCT FOR FEDERAL JUDGES   **SIDEBAR**

1. A judge should uphold the integrity and independence of the judiciary.
2. A judge should avoid impropriety and the appearance of impropriety in all activities.
3. A judge should perform the duties of the office impartially and diligently.
4. A judge may engage in extra-judicial activities to improve the law, the legal system, and the administration of justice.

5. A judge should regulate extra-judicial activities to minimize the risk of conflict with judicial duties.
6. A judge should regularly file reports of compensation received for law-related and extra-judicial activities.

Source: Judicial Conference of the United States

Only once has a Supreme Court Justice been impeached by the House. In 1804, Justice Samuel Chase fell victim to President Jefferson's attempt to control a federal judiciary largely comprised of Washington and Adams appointees. Justice Chase had irritated the Jeffersonians by his haughty and arrogant personality and his extreme partisanship. Nevertheless, there was no evidence that he was guilty of any crime. Consequently, Chase narrowly escaped conviction in the Senate. The Chase affair set an important precedent— a federal judge may not be removed simply for reasons of partisanship, ideology, or personality. Thus, despite strong support in conservative quarters for the impeachment of Chief Justice Earl Warren during the 1960s, there was never any real prospect of Warren's removal. Barring criminal conduct or serious breaches of judicial ethics, federal judges do not have to worry that their decisions might cost them their jobs.

Federal Magistrate Judges

Federal magistrate judges (formerly called federal magistrates) are appointed by the judges of the federal district courts for a period of eight years. Magistrate judges preside over pretrial proceedings in civil and criminal cases. They try misdemeanors and can preside over civil trials with the consent of both parties. The position of federal magistrate was created by Congress in 1968 to replace the ancient system of federal judicial commissioners. In 1990, Congress changed their title to "federal magistrate judge." Today, they tend to be experienced lawyers who are appointed based on the recommendations of merit selection committees. There are currently more than 500 federal magistrate judges.

State Court Systems

Each of the 50 states has its own court system, responsible for cases arising under the laws of that state. These include the state constitution, statutes enacted by the state legislature, orders issued by the governor, regulations promulgated by various state agencies, and ordinances (local laws) adopted by cities and counties. State courts have jurisdiction over most

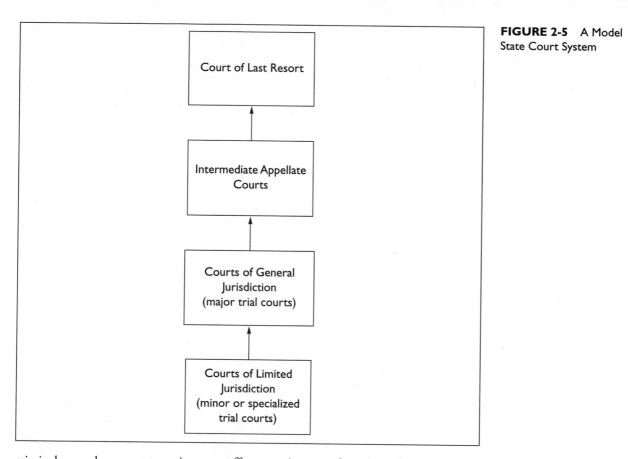

FIGURE 2-5 A Model
State Court System

criminal cases, because most crimes are offenses against state laws (see Chapter 4). State courts address most questions of property law, including real estate, probate, and inheritance questions (see Chapter 6). State courts handle most torts (see Chapter 5) and most contract disputes (see Chapter 7). Finally, state courts resolve almost all family law cases, including issues of divorce, child custody, guardianship, and juvenile delinquency (see Chapter 8). Indeed, the great majority of cases are not decided by the federal courts, but by state courts.

Although no two state court systems are identical, all of them contain trial and appellate courts (see figure 2-5). Trial courts go by many names: county court, superior court, district court, circuit court, court of common pleas, and so forth. The New York Supreme Court has both trial and appellate divisions, which sometimes is a source of confusion. Many states have trial courts of limited jurisdiction to handle minor or specialized matters. They too have many names: probate court, juvenile court, municipal court, sessions court, mayor's court, and so forth. Some states, such as Idaho, Illinois, Iowa, and South Dakota, have one consolidated trial court that handles all civil and criminal cases. Other states have multiple trial courts with specialized jurisdictions.

Each state has a **court of last resort,** usually called the **state supreme court,** which speaks with finality on matters of state law. Most states now have **intermediate appellate courts** to handle routine appeals, which allows the state supreme court to focus on the most important cases. However, the jurisdictional characteristics of appellate courts vary considerably. In Florida, for example, the district courts of appeal are ostensibly the intermediate appellate courts. But under Florida law they are final in most matters. The Florida Supreme Court only reviews district court decisions on constitutional issues or when the district courts are in conflict or certify a question as one of great public importance.

Selection and Retention of State Judges

State judges are selected in a variety of ways. Most are elected, though some run on partisan ballots and others run in nonpartisan races. Many state judges are appointed by governors, either directly or through a nominating process known as merit selection. Even appointed judges typically must face the voters eventually in a contested election or a merit-retention election in which voters are asked whether a judge should be given another term. Considerable controversy surrounds judicial selection and retention. Advocates of **judicial accountability** to the people usually support some sort of elective system. Proponents of **judicial independence** generally argue for an appointive process with life tenure (the federal model) or at least long terms of office. A compromise approach that has been steadily gaining acceptance since it was first adopted in 1940 is known as the **Missouri Plan.** It consists of three elements:

1. When a vacancy occurs, qualified persons submit applications to a nonpartisan judicial nominating commission. The commission reviews the applications, conducts interviews, and submits a "short list" to the governor.
2. The governor appoints an individual from the list submitted by the nominating commission.
3. When the judge's term of office expires, the judge faces the voters in a retention election. The voters are simply asked, "Should Judge X be retained in office for another term?"

By combining merit-based, appointive, and elective elements, the Missouri Plan attempts to balance the values of judicial competency, independence, and accountability. It is no guarantee of excellence, but at least incompetent or unsuitable prospects are screened out. Governors can often still use judicial appointments as patronage, which is something they have done historically. Finally, the voters can oust those judges whom they believe have abused their authority or acted unwisely. It is important to realize that the overwhelming majority of judges who stand for retention are retained; but sometimes the electorate can become aroused over an issue such as capital punishment and vote out of office judges they believe to be acting contrary to their preferences. Such was the case in 1986 when Chief Justice Rose Bird and two of her colleagues on the California Supreme Court were removed by the voters. In her decade-long tenure as chief justice, Bird voted to reverse the death sentence in all of the 64 death penalty cases that came before the court. Her ouster by the voters probably had an effect on the California judiciary, making judges more cautious in dealing with controversial issues. Critics of judicial elections saw the defeat of Chief Justice Bird as a real threat to judicial independence, whereas those of a more populist bent celebrated what they regarded as a victory for judicial accountability.

Judicial Discipline and Removal

Every state has some mechanism (other than the ballot box) by which judges who commit serious legal or ethical violations can be removed from office. Generally speaking, this process is impeachment and basically follows the federal model discussed below. In recent years, state legislatures have created **judicial disciplinary commissions** to reprimand, censure, and even suspend judges whose violations do not rise to the level where impeachment is warranted. In Tennessee, for example, this body is known as the Court of the Judiciary. Composed of judges, attorneys, and laypersons, the Court of the Judiciary reviews complaints about judicial conduct, often from disgruntled litigants or attorneys. When these complaints are determined to have merit, the Court of the Judiciary may issue a reprimand, issue a cease and desist order, suspend the offending judge for a period of 30 days, or recommend the judge's removal altogether. If the Court of the Judiciary recommends removal, the matter is referred to the Tennessee General Assembly for impeachment.

Judicial Administration, Rule Making, and Supervision of the State Judiciary

Most state courts have substantial, if not total, control over the process of making procedural rules for the courts. In most states, the state supreme court is the rule-making body for the state judiciary. Local courts usually have some authority to establish their own **rules of practice,** but these must not conflict with the rules of procedure that apply statewide. Typically, the state supreme court has administrative responsibility for the entire state court system, although in some states administration is still fairly decentralized. The state supreme court generally has supervisory power over the practice of law, which includes responsibility for disciplining attorneys who violate the code of professional responsibility.

How Cases Begin

Most court cases can be divided into two basic categories: **criminal prosecutions** and **civil suits.** Criminal cases begin when a federal or state prosecutor files criminal charges against a defendant. The defendant is brought before the appropriate court of law to answer the charges. Most criminal cases are resolved by guilty pleas, which are often obtained through **plea bargaining.** When the defendant pleads "not guilty," a **trial** is conducted to determine guilt or innocence. (For a detailed examination of criminal procedure, see Chapter 10.)

All noncriminal cases are by definition civil cases. A civil case typically begins when one party files suit against another, alleging some wrong and seeking some remedy. Many civil suits are settled through negotiation. Those that are not settled or dismissed result in a civil trial. (For a detailed examination of civil procedure, see Chapter 9.)

Powers of Courts

Courts have power to issue binding judgments in the civil and criminal cases. They can sentence persons convicted of crimes to a variety of punishments as allowed by law. They can award **damages** to persons who are the victims of civil wrongs. They can issue **injunctions** and **restraining orders** to prevent an injury from taking place or continuing. Courts also have power to issue a number of orders, writs, and decrees to effectuate their judgments. Common writs include:

- the **writ of mandamus,** requiring a judge or other public official to perform a nondiscretionary duty
- the **writ of habeas corpus,** ordering a party to show cause for holding a person in custody
- the **writ of prohibition,** ordering a lower court not to take jurisdiction in a particular case
- the writ of certiorari, calling up the record of a lower court proceeding so that it can be reviewed for error

The Power of Contempt

Courts can hold in **contempt** parties who disrupt court proceedings or refuse to comply with court orders. **Criminal contempt** is the offense of engaging in contemptuous behavior in the presence of the court or so close to the court as to interrupt or hinder the judicial proceedings. In 1968, the Supreme Court held that criminal contempt is a crime in the ordinary sense and may be punished by fine, imprisonment, or both.[29] Perhaps the most sensational use of the contempt power in recent memory occurred in 1999 when U.S. District Judge Susan Webber Wright cited President Clinton for contempt and fined him $100,000. Clinton was cited for giving false, evasive, and misleading testimony to a federal grand jury investigating allegations of his misconduct.

A **civil contempt** is a sanction imposed to coerce a recalcitrant person to obey a court order, for example a "deadbeat dad" who refuses to pay court-ordered support for his dependents. A judge may order this individual to be confined in jail until he agrees to comply. How long may the individual be held in custody? There is no set limit—the standard is one of "reasonableness" in the context of the situation.

An interesting example of the use of a civil contempt took place in Knoxville, Tennessee, in the early 1990s. An antiabortion protester was arrested for criminal trespass after he refused to remain outside the property of a clinic that performed abortions. At the police station and again when he was hauled into court, the defendant refused to reveal his true identity, giving his name only as Baby John Doe. A judge held him in contempt and ordered him jailed until he would cooperate. After several months the judge relented, noting that he had already served more time than he could serve if convicted of the trespass.

The Judicial Role

In their high school civics classes, students are taught that "legislatures make the law and judges interpret the law." Although this civics lesson is basically true, it represents an oversimplification of the role of the judge. Trial judges attempt to apply settled and clear principles of law to particular disputes. Unfortunately, the law is not always settled or clear and often trial judges must choose between conflicting interpretations of the law. When they make such choices, extra-legal factors may come into play. Of course, trial judges do not have the final say. Appellate courts review the interpretations of law rendered by trial courts.

Appellate judges attempt to clarify and settle the law, drawing on legislative intent, precedent, and tradition. Appellate judges, especially in the courts of last resort, are inevitably engaged in the process of "saying what the law is," to paraphrase Chief Justice John Marshall's opinion in *Marbury v. Madison*.[30] Because the process of legal interpretation is far from an exact science, the values, preferences, and biases of individual judges may enter into the interpretive process. Yet it is important to remember that appellate courts are all **collegial courts**, in that decisions are made by panels of judges and not individuals. Moreover, appellate courts justify their interpretation of the law by producing written **opinions**. The process is designed to maximize rationality and minimize subjectivity. Appellate judges strive for objectivity, even if it is never perfectly achieved.

THE ROLE OF THE CHIEF EXECUTIVE

Chief executives at all levels of government—mayors, governors, and presidents—play an important role in the American legal system. Chief executives can issue executive orders based on statutory provisions and, in some instances, direct constitutional authority. Executive orders have the force of law—they must be obeyed in the same way that statutes and court decisions command obedience.

CASE IN POINT

PRESIDENTIAL ENFORCEMENT OF JUDICIAL DECISIONS

United States Supreme Court
Cooper v. Aaron

358 U.S. 1, 78 S.Ct. 1401, 3 L.Ed.2d 5 (1958)

Undoubtedly one of the most important decisions of the Supreme Court in the modern era was **Brown v. Board of Education** (1954), where the Court said that states could no longer maintain racially segregated public schools. That decision touched off a firestorm of controversy in the South. In Arkansas, the governor called out the National Guard to block the court-ordered desegregation of Central High School in Little Rock in 1957. After meeting with President Eisenhower, Governor Orval Faubus withdrew the Guard, but an angry mob of white citizens attempted to prevent the African-American students from entering the school. President Eisenhower then ordered federal troops into Little Rock to enforce the court's desegregation order. The extreme situation led the local school board to petition the federal district court for a delay in the implementation of its desegregation order. In reviewing the case, the Supreme Court refused to allow the delay. In an unusual step, the Court produced an opinion coauthored by all nine justices. The Court reaffirmed its decision in **Brown** and rebuked Governor Faubus, reminding him of his duty to uphold the Constitution. Would the Court have been able to take this position if President Eisenhower, who had reservations about court-ordered desegregation, had decided not to send the troops to Little Rock? In using military force to implement a judicial decision about which he had doubts, Eisenhower was recognizing the authority of the Supreme Court to speak with finality on matters of constitutional interpretation. However, the ultimate decision to enforce the Court's authority belonged to the President. Accordingly, **Cooper v. Aaron** is more a testament to the importance of the executive than a bold assertion of judicial power.

Opinion of the Court . . .

COOPER V. AARON

358 U.S. 1, 78 S.Ct. 1401, 3 L. Ed. 2d 5 (1958)

Opinion of the Court by **The Chief Justice, Mr. Justice Black, Mr. Justice Frankfurter, Mr. Justice Douglas, Mr. Justice Burton, Mr. Justice Clark, Mr. Justice Harlan, Mr. Justice Brennan,** *and* **Mr. Justice Whittaker.**

. . . Article 6 of the Constitution makes the Constitution the "supreme Law of the Land." . . . Chief Justice Marshall . . . declared in *Marbury v. Madison:* . . . "It is emphatically the province and duty of the judicial department to say what the law is." This decision declared the basic principle that the federal judiciary is supreme in the exposition of the law of the Constitution, and that principle has ever since been respected by this Court and the Country as a permanent and indispensable feature of our constitutional system. . . . Every state legislator and executive and judicial officer is solemnly committed by oath taken pursuant to Article 6, clause 3, "to support this Constitution. . . ."

No state legislator or executive or judicial officer can war against the Constitution without violating his undertaking to support it. Chief Justice Marshall spoke for a unanimous Court in saying that: "If the legislatures of the several states may, at will, annul the judgments of the courts of the United States, and destroy the rights acquired under those judgments, the Constitution itself becomes a solemn mockery. . . ."

Presidents and governors can also veto bills enacted by their respective legislatures. For the U.S. Congress and most state legislatures to override a veto, more than a simple majority vote is required. This ensures that controversial legislation will not be enacted without a sufficiently strong consensus in the government.

Presidents and governors play more than a negative role in the legislative process. They also propose legislation. At the federal level, the president outlines a legislative agenda in the annual state of the union speech. Much of the effort expended by the White House on a day-to-day basis involves trying to persuade Congress to enact this agenda. Much the same thing happens at the state level.

Executives also perform a critical function in the enforcement of the law. Legislation and judicial decisions are not self-enforcing. Oftentimes the chief executive or other officials within the executive branch are called upon to carry out the will of courts and legislatures. Of course, in deciding how to implement statutes and court decisions, executive officials shape the law as it is applied in concrete circumstances.

REGULATORY AND ADMINISTRATIVE AGENCIES

The modern chief executive sits atop a massive bureaucracy—a panoply of departments, boards, commissions, and other agencies. These agencies have various functions. Some are law enforcement agencies that serve to investigate crimes, apprehend offenders, and assist in their prosecution. Others are purely **administrative agencies**—their job is to carry out government programs such as social security, Medicaid, or public housing programs. Still others are **regulatory agencies.** Their role is to create and enforce regulations in specific policy areas. They do this by invoking authority granted to them by the legislature, which has delegated power to agencies to act as, in effect, miniature legislatures. For example, Congress has created the Environmental Protection Agency and vested it with the authority to make and enforce regulations to give specific content to the nation's environmental laws. In making these regulations, EPA and other regulatory agencies follow a rule-making procedure outlined by Congress.

Agencies vary not only in their functions but in their relationship to the chief executive. Most agencies are located within the major departments of the executive branch, which means that the president or governor has a good deal of control over them. Others, called **independent agencies,** are freestanding entities over which presidents and governors have less control. These agencies are typically directed by boards whose members are appointed for set terms of office and can only be removed for good cause. Of course, there are mechanisms by which legislative bodies and chief executives can control the decisions of independent agencies, for example, through the budgetary process. All of the legal issues pertaining to the functions and processes of administrative and regulatory agencies are the subject of **administrative law,** which is dealt with in some detail in Chapter 12.

LAW ENFORCEMENT AGENCIES

In the United States today there are nearly 40,000 law enforcement agencies. Located within the executive branches of local, state, and federal governments, these agencies have the power to investigate criminal activity, to arrest suspects, and to detain arrested persons until their cases come before the appropriate courts of law. These agencies also play an important role in gathering evidence that prosecutors use in obtaining convictions. In addition to officers' testimony, these agencies provide arrest reports, statements made by persons who file complaints, witnesses' identification of perpetrators from lineups or mug shots, and many different types of **forensic evidence** obtained from victims or from crime scenes.

The role of law enforcement agencies goes well beyond investigating crime, arresting suspects, and assisting prosecutors. Society expects these agencies to prevent crimes from occurring, which is a much more demanding assignment. It also expects these agencies, especially those at the local level, to maintain public peace and order, a function that requires discretion and diplomacy and, when required, force and coercion. And, increasingly, under the rubric of **community-oriented policing,** law enforcement agencies are being viewed as social services agencies that must provide assistance to people in need and assist in resolving conflicts.

In carrying out their assigned functions, law enforcement agencies are subject to the limitations of the federal and state constitutions, in particular those clauses that protect citizens against unreasonable searches and seizures, arbitrary arrests, prolonged detentions, coerced confessions, and police brutality (see Chapter 10). In some instances, police misconduct may constitute a tort (see Chapter 5); in other instances it may even be criminal (see Chapter 4). In this country we expect law enforcement to abide by the rule of law even as it enforces the law. Of course, this is not always the case in practice, but when police violate the law, they too are subject to sanctions. They can be disciplined by internal affairs authorities within their agencies; they can be subject to civil suit and even prosecuted for crimes. Such was the case with four Los Angeles police officers who participated in the beating of Rodney King during an arrest in 1991. Although the officers were acquitted of criminal charges in state court, a federal grand jury indicted them under the federal civil rights laws. In 1993, a trial jury returned verdicts of guilty against two of the officers; the other two were acquitted. The two convicted officers were sentenced to 30 months in federal prison.[31]

Federal Agencies

The oldest federal law enforcement agency is the U.S. Marshal's Service, which was established by Congress in 1789. For most of the nineteenth century, federal marshals were the only law enforcement authorities on the western frontier. Today, federal marshals are responsible for executing warrants issued by federal courts, pursuing and arresting federal fugitives, transporting federal prisoners, and protecting federal judges and witnesses.

The Federal Bureau of Investigation

The **Federal Bureau of Investigation** (**FBI**) is the primary agency empowered to investigate violations of federal criminal laws. Located in the **Department of Justice,** the FBI is by far the most powerful of the federal law enforcement agencies, with broad powers to enforce the many criminal laws adopted by the Congress. The FBI is perhaps best known for its Ten Most Wanted Fugitives program, which was inaugurated by the FBI's long-time director, J. Edgar Hoover, in 1950. In the 1950s, the Ten Most Wanted list mainly included bank robbers and car thieves. Today, it features alleged terrorists, serial killers, international drug dealers, and organized crime kingpins.

Under J. Edgar Hoover, who served as director from 1924 until his death in 1972, the FBI was often excessive in its zeal to enforce federal law and protect national security. In the 1950s, the FBI concentrated on the "Communist menace." In the 1960s it turned its attention to the more radical elements of the antiwar movement. On numerous occasions the FBI was accused of exceeding the limits of the law and infringing the rights of citizens. Today, the FBI operates under tighter legal constraints, the result of congressional action, judicial decisions, and cultural changes within the agency itself.

Although its history is somewhat checkered, the FBI is generally regarded today as embodying the highest standards of professionalism in the law enforcement community. The FBI currently employs nearly 25,000 people, including more than 10,000 special agents spread out over 56 field offices in the United States and 21 foreign offices. The FBI uses the most sophisticated methods in crime prevention and investigation. Its crime laboratory assists state and federal law enforcement agencies; thus, it figures prominently in the prosecution of numerous crimes.

The Secret Service

Most students know that the **Secret Service** protects the president and vice president of the United States, their families, presidential candidates, and visiting heads of state. Many are not aware that the Secret Service also has an important law enforcement function. Located within the Treasury Department, the Secret Service was created by Congress in 1865 for the purpose of preventing counterfeiting of paper money, which had been introduced in this country during the Civil War. It was not until after the assassination of President William McKinley in 1901 that the Secret Service was assigned the function of protecting the president. Today, the Secret Service enforces federal laws against forgery of federal government checks and bonds. It also investigates credit and debit card fraud, computer fraud, and electronic fund transfer fraud.[32]

ATF and Federal Gun Control Laws

Another well-known but more controversial federal law enforcement agency is the **Bureau of Alcohol, Tobacco and Firearms (ATF)**. Located within the Department of Treasury, the ATF enforces federal laws pertaining to alcohol, tobacco, guns, and explosives. With respect to alcoholic beverages, ATF regulates distilleries, wineries, and breweries as well as importers and wholesalers. Regarding tobacco, ATF collects federal excise taxes on cigarettes and other tobacco products. It also licenses the manufacture and importation of such products. With regard to firearms, ATF enforces the regime of federal gun control laws. It was the exercise of this function that ultimately led to the catastrophic encounter between the ATF and the Branch Davidians in Waco, Texas, in April 1993. It was then that many Americans first became aware of the ATF and its law enforcement activities. The allegation that tear gas canisters fired by federal agents started the fire that destroyed the Branch Davidians' compound and killed 80 members of their group led to congressional investigations that basically exonerated federal agents. But the public's perception of the ATF was nevertheless marred.

Today, a debate rages in Congress and in the media over the adequacy of current federal gun control legislation. Advocates of gun control, for example, those who staged the Million Mothers March on Washington in May 2000, support tougher and more extensive federal gun laws. Others argue that existing laws need to be more vigorously enforced. The ATF contends that it needs more resources to enforce existing laws, but if new laws are passed, the responsibility for enforcing them will fall on the ATF, regardless of whether it gets more resources.

Federal Agencies Battling the War on Drugs

In the 1980s, the federal government declared war on drugs. Congress toughened the criminal laws prohibiting drug offenses; various federal agencies instituted drug-testing programs for their employees; efforts at interdiction were stepped up; more money was appropriated to fund agencies to enforce the drug laws; and a drug czar was appointed to coordinate federal policy and programs. Of course, despite some success in stemming the tide of illegal drugs flowing into this country and curtailing the consumption of illicit drugs by the American public, the drug problem remains an epidemic. Today, many people question the efficacy of the war on drugs; others lament the increased intrusiveness of law enforcement as it tries to ferret out drug smugglers, dealers, and users. Still others question the wisdom of incarcerating drug users.

At the front lines of the war on drugs is the Drug Enforcement Administration (DEA), which was established in 1973. Located within the Department of Justice, the DEA has more than 9,000 special agents and investigators. Its mission is to enforce federal drug laws and provide assistance to other federal agencies, such as the Immigration and Naturalization Service (INS), as well as state and local authorities involved in the war on drugs. The DEA's total budget for the 2000 fiscal year was $1.55 billion. In 1998, the DEA made 32,322 drug arrests.[33]

The INS and the Battle against Illegal Immigration

The Immigration and Naturalization Service, another agency located within the Department of Justice, is responsible for administering the process of legal immigration, apprehending and deporting those who enter the country illegally, and maintaining control of America's 8,000-mile-long border. Over the last two decades, the focus of INS attention has been the prevention of illegal immigration from Mexico, as Mexicans looking to improve their economic condition have streamed across the porous southern border to take agricultural and service jobs in California, Texas, and other states. In 1999 and 2000, the INS became the focus of national and international attention for its handling of the Elian Gonzales case (see Chapter 12).

State and Local Agencies

All 50 states have their own law enforcement agencies, although they vary quite a bit in how they are organized. Some states have their own counterpart to the FBI. For example, the Oklahoma Bureau of Investigation works with local law enforcement agencies to investigate crimes. Its criminalistics division provides forensic analysis including drug and alcohol testing, toxicology, fingerprints, DNA sampling, and ballistics. It also serves as the central repository for crime data and criminal history information. The principal statewide law enforcement agency in Oklahoma is the highway patrol, which is responsible for policing all state highways as well as lake and river shore lines. By way of contrast, Illinois has combined the investigative, enforcement, and forensic functions into one comprehensive agency: the Illinois State Police. Most states have multiple agencies charged with law enforcement in specific areas such as traffic safety, agricultural importation, casino gambling, alcoholic beverages, and hunting and fishing.

County Sheriffs

At the local level, we find both county and municipal law enforcement agencies. Nearly every county in America has a **sheriff**. The institution of sheriff dates from the reign of Alfred the Great in ninth-century England. The kingdom was divided into *shires,* which eventually became counties. The *shire reeve* was appointed by the king to represent the king in local affairs. As the English legal system evolved, sheriffs came to be responsible for arresting and detaining persons accused of crimes, serving summonses and subpoenas, and maintaining jails and workhouses. The institution of county sheriff was brought to America by the colonists. Early on, sheriffs were appointed by governors. In the early nineteenth century, states made this position elective, as it remains today. In some areas, particularly the urban Northeast, many of the powers traditionally exercised by sheriffs have been assumed by state or metropolitan police forces. However, in the rest of the country, especially in the rural areas, sheriffs (and their deputies) are the principal law enforcement agents at the county level.

Municipal Law Enforcement Agencies

The idea that a city should have its own professional police force is generally credited to Sir Robert Peel, who in 1829 persuaded Parliament to establish a metropolitan police force for the city of London.[34] Soon cities throughout the world emulated London's example. Today more than 20,000 cities and towns in the United States have their own police departments. Local police are charged with enforcing the criminal laws of their states as well as the ordinances enacted by their municipalities. Although the county sheriff usually has jurisdiction within the municipalities of the county, generally the sheriff concentrates enforcement efforts on those areas outside municipal boundaries.

Traditionally, police officers in America were apt to have low levels of education and were provided little in the way of formal job training. In the latter half of the twentieth century, law enforcement became much more professional. Most states now have standards for certification of officers based on their completion of training programs and meeting certain standards. Often attainment of these standards is the key to promotion. Increasingly, modern police agencies are seeking candidates who have completed college-level courses in criminal justice and other social sciences. Some police agencies subsidize community college–level courses for in-service officers.

PROSECUTORIAL AGENCIES

Whereas law enforcement agencies are the *gatekeepers* of the criminal justice system, **prosecutors** are central to the administration of criminal justice. They determine whether to bring charges against suspected criminals. They have enormous **prosecutorial discretion,** not only in determining whether to prosecute but also in determining what charges to file. Moreover, prosecutors frequently set the tone for plea bargaining and have a powerful voice in determining the severity of sanctions imposed on persons convicted of crimes. Accordingly, prosecutors play a crucial role in the criminal justice system.

The chief prosecutor at the federal level is the **attorney general,** who is the head of the Department of Justice. Below the attorney general are a number of **U.S. attorneys,** each responsible for prosecuting crimes within a particular federal district. The U.S. attorneys in turn have a number of assistants who handle most of the day-to-day criminal cases brought by the federal government. The attorney general and the U.S. attorneys are appointed by the President, subject to the consent of the Senate. The assistant U.S. attorneys are federal civil service employees.

In addition to the regular federal prosecutors, Congress has provided for the appointment of **independent counsel** (special prosecutors) in cases involving alleged misconduct by high government officials. By far the most infamous such case was the Watergate scandal (1972–1974), which resulted in the convictions of several high-ranking officials and the resignation of a president. But there have been numerous cases when, under congressional direction, a special prosecutor has been appointed. One of the best known recent examples of this was the appointment of former federal judge Kenneth Starr to investigate the Whitewater scandal that involved close associates of President Bill Clinton and First Lady Hillary Rodham Clinton. In 1998, Starr alleged, among other things, that President Clinton had given false and misleading statements to a federal grand jury. This led to President Clinton's impeachment by the House of Representatives, although he was acquitted after trial in the Senate. In the wake of the Starr investigation, Congress voted not to extend the law under which Starr was appointed, but Congress could provide for a new independent counsel at any time.

Each state likewise has its own attorney general and a number of assistant attorneys general, plus a number of district or **state's attorneys** at the local level. Generally speaking, local prosecutors are elected for set terms of office. In most states local prosecutors act autonomously and possess broad discretionary powers.

Cities and counties also have their own attorneys. These attorneys sometimes prosecute violations of city and county ordinances, but increasingly their function is limited to representing their cities or counties in civil suits and giving legal advice to local councils and officials. These city and county attorneys are generally appointed by the governing bodies they represent.

THE LEGAL PROFESSION

As noted in Chapter 1, the American legal profession has its roots in English common-law practice. In England, trial lawyers were (and are) called *barristers,* and attorneys who provided other legal services were (and are) known as *solicitors.* In the United States, we do not use that nomenclature, although the distinction between "trial lawyer" and "office lawyer" remains relevant. Indeed, lawyers in the United States have become extremely specialized. As in medicine, the general practitioner is becoming increasingly rare. Lawyers today specialize in torts, estate planning, taxation, civil rights, contracts, real estate, criminal defense work, and every other conceivable area of the law.

Legal Education and Admission to the Bar

About half the Framers of the U.S. Constitution were lawyers who "read law" and served apprenticeships with those who practiced law. A few states still allow some alternatives to formal study at a law school, but even when permitted such option is infrequently exercised. Today the path to becoming a lawyer is to successfully complete a three-year course from one of the 174 law schools accredited by the American Bar Association.[35] Indeed, all but a few states now require that to take a bar examination for admission to the practice of law an applicant must possess a Juris Doctor (J.D.) degree. Prior to the 1960s law schools awarded graduates a bachelor of laws (LL.B.) degree.

The number of applicants who annually seek admission to law schools has leveled off somewhat from the vast increase that occurred from the late 1960s to the 1970s, a time of social upheaval when many students were inspired to channel social and economic changes through law. A prospective law student must have a four-year college degree and generally score well on the Law School Aptitude Test (LSAT) and have a credible grade point average (GPA). Law schools are selective but do not demand that pre-legal education be in a particular field. Business, history, political science, and economics have been popular undergraduate majors. Admission committees often employ various criteria beyond LSAT and GPA scores to enroll a diverse group. Prior to 1960, women and minority students represented a very small percentage of law students. Today they represent a substantial percentage of the enrollment in most law schools.

Law schools usually require completion of basic courses in contracts, property, torts, criminal law, civil procedure, constitutional law, legal research and writing, evidence, and professional responsibility. Electives are available in fields such as estates and trusts, taxation, administrative and commercial law, and often include skills courses in trial and appellate advocacy and clinical training in client counseling. Some newer electives are in the fields of environmental, employment discrimination, and intellectual property law. Classes in alternate dispute resolution are becoming increasingly popular.

Since first introduced at the Harvard Law School in the 1870s, the *case method* has become the principal method of instruction in law schools. Casebooks today not only contain reported appellate court cases but also related materials. Professors frequently employ the *Socratic method* with students reciting cases and responding to in-depth questions posed concerning analysis of a case and its implications in the law. Use of the Socratic method has declined somewhat in recent years, particularly in classes beyond the basic required courses. In elective courses many professors now follow traditional college lecturing and discussion. Most basic law courses culminate in a written examination requiring a detailed analysis of hypothetical factual situations with discussion of applicable rules of law. Many law schools now place an increased emphasis on clinical and skills training in which students learn "to perform like lawyers" and are graded on their performance rather than on written examination.

The Organized Bar

Although we do not use the term *barrister* in the United States, we do refer to licensed attorneys as having been "admitted to the bar." State laws govern the admission requirements and require passage of a written bar examination before being admitted to practice in a particular state. Usually the highest court in the state has oversight of the bar admission policies and requires a thorough check of the applicant's background. Successful applicants take an oath to support the federal and state constitution and adhere to the ethical requirements of being a lawyer.

Some states have a **unified bar** which has been delegated authority to regulate the profession, usually under the oversight of the state's highest court. One who practices law in the state must be a dues-paying member of the state bar association. Dues furnish the administrative support for activities relating to disciplinary measures and continuing legal education. In some instances, however, a unified bar has used its funds to pay for lobbying to secure legislation favorable to causes advocated by bar leadership. Some members have disagreed with positions taken by unified bar associations, and in 1990 their disagreement came into sharp focus when the U.S. Supreme Court ruled that a bar member cannot be forced to pay dues to support political and ideological activities with which a lawyer–member disagrees.[36] In other states, bar association membership is optional. In either instance, lawyers usually form voluntary bar associations at the local level to further their social and professionals contacts, foster continuing legal education, and provide legal assistance to the poor.

Being admitted to the bar in one state does not permit a lawyer to practice in another state. Nevertheless, a lawyer can usually be admitted to practice in another state on a limited basis when accompanied by a lawyer admitted in that state. Admission to the practice of law in a state does not carry with it admission to practice in a federal court. Instead each federal trial and appellate court has its own requirements. These requirements are largely administrative but in some instances an oral examination is given.

Prior to 1975, bar associations often adopted minimum fee schedules designed to limit "cost cutting practitioners" that established lawyers deemed unethical in a learned profession. In 1975, the Supreme Court turned a deaf ear to such contentions and held that enforcement of a mandatory minimum fee schedule violated antitrust laws.[37]

Specialization and Certification

The law has grown exceedingly complex and the practice of law has become quite competitive. These factors and the Supreme Court's ruling in 1977 that protects the right of a lawyer to advertise under First Amendment protection of commercial speech have led to extensive advertising.[38] Advertising fosters specialization, which in turn has led to certification of lawyers to practice in a particular area. Certification is generally conferred by a state bar organization under the oversight of the state's highest court. It is achieved by having practiced in a given area for a stated period of time and having successfully completed a written examination of the law and procedures applicable to that area of the law. Board certified attorneys are deemed to have special knowledge and skill in their area of certification. Certification enables a lawyer to publicly announce his or her competency in a given field. Usually one who is certified must fulfill certain practice requirements and complete a number of continuing legal education courses in order to be periodically recertified.

Paralegals

Lawyers have long placed great responsibilities on their legal secretaries who often acquire considerable experience in assisting in drafting legal documents and in preparing cases for settlement or trial. With the increased specialization of the legal profession, in recent years the **paralegal** (sometimes referred to as a legal assistant) has come on the legal scene to work in conjunction with the attorney and the legal secretary. A paralegal is one who has been educated in basic legal studies and trained to assist attorneys in drafting legal documents and in preparing cases. The duties and responsibilities of a paralegal depend on the practice of the lawyer being assisted. For example, lawyers who specialize in handling personal injury cases often rely on paralegals to prepare suggested drafts of interrogatories to opposing parties, to assemble medical reports, and to keep track of a client's expenses that may be eligible for reimbursement. In real estate practice, a paralegal may obtain appraisals and title insurance commitments, handle property insurance transfers, draft routine legal documents for review by the lawyer, and prepare closing statements for transactions. Paralegal institutes now train individuals to become professionals and, in some instances, use this text for instruction in basic principles of law. In addition to the examples given, in probate, employment discrimination, criminal law, and other specialized areas, the paralegal has become an established professional in the delivery of legal services.

Finding a Lawyer

Although more than two-thirds of lawyers engage in private practice, a prospective client often finds it difficult to select a lawyer to serve the client's needs. Telephone books and local bar directories carry names and increasingly indicate a lawyer's area of practice. Yet, as in selecting a physician, a person must often depend on a referral. Historically, advertising by lawyers was prohibited and many members of the legal profession are disdainful of advertising, believing it to be unprofessional. Nonetheless, truthful advertising is permitted and can enable a prospective client to become informed about the qualifications and areas of practice of lawyers without the necessity of making repetitive calls to law offices. In some instances, membership organizations, prepaid legal insurance, and group legal plans assist in making referrals.

Some states have lawyer referral services whereby lawyers agree to hold a brief initial conference with a client for a modest fee. During the conference the client can either arrange to go forward with that lawyer or to receive a referral to one who practices in a specialized field. Still, the most common method of selection of a lawyer is probably based on a recommendation by a friend, business associate, fellow employee, or from an organization.

CASE IN POINT

LIMITATIONS ON ATTORNEY SOLICITATION

Florida Bar v. Went For It, Inc.

United States Supreme Court
515 U.S. 618, 115 S.Ct. 2371, 132 L.Ed.2d 541 (1995)

To practice law in Florida, an attorney must be a member of the Florida Bar and must abide by its rules of professional responsibility. One of these rules forbids personal injury lawyers from mailing solicitations to victims and their relatives for one month after an accident or disaster. G. Stewart McHenry, who operated an attorney referral service called Went For It, Inc., filed suit in federal district court challenging the bar's prohibition as a violation of the First Amendment. Reviewing the case on certiorari, the Supreme Court rejected the challenge. Writing for a sharply divided Court, Justice Sandra Day O'Connor recognized that the Florida Bar had "substantial interest both in protecting injured Floridians from invasive conduct by lawyers and in preventing the erosion of confidence in the profession that such repeated invasions have engendered." Writing for the four dissenters, Justice Anthony Kennedy observed that lawyers "who communicate their willingness to assist potential clients are engaged in speech protected by the First and Fourteenth Amendments." In his view, the Court's decision "undercuts this guarantee in an important class of cases and unsettles leading First Amendment precedents, at the expense of those victims most in need of legal assistance."

Legal Assistance for Indigent Persons

In most areas bar associations have established legal aid offices to assist persons of limited means to obtain legal advice. Assistance is often provided for persons of limited income. Congress has provided limited federal funds and state and local agencies, including bar associations, often assist in funding these offices. These offices often employ staff lawyers and law student interns. In many instances a legal aid office will refer a case to a practicing attorney who agrees to handle a case on a *pro bono* (for benefit of the public) basis without charge to the client. Of course, indigent criminal defendants are furnished legal counsel, a topic we examine in Chapter 10.

Professional Responsibility

Professional responsibility of lawyers has become a major topic. Lawyers are regulated by codes of professional conduct often patterned after the Model Code of Professional Conduct promulgated by the American Bar Association (ABA), a voluntary association of lawyers. The Model Code has no legal effect because the ABA is a private organization, but many state legislatures and the highest court of the states have adopted the ABA Model Code with some variations. Because lawyers are deemed to be "officers of the court," judges exercise inherent power to discipline them and even hold them in contempt of court for violations of ethical standards in the conduct of litigation.

Among the ethical concerns these codes of professional responsibility address are standards to be abided by lawyers concerning their duties to:

- charge reasonable fees (often with limitations on contingency fees)
- provide a client competent representation
- act with reasonable diligence in handling a client's interests
- be loyal to the client
- keep the client advised of the progress of legal matters undertaken
- avoid conflicts of interest
- exercise candor in dealings with courts and agencies

Bar associations customarily provide a mechanism for clients to file a grievance against an attorney whom the client believes to have violated the standards of professional responsibility. Grievances that have merit result in disciplinary action that ranges from a reprimand to suspension or disbarment. Moreover, a client may institute a malpractice suit against an attorney for misconduct or negligence in handling legal matters. If successful, the client may recover damages. Many attorneys carry liability insurance to protect both the client and lawyer. Finally, some bar associations have established client security funds to reimburse a client who suffers a financial loss due to a lawyer's misconduct.

The Changing Profession

In the latter half of the twentieth century the legal profession in the United States experienced rapid growth. Indeed, the prevailing attitude among the mass public today is that there are too many lawyers. In 1951, there were about 220,000 lawyers in the United States, but by

1995 that number had increased to more than 850,000. To put this in perspective, in 1951 there was one lawyer per 700 people; in 1995 the ratio was one per 300.[39] With one lawyer for every 24 persons, Washington, D.C., has the highest density of lawyers in the country.[40] In contrast, Arkansas has the lowest density of lawyers with one for every 556 persons.[41]

The demographics of the legal profession have also changed, especially with regard to gender. In 1951, there were about 5,500 female lawyers in the United States—less than 3 percent of the profession. By 1980 females constituted 8 percent of the profession, but by 1995 their representation had grown to 24 percent. In the 1950s, it was common for law school classes to be all male. By the 1997–1998 academic year, 45 percent of the law students were female. It is not uncommon today for women to outnumber men in law school classes.[42] The legal "fraternity" is rapidly vanishing. It is being replaced by a more diverse profession—one that is more representative of the population it serves.

THE ADVERSARIAL SYSTEM OF JUSTICE

The American court system follows the historic **adversarial system** this nation inherited from the English common law. Unlike the system that prevails in civil law countries (see Chapter 1), the adversarial system separates the function of gathering evidence from the judge's role in pretrial and trial processes. The theory is that by a judge not having participated in the investigative process assures the parties their case will be heard before a neutral decision maker.

In the adversary process the competing parties develop the evidence through investigation. Parties, usually through their lawyers, present their evidence and arguments in support of their positions and seek to demonstrate the weakness of the other side of the case. This affords each party an opportunity to have a lawyer-conducted examination and cross-examination of witnesses, and challenges to the evidence and argument presented by the opposing sides. An important aspect of the adversarial system is the development of detailed procedural rules that a judge must apply impartially, irrespective of the merits of a party's case.

Juries

Juries are not a necessary part of the legal system in civil law countries (see Chapter 1); however, in some civil law countries lay judges assist the professional judge in the decision-making processes. Although a jury is not essential to the functioning of the adversarial system, in America it is a vital component of the system. Juries are deeply rooted in Anglo-American tradition. In the late eighteenth century, William Blackstone called the jury a "strong barrier between the liberties of the people and the prerogative of the crown."[43] Today, Americans continue to regard the jury as an important check on government. Even though Americans are frequently frustrated by jury verdicts that seem unjust or even inexplicable, and are often annoyed by the inconvenience of jury duty, support for the institution remains strong.

In America, juries are selected from a cross section of the adult community without regard to educational attainments. Thus, a college professor may be seated next to an elementary school dropout. To assure an impartial jury, parties have the right to challenge jurors as to their basic qualifications to render a fair and impartial verdict. Although a prospective juror is not usually disqualified by having heard or read about a case, a juror who has formed an opinion about a pending case or who may have an interest in the litigation will be disqualified from serving. Juries decide the facts in a case and must apply the law as instructed by the presiding judge. Historically a juror was not permitted to ask questions, only to hear the evidence presented. The trend is to allow jurors to ask the presiding judge to have lawyers pose their questions to a witness. Where this is permitted, the judge has broad discretion in such matters. We explain the selection process of jurors and their functions in the decision-making process in later chapters.

Trial Procedures

We also explain the procedures in a civil and criminal trial in later chapters. Many of these adversary processes such as depositions and other discovery processes occur during pretrial phases of litigation, but for now it is helpful to become acquainted with the basic steps at trial.

1. Opening statements: The plaintiff's attorney or the prosecutor and the defendant's attorney outline their theories of the case and the evidence to be presented.
2. Direct examination by plaintiff or prosecutor: The plaintiff's attorney or prosecutor questions witnesses and presents documentary and physical evidence.
3. Cross-examination by defense: The defendant's attorney may cross-examine the plaintiff's or prosecutor's witnesses in an attempt to discredit their testimony.
4. Motions by defense: The judge rules on any defense motions to dismiss the plaintiff's case or to grant acquittal and discharge the defendant.
5. Direct examination by defense: The defendant's attorney proceeds along the lines outlined in step 2.
6. Cross-examination by the plaintiff or prosecutor: The plaintiff or prosecutor proceeds as outlined in step 3.
7. Closing arguments: The plaintiff or prosecutor and the defense attorney present their closing arguments summarizing the evidence and seeking to persuade the jury (or the court in a nonjury trial) of their respective positions.
8. Jury instructions: In a jury trial, the court instructs the jury members as to the law applicable to the case and their responsibilities in arriving at a verdict.
9. Verdict and judgment: The jury returns its verdict and the court subsequently enters a judgment in favor of the prevailing party in a civil case or enters a judgment of conviction and proceeds to sentence the defendant or to discharge the defendant if acquitted. In a nonjury case, the court makes a disposition of the case and enters judgment accordingly.

ALTERNATIVE DISPUTE RESOLUTION

Courts and regulatory agencies represent traditional means of formal conflict resolution. They focus on adjudicatory means of dispute resolution. With the increased involvement of government in the lives of individuals and businesses and the diminished role of informal dispute resolution in the family and religious institutions, many have seen a need for fair, efficient, economical, yet informal means of dispute resolution. These alternate methods of dispute resolution take several forms, some voluntary and some involuntary.

Private arbitration is a voluntary method of dispute resolution. It has historic roots. In an effort to ward off any possible litigation, President George Washington included an arbitration clause in his will to the effect that any disputes be decided "by three intelligent and impartial men known for their probity and good understanding." Today many construction, employment, and brokerage agreements include provisions requiring arbitration of any dispute arising out of the contract. Parties select an arbitrator or a panel of three arbitrators, usually persons who have experience in the area of the dispute. Each party has an opportunity to present various forms of proof including live witnesses. The proceedings are usually private and the procedure is informal with participants agreeing to be bound by the decision of the arbitrators. Judicial review is generally limited to issues of misconduct of the arbitrators.

To speed the resolution of court cases, a number of jurisdictions have recently adopted court-ordered **arbitration.** Usually neither party is bound to accept the results, however, the court may impose sanctions on a party who has rejected the results of arbitration and fails to obtain a more satisfactory result in court.

Negotiation remains the primary tool of **alternative dispute resolution** not involving adjudicatory procedures. Negotiation frequently takes place without court supervision. In other instances it may be a means of settling pending litigation trial. Much civil litigation is resolved through some form of negotiation undertaken by lawyers who are trained in evaluating the merits of positions taken by parties.

Mediation has become the most popular form of alternate dispute resolution. It is a process whereby a neutral third party acts as a facilitator in an informal and nonadversarial process to assist the disputants to reach a mutually agreeable settlement. Some jurisdictions have mediation training programs and prescribe competency and ethical standards for mediators. Mediation may take place irrespective of pending litigation, but most mediation occurs while litigation is pending. The mediator encourages parties to communicate freely with the understanding that communications are confidential and statements made cannot be used in court proceedings. The mediator will point out problems incident to each party's position, often in private conference with a party and that party's counsel. Voluntary mediators often serve in small claims courts to assist litigants, most of whom are not represented by counsel.

In family law disputes, personal injury cases, and other major legal controversies, parties often agree to mediation. The parties select and pay the fees of a mediator, which may be based on the mediator's expertise in a given field. Experienced lawyers are frequently called upon to serve as mediators. Legal counsel often represent parties, but the procedure remains informal. In some instances a court will order the parties to mediate a pending case and will appoint the mediator.

The ability of legal counsel to successfully negotiate becomes a key factor in mediation. Much of mediation proceeds on a give-and-take basis. It has the advantage of allowing parties to fashion an agreement with more flexibility than can often be obtained in court. Where agreement is reached it is reduced to writing and signed by the parties and mediator.

In cases when litigation is pending, the agreement is generally filed with the court and enforced as a resolution of the dispute. In family law matters, the court usually determines if the agreement is in the best interests of the parties when minor children are involved.

Although arbitration and mediation are more popular, other forms of alternate dispute resolution include a mini-trial or summary jury trial. In a mini-trial, the parties present their proofs in a summary manner in a private proceeding with the expectation that they can agree on a decision proposed by the advisor. In a summary jury trial, each side in a litigated case presents a summary of that party's case to a mock jury under relaxed rules of evidence and procedure. The jury renders an advisory verdict that is nonbinding but often accepted by the parties.

CONCLUSION

The American legal system is extremely complicated, due in large part to federalism: the division of political and legal authority among one national government and 50 state governments. No two sets of state laws are identical. Even when states have emulated laws of other states, there are likely to be nuances. No two state court systems are exactly alike. Even those that are superficially similar are likely to have significant jurisdictional, procedural, and administrative differences. The federal system is also quite unique in many respects.

The American legal system depends on the contributions of many different actors, most notably the legislators who write statutes, the chief executives and other executive officials who enforce them, and the judges who apply them to specific cases. The system also depends on litigants, people who are willing to subject their disputes to courts of law for orderly and peaceful resolution, as well as the lawyers who help litigants navigate a legal maze that can be at times frustrating. Other actors who are essential to the functioning of the legal system include legislative staffers, law clerks, research aides, bailiffs, sheriffs, jurors, stenographers, police officers, customs agents, postal inspectors, marshals, constables, corrections officers, secretaries, paralegals, and many more. Ultimately, though, the American legal system depends on the faith and support of average Americans who are asked to believe that our legal system represents a sincere effort to achieve the rule of law in this country.

SUMMARY OF KEY CONCEPTS

American government is complicated because it is a federal system with powers shared between national and state office holders. At the federal level, lawmaking is primarily a legislative function performed by elected members of the U.S. Senate and House of Representatives. At the state level, elected legislatures perform this function.

Federal and state judicial systems interpret the laws and sometimes fill in gaps in the law by "making law." Federal district courts are trial courts; the U.S. Courts of Appeals perform appellate review. State courts are structured similarly with trial and appellate courts. The U.S. Supreme Court sits at the apex of the judicial system. Its jurisdiction is almost entirely discretionary but its judgments, particularly those determining the constitutionality of federal and state laws, vitally affect the entire legal system. The President, with consent of the U.S. Senate, appoints judges of most federal courts for life; state court judges come into office by election or by various means of appointment.

Each level of government has an executive department. At the national level the President performs this function; at the state level, the governor. At local levels a mayor or commission chair serve as executives. The executive branch of each level of government functions largely through various regulatory and administrative agencies. Law enforcement agencies operate at the federal, state, and local levels, as do prosecutorial offices.

Lawyers serve as advocates in criminal and civil court proceedings in our adversary system of justice, which in many instances relies on juries to determine guilt and innocence in criminal cases and awards in civil cases. In addition, lawyers serve as counselors on the law, advising clients in a variety of legal matters. The American legal system is based on adversary practice. Today many citizens rely on negotiation, arbitration, and mediation as alternative dispute processes.

QUESTIONS FOR THOUGHT AND DISCUSSION

1. When seeking to determine the status of a federal or state law, what advantage is gained by consulting a set of annotated statutes?

2. What is meant by the term *police power* as it relates to state legislatures?

3. Why did the U.S. Congress never adopt the English common law?

4. What is the difference between the *delegate* and *trustee* models of representation? If you were elected to your state legislature, which of these models would you espouse?

5. Why do we have separate state and federal court systems?

6. Which mode of selecting judges makes more sense, gubernatorial appointment or popular election? How does the Missouri Plan combine elements of both?

7. Is a President required to enforce a decision of the U.S. Supreme Court that the president believes to be contrary to the U.S. Constitution?

8. Is the president constitutionally required to enforce or abide by a Supreme Court decision that he (or she) believes to be contrary to the Constitution?

9. When is mediation a more desirable method of dispute resolution in a civil case than to seek recourse through a jury in a trial court?

10. What are the basic procedural steps in a civil or criminal trial?

11. Should attorneys be permitted to advertise their services on television, radio, and the internet?

12. Explain the concept of a *unified bar*. What advantages or disadvantages do you find?

KEY TERMS

federalism	judicial review	enumerated powers
police power	legislators	implied powers
concurrent powers	delegates	oversight
legislature	trustees	veto
law enforcement agencies	Congress	U.S. Code

session laws

trial courts

appellate courts

federal question jurisdiction

diversity of citizenship jurisdiction

U.S. District Courts

U.S. Courts of Appeals

U.S. Supreme Court

original jurisdiction

concurrent jurisdiction

appellate jurisdiction

appeals of right

writ of certiorari

law clerks

rules of procedure

Tax Court

Court of Veterans' Appeals

Court of Federal Claims

tort claims

Court of International Trade

Uniform Code of Military Justice

courts-martial

U.S. Court of Appeals for the Armed Forces

impeachment

federal magistrate judges

court of last resort

state supreme court

intermediate appellate courts

judicial accountability

judicial independence

Missouri Plan

judicial disciplinary commissions

rules of practice

criminal prosecutions

civil suits

plea bargaining

trial

damages

injunctions

restraining orders

writ of mandamus

writ of habeas corpus

writ of prohibition

contempt

criminal contempt

civil contempt

collegial courts

opinions

administrative agencies

regulatory agencies

independent agencies

administrative law

forensic evidence

community-oriented policing

Federal Bureau of Investigation (FBI)

Department of Justice

Secret Service

Bureau of Alcohol, Tobacco and Firearms (ATF)

sheriff

prosecutors

prosecutorial discretion

attorney general

U.S. attorneys

independent counsel

state's attorneys

unified bar

paralegal

professional responsibility

adversarial system

arbitration

negotiation

alternative dispute resolution

mediation

ENDNOTES

[1]U.S. Const. Art. I, § 8.

[2]A major exception applies, however, to the third option: If Congress adjourns before the 10 days have expired and the president has still not signed the bill, it is said to have been subjected to a *pocket veto.*

[3]Students can access the U.S. Code on line at *http://www4.law.cornell.edu/uscode/.*

[4]1 Stat. 73.

[5]U.S. Const. Art. III, § 2.

[6]28 U.S.C.A. § 1331.

[7]28 U.S.C.A. § 1332.

[8]For provisions of the U.S. Code dealing with the district courts, see 28 U.S.C.A. §§ 81–132.

[9]See 28 U.S.C.A. §§ 151–158.

[10]There are also federal district courts in Guam, Puerto Rico, the Northern Marianna Islands, the Virgin Islands, and the District of Columbia.

[11]The U.S. District Court for the Eastern District of Tennessee is based in Knoxville. The Middle District is based in Nashville. The Western District is based in Jackson.

[12]California's four federal judicial districts are based in San Francisco (Northern), Sacramento (Eastern), Los Angeles

(Central), and San Diego (Southern). New York's four districts are based in Syracuse (Northern), Buffalo (Western), Brooklyn (Eastern), and Manhattan (Southern).

[13]Administrative Office of the United States Courts.

[14]Chief Justice William H. Rehnquist, *1999 Year End Report on the Federal Judiciary* (Administrative Office of the United States Courts, 2000).

[15]Administrative Office of the United States Courts, *Annual Report of the Director, 1982* (Administrative Office of the United States Courts, 1982).

[16]For provisions of the U.S. Code dealing with the U.S. Courts of Appeals, see 28 U.S.C.A. §§ 41–49.

[17]26 Stat. 828.

[18]Administrative Office of the United States Courts, *Annual Report of the Director, 1999* (Administrative Office of the United States Courts, 1999).

[19]For provisions of the U.S. Code dealing with the Supreme Court, see 28 U.S.C.A. §§ 1–6.

[20]U.S. Const. Art. III, § 2.

[21]The Supreme Court's jurisdiction is set forth in 28 U.S.C.A. §§ 1251–1259.

[22]See 28 U.S.C.A. § 2071.

[23]See 28 U.S.C.A. §§ 251–258; §§ 1581–1585; §§ 2631–2647.

[24]See 28 U.S.C.A. § 1295.

[25]See 10 U.S.C.A. §§ 801–940.

[26]U.S. Const. Art. III, § 1.

[27]U.S. Const. Art. I, § 2.

[28]U.S. Const. Art. I, § 3.

[29]*Bloom v. Illinois,* 391 U.S. 194, 88 S.Ct. 1477, 20 L.Ed.2d 522 (1968).

[30]5 U.S. 137, 2 L.Ed. 60 (1803).

[31]See *Koon v. United States,* 518 U.S. 81, 116 S.Ct. 2035, 135 L.Ed.2d 392 (1996).

[32]The law enforcement authority of the Secret Service is provided by 18 U.S.C.A. § 3056.

[33]Information available at the DEA website, located at *www.usdoj.gov/dea.*

[34]This is why London police officers are still referred to as "Bobbies."

[35]The *U.S. News and World Report* annually presents a magazine feature on what it considers the top 50 law schools and its classification of the remaining 124 law schools by second, third, and fourth tiers along with the criteria on which it bases its scale. Additionally, it identifies law schools that are highly ranked in particular areas of legal education.

[36]*Keller v. State Bar of California,* 496 U.S. 1, 110 S.Ct. 2228, 110 L.Ed.2d 1 (1990).

[37]*Goldfarb v. Virginia State Bar,* 421 U.S. 773, 95 S.Ct. 2004, 44 L.Ed.2d 572 (1975).

[38]*Bates v. State Bar of Arizona,* 433 U.S. 350, 97 S.Ct. 2691, 53 L.Ed.2d 810 (1977).

[39]See Carson, *The Lawyer Statistical Report, The U.S. Legal Profession in 1995* (1999).

[40]Id. at 61.

[41]Id. at 41.

[42]Id. at 4.

[43]W. Blackstone, *Commentaries on the Laws of England* 349–350 (T. Cooley 4th ed. 1896).

FOR FURTHER READING

Abraham, Henry J., *The Judiciary: The Supreme Court in the Governmental Process* (10th ed., Allyn and Bacon 1996).

Baum, Lawrence, *American Courts: Process and Policy* (4th ed., Houghton Mifflin 1998).

Baum, Lawrence, *The Supreme Court* (5th ed., Congressional Quarterly Press 1995).

Carp, Robert A., and Ronald Stidham, *The Federal Courts* (3rd ed., CQ Press 1998).

Coffin, Frank M., *The Ways of a Judge* (Houghton Mifflin 1980).

Kalven, Harry, and Hans Zeisel, *The American Jury* (University of Chicago Press 1966).

Lazarus, Edward, *Closed Chambers: The First Eyewitness Account of the Epic Struggles Inside the Supreme Court* (Times Books 1998).

Neely, Richard, *How Courts Govern America* (Yale University Press 1981).

Schwartz, Bernard, with Stephen Lesher, *Inside the Warren Court* (Doubleday 1983).

Wasby, Stephen, *The Supreme Court in the Federal Judicial System* (4th ed., Nelson-Hall 1993).

Woodward, Bob, and Scott Armstrong, *The Brethren: Inside the Supreme Court* (Simon and Schuster 1979).

PART II

The Substance of the Law

3

CONSTITUTIONAL LAW

Courtesy of National Archives and Records Administration

LEARNING OBJECTIVES

This chapter should enable the student to understand:

- the concept of judicial review and interpretive powers of courts
- legislative functions based on constitutionally enumerated and implied powers
- how executive powers have been expanded administratively and judicially
- how the principle of separation of powers and related system of checks and balances and federalism define American government
- how the Constitution protects civil rights and liberties
- the significance of the Fourteenth Amendment provisions and the judicial interpretations of "due process of law" and "equal protection of the laws"

CHAPTER OUTLINE

Introduction

Judicial Review

Legislative Power

Executive Power

Separation of Powers

Federalism

Civil Rights and Liberties

Conclusion

Summary of Key Concepts

Questions for Thought and Discussion

Key Terms

For Further Reading

INTRODUCTION

The federal government and each of the 50 state governments are based on written constitutions. Each of these constitutions sets forth the structure and powers of government as well as the rights of citizens. The term *constitutional law* refers to the judicial interpretation of these constitutions in the context of legal disputes. These disputes arise in both state and federal courts. Each of the 50 states has its own court system, responsible for interpreting its own state constitution and, in some instances, the federal constitution. Because of the variations in state constitutional law, this chapter focuses on federal constitutional law. It is important to understand, however, that because the federal constitution is the "supreme law of the land," state constitutions (as well as statutes and local ordinances) must conform to the principles of the U.S. Constitution. All federal courts interpret the U.S. Constitution, but because the U.S. Supreme Court sits at the apex of the federal judicial hierarchy, the Supreme Court is the most important developer of constitutional law.

Constitutional law has two basic components: the institutional component and the civil rights/civil liberties component. The former component embraces issues of congressional, presidential, and judicial power as well as questions of state versus national authority and problems of interstate relations. The latter component involves claims of personal freedom and legal and political equality, usually asserted in opposition to exercises of governmental power.

JUDICIAL REVIEW

In its most general sense, **judicial review** refers to the authority of a court of law to review a particular legal issue. In constitutional law, however, the term has more specific meaning. It refers to the power of courts to declare government actions invalid if they are determined to be contrary to constitutional principles. The U.S. Constitution does not explicitly grant the power of judicial review. However, in *Marbury v. Madison* (1803),[1] the Supreme Court assumed the power to strike down unconstitutional federal statutes. Later the Court extended the scope of judicial review to encompass executive actions[2] and state statutes.[3] Today, all actions of government, from the conduct of police officers on the street to orders issued by the President, are subject to judicial review. Judicial review has become a bedrock principle of the American legal and political systems. It is generally regarded as essential to preserve the ideal of constitutional supremacy.

Constitutional Interpretation

The exercise of judicial review requires courts to interpret the Constitution. When possible, courts rely on the plain meaning of the text, but the meaning of many constitutional provisions is not self-evident. Courts often seek to discern the **intentions of the Framers** of the

Constitution. In determining original intent, courts often rely on the debate that took place during the Constitutional Convention in 1787. They also look to essays by James Madison, Alexander Hamilton, and John Jay written during the debate over ratification of the Constitution and later published as *The Federalist Papers.*

The **doctrine of original intent** is not universally accepted. Many judges and commentators believe that the intentions of the Framers are impossible to discern on a number of issues. Others argue that original intent, even if knowable, should not control contemporary constitutional decision making. These commentators extoll the virtues of the **living Constitution,** whose meaning evolves according to what Justice Oliver Wendell Holmes called the "felt necessities" of the times. The Supreme Court has never resolved the issue of constitutional interpretation. Rather, the Court's numerous decisions reflect an ongoing debate over how the eighteenth century Constitution should be applied to contemporary circumstances.

Precedent

In the common-law tradition, courts rely on **precedent,** which means that they generally follow what courts have said and done in the past. This doctrine of *stare decisis,* which literally means "to stand by things decided," applies to constitutional law as well. Courts tend to interpret provisions of the Constitution in the same fashion that they have been interpreted by courts in previous cases. But the doctrine of precedent is by no means absolute, and courts will frequently overturn or abandon precedent in constitutional cases. As the Supreme Court has observed,

> Adhering to precedent "is usually the wise policy, because in most matters it is more important that the applicable rule of law be settled than it be settled right." . . . Nevertheless, when governing decisions are unworkable or are badly reasoned, "this Court has never felt constrained to follow precedent." . . . *Stare decisis* is not an inexorable command; rather, it "is a principle of policy and not a mechanical formula of adherence to the latest decision." . . . This is particularly true in constitutional cases, because in such cases "correction through legislative action is practically impossible."[4]

Perhaps the best known example of a long-standing precedent that was later overturned is the Supreme Court's decision in *Plessy v. Ferguson* (1896).[5] In *Plessy,* the Court upheld a Louisiana law that required racial segregation on passenger trains. The statute was merely one of many such "Jim Crow laws" that were common in the American South well into the twentieth century. The law was challenged as a violation of the Fourteenth Amendment, which forbids states from denying equal protection of the laws to persons within their jurisdiction. Under the pretense that segregation was not inherently unequal, the Supreme Court found no violation of equal protection and upheld the statute. Thus the "separate but equal" doctrine became the law of the land. Fifty-eight years later, in the landmark case of *Brown v. Board of Education,*[6] the Supreme Court repudiated the separate but equal doctrine in the context of public education. In later decisions during the 1950s and 1960s, the Court would abolish the separate but equal doctrine altogether.

Limiting Doctrines

Because judicial review is inherently counter-majoritarian, and because the exercise of judicial review can produce intense political conflict, courts tend to be cautious in exercising this authority. This caution is often referred to as **judicial self-restraint,** whereas the absence of caution is dubbed **judicial activism.** Judicial self-restraint is manifested in a number of doctrines limiting the exercise of judicial review. Judicial activism consists largely in ignoring or circumventing these limiting doctrines.

Perhaps the most fundamental limiting doctrine is the **presumption of constitutionality.** Under this doctrine, courts will presume a challenged statute or governmental action is valid until it is demonstrated otherwise. In other words, the party bringing the constitutional challenge carries the burden of persuasion. This doctrine is based on an appreciation for the counter-majoritarian character of judicial review and a fundamental respect for the legislative bodies in a democratic system. However, the Supreme Court has modified the doctrine of presumptive constitutionality with respect to laws discriminating against citizens on grounds of race or national origin. Such laws are now viewed as inherently suspect and are subjected to **strict judicial scrutiny.**[7] Similarly, laws abridging fundamental rights such as freedom of speech are not afforded the traditional presumption of validity.[8]

Another fundamental limiting doctrine is that of **standing.** A party seeking judicial review of a law must have standing to challenge that law, which means that the operation of the law must produce a substantial injury to the rights of the party seeking review. For example, a federal taxpayer who believes that a particular federal program is unconstitutional does not normally have standing to challenge the law on which the program is based.[9] However, a person who is prosecuted criminally under an arguably unconstitutional statute certainly has standing to challenge that statute.[10] In many instances one who is likely to be prosecuted or whose activities are chilled or deterred by the existence of a statute can bring a civil suit seeking to enjoin enforcement of the law. Such was the case in *Roe v. Wade* (1973),[11] in which a woman facing an unwanted pregnancy brought suit in federal court to challenge the constitutionality of a Texas law criminalizing most abortions. The Supreme Court's decision to strike down the Texas law, and thus effectively legalize abortion throughout the country, was perhaps the most controversial exercise of judicial review in the modern age.

In a concurring opinion in *Ashwander v. Tennessee Valley Authority* (1936),[12] Associate Justice Louis D. Brandeis set forth the basic limiting doctrines observed by courts in the exercise of judicial review:

1. The Court will not pass upon the constitutionality of legislation in a friendly, non-adversary, proceeding, declining because to decide such questions "is legitimate only in the last resort, and as a necessity in the determination of real, earnest, and vital controversy between individuals. It never was the thought that, by means of a friendly suit, a party beaten in the legislature could transfer to the courts an inquiry as to the constitutionality of the legislative act."
2. The Court will not "anticipate a question of constitutional law in advance of the necessity of deciding it."
3. The Court will not "formulate a rule of constitutional law broader than is required by the precise facts to which it is to be applied."

4. The Court will not pass upon a constitutional question although properly presented by the record, if there is also present some other ground upon which the case may be disposed of. . . . Thus, if a case can be decided on either of two grounds, one involving a constitutional question, the other a question of statutory construction or general law, the Court will decide only the latter.
5. The Court will not pass upon the validity of a statute upon complaint of one who fails to show that he is injured by its operation.
6. The Court will not pass upon the constitutionality of a statute at the instance of one who has availed himself of its benefits.
7. "When the validity of an act of the Congress is drawn in question, and even if a serious doubt of constitutionality is raised, it is a cardinal principle that this Court will first ascertain whether a construction of the statute is fairly possible by which the question may be avoided."

The so-called *Ashwander* **rules** obviously limit the exercise of judicial review and, accordingly, reduce the potential for political conflict flowing from an ill-advised or untimely use of judicial power. It must be pointed out, however, that the *Ashwander* rules are frequently honored in the breach. In the modern era, courts tend to be less cautious in their exercise of judicial review. Under Chief Justice Earl Warren (1953–1969) the Court was particularly active in its use of judicial review. The Warren Court rendered numerous decisions that contradicted public opinion and aroused the ire of politicians at all levels of government. Of course, because the courts function within the constitutional system of checks and balances, there are a number of external constraints on judicial power. These constraints prevent the courts from straying too far from mainstream opinion.

Restriction of the Court's Jurisdiction

The Supreme Court's original jurisdiction is fixed by Article III of the Constitution. *Marbury v. Madison* made clear that Congress may not alter the Court's original jurisdiction. Congress may, however, authorize lower federal courts to share the Court's original jurisdiction. The Supreme Court's appellate jurisdiction is another matter. Article III indicates that the Court " . . . shall have appellate Jurisdiction, both as to Law and Fact, with such Exceptions, and under such Regulations as the Congress shall make."

On only one occasion has Congress significantly limited the appellate jurisdiction of the Supreme Court. It happened during the turbulent Reconstruction period that followed the Civil War. Congress restricted the Court's appellate jurisdiction in a certain category of cases to prevent the Court from ruling on the constitutionality of the Reconstruction program. In *Ex Parte McCardle* (1869) the Court acquiesced in the curtailment of its jurisdiction, thus buttressing congressional control of the Court.[13]

Congress has, on several occasions, debated limitations on the Supreme Court's appellate jurisdiction. In the late 1950s, there was a movement in Congress to deny the Supreme Court appellate jurisdiction in cases involving national security, a reaction to Warren Court decisions protecting the rights of suspected Communists. Although the major legislative proposals were narrowly defeated, the Court retreated from some of its most controversial decisions.[14]

Does *Ex Parte McCardle* suggest that Congress could completely abolish the Court's appellate jurisdiction? Whatever the answer might have been in 1869, the answer today would certainly be no. It is highly unlikely that Congress would ever undertake such a radical measure, but if it did the Supreme Court would almost certainly declare the act invalid. Because the Court's major decision-making role is a function of its appellate jurisdiction, any serious curtailment of that jurisdiction would in effect deny the Court the ability to perform its essential function in the constitutional system.

In the early 1980s, a flurry of activity in Congress was aimed at restricting Supreme Court jurisdiction to hear appeals in cases dealing with abortion and school prayer. A number of proposals surfaced, but none was adopted. The constitutionality of such proposals is open to question, in that they might be construed as undermining the Court's ability to protect fundamental constitutional rights. The question remains academic, however, as Congress has not enacted such a restriction on the Court. Denial of jurisdiction as a limiting strategy depends greatly on the substantive issue-area involved, what the Court has done in the area thus far, and what it is likely to do in the future. As retaliation against the Court for one controversial decision, the curtailment of appellate jurisdiction is not likely to be an effective strategy.

Constitutional Amendment

From time to time Congress will attempt to overturn, evade, or modify a Supreme Court decision through the enactment of legislation. The Court will generally not permit this, as it reserves to itself the final word in matters of constitutional interpretation.[15] The only conclusive means of overruling a Supreme Court or any federal court decision is through adoption of a constitutional amendment. If Congress disapproves of a particular judicial decision, it may be able to override that decision through a simple statute, but only if the decision was based on statutory interpretation. It is much more difficult to override a federal court decision that is based on the U.S. Constitution. Congress alone cannot do so. Ever since *Marbury v. Madison,* our system of government has conceded to the courts the power to authoritatively interpret the nation's charter. A Supreme Court decision interpreting the Constitution is therefore final unless and until one of two things occurs. First, the Court may overrule itself in a later case. This has happened numerous times historically. The only other way to overturn a constitutional decision of the Supreme Court is through constitutional amendment. This is not easily done, since Article V of the Constitution prescribes a two-thirds majority in both houses of Congress followed by ratification by three-fourths of the states. Yet on at least four occasions in our history specific Supreme Court decisions have been overturned in this manner.[16]

Over the years numerous unsuccessful attempts have been made to overrule Supreme Court decisions through constitutional amendments. In 1983, an amendment providing that "[t]he right to an abortion is not secured by this Constitution," obviously aimed at *Roe v. Wade,* failed to pass the Senate by only one vote. The most recent example of a proposed constitutional amendment aimed at a Supreme Court decision dealt with the emotional public issue of flag burning. In 1989, the Court held that burning the American flag as part of a public protest was a form of symbolic speech protected by the First Amendment.[17]

Many, including President Bush, called on Congress to overrule the Court. Congress considered an amendment that read, "The Congress and the States shall have power to prohibit the physical desecration of the flag of the United States." Votes were taken in both houses, but neither achieved the necessary two-thirds majority. As recently as 1997, the U.S. House of Representatives passed another proposed constitutional amendment designed to overrule the Court's flag-burning decisions. However, this measure was not approved by the requisite two-thirds vote in the Senate.

The Appointment Power as a Check on the Courts

As discussed in Chapter 2, all federal judges are appointed by the President subject to the consent of the Senate. Normally, the Senate consents to presidential judicial appointments with a minimum of controversy. However, senatorial approval is by no means automatic, especially when the opposing political party controls the Senate. The shared presidential/senatorial power of appointing federal judges is an important means of influencing the judiciary. For example, President Richard Nixon made a significant impact on the Supreme Court and on American constitutional law through his appointment of four justices. During the 1968 presidential campaign, Nixon criticized the Warren Court's decisions, especially in the criminal law area, and promised to appoint "strict constructionists" to the bench. President Nixon's first appointment came in 1969 when Warren E. Burger was selected to succeed Earl Warren as chief justice. Nixon would appoint three more justices to the Court: Lewis Powell, Harry Blackmun, and William Rehnquist (who was elevated to chief justice by President Reagan in 1986). The four Nixon appointments had a moderating influence on the Supreme Court and set the stage for the emergence of the more conservative Rehnquist Court in the 1980s. This shows how the appointment process provides an indirect democratic control on the courts, ensuring that judicial interpretation of the Constitution will not move too far from a national consensus.

LEGISLATIVE POWER

Having discussed the power of judicial review and its exercise under the system of checks and balances, we turn now to the substance of constitutional law, beginning with the interpretation of Article I, which defines the legislative power.

Article I, Section 1 of the Constitution provides that "[a]ll legislative powers herein granted shall be vested in a Congress of the United States, which shall consist of a Senate and a House of Representatives." Article I delineates the composition of both houses of Congress, indicates minimal qualifications for members, specifies how members are to be chosen, grants broad authority to each house to determine its own procedures, and extends certain privileges to members of Congress. Article I also defines the legislative powers of Congress, although grants of congressional authority are also found elsewhere in the Constitution.

Enumerated Powers

Most of the **enumerated powers** of Congress are located in Article I, Section 8, which consists of 17 brief paragraphs enumerating specific powers followed by a general clause permitting Congress to "make all laws which shall be necessary and proper for carrying into Execution the foregoing powers, and all other powers vested by this Constitution in the Government of the United States. . . ." The powers enumerated in Article I, Section 8 authorize Congress to lay and collect taxes; borrow money; regulate commerce among the states; control immigration and naturalization; regulate bankruptcy; coin money; fix standards of weights and measures; establish post offices and post roads; grant patents and copyrights; establish tribunals "inferior to the Supreme Court;" declare war; raise and support an army and a navy; regulate the militia when called into service; and perform other more restricted functions.

In reading Article I, Section 8, one will note that, although Congress is empowered to "provide for the common defense and general welfare of the United States," there is no general grant of police power to Congress. The power to make any and all laws deemed necessary for the protection of the public health, safety, welfare, and morals is thus reserved to the states under the Tenth Amendment. Yet Congress exercises substantial legislative power by linking laws to the specific powers contained in Section 8. For example, Congress is not empowered to prohibit prostitution per se, but it can make it a crime to transport persons across state lines for "immoral purposes" by drawing on its broad power to regulate "commerce among the states."[18] Over the years, the power to regulate interstate commerce has been invoked to justify a wide range of federal legislation, including laws relating to telecommunications, the natural environment, civil rights, and organized crime. One is tempted to argue that Congress has acquired a police power through its reliance on the Commerce Clause and the courts' willingness to interpret the clause liberally. However, in 1995, the Supreme Court held that the Commerce Clause is not boundless and does not confer a general police power on the Congress. In *United States v. Lopez,* the Court struck down a federal law making it a crime to possess a firearm in close proximity to a school.[19] Noting that most states already had similar prohibitions, the Court held that the mere act of possessing a firearm was not sufficiently related to interstate commerce to permit Congress to reach this activity. In a similar vein, the Court in 2000 struck down the Federal Violence against Women Act of 1994 on the ground that Congress had exceeded its power under the Commerce Clause (see Case in Point on p.81).

Implied Powers

It is obvious that Congress today exercises far more powers than are specifically enumerated in the Constitution. Over the years, the American people have come to expect, even demand, as much. Yet arguably Congress has remained within the scope of powers delegated to it by the Constitution. The linchpin of this argument is the Necessary and Proper Clause (Article I, Section 8, clause 18) and the related doctrine of **implied powers**. In fact, the Necessary and Proper Clause is today, along with the Commerce, Taxing, and Spending Clauses, one of the key sources of congressional power.

CASE IN POINT

THE CONSTITUTIONALITY OF THE FEDERAL VIOLENCE AGAINST WOMEN ACT OF 1994

United States v. Morrison

United States Supreme Court
529 U.S. 598, 120 S.Ct. 1740, 146 L.Ed.2d 658 (2000)

After allegedly being raped by two members of the football team, a female student at Virginia Tech filed suit under 42 U. S. C. § 13981. Known as the Federal Violence against Women Act of 1994, this statute provided a federal civil remedy for the victims of gender-motivated violence. The defendants moved to dismiss, challenging the constitutionality of the statute. The U.S. Justice Department intervened to defend the statute's constitutionality. In dismissing the complaint, the district court held that Congress lacked authority to enact §13981 under either the Commerce Clause or the Fourteenth Amendment. The U.S. Court of Appeals for the Fourth Circuit affirmed, as did the Supreme Court on certiorari. Writing for the Court, Chief Justice Rehnquist observed that, "If the allegations here are true, no civilized system of justice could fail to provide her a remedy for the conduct.... But under our federal system that remedy must be provided by the Commonwealth of Virginia, and not by the United States." The Court's decision showed that the Court was unwilling to allow Congress to use the Commerce Clause as a boundless source of legislative authority, especially in areas traditionally left to the states.

The doctrine of implied powers was firmly established in the landmark case of *McCulloch v. Maryland* (1819).[20] The doctrine holds that Congress may enact laws that are reasonably related to its enumerated powers, as long as Congress does not violate a specific prohibition of the Constitution. Under the doctrine of implied powers, scarcely any area exists in which Congress is absolutely barred from acting, since most problems have a conceivable relationship to the broad powers and objectives contained in the Constitution.

Congress has many sources of constitutional authority. Some of these are quite explicit, as the list of enumerated powers in Article I, Section 8 makes clear. Others are implicit, open-ended, and subject to no complete or conclusive definition. These implied powers are fully recognized, however, in the Necessary and Proper Clause and in the enforcement provisions of several constitutional amendments, most notably the Thirteenth, Fourteenth, and Fifteenth. Within this broad range of explicit and implicit powers, Congress has ample latitude to address the major problems, needs, and goals of the nation, as perceived by succeeding generations of Americans during two centuries of constitutional history.

The Power to Investigate

Although legislation is a principal function of Congress, **oversight** of the executive branch is also an important responsibility. To this end, congressional committees conduct investigations in which they hold hearings and call witnesses to testify. Sometimes these investigations have been great public events, such as the Watergate hearings of 1973 and 1974, which led to the demise of the Nixon presidency. However, Article I makes no mention of Congress having the **power to investigate**. In 1881, the Supreme Court confronted this problem.[21] It held that congressional power to investigate is a necessary auxiliary of the legislative function.

Opinion of the Court . . .

McCULLOCH v. MARYLAND
4 Wheat. (17 U.S.) 316; 4 L. Ed. 579 (1819)

Mr. Chief Justice Marshall delivered the opinion of the Court.

...This government is acknowledged by all to be one of enumerated powers. . . . That principle is now universally admitted. But the question respecting the extent of the powers actually granted, is perpetually arising, and will probably continue to arise, as long as our system shall exist. . . .

We admit, as all must admit, that the powers of the government are limited, and that its limits are not to be transcended. But we think the sound construction of the Constitution must allow to the national legislature that discretion, with respect to the means by which the powers it confers are to be carried into execution, which will enable the body to perform the high duties assigned to it, in the manner most beneficial to the people. Let the end be legitimate, let it be within the scope of the Constitution, and all means which are appropriate, which

are plainly adapted to that end, which are not prohibited, but consist with the letter and spirit of the Constitution, are constitutional.

. . . Should Congress, in the execution of its powers, adopt measures which are prohibited by the Constitution; or should Congress, under the pretext of executing its powers pass laws for the accomplishment of objects not entrusted to the government, it would become the painful duty of this tribunal, should a case requiring such a decision come before it, to say that such an act was not the law of the land. But where the law is not prohibited, and is really calculated to effect any of the objects entrusted to the government, to undertake here to inquire into the degree of its necessity, would be to pass the line which circumscribes the judicial department, and to tread on legislative ground. This court disclaims all pretensions to such a power. . . .

Yet the implied power to investigate is not unlimited. It must be exercised only in relation to potential legislation. Today, there are few areas in which Congress may not potentially legislate; thus, there are few areas off limits to congressional investigation. Still, an investigation purely for its own sake is subject to judicial challenge.[22]

EXECUTIVE POWER

Article II, Section 1 of the Constitution provides that the "executive power shall be vested in a President of the United States." Sections 2 and 3 enumerate specific powers granted to the President. These include authority to appoint judges and ambassadors, veto legislation, call Congress into special session, grant pardons, and serve as commander in chief of the armed forces. Each of these designated powers is obviously a part of **executive power,** but that general term is not defined in Article II. Thus, it is debatable whether the opening statement of Article II was intended to be merely a summary of powers later enumerated in the article or, as Alexander Hamilton argued, an independent grant of power to the President.

CASE IN POINT

IS EXECUTIVE PRIVILEGE ABSOLUTE?

United States v. Nixon

United States Supreme Court
418 U.S. 904, 94 S.Ct. 3193, 41 L.Ed.2d 1152 (1974)

This case stems from President Nixon's refusal to comply with a *subpoena duces tecum* (an order to produce documents or other physical evidence) obtained by Watergate Special Prosecutor Leon Jaworksi. The subpoena directed President Nixon to produce the infamous Watergate Tapes on which were recorded conversations that took place in the Oval Office between President Nixon and his advisers. In refusing to honor the subpoena, President Nixon argued that the tapes were protected by executive privilege. Indeed, the president's counsel asserted that executive privilege is absolute and not subject to subpoena. The U.S. District Court for the District of Columbia, which had issued the subpoena, rejected the president's arguments and ordered him to produce the tapes. The president appealed to the Court of Appeals, but before the Circuit Court could act the Supreme Court granted Leon Jaworksi's petition for certiorari, citing great public importance of the matter and the need for prompt resolution of the conflict. On the merits, the Supreme Court ruled in favor of the special prosecutor. Writing for a unanimous Court, Chief Justice Warren E. Burger (a Nixon appointee) concluded that "when the ground for asserting privilege as to subpoenaed materials sought for use in a criminal trial is based only on the generalized interest in confidentiality, it cannot prevail over the fundamental demands of due process of law in the fair administration of criminal justice." President Nixon reluctantly complied with the Supreme Court's decision, surrendered the incriminating tapes, and resigned as president. *United States v. Nixon* is generally regarded as a vindication of the rule of law over political power and a fundamental reaffirmation of our constitutional democracy.

For the most part, Hamilton's argument has prevailed, as the Supreme Court has generally acquiesced in the expansion of executive authority beyond the powers enumerated in Article II. It would be naive to expect the Court to stem the flow of power into the executive branch, given the fundamental economic, social, technological, and military needs that have led to concentration of power in the presidency. There are cases in which the Court has invalidated particular exercises of executive power—for example, the Steel Seizure Case in 1952[23] and the Watergate Tapes Decision of 1974,[24] but the overall trend has been to legitimize broad presidential power. For example, in 1936, the Supreme Court placed its stamp of approval on presidential primacy in the realm of foreign affairs, referring to the President as the "sole organ of the federal government in the field of international relations."[25]

SEPARATION OF POWERS

The Constitution allocates the legislative, executive, and judicial functions of the national government to separate branches. Moreover, each branch has the means to resist encroachments and to check excesses by the other branches. The Framers of the Constitution viewed the constitutional principle of **separation of powers** and the related system of **checks and balances** as essential to the maintenance of limited government and, ultimately, individual liberty. As James Madison observed in *The Federalist* No. 47, "[t]he accumulation of all powers, legislative, executive, and judiciary, in the same hands . . . may justly be pronounced the very definition of tyranny."

Of course, the separation of powers is not absolute and the courts have on many occasions recognized exceptions to the principle. But in general the following rules apply. Congress may not exercise the appointment power, for that power is reserved to the president.[26] Congress may not invest itself, its members, or its agents with executive power.[27] Nor can Congress delegate wholesale legislative power to the executive branch.[28] However, as long as Congress "shall lay down by legislative act an intelligible principle to which the person or body authorized to [exercise the delegated power] is directed to conform, such legislative action is not a forbidden delegation of legislative power."[29] In the modern era, the Supreme Court has tended to be somewhat permissive in applying this principle, which has facilitated substantial delegations of power to federal regulatory agencies. The Court has observed that "in our increasingly complex society, replete with ever changing and more technical problems, Congress simply cannot do its job absent an ability to delegate power under broad general directives."[30]

One of the more difficult separation of powers issues came to the Supreme Court in 1988. *Morrison v. Olson*[31] tested the constitutionality of the independent counsel provisions of the Ethics in Government Act of 1978.[32] A legacy of the Watergate scandal, this act allowed for the appointment of an **independent counsel** to investigate and, if appropriate, prosecute certain high-ranking government officials for violations of federal criminal laws. The issue before the Court was whether the appointment of the independent counsel could be vested in a panel of federal judges rather than the President. The Court upheld the provision, saying that "we do not think that the Act 'impermissibly undermine[s]' the powers of the Executive Branch . . . or 'disrupts the proper balance between the coordinate branches [by] prevent[ing] the Executive Branch from accomplishing its constitutionally assigned functions'. . . ." Dissenting, Justice Scalia observed that "the President's constitutionally assigned duties include complete control over investigation and prosecution of violations of the law. . . . " In Scalia's view, vesting the appointment of the independent counsel in the courts deprived the President of such control.

The competing views in *Morrison v. Olson* are interesting in light of the 1994 appointment of Kenneth Starr to investigate allegations of misconduct by President Clinton. This investigation led to President Clinton's impeachment by the House of Representatives in 1998. Like federal judges, presidents can be removed from office upon conviction of "high crimes and misdemeanors." President Clinton was charged with perjury and obstruction of justice, but was acquitted by the Senate in early 1999. Later that year Congress decided not to renew the independent counsel statute under which Starr was appointed.

FEDERALISM

Separation of powers is one of the two basic structural characteristics of the American constitutional system, the other being **federalism.** In a federal system, power is divided between a central government and a set of regional governments. A **unitary system,** by contrast, vests all authority in the central government. In the American context, federalism refers to the division of power between the national government on the one hand and the state and local governments on the other.

Historically, the states preceded the nation as political communities. After the Revolutionary War, citizens thought of themselves primarily as Virginians, New Yorkers, Rhode Islanders, and so forth, and only secondarily as Americans. The **Articles of Confederation,** under which this country was governed between the end of the Revolution and the time the Constitution was ratified in 1788, created a loose confederation of states held together by a weak central government. The Framers of the Constitution sought to create an effective but limited national government. Still, during the debate over ratification, critics charged that the new national government might become too powerful and intrude on the rights of the states. Thus, the Tenth Amendment was adopted in 1789, which reserved to the states all powers not delegated to the national government.

In the early days of the republic, the national government played a fairly limited role. However, under Chief Justice John Marshall (1801–1835), the Supreme Court established the fundamental principle that state policies may not contravene policies of the national government, assuming the latter are consistent with the Constitution.[33] The opposing doctrine, that states could "nullify" actions of the federal government they believed to be unconstitutional, and could even secede from the Union, was defeated on the battlefields of the Civil War.[34]

The Civil War, the Industrial Revolution, the Great Depression, and two world wars had a profound impact on American political culture. In the twentieth century, people came to think of themselves first and foremost as Americans. Increasingly, they looked to the national government to solve problems the state and local governments could not, or would not, address. This cultural change produced a corresponding change in constitutional law. Whereas in the late nineteenth and early twentieth centuries, the Supreme Court adopted a conservative model known as **dual federalism,**[35] in the wake of the Great Depression the

CASE IN POINT

CAN THE FEDERAL GOVERNMENT COMMAND LOCAL OFFICIALS TO IMPLEMENT A FEDERAL GUN CONTROL PROGRAM?

Printz v. United States

United States Supreme Court
521 U.S. 898, 117 S.Ct. 2365, 138 L.Ed. 2d 914 (1997)

The Supreme Court struck a blow to congressional power by invalidating a provision of the Brady handgun control law. The offending provision required local law enforcement officials to perform background checks on prospective handgun purchasers. According to Justice Scalia's opinion for the sharply divided Court, this provision violated "the very principle of separate state sovereignty," which Scalia characterized as "one of the Constitution's structural protections of liberty." The *Printz* decision suggests that Congress cannot require state and local officials to assist in the administration of federal programs. Of course, there are many joint federal–state programs, but most of them involve voluntary cooperation by the states.

Court embraced a more progressive model of federalism in which the national government was clearly recognized as the paramount authority.[36]

Over the two centuries since the republic was founded, the relationship between the national government and the states has changed dramatically. Today, there is no question of the dominance of the national government in most areas of policy making. There is also considerable interaction between federal and state agencies, an arrangement often referred to as **cooperative federalism.** In the contemporary age, the federal government often uses its superior fiscal resources to prod the states into adopting policies they might not otherwise adopt. A good example of this sort of **coercive federalism** was the congressional decision in the early 1980s to force the states to raise the legal drinking age to 21 by threatening to cut off badly needed federal highway funds.[37] Despite clear federal dominance, states remain viable actors in the political system; and the courts continue to take the concept of federalism seriously.[38] Thus, as a constitutional principle, federalism retains considerable vitality.

CIVIL RIGHTS AND LIBERTIES

One of the principal objectives of the U.S. Constitution, as stated in its preamble, is "to secure the Blessings of Liberty to ourselves and our Posterity." The Framers of the Constitution thus recognized the protection of individual liberty as a fundamental goal of constitutional government. The Framers sought to protect liberty by creating a system of government that would be inherently restricted in power, hence limited in its ability to transgress the rights of the individual. However, the original Constitution contained few explicit protections of individual rights. This was not because the Framers did not value rights but because they thought it unnecessary to deal with them explicitly. Significantly, most of the state constitutions adopted during the American Revolution contained fairly detailed bills of rights placing limits on state and local governments. The Framers did not anticipate the growth of a pervasive national government and thus did not regard the extensive enumeration of individual rights in the federal Constitution as critical. They did, however, recognize a few important safeguards in the original Constitution, most notably the guarantee of **habeas corpus** and the prohibition against **bills of attainder** and **ex post facto laws.**

Habeas Corpus

Article I, Section 9 of the Constitution states, "the privilege of the Writ of Habeas Corpus shall not be suspended, unless when in Cases of Invasion or Rebellion the public Safety may require it." Grounded in English common law, the writ of habeas corpus gives effect to the all-important right of the individual not to be held in unlawful custody. Specifically, habeas corpus enables a court to review a custodial situation and order the release of an individual who is being held in custody illegally. Although the right has many applications, the most common is in the criminal context, when an individual is held in custody but denied due process of law.[39] Indeed, the writ of habeas corpus is an important and controversial element of modern criminal procedure (see Chapter 10).

Ex Post Facto Laws and Bills of Attainder

Article I, Section 9 of the Constitution prohibits Congress from passing ex post facto laws. Article I, Section 10 imposes the same prohibition on state legislatures. Ex post facto laws are laws passed after the occurrence of an act that alter the legal status or consequences of that act. The ex post facto clauses apply to criminal but not to civil laws.[40] For an act to be invalidated as an ex post facto law, two key elements must exist. First, the act must be retroactive—it must apply to events that occurred before its passage. Second, it must seriously disadvantage the accused, not merely by changes in procedure but by means that render conviction more likely or punishment more severe.

Article I, Sections 9 and 10 also prohibit Congress and the states, respectively, from adopting bills of attainder. A bill of attainder is a legislative act that imposes punishment upon a person without benefit of a trial in a court of law. After the Civil War, the Supreme Court struck down a federal statute forbidding attorneys from practicing before federal courts unless they took an oath that they had not supported the Confederacy.[41] The Court also invalidated a provision of the Missouri Constitution that required a similar oath of all persons who wished to be employed in a variety of occupations, including the ministry.[42] The Court found that these laws violated both the bill of attainder and ex post facto provisions of Article I.[43]

The Contract Clause

A principal motivation behind the Constitutional Convention of 1787 was the desire to secure overriding legal protection for contracts. Thus, Article I, Section 10 prohibits states from passing laws "impairing the obligation of contracts." The Contract Clause must be counted among the provisions of the original Constitution that protect individual rights—in this case, the right of individuals to be free from governmental interference with their contractual relationships. By protecting contracts, Article I, Section 10 performed an important function in the early years of American economic development. Historically, the Contract Clause was an important source of litigation in the federal courts. In modern times, it is seldom interpreted to impose significant limits on the states in the field of economic regulation.

Adoption of the Bill of Rights

The omission of a bill of rights from the original Constitution was regarded as a major defect by numerous critics and even threatened to derail ratification in some states. Thomas Jefferson, who had not participated in the Constitutional Convention due to his diplomatic duties in France, was among the most influential critics. In a letter to his close friend, James Madison, Jefferson argued, "You must specify your liberties, and put them down on paper." Madison, the acknowledged father of the Constitution, thought it unwise and unnecessary to enumerate individual rights, but Jefferson's view eventually prevailed. Honoring a gentleman's agreement designed to secure ratification of the Constitution in several key states, the First Congress considered a proposed bill of rights drafted by Madison. Madison's original bill of rights called for limitations on the states as well as the federal government, but this proposal was defeated by states' rights advocates in Congress. The Bill of Rights was adopted by Congress in September 1789 and was ratified in November 1791.

The **Bill of Rights** was adopted as a set of limitations on the new federal government; it was not intended to apply to the states.[44] Accordingly, citizens had to look to their respective state constitutions and state courts for protection against actions by their state governments. That situation changed beginning in the late nineteenth century, as the Supreme Court held that various provisions of the Bill of Rights were applicable to the states as well. Today, virtually all provisions of the Bill of Rights apply with equal force to all levels of government. (To learn how this was accomplished, see "Adoption of the Fourteenth Amendment" later in this chapter.)

The First Amendment: Freedom of Religion

The First Amendment provides a number of crucial guarantees of freedom. The Establishment Clause prohibits Congress from making laws "respecting an establishment of religion," whereas the Free Exercise Clause enjoins the national government from "prohibiting the free exercise thereof." These first two clauses demonstrate the fundamental character of the Founders' devotion to freedom of religion.

The Free Exercise Clause provides virtually absolute protection for the right to express one's religious beliefs and to assemble with other believers. It also protects people's right to solicit funds and proselytize on behalf of religious organizations, although these rights are subject to reasonable time, place, and manner restrictions.[45] The Free Exercise Clause prohibits government from adopting laws or regulations aimed specifically at the practices of one religious sect.[46] It does not, however, generally permit citizens to flout applicable criminal laws that apply to everyone.[47]

Separation of Church and State

The Supreme Court has said that the Establishment Clause was intended to erect a "wall of separation between church and state."[48] Of course, many people disagree as to how high or thick the wall of separation should be. Nowhere is the debate more intense than in the context of public education, where the courts have dealt with such emotional issues as prayer and the teaching of "creation science" in the public schools.[49] With respect to both these issues, the Supreme Court has taken the position that the Constitution requires strict **separation of church and state.** In the early 1960s, the Supreme Court under Chief Justice Warren invalidated the long-standing practice of prayer and Bible reading in the public schools.[50] That position has been reaffirmed by the Supreme Court many times since then and indeed has been made more stringent.[51] In a controversial holding in June 2000, the Court struck down a public high school practice in which an elected student "chaplain" delivered a prayer over the public address system before each home football game.[52]

On the other hand, the Court has permitted states and communities to provide assistance to children in religious schools as long as it is part of a general program of assistance that benefits all schoolchildren. For example, in 1997 the Court upheld a New York City program that placed public school teachers in parochial schools for the purpose of providing federally financed remedial courses to disadvantaged students. In her opinion for the Court, Justice Sandra Day O'Connor stressed the neutrality of the remedial instruction and noted that this program could not reasonably be viewed as an endorsement of religion by the city.[53] In a sim-

CASE IN POINT

IS A LAW REQUIRING A MOMENT OF SILENCE IN THE PUBLIC SCHOOLS A VIOLATION OF THE PRINCIPLE OF SEPARATION OF CHURCH AND STATE?

Wallace v. Jaffree

United States Supreme Court
472 U.S. 38, 105 S.Ct. 2479, 86 L.Ed.2d 29 (1985)

Ishmael Jaffree brought suit against Alabama Governor George Wallace and other public officials to challenge the constitutionality of the state "moment of silence" law. Specifically, the statute provided: "At the commencement of the first class each day in the first through the sixth grades in all public schools, . . . a period of silence, not to exceed one minute in duration, shall be observed for meditation or voluntary prayer." The Supreme Court, splitting 6–3, invalidated the statute as a violation of the Establishment Clause. The Court concluded that the purpose of the statute was to "convey a message of State-approval of prayer activities in the public schools." Dissenting, Justice Rehnquist argued: "Nothing in the Establishment Clause of the First Amendment, properly understood, prohibits any such generalized 'endorsement' of prayer."

ilar vein, the Court in June 2000 upheld Chapter 2 of the Education Consolidation and Improvement Act of 1981, under which the federal government makes grants to state and local agencies that provide materials and equipment to public and private schools, including religious schools.[54] As long as government is merely aiding the education of all children in secular subjects on a nondiscriminatory basis, the Establishment Clause is not breached.

The Supreme Court has fashioned a three-part test to determine whether a challenged law or policy violates the Establishment Clause. It is referred to as the *Lemon* test, as it was first articulated in the Court's 1971 decision in *Lemon v. Kurtzman*.[55] To pass muster, the law or policy (1) must have a secular legislative purpose; (2) its principal or primary effect must be one that neither advances nor inhibits religion; and (3) it must not foster an excessive government entanglement with religion. Of course this test is not self-executing. Judges often disagree about what constitutes a "secular purpose," "principal or primary effect," and "excessive entanglement." A number of commentators and even some of the justices of the Supreme Court have questioned the value of the *Lemon* test; but the Court has maintained it for lack of a superior alternative formulation.

The First Amendment: Freedom of Expression

The First Amendment also protects freedom of speech and freedom of the press, often referred to jointly as **freedom of expression.** One can argue that freedom of expression is the most vital freedom in a democracy, in that it permits the free flow of information between the people and their government. Certainly the Framers of the Bill of Rights were aware of its fundamental importance, which is why the freedoms of speech and press were placed in the First Amendment. Finally, the First Amendment protects the "right of the people peaceably to assemble and petition the Government for a redress of grievances." Freedom of assembly remains an important right, and one that is often controversial, as when an extremist group such as the Ku Klux Klan stages a public rally. The freedom to petition government for a redress of grievances is no less important. Today, it is referred to as *lobbying*, a principal activity of interest groups.

Legitimate Restrictions on Expression

Freedom of expression is not absolute. As Justice Oliver Wendell Holmes, Jr. observed in 1919, it does not give a person the right to falsely shout "Fire" in a crowded theater.[56] Thus was born the **clear and present danger doctrine**, which marks the outer limits of First Amendment protection (see Case in Point below). Expression that creates a clear and present danger of producing a condition that the government has a right to prevent is not protected by the First Amendment. In 1969, the Supreme Court said that clear and present danger means **imminent lawless action**, that is, a condition in which violence or lawbreaking is about to take place.[57]

Expression in the public forum is subject to reasonable **time, place, and manner regulations**, although such regulations may not be employed on a discriminatory basis or invoked only to suppress particular messages that authorities deem undesirable. A valid time, place, and manner regulation must be "narrowly tailored" to serve the state's legitimate interests and must leave open ample alternative channels of communication.[58]

Freedom of expression does not include the right to commit libel or slander, although the Supreme Court has made it very difficult for public officials and other "public figures" to sue their detractors for **defamation**.[59] **Obscenity** is not protected by the First Amendment;[60] however, most pornography falls outside the current definition of obscen-

CASE IN POINT

ESTABLISHMENT OF THE CLEAR AND PRESENT DANGER DOCTRINE

Schenck v. United States

United States Supreme Court
249 U.S. 47, 39 S.Ct. 247, 63 L.Ed. 470 (1919)

Charles T. Schenck, general secretary of the Socialist Party, was convicted under the Espionage Act of 1917 for interfering with military recruitment by conspiring to print and circulate leaflets "to men who had been called and accepted for military service." The leaflets urged resistance to the draft on the ground that it violated the Thirteenth Amendment of the Constitution. Although sharply critical of the war effort, the Socialists' message was confined to the advocacy of peaceful measures such as petition for repeal of the draft. No disruption or actual draft resistance occurred as a result of Schenck's efforts; however, the U.S. Supreme Court unanimously upheld his conviction on the ground that speech intended to obstruct the war effort was not entitled to constitutional protection. Writing for the Court, Justice Oliver Wendell Holmes Jr. reasoned that "the character of every act depends upon the circumstances in which it is done. The most stringent protection of free speech would not protect a man in falsely shouting fire in a theater, and causing a panic. . . . The question in every case is whether the words used are used in such circumstances and are of such a nature as to create a clear and present danger that they will bring about the substantive evils that Congress has a right to prevent."

ity and prosecutorial efforts focus almost exclusively on child pornography. Expressions of hatred and bigotry are protected by the First Amendment, except when such expression constitutes **fighting words,** that is, threats or insults that are inherently likely to incite violence. The Supreme Court's First Amendment jurisprudence is based on the premise that "debate on public issues should be uninhibited, robust, and wide-open."[61]

The Prior Restraint Doctrine

One reason why the Framers of the Bill of Rights saw the need for the First Amendment was that the English common law provided little protection to personal expression. However, one common-law doctrine has been grafted onto the First Amendment through judicial interpretation: the rule against **prior restraint.** The concept was first discussed by the Supreme Court in 1931 in a case involving a dispute over publication of a newspaper.[62] The case involved a state law that permitted public officials to seek an injunction to stop publication of any "malicious, scandalous and defamatory newspaper, magazine or other periodical." Writing for the Court, Chief Justice Charles Evans Hughes characterized this law as "the essence of censorship" and declared it unconstitutional. Chief Justice Hughes acknowledged that the rule against prior restraint would not, for example, prevent government in time of war from prohibiting publication of "the sailing dates of transports or the number and location of troops." In these and related situations, national security interests are almost certain to prevail over freedom of the press. But where is the line to be drawn? How far can the "national security" justification be extended in suppressing publication?

The Court revisited the question of prior restraint on the press in the much-heralded Pentagon Papers case of 1971.[63] Here, the federal government attempted to prevent the *New York Times* and the *Washington Post* from publishing excerpts from a classified study entitled "History of U.S. Decision-Making Process on Viet Nam Policy," better known as the Pentagon Papers. By a 6-to-3 vote, the Supreme Court held that the government's effort to block publication of this material amounted to an unconstitutional prior restraint. The majority was simply not convinced that such publication—several years after the events and decisions discussed in the Pentagon Papers—constituted a significant threat to national security.

Freedom of Association

The First Amendment makes no mention of the right to associate freely with people of one's own choosing, but the courts have recognized that this right is implicit in the First Amendment. In recent years, this implicit **freedom of association** has come into conflict with government efforts to eliminate various forms of social discrimination. In one case, a unanimous Supreme Court found that Minnesota's interest in eradicating sex discrimination was sufficiently compelling to justify a decision of its human rights commission requiring local chapters of the Jaycees to admit women. The Court rejected the Jaycees' argument that their First Amendment rights were being violated.[64] However, in June 2000, the Court ruled that the Boy Scouts of America (BSA) had a constitutional right to prohibit openly gay men from serving as scout leaders. This controversial ruling came in a case where the New Jersey courts had prohibited the BSA from engaging in such discrimination under that state's civil rights laws.[65] The 5–4 decision by the Supreme Court was denounced by leaders of the gay rights movement, but hailed by those who wish to see private organizations protected from governmental intrusion.

The Second Amendment: The Right to Keep and Bear Arms

Most Americans believe that the Constitution protects their **right to keep and bear arms.** Yet the Second Amendment refers not only to the keeping and bearing of arms but also to the need for a well-regulated militia. The Second Amendment provides: "A well-regulated Militia, being necessary to the security of a free state, the right of the people to keep and bear arms shall not be infringed." The Supreme Court has held that the Second Amendment guaranteed states the right to maintain militias but did not guarantee to individuals the right to possess guns.[66] Accordingly, the Court has uniformly upheld federal **gun control legislation.**[67] As currently interpreted, the Second Amendment does not pose a significant constitutional barrier to the enactment or enforcement of gun control laws, whether passed by Congress, state legislatures, or local governments.

The Third Amendment: Protecting Citizens' Homes from the Military

The Third Amendment prohibits military authorities from quartering troops in citizens' homes without their consent. This was a matter of serious concern to the Founders, because English troops had been forcibly billeted in colonists' homes during the Revolutionary War. Today, the Third Amendment is little more than a historical curiosity, since it has not been the subject of any significant litigation.

The Fourth Amendment: Prohibition of Unreasonable Searches and Seizures

The Fourth Amendment protects citizens from **unreasonable searches and seizures** conducted by police and other government agents. Reflecting a serious concern of the Founders, the Fourth Amendment remains extremely important today, especially in light of the pervasiveness of crime and the national war on drugs. In the twentieth century, the Fourth Amendment was the source of numerous important Supreme Court decisions and generated a tremendous and complex body of legal doctrine. For example, the Supreme Court under Chief Justice Warren expanded the scope of Fourth Amendment protection to include wiretapping, an important tool of modern law enforcement.[68] The Burger and Rehnquist Courts were decidedly more conservative in this area, facilitating police efforts to ferret out crime. (For additional discussion see Chapter 10.)

The Fifth Amendment: Rights of the Accused

The Fifth Amendment contains a number of important provisions involving the rights of persons accused of crime. It requires the federal government to obtain an **indictment** from a **grand jury** before trying someone for a major crime. It also prohibits **double jeopardy,** that is, being tried twice for the same offense. Additionally, the Fifth Amendment protects persons against **compulsory self-incrimination,** which is what is commonly meant by the phrase "taking the Fifth." (For additional discussion see Chapter 10.)

The Fifth Amendment: Property Rights and Due Process

The Fifth Amendment also protects people against arbitrary use of **eminent domain,** the power of government to take private property for public use. The Just Compensation Clause forbids government from taking private property without paying **just compensation** to the owner. Finally, the Fifth Amendment prohibits the federal government from depriving persons of life, liberty, or property without **due process of law.** A virtually identical clause is found in the Fourteenth Amendment, which applies specifically to the states. The Due Process Clauses have implications both for civil and criminal cases, as well as for a variety of relationships between citizen and government. Due process is the broadest and most basic protection afforded by the Constitution.

The Sixth Amendment: Rights of the Accused

The Sixth Amendment is concerned exclusively with the **rights of the accused.** It requires, among other things, that people accused of crimes be provided a "speedy and public trial, by an impartial jury. . . ." The right of **trial by jury** is one of the most cherished rights in the Anglo-American tradition, predating the Magna Carta of 1215. The Sixth Amendment also grants defendants the right to confront, or cross-examine, witnesses for the prosecution and the right to have **compulsory process** (the power of subpoena) to require favorable witnesses to appear in court. Significantly, considering the incredible complexity of the criminal law, the Sixth Amendment guarantees that accused persons have the "Assistance of Counsel" for their defense. The Supreme Court has regarded the **right to counsel** as crucial to a fair trial and, since 1963, has held that defendants who are unable to afford private counsel must be afforded counsel at public expense.[69] (For additional discussion see Chapter 10.)

The Seventh Amendment: The Right to a Jury Trial in Civil Suits

The Seventh Amendment guarantees the right to a jury trial in federal civil suits "at common law" where the amount at issue exceeds $20. Originally, it was widely assumed that the Seventh Amendment required jury trials only in traditional common-law cases, for example, actions for libel, wrongful death, and trespass. But over the years, the Supreme Court expanded the scope of the Seventh Amendment to encompass civil suits seeking enforcement of statutory rights;[70] however, the Seventh Amendment does not apply to the adjudication of certain issues by administrative or regulatory agencies.[71] Although at common law a jury in a civil trial consisted of 12 jurors, the Supreme Court has approved the use of six-person juries in civil cases.[72]

The Eighth Amendment: Prohibitions of Excessive Bail, Excessive Fines, and Cruel and Unusual Punishments

The Eighth Amendment protects persons accused of crimes from being required to post **excessive bail** to secure **pretrial release.** The Supreme Court held that bail is excessive if it is higher than is reasonably necessary to ensure a defendant's appearance for trial.[73] But it has also said that the Eighth Amendment does not require that defendants be released on bail, only that, if the court grants bail, it must not be "excessive."[74]

The Eighth Amendment also forbids the imposition of **excessive fines.** Recently, the Supreme Court held that this prohibition also applies to forfeitures of property used in illicit activities. Federal law allows the government to sue to recover property used to facilitate criminal offenses. The Court ruled that **forfeitures,** although they are not technically criminal proceedings, are subject to the Excessive Fines Clause of the Eighth Amendment.[75]

Finally, the Eighth Amendment prohibits the infliction of **cruel and unusual punishments** on persons convicted of crimes. Originally designed to proscribe torture, the Cruel and Unusual Punishments Clause now figures prominently in the ongoing national debate over the **death penalty.**[76] The Supreme Court has said that the Cruel and Unusual Punishments Clause "must draw its meaning from the evolving standards of decency that mark the progress of a maturing society."[77] (For additional discussion see Chapter 10.)

The Ninth Amendment: Rights Reserved to the People

The Ninth Amendment was included in the Bill of Rights as a solution to a problem raised by James Madison; namely, that the specification of particular liberties might suggest that individuals possessed only those specified. The Ninth Amendment makes it clear that individuals retain a reservoir of rights and liberties beyond those listed in the Constitution by stating that "[t]he enumeration in the Constitution, of certain rights, shall not be construed to deny or disparage others retained by the people." This amendment reflects the dominant thinking of late-eighteenth-century America: Individual rights precede and transcend the power of government; individuals possess all rights except those that have been surrendered to government for the protection of the public good.

Although they have seldom relied explicitly on the Ninth Amendment, federal and state courts have over the years recognized a number of rights that Americans take for granted but which are not specifically enumerated in the Constitution. The right to marry, to determine how one's children are to be reared and educated, to choose one's occupation, to start a business, to travel freely across state lines, to sue in the courts, and to be presumed innocent of a crime until proven guilty are all examples of individual rights that have been recognized as constitutional, despite their absence from the text of the Constitution. Quite often these rights have been recognized under the broad Due Process Clauses of the Fifth and Fourteenth Amendments.

The Tenth Amendment: The States' Rights Amendment

The Bill of Rights is generally considered to be the first 10 amendments to the Constitution; but the Tenth Amendment is of a fundamentally different character than the amendments that precede it. The Tenth Amendment provides: "The powers not delegated to the United States by the Constitution, nor prohibited by it to the States, are reserved to the States respectively, or to the people."

Unlike other provisions of the Bill of Rights, and despite its reference to "the people," the Tenth Amendment recognizes the powers of the states vis-à-vis the federal government and does not directly address individual rights. Accordingly, the Tenth Amendment is largely unrelated to civil rights and liberties. Rather, it pertains to the topic of federalism.

Adoption of the Fourteenth Amendment

Without question, the most important amendment to the Constitution outside of the Bill of Rights is the Fourteenth Amendment. Ratified in 1868, the principal objective of the Fourteenth Amendment was to protect the civil rights and liberties of African-Americans. Although slavery had been formally abolished by the Thirteenth Amendment, ratified in 1865, questions remained about the legal status of the former slaves. In *Dred Scott v. Sandford* (1857),[78] the Supreme Court had not only defended the institution of slavery but also indicated that blacks were not citizens of the United States and possessed "no rights or privileges but such as those who held the power and the Government might choose to grant them." Section 1 of the Fourteenth Amendment made clear that *Dred Scott* was no longer the law of the land:

> All persons born or naturalized in the United States, and subject to the jurisdiction thereof, are citizens of the United States and of the State wherein they reside. No state shall make or enforce any law which shall abridge the privileges or immunities of citizens of the United States; nor shall any State deprive any person of life, liberty, or property, without due process of law; nor deny to any person within its jurisdiction the equal protection of the laws.

Due Process of Law

The Fourteenth Amendment prohibits states from depriving persons within their jurisdiction of life, liberty, or property without due process of law. In its most generic sense, due process refers to the exercise of governmental power under the rule of law with due regard for the rights and interests of individuals. The concept of procedural due process embraces government's obligation to provide **fair notice** and a **fair hearing** to individuals before depriving them of "life, liberty or property." Thus, for example, in 1967 the Supreme Court relied on the Due Process Clause of the Fourteenth Amendment in a landmark decision revolutionizing the juvenile justice system, holding that juveniles must be afforded certain procedural protections before they can be judged "delinquent" and sent to a reformatory.[79] Similarly, the Supreme Court has invoked due process to say that police may not use methods that "shock the conscience" in attempting to gather evidence of criminal wrongdoing.[80]

Historically, the concept of due process was extremely important in defending private property rights from government regulation. More recently, the courts have recognized government employment and government benefits as "property interests" subject to the requirements of due process. Thus, while there is no constitutional right to receive welfare assistance, government may not terminate a person's welfare benefits without observing certain procedural safeguards.[81]

Incorporation of the Bill of Rights

One of the most important consequences of the Fourteenth Amendment has been to make the Bill of Rights applicable to the states. Although it is unclear whether the Framers of the Fourteenth Amendment intended this result, the Supreme Court has interpreted the Due Process Clause to this effect. In 1897, the Supreme Court held that the Fifth Amendment's Just Compensation Clause is incorporated within the concept of due process and thereby enforceable against the states.[82] In 1937, the Court said that those protections of the Bill of Rights that are essential to "a scheme of ordered liberty" are enforceable against the states via the Fourteenth Amendment.[83] Over the years the Court used this **doctrine of incorporation** to apply most of the other provisions of the Bill of Rights to the states.[84] This helps explain why the federal courts have assumed something of a supervisory role with regard to the state and local governments.

Substantive Due Process

In addition to providing procedural protections against arbitrary and capricious government action, due process has been held to impose substantive limits on government policies as well. Under the concept of **substantive due process,** government is barred from enforcing policies that are irrational, unfair, unreasonable, or unjust, even if such policies do not run counter to other specific constitutional prohibitions. For almost 50 years (roughly 1890 to 1937), the Supreme Court relied on substantive due process to invalidate a variety of state and federal laws regulating aspects of economic life. For example, in the leading case of the era, *Lochner v. New York* (1905),[85] the Court struck down a state law setting maximum working hours in bakeries. The Court held that the restriction violated both the employer's and the employee's liberty of contract, a right not specifically enumerated in the Constitution but held to be embraced within the substantive prohibitions of the Due Process Clause of the Fourteenth Amendment. While the liberty of contract version of substantive due process has been repudiated by the modern Supreme Court, substantive due process lives on under the rubric of the constitutional **right of privacy.**

The Right of Privacy

First recognized in *Griswold v. Connecticut* (1965),[86] the right of privacy is not found in any specific provision of the Bill of Rights. Nevertheless, the Supreme Court has held that privacy is a fundamental right enforceable against the state governments via the Due Process Clause of the Fourteenth Amendment. In *Griswold,* the right of privacy was invoked to invalidate a state law prohibiting the use of birth control devices. Eight years later, in *Roe v.*

Wade (1973),[87] the right of privacy was held to be broad enough to include a woman's decision to have an abortion, touching off a constitutional debate that continues to rage. The *Roe* decision remains one of the most hotly debated decisions of the modern Supreme Court. The Court, however, has reaffirmed its *Roe* decision on several occasions, most recently in June 2000.[88]

The right of privacy has been applied to a number of other controversial questions of social policy. The Supreme Court has recognized that terminally ill patients have a **right to die,** that is, to refuse artificial means of prolonging life;[89] but the Court has refused to extend the right to encompass physician-assisted suicide.[90] It has also refused to strike down laws prohibiting homosexual sodomy, much to the chagrin of the gay rights movement.[91] Meanwhile, state courts can recognize broader privacy rights under their own constitutions and many have done so. A number of state courts have gone considerably further than the U.S. Supreme Court in recognizing various applications of the right of privacy. For example, a number of state appellate courts have struck down state laws criminalizing private homosexual conduct, something that the U.S. Supreme Court has been unwilling to do.

CASE IN POINT

ABORTION AS A CONSTITUTIONAL RIGHT

Roe v. Wade

United States Supreme Court
410 U.S. 113, 93 S.Ct. 705, 35 L.Ed.2d 147 (1973)

Norma McCorvey, a.k.a. Jane Roe, was a 25-year-old unmarried Texas woman who was faced with an unwanted pregnancy. Because abortion was illegal in Texas, Roe brought suit in federal court against District Attorney Henry Wade to challenge the constitutionality of the state's antiabortion statute. The District Court declared the Texas law unconstitutional, but refused to issue an injunction barring its enforcement. On appeal, the Supreme Court handed down a 7–2 decision striking down the Texas law. Justice Harry Blackmun wrote the majority opinion, concluding that the right of privacy was broad enough to encompass a woman's decision to terminate her pregnancy. However, Blackmun noted, "the right [to abortion] is not unqualified and must be considered against important state interests ..." Although a fetus was not, in theCourt's view, a "person" within the language of the Constitution, states would be permitted (except in cases when the mother's life was endangered by carrying the fetus to term) to ban abortion after *viability* (that point in gestation when the fetus is capable of surviving outside the mother's womb). Dissenting, Justice Rehnquist wrote that "the fact that a majority of the States ... have had restrictions on abortion for at least a century is a strong indication ... that the right to an abortion is not 'so rooted in the traditions and conscience of our people to be ranked as fundamental.' " Although the Supreme Court has reaffirmed *Roe v. Wade* several times, most recently in 2000, the abortion issue remains the most divisive constitutional question of our age.

In January 2001, the abortion issue came to the political forefront once again when President George W. Bush nominated John Ashcroft to be Attorney General. Although the Senate ultimately confirmed the nomination, there was considerable conflict over the question of whether Ashcroft, a conservative with strong pro-life views, would lead the charge to have Roe v. Wade overturned.

Equal Protection of the Laws

One of the philosophical foundations of American democracy is the idea that all individuals are equal before the law. This ideal is expressed both in the Declaration of Independence and in the Equal Protection Clause of the Fourteenth Amendment, which provides that no state shall "deny to any person within its jurisdiction the **equal protection of the laws.**" The Equal Protection Clause prohibits states from denying any person or class of persons the same protection and rights that the law extends to other similarly situated persons or classes of persons.

In the late nineteenth century, the Supreme Court declared that the word *person* in the Equal Protection Clause included corporations.[92] Occasionally, the Clause was employed as a basis for invalidating discriminatory business regulation.[93] In the modern era, the federal courts have relied heavily on the Equal Protection Clause of Section 1 in advancing the civil rights of African-Americans and other minority groups. The "case of the century," *Brown v. Board of Education* (1954),[94] in which the Supreme Court abolished racial segregation in the public schools, was based squarely on the Equal Protection Clause.

Like other rights guaranteed by the post–Civil War amendments, the Equal Protection Clause was motivated in large part by a desire to protect the civil rights of African-Americans recently freed from slavery. However, the text of the clause makes no mention of race; rather, it refers to any person within the jurisdiction of a state. Although in 1873 the Supreme Court attempted to limit the scope of the Equal Protection Clause to discrimination claims brought by African-Americans,[95] the clause has been developed into a broad prohibition against unreasonable governmental discrimination directed at any identifiable group. From the 1970s through the 1990s, advocates for women's rights successfully used the Equal Protection Clause to combat sex discrimination.[96] More recently, gay rights activists have employed the Equal Protection Clause to attack discrimination based on sexual orientation.[97]

CASE IN POINT

IS AN ALL-MALE STATE MILITARY ACADEMY CONSTITUTIONAL?

United States v. Virginia

United States Supreme Court
518 U.S. 515, 116 S.Ct. 2264, 135 L.Ed.2d 735 (1996)

In this widely publicized decision, the U.S. Supreme Court struck down the male-only admissions policy of the Virginia Military Academy (VMI). The lawsuit had been brought by the Justice Department, after a complaint was filed by a female high school student who wanted to go to VMI but was barred from doing so by the institute's absolute prohibition against admitting women. In a 7–1 decision, the Supreme Court, speaking through Justice Ginsburg, ruled that the state of Virginia had "fallen far short of establishing the 'exceedingly persuasive justification,' that must be the solid base for any gender-defined classification. . . ." In a scathing dissent, Justice Scalia questioned the majority's "amorphous 'exceedingly persuasive justification' phrase" and lamented the fact that the Court had, in his view, "shut down an institution that has served the people of the commonwealth of Virginia with pride and distinction for over a century and a half." He ended by observing that "I do not think any of us, women included, will be better off for its destruction."

Earl Warren believed that the most important decisions rendered by the Supreme Court during his tenure as chief justice were those in which the Court used the Equal Protection Clause to require **reapportionment** of state legislatures. For many years, wide population disparities among legislative districts meant that rural districts had disproportionate influence over state legislatures. In 1964, the Supreme Court held that these districts had to be reapportioned on the principle of "one person, one vote."[98] American politics changed dramatically as a result.

The Fourteenth Amendment prohibits **state-sponsored discrimination**. Discrimination by private actors is beyond the reach of the Equal Protection Clause.[99] Of course, private discrimination can be addressed by federal, state, and local civil rights legislation. The best known example of this is Title II of the Civil Rights Act of 1964, which prohibits racial discrimination by privately owned places of public accommodation (businesses that open their doors to the general public) (see Chapter 11).

Today, one of the most difficult equal protection problems involves the controversial policy of **affirmative action**, a broad term referring to a variety of efforts designed to assist women and minority groups in employment, government contracting, and higher education. Affirmative action has been a major source of litigation, as it is often characterized by its critics as "reverse discrimination." In the 1970s, the Supreme Court sought middle ground in the affirmative action area, approving the basic concept but rejecting the policy of using numerical quotas.[100] In recent years the Court has taken a more negative view of affirmative action but has not repudiated the concept altogether.[101]

Voting Rights

Although the Fourteenth Amendment is the broadest and most important source of protection for civil rights and liberties outside of the Bill of Rights, a number of other constitutional amendments address specific civil rights issues. These Amendments (Fifteenth, Nineteenth, Twenty-fourth, and Twenty-sixth) focus on the **right to vote,** which is arguably the most essential right in a democracy. The original Constitution left the matter of voting rights to the states. In 1787, voting in the United States was confined for the most part to *freeholders,* that is, white male landowners above the age of 21. As our society has become progressively more democratic, the Constitution has been amended to make the franchise more inclusive. Moreover, Congress has enacted legislation to protect access to registration and voting, most significantly the Voting Rights Act of 1965 (see Chapter 11).

CONCLUSION

After the new Americans won their freedom, the Articles of Confederation that attempted to tie together the citizens of the new American states proved unworkable. The U.S. Constitution created a workable framework that enabled a loosely knit group of states to become a nation. The Framers incorporated into the Constitution a process for orderly, albeit difficult, amendment. In allocating powers, the Framers painted with a broad brush.

Congress and the president have the ability to make and execute laws. The Supreme Court exercises the power to interpret the constitutional aspects of government in light of the vast social, economic, and political differences that have evolved in our society since ratification of the Constitution in 1789. Thus, the Constitution has provided an enduring basis for the American political system for over two centuries.

Rather than becoming a mere document to be outdated by generations that followed its ratification, the new Constitution was promptly followed by a Bill of Rights. The concepts of separation of powers, **judicial independence,** and federalism have bolstered the enduring quality of the Constitution. But the Constitution became the bulwark of civil liberties through adoption of the Bill of Rights. While designed to protect the rights and liberties of citizens from actions of the federal government, over time these guarantees largely have been applied against the states as well.

Today the constitutional makeup embraces not only the original constitution and the Bill of Rights, but significantly the Fourteenth Amendment, which prohibits states from depriving any citizen from life, liberty, or property without due process of law or from denying any citizen the equal protection of the laws. Through the Constitution, as amended, and as interpreted, Americans have become national citizens in a sovereign nation with 50 sovereign states that has expanded from a framework for government to include a charter for a democracy to protect the rights and liberties of the citizens of the new republic.

SUMMARY OF KEY CONCEPTS

In this chapter we have endeavored to portray the significance of the U.S. Constitution, the Bill of Rights, and later amendments. Central to comprehending constitutional law is an understanding of how the Supreme Court developed the doctrine of judicial review and how the exercise of interpretive powers of the courts have given continued viability to the Constitution. In interpreting the Constitution, the Supreme Court has generally followed the doctrine of precedent, at times with judicial restraint while at other times displaying judicial activism.

The Constitution stands as the bedrock for operation of the government. Its meaning has been expanded not only through the processes of amendment and judicial interpretation but also through the exercise of enumerated and implied powers of Congress. Through judicial deference to the exercise of implied powers, the legislative branch is enabled to enact laws providing for the economic and social development of the nation.

Two characteristics define the basic structure of American constitutional government. First, the principle of separation of powers and related checks and balances are essential to the maintenance of limited government and ultimately to individual liberty. Second, the concept of federalism allows the power to govern to be shared between the national and the state and local governments.

A variety of constitutional provisions protect civil rights and liberties in the United States. Basic are constitutional guarantees of the writ of habeas corpus, the prohibition of bills of attainder, and the clause that prevents impairment of contracts. But to most Americans the guarantees of the Bill of Rights characterize freedom in everyday life in

America. These include the freedom of expression and religion, protections against unreasonable searches and seizures, the many rights afforded an accused, the right to trial by jury, and the right to just compensation when private property is taken for public use.

In contemporary America, the Supreme Court has amplified these specifically defined rights by developing a right of privacy and by broadly interpreting provisions of the Fourteenth Amendment that guarantee all citizens "due process of law" and "equal protection of the laws." We will discuss these protections further, but the student who grasps these basic concepts of constitutional law at this point will better understand the American legal system as developed in later chapters.

QUESTIONS FOR THOUGHT AND DISCUSSION

1. What is judicial review and how did it become a part of our constitutional fabric?
2. To what extent, if at all, can Congress restrict the jurisdiction of the U.S. Supreme Court?
3. What process must be followed before an amendment to the U.S. Constitution can become effective?
4. How has the Supreme Court's 1819 decision in *McCulloch v. Maryland* affected the lawmaking role of Congress?
5. Explain the constitutional principle of federalism. How has this principle affected governmental policymaking over the last two centuries?
6. What are the two prongs of the First Amendment in relation to freedom of religion? Give an example of state action that would likely violate each of these proscriptions.

7. Do you think the Eighth Amendment to the U.S. Constitution provides a basis for the Supreme Court to conclude that in our contemporary society death by electrocution constitutes a "cruel and unusual punishment?" Why or why not?
8. What is the basis of the authors' statement that "the most important amendment to the Constitution outside of the Bill of Rights is the Fourteenth Amendment?" How has the Supreme Court expanded the role of the Fourteenth Amendment?
9. What are the two basic requirements of procedural due process of law?
10. What is meant by "substantive due process of law?" Give an example.

KEY TERMS

judicial review	standing	federalism
intentions of the Framers	*Ashwander* rules	unitary system
doctrine of original intent	enumerated powers	Articles of Confederation
living Constitution	implied powers	dual federalism
precedent	oversight	cooperative federalism
stare decisis	power to investigate	coercive federalism
judicial self-restraint	executive power	habeas corpus
judicial activism	separation of powers	bills of attainder
presumption of constitutionality	checks and balances	ex post facto laws
strict judicial scrutiny	independent counsel	Bill of Rights

separation of church and state	grand jury	cruel and unusual punishments
freedom of expression	double jeopardy	death penalty
clear and present danger doctrine	compulsory self-incrimination	fair notice
imminent lawless action	eminent domain	fair hearing
time, place, and manner regulations	just compensation	doctrine of incorporation
defamation	due process of law	substantive due process
obscenity	rights of the accused	right of privacy
fighting words	trial by jury	right to die
prior restraint	compulsory process	equal protection of the laws
freedom of association	right to counsel	reapportionment
right to keep and bear arms	excessive bail	state-sponsored discrimination
gun control legislation	pretrial release	affirmative action
unreasonable searches and seizures	excessive fines	right to vote
indictment	forfeitures	judicial independence

ENDNOTES

[1] *Marbury v. Madison,* 5 U.S. 137, 2 L.Ed. 60 (1803).

[2] The Prize Cases, 67 U.S. 635, 17 L.Ed. 459 (1862).

[3] *Fletcher v. Peck,* 10 U.S. 87, 3 L.Ed 162 (1810).

[4] *Payne v. Tennessee,* 501 U.S. 808, 827-828, 111 S.Ct. 2597, 2609-2610, 115 L.Ed. 2d 720, 737 (1991).

[5] *Plessy v. Ferguson,* 163 U.S. 537, 16 S.Ct. 1138, 41 L.Ed. 256 (1896).

[6] *Brown v. Board of Education,* 347 U.S. 483, 74 S.Ct. 686, 98 L.Ed. 873 (1954).

[7] *Korematsu v. United States,* 323 U.S. 214, 65 S.Ct. 193, 89 L.Ed. 194 (1944).

[8] *Shapiro v. Thompson,* 394 U.S. 618, 89 S.Ct. 1322, 22 L.Ed.2d 600 (1969).

[9] *Frothingham v. Mellon,* 262 U.S. 447, 43 S.Ct. 597, 67 L.Ed. 1078 (1923).

[10] See, for example, *Texas v. Johnson,* 491 U.S. 397, 109 S.Ct. 2533, 105 L.Ed.2d 342 (1989).

[11] *Roe v. Wade,* 410 U.S.113, 93 S.Ct. 705, 35 L.Ed.2d 147 (1973).

[12] *Ashwander v. Tennessee Valley Authority,* 297 U.S. 288, 56 S.Ct. 466, 80 L.Ed. 688 (1936).

[13] 74 U.S. 506, 19 L.Ed. 264 (1869).

[14] In this regard, it is instructive to compare *Pennsylvania v. Nelson,* 350 U.S. 497, 76 S.Ct. 477, 100 L.Ed. 640 (1956) and *Watkins v. United States,* 354 U.S. 178, 77 S.Ct. 1173, 1 L.Ed. 2d 1273 (1957) with *Uphaus v. Wyman,* 360 U.S. 72, 79 S.Ct. 1040, 3 L.Ed.2d 1090 (1959) and *Barenblatt v. United States,* 360 U.S. 109, 79 S.Ct. 1081, 3 L.Ed.2d 1115 (1959).

[15] See, for example, *United States v. Eichman,* 496 U.S. 310, 110 S.Ct. 2404, 110 L.Ed.2d 287 (1990); *City of Boerne v. Flores,* 521 U.S. 507, 117 S.Ct. 2157, 138 L.Ed.2d 624 (1997).

[16] The Eleventh Amendment was adopted to overturn the Supreme Court's decision in *Chisholm v. Georgia,* 2 U.S. 419, 1 L.Ed. 440 (1793). The infamous *Dred Scott* decision of 1857 was effectively overruled by adoption of the Thirteenth Amendment, abolishing slavery, and the Fourteenth Amendment, granting citizenship to all persons born or naturalized in the United States. The Sixteenth Amendment, granting Congress the power to "lay and collect" income taxes, overruled *Pollock v. Farmer's Loan and Trust,* 157 U.S. 429, 15 S.Ct. 673, 39 L.Ed. 759 (1895), in which the Court had declared a federal income tax law unconstitutional. Finally, In *Oregon v. Mitchell,* 400 U.S. 112, 91 S.Ct. 260, 27 L.Ed.2d 272 (1970), the Supreme Court ruled that Congress had no power to regulate the voting age in state elections. The

Twenty-Sixth Amendment, ratified in 1971, accomplished what Congress was not permitted to do through statute. The Amendment provides: "The right of citizens of the United States, who are eighteen years of age or older, to vote shall not be denied or abridged by the United States or by any State on account of age."

[17] *Texas v. Johnson,* 491 U.S. 397, 109 S.Ct. 2533, 105 L.Ed.2d 342 (1989).

[18] See *Hoke v. United States,* 227 U.S. 308, 33 S.Ct. 281, 57 L.Ed. 523 (1913).

[19] *United States v. Lopez,* 514 U.S. 549, 115 S.Ct. 1624, 131 L.Ed.2d 626 (1995).

[20] *McCulloch v. Maryland,* 17 U.S. (4 Wheat.) 316, 4 L.Ed. 579 (1819).

[21] *Kilbourn v. Thompson,* 103 U.S. 168, 26 L.Ed. 377 (1881).

[22] See, for example, *Watkins v. United States,* 354 U.S. 178, 77 S.Ct. 1173, 1 L.Ed. 2d 1273 (1957).

[23] *Youngstown Sheet & Tube Company v. Sawyer,* 343 U.S. 579, 72 S.Ct. 863, 96 L.Ed 1153 (1952).

[24] *United States v. Nixon,* 418 U.S. 683, 94 S.Ct. 3090, 41L.Ed.2d 1039 (1974).

[25] *United States v. Curtiss-Wright Export Corporation,* 299 U.S. 304, 320, 57 S.Ct. 216, 221, 81 L.Ed. 255, 262 (1936).

[26] *Buckley v. Valeo,* 424 U.S. 1, 96 S.Ct. 612, 46 L.Ed.2d 659 (1976).

[27] *Bowsher v. Synar,* 478 U.S. 714, 106 S.Ct. 3181, 92 L.Ed.2d 583 (1986).

[28] *A.L.A. Schechter Poultry Corporation v. United States,* 295 U.S. 495, 55 S.Ct. 837, 79 L.Ed. 1570 (1935).

[29] *J. W. Hampton, Jr., & Co. v. United States,* 276 U.S. 394, 409, 48 S.Ct. 348, 352, 72 L.Ed. 624, 630 (1928).

[30] *Mistretta v. United States,* 488 U.S. 361, 372, 109 S.Ct. 647, 655, 102 L.Ed.2d 714, 731 (1989).

[31] *Morrison v. Olson,* 487 U.S. 654, 108 S.Ct. 2597, 101 L.Ed.2d 569 (1988).

[32] The Act was codified at 28 U.S.C.A. 591–599.

[33] *McCulloch v. Maryland,* 17 U.S. 316, 4 L.Ed. 579 (1819); *Gibbons v. Ogden,* 22 U.S. 1, 6 L.Ed. 23 (1824).

[34] In *Texas v. White,* 74 U.S. 700, 19 L.Ed. 227 (1869), the Supreme Court formally rejected the doctrine of secession.

[35] See, for example, *Hammer v. Dagenhart,* 247 U.S. 251, 38 S.Ct. 529, 62 L.Ed. 1101 (1918), in which the Court struck down federal child labor legislation on the ground that it intruded on an area reserved to the states.

[36] For example, in *United States v. Darby Lumber Company,* 312 U.S. 100, 61 S.Ct. 451, 85 L. Ed. 609 (1941), the Supreme Court relegated the status of the Tenth Amendment to that of a mere "truism" rather than a meaningful limitation on the power of the national government. Although the Court has on occasion resurrected the Tenth Amendment, see for example, *National League of Cities v. Usery,* 426 U.S. 833, 96 S.Ct. 2465, 49 L. Ed. 2d 245 (1976), the classical model of federalism belongs to a bygone era.

[37] See *South Dakota v. Dole,* 483 U.S. 203, 107 S.Ct. 2793, 97 L.Ed. 2d 171 (1987).

[38] See, for example, *Printz v. United States,* 521 U.S. 898, 117 S.Ct. 2365, 138 L.Ed.2d 914 (1997).

[39] See, for example, *Felker v. Turpin,* 518 U.S. 651, 116 S.Ct. 2333, 135 L.Ed.2d 827 (1996).

[40] *Calder v. Bull,* 3 U.S. 386, 1 L.Ed. 648 (1798).

[41] *Ex parte Garland,* 71 U.S. 333, 18 L.Ed. 366 (1867).

[42] *Cummings v. Missouri,* 71 U.S. 277, 18 L.Ed. 356 (1867).

[43] Since World War II, the Supreme Court has declared only two acts of Congress invalid as bills of attainder. The first instance was *United States v. Lovett,* 328 U.S. 303, 66 S.Ct. 1073, 90 L.Ed. 1252 (1946), in which the Court struck down a rider to an appropriations measure that prohibited three named federal employees from receiving compensation from the government. The three individuals had been branded by the House Committee on Un-American Activities as "subversives." The Court said that legislative acts "that apply either to named individuals or to easily ascertainable members of a group in such a way as to inflict punishment on them without a judicial trial are bills of attainder prohibited by the Constitution." In *United States v. Brown,* 381 U.S. 437, 85 S.Ct. 1707, 14 L.Ed.2d 484 (1965), the Court invalidated a law that prohibited members of the Communist party from serving as officers in trade unions, saying that Congress had inflicted punishment on "easily ascertainable members of a group."

[44] *Barron v. Baltimore,* 32 U.S. 243, 8 L.Ed. 672 (1833).

[45] *Heffron v. Int'l Society for Krishna Consciousness,* 452 U.S. 640, 101 S.Ct. 2559, 69 L.Ed.2d 298 (1981).

[46] *Church of the Lukumia Babalu Aye v. City of Hialeah,* 508 U.S. 520, 113 S.Ct. 2217, 124 L.Ed.2d 472 (1993).

[47] *Employment Division v. Smith,* 494 U.S. 872, 110 S.Ct. 1595, 108 L.Ed.2d 876 (1990).

[48] *Everson v. Board of Education,* 330 U.S. 1, 67 S.Ct. 504, 91 L.Ed. 711 (1947).

[49] See *Edwards v. Aguillard,* 482 U.S. 578, 107 S.Ct. 2573, 96 L.Ed.2d 510 (1987).

[50]See, for example, *School District of Abington Township v. Schempp,* 374 U.S. 203, 83 S.Ct. 1560, 10 L.Ed.2d 844 (1963).

[51]See, for example, *Lee v. Weisman,* 505 U.S. 577, 112 S.Ct. 2649, 120 L.Ed.2d 467 (1992).

[52]*Santa Fe Independent School District v. Doe,* No. 99–62 (June 19, 2000).

[53]*Agostini v. Felton,* 521 U.S. 203, 117 S.Ct. 1997, 138 L.Ed.2d 391 (1997).

[54]*Mitchell v. Helms,* No. 98–1648 (June 28, 2000).

[55]*Lemon v. Kurtzman,* 403 U.S. 602, 91 S.Ct. 2105, 29 L.Ed.2d 745 (1971).

[56]*Schenck v. United States,* 249 U.S. 47, 39 S.Ct. 247, 63 L.Ed. 470 (1919).

[57]*Brandenburg v. Ohio,* 395 U.S. 444, 89 S.Ct. 1827, 23 L.Ed.2d 430 (1969).

[58]See, for example, *Ward v. Rock Against Racism,* 491 U.S. 781, 109 S.Ct. 2746, 105 L.Ed.2d 661 (1989).

[59]*New York Times v. Sullivan,* 376 U.S. 254, 84 S.Ct. 710, 11 L.Ed.2d 686 (1964); *Curtis Publishing Co. v. Butts,* 388 U.S. 130, 87 S.Ct. 1975, 18 L.Ed.2d 1094 (1967).

[60]*Miller v. California,* 413 U.S. 15, 93 S.Ct. 2607, 37 L.Ed.2d 419 (1973).

[61]*New York Times v. Sullivan,* supra, 376 U.S. at 270, 84 S.Ct. at 721, 11 L.Ed.2d at 701.

[62]*Near v. Minnesota,* 283 U.S. 697, 51 S.Ct. 625, 75 L.Ed. 1357 (1931).

[63]*New York Times Company v. United States,* 403 U.S. 713, 91 S.Ct. 2140, 29 L.Ed.2d 822 (1971).

[64]*Roberts v. United States Jaycees,* 468 U.S. 609, 104 S.Ct. 3244, 82 L.Ed.2d 462 (1984).

[65]*Boy Scouts of America v. Dale,* No. 99–699 (June 28, 2000).

[66]*United States v. Cruikshank,* 92 U.S. 542, 23 L.Ed. 588 (1875).

[67]See, for example, *United States v. Miller,* 307 U.S. 174, 59 S.Ct. 816, 83 L.Ed. 1206 (1939); *Lewis v. United States,* 445 U.S. 55, 100 S.Ct. 915, 63 L.Ed.2d 198 (1980).

[68]*Katz v. United States,* 389 U.S. 347, 88 S.Ct. 507, 19 L.Ed.2d 576 (1967).

[69]*Gideon v. Wainwright,* 372 U.S. 335, 83 S.Ct. 792, 9 L.Ed.2d 799 (1963).

[70]*Curtis v. Loether,* 415 U.S. 189, 94 S.Ct. 1005, 39 L.Ed.2d 260 (1974).

[71]*Thomas v. Union Carbide,* 473 U.S. 568, 105 S.Ct. 3325, 87 L.Ed.2d 409 (1985).

[72]*Colgrove v. Battin,* 413 U.S. 149, 93 S.Ct. 2448, 37 L.Ed.2d 522 (1973).

[73]*Stack v. Boyle,* 342 U.S. 1, 72 S.Ct. 1, 96 L.Ed. 3 (1951).

[74]*United States v. Salerno,* 481 U.S. 739, 107 S.Ct. 2095, 95 L.Ed.2d 697 (1987).

[75]*Austin v. United States,* 509 U.S. 602, 113 S.Ct.2801, 125 L.Ed.2d 488 (1993).

[76]See, for example, *Furman v. Georgia,* 408 U.S. 238, 92 S.Ct. 2726, 33 L.Ed.2d 346 (1972); *Gregg v. Georgia,* 428 U.S. 153, 96 S.Ct. 2909, 49 L.Ed.2d 859 (1976).

[77]*Trop v. Dulles,* 356 U.S. 86, 78 S.Ct. 590, 2 L.Ed.2d 630 (1958).

[78]*Scott v. Sandford,* 60 U.S. 393, 15 L.Ed. 691 (1857).

[79]*In re Gault,* 387 U.S. 1, 87 S.Ct. 1428, 18 L.Ed.2d 527 (1967).

[80] *Rochin v. California,* 342 U.S. 165, 72 S.Ct. 205, 96 L.Ed. 183 (1952).

[81] *Goldberg v. Kelly,* 397 U.S. 254, 90 S.Ct. 1011, 25 L.Ed.2d 287 (1970).

[82]*Chicago, Burlington and Quincy RR v. City of Chicago,* 166 U.S. 226, 17 S.Ct. 581, 41 L.Ed. 979 (1897).

[83]*Palko v. Connecticut,* 302 U.S. 319, 58 S.Ct. 149, 82 L.Ed. 288 (1937).

[84]The only provisions of the Bill of Rights that have not been made applicable to the states are the Second Amendment, the Third Amendment, the grand jury clause of the Fifth Amendment, the Seventh Amendment, and the excessive bail and excessive fines clauses of the Eighth Amendment.

[85]*Lochner v. New York,* 198 U.S. 45, 25 S.Ct. 539, 49 L.Ed. 937 (1905).

[86]*Griswold v. Connecticut,* 381 U.S. 479, 85 S.Ct. 1678, 14 L.Ed.2d 510 (1965).

[87]*Roe v. Wade,* 410 U.S.113, 93 S.Ct. 705, 35 L.Ed.2d 147 (1973).

[88]*Stenberg v. Carhart,* No. 99–830 (June 28, 2000).

[89]*Cruzan v. Director, Missouri Dept. of Health,* 497 U.S. 261, 110 S.Ct. 2841, 111 L.Ed.2d 224 (1990).

[90]*Washington v. Glucksberg,* 521U.S. 702, 117 S.Ct. 2258, 138 L.Ed 772 (1997).

[91]*Bowers v. Hardwick,* 478 U.S. 186, 106 S.Ct. 2841, 92 L.Ed.2d 140 (1986).

[92]*Santa Clara County v. Southern Pacific Railroad Company,* 118 U.S. 394, 6 S.Ct. 1132, 30 L.Ed. 118 (1886).

[93]See, for example, *Yick Wo v. Hopkins,* 118 U.S. 356, 6 S.Ct. 1064, 30 L.Ed. 220 (1886).

[94]*Brown v. Board of Education,* 347 U.S. 483, 74 S.Ct. 686, 98 L.Ed. 873 (1954).

[95]The Slaughterhouse Cases, 83 U.S. 36, 21 L.Ed. 394 (1873); *Strauder v. West Virginia,* 100 U.S. 303, 25 L.Ed. 664 (1880).

[96]See, for example, *Craig v. Boren,* 429 U.S. 190, 97 S.Ct. 451, 50 L.Ed.2d 397 (1976); *Mississippi University for Women v. Hogan,* 458 U.S. 718, 102 S.Ct. 3331, 73 L.Ed.2d 1090(1983); *United States v. Virginia,* 518 U.S. 515, 116 S.Ct. 2264, 135 L.Ed.2d 735 (1996).

[97]In *Romer v. Evans,* 517 U.S. 620, 116 S.Ct. 1620, 134 L.Ed.2d 855 (1996), the Court struck down an amendment to the Colorado Constitution that precluded "all legislative, executive, or judicial action at any level of state or local government designed to protect the status of persons based on their 'homosexual, lesbian or bisexual orientation, conduct, practices or relationships.' " Writing for the Court, Justice Kennedy observed: "It is not within our constitutional tradition to enact laws of this sort. Central both to the idea of the rule of law and to our own Constitution's guarantee of equal protection is the principle that government and each of its parts remain open on impartial terms to all who seek its assistance." 517 U.S. at 634, 116 S.Ct. at 1628, 134 L.Ed.2d at 866.

[98]*Reynolds v. Sims,* 377 U.S. 533, 84 S.Ct. 1362, 12 L.Ed.2d 506 (1964).

[99]The Civil Rights Cases, 109 U.S. 3, 3 S.Ct. 18, 27 L.Ed. 835 (1883).

[100]See, for example, *Regents of the University of California v. Bakke,* 438 U.S. 265, 98 S.Ct. 2733, 57 L.Ed.2d 750 (1978).

[101]See *Adarand Constructors v. Peña,* 515 U.S. 200, 115 S.Ct. 2097, 132 L.Ed.2d 158 (1995).

FOR FURTHER READING

Abraham, Henry J., and Barbara A. Perry, *Freedom and the Court: Civil Rights and Liberties in the United States* (6th ed., Oxford University Press 1994).

Amar, Akhil Reed, *The Bill of Rights: Creation and Reconstruction* (Yale University Press 1998).

Berger, Raoul, *Government by Judiciary: The Transformation of the Fourteenth Amendment* (Harvard University Press 1977).

Carter, Lief H., *Contemporary Constitutional Lawmaking: The Supreme Court and the Art of Politics* (Pergamon Press 1985).

Ely, John Hart, *War and Responsibility: Constitutional Lessons of Vietnam and Its Aftermath* (Harvard University Press 1993).

Fisher, Louis, *The Politics of Shared Power: Congress and the Executive* (Congressional Quarterly Press 1987).

Irons, Peter, *May It Please the Court: The First Amendment* (The New Press 1997).

Kelly, Alfred H., Winfred A. Harbison, and Herman Belz, *The American Constitution: Its Origins and Development* (7th ed., 2 vols., Norton 1991).

McDonald, Forrest, *Novus Ordo Seclorum: The Intellectual Origins of the Constitution* (University of Kansas Press 1985).

Swisher, Carl Brent, *American Constitutional Development* (2d ed., Houghton-Mifflin 1954).

4

CRIMINAL LAW

photodisc.com

LEARNING OBJECTIVES

This chapter should enable the student to understand:

- the role of federal, state, and local legislative bodies in defining criminal laws
- constitutionally imposed limitations on defining criminal conduct
- the essential elements of crimes and classification of parties to crimes
- the rationale for and definition of inchoate offenses
- how common-law crimes evolved into statutory offenses against persons, property, public order, justice, and the environment
- the American statutory assault on white-collar and organized crime and vice

CHAPTER OUTLINE

Introduction

The Origin and Sources of Criminal Law

Constitutional Limitations on Criminal Law

Elements of Crimes

Parties to Crimes

Inchoate Offenses

Crimes against Persons

Property Crimes

White-Collar Crime

Organized Crime

Vice Crimes

Offenses against Public Order and Safety

INTRODUCTION

Criminal law is that branch of the law that deals with crimes and punishments. **Substantive criminal law** defines crimes and establishes penalties. **Procedural criminal law** regulates the enforcement of the substantive law, the determination of guilt, and the punishment of those found guilty of crimes. In this chapter, we examine the substantive criminal law. We examine criminal procedure in Chapter 10.

Crime and the Evolving Social Consensus

The law distinguishes between serious crimes, known as **felonies,** and less serious offenses, called **misdemeanors.** The distinction between felonies and misdemeanors is that the former carry terms of incarceration for a year or more, whereas the latter usually are punishable by shorter terms of confinement. Most felonies are considered *mala in se,* or evils in themselves. These crimes, which include such offenses as murder, rape, robbery, theft, kidnapping, and arson, are universally condemned by civilized societies. Misdemeanors, on the other hand, are generally considered *mala prohibita*—they are wrong because the law has declared them to be incompatible with the public good. Many so-called victimless crimes, such as gambling, prostitution, and possession of marijuana, are considered *mala prohibita* and are punished as misdemeanors. However, possession of even a small quantity of cocaine is a felony in most American jurisdictions, even though this behavior is *malum prohibitum;* and petit theft is a misdemeanor, even though larceny or grand theft is *malum in se.*

Cocaine possession is a crime because our society has made a collective judgment that cocaine use is inimical to the public welfare. Obviously, this is not a unanimous judgment. Many people believe that criminalizing cocaine and other "recreational" drugs is unwise public policy. But our federal and state legislative bodies have come to the opposite conclusion.

Of course, our system is a constitutional democracy, which means that legislation must conform to the requirements of the federal and state constitutions. Some would argue that laws prohibiting the private recreational use of cocaine and other drugs infringe the constitutionally protected liberty of the individual, but this argument has not prevailed in the courts.[1]

As society evolves and its standards change, behaviors that were once *mala prohibita* are no longer subject to criminal sanction. Sexual offenses are a good example. Not long ago the law criminalized sexual relations outside of marriage. Today, adultery and fornication are not even crimes in most jurisdictions, and in states where such prohibitions remain on the books they are no longer enforced. Once a particular criminal prohibition no longer is supported by societal consensus, it is apt to go unenforced or be stricken from the laws. By the same token, new prohibitions are enacted as society comes to recognize certain behaviors as harmful. Recent years have seen the establishment of many new criminal prohibitions, including smoking in public buildings, transmission of HIV, failure to wear seat belts, and improper disposal of sewage.

Crime: An Offense against Society

Our legal system regards crimes not merely as wrongs against particular victims but as offenses against the entire society. Indeed, there does not have to be an individual victim for there to be a crime. For example, it is a felony to possess cocaine, even though it is unlikely that a particular individual will claim to have been victimized by another person's use of the drug.

Because crime is an injury against society, it is government, as society's legal representative, that brings charges against persons accused of committing crimes. In the United States, we have a federal system, that is, a division of power and responsibility between the national and state governments. Both the national government and the states enact their own criminal laws. Thus, both the national and state governments may prosecute persons accused of crimes. The national government initiates a prosecution when a federal law has been violated; a state brings charges against someone who is believed to have violated one of its laws.

The Role of the Crime Victim

The principal parties in a criminal case are the prosecution (i.e., the government) and the defendant (i.e., the accused person). Crime victims play a very limited role. Even when a crime victim files a complaint with a law enforcement agency that leads to prosecution, once the prosecution begins, the victim's participation is primarily that of being a witness. Victims often complain that the system is insensitive to their interests, and states have begun to address their concerns in several ways. Some states now provide for notice to enable a victim to observe how a case is handled at the trial and sentencing stages. Increasingly, courts order convicted defendants who are placed on probation to make restitution to their victims. Several states have enacted statutes providing compensation to victims who suffer direct financial losses as a result of crime. Finally, a civil suit to recover damages for losses or injuries is available, but all too often the defendant is financially unable to respond to an award of damages to a victim.

Criminal Responsibility

The criminal law, indeed our entire legal system, rests on the idea that individuals are responsible for their actions and must be accountable for them. This is the essential justification and rationale for imposing punishments on persons convicted of crimes. On the other hand, society recognizes that certain individuals (for example, young children) lack the capacity to appreciate the wrongfulness of their conduct. Similarly, factors beyond individuals' control may lead them to commit criminal acts. In such instances the law exempts individuals from responsibility. Moreover, in certain situations, acts that would otherwise be crimes may be justified. The best example of this is committing a homicide in self-defense. There are a host of defenses that individuals may invoke beyond a simple denial of guilt. We discuss the topic of criminal responsibility and defenses later in this chapter.

THE ORIGIN AND SOURCES OF CRIMINAL LAW

American criminal laws basically came from the **English common law** as it existed at the time that America proclaimed its independence in 1776. After independence, the new American states adopted the English common law to the extent that it did not conflict with the new state and federal constitutions. The federal government, however, did not adopt the common law of crimes. From the outset, statutes passed by Congress defined federal crimes. Of the 50 states in the Union, Louisiana is the only one whose legal system is not based on the common law. Rather, it is based on the Napoleonic Code of France.

The new American judges and lawyers were greatly aided by *Blackstone's Commentaries,* published in 1769, in which Sir William Blackstone, a professor at Oxford, codified the principles of the common law. Blackstone's seminal effort was a noble undertaking, but it had the effect of demystifying English law. Consequently, Blackstone's encyclopedic treatment of the law was less than popular among English barristers, who by this time had developed a close fraternity and took great pride in offering their services to "discover the law." In America, however, *Blackstone's Commentaries* became something of a legal bible.

State and Local Authority to Enact Criminal Prohibitions

At the time of the American Revolution, the English common law constituted the criminal law of the new United States. Eventually, most common-law definitions of crimes were superseded by legislatively defined offenses in the form of statutes adopted by the state legislatures. Today, the state legislatures are the principal actors in defining crimes and punishments. For the most part, modern criminal statutes retain the *mala in se* offenses defined by the common law, but many of the old common-law crime definitions have been modified to take into account social and economic changes. As we shall see, modern criminal statutes often go far beyond the common law in prohibiting offenses that are *mala prohibita.*

When authorized by state constitutions or acts of state legislatures, cities and counties may adopt ordinances that define certain criminal violations. Local ordinances typically deal with traffic offenses, animal control, land use, building codes, licensing of businesses, and so forth. Usually these offenses are prosecuted in courts of limited jurisdiction such as municipal or county courts.

Federal Authority to Define Crimes

The national government's responsibility in the criminal justice area has always been more limited than that of the states. Yet Congress has adopted statutes defining criminal offenses that relate to its legislative powers and responsibilities. Thus, there are federal criminal laws that relate to military service, immigration and naturalization, use of the mail, interstate commerce, civil rights violations, and so forth. Criminal offenses may also be defined by federal regulatory agencies when Congress has specifically delegated such authority and provided sufficient guidelines. Persons who commit federal crimes are subject to prosecution in the federal courts.

The Model Penal Code

The American Law Institute (ALI) is an organization of distinguished judges, lawyers, and academics who have a strong professional interest in drafting model codes of laws. In 1962, after a decade of work that produced several tentative drafts, the ALI published its proposed official draft of the **Model Penal Code (MPC).** The MPC consists of general provisions concerning criminal liability, sentences, defenses, and definitions of specific crimes. The MPC is not law; rather, it is designed to serve as a model code of criminal law for all states. It has had a significant impact on legislative drafting of criminal statutes, particularly during the 1970s when the majority of the states accomplished substantial reforms in their criminal codes. Additionally, the MPC has been influential in judicial interpretation of criminal statutes and doctrines, thereby making a contribution to the continuing development of the decisional law.

The Role of Courts in Developing the Criminal Law

Although substantive and procedural criminal law are often modified by the adoption of federal and state statutes, courts play an equally important role in the development of law. Trial courts make factual determinations, apply settled law to established facts, and impose sanctions. In reviewing the decisions of trial courts, appellate courts must interpret the federal and state constitutions and statutes. The federal and state constitutions are replete with majestic phrases such as "equal protection of the laws" and "privileges and immunities" which require interpretation. That is, courts must define exactly what these grand phrases mean within the context of particular legal disputes. Likewise, federal and state statutes often use vague language such as "affecting commerce" or "reasonable likelihood." Courts must assign meaning to these and a multitude of other terms. Although the majority of states have abolished all, or nearly all, common-law crimes, and replaced them with statutorily defined offenses, the common law remains a valuable source of statutory interpretation, because legislatures frequently use terms known to the common law without defining such terms. For example, in proscribing burglary, the legislature may use the term *curtilage* without defining it. In such an instance, a court would look to the common law, which defined the term to mean "an enclosed space surrounding a dwelling."

In rendering interpretations of the law, appellate courts generally follow precedent, in keeping with the common law doctrine of *stare decisis;* however, in our rapidly changing society, courts often encounter situations to which precedent arguably does not or should not apply. In such situations courts will sometimes deviate from or even overturn precedent. Moreover, when there is no applicable precedent, appellate courts often perform an important lawmaking function as well as an error-correction function.

CONSTITUTIONAL LIMITATIONS ON CRIMINAL LAW

Because it is the "supreme law of the land," the U.S. Constitution limits the power of Congress and the state legislatures to enact criminal statutes. For example, Article III, Section 3 provides that the crime of **treason** against the United States "shall consist only in levying War against them, or in adhering to their Enemies, giving them Aid and Comfort." Incidentally, treason is the only crime actually defined in the Constitution; all other crimes are defined by the common law, state and federal statutes, or both. Other constitutional limitations on the criminal law include the prohibitions against bills of attainder and ex post facto laws contained in Article I, Sections 9 and 10 and many of the provisions of the Bill of Rights (see Chapter 3).

First Amendment Limitations

Among the most significant protections of the Bill of Rights in the criminal law context are the First Amendment freedoms of religion, speech, and assembly. The following cases represent several well-known instances in which the U.S. Supreme Court struck down or limited the enforcement of criminal statutes on First Amendment grounds:

- *Brandenburg v. Ohio* (1969).[2] Here the Court struck down an Ohio statute prohibiting "criminal syndicalism." The law made it a criminal act to advocate violence as a means of political change. The Court held that it is unconstitutional to punish someone merely for advocating violence unless there is "imminent lawless action."
- *Wisconsin v. Yoder* (1972).[3] In this case, members of the Old Order Amish religion were convicted of violating a state law requiring school attendance through age 16. The Amish argued that sending their children to school beyond the eighth

grade would be psychologically and spiritually damaging to them and would ultimately have a destructive effect on their tight-knit community. The Supreme Court held that the compulsory school attendance law as applied to the Amish was a violation of the Free Exercise Clause.

- *Texas v. Johnson* (1989).[4] After burning an American flag as part of a public protest, Gregory Lee Johnson was convicted of desecrating a flag in violation of Texas law. The Texas Court of Criminal Appeals reversed the conviction, holding that the statute under which Johnson was convicted was unconstitutional as applied to his particular conduct. The State of Texas petitioned the U.S. Supreme Court for certiorari. The Supreme Court, in a highly controversial 5–4 decision, upheld the Texas Court of Criminal Appeals. Writing for the Court, Justice Brennan observed that punishing desecration of the flag would dilute the freedom that it represents.

- *Reno v. American Civil Liberties Union* (1997).[5] In 1996, Congress adopted the Communications Decency Act, which made it a crime to display "indecent" material on the internet in a manner that might make it available to minors. In *Reno v. ACLU* the Court declared this statute unconstitutional as an abridgment of freedom of speech. Speaking for the Court, Justice Stevens concluded that the interest in freedom of expression in a democratic society outweighs any benefits achieved by trying to censor the internet.

Of course, as noted in Chapter 3, the protections of the First Amendment are not absolute, and in numerous cases the Court has rejected First Amendment claims and allowed criminal statutes to be enforced.

Due Process and Equal Protection of the Laws

The due process clauses of the Fifth and Fourteenth Amendments also provide important constraints on the criminal law, as does the Equal Protection Clause of the Fourteenth Amendment. Due process requires, among other things, that criminal statutes be written in such a way that a person of ordinary intelligence has a reasonable opportunity to know what is prohibited. As the Supreme Court observed in 1948, "Legislation may run afoul of the Due Process Clause because it fails to give adequate guidance to those who would be law-abiding, to advise defendants of the nature of the offense with which they are charged, or to guide courts in trying those who are accused."[6] When legislatures fail to meet this obligation, they have succumbed to the **vice of vagueness.**

Equal protection prohibits legislatures from criminalizing conduct only for certain groups of people, at least not without a very strong justification. For example, in 1976, the Supreme Court declared unconstitutional as a violation of equal protection an Oklahoma law that prohibited 18 to 20-year-old men from consuming 3.2 percent beer but did not apply the same prohibition to women of the same age.[7] The Court concluded that the state lacked a sufficient justification for discriminating between the sexes in the availability of the contested beverage.

Although courts cannot prevent legislatures from enacting unconstitutional criminal laws, they can enjoin their enforcement. They can also reverse convictions of persons who are prosecuted under such laws. Of course, the burden is on the defendant to raise a constitutional objection to the enforcement of a criminal statute.

Opinion of the Court . . .

GRAYNED V. CITY OF ROCKFORD

408 U.S. 104, 92 S.Ct. 2294, 33 L.Ed.2d 222 (1972)

Mr. Justice Marshall delivered the opinion of the Court.

. . . It is a basic principle of due process that an enactment is void for vagueness if its prohibitions are not clearly defined. Vague laws offend several important values. First, because we assume that man is free to steer between lawful and unlawful conduct, we insist that laws give the person of ordinary intelligence a reasonable opportunity to know what is prohibited, so that he may act accordingly. Vague laws may trap the innocent by not providing fair warning. Second, if arbitrary and discriminatory enforcement is to be prevented, laws must provide explicit standards for those who apply them. A vague law impermissibly delegates basic policy matters to policemen, judges, and juries for resolution on an ad hoc and subjective basis, with the attendant dangers of arbitrary and discriminatory application. Third, but related, where a vague statute "abut[s] upon sensitive areas of basic First Amendment freedoms," it "operates to inhibit the exercise of [those] freedoms." Uncertain meanings inevitably lead citizens to " 'steer far wider of the unlawful zone' . . . than if the boundaries of the forbidden areas were clearly marked." . . .

ELEMENTS OF CRIMES

To constitute a crime there must be a **wrongful act or omission** *(actus reus)* accompanied by **criminal intent** *(mens rea).* The criminal law requires a wrongful act because it is concerned with infliction of harm and not simply with someone's evil thoughts. Thinking about killing someone may be sinful, but the evil thought is not in and of itself a crime. But an actual homicide is an evil act unless it is justifiable or excusable.

Even an omission may constitute the required act, but only when there is a duty to act. For example, a physician who undertakes surgery has a duty to complete the necessary operation. And while there is ordinarily no duty to come to the aid of a stranger who is drowning, parents have a duty to take care of their children and their failure to perform, for example, failure to furnish them nourishment, can suffice as a criminal act.

The second element of a crime is the mental state or criminal intent. The common law described this as either **general intent** or **specific intent.** A person who performs an act without an intent to do a particular type of injury is said to act with a general intent, whereas one who acts to accomplish some specific harmful result is said to act with a specific intent. For example, a person who voluntarily sets fire to a building commits an act with an awareness of the general consequences and has acted with a general intent. One who then files a false claim to require an insurance company to pay damages for the loss of the building commits an act with a specific intent, that is, the intent to defraud the insurer.

The Model Penal Code classifies culpability for crimes by using a different terminology. Under the MPC classification a person acting recklessly or negligently would equate generally with the common-law designation of general intent. One who acts purposely or knowingly as to a result would equate generally with the common-law designation of specific intent. Students should become familiar with these newer classifications; however, in this text we generally refer to crimes as involving general or specific intent.

In certain instances one may be held criminally responsible irrespective of intent. Crimes of this nature are classified as **strict-liability offenses.** The classic example of a strict liability offense is statutory rape, where a person who has sexual intercourse with a minor is guilty irrespective of intent. Another example of a strict liability offense is selling liquor to a minor. Most minor traffic offenses fall into this category of offenses.

In addition to the essential elements of *actus reus* and *mens rea,* the concept of **causation** becomes important when an offense is defined in a manner that a specific result must occur. For example, the various degrees of homicide require that to be guilty of murder or manslaughter the defendant's conduct must have resulted in the death of a human being. Sometimes causation is referred to as **proximate cause,** a requirement satisfied if the result that occurs was foreseeable.

PARTIES TO CRIMES

Historically, the common law classified parties to crimes as either **principals** or **accessories.** A person directly involved in committing a felony was classified as a principal; a person whose conduct did not involve direct participation was classified as an accessory. Principals were further classified by the degree of their participation. A person who directly or through the acts of an innocent agent actually committed the crime was a principal in the first degree. A principal in the second degree was a person not directly involved but actually or constructively present at the commission of the crime who aided and abetted the perpetrator. The concept of actual presence is self-explanatory; however, the concept of constructive presence requires further explanation. To be constructively present, one had to be sufficiently close to render assistance to the perpetrator. For example, suppose a man led a woman's escort away from her so that another man could sexually attack the woman. The man who led the escort away would probably be constructively present at the crime and would be classified as a principal in the second degree because he was **aiding and abetting** a crime. Aiding and abetting another in the commission of a crime means assenting to an act or lending countenance or approval, either by active participation in it or by encouraging it in some other manner.

An accessory at common law was classified as either an accessory before or after the fact. An accessory before the fact procured or counseled another to commit a felony, but was not actually or constructively present at commission of the offense. An accessory after the fact knowingly assisted or gave aid or comfort to a person who had committed a felony.

Because misdemeanors were far less serious than felonies, the common law found no necessity to distinguish between participants. As in the case of treason, all participants in misdemeanor offenses were regarded as principals. Accessories to felonies were not regarded as being as culpable as the principals, so they were punished less severely at common law.

The trend in American criminal law has been to abolish both the distinctions between principals and accessories before the fact. Federal law stipulates that "Whoever commits an offense against the United States or aids, abets, counsels, commands, induces, or procures its commission, is punishable as a principal. . . ."[8] The federal statute reflects the law of most of the states insofar as it abolishes the distinction between principals and accessories before the fact.

Even though the common-law distinction between principals and accessories before the fact has been largely abolished, the concept of accessory after the fact as a separate offense has been retained by many jurisdictions. Modern statutes view an accessory after the fact as less culpable than someone who plans, assists, or commits a crime. Thus, statutes generally define accessory after the fact as a separate offense and provide for a less severe punishment.[9] In most states, a lawful conviction as an accessory after the fact requires proof that the defendant knew that the person that he or she assisted had committed a felony. The gist of being an accessory after the fact lies essentially in obstructing justice, and a person is guilty who knows that an offense has been committed and receives, relieves, comforts, or assists the offender in order to hinder his or her apprehension, trial, or punishment.[10] Federal law, however, does not distinguish whether the person assisted has committed a felony or a misdemeanor.[11]

Because of a wife's duty at common law to obey her husband, a woman who gave aid and comfort to her husband was exempt from the law governing accessories after the fact. While this exemption no longer prevails, some state statutes exempt spouses and other classes of relatives from penalty for being accessories after the fact. For example, Florida law prevents the prosecution as an accessory after the fact of any person standing in the relation of husband or wife, parent or grandparent, child or grandchild, brother or sister, either by blood or marriage.[12]

INCHOATE OFFENSES

The word *inchoate* means underdeveloped or unripened. Thus, an **inchoate offense** is one involving activity or steps directed toward the completion of a crime. There are three such offenses: **attempt, solicitation,** and **conspiracy.** Although preparatory to commission of other offenses, they are separate and distinct crimes. During the 1800s each was recognized as a misdemeanor at common law, too late to become a part of the common law under the reception statutes adopted by most new American states. Most American jurisdictions now define these offenses by statute, frequently classifying them as felonies.

Inchoate offenses were originally created by the courts in response to the need to prevent commission of serious crimes. The development of the law in this area has been primarily through the courts. Frequently the courts have found difficulty in determining when mere noncriminal activity has reached the stage of criminal conduct. Yet, by making certain inchoate conduct illegal, the law affords law enforcement officers an opportunity to terminate such conduct at an early stage.

Attempt

Attempt is the most frequently charged of the inchoate crimes. A criminal attempt consists of an intent to commit a specific offense coupled with an act that goes beyond mere preparation toward the commission of that offense. No particular federal statute proscribes the offense of attempt. In general, federal courts have recognized the requisite elements of attempt as (1) an intent to engage in criminal conduct, and (2) the performance of an act that constitutes a substantial step toward the completion of the substantive offense.[13] State penal codes often specifically provide for attempts to commit the most serious crimes such as murder. A general attempt statute then covers the remaining offenses. A typical statute that covers all attempts provides "Whoever attempts to commit an offense prohibited by law and in such attempt does any act toward the commission of such an offense, but fails in the perpetration or is intercepted or prevented in the execution of the same, commits the offense of criminal attempt."[14] The "act" requirement contemplates an overt act that constitutes a substantial step toward commission of an offense. While the quoted statute makes no distinction between felony or misdemeanor offenses, statutes in some states limit the crime of attempt to attempts to commit felonies or certain specified crimes.

The Model Penal Code distinguishes preparatory conduct from an attempt. It allows conviction for the crime of attempt where the actor engages in "an act or omission constituting a substantial step in a course of conduct planned to culminate in the commission of the crime." Federal courts apply this test.[15] It is possible that when there are multiple intentions underlying an act, one act may establish several different criminal attempts.

To find a defendant guilty of the crime of attempt, most courts require the prosecution to prove that the defendant had a specific intent to commit the intended offense, frequently referred to as the **target crime.** Most courts reason that one cannot attempt to do something without first forming the specific intent to accomplish that particular act. The rationale for this majority view seems to be that an attempt involves the concept of intended consequences by the actor. In any event, courts require at least the level of intent that must be established in proof of the target crime.

When a criminal attempt completes a substantive crime, the attempt usually merges into the target offense. The actor is then guilty of the substantive crime, rather than merely an attempt to commit it. Thus, a person who is successful in an attempt to commit murder is guilty of murder. However, there can be no attempt to commit certain crimes because some substantive offenses by definition embrace an attempt. To illustrate, the statutory crime of uttering a forged instrument is usually defined as including an attempt to pass a forged instrument to someone to obtain something of value. Therefore, one who makes such an attempt would be guilty of uttering a forged instrument, not merely an attempt to do so. In effect, the attempt is subsumed by the very definition of the substantive crime. Needless to say, it would be redundant to charge someone with attempting to attempt to commit a given crime.

Some jurisdictions have laws providing that it is a defense to the crime of attempt if the defendant abandons an attempt to commit an offense or otherwise prevents its consummation.[16] If recognized as a defense, abandonment must be wholly voluntary. It cannot be the result of any outside cause such as the appearance of the police on the scene.

Solicitation

By the 1800s, the English common law specified that a person who counseled, incited, or solicited another to commit either a felony or a misdemeanor involving breach of the peace committed the offense of solicitation. A person who solicited another to commit a crime was guilty of solicitation even if the crime counseled, incited, or solicited was not committed. The offense of solicitation is now defined by statute in most American jurisdictions. The statutory definition of solicitation in Illinois is typical: "A person commits solicitation when, with intent that an offense be committed, other than first-degree murder, he commands, encourages, or requests another to commit the offense."[17] The gist of the offense remains the solicitation, so the offender may be found guilty irrespective of whether the solicited crime is ever committed. Conviction under federal law requires the solicitation to be of a federal offense.[18]

The offenses of solicitation and attempt are different crimes, analytically distinct in their elements. Although each is an inchoate offense, solicitation is complete when the request or enticement to complete the intended offense is made; and it is immaterial if the solicitee agrees, if the offense is carried out, or if no steps were taken toward consummation of the offense. Mere solicitation is generally not sufficient to constitute an attempt, because attempt requires proof of an overt act to commit the intended criminal act.

Generally, the fact that the solicitor countermands the solicitation is not a defense to the crime of solicitation. Nor is the fact that it was impossible for the person solicited to commit the crime a defense. The Model Penal Code provides that a timely, complete, and voluntary renunciation of the accused's criminal purpose is a defense to a charge of solicitation.[19] Some states have adopted this position. For such a defense to prevail, a defendant would have to affirmatively establish that after soliciting another person to commit an offense, the defendant prevented commission of the crime under circumstances manifesting a complete and voluntary renunciation of any criminal purpose.

Conspiracy

At common law, conspiracy consisted of an agreement by two or more persons to accomplish a criminal act or to use unlawful means to accomplish a noncriminal objective. The gist of the offense was the unlawful agreement between the parties, and no overt act was required. The common law regarded a husband and wife as one person for most purposes; therefore, a husband and wife could not be guilty of conspiring with one another. Since the trend of the law in recent years has been to recognize the separate identities of the spouses, there appears to be no valid reason to continue the common-law approach.

Today the offense of conspiracy is defined by statute in all jurisdictions. Most state laws define the elements of the offense along the lines of the common law. Thus, under Florida law, both an agreement and an intention to commit an offense are necessary elements to support a conviction for conspiracy.[20] On the other hand, federal law (with some exceptions) requires an overt act in a conspiracy to commit an offense or defraud the United States.[21] A number of states also require proof of an overt act in order to convict someone for conspiracy. Texas law, for example, provides: "A person commits criminal conspiracy if, with intent that a felony be committed, (1) he agrees with one or more persons they or one or more of them engage in conduct that would constitute the offense, and (2) he or one or more of them performs an overt act in pursuance of the agreement."[22] Note that the Texas statute also requires an intent that a felony be committed, whereas in many states it is only necessary to prove an intent to commit a criminal offense.

The range of conspiracies cuts across socioeconomic classes in society. Traditionally, state prosecutions for conspiracy have been directed at criminal offenses such as homicide, arson, perjury, kidnapping, and various offenses against property. In recent years an increasing number of both state and federal conspiracy prosecutions have been related to illicit drug trafficking. In addition to the large number of narcotics violations, federal prosecutions include a variety of conspiracies not found under state laws. Among these are customs violations, counterfeiting of currency, copyright violations, mail fraud, lotteries, and violations of antitrust laws and laws governing interstate commerce and other areas of federal regulation.

Wharton's Rule, named after Francis Wharton, a well-known commentator on criminal law, provides an exception to the principle that two or more persons can commit a conspiracy. Wharton's Rule holds that two people cannot conspire to commit a crime such as incest or bigamy because these offenses require only two participants. The rationale is that, unlike the usual conspiracy (often viewed as a wheel with many spokes or as a chain of circumstances), the offenses named do not endanger the public generally. Wharton's Rule has been applied in many state and federal courts, but it has its limitations. In holding the rule inapplicable to various federal gambling offenses under the Organized Crime Control Act of 1970, the Supreme Court pointed out that the rule itself is simply an aid to determination of legislative intent and must defer to a discernible legislative judgment.[23]

There has been an increased tendency in recent years to prosecute defendants for conspiracies as well as target crimes. The offense of conspiracy is a potent weapon in the hands of the prosecutors, particularly in coping with the problem of organized crime; but because the intent requirement and the form of agreement required are somewhat imprecise, a conspiracy is easier to prove than specific substantive crimes. On this basis, some critics argue that prosecutors, judges, and juries are given too wide latitude in finding a defendant guilty. Other critics point to the fact that conspiracy prosecutions may chill or effectively abolish First Amendment rights of free expression.

In some states, statutes specifically provide for a defense of withdrawal from and renunciation of a conspiracy. As an illustration, Missouri law specifies: "No one shall be convicted of conspiracy if, after conspiring to commit the offense, he prevented the accomplishment of the objectives of the conspiracy under circumstances manifesting a renunciation of his criminal purpose."[24]

In the absence of statutory authority, courts have been reluctant to approve a person's withdrawal as a defense. One difficulty in approving withdrawal as a defense is that even though a conspirator withdraws, the criminal objective of the conspiracy may proceed. Therefore, it seems reasonable to require that a person who would rely on such defense not only renounce any criminal purpose, but also take the necessary steps to thwart the objective of the conspiracy. To accomplish this result, the conspirator would probably have to notify law enforcement authorities of the pertinent details of the conspiracy. If the accused is allowed to offer such a defense, the defendant has the burden of establishing a withdrawal from the conspiracy.

CRIMES AGAINST PERSONS

The protection of people from others who would do them harm is the fundamental mission of the criminal law. Offenses against persons can be divided into five basic categories:

1. assaultive offenses
2. homicide
3. rape and sexual battery
4. false imprisonment and kidnapping
5. abusive offenses

Assaultive Offenses

Assault and battery, terms familiar to everyone, derive from the common law. An **assault** is an attempt or threat to inflict bodily injury upon another person. An **aggravated assault** is an assault involving a weapon capable of inflicting death or serious bodily injury. Simple assault is a misdemeanor; aggravated assault is a felony. **Battery** is the unlawful use of force against another person that entails some injury or offensive touching. **Aggravated battery** entails the infliction of serious bodily injury. In some jurisdictions, assault and battery is one offense, which is to say that battery is subsumed under assault. The common law developed an offense called **mayhem,** which involves the severing of a limb or the putting out of an eye, such that the victim was rendered less able to fight. Today, some jurisdictions retain mayhem as an offense, but others consider mayhem to be aggravated battery.

Another assaultive offense is **stalking.** A relatively new development, stalking is typically defined as "willfully, maliciously, and repeatedly following or harassing another and making a credible threat against that person." Usually a stalking statute defines a general-intent crime. Most complainants are women targeted by men. Some commentators have criticized stalking laws as being excessively vague.

Homicide

The common law recognized **murder** and **manslaughter** as criminal homicide. Murder was the "unlawful killing of another with malice aforethought." Manslaughter was an unlawful killing that did not involve malice. There were two categories of manslaughter: involuntary (unintentional) and voluntary (intentional). The common law also recognized **justifiable homicide** and **excusable homicide.** Homicide was justifiable if a killing resulted from self-defense or by a command or permission of the law. It was excusable where committed through accident or misfortune.

Criminal homicide involves actions that result in the death of a human being and is generally classified according to degrees. **First-degree murder** is usually defined as requiring proof of malice aforethought or premeditation; hence, it is a specific-intent crime. Other homicidal offenses are usually general-intent crimes. **Second-degree murder** commonly requires proof of a defendant's depraved indifference to human life or imminently dangerous or outrageous conduct. A few statutes proscribe an offense requiring a lesser level of culpability known as third-degree murder.

Modern penal codes preserve manslaughter as criminal homicide; however, some jurisdictions combine voluntary and involuntary manslaughter into one offense. Manslaughter today frequently embraces responsibility for omissions as well as commissions when there is a legal duty to act. Manslaughter usually requires proof of gross or culpably negligent conduct that results in another's death. Provocation that would cause a reasonable person to lose control may be sufficient to convert an otherwise intentional killing of another to manslaughter. Mere words, however gross or insulting, are not sufficient to constitute provocation. It must generally be shown that the provocation was sufficient to excite in the defendant's mind such anger, rage, or terror as to obscure an ordinary person's reasoning and render the person incapable of cool reflection. Often there is a fine line between a conviction for second-degree murder and manslaughter. In some instances a verdict finding a defendant guilty of manslaughter results from a jury's desire to mitigate the seriousness of a defendant's offense.

Vehicular homicide involves death resulting from the negligent operation of a vehicle or driving while in the commission of an unlawful act not amounting to a felony. The offense usually carries a lesser penalty than the crime of manslaughter. Prosecutors often charge a defendant with vehicular homicide rather than manslaughter when the evidence shows the defendant was negligent but not necessarily grossly negligent.

Felony murder consists of an unintentional killing that occurs during the commission or attempted commission of another serious felony. Developed at common law when felonies were punishable by death, the doctrine has been incorporated into most criminal codes in the United States. Today, capital punishment is far more restricted, and there is considerable criticism of the doctrine.

Homicide is generally considered excusable when committed by accident or misfortune or in doing any other lawful act by lawful means, with usual and ordinary caution, and without any unlawful intent. Homicide may also be excusable when committed in the heat of passion, or on sudden and sufficient provocation, or on sudden combat where no dangerous weapon is used and the killing is not done in a cruel or unusual manner. A death that results from a vehicular accident where the driver is not negligent is an example of excusable homicide.

In justifiable homicide the intent to cause death is often present. When death is inflicted by public officers in obedience to a court judgment or in discharge of certain other legal duties, or when necessarily committed in apprehending felons, it is considered justifiable homicide.

The prosecution must prove that the victim was alive before the homicidal act, that the victim was killed by a criminal act or agency of another (*corpus delicti*), and that the victim's death was proximately caused by the defendant. At common law, the victim's death had to occur within a year and a day of the defendant's act. Modern technology has caused courts and legislatures to recede from this inflexible requirement. While cessation of heartbeat was the classic definition of death, many jurisdictions have legislatively or judicially supplemented the classic requirement of when death occurs by a new definition of "brain death."

Defenses to homicidal crimes often involve pleas of self-defense and, sometimes, insanity, as well as claims that the victim's death resulted from an accident or through actions taken in the heat of passion.

Suicide

Early English common law defined the offense of suicide as "the intentional taking of one's life by self-destruction." Suicide was not only regarded as being contrary to nature, it was looked upon as an offense against the biblical commandment, "Thou shalt not kill." Suicide was punishable by forfeiture of the decedent's goods and chattels because it deprived the king of one of his subjects.

The thrust of statutory criminal law has been to make it an offense for anyone to cause or aid another person to commit suicide. After several unsuccessful attempts to convict Dr. Jack Kevorkian for assisting terminally ill individuals to commit suicide, in 1999 the state of Michigan successfully prosecuted Kevorkian for second-degree murder in the death of a man suffering from Lou Gehrig's disease.

In 1997, in *Washington v. Glucksberg*, the U.S. Supreme Court upheld a Washington statute making it a crime to assist another in committing suicide.[25] Writing for a unanimous Court, Chief Justice Rehnquist discussed the historical and cultural background of laws prohibiting **assisted suicide**. He pointed out that in almost every state it is a crime to assist in a suicide, and that the statutes banning assisted suicide are longstanding expressions of the states' commitment to the protection and preservation of all human life. The Court's opinion analyzed the interests that come into play in determining whether a statute banning assisted suicide passes constitutional muster. The Court rejected any parallel between a person's right to terminate medical treatment and the 'right' to have assistance in committing suicide.

Laws against assisted suicide bring into play significant policy issues and require legislatures to carefully balance competing claims of individual liberty, ethics, and the interest of society. Some proponents of allowing assisted suicide argue that it simply enables a person who has a rational capacity to make a fundamental life choice that should be within his or her domain of decision making. Those who reject this view urge that the state has an interest in the preservation of life and that some individuals may die needlessly as a result of misdiagnosis. Moreover, they argue that allowing assisted suicide leads to an indifference to the value of life.

The Supreme Court's decision in *Washington v. Glucksberg* effectively leaves the question of doctor-assisted suicide in the hands of state legislators and voters. In 1994, Oregon voters narrowly approved a law allowing a doctor to assist terminally ill persons in committing suicide under specified circumstances.

Rape and Sexual Battery

At common law, **rape** was "the unlawful carnal knowledge of a female by force and against her will." Later it became a statutory offense for a male to have carnal knowledge (sexual intercourse) of a female child under age 10 irrespective of her consent. There was a conclusive presumption at common law that a male under age 14 could not commit rape. Because common-law rape required that the carnal knowledge be unlawful, under Hale's Rule, a husband could not be found guilty of raping his wife.

American courts generally followed the common-law definition of rape but rejected the presumption that a male under age 14 could not commit the offense. Moreover, most legislatures classified intercourse with females under 16 or 18, irrespective of consent, as statutory rape. All courts recognized that to constitute common-law rape, sexual intercourse had to be without the female's consent. But many American courts struggled with the requirements of force and in determining what constituted consent. Some judges instructed juries that "in order for the defendant to be found guilty of rape, you must find that the woman resisted to her utmost." Courts commonly admitted evidence of a female victim's reputation, allowed inquiry concerning her prior sexual experiences, and some courts admonished juries to rigidly scrutinize the testimony of female victims.

Later cases recognized that it was not necessary for a female victim to resist to the utmost; rather, the degree of resistance came to be regarded as a relative matter dependent on all the circumstances surrounding the incident. Courts have divided on the issue of whether sexual battery laws require proof of a general or specific intent, the wording of the statute proscribing the offense generally determining the intent requirement.

Since the late 1970s the offense of rape has evolved as a gender-neutral offense proscribing not only rape as defined by the common law, but all types of sexual impositions and, in some instances, permitting prosecution of a husband for spousal rape. Additionally, modern sexual battery laws often classify sexual battery by degree according to the conduct involved, the character and extent of force, and the age and vulnerability of the victim.

By the early 1990s, about half of the states had either abrogated or modified the marital exemption in Hale's Rule. Some states created a new offense of spousal rape carrying lesser penalties than the traditional rape statutes. A few states will allow prosecution of a husband for rape of his wife only if the wife has filed for divorce or other termination of their legal relationship and the couple is living apart.

One of the most significant legal reforms concerning rape has been the enactment of **rape shield laws** by a majority of the states. In a prosecution for rape (or sexual battery), these laws preclude presentation of evidence of a victim's prior sexual activity with anyone other than the defendant on the theory that a victim's prior sexual activity is not probative of whether the victim has been violated. Even when the defendant seeks to introduce evidence of prior relations with a victim, some statutes require such evidence to be first presented to the court *in camera* to determine whether evidence of the defendant's prior relationship with the victim is relevant to the victim's consent.

The term **rape trauma syndrome** was coined in the early 1970s to describe a recurring pattern of physical and emotional symptoms experienced by rape victims. Since then prosecutors have sought to introduce expert testimony at rape trials to establish that a victim's symptoms are consistent with the syndrome. This type of evidence has particular relevance to a prosecution where the defendant claims consent of the victim as a defense. On review of convictions, appellate courts have disagreed on whether such evidence is admissible.

Megan's law refers to a new type of statute that requires convicted sex offenders who are released from prison to register with local law enforcement agencies. This information is then made available to the public. Failure to comply with the registration requirement is a criminal offense. The initial law was enacted in New Jersey, but now federal legislation has been enacted encouraging states to adopt similar laws.

Beyond a general denial, the most common defense in sexual battery cases is that the victim consented to have sex with the defendant. However, the offense of statutory rape is generally held to be a strict-liability offense to which the defense of consent is unavailable.

False Imprisonment and Kidnapping

At common law, **false imprisonment** consisted of confining someone against that person's will; **kidnapping** involved forcibly abducting and taking a person to a foreign country. The modern statutory definition of false imprisonment is similar to the common-law definition. Most statutes require proof of a general intent. To prove the offense, the prosecution must show the confinement or movement was not merely incidental to another crime.

False imprisonment is no longer a frequently charged offense. Serious cases of false imprisonment frequently result in kidnapping prosecution, while others result in civil suits. In contrast to false imprisonment, kidnapping has become a far more serious offense and is universally proscribed by state and federal statutes. Unlike the common law, statutes now usually define kidnapping as "the unlawful taking and carrying away (asportation) of a victim without that person's consent." Most require proof of a general intent. Many states distinguish between simple kidnapping and kidnapping for ransom whereas others classify kidnapping by degree according to the seriousness of the acts attendant to the crime.

Federal law plays a prominent role in the prosecution of kidnapping. Federal statutes presume that a kidnapping victim who has not been returned within 24 hours has been taken across state lines, thus providing a basis for federal jurisdiction. The intent requirement in kidnapping is dependent upon the language of the particular statute. Recent federal statutes also criminalize hostage taking.

The term *child snatching* is now commonly applied to situations in which one parent seizes his or her child from the custody of the other. The Uniform Child Custody Jurisdiction Act (UCCJA), now in force in 35 states, and the Parental Kidnapping Prevention Act (PKPA), enacted by Congress in 1980, address the problem of interstate child abduction.

An officer, or even a private citizen, who makes a lawful arrest or a jailer who detains a prisoner lawfully committed to custody or a parent or a teacher who reasonably restrains a child would not be guilty of false imprisonment. Consent can be a defense to false imprisonment or kidnapping, but it must have been given by a competent person and must not have been induced by threat, coercion, or misrepresentation. A person who relies on consent as a defense has the burden of establishing its validity. Finally, defendants frequently challenge whether there was sufficient movement of the victim to constitute the asportation element of kidnapping.

Abusive Offenses

Many cases of abusive conduct involve commission of assault or battery (or aggravated categories thereof), or some category of sexual battery. Nevertheless, with the rise of neglect, abuse, and violence against children, many states have enacted specific child abuse laws to cover a broader range of abusive behavior. Statutes now commonly require medical professionals and social workers to report instances of suspected child abuse to enforcement authorities. Child abuse cases often involve issues as to whether parents, social workers, and others who discuss these matters with an abused child are to be permitted to testify in court concerning communications with the child. Moreover, expert testimony by physicians, psychologists, and social workers is often relied upon to explain a child's sometimes-curious behavior that may grow out of certain types of abuse.

Many abuses of spouses and the elderly constitute criminal violations of traditional statutes previously discussed; however, laws have been enacted in many states to provide for issuance of court injunctions to protect spouses from domestic violence and provide for arrest of those who violate these orders. Additionally, legislatures frequently have provided for enhanced penalties for those who commit crimes of violence against elderly persons.

PROPERTY CRIMES

If the most important goal of the criminal law is to protect persons, the next most important goal is the protection of property. The Anglo-American legal tradition places a premium on private property rights, and this emphasis can be seen in the many criminal prohibitions relative to economic and property crimes.

Theft

The basic common-law offense against someone taking another's personal property was **larceny**. The crime consisted of (1) the wrongful taking and carrying away of (2) the personal property of another (3) with the intent to permanently deprive the other person of the property. The taking was called the "caption"; the carrying away, the "asportation." The wrongful act was a "trespass" and to convict a defendant of larceny required proof of the defendant's specific intent to permanently deprive the victim of possession of the property.

Because of the many technical distinctions in larceny, the English Parliament developed two statutory offenses, **false pretenses** and **embezzlement**. False pretenses made it a misdemeanor for a seller to obtain someone else's property by false pretenses. This statute was adopted in 1757 and became a part of the common law of most new American states. Embezzlement occurred when a person who had lawful possession of another's property wrongfully appropriated that property. This statute was aimed at brokers, bankers, lawyers, trustees, and others who abused their positions of trust. Parliament enacted the offense of embezzlement in 1799, too late to be received by the new American states as part of the common law.

Most states originally followed the common law of larceny, receiving stolen property, and false pretenses, and enacted statutes making embezzlement of intangible and tangible items a crime. During the ensuing years states passed a variety of statutes that proscribed stealing in its various forms. Since the 1970s the trend has been for the states to replace their disparate statutes defining various aspects of stealing with an omnibus statute proscribing theft in comprehensive terms. These newer statutes replace the narrow common-law concept of what constitutes a taking, carrying away, and trespass. Most retain the specific-intent requirement, but generally define it as the "intent to steal" rather than the intent to permanently deprive another of his or her property.

The newer state statutes defining theft make it unlawful for a person to commit any of the common-law offenses and also mention various other crimes. Theft statutes usually classify the seriousness of the offense based on the value of the goods or services stolen, an element the prosecution must establish by proving the market value of the goods or services taken. Frequently theft of certain articles (for example, firearms, a fire extinguisher, a person's last will and testament), is classified as a more serious offense, irrespective of the articles market value. Likewise, some states classify the degree of theft on the basis of local economic interests such as theft of livestock, citrus fruit, or building materials.

Most **computer crimes** violate one or more laws defining theft, fraud, embezzlement, and similar offenses at the state level, and often, mail fraud at the federal level. Nevertheless, nearly every state has adopted some laws defining such offenses as computer fraud, computer trespass, and theft of computer services. These new laws define such terms as *access, computer program, software, database, hacking,* and other computer parlance, and address computer manipulation, theft of intellectual property, telecommunications crimes, and software piracy. Depending on the value of property or services actually obtained, these offenses are graded as felonies or serious misdemeanors.

Robbery

At common law, **robbery** was a felony consisting of (1) a taking of personal property (2) from another person's possession (3) by force or placing a person in fear (4) with the intent to permanently deprive the victim of the property. Thus, in reality robbery is both a property crime and a crime against a person. Robbery became a statutory offense in all American jurisdictions. Federal statutes apply to post offices, military installations, and banks where deposits are insured by the federal government. Federal law varies from the common-law requirements by not requiring the prosecution to establish the defendant's specific intent.

Most states define robbery much as did the common law, however, many now classify the offense by degrees depending on whether the accused is armed, the extent of force used or injury inflicted and, in some instances, the vulnerability of the victim based on the victim's age or disabilities. A contemporary issue in robbery is whether the element of force or placing the victim in fear must occur prior to or contemporaneous with the taking of the victim's property.

Recognizing the serious threat that forcible auto theft poses to persons and their motor vehicles, and after a nationwide spree of "carjacking," Congress in 1994 enacted a law providing that:

> Whoever, with the intent to cause death or serious bodily harm takes a motor vehicle that has been transported, shipped, or received in interstate or foreign commerce from the person or presence of another by force and violence or by intimidation or attempts to so shall be [fined or imprisoned].[26]

Many states have also adopted **carjacking** statutes. For example, a Tennessee law enacted in 1995 follows the federal law by defining carjacking as "the intentional or knowing taking of a motor vehicle from the possession of another by use of: (1) a deadly weapon; or (2) force or intimidation."[27]

Forgery and Uttering a Forged Instrument

At common law, **forgery** was a misdemeanor that consisted of "the fraudulent making or alteration of a writing to the prejudice of another man's rights." To convict, the prosecution had to establish the defendant's specific intent to defraud the victim. A separate and distinct misdemeanor, **uttering a forged instrument,** involved the publishing or passing of a forged instrument. The status of forgery offenses as misdemeanors attests to the lesser importance of commercial matters at common law.

The chief difference between common law and statutory forgery lies not in the definition of the offense but in the broader scope of the latter and the more serious punishments now imposed by statutes. Federal and state statutes classify forgery as a felony. Federal law provides that "[w]hoever, with intent to defraud, falsely makes, forges, counterfeits, or alters any obligation or other security of the United States" commits forgery, thus retaining the specific–intent requirement. Numerous federal statutes describe instruments subject to forgery.

Most states have substantially adopted the common-law definition of forgery requiring either the intent to defraud or to injure, and have enacted statutes proscribing the uttering of forged instruments.

Worthless Checks and Credit Card Fraud

As commercial banking developed, the passing of bad checks became a serious problem. In early cases the issuance of a check without funds in the bank was prosecuted as the use of a "false token" under statutes proscribing the use of false pretenses to obtain property. Now a variety of statutes make it unlawful to issue checks with insufficient funds to cover payment. Earlier statutes often provided that to be guilty a person had to fraudulently obtain goods. With the widespread use of commercial and personal banking, legislatures enacted worthless check statutes usually classifying such an offense as a misdemeanor. Often these statutes allow an offender to avoid prosecution by making prompt restitution.

One who makes a purchase through use of a stolen or otherwise fraudulently obtained credit card is guilty of **credit card fraud** and may be prosecuted under most modern larceny and theft statutes. Credit cards, however, are now in such widespread use that many states have enacted laws creating specific offenses for their improper use.

Habitation Offenses: Burglary and Arson

The common-law offenses of **burglary** and **arson** protected not only the dwelling house but also the buildings within the *curtilage,* the enclosure that typically included the cookhouse and other outbuildings. At common law burglary consisted of (1) breaking and entering of (2) a dwelling of another (3) during the nighttime (4) with the intent to commit a felony therein.

In the United States all jurisdictions enacted statutes to eliminate the common-law requirement that the offense take place in the nighttime. Most statutes retain the requirement for a specific intent, usually providing that the entry be made "with the intent to commit a felony," however, some have added "or theft" to broaden the coverage. Today burglary statutes usually proscribe the breaking and entering of all types of private and commercial structures as well as vehicles, aircraft, and vessels of all types. Retaining the common-law tradition of the sanctity of the home, statutes commonly impose enhanced punishment for burglary of a dwelling. Most statutes use the term *curtilage,* but courts construe it in a modern way to protect reasonable enclosures surrounding a dwelling and in some instances even commercial structures.

Many states have also enacted statutes making the possession of burglar's tools a crime. Because burglar's tools may consist of common household items, to obtain a conviction the prosecution is usually required to prove that the defendant knew the tools could be used for a criminal purpose and intended to use them for such purpose.

Arson at common law consisted of (1) the willful and malicious burning (2) of a dwelling (3) of another. There was no requirement that the dwelling be destroyed; charring was sufficient. The requirement of "malice" was fulfilled by proof that the burning was deliberate, hence the offense only required proof of the defendant's general intent to commit the crime.

As with burglary, modern statutes extend the offense of arson to include the intentional burning of buildings, structures, and vehicles of all types. Many statutes now provide that use of explosives to damage a structure constitutes arson. Therefore, arson can no longer be considered strictly a habitation offense. In contrast to the common law, many modern statutes provide that damage by smoke or scorching is sufficient to constitute arson. The modern approach is to classify arson by categories and provide penalties accordingly with the most serious offense being arson of a dwelling.

Statutes often make it an offense to burn (and sometimes to otherwise destroy or injure) structures or personal property with the intent to defraud an insurer of the property. By definition this offense requires proof of the defendant's specific intent to defraud.

Malicious Mischief

Malicious mischief was the common-law misdemeanor of intentionally and maliciously causing damage to another's real or personal property. Modern statutes define the offense much as did the common law, often identifying it as **vandalism.** The punishment under contemporary statutes is often based on the value of property injured or destroyed.

Extortion

At common law, **extortion** involved the "taking by color of an office of money or other thing of value, that is not due, before it is due, or more than is due." Some modern statutes rather closely parallel the common law, but others equate with the common concept of *blackmail.* The gist of the modern offense is obtaining something of value from someone induced by fear of accusing or exposing the victim to some form of injury, embarrassment, or disgrace.

WHITE-COLLAR CRIME

White-collar crimes are offenses committed in the course of a person's occupation or profession and frequently include **prostitution, gambling, obscenity,** and offenses relative to the importation, manufacture, and supply of illegal drugs and alcohol. Environmental crimes and violations of the federal food and drug acts are often included in the white-collar crime category, as are **obstruction of justice** and other offenses against the administration of justice. Sometimes **violations of civil rights** are also categorized as white-collar crimes. In addition, a number of federal statutes (and to a lesser extent various state statutes) proscribe acts uniquely referred to as white-collar crimes. These include **antitrust violations, bid rigging, price fixing, money laundering, insider trading, tax fraud,** and various other offenses. Essentially, these offenses involve the use of deceit and concealment (as opposed to force or violence) to obtain economic benefits or advantages. Many crimes, for example, assaultive and homicidal offenses, are not usually considered white-collar crimes although they are committed by "white-collar persons."

ORGANIZED CRIME

Organized crime involves offenses committed by persons or groups who conduct their business through illegal enterprises. Organized crime figures often attempt to gain political influence through graft and corruption, and they frequently resort to threats and acts of violence in commission of white-collar offenses. Organized crime gained its greatest foothold during the period when the Eighteenth Amendment to the U.S. Constitution prohibiting the sale and distribution of alcoholic beverages was extant. By the time Prohibition was repealed in 1933, organized crime had become involved in many phases of our economy, often pursuing its interests through such illegal activities as loan sharking, gambling, prostitution, and drug trafficking. Protection rackets and other forms of racketeering have become the methodology of organized crime as it has infiltrated many legitimate business operations. There is often an overlap between white-collar crime and organized crime.

Under its power to regulate foreign and interstate commerce, Congress enacted the Organized Crime Control Act of 1970. Title IX of the act is entitled "Racketeer Influenced and Corrupt Organizations" and is commonly referred to by the acronym **RICO.** The law prohibits infiltration of legitimate organizations by racketeers where foreign or interstate commerce is affected. In addition to increased criminal penalties, the new RICO statute provides for forfeiture of property used in criminal enterprises and permits the government to also bring civil actions against such enterprises.

RICO makes it a crime for any person "who has received any income derived, directly or indirectly, from a pattern of racketeering activity or through collection of an unlawful debt . . . to use or invest [in] any enterprise which is engaged in interstate or foreign commerce." Second, it makes it unlawful for any such person to participate, directly or indirectly, in the conduct of the enterprise's affairs through a "pattern of racketeering." Third, it makes it a crime for any person "employed by or associated with any enterprise engaged in, or the activities of which affect, interstate or foreign commerce, to conduct or participate, directly or indirectly, in the conduct of such enterprise's affairs through a pattern of racketeering activity or collection of unlawful debt." This latter subsection of the act making it unlawful to conduct the affairs of an enterprise through a pattern of racketeering has become the most frequently relied upon provision by prosecutors. Finally, the act prohibits conspiracies to violate any of these proscriptions.

VICE CRIMES

The common law of crimes developed based on the shared experiences of the English people. Customs were greatly influenced by the Bible and church doctrine. These concepts, in turn, became the foundation of pre-Revolutionary criminal law in America. Later, as legislative bodies began defining crimes, they took a more secular approach in the exercise of their police power, which is their authority to proscribe conduct that threatens the public health, safety, and morals. Today, there is considerable debate about whether the government should criminalize vices such as prostitution, obscenity, gambling, and illicit drugs. Certainly these prohibitions are among the most widely violated.

Prostitution

A prostitute is one who engages in indiscriminate sexual activity for hire. Although it was not a crime at common law, historically prostitution has been prohibited by most American penal codes. Traditionally directed at females, laws proscribing prostitution are now directed at both females and males. Increasingly the police arrest customers who solicit prostitutes.

Obscenity

At common law the use of vulgar and obscene language and indecent public exhibitions was considered a private nuisance and punishable as a misdemeanor. Historically both the federal and state governments proscribed obscenity. With the development of mass communications in the 1950s, a flood of erotic material inundated the market. Statutes and ordinances proscribing obscenity seldom defined it. Typically laws simply proscribed the "buying, selling, giving or showing any obscene, indecent or impure book, paper or picture" without any definition of "obscene." Courts usually defined obscenity as being "repulsive" to the senses. Producers of sexually oriented materials and law enforcement officers lacked a guide to determine whether particular materials were obscene.

In 1957, the U.S. Supreme Court in *Roth v. United States,* after first ruling that obscene materials had no First Amendment protection, declared that the test of obscenity was "whether to the average person applying contemporary community standards, the dominant theme of the material taken as a whole, appeals to the prurient interest."[28] In the ensuing years the Court reviewed a number of lower court decisions culminating in 1973 in its review of the seminal case, *Miller v. California*. In *Miller* the Court clarified its *Roth* test by defining "community" so as to permit local juries to base their judgments on local and not national standards. Then the Court redefined the standards for determining obscenity, saying that the basic guidelines for the trier of fact must be (a) whether "the average person, applying contemporary community standards" would find that the work, taken as a whole, appeals to the prurient interest; (b) whether the work depicts or describes, in a patently offensive way, sexual conduct specifically defined by the applicable state law; and (c) whether the work, taken as a whole, lacks serious literary, artistic, political, or scientific value. The Court expressly rejected any requirement that the challenged materials must be found to be "utterly without redeeming social importance," and gave examples of the type of materials that would be considered "patently offensive."[29]

In 1982, in *New York v. Ferber*, the Supreme Court unanimously held that child pornography, like obscenity, is unprotected by the First Amendment.[30] Then, in 1987, the Court said that while application of "contemporary community standards" is appropriate in evaluating the first two prongs of the *Miller* test, the third prong concerning the work's value must be gauged by the "reasonable person" test.

Although most states proscribe obscenity along the lines of the federal constitutional definitions, states are free to grant greater freedom of expression than allowed under the current federal constitutional interpretations. Indeed, some have chosen to do so. Police and prosecutors experience difficulties chiefly in determining what is obscene based on "contemporary community standards" and in coping with Fourth Amendment problems relative to search and seizure of allegedly obscene materials. Thus obscenity prosecutions frequently fail.

Gambling

To gamble means to risk money on an event, chance, or contingency in the expectation of realizing a gain. The common law did not regard gambling as an offense; however, the new American states made all or certain forms of gambling illegal. Today federal laws and a variety of state statutes and local ordinances prohibit various forms of gambling. Bingo, craps, baccarat, poker, raffles, bookmaking, and slot machines are examples of common forms of gambling. However, the trend in America is toward legalization of gambling and there now exist numerous opportunities for legal gambling.

Courts generally agree that to convict a defendant for a violation of a gambling law the prosecution must establish three elements: (1) a consideration, (2) a prize, and (3) a chance. Where gambling is prohibited, laws customarily make it unlawful to possess gambling devices and provide for their confiscation.

An analysis of the gambling laws extant in the United States is difficult because laws often authorize certain forms of gambling by certain organizations (usually church, fraternal, or other nonprofit activities) while forbidding others to do the same acts. State statutes often create exceptions for retail merchandising promotions and permit charitable, nonprofit, and veterans' organizations to conduct bingo games. Indeed, many states now promote lotteries to supplement tax revenues. Betting on sports events is widespread, but because of the private consensual nature of such activity any attempt to enforce laws against participants is usually futile. Gambling laws present a paradox and enforcement must be directed primarily toward organized gambling under control of crime syndicates.

If the statute prohibiting gambling makes intent an element of the offense, the prosecution must prove the defendant's intent; otherwise, it is sufficient merely to prove the act of gambling. In some instances statutes provide that it is a defense if the actor reasonably believed that the gambling conduct was permitted under bingo or charitable raffle laws. Defendants frequently raise constitutional issues relating to search and seizure problems and in some instances a defendant charged with gambling might succeed in establishing entrapment.

Drug and Alcohol Offenses

The misuse of drugs and alcohol are among the oldest vices in society. The common law had little to say about the abuse of alcohol and did not address illicit drugs. Consequently, these offenses are based on statutory enactments reflecting the adverse social consequences of alcohol and drug abuse.

The Federal Controlled Substances Act[31] establishes schedules classifying controlled substances according to their potential for abuse and provides penalties for offenses involving the manufacture, sale, distribution, and possession of controlled substances. All states provide similar proscriptions, often setting mandatory penalties for those who sell large quantities of contraband or controlled substances with a high potential for abuse. Although most narcotics offenses are felonies, it has become common for states to provide that when possession of a very small quantity of marijuana is involved, the offense is reduced to a misdemeanor. Despite numerous challenges, drug laws generally have been upheld, as courts are generally reluctant to reassess legislative judgments in this area.

All states prohibit operating a vehicle in public while intoxicated (DWI) or while under the influence of intoxicating liquors or drugs (DUI). Many states prohibit driving with an unlawful blood alcohol level (DUBAL). Most states set 0.10 percent or more alcohol in the bloodstream as the criterion for determining intoxication. By 2000, 18 states and the District of Columbia had decreased the level of blood alcohol required to establish legal intoxication to .08 percent or less. This nationwide trend was promoted by an act of Congress passed in the summer of 1998 under which states receive lucrative federal grants for lowering the prohibited blood-alcohol level to .08 percent.

OFFENSES AGAINST PUBLIC ORDER AND SAFETY

Government has an obligation to protect the public order and safety. Virtually all governments seek to achieve this goal by criminalizing acts that threaten society's interests in order and safety. The contemporary American offenses against public order have their roots in the English common law and include several misdemeanor offenses. **Unlawful assembly, riot, and disorderly conduct** were designed to preserve order, and **vagrancy** (going about without visible means of support) was designed to punish idleness and to control suspicious persons. Traffic violations and weapons offenses, while unknown to the common law, exist by virtue of modern legislation aimed at protecting the public safety.

CASE IN POINT

**THE SUPREME COURT INVALIDATES A CHICAGO LOITERING
ORDINANCE AIMED AT STREET GANGS**

Chicago v. Morales

United States Supreme Court
527 U.S. 41, 119 S.Ct. 1849, 144 L.Ed.2d 67 (1999)

In 1992, the Chicago City Council enacted an ordinance prohibiting criminal street gang members from loitering in any public place. Over the next three years, the police issued over 89,000 dispersal orders and arrested more than 42,000 people for violating the new law. In 1999, the U.S. Supreme Court declared the ordinance unconstitutional. Writing for the Court, Justice John P. Stevens concluded that the ordinance did not provide "sufficiently specific limits on the enforcement discretion of the police" and failed to meet "constitutional standards for definiteness and clarity." The Court found that the ordinance succumbed to the vice of vagueness—that the city council had failed to meet its obligation to specify the criminal law with reasonable precision.

Following the common law, most states have enacted statutes proscribing unlawful assembly, riot, and disorderly conduct. Cities frequently supplement these prohibitions by enacting ordinances against disturbing the peace and excessive noise. The old common-law offense of vagrancy has been replaced in most states and communities by laws that prohibit loitering. Crimes against public order are often attacked as being violations of First Amendment freedoms of expression and assembly. Vagrancy has been assailed as an inherently vague offense and courts have struck down vagrancy laws as violations of due process.[32]

Motor Vehicle Violations

States, and often municipalities, have adopted laws defining a wide range of motor vehicle violations. These are generally strict-liability offenses, and thus have no requirement to prove criminal intent to find a defendant guilty of a traffic violation. Among other offenses, these laws proscribe speeding; failing to yield the right-of-way; failing to observe traffic officers, signs and signals; and driving without required equipment. During the 1970s and 1980s, states adopted a number of model laws, so that traffic offenses are highly uniform across the states. This uniformity is both necessary and desirable given the mobility of today's populace and the volume of traffic on the nation's highways.

Weapons Offenses

The Second Amendment to the U.S. Constitution provides that "a well regulated Militia, being necessary to the security of a free state, the right of the people to keep and bear Arms, shall not be infringed." Nevertheless, there are numerous state and federal statutory prohibitions against the manufacture, sale, possession, and use of firearms and other weapons. For example, states commonly enact statutes making it unlawful to carry a concealed weapon. The Federal Gun Control Act of 1968 established a fairly comprehensive regime governing the distribution of firearms.[33] For example, federal law prohibits the sale, possession, and use of machine guns and other automatic weapons. The Supreme Court has said that federal gun control laws do not violate the Second Amendment, because the amendment only protects the keeping and bearing of arms in the context of a well-regulated militia.[34] State courts have also been unsympathetic to challenges to state gun control laws based on state constitutional provisions. Today, in the wake of school shootings and other acts of senseless gun violence, a great debate rages in the land over the need for tougher gun control legislation and/or increased enforcement of existing prohibitions.

OFFENSES AGAINST THE ADMINISTRATION OF JUSTICE

The common law recognized the need to deter and, if necessary, to punish those who corrupt the orderly processes of government and the administration of justice. In the United States, federal and state statutes proscribe such offenses as **bribery, perjury, subornation of perjury,** obstruction of justice, **resisting arrest, flight to avoid prosecution, compounding a crime,** and **escape** (See glossary for definitions of these offences). Statutory offenses expand the common law and generally increase the severity of these offenses from misdemeanors to felonies.

Courts have the power to hold a person in either civil or criminal **contempt.** Civil contempt is a sanction imposed to coerce a recalcitrant person to obey a court order, for example, for failing to pay court-ordered support for dependents. A court imposes criminal contempt to punish an offender whose deliberate conduct is calculated to obstruct or embarrass the court or to degrade a judicial officer in the role of administering justice.

ENVIRONMENTAL CRIME

Unlike common-law crimes, offenses against the public health and the environment are defined by statutes enacted by the federal and state legislatures. Although not faced with the severe environmental problems of our age, the common law did regard wildlife, game, and fish as resources to be preserved. In the United States, the state and federal governments have for many years enacted regulations and imposed criminal sanctions on poachers to protect these resources for the benefit of the public. Many offenses relating to public health developed during the industrial revolution as a result of the widespread distribution of food, drugs, and cosmetics and the need to control communicable diseases. By the early 1900s, municipalities perceived the need for zoning to control nuisances and to regulate land use. Since the middle of the twentieth century, pollution of the ground, water, and air has been recognized as a major threat to the health and welfare of the people and, indeed, to the ecological balance of the earth.

Enforcement of regulations in these fields is accomplished largely by regulatory agencies and through measures imposing civil liability. Nevertheless, legislatures have found it necessary to impose criminal sanctions to effectively enforce standards and to deter violators. In contrast to the typical common-law crimes, **environmental crimes** often involves an offender's neglect to comply with required standards or failure to take action required by law. These are *mala prohibita* offenses, and statutes criminalizing conduct in these areas generally contemplate a lower level of intent, frequently imposing a standard of strict liability.

DEFENSES

Defenses are arguments that defendants use to deny criminal responsibility. Like crimes, most defenses have their roots in the English common law, though they have been modified over the years by constitutional provisions and statutes and judicial interpretations thereof.

The most common defense asserted by defendants is a general denial, often accompanied by an **alibi.** Defendants may simply deny the factual allegations of the prosecutor. A defendant who pleads alibi simply says, "I was elsewhere when the offense was committed." The Supreme Court has ruled that when the state law requires that a defendant who pleads an alibi must notify the prosecution in advance of trial and furnish the names of witnesses the defendant intends to use to support the alibi, the prosecution must make similar disclosures to the defendant concerning refutation of the evidence the defendant furnishes.[35]

Denial and alibi are examples of **negative defenses** in that they seek to negate the charge that the defendant committed a wrongful act. **Affirmative defenses,** on the other hand, do not dispute that the act took place, but deny the defendant's criminal responsibility for the act or assert other limitations on the authority of government to prosecute the defendant. Affirmative defenses to crimes may be divided into five categories:

1. those asserting lack of capacity
2. those asserting excuse or justification
3. those justifying the use of force
4. those relying on constitutional or statutory rights
5. those assailing governmental conduct

Defenses Asserting Lack of Capacity to Commit a Crime

Except in cases of strict liability, it is necessary to prove the defendant's criminal intent as well as the commission of an evil act. This first set of affirmative defenses involves the claim that the defendant lacks the capacity to form criminal intent due to **infancy, intoxication, insanity,** or **automatism.**

Infancy

The common law protected very young children from the harshness of the law by presuming a child under age 7 to be incapable of forming criminal intent. This presumption of incapacity was rebuttable for a child over 7 but under 14, with the prosecution having to demonstrate that a child under 14 was capable of comprehending the wrongdoing involved in commission of an offense. Children over age 14 were treated as adults. In many American jurisdictions these presumptions are no longer viable, because legislatures have provided that children under certain ages are subject to the jurisdiction of juvenile courts where procedures are tailored toward less mature offenders. Under federal law, a juvenile is a person who has not attained age 18 at the time of the commission of an offense.[36]

Intoxication

English common law did not excuse a person who voluntarily became intoxicated from responsibility for criminal conduct. American courts distinguish voluntary intoxication from involuntary intoxication. In most jurisdictions, voluntary intoxication may be considered in determining whether a defendant can formulate the specific intent required in such crimes as larceny, burglary, and premeditated murder. A few courts will not even permit a jury to consider voluntary intoxication on the issue of specific intent. Courts generally reject the defense of voluntary intoxication in respect to general-intent crimes such as voluntary manslaughter and most sexual offenses. Involuntary intoxication rarely occurs, but when it does, it relieves the criminality of an act committed under its influence if, as a result of intoxication, the defendant no longer knows right from wrong.

Insanity

All persons are presumed sane unless previously adjudicated insane. The concept of mental responsibility has historic roots in Anglo-American law because common-law crimes included a *mens rea,* the mental element. The *M'Naghten Rule* developed at common law provides "it must be clearly proved that, at the time of committing the act, the party accused as labouring under such a defect of reason, from disease of the mind, as not to know the nature and quality of the act he was doing; or, if he did know it, that he did not know what he was doing was wrong."[37] By the mid-1800s, the *M'Naghten Rule* had become the test for insanity used in both federal and state courts in the United States.

In 1962, the American Law Institute (ALI), proposed a new standard sometimes referred to as the **substantial capacity test.** It provides that "a person is not responsible for criminal conduct if at the time of such conduct, as a result of mental disease or defect, a person lacks substantial capacity either to appreciate the wrongfulness of his conduct or to conform his conduct to the requirements of the law." Most federal courts adopted the ALI standard. The defense of insanity has never been popular with the public, sometimes being called "a rich person's defense," because defendants who invoke it frequently expend considerable financial resources to present psychiatric testimony.

Few cases have caused as great a concern over the functioning of the criminal justice system in the United States as the verdict of "not guilty by reason of insanity" in the federal court trial of John Hinckley for the 1981 shooting of then President Ronald Reagan, his press secretary, and two law officers. The Hinckley verdict motivated Congress and several state legislatures to review the status of insanity defenses. Dissatisfied with the ALI test, which was applied in the Hinckley trial, Congress decided to eliminate the volitional prong in the federal test for insanity and to revert substantially to the *M'Naghten Rule* when it enacted the Insanity Defense Reform Act of 1984. This act provides that in federal courts:

> It is an affirmative defense to a prosecution under any Federal statute that, at the time of the commission of the acts constituting the offense, the defendant, as a result of a severe mental disease or defect, was unable to appreciate the nature and quality or the wrongfulness of his acts. Mental disease or defect does not otherwise constitute a defense.[38]

Additionally, the act stipulates: "The defendant has the burden of proving the defense of insanity by clear and convincing evidence."[39] The clear and convincing evidence standard is higher than the usual civil evidentiary standard of preponderance of the evidence but somewhat lower than the standard of beyond a reasonable doubt, the evidentiary standard required for criminal convictions.

Under the Insanity Defense Reform Act, psychiatric evidence of impaired volitional control is not admissible to support an insanity defense; however, in 1990, the U.S. Court of Appeals for the Eleventh Circuit ruled that the language of the new federal act does not bar the use of psychiatric evidence to negate specific intent where that level of intent is an element of the offense charged by the government.[40]

Although Congress has placed the burden on defendants who plead insanity in federal courts to prove their defense, state courts are divided on the issue. In some states where insanity is classified as an affirmative defense, the defendant bears the burden of proof of insanity, usually by a preponderance of the evidence. In other states, when a defendant pleads insanity and introduces some evidence of insanity, the state must then establish the defendant's sanity, usually by proof beyond a reasonable doubt, the standard required for establishing a defendant's guilt. Courts permit laypersons as well as expert witnesses to testify on the issue of a defendant's insanity.

Unlike a defendant who is simply found not guilty, a defendant found not guilty by reason of insanity may, in some circumstances, be committed to a mental institution if the trial judge determines that protection of the public requires that the defendant be confined.

Some states have recently resorted to verdicts of guilty but mentally ill in cases when the defendant's insanity has been established. Several states have abolished the defense of insanity. Although the Supreme Court has not settled the issue, its action suggests that the U.S. Constitution does not require that states allow a defendant to plead insanity.

Automatism

Traditionally, defendants claiming that their unlawful acts were committed because of an involuntary condition such as somnambulism (i.e., sleepwalking) were treating the same as those making an insanity plea. Newer cases tend to classify such involuntary actions as automatism and view them as a basis for an affirmative defense independent from insanity. The defense is usually limited to a situation where criminal conduct is beyond a person's knowledge and control. Generally there are no follow-up consequences such as institutionalization, which often occurs in an acquittal by reason of insanity.

Defenses Asserting Excuse or Justification

A defendant who asserts an excuse admits the offense but claims that under the circumstances such conduct should not result in punishment. A defendant who asserts a justification for conduct says, in effect, that it was justified under the circumstances. The five principal defenses based on a defendant asserting an excuse or justification are **duress, necessity, consent, mistake of law,** and **mistake of fact.**

Duress

The common law recognized that duress can be a defense to criminal charges if the coercion exerted involved the use of threats of harm that were "present, imminent and pending" and "of such nature as to include well grounded apprehensions of death or serious bodily harm if the act was not done." Not even the threat of imminent death was sufficient to excuse the intentional killing of an innocent human being. The defense of duress, sometimes referred to as "coercion, compulsion, or duress," is recognized today either by statute or decisional law. American courts have generally ruled that a threat of future harm is not sufficient to constitute duress. Duress has been asserted most frequently by defendants who have committed robberies and thefts and by prisoners who have escaped from custody.

Necessity

Early common-law cases recognized the defense of necessity. Suppose several people are shipwrecked on a cold night. One person swims to shore, breaks into an unoccupied beach cottage, and takes food and blankets to assist the injured until help can be secured. Prosecution in such an event would be unlikely, but if prosecuted, the defendant would properly plead the defense of necessity. American courts hold that if there is a reasonable legal alternative to violating the law, the defense of necessity fails.

Recently defendants have attempted to justify actions involving "civil disobedience" on the ground of necessity in instances when they have forcefully asserted their personal or political beliefs. In most, but not all cases, the necessity defense has been unavailing to defendants espousing social and political causes. For example, several defendants were charged with criminal trespass when they refused to leave an abortion clinic in Anchorage, Alaska. They claimed their actions were necessary to avert the imminent peril to human life that would result from abortions being performed. In rejecting their contention, the Alaska Supreme Court outlined three requirements that must be met by a person who pleads the defense of necessity: (1) The act charged must have been done to prevent a significant evil; (2) there must have been no adequate alternative; and (3) the harm caused must not have been disproportionate to the harm avoided.[41]

Consent

Because a victim may not excuse a criminal act, historically courts have said that consent is not a defense to a criminal prosecution. But there are exceptions to this general statement. For example, where lack of consent is an element of the offense, as in larceny, consent is a defense. This may be true in a prosecution for rape, but only when competent adults freely consent before having sexual relations. Consent is commonly given to physicians who perform surgery. In contact sports, such as football and boxing, consent is implied and may be a defense to reasonable instances of physical contact that may otherwise be regarded as batteries. Of course, a valid consent presupposes that it is voluntarily given by a person legally competent to do so.

Mistake of Law

One of the oft-quoted maxims of the law is that "ignorance of the law is no excuse." But in some instances a defendant's honest, but mistaken, view of the law may be accepted as a defense. One example is when such a mistake negates the specific-intent element of a crime.

Thus, a mistake of law may be asserted as a defense in a larceny case where there is a technical question of who has legal title to an asset. Likewise, a defendant's good faith, but mistaken trust in the validity of a divorce has been held to be a defense to a charge of bigamy. A court will never recognize a dishonest pretense of ignorance of the law as a defense.

Mistake of Fact

In contrast to the ancient common-law maxim that "ignorance of the law is no excuse," at common law ignorance or mistake of fact, guarded by an honest purpose, afforded a defendant a sufficient excuse for a supposed criminal act. American courts have agreed, but have generally said that a mistake of fact will not be recognized as a defense to a general-intent crime unless the mistake is a reasonable one for a person to make under the circumstances. However, even an unreasonable mistake may be asserted as a defense to a crime that requires a specific intent.

In strict-liability offenses, the defense of mistake of fact is unavailing since these offenses are not based on intent. Having consensual sexual relations with a minor is generally considered a strict-liability offense and a mistake of fact as to a minor's age is generally not a defense. Even if a court finds that a statutory rape statute requires proof of a general criminal intent to convict, a defendant's reasonable mistake of fact concerning a female's age is generally not available as a defense. In the past decade, trial courts have rejected the contention that because a minor female can consent to an abortion, she should be able to consent to sexual intercourse. Yet some judges have questioned the need to employ a strict-liability standard in consensual sexual relationships where a minor represents herself as an adult.

Defenses Justifying the Use of Force

The use of force may be a defense to a criminal charge that the defendant caused injury or death to another. Therefore, the defense of **justifiable use of force** is applicable to the assaultive and homicidal offenses when the defendant claims that the use of force was justified under the circumstances.

In general, the use of **deadly force** in self-defense requires that the person using such force (1) be in a place where the person has a right to be; (2) act without fault; and (3) act in reasonable fear or apprehension of death or great bodily harm. In evaluating whether the use of deadly force is reasonable, courts consider numerous factors. Among these are the sizes, ages, and physical abilities of the parties, whether the attacker was armed, and the attacker's reputation for violence. Ordinarily, a person may use whatever degree of nondeadly force appears reasonably necessary under the circumstances.

Self-Defense

At common law, a person attacked had a duty "to retreat to the wall" before using deadly force in **self-defense**. A majority of courts reject the common-law doctrine of requiring a person to retreat to the greatest extent possible before meeting force with force. Rather, they say that a person attacked or threatened may stand one's ground and use any force reasonably necessary to prevent harm. A substantial minority of courts, however, has adopted the principle that a person who can safely retreat must do so before using deadly force. Courts that follow the retreat rule have generally adopted the principle that a person does not have to retreat in one's own dwelling.

In recent years the concept of self-defense by women has been expanded where a woman claims to have been continually battered by a man. **Battered-woman syndrome (BWS)** refers to a pattern of psychological and behavioral symptoms of a woman living with a male in a battering relationship. Some courts now permit a female in that situation who is charged with assaulting or killing a man to show that even though she did not face immediate harm, her plea of self-defense should be recognized because her actions were a response to constant battering by the man with whom she lived. Relatively little decisional law from the higher courts has developed in this area. The trend seems to be to allow such evidence, either by judicial decision or statute.

Following the same rationale, if there is evidence that a child has been abused continually over an extended period, there is a movement now to assert the **battered-child syndrome (BCS)** in defense of a child accused of assaulting or killing a parent. In a much-discussed opinion, a Washington appellate court held: "Neither law nor logic suggest any reason to limit to women recognition of the impact a battering relationship may have on the victim's actions or perceptions. . . . the rationale underlying the admissibility of testimony regarding the battered women syndrome is at least as compelling, if not more so, when applied to children."[42]

Defense of Others

At common law a defender had the right to use reasonable force to prevent commission of a felony or to protect members of the household who were endangered. The trend in American jurisdictions is to allow a person "to stand in the shoes of the victim" and to use such reasonable force as is necessary to defend anyone from harm, irrespective of relationship. Courts in many states limit a person's right to defend another individual from harm to those persons who "reasonably believe" that force is necessary to protect another. Some courts take a more restrictive view and hold that an intervener is justified in using force to defend another only if the party being defended would have been justified in using the same force in self-defense. Of course, under either standard, the right to go to the defense of another does not authorize a person to resort to retaliatory force.

Defense of Habitation

The common law held that "a man's home is his castle" and placed great emphasis on the security of a person's dwelling and permitted the use of deadly force against an intruder. This is sometimes referred to as the **castle doctrine.** While a householder may, under some circumstances, be justified in using deadly force, the householder would not be justified in taking a life to repel a mere trespass. Courts have said that the use of deadly force is generally justified to prevent a forcible entry into the habitation in circumstances such as threats or when the occupant reasonably apprehends death or great bodily harm to self or other occupants or reasonably believes the assailant intends to commit a felony. The courts have generally applied the castle doctrine against trespassers, but they have divided on whether this doctrine applies to co-occupants or others legally on the premises.

Defense of Property

The right to defend your personal property is more limited than the right to defend your home place or yourself. The common law allowed a person in lawful possession of property to use reasonable, but not deadly, force to protect it. Today, the use of force to protect a person's property is often defined by statute. Typically, Iowa law provides that "[a] person is justified in the use of reasonable force to prevent or terminate criminal interference with his or her possession or other right to property."[43] The quoted statutory language generally represents contemporary decisional law even in absence of a statute.

Defenses Based on Constitutional and Statutory Authority

Everyone is familiar with the scenario of the witness who invokes the constitutional privilege against self-incrimination based on the Fifth Amendment to the Constitution that provides that "[N]o person . . . shall be compelled in any criminal case to be a witness against himself." The privilege against self-incrimination is applicable to the states through the Fourteenth Amendment. The privilege against self-incrimination guaranteed by the federal Constitution is a personal one that applies to natural persons but not corporations. A strict reading of the clause would limit the privilege to testimony given in a criminal trial. The Supreme Court, however, has held that an individual may refuse to answer official questions posed in any proceeding, civil or criminal, formal or informal, where the answers might be incriminating. A classic example is the privilege of suspects in police custody to invoke their *Miranda* rights, a subject we discuss in Chapter 10.

Immunity

A witness compelled to give incriminating testimony receives **use immunity** (i.e., the testimony given cannot be used against the witness). This form of immunity meets the demands of the Constitution.[44] In some states a witness who testifies under a grant of immunity is given **transactional immunity**, a broader protection than required under the federal Constitution. Transactional immunity protects a witness from prosecution for any activity mentioned in the witness's testimony. Despite a grant of immunity, a witness may be prosecuted for making material false statements under oath.

Sometimes a prosecutor, with approval of the court, grants a witness **contractual immunity** to induce a suspect to testify against someone and thereby enable the prosecution to obtain a conviction not otherwise obtainable because of constitutional protection against self-incrimination. This type of immunity is rarely granted if other available evidence will lead to a conviction. The authority to grant immunity in federal courts is vested in the U.S. attorney with approval of the attorney general or certain authorized assistants.[45] At the state level such authority is generally vested in the chief prosecuting officer (i.e., the district or state attorney).

Under international law, a person who has diplomatic status and serves as a part of a diplomatic mission, as well as members of the diplomat's staff and household, is immune from arrest and prosecution, thus enjoying **diplomatic immunity.**

Double Jeopardy

The concept of forbidding retrial of a defendant who has been found not guilty developed under English common law. The Fifth Amendment to the U.S. Constitution embodies the principle by stating "[N]or shall any person be subject for the same offence to be twice put in jeopardy of life or limb." The Double Jeopardy Clause forbids a second prosecution for the same offense after a defendant has been acquitted or even after a conviction.[46] But, if a defendant appeals from a conviction and prevails, it is not **double jeopardy** for the prosecution to retry the defendant, unless the appellate court rules that there was insufficient evidence to sustain the defendant's conviction.[47] Nor is it double jeopardy to retry a defendant if the trial court, at the defendant's request, has declared a mistrial.[48] If, however, the government moves for a mistrial, the defendant objects, and the court grants the mistrial, the prosecution must establish a manifest necessity for the mistrial for a retrial to be permitted.

Some offenses are crimes against both the federal and state governments. The policy, and in some instances state law, forbids a second prosecution once an offender has been prosecuted in a different jurisdiction. Nevertheless, under the federal system the double jeopardy clause does not preclude a prosecution by both the federal and state governments, since separate sovereigns are involved.[49] Yet, this principle does not allow two courts within a state to try an accused for the same offense.[50] In addition to protecting against a second prosecution for the same offense after conviction or acquittal, the Double Jeopardy Clause protects against multiple punishments for the same offense.[51] The Constitution, however, does not define "same offense." In *Blockburger v. United States* (1932), the Supreme Court said that "[t]he applicable rule is that, where the same act or transaction constitutes a violation of two distinct statutory provisions, the test to be applied to determine whether there are two offenses or only one is whether each provision requires proof of an additional fact which the other does not."[52]

The *Blockburger* test compares the elements of the crimes in question and examines the elements, not the facts. Not all courts have regarded *Blockburger* as the exclusive method of determining whether successive prosecutions violate the principle of double jeopardy. Indeed, some courts look also to the evidence to be presented to prove those crimes.

Statutes of Limitations

A **statute of limitations** is a legislative enactment that places a time limit on the prosecution of a crime. Common law placed no time limits on prosecution. There is no federal constitutional basis to limit the time in which a prosecution can be initiated. Nonetheless, the federal government and almost all states have laws that prescribe certain time limits for prosecution of most offenses, except murder. There are two primary public policy reasons for enacting statutes of limitations on the prosecution of crimes. First, it is generally accepted that a person should not be under threat of prosecution for too long a period. Second, after a prolonged period, proof is either unavailable or, if available, perhaps not credible.

Statutes of limitations seldom place time limits on prosecutions for murder and other very serious offenses. This fact was dramatized in 1994 when Byron De La Beckwith was convicted for the June 1963 murder of Medgar Evers. Evers was an official of the National Association for the Advancement of Colored People, and his death galvanized support for the enactment of civil rights laws in the 1960s. Two trials in 1964 ended in deadlocked juries;

but after extended litigation, and a lapse of more than 30 years since the victim's death, a Mississippi jury found Beckwith guilty of killing Evers.

Under most statutes of limitation, the period for prosecution begins when a crime is committed, and not when it is discovered. The period ends when an arrest warrant is issued, an indictment is returned, or an information is filed. The period of limitations is interrupted while a perpetrator is a fugitive or conceals one's self from authorities. This cessation of the statute of limitations is often referred to as the "tolling" of the statutory period.

Federal statutes of limitations provide a five-year limitation on prosecution of noncapital crimes.[53] Although limitations periods vary among the states, most provide five-to-seven-year limitations on the prosecution of felonies other than murder, one to two years on major misdemeanors, and a year or less on minor misdemeanors

Defenses Based on Improper Government Conduct

Law enforcement officers may provide an opportunity for a predisposed person to commit a crime, but they are not permitted to *manufacture* crime by implanting criminal ideas into innocent minds. Therefore, a person who has been induced to commit an offense under these latter circumstances may plead the defense of **entrapment.** A defendant who claims to have committed an offense as a result of inducement by an undercover police officer or a confidential police informant often asserts the defense of entrapment. It is not available to a defendant who has been entrapped by a person not associated with the government or police.

Entrapment was not a defense under the common law, and strictly speaking, it is not based on the Constitution. Nevertheless, it has long been recognized in federal and state courts in the United States. In a landmark case arising during Prohibition days, the Supreme Court held that a federal officer had entrapped a defendant by using improper inducements to cause him to buy illegal liquor for the officer. The Court observed that the evidence revealed that the defendant, Sorrells, had not been predisposed to commit a crime but had been induced by the government agent to do so. The Court opined that entrapment occurs when criminal conduct involved is "the product of the creative activity of [law enforcement officers]."[54] In *Sorrells,* the majority of the justices viewed entrapment as whether the defendant's criminal intent originated in the mind of the officer or whether the defendant was predisposed to commit the offense. This focus on the predisposition of the defendant has come to be known as the subjective test of entrapment. A minority of justices in *Sorrells* would have applied what is now known as the objective test of entrapment. Under this view, the court would simply determine whether the police methods were so improper as likely to induce or ensnare a person into committing a crime.

Most courts follow the subjective view. Thus, a person who pleads entrapment is held to have admitted commission of the offense. A jury then determines whether the defendant committed the crime because of predisposition, or if the defendant was improperly induced to do so by the police. Where courts follow the objective view, the judge, not the jury, determines whether the police methods were so improper as to constitute entrapment. Some

CASE IN POINT

ENTRAPMENT IN A CHILD PORNOGRAPHY CASE

Jacobson v. United States

United States Supreme Court
503 U.S. 540, 112 S.Ct. 1535, 118 L.Ed.2d 174 (1992)

In 1987, Keith Jacobson was indicted for violating the Child Protection Act of 1984, which criminalizes the knowing receipt through the mails of a "visual depiction [that] involves the use of a minor engaging in sexually explicit conduct." At trial Jacobson contended the government entrapped him into committing the crime. A jury found him guilty, and his conviction was affirmed by the Court of Appeals. The U.S. Supreme Court granted review. In evaluating the evidence at Jacobson's trial, the Supreme Court found that while it was still legal to do so, Jacobson ordered some magazines containing photos of nude boys. After Congress enacted the Child Protection Act making this illegal, two government agencies learned that Jacobson had ordered the magazines. The agencies sent mail to Jacobson through fictitious organizations to explore his willingness to break the law. He was literally bombarded with solicitations, which included communi-

cations decrying censorship and questioning the legitimacy and constitutionality of the government's efforts to restrict availability of sexually explicit materials. He finally responded to an undercover solicitation to order child pornography and was arrested after a controlled delivery of the explicit sexual materials. After pointing out that for 26 months the government agents had made Jacobson the target of repeated mailings, the Court held that the prosecution failed to produce evidence that Jacobson was predisposed to break the law before the government directed its efforts toward him. Adding that government agents may not implant a criminal design in an innocent person's mind and then induce commission of a crime, the Court reversed his conviction, observing that Congress had not intended for government officials to instigate crime by luring persons otherwise innocent to commit offenses.

federal courts have simply said that when police conduct is outrageous, it becomes a question of law for the judge to determine if governmental misconduct is so shocking as to be a due process of law violation. In courts that strictly follow the objective view, the defendant's predisposition to commit an offense is irrelevant.

Two principal reasons account for the increased assertion of the defense of entrapment in recent years. First, a large number of violations of narcotics laws have been prosecuted on the basis of undercover police activity and evidence given by confidential police informants. Second, there has been increased attention to prosecuting corruption involving government officials.

Selective Prosecution

Selective enforcement of the criminal law is not itself a constitutional violation, and therefore, without more, it does not constitute a defense.[55] To prevail on the defense of **selective prosecution,** a defendant must demonstrate that other similarly situated persons have not been prosecuted for similar conduct, and that prosecution was based on some impermissible ground such as race, religion, or exercise of the First Amendment rights of free speech.

Nontraditional Defenses

Although they are rarely successful, defendants sometimes employ novel and innovative defenses. When a novel defense leads to an acquittal, appellate courts do not have an opportunity to evaluate the legal basis of the defense so precedent is slow to develop. Such defenses have alleged victim's negligence, premenstrual syndrome (PMS), compulsive gambling, post-traumatic stress syndrome (PTSS) (refers to the unique stresses suffered during combat), the junk food defense, and pornographic and television intoxication. From time to time claims are asserted defensively of urban survival syndrome, XYY chromosome abnormality, black rage, and multiple personalities.

PUNISHMENT OF OFFENDERS

Law and society both demand that criminals be punished for their offenses. Defendants who are convicted face a variety of punishments, depending on the nature and severity of their crimes. These punishments are designed to meet one or more of the basic goals of the criminal justice system: retribution, deterrence, rehabilitation, and incapacitation.

- **Retribution.** Literally, this term refers to something demanded as payment. In criminal justice, retribution is the idea that the criminal must pay for wrongs perpetrated against society. The biblical phrase "an eye for an eye" is often invoked in this regard.[56] Another oft-used phrase is that criminals must be given their "just deserts." Some people question whether retribution, or legalized vengeance, is a legitimate goal of criminal justice. The answer is that the desire for revenge is deep-seated in the human psyche and that if the state does not exact vengeance individuals will resort to vigilantism. Another defense of retribution focuses on the need for expiation of guilt—criminals must suffer in order to atone for their wrongs. Finally, defenders of retribution note that it involves **proportionality**— offenders are punished, but punishment must fit the crime.
- **Deterrence.** This is the idea that punishing persons who commit crimes will prevent other similarly disposed individuals from committing like offenses. Criminals must be punished to the degree necessary to impress those who would emulate them of the undesirable consequences of crime. This assumes, of course, that potential criminals are rational calculators of costs and benefits associated with particular courses of action. In many cases, this may be basically true, but it certainly does not apply to crimes of passion. Another problem with deterrence theory is that people discount the negative consequences of crime by the improbability of being caught. To be an effective deterrent, punishment would have to be so severe that even those who did not believe that they were going to be caught would not take the risk. We could, for example, increase compliance with speed limits by executing those who are caught speeding, but such a punishment would be unthinkable. In practice, the criminal justice system strives to achieve deterrence, but not at the expense of proportionality in punishment.

- **Rehabilitation.** Perhaps the loftiest goal of the criminal justice system, rehabilitation means changing the offender to function in civil society without resorting to criminal behavior. On its face, this is the most appealing theory of criminal punishment. We would like to believe that by punishing people we can improve them. Of course, rehabilitation involves more than punishment. It entails various sorts of programs and therapies, each of which is based on its own theory of what causes criminal behavior. Today, high **recidivism** (repeat offending) rates among those convicted of felonies have made society much less sanguine about its ability to rehabilitate "hardened criminals."
- **Incapacitation.** The idea here is that that punishment should prevent criminals from committing additional crimes. Contemporary American society resorts to imprisonment or, in extreme cases, execution to rid itself of seriously threatening behavior. Although nearly everyone favors incapacitation of violent offenders, in practice incapacitation extends beyond the execution or incarceration of violent criminals. For instance, when the state revokes the driver's license of someone convicted of driving while intoxicated, the purpose is primarily incapacitation. Similarly, some states have laws offering convicted rapists the option of taking a drug to render them incapable of committing rape.

Each of these goals or justifications of punishment is somewhat controversial, and there is not a consensus as to which should be paramount. As we examine particular punishments, the student should reflect on which of these goals is being served.

Historical Background

Under English common law, persons convicted of misdemeanors were generally subjected to **corporal punishment** such as flogging. The misdemeanant was taken into the public square, bound to the whipping post, and administered as many lashes as were prescribed by law for the offense. At common law, felonies were punishable by death. In the early days of the common law, nobles who committed **capital crimes** were shown mercy by simply being beheaded. Commoners who were sentenced to death were often subjected to more grisly forms of punishment—they were broken on the wheel, burned at the stake, or drawn and quartered. Eventually, the comparatively humane method of hanging was adopted as the principal means of execution in England.

In colonial America, criminal punishment followed common-law practice, although the Massachusetts Code of 1648 mandated the **death penalty** in cases of witchcraft, blasphemy, sodomy, adultery, and "man stealing," as well as the common-law capital crimes. During the colonial period of American history, and indeed well into the nineteenth century, the death penalty was often inflicted for a variety of felonies including rape, arson, and horse theft; and corporal punishment, primarily flogging, was widely used for a variety of crimes, including many misdemeanors

The American Bill of Rights, ratified in 1791, prohibited the imposition of "cruel and unusual punishments." The Framers of the Bill of Rights sought to prevent the use of torture, which had been common in Europe as late as the eighteenth Century. They did not intend, however, to outlaw the death penalty or abolish all forms of corporal punishment;

however, the meaning of cruel and unusual punishment has changed markedly since 1791. As the Supreme Court noted in 1958, the Cruel and Unusual Punishments Clause must draw its meaning from the "evolving standards of decency that mark the progress of a maturing society."[57]

In the early nineteenth century, reformers introduced the concept of the **penitentiary,** literally, "a place to do penance." The idea was that criminals could be reformed through isolation, Bible study, and hard labor. These gave rise to the notion of rehabilitation, the belief that the criminal justice system could reform criminals and reintegrate them into society. Many of the educational, occupational training, and psychological programs found in modern prisons are based on this theory.

By the twentieth century, **incarceration** replaced corporal punishment as the mainstay of criminal sentencing. All states, as well as the federal government, constructed prisons to house persons convicted of felonies. Even cities and counties constructed jails for the confinement of persons convicted of misdemeanors. The death penalty remained in wide use, however, for the most serious violent felonies. But the gallows were replaced by the firing squad, the gas chamber, the electric chair, and, eventually, lethal injection.

The Death Penalty

By the 1960s, it appeared that the death penalty was on the way out. Public opinion no longer favored it and a number of states had abolished it. In those that had not, the courts began to impose restrictions on its use. When the Supreme Court declared Georgia's death penalty law unconstitutional in *Furman v. Georgia* (1972),[58] many observers thought it signaled the demise of the death penalty nationwide. That decision striking the Georgia death penalty focused on the virtually unlimited discretion the state placed in trial juries empowered to impose death sentences for a number of felonies. According to Justice Stewart's concurring opinion in *Furman,* Georgia's administration of the death penalty was unpredictable to the point of being "freakishly imposed." In the wake of the *Furman* decision, Georgia and most other states revised their death penalty laws to address the concerns raised by the Court. In *Gregg v. Georgia* (1976),[59] the Supreme Court upheld Georgia's revised death penalty statute, thus effectively ending a four-year moratorium on capital punishment (for further discussion, see Chapter 10).

Capital punishment officially returned to America in 1977 when the state of Utah placed convicted murderer Gary Gilmore in front of a firing squad. Since then, the administration of the death penalty has become more common. Currently, 39 states as well as the federal government have statutes providing for capital punishment.

The Anti-Drug Abuse Act of 1988 allows the death penalty for so-called drug kingpins who control "continuing criminal enterprises" whose members intentionally kill or procure others to kill in furtherance of the enterprise.[60] Moreover, the Violent Crime Control and Law Enforcement Act of 1994, better known as the Federal Crime Bill, dramatically increased the number of federal crimes eligible for the death penalty. Federal law now permits capital punishment for a number of crimes, including treason, murder of a federal law enforcement official, as well as kidnapping, carjacking, child abuse, and bank robbery that result in death.

In August 1997, Timothy McVeigh was sentenced to death for his role in the 1995 bombing of the federal building in Oklahoma City. After requesting his appeals be halted, McVeigh's execution was scheduled for May 16, 2001. As that date approached, the FBI disclosed it had failed to release to McVeigh's attorneys several thousand pages of documents concerning the case. Attorney General John Ashcroft postponed the execution to allow review of the documents. McVeigh's lawyers then sought additional delays to conduct a further study, but while lamenting the FBI's dereliction, U.S. District Judge Richard P. Matsch found the documents had no bearing on McVeigh's guilt; a federal appeals court agreed. McVeigh declined to pursue further appeals and was executed by lethal injection on the morning of June 11, 2001 at the federal prison at Terre Haute, Indiana.

Even though the death penalty is supported both by law and public opinion, it remains the object of intense debate. Objections to the death penalty include moral, constitutional, and practical arguments. Some believe that state-sponsored execution is nothing more than legalized murder, although the traditional legal justification of capital punishment is that it, like war and self-defense, involves justifiable homicide. Others argue that the death penalty today is "cruel and unusual punishment" in that it is relatively infrequently applied and the United States is one of the few countries that have not abolished it. The opponents of the death penalty often see it as barbaric and believe it is inconsistent with a civilized society. Others claim that the death penalty has no appreciable deterrent value, a claim buttressed by the fact that states that have abolished the death penalty do not have higher murder rates. Whatever the theoretical deterrence value of the death penalty, its actual deterrent effect is no doubt attenuated by the years of delay between sentencing and execution.

Since the reinstatement of capital punishment in 1976, the courts have continued to wrestle with the death penalty issue. While generally upholding state death penalty statutes and only infrequently reversing death sentences, the Supreme Court has imposed a number of additional limitations on the ultimate punishment. For example, the Court has disallowed the death penalty in cases of rape.[61] It has held that persons cannot be sentenced to death if they were under the age of 16 at the time they committed their capital crimes.[62] It has also said that prisoners who become insane while on death row cannot be put to death until their sanity is restored.[63] The Court opined that executing a prisoner who is unable to comprehend what is taking place and why it is taking place is nothing more than mindless vengeance, which the Eighth Amendment prohibits.

Is the Death Penalty Racially Discriminatory?

In *McCleskey v. Kemp* (1987), the Supreme Court upheld the death sentence imposed on Warren McCleskey, an African-American who killed a white police officer during an armed robbery.[64] In challenging his death sentence, McCleskey relied on a sophisticated statistical study that purported to demonstrate that capital punishment in Georgia was infected by pervasive racial discrimination. The study showed that, while black defendants were more likely to receive the death penalty, the real disparity pertained to the race of the victim. Defendants who killed whites were much more likely to receive the death penalty than were defendants who killed African-Americans. The Court took the view that, even assuming the statistical validity of the study, McCleskey had not shown that his sentence was the result of racial discrimination. Moreover, in what some commentators viewed as a revealing statement, the Court expressed the view that if it accepted McCleskey's claim, the entire system of criminal sentencing might be vulnerable to attack on equal protection gounds. Since the Georgia study was conducted, criminologists have conducted similar studies in other states and most of them have reached similar conclusions. Although the Supreme Court has chosen not to regard this as a viable equal protection issue, the debate over the discriminatory impact of the death penalty rages on.

Methods of Execution

Today, one of the most heated controversies over the death penalty involves the method by which it is carried out. There are currently five methods of execution extant in the United States: the electric chair, lethal injection, the gas chamber, the firing squad, and hanging. Hanging is by far the least common and, with the possible exception of the gas chamber, it is also the least humane mode of capital punishment. Nevertheless, a federal appeals court ruled in 1994 that hanging, as it is administered by the state of Washington, is not cruel and unusual punishment.[65] The gas chamber has also been the subject of legal challenge, but that issue has yet to be resolved.[66]

The electric chair was introduced in the 1890s as a "humanitarian" alternative to the gallows. This method of execution subjects the inmate to approximately 2,000 volts of electricity conducted through copper electrodes attached to the head. Usually, the first jolt of electricity causes death by cardiac arrest and respiratory paralysis, although there have been a number of instances when multiple jolts have had to be applied. In September 1999, the Florida Supreme Court divided 4–3 in upholding the use of the electric chair.[67] A dissenting justice took the unusual step of including photos of actual executions in an appendix to his opinion.

Incarceration

Today incarceration is the conventional mode of punishment prescribed for persons convicted of felonies. Under federal and state law, felonies are classified by their seriousness, and convicted felons may be imprisoned for periods ranging from one year to life. Incarceration is usually available as a punishment for those convicted of the more serious misdemeanors, but for only up to one year in most jurisdictions. While it was originally thought to be an effective means of rehabilitation, most criminologists now view incarceration simply as a means of isolating those persons who pose a serious threat to society. In 1999, the U.S. Department of Justice reported that by mid-1998 the number of inmates in federal and state prisons reached an all-time high, with 1,277,866 persons incarcerated.[68] Indeed, prison populations more than tripled in the last two decades. This tremendous increase reflects the fact that during the 1980s and 1990s federal and state sentencing laws were amended to increase the length of prison terms given to convicted felons. Unfortunately, many prisons are now seriously overcrowded to the point that courts must limit the number of inmates that can be confined.

Prisoners' Rights

The federal courts have made it clear that the Eighth Amendment's prohibition of "cruel and unusual punishments" imposes obligations on prison administrators to maintain certain standards of confinement. Traditionally, courts adopted a "hands-off" policy, allowing prison officials free rein. In the late 1960s, that situation began to change, as federal and state tribunals came to examine prison conditions and policies. As the courts signaled their willingness to scrutinize the prisons, litigation mushroomed. In the past two decades litigation in the federal courts by prisoners has increased dramatically, often challenging conditions of prison overcrowding. Although the Supreme Court has said, "the Constitution does not mandate comfortable prisons,"[69] lower federal courts have intervened to limit the number of inmates than can be housed in some prisons.

A sizable number of state prison systems have been or are currently under court orders to improve conditions of confinement or reduce overcrowding. In recent years some state courts have begun to focus their attention on the deplorable conditions existing in many city and county jails. As currently interpreted, the Eighth Amendment requires that prisoners must be provided with reasonably adequate food, clothing, shelter, medical care, and sanitation and that there must be a reasonable assurance of their personal safety. In 1992, the Supreme Court held that a prisoner who is beaten maliciously by guards may bring a civil action for damages based on a claim of cruel and unusual punishment, even if the prisoner does not suffer "significant injuries."[70]

The courts have held that a prison inmate retains those First Amendment rights "that are not inconsistent with his status as a prisoner or with the legitimate penological objectives of the corrections system."[71] For example, under the Free Exercise Clause of the First Amendment, courts are generally receptive to prisoners' rights to possess bibles, prayer books, and other religious materials, as well as inmates' rights to be visited by the clergy. On the other hand, courts have generally upheld restrictions on religious exercises if they disrupt prison order or routine.[72]

One of the most firmly established **rights of prisoners** is the right of access to the courts. The Supreme Court made it clear decades ago that prison officials may not deny inmates access to the courts, nor penalize them for utilizing that access.[73] Similarly, courts have held that indigent inmates must be furnished writing materials and notarial services to assist them in filing petitions and seeking writs from courts. Courts have generally upheld the right of prisoners to meet with counsel in private and, in the absence of other forms of legal assistance, to have access to law libraries.[74]

The courts have also recognized that prisoners retain a limited right to communicate with the outside world via the mails, although prison officials may limit and censor the mail prisoners send and receive, provided there is no interference with attorney–client relationships. Prison officials also have broad latitude to restrict visitation privileges if there is reason to believe that an inmate is receiving smuggled contraband from visitors.[75] Likewise, prison regulations impinging on inmates' interests in free assembly and association have been consistently upheld. The federal courts have imposed limits on prison disciplinary measures such as corporal punishment and the extended use of punitive isolation. Today, prison discipline is largely accomplished by the granting and removal of **good-time credit,** that is, early release for good behavior.

Parole

Traditionally most states have provided for early release from prison on **parole** for those inmates who can demonstrate to the satisfaction of a **parole board** their willingness to conform their conduct to the requirements of the law.[76] Persons released on parole must submit to a number of conditions (see sidebar). If these conditions are violated, parole can be revoked and the offender returned to prison to serve the remainder of the original sentence. The

Federal Sentencing Reform Act of 1984 abolished parole for federal offenders who commit offenses on or after November 1, 1987. Many states have followed the lead of the federal government and have abolished or restricted parole.

Alternatives to Incarceration

Although society must be protected from violent offenders who have shown no inclination toward reform, today we recognize that imprisonment is not the appropriate punishment for all convicted felons. Moreover, the overcrowding of penal institutions mandates the consideration of alternatives. Of course, there are other means of punishing nonviolent offenders, first-time offenders, and those who have potential for rehabilitation. One of the most common of these is **probation**, where the convicted person is not incarcerated in a penal institution but remains under the close supervision of authorities. About 3 million adults are on probation in the United States. Probation is usually conditioned on restrictions on the probationer's everyday conduct (see sidebar). The most extreme limitations on conduct and movement take the form of **house arrest**. Unfortunately, the success of probation has often been hindered by inadequate staffing, resulting in inadequate supervision of probationers. Increasingly probationers are being monitored through the use of electronic ankle bracelets that allow officials to track their whereabouts.

Boot Camps
In recent years, state legislatures have experimented with military-style **boot camps** as an alternative to prison. Boot camps are designed to instill discipline in young offenders who have committed nonviolent offenses, often brought about by their drug abuse. In lieu of a prison sentence, they elect to undergo three to six months of training that often includes drug rehabilitation and work on public projects. Although boot camps have produced some notable success stories, there is little evidence that they are superior to conventional incarceration in terms of reducing the rates of recidivism.

Community Service
The requirement that an offender perform community service is becoming more attractive as a punishment for less serious crimes, especially for juveniles and first-time offenders. **Community service** is generally regarded as a more meaningful sanction than the imposition of a fine. It is also viewed as less likely than incarceration to promote future criminal behavior. The theory underlying community service is that an offender will become aware of obligations to the community and how criminal conduct violates those obligations. Community service is often imposed as a condition of probation or as part of a pretrial diversion program in which first-time nonviolent offenders are offered the opportunity to avoid prosecution by completing a program of counseling or service.

Restitution
As society becomes more cognizant of the rights of crime victims, courts are increasingly likely to require that persons convicted of crimes pay sums of money to their victims by way

STANDARD CONDITIONS OF PROBATION FOR U.S. CODE OFFENDERS

SIDEBAR

1. You shall go directly to the district shown on this CERTIFICATE OF RELEASE (unless released to the custody of other authorities). Within three days after your arrival, you shall report to your parole advisor if you have one, and the United States Probation Officer whose name appears on this Certificate. If in any emergency you are unable to contact your parole advisor, or your Probation Officer or the United States Probation Office, you shall communicate with the United States Parole Commission, Department of Justice, Chevy Chase, Maryland 20815.

2. If you are released to the custody of other authorities, and after your release from physical custody of such authorities, you are unable to report to the United States Probation Officer to whom you are assigned within three days, you shall report instead to the nearest United States Probation Officer.

3. You shall not leave the limits fixed by this CERTIFICATE OF RELEASE without written permission from your Probation Officer.

4. You shall notify your Probation Officer within 2 days of any change in your place of residence.

5. You shall make a complete and truthful written report (on a form provided for that purpose) to your Probation Officer between the first and third day of each month, and on the final day of parole. You shall also report to your Probation Officer at other times as your Probation Officer directs, providing complete and truthful information.

6. You shall not violate any law. Nor shall you associate with persons engaged in criminal activity. If you are arrested or questioned by a law-enforcement officer, you shall within 2 days report such contact to your Probation Officer or the United States Probation Office.

7. You shall not enter into any agreement to act as an "informer" or special agent for any law-enforcement agency.

8. You shall work regularly unless excused by your Probation Officer, and support your legal dependents, if any, to the best of your ability. You shall report within 2 days to your Probation Officer any changes in employment.

9. You shall not drink alcoholic beverages to excess. You shall not purchase, possess, use or administer marijuana or narcotic or other habit-forming or dangerous drugs, unless prescribed or advised by a physician. You shall not frequent places where such drugs are illegally sold, dispensed, used or given away.

10. You shall not associate with persons who have a criminal record unless you have permission of your Probation Officer.

11. You shall not possess a firearm/ammunition or other dangerous weapons.

12. You shall permit confiscation by your Probation Officer of any materials which your Probation Officer believes may constitute contraband in your possession and which your Probation Officer observes in plain view in your residence, place of business or occupation, vehicle(s) or on your person.

13. You shall make a diligent effort to satisfy any fine, restitution order, court costs or assessment, and/or court ordered child support or alimony payment that has been, or may be, imposed, and shall provide such financial information as may be requested, by your Probation Officer, relevant to the payment of the obligation. If unable to pay the obligation in one sum, you will cooperate with your Probation Officer in establishing an installment payment schedule.

14. You shall submit to a drug test whenever ordered by your Probation Officer.

Source: United States Parole Commission

of **restitution.** Typically, requirements to make restitution are imposed in property crimes cases where victims have suffered some sort of economic loss. Often the requirement to pay restitution is one of several conditions that must be met in order for the offender to gain release via probation. The term *restitution* should not be confused with *retribution,* which, as noted previously, is one of the classic justifications for imposing criminal punishments.

Fines and Forfeitures

Monetary **fines** are by far the most common punishment for those convicted of misdemeanors. Felons are likewise often subject to fines in addition to, or instead of, incarceration. Usually, the law allows the sentencing judge to impose a fine, a jail term, or some combination of the two. A number of felonies, especially serious economic crimes, now carry very heavy fines. For example, violations of federal banking and securities laws are punishable by fines running into the millions of dollars. The Eighth Amendment to the United States Constitution prohibits "excessive fines," and many state constitutions contain similar protections. But appellate courts rarely overturn criminal fines on this basis.

Federal law provides for **forfeiture** of the proceeds of a variety of criminal activities. Under federal law a "conveyance," which includes aircraft, motor vehicles, and vessels, is subject to forfeiture if it is used to transport controlled substances.[77] Real estate may be forfeited if it is used to commit or facilitate commission of a drug-related felony.[78] Many states have similar statutes. Though technically this kind of forfeiture is a civil, and not a criminal sanction, the U.S. Supreme Court has recognized that forfeiture constitutes significant punishment and is thus subject to constitutional limitations under the Eighth Amendment.[79] The Court, however, left it to state and lower federal courts to determine the tests of "excessiveness" in the context of forfeiture.

CONCLUSION

The criminal law expresses society's collective judgment that certain forms of conduct are inimical to social welfare and must not be permitted. Many of these proscriptions are ancient and universal. From the beginning of civilization people everywhere have condemned murder, rape, arson, perjury, burglary, and theft. Of course, our modern criminal law applies to many activities that are not *mala in se,* such as motor vehicle infractions, drug and alcohol offenses, white-collar crimes, and offenses against public health and the natural environment. The changing prohibitions of the criminal law reflect the appearance of new social problems as well as the evolving values of a maturing society. Behaviors that were permissible on the American frontier of the nineteenth century are no longer considered appropriate in a postindustrial, urbanized culture.

Crimes are deemed to be offenses against the entire society, which is why they are prosecuted in the name of the state or the people. The criminal law is most successful when its prohibitions are supported by a strong social consensus. This social consensus does as much to deter crime as do the penalties associated with criminal prosecution. When the criminal law deviates from social consensus, lawbreaking inevitably increases and respect for the criminal justice system is diminished.

The criminal law assumes that people are responsible for their actions, yet advances in medicine, psychology, and the social sciences have made us aware that human behavior is influenced by a variety of internal and external factors. One of the greatest challenges to criminal law today is how to maintain the norm of criminal responsibility in the face of novel defenses that seek to deflect blame away from the defendant.

There is a consensus that criminals should be punished, although there is considerable disagreement as to the nature and degree of punishment that particular crimes warrant. Courts of law inevitably face the philosophical questions associated with criminal punishment as they interpret the sentencing laws enacted by legislatures and the limitations that the federal and state constitutions impose on the criminal justice system. In so doing they tend to reflect the dominant values of the society. Thus, courts have not hesitated to invalidate torture and flogging as cruel and unusual punishments forbidden by the Eighth Amendment, yet they have been extremely reluctant to reach similar conclusions regarding the death penalty. As social norms change, judicial decisions interpreting and applying the criminal law will also evolve.

SUMMARY OF KEY CONCEPTS

To understand the criminal law one must understand its social and political aspects and its historical development. It was against this historic common-law background that the federal government and the states have enacted statutes that refine the common-law crimes and define new offenses as the social, economic, and political development of this nation has developed.

Federal, state, and local legislative bodies define crimes and courts interpret these legislatively enacted laws. But in each instance the U.S. Constitution requires crimes to be defined precisely. A crime ordinarily involves two essential elements: an act and an intent; however, increasingly governments have enacted strict-liability offenses where a violator's intent is irrelevant. A violator's culpability may depend upon that person's role in the offense; however, under federal and state laws one who aids and abets the commission of a crime is regarded as a principal of that offense. In some instances an accessory after the fact is treated differently today.

In reviewing this chapter the student should grasp a basic understanding of the inchoate crimes, crimes against persons and property, offenses against public order, justice, and the environment. These are the basic building blocks of the criminal law. But the criminal law in America has expanded to proscribe white-collar offenses and is making a concerted effort to combat organized crime. Responses to governmental assault on vice have been mixed, yet there is support for legalized protection of the most core moral values.

Historic defenses of alibi, use of force, and excuses and justifications for commission of criminal acts remain. In recent decades the approaches to infancy and intoxication have often been modified to allow special treatment for juveniles and intoxicated persons. Yet there has been a trend to take a firmer approach to pleas of insanity. The American penchant for timely action against a wrongdoer has brought about the statute of limitations defense and the U.S. Constitution has brought about defenses against double jeopardy and wrongful conduct by government.

Finally, at this stage it is relevant to recognize the roles that retribution, deterrence, and rehabilitation have played in inflicting punishment on wrongdoers through the death penalty, incarceration, and the growing reliance on community-based alternatives. The U.S. Constitution again appears in the punishment phase of the criminal justice system in its evolving considerations against cruel and unusual punishments and the requirement that prisoners are not deprived of the most fundamental constitutional rights.

QUESTIONS FOR THOUGHT AND DISCUSSION

1. Why was the English common law important in the development of the American criminal law?
2. What purpose is served by criminalizing inchoate conduct?
3. Is it good public policy to criminalize vices such as gambling, prostitution, and drug abuse? Why or why not?
4. What are the arguments for and against making assisted suicide a crime?
5. Give an example of a scenario when a defendant might assert the defenses of (a) duress and (b) necessity.
6. Under what circumstances does the law generally allow a person to use deadly force in defense of an attack?
7. Why has the defense of entrapment been asserted more frequently in recent years?
8. Under what circumstances should a court impose a fine in lieu of imprisonment on a defendant convicted of a felony?
9. Do you think that a judge who places a convicted defendant on probation should impose a community service obligation as a condition of probation? Support your view.
10. What is the rationale for enactment of a statute of limitations on the prosecution of crime?

KEY TERMS

substantive criminal law

procedural criminal law

felonies

misdemeanors

mala in se

mala prohibita

English common law

Model Penal Code (MPC)

treason

vice of vagueness

wrongful act or omission

actus reus

criminal intent

mens rea

general intent

specific intent

strict-liability offenses

causation

proximate cause

principals

accessories

aiding and abetting

inchoate offense

attempt

solicitation

conspiracy

target crime

assault

aggravated assault

battery

aggravated battery

mayhem

stalking

murder

manslaughter

justifiable homicide

excusable homicide

first-degree murder

second-degree murder

vehicular homicide

felony murder

corpus delicti

assisted suicide

rape

rape shield laws

in camera

rape trauma syndrome

Megan's law

false imprisonment

kidnapping

larceny

false pretenses

embezzlement

computer crimes

robbery

carjacking

forgery

uttering a forged instrument

credit card fraud

burglary

arson

malicious mischief

vandalism

extortion

white-collar crimes

prostitution

gambling

obscenity

obstruction of justice

violations of civil rights

antitrust violations

bid rigging

price fixing

money laundering

insider trading

tax fraud

organized crime

RICO

unlawful assembly

riot

disorderly conduct

vagrancy

bribery

perjury

subornation of perjury

resisting arrest

flight to avoid prosecution

compounding a crime

escape

contempt

environmental crimes

alibi

negative defenses

affirmative defenses

infancy

intoxication

insanity

automatism

M'Naghten Rule

substantial capacity test

duress

necessity

consent

mistake of law

mistake of fact

justifiable use of force

deadly force

self-defense

battered-woman syndrome (BWS)

battered-child syndrome (BCS)

castle doctrine

use immunity

transactional immunity

contractual immunity

diplomatic immunity

double jeopardy

statute of limitations

entrapment

selective prosecution

retribution

proportionality

deterrence

rehabilitation

recidivism

incapacitation

corporal punishment

capital crimes

death penalty

penitentiary

incarceration

rights of prisoners

good-time credit

parole

parole board

probation

house arrest

boot camps

community service

restitution

fines

forfeiture

ENDNOTES

[1] Two interesting exceptions are *People v. Woody,* 394 P.2d 813 (Cal. 1964); and *Ravin v. State,* 537 P.2d 494 (Alaska 1975).

[2] 395 U.S. 444, 89 S.Ct. 1827, 23 L.Ed.2d 430 (1969).

[3] 406 U.S. 205, 92 S.Ct. 1526, 32 L.Ed.2d 15 (1972).

[4] 491 U.S. 397, 109 S.Ct. 2533, 105 L.Ed.2d 342 (1989).

[5] 521 U.S. 844, 117 S.Ct. 2329, 138 L.Ed.2d 874 (1997).

[6] *Musser v. Utah,* 333 U.S. 95, 97, 68 S.Ct. 397, 398, 92 L.Ed. 562, 565 (1948).

[7] *Craig v. Boren,* 429 U.S. 190, 97 S.Ct. 451, 50 L.Ed.2d 397 (1976).

[8] 18 U.S.C.A. § 2(a).

[9] See, e.g., West's Ann. Cal. Penal Code § 33.

[10] *United States v. Barlow,* 470 F.2d 1245 (D.C. Cir. 1972).

[11] 18 U.S.C.A. § 3

[12] West's Fla. Stat. Ann. § 777.03.

[13] See *United States v. Manley,* 632 F.2d 978 (2d Cir. 1980), cert. denied, 449 U.S. 1112, 101 S.Ct. 922, 66 L.Ed.2d 841 (1981).

[14] West's Fla. Stat. Ann. § 777.04(1).

[15] *United States v. Mandujano,* 499 F.2d 370, 376 (5th Cir. 1974).

[16] See, for example, Vernon's Tex. Ann. Penal Code § 15.04(a).

[17] Illinois S.H.A. 720 ILCS 5/8–1.

[18] *United States v. Korab,* 893 F.2d 2122 (9th Cir. 1989).

[19] M.P.C. § 5.02(3).

[20] *Webster v. State,* 646 So.2d 752 (Fla. App. 1994).

[21] 18 U.S.C.A. § 371.

[22] Vernon's Tex. Penal Code Ann. § 15.02(a).

[23] *Iannelli v. United States,* 420 U.S. 770, 786, 95 S.Ct. 1284, 1294, 43 L.Ed.2d 616, 628 (1975).

[24] Vernon's Mo. Ann. Stat. § 564.016(5)(1).

[25] 521 U.S. 702, 117 S.Ct. 2258, 138 L.Ed.2d 772 (1997).

[26] 18 U.S.C.A. § 2119.

[27] Tennessee Code Annotated § 39–13–404.

[28] 354 U.S. 476, 489, 77 S.Ct. 1304, 1311, 1 L.Ed.2d 1498, 1509 (1957).

[29] 413 U.S. 15, 24, 93 S.Ct. 2607, 2613, 37 L.Ed.2d 419, 413 (1973).

[30] 458 U.S. 747, 102 S.Ct. 3348 73 L.Ed.2d 1113 (1982).

[31] 21 U.S.C.A. § 801 et seq.

[32] See, e.g., *Papachristou v. City of Jacksonville,* 405 U.S. 156, 92 S.Ct. 839, 31 L.Ed.2d 110 (1972).

[33] 18 U.S.C.A. § 921 et seq.

[34] See *United States v. Miller,* 307 U.S. 174, 59 S.Ct. 816, 83 L.Ed. 1206 (1939); *Lewis v. United States,* 445 U.S. 55, 100 S.Ct. 915, 63 L.Ed.2d 198 (1980).

[35] *Wardius v. Oregon,* 412 U.S. 470, 93 S.Ct. 2208, 37 L.Ed.2d 82 (1973).

[36] 18 U.S.C.A. § 5031.

[37] *M'Naghten*'s Case, 8 Eng. Rep. 718 (1843).

[38] 18 U.S.C.A. § 17(a).

[39] 18 U.S.C.A. § 17(b).

[40] *United States v. Cameron,* 907 F.2d 1051, 1063 (11th Cir. 1990).

[41] *Cleveland v. Municipality of Anchorage,* 631 P.2d 1073, 1078 (Alaska 1981).

[42] *State v. Janes,* 822 P.2d 1238, 1243 (Wash. App. 1992).

[43] Iowa Code Ann. § 704.4.

[44] *Kastigar v. United States,* 406 U.S. 441, 92 S.Ct. 1653, 32 L.Ed.2d 212 (1972).

[45] 18 U.S.C.A. § 6003.

[46] *United States v. Wilson,* 420 U.S. 332, 95 S.Ct. 1013, 43 L.Ed.2d 232 (1975).

[47] *Burks v. United States,* 437 U.S. 1, 98 S.Ct. 2141, 57 L.Ed.2d 1 (1978).

[48] *Oregon v. Kennedy,* 456 U.S. 667, 102 S.Ct. 2083, 72 L.Ed.2d 416 (1982).

[49] *Bartkus v. Illinois,* 359 U.S. 121, 79 S.Ct. 676, 3 L.Ed.2d 684 (1959).

[50] *Waller v. Florida,* 397 U.S. 387, 90 S.Ct. 1184, 25 L.Ed.2d 435 (1970).

[51] *North Carolina v. Pearce,* 395 U.S. 711, 89 S.Ct. 2072, 23 L.Ed.2d 656 (1969).

[52]284 U.S. 299, 304, 52 S.Ct. 180, 182, 76 L.Ed. 306, 309 (1932).

[53]18 U.S.C.A. § 3282 et seq.

[54]*Sorrells v. United States,* 287 U.S. 435, 451, 53 S.Ct. 210, 216, 77 L.Ed. 413, 422 (1932).

[55]*Oyler v. Boles,* 368 U.S. 448, 82 S.Ct. 501, 7 L.Ed.2d 446 (1962).

[56]Leviticus 24:17–20.

[57]*Trop v. Dulles,* 356 U.S. 86, 101, 78 S.Ct. 590, 598, 2 L.Ed.2d 630, 642 (1958).

[58]408 U.S. 238, 92 S.Ct. 2726, 33 L.Ed.2d 346.

[59]428 U.S. 153, 96 S.Ct. 2909, 49 L.Ed.2d 859.

[60]21 U.S.C.A. § 848(e).

[61]*Coker v. Georgia,* 433 U.S. 584, 97 S.Ct. 2861, 53 L.Ed.2d 982 (1977).

[62]*Stanford v. Kentucky,* 492 U.S. 361, 109 S.Ct. 2969, 106 L.Ed.2d 306 (1989).

[63]*Ford v. Wainwright,* 477 U.S. 399, 106 S.Ct. 2595, 91 L.Ed. 2d 335 (1986).

[64]*McCleskey v. Kemp,* 481 U.S. 279, 107 S.Ct. 1756, 95 L.Ed.2d 262 (1987).

[65]*Campbell v. Wood,* 978 F.2d 1502 (9th Cir. 1994).

[66]In 1996, the Ninth Circuit Court of Appeals invalidated the use of the gas chamber. *Fierro v. Gomez,* 77 F.3d 301 (9th Cir. 1996). Later that year, however, the Supreme Court granted certiorari and remanded the case to the ninth circuit for reconsideration. *Gomez v. Fierro,* 519 U.S. 918, 117 S.Ct. 285, 136 L.Ed.2d 204 (1996). On remand, the court held that the case was not ripe for review, as no inmate in California was then subject to execution by lethal gas as the legislature had passed a law giving condemned prisoners the option of dying by lethal injection. *Fierro v. Terhune,* 147 F.3d 1158 (9th Cir. 1998).

[67]*Provenzano v. Moore,* 744 So.2d 413 (Fla. 1999).

[68]U.S. Dept. of Justice, Bureau of Justice Statistics, *Prison and Jail Inmates at Midyear 1998,* Washington, DC, U.S. Dept. of Justice, March 1999, p. 3.

[69]*Rhodes v. Chapman,* 452 U.S. 337, 101 S.Ct. 2392, 69 L.Ed.2d 59 (1981).

[70]*Hudson v. McMillian,* 503 U.S. 1, 112 S.Ct. 995, 117 L.Ed.2d 156 (1992).

[71]*Pell v. Procunier,* 417 U.S. 817, 822, 94 S.Ct. 2800, 2804, 41 L.Ed.2d 495, 501 (1974).

[72]*O'Lone v. Estate of Shabazz,* 482 U.S. 342, 107 S.Ct. 2400, 96 L.Ed.2d 282 (1987).

[73]*Ex parte Hull,* 312 U.S. 546, 61 S.Ct. 640, 85 L.Ed. 1034 (1941).

[74]*Bounds v. Smith,* 430 U.S. 817, 97 S.Ct. 1491, 52 L.Ed.2d 72 (1977).

[75]*Kentucky Department of Corrections v. Thompson,* 490 U.S. 454, 109 S.Ct. 1904, 104 L.Ed.2d 506 (1989).

[76]The Sentencing Reform Act of 1984 abolished parole eligibility for federal offenders other than military offenders who commit offenses on or after November 1, 1987. It also provided for the abolition of the U.S. Parole Commission on November 1, 1992. However, Congress subsequently extended the Commission in five-year increments through November 2002.

[77]21 U.S.C.A. § 881(a)(4).

[78]21 U.S.C.A. § 881(a)(7).

[79]*Austin v. United States,* 509 U.S. 602, 113 S.Ct. 2801, 125 L.Ed.2d 488 (1993).

FOR FURTHER READING

Bacigal, Ronald J., *Criminal Law and Procedure: An Introduction* (West Publishing Co. 1996).

Dershowitz, Alan M., *The Best Defense* (Random House 1982).

Gardner, Thomas J., and Terry M. Anderson, *Criminal Law* (7th ed., West/Wadsworth 2000).

Samaha, Joel, *Criminal Law* (6th ed., West/Wadsworth 1999).

Scheb, John M., and John M. Scheb II, *American Criminal Law* (2nd ed., West/Wadsworth 1999).

Scheingold, Stuart A., *The Politics of Law and Order: Street Crime and Public Policy* (Longman 1984).

White, Welsh., *The Death Penalty in the Eighties* (University of Michigan Press 1988).

5

TORTS

photodisc.com

LEARNING OBJECTIVES

This chapter should enable the student to understand:

- the definition of a tort, its historical development, and the purpose of tort law
- the basic elements of negligence: duty, breach, causation
- defenses to actions based on negligence
- categories of intentional torts
- defenses to torts against persons and property
- the doctrine of strict liability applicable to products and to dangerous activities
- the applicability of vicarious liability in tort law

CHAPTER OUTLINE

INTRODUCTION

The word **tort** comes from the Latin *tortus,* which means "twisted or wrong." Thus, a tort is a wrongful act committed by a person or an entity, known as the **tortfeasor,** resulting in injury or loss to the victim. But a tort is not always a wrongful act, because in certain instances the law imposes liability for activities that are not necessarily wrongful yet result in injury or damage.

The law of torts emanates from the English common law. In the United States, tort law has developed over the years largely by judicial decisions, but also through legislative action restricting or expanding tort liability. The American Law Institute (ALI), an organization of scholarly lawyers and judges, has published three editions of the *Restatement of Torts.* The *Restatement* is not law; however, it purports to restate principles of contemporary American law and is often relied on by courts in interpreting the law. In this chapter we refer to certain sections of the *Restatement.* We refer to a person who allegedly suffers as a result of someone's negligence or intentional act as the *plaintiff* and to the alleged tortfeasor as the *defendant.*

Tort law is designed to protect persons from injury to their person, property, and reputation. One who suffers a tort may bring a civil action for damages to obtain redress of the injury or loss caused by the torfeasor's actions. There are three basic types of torts:

1. **Negligent acts or omissions.** Negligence is the failure to exercise reasonable care. A tortfeasor's negligent driving that causes injuries to a person or damage to someone's vehicle, or a physician or lawyer whose performance falls below the required standard of care, are common examples of the tort of negligence. In some instances failure to perform an act (omission) may be a tort.

2. **Intentional acts.** These are torts committed by someone who intends to do something that the law has declared wrongful, such as assault, battery, defamation, false imprisonment, trespass, or fraud. Striking someone with a stick is a battery and is a classic example of an intentional tort, unless one happens to be participating in a karate tournament.

3. Acts for which the law imposes strict liability. This means that one is held liable for an injury regardless of one's intent or negligence. Historically one who keeps wild animals or who stores or uses explosives has been held strictly liable even where damage occurs through no fault of the tortfeasor. Today strict liability is imposed on those who engage in abnormally dangerous activities and can be imposed on designers and manufacturers of products.

Under certain circumstances a person or an entity can be held responsible for the tortious acts of another, called **vicarious liability**. The most common example of vicarious liability is when an employer is held liable for acts of an employee committed within the scope of employment.

Tort law is a very dynamic area and its development has closely paralleled the social and economic changes in society. In recent years legislative bodies and courts began to recognize a tort action to protect a person's privacy. Thus, the tort of **invasion of privacy** came into being. By the 1970s as society began to seriously address environmental concerns, courts recognized **toxic torts**. Courts are now being asked to impose tort liability on tobacco companies whose products allegedly have caused serious injuries to smokers and on gun manufacturers whose products have been used to kill or injure people.

NEGLIGENCE

Most contemporary law actions involving torts are based on the tort of **negligence**. Negligence is the failure of a person or entity to use reasonable care that results in injury to persons or damage to property. People frequently commit negligent acts or negligently omit to perform certain acts. But before a defendant can be held liable for commission of a negligent act or omission, the plaintiff must prove by the preponderance (greater weight) of the evidence these four basic elements:

- First, there must be a **duty** to act in such a manner as not to expose the plaintiff to an unreasonable risk.
- Second, there must be a **breach of duty** on the part of the defendant.
- Third, there must be a causal connection (called **proximate cause**) between the defendant's failure to abide by the duty to act in a reasonable and prudent manner and the plaintiff's loss, and the result must have been reasonably **foreseeable** by the defendant.
- Fourth, the defendant's negligent act or omission must result in injury or loss to the plaintiff.

Duty and the Required Standard of Care

A plaintiff who initiates a tort action must initially show that the defendant owed the plaintiff a duty. People must conduct their activities in ways not to create unreasonable risks of harm to others. The standard of care that a defendant must observe is based on an objective standard of what a **reasonable person** would observe under the circumstances. The hypothetical reasonable person is not held to a perfect standard in making judgments but is held to exercise the ordinary care that a reasonable person would have exercised under the circumstances. Consequently, one who drives a vehicle is held to the standard of care of a reasonable driver.

To establish a defendant's standard of care, plaintiffs often submit evidence of the standard of performance or the safety practices customarily followed in a particular industry or business. A defendant who engages in a profession that requires special education or training is held to the standard of a reasonably competent person who performs in that area; thus, a physician, lawyer, engineer, and accountant are held to the standard of a reasonably skilled practitioner in that profession. An aspect of a professional's duty of care is the responsibility to effectively inform clients of potential risks. Thus, before undertaking nonemergency surgery, a physician generally explains the risks involved and asks the patient to sign a consent form. **Informed consent** is given by a patient after receiving an explanation of the risks and possible outcomes of the treatment or surgery.

Courts continue to review the required duty and standard of care of professionals. In 1976, in *Tarasoff v. Regents of University of California,* the Supreme Court of California ruled that when a psychotherapist determines, or pursuant to the standards of his or her profession should determine, that a patient presents a serious danger of violence to another the therapist must use reasonable care to protect the intended victim against such danger.[1] The court held that discharge of such duty may require the therapist to warn the intended victim or others of the danger, notify the police, or take whatever steps reasonably necessary under the circumstances. *Tarasoff* was considered a far-reaching development in tort law, yet some 20 years later the Supreme Court of Ohio observed that the majority of courts now follow the ruling and have extended it to psychiatrists, mental health clinics, and even social workers.[2]

Emergency Situations

In emergency situations courts view the defendant's conformity to the required standard of care based on the circumstances that exist at the time of an event. Of course, a defendant must observe ordinary care in anticipating certain emergencies such as a theater owner providing sufficient exits in event of an emergency.

Children

Historically children have been held liable for their own torts; however, some courts hold that a child under age seven is incapable of committing a tort.[3] The law recognizes that children are generally incapable of meeting the standard of care for adults. Thus, it tends to judge what is reasonable conduct for a child based on the child's age, intelligence, and experience and to look subjectively at the level of care observed by a minor plaintiff or defendant.[4] Nevertheless, when a child engages in an adult activity such as driving an automobile, courts generally hold the child to an adult standard.

Persons Suffering Physical and Mental Infirmities

The law recognizes that a person who suffers from physical infirmities may not meet the objective requirement of acting as a reasonably prudent person, yet such a person must act in accordance with the standard of a reasonable person with such a disability and must not take unreasonable risks. In contrast, those suffering from mental and emotional deficiencies or from voluntary intoxication may not be able to act as the hypothetical reasonable person, yet they are generally held to the standard of the reasonably prudent individual. Here the law must strike a balance between the rights of a plaintiff who has suffered a loss and a defendant whose disability may have been a contributing factor in causing the plaintiff's loss.

Breach of Duty

Once a plaintiff establishes that the defendant owes a duty to the plaintiff, to present a prima facie case the plaintiff must establish a breach of that duty by the defendant. The plaintiff can do this by showing that the plaintiff's act or failure to act violated the standard of care that a reasonable person should observe under the circumstances.

Violation of duties imposed by statutory laws, ordinances, and governmental regulations may indicate negligence. This is a very technical area. If the particular statute or regulation is designed to specifically protect the plaintiff against the harm caused by the defendant's violation, such violation may constitute **negligence per se**; that is, the defendant's conduct may be treated as negligence without regard to any surrounding circumstances. In other instances such violation may simply be evidence of negligence to be considered along with all other circumstances.[5]

In rare instances a plaintiff may be aided in proving breach of the defendant's duty by a legal doctrine called *res ipsa loquitur* ("the thing speaks for itself"). In such cases, negligence is inferred from the simple fact that the injury occurred. For example, an Ohio court upheld use of the doctrine in a case where personal injuries resulted from explosion of a bottle of beer.[6] The bottle of beer would not have exploded if it had not been defective. Another example would be an operation in which a surgeon erroneously removes a patient's gall bladder instead of her appendix. The thing speaks for itself. If the doctrine is properly invoked, a court may instruct the jury that it may infer the defendant's negligence.

Causation—The Proximate or Legal Cause

To establish the defendant's liability, the plaintiff must prove that the defendant's act or omission (breach of duty) caused the plaintiff's injury. The actual cause of the plaintiff's injury is often determined by the **"but for" test,** with the court asking whether the plaintiff would have been injured *but for* the defendant's act or omission. In other instances the court may seek to determine if the defendant's act or omission was a substantial factor in causing the plaintiff's injury. But simply proving factual cause is not sufficient. Courts look not only to the actual cause of the plaintiff's injury but also to determine if the cause was the *proximate* or *legal* cause of that injury. The element of proximate cause involves proof that the natural or reasonably foreseeable consequence of the defendant's act or omission resulted in the plaintiff's injury.

A classic case that every law student studies is *Palsgraf v. Long Island Railroad.*[7] In *Palsgraf,* two railroad employees assisted a passenger in boarding a train. In assisting the passenger, the employees dislodged a package containing fireworks the passenger was carrying.

The fireworks exploded and caused a scale some distance away to fall and injure Mrs. Palsgraf, a bystander. The New York Court of Appeals reversed a judgment for damages against the railroad in favor of Mrs. Palsgraf. The majority opinion of the court held that the injury to Mrs. Palsgraf was not a foreseeable result of the actions by the railroad's employees. This classic decision has been argued in hundreds of cases with lawyers parsing its language that requires that a defendant be held liable only where the injury is foreseeable. Moreover, if there is an **intervening act** by someone after a defendant's negligent act and that act causes the plaintiff's injury, courts generally hold that the intervening party is responsible, unless the intervening act itself was foreseeable.

Damages

Finally, to establish a prima facie case in a negligence action the plaintiff must prove an entitlement to damages. Most negligence actions are based on what the law terms as "ordinary" negligence and a successful plaintiff may recover **compensatory damages.** In most negligence cases, a jury determines the amount of damages to be awarded. Compensatory damages are designed to attempt to "make whole" the plaintiff who has suffered economic and noneconomic losses. Loss of wages, medical bills, and damage to property are examples of economic damages. Noneconomic damages may consist of pain and suffering resulting from an accident and the inability to continue one's usual lifestyle. Although economic damages can be measured in dollars, it is often difficult to place a dollar value on such items as the loss of one's ability to pursue sports or hobbies. A plaintiff's spouse may be awarded compensatory damages for the loss of the injured spouse's services and companionship.

In addition to awarding compensatory damages to a plaintiff, some courts allow **punitive damages** to punish a defendant whose conduct evidences **gross negligence.** Gross negligence is generally defined as the intentional failure to perform an act required by law or the outrageous disregard of the rights of others. To illustrate, an intoxicated driver who drives in the lane of oncoming traffic and causes a vehicular accident would be considered grossly negligent. (See Chapter 9 for a further discussion of compensatory and punitive damages.)

Defenses to Negligence Actions

The most common defense in negligence cases is the defendant's denial of negligence. Beyond this, defendants commonly assert an affirmative defense, that is, a defense that the defendant is required to prove. Affirmative defenses commonly include **assumption of risk, contributory negligence,** and **comparative negligence.**

Assumption of Risk

Historically courts have held that a plaintiff who voluntarily consents to a known risk assumes the consequences of such risk. Thus, courts have allowed a defendant to assert assumption of risk as a defense against actions brought on the theory that the defendant is negligent. Consequently, one who expressly agrees to assume a known risk is generally barred from recovery of damages for the tort of negligence.

Often consent to a defendant's conduct is manifested by a document the plaintiff has signed agreeing to relieve the defendant from the consequences of negligence. The permission slip signed by parents allowing their child to go on a school field trip is one example. A more formal consent may take the form of an exculpatory agreement whereby a person expressly agrees not to hold another party liable for any injury or damage from a given activity. Courts view such documents cautiously and before a party can be relieved of negligent acts the exculpatory language of the document must be very clear and explicit. Even if valid, such a document would not ordinarily relieve a person from liability for commission of an intentional tort or for conduct amounting to gross negligence.

Another type of assumption of risk is called an **implied consent.** A person's conduct may imply an assumption of risk. For example, a person who attends an athletic event and sits in a place where spectators are prohibited and is injured may be said to have assumed the risk of injury.[8] A player who willingly participates in a football game impliedly consents to being tackled and possibly being injured under the rules of the game. In one well-known case, a woman who willingly raised her arm for a nurse to administer an immunization shot was held to have impliedly consented to receiving the immunization.

Contributory and Comparative Negligence

During the early 1800s the courts developed a doctrine that barred a plaintiff who brought suit from recovering damages if the defendant could show the plaintiff's own actions contributed to his or her injuries or losses. Courts began to universally apply this defense, called contributory negligence. By the mid-twentieth century, courts increasingly criticized the doctrine, particularly as related to manufacturers of products and owners and drivers of vehicles. In recent years, through legislation or judicial decision,[9] many states have adopted the doctrine of comparative negligence extant in civil law countries.

Comparative negligence seeks to assess damages based on the amount of negligence of the parties. Some jurisdictions apply the doctrine in its purest form and allow a plaintiff to recover damages against a negligent defendant irrespective of the amount of the plaintiff's own negligence. Thus, a plaintiff found to be 80 percent negligent could recover damages for the 20 percent of negligence attributable to the defendant. Other jurisdictions apply a modified form of comparative negligence and a plaintiff may not recover any damages if found to be 50 percent or more negligent. Most commentators believe the doctrine of comparative negligence is a more equitable approach to assessing liability. Nevertheless, the shift from contributory negligence has resulted in complexities particularly when multiple parties are involved or when traditionally the law allowed a defendant to assert that a plaintiff assumed the risk of injury or loss. These changes pose problems to the insurance industry, which underwrites liability protection for defendants in the majority of major tort actions based on negligence.

INTENTIONAL TORTS

An intentional tort consists of a willful act that a tortfeasor knows or is substantially certain will cause injury to another, interferes with another's property, injures a person's reputation, or wrongfully invades someone's privacy. Intent is a state of mind and is usually proved by the circumstances surrounding a person's action. Intent is distinguished from motive in that intent is the desire to cause certain immediate consequences or knowledge that they will occur, whereas motive is the actor's conscious reason for acting. The law presumes that a person intends the natural and probable consequences of one's acts. Therefore, to establish a prima facie case, a plaintiff must prove that a defendant committed a voluntary tortious act directed against a plaintiff or the plaintiff's legally protected interest. In some instances a defendant's intent is transferred from the intended victim to an unintentional victim. For example, if A fires a pistol at B, but instead the bullet hits C, A's intent to kill or injure B is transferred to C who has a tort action against A.

We discuss intentional torts in four categories:

1. Assault, battery, and false imprisonment are examples of intentional torts that involve interference with a person's body.
2. Defamation is a tort that injures another's reputation.
3. Infliction of emotional distress and invasion of privacy are newer torts against persons.
4. Trespass to land or taking, misusing, or conversion of personal property belonging to another, and misrepresentation,[10] concealment, and fraud, are intentional torts that involve interference with someone's property.

Assault, Battery and False Imprisonment

Assault and **battery** frequently coexist; however, each is a distinct tort. An assault occurs when a person with apparent ability places another person in apprehension of injury or unwanted physical contact. An assault requires an overt act but does not require physical contact, and although an assault is often accompanied by threatening words, words alone do not constitute an assault. A missed punch is a classic example of an assault.

A battery is the act of physically injuring someone, but even an unwanted and unreasonable touching of another without that person's consent can constitute a battery. Thus, striking someone with a ball bat or hurling a stone and hitting someone is a battery. Even a male's offensively touching a female's body without her consent could constitute a battery.

An assault does not necessarily culminate in a battery, but more frequently an assault and a battery will be committed simultaneously. For example, an aggressor who threatens to beat up another person and then proceeds to physically attack the victim has committed an assault and battery. Of course, a battery may exist without commission of an assault; for instance, a person who is struck from behind may never have anticipated an injury.

False imprisonment consists of intentionally restraining a person's freedom or confining a person without that person's consent or without legal authority. An amorous suitor who locks the door to prevent the object of affection from leaving the room, or the jailer who refuses to release a prisoner once the prisoner has served a prescribed term, commits false imprisonment. Security personnel in a store may commit false imprisonment by preventing a customer from leaving the store; however, statutes generally allow temporary detention of a suspected shoplifter when the security personnel have a reasonable basis to believe a customer has shoplifted merchandise. In such an instance it would not be false imprisonment if the security personnel detained the suspected shoplifter in a reasonable manner until police arrive.[11]

As discussed in Chapter 4, assault, battery, and false imprisonment are crimes as well as torts. Such conduct is prosecuted as a crime to vindicate the right of the state, punish the offender, and deter others from like conduct. Irrespective whether the state chooses to prosecute the wrongdoer, the victim may bring a civil legal action to recover monetary damages for injuries or losses resulting from commission of a tort. Actions for intentional torts are far less frequent than lawsuits alleging negligence where the defendant likely carries liability insurance. Liability insurance does not generally cover intentional torts, except in cases of vicarious liability (discussed later in this chapter). Consequently a plaintiff who is successful in a suit based on an intentional tort may not have any assurance of collecting damages.

Defamation

Defamation consists of publishing communications that cause another person to be held in ridicule, or that injure another's reputation or business interests. Oral defamation is called **slander;** written or printed defamation is called **libel.** Courts differ on whether defamation by radio or television is slander or libel, but the difference is primarily a matter of form as essentially the same principles of law apply to each.

In 1999, quoting from the second edition of *Restatement of Torts,* Section 559, the Indiana Supreme Court stated that a defamatory communication is one that "tends so to harm the reputation of another as to lower him in the estimation of the community or to deter third persons from dealing with him." The court explained that whether a communication is defamatory depends, among other things, upon the temper of the times and contemporary public opinion, with the result that words, harmless in one age, in one community, may be highly damaging to a person's reputation at another time or in another place.[12]

To recover damages for defamation, the plaintiff must usually prove a financial loss; however, some forms of defamation give rise to an action against the tortfeasor irrespective of loss. These include such accusations as falsely imputing perjury or treason, or that a person is guilty of a crime or has a loathsome disease, or falsely alleging that a person is having deviate sexual relations with a minor.

In 1964, the U.S. Supreme Court held that the First Amendment to the U.S. Constitution precludes **public officials** from recovering damages for defamatory falsehoods related to their official conduct unless they can prove "that the statement was made with . . . knowledge that it was false or with reckless disregard whether it was false or not."[13] The Court later expanded the principle to apply to all **public figures** that sue for libel.[14] The theory underlying this holding is that public figures have sufficient access to the mass media to defend themselves against false accusations and thus do not require the assistance of libel suits.

The "public figure" doctrine has made it difficult for celebrities to prevail in libel suits against the tabloid press. A notable exception occurred in 1981 when Carol Burnett prevailed in a libel suit against *The National Enquirer.* The tabloid had run a brief item asserting that a "boisterous" Carol Burnett had a loud argument with Henry Kissinger in a Washington restaurant. According to the article, "she traipsed around the place offering everyone a bite of her dessert." The article implied that Burnett was drunk. Burnett sued for defamation. The jury awarded her $300,000 in compensatory damages and $1.3 million in punitive damages. The trial judge reduced the award to $50,000 compensatory and $750,000 punitive damages. An appeals court remanded the case, holding that the punitive damages were excessive.[15] In 1986, Burnett agreed to settle the case.

Intentional Infliction of Emotional Distress and Invasion of Privacy

The tort of **intentional infliction of emotional distress** consists of willfully committing outrageous acts directed against another person. Historically, infliction of emotional distress upon another person was considered an actionable tort only if accompanied by another tort such as assault, battery, or false imprisonment. The trend is for courts to allow emotional distress to stand as a separate tort where the conduct of the tortfeasor is particularly reprehensible. Virginia law illustrates the high standard of proof imposed on a plaintiff who seeks to recover damages in an action for intentional infliction of emotional distress. It requires the plaintiff to establish that the defendant's conduct is intentional or reckless; that it offends generally accepted standards of decency or morality; that it is causally connected with the plaintiff's emotional distress, and that the defendant's conduct caused the plaintiff to suffer severe emotional distress.[16]

Hustler Magazine featured a parody of an advertisement that portrayed Rev. Jerry Falwell, a nationally known minister active in politics and public affairs, as having engaged in a drunken incestuous rendezvous with his mother in an outhouse. Rev. Falwell sued and recovered damages based on the tort of emotional distress. The victory was short lived for in 1988 the U.S. Supreme Court reversed the judgment.[17] The Court held that, as in defamation, a public figure is precluded from recovering damages for the tort of intentional infliction of emotional distress without showing that publication of a false statement of fact was made with actual malice.[18]

Opinion of the Court . . .

HUSTLER MAGAZINE V. FALWELL
485 U.S. 46, 108 S.Ct. 876, 99 L. Ed.2d 41 (1988)

Chief Justice Rehnquist delivered the opinion of the Court.

. . . The sort of robust political debate encouraged by the First Amendment is bound to produce speech that is critical of those who hold public office or those public figures who are "intimately involved in the resolution of important public questions or, by reason of their fame, shape events in areas of concern to society at large." . . . Such criticism, inevitably, will not always be reasoned or moderate; public figures as well as public officials will be subject to "vehement, caustic, and sometimes unpleasantly sharp attacks." . . .

. . . [A] public figure may hold a speaker liable for the damage to reputation caused by publication of a defamatory falsehood, but only if the statement was made "with knowledge that it was false or with reckless disregard of whether it was false or not." False statements of fact are particularly valueless; they interfere with the truth-seeking function of the marketplace of ideas, and they cause damage to an individual's reputation that cannot easily be repaired by counter speech, however persuasive or effective. . . . But even though falsehoods have little value in and of themselves, they are "nevertheless inevitable in free debate," . . . and a rule that would impose strict liability on a publisher for false factual assertions would have an undoubted "chilling" effect on speech relating to public figures that does have constitutional value. "Freedoms of expression require 'breathing space.'" This breathing space is provided by a constitutional rule that allows public figures to recover for libel or defamation only when they can prove both that the statement was false and that the statement was made with the requisite level of culpability.

As mentioned in the introductory remarks, invasion of privacy is one of the newer torts. In 1983, in recognizing this tort, the Alabama Supreme Court explained that it consists of four distinct wrongs: (1) intrusion upon plaintiff's physical solitude or seclusion; (2) publicity which violates ordinary decencies; (3) putting the plaintiff in a false, but not necessarily defamatory position in the public eye; and (4) appropriation of some element of plaintiff's personality for commercial use. The court went on to hold that the defendant's intrusive demands and threats, and inquiry into the nature of sex between the plaintiff and her husband, supported a claim for invasion of privacy.[19] A public official or public figure who claims to have been placed in a false light in regard to a matter of public concern bears the burden of proof required in defamation under the previously discussed rule in *New York Times v. Sullivan.*[20]

Interference with Property

As discussed in Chapter 1, the English common law developed largely in an agrarian economy. Consequently, the common law placed great emphasis on a person's interest in land. Today torts involving interference with someone's property may take several forms. Going on another's land or into another's buildings without permission are classic examples of the tort of **trespass to land.** But trespass to land also extends to the use of one's own land in such a way as to damage or to create a **nuisance** affecting another's land. The tort of nuisance developed from a landowner's use of property in such a way as to adversely affect the plaintiff's land. For example, in an early case the Georgia Supreme Court held that the unlawful diversion of water from a stream to the deprivation of the lower riparian owner constituted a trespass.[21] In recent years plaintiffs have employed trespass and nuisance actions to recover damages where pollution has caused damages, for example, to a farmer's crops.[22]

The theft of someone's personal property, failure to return that property, or damaging or depreciating the property so as to deprive the owner or rightful possessor of the use or enjoyment of the property constitutes the tort of **conversion.**

Fraud and Misrepresentation

At common law the torts of **fraud** and **misrepresentation** consisted of (1) a false statement of a material fact, (2) knowledge by the person making the statement that the representation is false, (3) intent by the person making the statement that the representation will induce another to act, and (4) justifiable reliance on the representation to the injury of the other party.[23] Today many statutes define fraud and misrepresentation in context of various areas of commerce and may include concealment as a fraudulent act. Most of these statutes include the common-law elements of fraud. When considering whether an action is fraudulent one must remember that in business dealings there is a significant difference between "puffing" or "sales talk" ("This is the finest used car you will find in this town!") for which there is no liability and fraudulent misrepresentation of material facts that meet the above requirements.

The sale of securities is a prime example where both federal and state laws protect persons from fraud and misrepresentations. But despite establishing other elements of a cause of action for fraud, often the plaintiff falls short of proving that he or she justifiably relied on the seller's representations. In 1983, the U.S. Court of Appeals for the Tenth Circuit reviewed a case where a plaintiff who purchased stock, suffered a financial loss, and then sued the company that issued the securities claiming violations of federal securities laws.[24] The president and vice president of the company had described an investment in the stock as a "good opportunity" and assured investors there were no risks and that the investment would achieve the potential benefits illustrated by their oral and written projections. Nevertheless, they furnished the plaintiff a private placement memorandum, a written document that explained the details concerning the securities being offered for sale and that clearly outlined the risks involved. Moreover, before purchasing the stock the plaintiff signed a subscription agreement stating the investment was subject to the risks set forth in the memorandum. Yet the plaintiff never read the memorandum. After suffering a financial loss the plaintiff sued and recovered a judgment for damages. Observing that the plaintiff had never read the memorandum furnished him, the court reversed the plaintiff's judgment and held that "knowledge of a prospectus or an equivalent document authorized by statute or regulation should be imputed to investors who fail to read such documents."[25]

Defenses to Intentional Torts against a Person

There are three common defenses to intentional conduct that results in injury or damage to another person: **consent, self-defense** (including **defense of a third person**), and **authority of the law.**

Consent

The most common defense to an intentional tort to a person is that the plaintiff consented to the defendant's actions. Consent may be communicated expressly by words or impliedly by actions, and in some instance by a person's silence. A person who is intoxicated or unconscious is not competent to give consent and fraud or coercion vitiates a person's consent and can render the offending party liable for committing a battery. Moreover, where statutes are enacted to protect certain classes of persons, such as minors, consent is not valid. Statutes defining statutory rape and making it a crime to have sexual relations with a minor irrespective of the minor's consent illustrate this principle.

Self-Defense

When a person reasonably believes that it is necessary to use force to protect against a threat to one's person, it is proper to defend by use of **reasonable force.** Self-defense can be a defense against such torts as assault and battery. Of course, one may not become the aggressor during self-defense. Most courts extend self-defense to allow defense of a third person; however, the Ohio Supreme Court has pointed out that one who uses force to intervene on behalf of another person may not invoke the privilege of self-defense if the person defended was the aggressor in the conflict.[26]

Authority of Law

One who acts under authority of law may also have a defense to the tort of false imprisonment. Generally, the officer who makes a legal arrest or the schoolteacher who keeps a pupil after school for a reasonable period of time could assert such a defense.

Defenses against Defamation

Truth is a defense against slander and libel. Public policy also dictates that in certain instances a person is privileged to make statements that may be defamatory. This defense of **privilege** may apply to statements made by public officials in the course of their duties and is applicable to those testifying in judicial proceedings. In other instances the defense of **qualified privilege** may apply. For example, an employer has a qualified privilege to inform a prospective employer of a former employee's poor performance at work as long as the report is not made with malice. Likewise, a person who has a reasonable belief that someone has stolen his or her property and makes such a report to the police is exercising a qualified privilege.

Defenses to Torts against Property

A defendant sued for committing a tort against property will first seek to defend on the basis that the allegations of conduct do not constitute a tort or by a general denial of the allegations. There are, however, two classic defenses: reasonable use of force and **necessity.**

Use of Force

A possessor of property is justified in defending that property against trespass and may use such reasonable force as is necessary to prevent trespass or to remove a trespasser. Ordinarily a person must first request an intruder to desist. **Deadly force** cannot be used simply to protect property. There must be a threat of serious harm to the owner or possessor and even then in many jurisdictions courts require that a person threatened who can safely retreat must do so. Our common-law heritage regarded that "a man's home is his castle" and rarely do courts require a person to retreat within one's own home.

Courts have approved the use of guard dogs and electronically charged fences to protect property. Historically courts permitted the use of spring guns and other mechanical devices to protect property, but modern courts have generally disallowed such means of defense. Most courts now hold that one who sets up a spring gun or other mechanical device designed to kill or injure a trespasser will be held liable for the death or injury to the trespasser. Indeed, today the use of a spring gun could under certain circumstances result in the user being charged with a crime.

Necessity

Necessity is a defense that can be asserted by one who commits a tort of trespass or conversion in order to prevent greater harm to a person or the public generally. An example could be where it is necessary to destroy property to prevent the spread of fire. The defense applies only in the direst calamities. Even then, it does not shield one from a duty to compensate for harm caused where the defense of necessity is invoked to protect a person's private interest as opposed to protection of the public interest.

STRICT LIABILITY

Strict liability, sometimes referred to as liability without fault, is imposed by courts based on a defendant's activities rather than fault due to a defendant's intent or negligence. The doctrine originated in early English common law, which imposed strict liability on keepers of dangerous animals. In 1868 in a landmark decision, *Rylands v. Fletcher,* an English court applied strict liability in a case where the waters from the defendant's reservoir flooded the plaintiff's coal mine.[27] Thus the English courts broadened the doctrine of strict liability to hold liable those engaged in a particularly dangerous activity such as storing dynamite, blasting, or handling of dangerous chemicals. Over the years a majority of American courts have accepted the principle of strict liability. In determining whether to apply strict liability, courts today consider such factors as the inappropriateness of an activity and degree of risk involved. Of course, a defendant is held strictly liable only for those activities that are abnormally dangerous while the defendant's other activities would be subject to ordinary tort liability.

In 1975, in a significant environmental ruling a Florida appellate court held that impounding of phosphate slime in connection with phosphate mining operations constituted a "nonnatural use of land."[28] This enabled the state of Florida to invoke the doctrine of strict liability against the operator of a phosphate mine for damages to the public waters resulting from phosphate wastes.

Products Liability

Products liability refers to the legal responsibility of those who supply goods whose defects cause injuries or losses to others. American courts originally accepted the English doctrine of **caveat emptor** ("let the buyer beware") but during the twentieth century they began discussing the doctrine of strict liability mentioned above in reference to manufacturers of products. At first, a manufacturer was liable for negligence only to the immediate purchaser of a product who was usually a dealer from whom the ultimate consumer purchased. Consequently the ultimate purchaser or user of a product could not recover damages against the manufacturer.

But in 1916 in its seminal decision, *MacPherson v. Buick Motor Car Company,* which every law student studies, the New York Court of Appeals held a manufacturer of an automobile was liable to a person injured as a result of the vehicle's defective wheel.[29] The court made legal history by holding the manufacturer liable to the ultimate purchaser, and its decision was eventually adopted by all American jurisdictions. Later courts extended the doctrine to hold the seller of a product liable for damages to all persons who used the product whom the manufacturer or seller could reasonably have foreseen as users or consumers of the product. The manufacturer, seller, or supplier of the defective product became responsible not only to the purchaser but also to the users and even bystanders who suffer injuries because of the defect.

Today a plaintiff whose person or property suffers injury causally related to an unsafe product may opt to bring suit for negligence or breach of warranty or, in most states, may have a cause of action for "products liability" based on the doctrine of strict tort liability. The rationale for imposing such liability is that it will increase the level of safety. Moreover, manufacturers and distributors can cover most risks of this type by liability insurance.

To recover for damages resulting from a defective product, the plaintiff must establish that the injuries or losses that have accrued are the proximate result of the defective product. In general, the defendant can prevail by establishing that the product was used in a way not reasonably foreseeable or that it was used once the plaintiff had knowledge of the defective condition.

Many products liability cases involve claims of defective design of products, and until recently the comments to §402A *Restatement of Torts,* second edition, stated that a warning could insulate a manufacturer from liability in certain instances. As previously noted, tort law is dynamic and the *Restatement of Torts,* third edition, adopted in 1997[30] notes that warnings are not "a substitute for the provision of a reasonably safe design" of a product.

Following this view, a federal appeals court in May 1998 upheld a verdict for $16.7 million in damages. The court ruled that an adequate warning by itself does not "immunize a manufacturer from any liability caused by its defectively designed product."[31]

VICARIOUS LIABILITY

Vicarious liability means that one person is held liable for the acts of another based on a relationship between the parties. Courts justify the imposition of vicarious liability based on one party exercising control over the other. Not surprisingly, vicarious liability most frequently applies in a relationship known at common law as a master/servant. Today this type of relationship is more commonly characterized as an employer–employee relationship and the employer may be held liable for torts committed by employees acting within the scope of their duties. Being vicariously liable for employees gives an employer an incentive to carefully select and train employees. Employees remain liable for their own torts; however, plaintiffs generally seek recourse against the employer who is likely to carry liability insurance to cover such claims.

Typically an employer–employee relationship is created where an employer furnishes necessary tools and directly supervises a person working on an hourly basis or a salary. One must distinguish the employer–employee relationship from one who contracts with an **independent contractor.** An independent contractor is generally a party hired to accomplish a certain result for a stipulated payment. For example, an independent contractor relationship generally arises when a party employs a roofing company to repair a roof and the roofer brings the equipment and workers and directs the performance of their work. Ordinarily one who employs an independent contractor is not held liable for the torts of such contractor. There are exceptions. For example, a party who contracts to have dangerous work performed can be held vicariously liable for an independent contractor's torts that are inherent and foreseeable in the work to be accomplished. A good example of this would be a contract to perform blasting with explosives. Other technical exceptions include duties imposed by contract or by laws and regulations.

Employer Hiring Practices

Historically an employer was vicariously liable for acts of an employee committed within the scope of employment, but the trend of court decisions has been to broaden that liability. In 1980, a Pennsylvania appellate court ruled that employers are liable for acts of violence committed by their employees if the employer knew, or should have known, of the employee's propensity for violence.[32] Since that time, courts have held that an employer is liable for the willful tort of an employee committed against a third person if the employer knew or should have known that the employee was a threat to others. These principles have brought about the tort known as **negligent hiring** in many jurisdictions. In an interesting application of the doctrine of negligent hiring, an occupant of a townhouse sued the developer for injuries sustained when she was assaulted by one of the developer's employees who was permitted to enter the townhouses to perform maintenance. The plaintiff was unsuccessful in the trial court, but a Florida appellate court remanded the case for trial based on the principle that when the developer permits an employee to have access to the townhouses, the developer is charged with such information concerning the employee's background as it could have obtained upon reasonable inquiry.[33]

Owners and Drivers of Motor Vehicles

A driver whose negligence causes an automobile accident is liable; however, frequently the owner of the vehicle is in a better financial position (often by virtue of liability insurance) to respond in damages. Yet under traditional tort law an owner of an automobile who permits another person to drive was not liable to a party injured as a result of the driver's negligence unless the driver was an agent of the owner or was acting within the scope of employment, or if the owner had negligently entrusted the vehicle to a person not competent to operate it. Through different legal devices states have created doctrines of law to assess liability against the owner. Some states have enacted statutes or courts have ruled that the driver is presumed to be the owner's agent, thereby making the owner liable for the negligence of anyone operating the vehicle with the owner's consent. Others treat a family much like a business and hold that an owner is liable for negligent operation of a vehicle by members of the owner's family. Very early in the history of automobiles the Florida Supreme Court, in a landmark decision, declared that an automobile is a **dangerous instrumentality** and therefore the owner is liable for the negligence of a driver permitted to use the vehicle.[34]

SPECIAL TORT SITUATIONS

Tort law is a complex and highly dynamic area, and a number of special situations do not fit neatly into the categories we have been discussing. These include the liability of owners and possessors of real estate, negligent infliction of emotional distress, survival actions, wrongful death actions, preconception torts, torts involving alcoholic beverages, toxic torts, and torts involving the deprivation of constitutional rights.

Owners and Possessors of Real Estate

Tort liability of owners or possessors of land or buildings depends on the duty the law imposes on such owner or occupier. Generally an owner who leases property to a tenant is not liable to the tenant or to third parties for injuries occurring on the leased premises unless the owner knows or has reason to know of some concealed danger on the premises.

Most courts determine the possessor's duty based on whether the plaintiff is an **invitee, licensee,** or **trespasser.** The duty to an invitee is to exercise reasonable care for a person's safety. Therefore, it is not uncommon for a supermarket to be held liable to a person who slips on a green pea or banana peel. This usually occurs where the evidence shows the supermarket was aware of the existence of a dangerous situation or that the condition existed a sufficient length of time for the store to be on what is called **constructive notice** of the situation. Courts hold that an owner or possessor of property has a somewhat lesser standard of care to social guests and household occupants. This class of persons has historically been classed as licensees. The trend in recent years has been for courts to hold a landowner or possessor to a reasonable standard of care to all classes of persons.[35] Some states have enacted statutes limiting the liability of an owner or possessor who makes land available to the public without charge for recreational use.

Most courts take the position that a trespasser must take the property as it is found and generally require only that the owner or possessor of the premises not commit an intentional tort against the trespasser. Courts, however, have imposed special rules in respect to trespassing children who are injured by an artificial condition on the land if the owner or possessor knows or has reason to know that children are likely trespassers. This is especially true when the possessor has created something that particularly attracts very young children. Some courts term such a condition an **attractive nuisance.**[36]

Most American courts have adopted the English common-law doctrine called the **firefighter's rule,** which treats a firefighter or police officer as a licensee thereby limiting a landowner's or possessor's liability to a firefighter or police officer injured as a result of the condition of premises they enter. The rationale for the rule is that those whose occupations call for them to enter premises as part of their duties assume the risks incident thereto. Yet some courts have held that this rule should not be applied to prevent a firefighter or police office from recovering damages against someone that intentionally injures or causes injuries to an officer on the scene.[37]

Negligent Infliction of Emotional Distress

As discussed, the tort of intentional infliction of emotional distress consists of willfully committing outrageous acts directed against another person. In the past four decades, most courts have extended the tort of intentional infliction of emotional distress to include **negligent infliction of emotional distress.** With some variations in the states, most courts allow plaintiffs to recover for negligent infliction of emotional distress if they suffer demonstrable physical consequences from fright or shock resulting from exposure to physical danger.

Survival Actions

Under the English common law the right to bring a law action for personal injuries terminated at the death of either the victim or the tortfeasor. In the United States **survival statutes** provide that most tort actions survive both the plaintiff and defendant; however, some jurisdictions stipulate that a cause of action for defamation does not survive a deceased plaintiff. The right to continue a deceased victim's cause of action is transferred to the personal representative of the victim's estate, or in some instances to designated family members. Any defenses that would have been available to a defendant had the decedent lived continue to be available to the defendant's estate.[38]

Wrongful Death Acts

The English common law did not provide for a civil suit against one who caused another's death. Thus, a tortfeasor who caused someone's death was in the anomalous position of not suffering the economic consequences of one who merely injured the victim. Eventually this restriction was eliminated in England by passage in 1846 of Lord Campbell's Act.[39] In the United States all states now have **wrongful death acts** that allow an action for wrongful death. Because many of these state statutes are patterned after the English legislation, these acts are commonly referred to as Lord Campbell Acts. In some states the personal representative of the decedent's estate is the plaintiff; in other states members of the decedent's family who were dependent on the decedent can bring the action. The class of persons who may recover and the elements of damage recoverable vary among the states. Usually a decedent's spouse and children are permitted beneficiaries, but in some instances it is the decedent's estate that is entitled to certain elements of damage. Some statutes simply specify the action is for the benefit of the decedent's heirs. But courts have denied a "live-in cohabitant" the right to recover even though such person may have been dependent on the decedent for support.[40]

Wrongful Birth, Wrongful Life, Preconception Torts

The dynamic character of tort law is illustrated by recent decisions recognizing a rather distinct species of medical malpractice. The tort of **wrongful birth** is a species of medical malpractice in which parents give birth to an impaired or deformed child where negligent treatment or advice deprived them of the opportunity to avoid or terminate the pregnancy. For example, a child is born with severe defects because the mother contracted a serious illness. In jurisdictions that permit an action for wrongful birth, the plaintiff can generally recover those extra expenses associated with the birth defect. Some courts have permitted a child's parent to sue a physician for negligence in performing sterilization procedures that resulted in the birth of a child.

The tort of **wrongful life** refers to an action brought on behalf of a child born with birth defects when the birth would not have occurred but for the negligent medical advice or treatment. Most courts today recognize the tort of wrongful birth[41] and some recognize the tort of wrongful life.[42] This area of the law is now developing with courts in wrongful life cases generally limiting damages to medical expenses rather than the cost of raising a child.

A recent decision by the Indiana Court of Appeals is another example of law developing in this area. In 1992, the court ruled that a child's complaint alleging that he suffered injuries, including mental retardation, as a result of the defendant physician's failure to determine that his mother had Rh negative blood and to administer a "Rho GAM" injection during his mother's pregnancy stated a claim for a **preconception tort** against the hospital and the physician.[43]

Alcoholic Beverages

Under the English common law a vendor of intoxicating beverages was not liable to persons injured by the intoxicated purchaser. The trend in American courts in recent years has been to allow a tort action against the seller of intoxicated beverages, particularly if the seller violated a statute imposing liability on vendors who sell intoxicating beverages to a minor.

These statutes, often called **dram shop acts** (a dram shop is a place of business that dispenses alcoholic beverages) eliminate the proximate cause requirement and allow a person injured by the intoxicated individual to recover damages against the vendor. Some courts have held that an injured party has a claim against the vendor under a dram shop act even though a minor with whom the purchasing minor shared the alcoholic beverage caused the injuries. In 1998, the Washington Supreme Court ruled that a vendor who illegally sold alcoholic beverages to the minor, who in turn furnished the alcoholic beverage to another minor, could be held liable for foreseeable alcohol-related injuries that arose from the initial sale.[44]

The so-called dram shop acts generally are not applicable to a **social host** who furnishes alcoholic beverages to a guest. Legislatures and courts are beginning to address whether a social host can be held responsible for furnishing alcoholic beverages to a guest who becomes intoxicated and causes injury or death to another person. In 1990, a state supreme court ruled that parents may be held liable if they know their children are planning a party where underage drinking is likely even if the parents are not at home at the time of the party.[45]

Toxic Torts

One of the newest tort actions is based on claims resulting from toxic torts. Toxic tort actions involve claims of human or property exposure through absorption, contact, ingestion, inhalation, implantation, or injection of toxins. Plaintiffs have charged that asbestos, various chemical compounds, silicone breast implants, and disposal of hazardous wastes, to name a few, have caused injuries to health or the environment. Many of the substances involved in toxic tort actions are regulated by such federal agencies as the Food and Drug Administration (FDA), the Environmental Protection Agency (EPA), and the Occupational Safety and Health Administration (OSHA).

Among the legal problems that arise in this area is whether exposure to a toxic substance (e.g., asbestos), where the symptoms remained latent until after the right to bring suit, is barred by a **statute of limitations.** Another problem concerns the legal theory available for recovery and what defenses may be available to a defendant. In 1973, the U.S. Court of Appeals for the Fifth Circuit applied the principles of strict product liability and held a manufacturer liable for failure to adequately warn the plaintiff of the hazards of products that contained asbestos at his work.[46]

In 1991, the Supreme Court of California reviewed a case where a shipyard worker brought a toxic tort action based on strict liability.[47] The plaintiff alleged that while working he contracted lung ailments through exposure to asbestos and asbestos products. The issue before the state supreme court was whether in a strict products liability action, based on an alleged failure to warn of a risk of harm, a defendant could present evidence of the state-of-the-art, that is, evidence that the particular risk was neither known nor knowable by the application of scientific knowledge available. The court recounted that it had previously concluded that a manufacturer of prescription drugs is exempt from strict liability for defects in design and is not strictly liable for injuries caused by scientifically unknowable dangerous propensities in prescription drugs. This principle, the court said, should allow a defendant to present state-of-the-art evidence at trial.

THE LAW IN ACTION

TOXIC TORTS

Recent years have seen a surge in toxic tort litigation involving claims arising from injuries or illnesses caused by exposure to toxic chemicals, radiation, or other hazardous materials such as asbestos. Perhaps the best-known toxic tort case was that stemming from the 1984 accident at the Union Carbide plant in Bhopal, India. Over 10,000 people died and more than 300,000 people were injured as the result of exposure to a cloud of methyl isocyanate and other toxic chemicals that were accidentally released from the plant. Union Carbide paid $470 million to settle the case out of court.

Other well-known examples of toxic tort litigation include the Love Canal case in Niagara Falls, New York, the Times-Beach Case in Missouri, and the W.R. Grace case in Massachusetts, which was the subject of the book and film, *A Civil Action.*

Toxic tort litigation was also the subject of one of the biggest films of 2000. Based on a true story, *Erin Brockovich* features Julia Roberts as a legal secretary who investigated water contamination in the small desert community of Hinckley, California. The resulting lawsuit brought by 652 Hinckley residents against Pacific Gas & Electric Company resulted in a $333 million out-of-court settlement in 1996.

Toxic tort claims usually involve claims of negligence or strict liability. This type of litigation also typically involves complex factual issues. Thus, plaintiffs and defendants tend to rely heavily on expert witnesses.

In toxic tort litigation, courts must resolve disputes involving complex problems of science and technology. These actions present a problem to the legal system when they involve an issue of when a statute of limitations begins to run where the plaintiff alleges latent injuries. Often thousands of plaintiffs are involved in tort claims involving toxic torts resulting from massive accidents, and not infrequently multiple defendants are charged with the responsibility for such massive occurrences. Generally claims in mass torts are handled through class action lawsuits (see Chapter 9).

Employer–Employee Relationships

Under the common law employers were rarely found liable for injuries to their employees, because they were allowed to assert defenses that usually insulated them from liability. An employer was exonerated if the court found that the employee assumed the risk of injury incident to a particular job (assumption of risk), if another employee caused the injury (fellow servant rule), or if the worker's carelessness contributed to the injury (contributory negligence).

These common-law doctrines were unsuitable to an industrial age, and in the early 1900s Congress and the state legislatures enacted laws, which today are called **workers' compensation acts.** These acts provide that if an injury occurs "in the course of employment," and "arises out of the employment," an injured worker is compensated according to a statutory schedule that covers medical expenses, loss of wages, and temporary and permanent disabilities. Dependents can recover benefits if the employee's death stemmed from the employment situation. These acts are beneficial to both employers and employees. Employers gain the advantage of averting litigation and being able to budget to pay insurance premiums for necessary coverage. Employees obtain compensation promptly without the necessity of proving fault, yet the benefits to the employee do not include compensation for pain and suffering. The Federal Employees Liability Act provides somewhat similar benefits for railroad workers; another federal statue, the Jones Act, covers maritime employees.

Deprivation of Constitutional Rights— A Quasi-Tort

A federal statute passed after the Civil War, 42 U.S.C.A. § 1983, creates a cause of action for an **intentional tort committed under color of authority of law** that deprives a person of federal constitutional rights or rights under federal laws. The basic purpose of the law is to deter state actors from using their authority to deprive individuals of their federally guaranteed rights. Section 1983 provides:

> Every person, who under color of any statute, ordinance, regulation, custom, or usage, of any State or Territory, subjects or causes to be subjected, any citizen of the United States or other person within the jurisdiction thereof the deprivation of any rights, privileges, or immunities secured by the Constitution and laws, shall be liable to the party injured in action at law, and in equity, or other proper proceeding for redress.

The statute is the basis for actions, commonly referred to as § 1983 suits, against state and local officials in both federal and state courts. Section 1983 does not create a basis for a tort action against a federal official; nevertheless, the U.S. Constitution is the basis for actions against federal officials whose conduct fits within the act under color of federal law.

Tort actions based on § 1983 span a variety of situations in employment, education, housing, and public facilities as well as prisoners' rights, voting rights, and other areas. Many § 1983 actions focus on law enforcement activities. Because negligence does not constitute a violation of constitutional rights, a negligent shooting death of an individual by a police officer would not ordinarily constitute a violation of § 1983. But a complaint alleging that police officers illegally arrested a black man, contrived charges to justify his arrest, falsified police reports, and initiated prosecution in bad faith, all with racial animus and pursuant to official policy, was held to state a claim for deprivation of equal protection of the law under § 1983.[48]

Perhaps the most famous § 1983 case was the suit brought by Rodney King, who alleged that Los Angeles police officers had used excessive force in violation of the federal constitution when they stopped King's car after a high-speed chase in 1991. The officers were charged criminally in a California court but were acquitted, which spawned the Los Angeles riot of 1992. The officers were subsequently convicted of federal civil rights violations and went to prison. In the related civil action, King won a $3.8 million judgment from the City of Los Angeles.

Section 1983 is not itself a source of substantive rights, but rather is a method for vindicating rights recognized by the U.S. Constitution or conferred by federal statutes. Thus, the first issue in a § 1983 lawsuit is to identify the substantive right allegedly infringed. An interesting recent case in this regard is *Board of County Commissioners, Wabaunsee County, Kansas v. Umbehr*.[49] The case began when a county commission terminated a garbage collection contract with a company whose owner had been extremely critical of the commission. The owner, Umbehr, claimed that the commission had violated his First Amendment rights by retaliating against him economically. The federal district court dismissed the suit, holding that the First Amendment does not prohibit government from considering a contractor's expression as a factor in deciding not to continue the contract. The court reasoned that, as an independent contractor, Umbehr was not entitled to the First Amendment protection that is afforded public employees.[50] The Supreme Court reinstated the complaint,

ARE MUNICIPALITIES IMMUNE FROM FEDERAL CIVIL RIGHTS LAWSUITS?

Monell v. New York City Department of Social Services

United States Supreme Court
436 U.S. 658, 98 S.Ct. 2018, 56 L.Ed.2d 611 (1978)

Female employees of the New York City Department of Social Services brought suit under 42 U.S.C. § 1983 against the department and a number of local officials. The essence of their complaint was that the department had compelled pregnant employees to take unpaid leaves of absence before they were medically necessary. Relying on precedent, the federal district judge held that local governments were immune from suits for damages under 42 U.S.C. § 1983 and that local officials were cloaked with this immunity. The court of appeals affirmed. The U.S. Supreme Court reversed, holding that local governments and local government officials can be sued under § 1983 in situations when employees' constitutional rights are deprived as a matter of policy or custom. The Court said that Congress did not intend for municipalities to be immune from lawsuits seeking to vindicate constitutional rights.

recognizing "the right of independent government contractors not to be terminated for exercising their First Amendment rights."[51] Thus, the existence of an "injury" in a § 1983 case depends on whether courts are willing to recognize a plaintiff's constitutional claims.

IMMUNITIES FROM LIABILITY

Under the English common law no action could be brought against the Crown because "the King could do no wrong." As early at the thirteenth century, the common law held that the king could not be sued in his own courts. This doctrine of **sovereign immunity** was received by the American courts and became a part of the American common law. The doctrine holds that the United States as a sovereign nation and the states as sovereign states cannot be sued without their consent. In a democratic society based on the principle that government is subject to the rule of law, the principle of sovereign immunity is difficult to defend. Of course, Congress and the state legislatures can, and often do, waive sovereign immunity in whole or in part.

Federal Tort Liability

To prevent injustices to those who suffer injuries or losses at the hands of the federal government, in 1946 Congress enacted the Federal Tort Claims Act.[52] The act waives the federal government's sovereign immunity for "negligent or wrongful acts or omissions"; therefore, the federal government is not liable under the doctrine of strict tort liability. Claims must first be presented to the appropriate federal agency before an injured party can file suit in the U.S. Court of Claims. The act contains numerous exceptions, for example, claims in respect to postal matters, intentional torts against a person, misrepresentation, fraud and deceit, defamation, interference with contract rights, and monetary matters involving the U.S. Treasury.

State and Local Tort Liability

In 1793, in *Chisholm v. Georgia,* the U.S. Supreme Court ruled that sovereign immunity did not apply to states when sued in federal court.[53] The Eleventh Amendment to the U.S. Constitution was promptly ratified and effectively nullified the Court's decision in *Chisholm.* The Eleventh Amendment provides: "The Judicial power of the United States shall not be construed to extend to any suit in law or equity, commenced or prosecuted against one of the United States by Citizens of another State, or by Citizens or Subjects of any Foreign State." The Supreme Court has said that the Eleventh Amendment exists both to prevent federal court judgments that must be paid out of state funds and to protect states from the coercion of the federal courts.[54]

Through a variety of constitutional and statutory provisions the states have provided various means for asserting claims and filing suits for torts. In some instances there are limits to amounts recoverable, in others claimants are limited to coverage provided by the state's liability insurance. Tort claims against the state and local units of government are usually limited to **proprietary or operational activities** and the states generally retain their sovereign immunity for such **discretionary activities** that are incident to governance. Utilities and road maintenance often are classified as operational activities while passage of laws and ordinances and planning activities generally fall within the area of discretionary activities.

With the availability of liability insurance, the trend is to abolish or restrict immunities of state and local governments. In some instances state and local governments waive their immunity to the extent that they have liability insurance coverage.

Interspousal and Parent–Child Immunity

The English common law identified spouses as one; thus, one spouse could not sue the other. By the middle of the nineteenth century, statutes and court decisions in the United States began to recognize married women as having a separate legal identity; however, most jurisdictions still maintained that one spouse could not sue the other for a tort. Courts said this doctrine of **interspousal immunity** was justified by the need to preserve marital harmony and to protect defendants and their liability insurers from the prospect of collusive lawsuits. Today, most states have abolished interspousal immunity, either by statute or court decision.

Historically courts refused to allow a parent–child tort action largely on the ground that such an action would undermine parental authority and lead to vexatious and possibly collusive lawsuits. Courts generally continue to hold there is no liability of a parent to an unemancipated child regarding issues of supervision, provision of basic necessities, and health care. Today, there is a trend toward abolition of parent–child immunity; however, the issue is unsettled with regard to automobile accidents.

Charitable Immunity

Historically nonprofit organizations conducting charitable activities were immune from liability under the doctrine of **charitable immunity.** In 1942, the U.S. Court of Appeals for the District of Columbia in a landmark decision rejected the doctrine of charitable immunity.[55]

Some courts have ruled there is no immunity; others have upheld immunity for certain types of charitable institutions, sometimes making a distinction between paying and nonpaying parties. With the increasing availability of liability insurance most courts now hold charitable organizations liable to the same extent as individuals and private corporations.

NEW DEVELOPMENTS IN TORT LAW

In our litigious society, there are always new developments in tort law. Increasingly, governments and interest groups are relying on tort law as a way of addressing social problems. Some of the more important recent developments include the following:

- Suits against the tobacco industry brought by smokers who have become ill and by states seeking to recover costs associated with treating illnesses due to smoking
- Suits against manufacturers of firearms brought by governments seeking to recover costs associated with gun violence
- Suits against pharmacists for failing to warn customers about possible dangers of prescription drugs

Tobacco Litigation: A Reversal of Judicial Attitudes

Before the 1990s, tobacco companies were generally successful in their defense of suits for damages by smokers who claimed to have developed tobacco-related illnesses, but the defense of such claims was greatly undermined by the U.S. Supreme Court's 1992 decision in *Cipollone v. Liggett Group, Inc.*[56] There the Court held that the federal law which established cigarette warnings in advertising did not bar a claimant from seeking damages under state laws. In later litigation, tobacco companies were ordered to produce documents that revealed scientific evidence concerning the adverse health consequences to tobacco users. In a number of instances appellate courts have reversed jury verdicts awarding damages to plaintiffs.

In 1997, the attorneys general of many states successfully negotiated settlements with tobacco companies in Medicaid reimbursement lawsuits. Nevertheless, by 1999, individual and class action suits were filed on behalf of smokers and the estates of deceased smokers seeking both compensatory and punitive damages for illnesses and death alleged to have resulted from smoking. Substantial verdicts have been rendered against major tobacco companies. For example, in March 2000, a San Francisco jury awarded $1.7 million in compensatory damages and $20 million in punitive damages to a terminally ill woman who smoked cigarettes for several decades. In April 2000, a Miami jury found a cigarette manufacturer liable in a class action suit and awarded $12.7 million in compensatory damages. The rules of law that will develop from such litigation will eventually be crystallized in the appellate courts.

Are Manufacturers of Firearms to Be Held Liable for Acts of Violence?

In the aftermath of the tragic deaths of the increasing number of victims of firearms violence, several cities and counties have filed lawsuits against gun manufacturers. These plaintiffs are seeking to recover millions of dollars spent on medical care and police protection incident to violence, which the local governments attribute to use of guns. Some plaintiffs claim the sale of guns to criminals constitutes a public nuisance, while others seek to recover on product liability theories or claims that the manufacturers have been negligent in failing to incorporate safety features into their products. In many instances trial courts have dismissed these suits; however, they raise novel issues of law. Appellate courts are destined to address these issues during this decade.[57]

Are New Duties on Pharmacists on the Horizon?

Traditionally pharmacists were liable only if they failed to accurately fill a prescription, but a June 1999 article in the *American Bar Association Journal* states, "Most states still do not hold pharmacists liable for failure to warn of possible drug hazards, but that may be changing."[58] The author cites two cases in point. In 1992, the Arizona Court of Appeals found that a pharmacist has a duty to warn patients about the possible adverse side effects of prescription medications or the combining of different ones.[59] In 1996, the Michigan Court of Appeals ruled that a pharmacy assumed a duty of care when it advertised that its computers could detect harmful drug interactions.[60] Again, this is a developing area of tort law.

TORT REFORM

In the early twentieth century, state and federal legislative bodies enacted laws that provide a uniform schedule of compensation to employees injured in the course of their employment. This usually takes the form of workers' compensation laws previously discussed. These laws have been modified frequently, the trend being to provide more generous benefits to injured workers. In the latter part of the twentieth century, legislative bodies began to seriously revise the laws concerning tort liability in respect to motor vehicle accidents.

No-Fault Automobile Insurance Laws

As automobile liability insurance became commonplace, litigation became increasingly costly and often subject to great delays. In the latter part of the twentieth century, reformers who pointed to uncertainties, delays, and costs to victims to obtain a fair award in automobile accident litigation persuaded a number of states to enact **no-fault automobile insurance laws.**

THE INFAMOUS MCDONALD'S COFFEE CASE   SIDEBAR

A popular example of an allegedly excessive jury award is the $2.7 million "scalding coffee award" against McDonald's in 1997. Stella Liebeck ordered coffee from the drive-through at a McDonald's restaurant in Albuquerque, New Mexico, in 1992. As she removed the lid, the coffee, which was more than 180 degrees Fahrenheit, spilled into her lap causing third-degree burns. Liebeck was hospitalized for eight days, during which time she received skin grafts. Evidence at trial showed that similar injuries had occurred in the past and that McDonald's was aware of the danger of maintaining its coffee at a high temperature. McDonald's argued that its customers preferred coffee to be served hot and were aware of the risks associated with hot liquids. The jury awarded Liebeck $160,000 in compensatory damages and $2.7 million in punitive damages. The trial court subsequently reduced the punitive award to $480,000. The case was eventually settled for an undisclosed amount. Nevertheless, the facts that the jury was willing to make such an immense award of punitive damages provided impetus to the movement to reform tort laws.

These laws provide for reimbursement to injured parties irrespective of fault. Thus, an injured party collects from his or her own insurance company instead of asserting a claim against the party alleged to be at fault. There are variations among no-fault laws, with some applying to property damage as well as personal injuries. In general these laws allow an injured party to collect for medical expenses, loss of wages, and other economic losses. Some no-fault laws allow traditional tort actions when an injured party suffers permanent injury or disability or when medical expenses and loss of income exceed certain threshold amounts. These laws are still a "work in progress" in the halls of state legislatures and in the courts.

As noted, courts and legislative bodies have limited or abolished the historic immunity of governmental bodies and charitable institutions. Moreover, they have formulated new torts, particularly in the areas of products and environmental liability. Many reformers argue that some juries have awarded excessive amounts to injured plaintiffs.

The Focal Points of Tort Reform Today

Present advocacy for tort reform centers largely on six areas.

1. *Joint and several liability.* Historically when joint tortfeasors are involved, an award of damages is issued on a **joint and several liability** basis. This means that when more than one tortfeasor is found responsible, each is liable to the plaintiff for the entire damage award. This allows a successful plaintiff to collect the entire judgment from one tortfeasor if the others are unable to pay. There is considerable criticism of the joint and several doctrine and some states have adopted laws to provide that joint and several liability is either not applicable, or applicable only in respect to awards under a certain amount, say $50,000.

2. *Collateral sources.* Legislatures have frequently modified the **collateral source rule,** which historically prohibited juries from hearing about the sources available to a plaintiff to receive reimbursement for losses, for example, personal disability insur-

ance. When the common-law collateral source rule has been overridden by legislation, the court instructs the jury that in awarding damages it must take into consideration the amount of compensation a plaintiff receives from personal insurance or other sources.

3. *Noneconomic damages.* Legislatures in a number of states have enacted laws (and in some instances the voters have amended their state constitutions), to provide caps on noneconomic awards, that is, amounts awarded to compensate a victim for pain and suffering.

4. *Punitive damages.* Legislatures in a majority of the states have placed some caps on the award of punitive damages, the so-called smart money (see Chapter 9) that juries have been permitted to award if they find the tortfeasor's conduct to be outrageous.

5. *Statutes of limitations.* Some legislatures have enacted laws shortening the time that plaintiff's are allowed to bring suit, particularly in the fields of professional malpractice, construction defects, and product liability claims.

6. *Restrictions on legal fees.* Lawyers frequently handle personal injury claims and lawsuits for plaintiffs on a **contingent fee** based on the amount of damages recovered. This arrangement enables injured plaintiffs who otherwise may not be able to afford legal counsel to effectively assert their rights. If the lawyer is unsuccessful in recovering damages, the plaintiff's obligation to the lawyer is generally limited to payment of necessary court costs. Lawyers who handle personal injury suits argue that contingent fees are essential to "level the playing field" between plaintiffs and defendants. Critics of contingent fee arrangements claim they lead to unnecessary litigation and are subject to abuse by lawyers. Some states have enacted laws to limit an attorney to a stated percentage of a plaintiff's recovery, often providing for a lesser percentage for recovery through out-of-court settlements.

Congress has been unable to agree on any major tort reforms in recent years. In contrast, state legislation in the above areas has been prolific, meeting varied reactions from the courts. In a number of states the highest courts have upheld various state laws initiating tort reforms. Many, however, have struck down, in whole or in part, laws capping tort awards and shortening statutes of limitation. Courts have often found such reforms contrary to state constitutional provisions guaranteeing the right to trial by jury in civil cases. Despite reformers having made gains in state legislatures, proponents of restrictions on tort suits now are fighting in the courts to protect their gains.

Some laws that have been invalidated have been unclear as to how they are to be applied by judges and juries. Many advocates of tort reform contend that courts are more likely to sustain reform legislation where the laws provide clear outlines for making awards of damages. One thing is certain: Tort reform will remain viable with legislative and judicial activity continuing to demonstrate the dynamic qualities of this area of the law.

CONCLUSION

The basic function of tort law is to compensate those who are injured or who suffer economic losses as a result of someone else's intentional or negligent conduct or unreasonably dangerous activity. But it also serves to deter persons from improper conduct, and, in some instances, to punish wrongdoers. Moreover, the availability of tort remedies is designed to prevent those who suffer injuries or loses from resorting to retaliation or self-help against those perceived to be at fault.

Although of common-law origin, the development of tort law has paralleled the dynamics of American society and the principle of fairness has played an increasing role in determining standards of care. Liability based on negligence rather than strict liability in most cases, the economic distribution of risks through workers' compensation, and the availability of liability insurance allowed America to become the world's greatest industrial nation.

As ownership of motor vehicles became almost universal, many states have replaced the doctrine of contributory negligence with a fairer doctrine of comparative negligence, and the trend has been to distribute risks among motorists under a no-fault concept. Modern technology enables manufacturers to produce safer products. Courts have responded by holding manufacturers and sellers of products to strict liability for damages resulting from defective products. The information age will present new and exciting problems in tort law.

Old immunities of governmental and charitable institutions have been severely limited, as insurance has provided a method of risk management compatible with modern conditions.

Legislatures and courts will continue to struggle to enact reasonable reforms to fairly compensate those who suffer injuries and losses while not unfairly penalizing those whose actions cause those injuries and losses. These are the dynamics of tort law.

SUMMARY OF KEY CONCEPTS

A tort is a wrongful act that results in injury or loss to the victim. The most common tort today is the tort of negligence based on a tortfeasor's wrongful act or omission and is illustrated by negligent operation of a motor vehicle. Another prominent example is malpractice by a professional. One simple way of remembering the required elements of the tort of negligence are four key words: duty, breach, causation, and damages. Defenses to actions based on negligence include contributory or comparative negligence of a plaintiff or a plaintiff's consent or assumption of risk.

Intentional torts against persons or property include such common examples as assault, battery, false imprisonment, trespass to land or personal property, defamation, fraud, and misrepresentations. Among the defenses commonly asserted by defendants sued for intentional torts against a person are consent, self-defense, and authority of the law. In actions based on torts against property, defendants often assert reasonable use of force and necessity as defenses. In an action for defamation, a defendant may assert the defense of statements made being the truth or being privileged.

A species of historic torts now broadened in the American legal system is known as strict liability. Originally applied against keepers of dangerous animals and persons conducting such inherently dangerous activities as blasting, the doctrine has been made applicable to those who supply goods whose defects cause injuries or losses to others. In another social development, workers' compensation insurance has largely replaced the uncertainties associated with suits by employees against their employers.

Tort law also provides a party may be vicariously liable; that is, one person is held legally responsible for actions of another person based on control over someone's activities. The most common example is an employer being held liable for acts of an employee committed within the scope of employment. In many instances legislatures and courts have imposed vicarious liability on owners of motor vehicles who permit others to operate their vehicles.

The student should gain an awareness of the many special tort situations such as survival actions, wrongful death, wrongful birth and life, and preconception torts as well as the growing field of toxic torts, and the quasi-tort involving liability for deprivation of a person's constitutional rights. These torts and the elimination of traditional immunities based on sovereignty and the relationship of parties illustrate this very dynamic area of the law. The newest areas of developing tort law concern no-fault automobile insurance laws and attempts to establish new principles of tort law concerning tobacco and firearms.

Finally, the student should become conversant with the legislative and judicial trends in tort reform. Attempts to limit noneconomic damages and awards of punitive damages awards and to shorten some statutes of limitations and limit joint and several liability are now underway in many states.

QUESTIONS FOR THOUGHT AND DISCUSSION

1. Give an example of conduct that might give rise to (a) a claim for damages based on the tort of invasion of privacy; and (b) a claim based on intentional infliction of emotional distress.

2. Would a court likely hold an owner liable to a person injured by a mechanical device such as a spring gun that was actuated when a trespasser came on the owner's premises?

3. What elements must a plaintiff establish in order to recover damages for injuries or losses suffered as a result of a defendant's alleged negligence?

4. Explain the differences between the defenses of contributory negligence and comparative negligence. Which doctrine do you find to be fairer and more practical? Why?

5. A seven-year-old boy enters an unfenced lot in his neighborhood without the owner's permission. The child drowns when he falls into a small vat of water that the owner left when the house that formerly stood on the land was demolished. Under what theory might the child's parents bring an action against the landowner?

6. Name the defenses that employers were allowed to assert in an employee's common-law tort action to recover damages for job-related injuries? What development in the law brought about a compensation system of employees injured in job-related activities?

7. How has the action for products liability developed from the common-law concept of strict liability? To what extent has its development been influenced by the *Restatement of Torts*?

8. Give an example of an action by a state official that would likely be a violation of 42 U.S.C.A.§ 1983.

9. Why have courts tended to limit tort liability of local government entities to operational activities thereby excluding liability for discretionary activities?

10. Evaluate the validity and fairness of tort reform legislation that would (a) shorten the statutes of limitation; (b) abolish the collateral source rule; and (c) place caps on noneconomic and punitive damages.

KEY TERMS

tort

tortfeasor

negligent acts or omissions

intentional acts

strict liability

vicarious liability

invasion of privacy

toxic torts

negligence

duty

breach of duty

proximate cause

foreseeable

reasonable person

informed consent

negligence per se

res ipsa loquitur

"but for" test

intervening act

compensatory damages

punitive damages

gross negligence

assumption of risk

contributory negligence

comparative negligence

implied consent

assault

battery

false imprisonment

defamation

slander

libel

public officials

public figures

intentional infliction of emotional distress

trespass to land

nuisance

conversion

fraud

misrepresentation

consent

self-defense

defense of a third person

authority of the law

reasonable force

privilege

qualified privilege

necessity

deadly force

products liability

caveat emptor

independent contractor

negligent hiring

dangerous instrumentality

invitee

licensee

trespasser

constructive notice

attractive nuisance

firefighter's rule

negligent infliction of emotional distress

survival statutes

wrongful death acts

wrongful birth

wrongful life

preconception tort

dram shop acts

social host

statute of limitations

workers' compensation acts

intentional tort committed under color of authority of law

sovereign immunity

proprietary or operational activities

discretionary activities

interspousal immunity

charitable immunity

no-fault automobile insurance laws

joint and several liability

collateral source rule

contingent fee

ENDNOTES

[1] 551 P.2d 334 (Cal. 1976).

[2] *Estate of Morgan v. Fairfield Family Counseling Center,* 673 N.E.2d 1311 (Ohio 1997).

[3] See, for example, *DeLuca v. Bowden,* 329 N.E. 2d 109 (Ohio 1975).

[4] See, for example, *Dunn v. Teti,* 421 A.2d 782 (Pa. Super. 1980).

[5]See, for example, *Sanchez v. Galey,* 733 P.2d 1234 (Idaho 1986).

[6]*Fick v. Pilsener Brewing Co.,* 86 N.E. 2d 615 (Ohio Com. Pl. 1949).

[7]162 N.E. 99 (N.Y. 1928).

[8]See *Dusckiwicz v. Carter,* 52 A.2d 788 (Vt. 1947).

[9]See, for example, *Hoffman v. Jones,* 280 So.2d 431 (Fla. 1973).

[10]There also can be instances of negligent misrepresentation.

[11]See, for example, *Vaughan v. Wal-Mart Stores, Inc.,* 734 So.2d 156 (La. App. 1999).

[12]*Journal Gazette Co., Inc. v. Bandido's Inc.,* 712 N.E.2d 446 (Ind. 1999).

[13]*New York Times v. Sullivan,* 376 U.S. 254, 84 S.Ct. 710, 11 L.Ed.2d 686 (1964).

[14]*Curtis Publishing Co. v. Butts,* 388 U.S. 130, 87 S.Ct. 1975, 18 L.Ed.2d 1094 (1967) (declaring Wally Butts, a well-known football coach, to be a public figure).

[15]*Burnett v. National Enquirer, Inc.,* 144 Cal. App. 3d 991 (1983).

[16]*Womack v. Eldridge,* 210 S.E. 2d 145 (Va. 1974).

[17]*Hustler Magazine v. Falwell,* 485 U.S. 46, 108 S.Ct. 876, 99 L.Ed.2d 41 (1988).

[18]485 U.S. at 55, 108 S.Ct. at 882, 99 L.Ed.2d at 52.

[19]*Phillips v. Smalley Maintenance Services, Inc.,* 435 So.2d 705 (Ala. 1983).

[20]376 U.S. 254, 84 S.Ct. 710, 11 L.Ed.2d 686 (1964).

[21]*McNabb v. Houser,* 156 S.E. 595 (Ga. 1931).

[22]See, for example, *Borland v. Sanders Lead Co., Inc.,* 369 So.2d 523 (Ala. 1979).

[23]See *First Union Discount Brokerage Services, Inc. v. Milos,* 997 F.2d 835 (11th Cir. 1993).

[24]*Zobrist v. Coal-X, Inc.,* 708 F.2d 1511 (10th Cir. 1983).

[25]708 F.2d at 1519.

[26]*Ellis v. State,* 596 N.E. 2d 428 (Ohio 1992).

[27]L.R. B.H.L. 330 (1868).

[28]*Cities Service Co. v. State,* 312 So.2d 799 (Fla. App. 1975).

[29]111 N.E. 1050 (1916).

[30]American Law Institute, St. Paul, Minn. (1998).

[31]*Rogers v. Ingersoll-Rand Co.,* 144 F.3d 841 (D.C. Cir. 1998).

[32]*Coath v. Jones,* 419 A. 2d 1249 (Pa. Super. 1980).

[33]*Williams v. Feather Sound, Inc.,* 386 So.2d 1238 (Fla. App. 1980).

[34]*Southern Cotton Oil Co. v. Anderson,* 86 So. 629 (Fla. 1920).

[35]See, for example, *Rowland v. Christian,* 443 P.2d 561 (Cal. 1968).

[36]See, for example, *Banker v. McLaughlin,* 208 S.W.2d 843 (Tex. 1948).

[37]See *Lang v. Glusica,* 393 N.W. 2d 181 (Minn. 1986).

[38]See, for example, *Wright v. Davis,* 53 S.E.2d 335 (W.Va. 1949).

[39]9 and 10 Vict. C. 93 (1846).

[40]See, for example,*Cassano v. Durham,* 436 A.2d 118 (N.J. Super. 1981).

[41]See, for example, *Kush v. Lloyd,* 616 So.2d 415 (Fla. 1992).

[42]See, for example, *Procanik v. Cillo & Sherman,* 478 A.2d 755 (N.J. 1984).

[43]*Yeager v. Bloomington Obstetrics and Gynecology, Inc.,* 585 N.E. 2d 696 (Ind. App. 1992).

[44]*Schooley v. Pinch's Deli Market, Inc.,* 951 P.2d 749 (Wash. 1998).

[45]*Huston v. Konieczny,* 556 N.E.2d 505 (Ohio 1990).

[46]*Borel v. Fibreboard Paper Products Corp.,* 493 F.2d 1076 (5th Cir. 1973).

[47]*Anderson v. Owens-Corning Fiberglass Corp.,* 810 P.2d 549 (Cal. 1991).

[48]*Usher v. Los Angeles,* 828 F.2d 556 (9th Cir. 1987).

[49]518 U.S. 668, 116 S.Ct. 2342, 135 L.Ed.2d 843 (1996).

[50]*Umbehr v. McClure,* 840 F. Supp. 837, 839 (D. Kan. 1993).

[51]518 U.S. at 686, 116 S.Ct. at 2352, 135 L.Ed.2d at 858.

[52]28 U.S.C.A. §1346 et seq.

[53]*Chisholm v. Georgia,* 2 U.S. 419, 1 L.Ed. 440 (1793).

[54]*Seminole Tribe v. Florida,* 517 U.S. 44, 116 S.Ct. 1114, 134 L.Ed.2d 252 (1996).

[55]*President and Directors of Georgetown College v. Hughes,* 130 F.2d 810 (D.C. Cir. 1942).

[56]505 U.S. 504, 112 S.Ct. 2508, 120 L.Ed2d 407 (1992).

[57]See J. Gibeaut, "Gunning for Change," *ABA Journal,* March 2000, p. 48.

[58]P. Barnes, "Prescription for Liability," *ABA Journal,* June 1999, p. 40.

[59]*Lasley v. Shrake's Country Club Pharmacy,* 880 P.2d 1129 (Ariz. App. 1994).

[60]*Baker v. Arbor Drugs, Inc.,* 544 N.W.2d 727 (Mich. App. 1996).

For Further Reading

Keeton, W. Page, *Prosser & Keeton on the Law of Torts* (5th ed., West Publishing Co. 1984).

Kionka, Edward J., *Torts: Injuries to Persons and Property* (West Group 1999).

Lewis, Anthony, *Make No Law: The* Sullivan *Case and the First Amendment* (Vintage Books 1992).

Litan, Robert E., and Clifford Winston (eds.), *Liability: Perspectives and Policy* (Brookings Institution 1988).

O'Connell, Jeffrey, *The Injury Industry* (University of Illinois Press 1971).

Olson, Walter (ed.), *New Directions in Liability Law* (Academy of Political Science 1988).

Posner, Richard A. (ed.), *Tort Law: Cases and Economic Analysis* (Little Brown 1977).

Rabin, Robert L. (ed.), *Perspectives on Tort Law* (Little Brown 1976).

Schuck, Peter H. (ed.), *Tort Law and the Public Interest* (W.W. Norton 1991).

Shavell, Steven, *Economic Analysis of Accident Law* (Harvard University Press 1987).

6

PROPERTY LAW

photodisc.com

LEARNING OBJECTIVES

This chapter should enable the student to understand:

- the historical background of private property, and the distinctions between personal and real property

- the forms of property ownership; how real estate is acquired, mortgaged, and transferred; and what constitutes nonpossessory interests in land

- the historic and modern-day concepts of the lessor–lessee relationship

- how the use of land is restricted by deed covenants and land-use zoning regulations

- the government's power of eminent domain and what constitutes a "taking" of property

- how living and testamentary trusts are created and their uses in estate planning

CHAPTER OUTLINE

Introduction

Personal Property

Real Estate

The Lessor–Lessee Relationship

Regulation of Real Property Use

Eminent Domain

Trusts

Wills and Intestate Succession

Estate, Gift, and Inheritance Taxes

Guardianship to Protect Property Rights

Conclusion

Summary of Key Concepts

Questions for Thought and Discussion

INTRODUCTION

Although property may be classified as either private or public, this chapter focuses on private property, a cornerstone of American political philosophy. The Fifth Amendment to the U.S. Constitution concludes with the proviso: "nor shall private property be taken for public use without just compensation." In 1897, the U.S. Supreme Court incorporated this clause into the Fourteenth Amendment, making it applicable to the states as well as the federal government.[1]

Property concepts and the language of property law are based primarily on the English common law. The somewhat archaic language of property law reflects its feudal origins. Perhaps more than any other area of the law, property law bears out Justice Oliver Wendell Holmes, Jr.'s oft-cited observation that "a page of history is worth more than a volume of logic."

Today, property law reflects the changes in the American economy. As protecting our natural resources and environment has become a greater priority, Congress, state legislatures, and local governmental bodies have responded by enacting various regulatory measures that limit private control of property. Indeed, the U.S. Supreme Court has held that laws may be enacted to require property owners to use their property in ways not to injure the property rights of others.[2] In recent decades, laws enacted at the national and state levels and land-use zoning ordinances and building codes adopted at the local level have diminished the extent of private control over property.

Real and Personal Property

Property is basically classified as **real property** or **personal property.** Real property consists of land and the structures that are built upon or attached to the land, growing timber and crops, airspace above the land, and the minerals underneath the surface of the land. All other types of property are considered personal property. Questions may arise as to whether some types of property, for example, window blinds installed in a building, are real or personal. The determination is based on the character of the property; how it is affixed to the building; and the intent of the parties and their legal relationship, that is, whether the parties are mortagor–mortagee or lessor–lessee and so forth. Some items of property that are personal,

CASE IN POINT

IS A MODULAR HOME REAL OR PERSONAL PROPERTY?

Far West Modular Home Sales, Inc. v. Proaps

Court of Appeal of Oregon
604 P.2d 452 (Oregon App. 1979)

As a result of a dispute over the price of a modular home the plaintiff sold to the defendants, the plaintiff filed a suit for replevin (an action to recover personal property) against the defendants, who purchased a modular home from the plaintiff. Upon purchasing the modular home, the defendants had it bolted to a concrete foundation and connected to utility lines and it became the family residence. The trial court concluded that the modular home sold to the defendants was personal property, and allowed the plaintiff's action for replevin. The defendants appealed, contending that their home was so annexed to their real property that it lost its character as personal property, and, therefore, was not subject to the replevin action. The appellate court agreed with the defendants and reversed the trial court's judgment.

In ruling for the defendants, the appellate court observed that the paramount factor to be considered is the objective intent of the annexor to make the item a permanent accession of the freehold. The court explained that the annexor's intent can be inferred from "the nature of the article, the relation of the party annexing, the policy of law in relation thereto, the structure and mode of annexation, and the purpose and use for which the item was annexed." The court concluded "the fact that this chattel is a home, coupled with evidence that it was bolted and nailed to a foundation and connected to all utilities, established that it was annexed to defendants' real property." Thus the modular home was no longer personal property and not subject to the plaintiff's action for replevin to regain possession of the home.

such as a mobile home, become real property when permanently affixed to the land. On the other hand, growing trees are considered real property, but once severed from the land they become personal property.

Ownership in respect to property is a generic rather than a legal term. The law attempts to define property rights with more precision. Because there are often different rights to the same property, law professors suggest students visualize ownership of property as a "bundle of sticks." A person's residence is generally classified as real property, and one who receives a deed to the property is generally regarded as the owner. But, if there is a mortgage on the property, the lender (mortgagee) also has a property interest. If the home was recently remodeled and the owner did not pay the contractor or the lumber company in full, the law provides that either or both may have a **lien** against the property. This, too, is a property interest. And if the owner leases the property to others, they, too, have a property interest called a **leasehold.** These are some of the "sticks" in the bundle of property rights.

Personal property may either be tangible, that is, something that is personal and movable, or intangible, something that evidences a property interest. A person's car, furniture, golf clubs, and clothing are classified as **tangible personal property.** Shares of stock in a corporation, a promissory note, a government or corporate bond are **intangible personal property.** Another species of intangible property is the **chose in action,** which is illustrated by one having a legal right to enforce a contract or bring an action for a tort. (We discussed torts in Chapter 5; contracts are discussed in Chapter 7.)

Patents, Copyrights, and Trademarks

Patents, copyrights, and trademarks are also forms of intangible property rights. The U.S. Constitution authorizes Congress "to promote Progress of Science and useful Arts, by securing for limited times to Authors and Inventors the exclusive Right to their respective Writings and Discovery."[3] A patent is a government grant for the exclusive right to make and sell an invention. The U.S. Patent and Trademark Office grants patents upon an applicant's proof that the machine or method is original and useful. Currently patent protection extends for 20 years in most instances.[4]

A copyright is an exclusive right granted to an author of literary, musical, photographic, video, or artistic work. A work created on or after January 1, 1978, is protected by statutory copyright for the life of the author plus 50 years postmortem.[5] Although registration is not required, it can be accomplished by depositing copies of an original work with the U.S. Copyright Office. It is essential to register a copyright before filing suit for infringement.

A trademark may also be registered with the Copyright Office. A trademark must be a distinctive emblem or device used to identify goods in the marketplace. Everyday common names have no trademark protection. Although federal and state laws allow registration of trademarks, it is the use of the trademark that is important. Registration, however, can establish the user's priority.

PERSONAL PROPERTY

To "own" personal property one must have **dominion and control** over it. Usually this is accomplished by possession of the tangible item that a person has either created or produced or acquired by purchase or gift. One who paints a picture or who grows crops has created or produced property. Acquisition by purchase is a simple concept, but sometimes controversies arise as to whether a **donor** has made a legal gift to a **donee**. To determine if a gift has been made, courts examine evidence of the donor's intent and whether a delivery of the gift has been made by the donor and accepted by the donee. If the size of the item permits, a gift should ordinarily be delivered manually; if too large to be manually delivered, something symbolic of the gift, for example, the keys to an automobile, should be given to the donee.

In addition to dominion and control, some items of personal property, such as motor vehicles, airplanes, and boats require a certificate of title in order for a person to have an ownership interest that can be transferred. Items of intangible property such as cash in a checking account, a promissory note, or shares of stock in a corporation are usually transferred by check, endorsement, or a written assignment, respectively.

Possession and Ownership of Personal Property

Personal property may be in someone's **actual possession** or **constructive possession**. A person is in actual possession of a finger ring or the clothes being worn, but may also "own" items not in actual possession. For example, a person who has the only key to a safe deposit box containing a gold watch or diamond ring is said to be in constructive possession of those items and thus may own those items in the box.

In addition to individual ownership, personal property may be owned as **tenants in common** by two or more persons, each owning an undivided interest. Or, individuals may own such property in **joint tenants with right of survivorship.** In this way upon the death of one party, the surviving party or parties becomes the sole owner(s). A bank or securities customer may see this designated as "JTROS" on bank signature cards and stock certificates. In some states the fact that a husband and wife own property jointly determines as a matter of law that upon death of one spouse the surviving spouse becomes the sole owner of the property.

Personal property may be pledged as **collateral** to secure repayment of a loan. The debtor signs a **security agreement** and the secured party (creditor) acquires a **security interest** in the personal property. Upon default by the debtor, the secured creditor has the right to the collateral and the debtor has the right to any surplus proceeds realized upon disposition of the collateral. The debtor may be liable for any deficiency remaining after the collateral is sold. These matters are generally governed by the Uniform Commercial Code and are discussed in more detail in Chapter 7.

Lost and Abandoned Property

Personal property is sometimes either lost or abandoned. If property is lost, the true owner continues to be the owner; but a finder of **lost property** has a right to it against everyone but the true owner. Lost property is property lost through inadvertence or neglect. **Abandoned property** is property that an owner voluntarily parts with having no intention to reclaim it. If a person finds lost or abandoned property, the finder who first exercises control over the property with intent to claim it usually becomes the owner. We say "usually" because in certain instance someone else may have an entitlement. For example, an employer may be entitled to lost or abandoned property found by an employee within the scope of employment. An Ohio appellate court required a hospital receptionist to return to the hospital jewelry found in an eyeglass case on top of the information desk. The hospital was directed to hold the jewelry as a gratuitous bailee for the rightful owner.[6]

Bailments

Another instance when a party receives possession or custody of personal property without acquiring an ownership interest is called a **bailment.** A bailment is created where one party, the **bailor** (usually but not necessarily the owner), delivers temporary possession of personal property to another party, the **bailee,** who accepts the property. Any type of personal property may be the subject of a bailment. The two basic types of bailments are **gratuitous bailments** and **mutual benefit bailments.** The rights and duties of parties to a bailment are often defined by contract, but in the absence of such an agreement the law provides for the rights and duties depending on the type of bailment and the relationship of the parties.

A gratuitous bailment is usually an informal arrangement where the transfer of possession of property is without any compensation. It can refer to a bailment that benefits only the bailor, for example, when a bailee agrees to store property for the bailor; or, it can refer to a bailment that benefits only the bailee, for example, a homeowner who lends a lawn mower to a neighbor is a bailor and the neighbor who borrows it is a bailee. If a gratuitous bailment is solely for the benefit of the bailor, the bailee's standard of care is minimal. If a gratuitous bailment is for benefit of the bailee, however, the bailee must exercise reasonable care and return the property to the bailor in good condition.

A more formal example is the mutual benefit bailment that is common in commercial relationships. There one party receives a benefit and another party receives compensation. Examples include a bailor who delivers an automobile to a mechanic for repairs or who stores goods in a commercial warehouse. In each instance the bailor pays a fee for services. If hidden dangers exist in the bailed property, the bailor must inform the bailee. The bailee must handle the property according to the bailor's instructions and owes the bailor the duty of exercising ordinary care. Upon payment for services, the bailee must return the bailed items to the bailor. Although the bailee is not an insurer of the property bailed, if the bailee is negligent and such negligence is the proximate cause of damage to the bailor's goods, courts hold the bailee liable.

A lease of personal property that expressly or impliedly requires the lessee to return the property to the lessor at the termination of the lease is, in effect, a bailment.[7] Likewise, the usual commercial lease of an automobile is generally considered a bailment for mutual benefit.

Parking an automobile in a commercial parking facility is a common experience. If the car is delivered to the parking attendants who retains the owner's keys and who has authority to move the owner's car, a bailment is often created. In contrast, a Missouri appellate court found that no bailment was created between the owner of a self-service parking lot and automobile owner. The owner parked an automobile, locked it, and retained control of the ignition keys. The access card to the parking lot stated that the owner of the parking lot was not liable for personal property stolen from the automobile. The court held the automobile owner merely had a license to park.[8]

Confusion and Accession

Where personal property of different owners is commingled and cannot be separated, laws relating to **confusion** apply and courts attempt to determine the proportionate interest of those who contributed to the confusion of the property. For example, when farmers combine their grain, the product owned by each loses its identity and each then has a proportionate interest in the confused product. **Accession** occurs when an owner's personal property enjoys a natural increase. Thus, one who owns a cow becomes owner of the calf born to the cow . . . as well as any milk the cow produces.

Can a Thief Transfer Title?

Despite acquiring possession, a thief does not acquire title to property. In the area of property law, the general rule is that a person can transfer no better title to personal property than the transferor has. Thus, one who has acquired possession of property by theft cannot confer title by a sale, even to a **bona fide purchaser.**

REAL ESTATE

Under early English law, the King was considered as the dominant owner of the lands of the country. The King made certain grants to feudal lords who possessed various tracts of land referred to as manors. In the manorial system of land holding, the lord of the manor, in turn, would grant his tenants certain rights in the land accompanied by certain obligations of the tenant to the lord. This system was known as **land tenure.** Among the several types of tenure, three were of primary use. One who had a **fee simple estate** could dispose of it at will. Those who had **fee tail estates** could only dispose of their estates within their family, and those who had simply **life estates** or **estates during the life of another** were further restricted in transfer of their interests. A significant development occurred in 1290 by enactment of the Statute of Quai Empotores. This English statute allowed freemen to transfer their estates in real property to another with the new possessor to have the same obligations to the lord of the manor.

The early English system of land conveyancing became part of the common law and was adopted by the new American states. Even today we speak of fee simple ownership to indicate the highest estate in land. Today, sales of real estate are completed by a deed, a written document by which an owner transfers title. Gifts of real estate occur by a deed, by a **will** upon an owner's demise, or by the laws of inheritance. Indeed, while most deeds or devises under a decedent's will transfer fee simple title, a deed or will may transfer a life estate, that is, ownership rights to the property during the owner's lifetime. A **life tenant** must maintain the improvements on the property and ordinarily must pay the real estate taxes assessed against the property. The life tenant of the property must protect the value of the property for benefit of the person who becomes the owner upon decease of the life tenant. At that time another party (called a **remainderman**) designated in the deed or will usually becomes the owner.

Acquiring and Transferring Title to Real Property

When real estate is sold, the buyer generally requires the seller, often referred to as the **grantor,** to transfer the title to the property by a **warranty deed.** A warranty deed is a document that contains promises, called **covenants,** to protect the buyer, or **grantee,** and to require the seller, if necessary, to defend the validity of the buyer's new title. In most states there is a form of warranty deed that by reference to the state law includes various common-law covenants, including the covenant of warranty. To be effective, a deed must not only be executed, but also delivered to the grantee by or with the grantor's permission. A deed recorded in the public records is presumed to have been delivered and accepted.

Early English common law regarded the title to land as extending "from the heavens to the center of the earth." In modern times, of course, the title to land must be balanced against the rights of the population. Hence, American courts have long recognized the right of aircraft to fly over lands to the extent permitted by federal regulations of aircraft.[9] Moreover, in some areas of the United States it is not uncommon for the seller of real estate to reserve certain interests, for example, the right to gas, oil, and other minerals.

When real estate is transferred to a buyer it is generally described in the deed of conveyance by its boundaries or by lot and block numbers with reference to a map or subdivision plat recorded in the county land records. For the protection of the new owner, a deed transferring real estate is recorded in the public records of the city or county where the property lies.

Another common form of deed is known as a **quitclaim deed.** This form of deed is often used to clear the title to real estate of some possible adverse claim. In a quitclaim deed the grantor makes no representation as to having an interest in the property, but simply releases any such possible interest. Therefore, if the grantee does not acquire any interest in property as a result of the quitclaim deed, the grantor has no liability.

WARRANTY DEEDS   SIDEBAR

Under the common law a warranty deed would set out a number of covenants by the grantor. State statutes often prescribe a form of warranty deed that is deemed to include such covenants if drafted substantially as provided by the statute. For example § 689.02, Florida Statute prescribes the following form:

* * * * *

This indenture, made this day of _____ A.D. _____ between _____ of the County of _____ in the State of _____, party of the first part, and _____ of the County of _____ in the State of _____, party of the second part,

Witnesseth:

That the said party of the first part, for and in consideration of the sum of _____ dollars, to her or him in hand paid by said party of the second part, the receipt whereof is hereby acknowledged, has granted, bargained and sold to the said party of the second part, her or his heirs and assigns forever, the following described land, to wit: _____.

And the said party of the first part does hereby fully warrant the title to said land, and will defend the same against the lawful claims of all person whomsoever.

* * * * *

Section 689.02, Florida Statutes provides that "A conveyance executed substantially in the foregoing form shall be held to be a warranty deed with full common-law covenants, and shall just as effectually bind the grantor, and the grantor's heir, as if said covenants were specifically set out herein."

Other statutes provide for the proper signing of the deed and the requirements for witnesses to the signers' signatures and for acknowledgment of the signers before a notary public or other officer for the deed to be recorded in the public records.

Mortgages

One who borrows money using real property as collateral signs a promissory note payable to the lender providing for repayment of the loan and interest according to the terms of the note. The borrower secures payment of the note by executing a contractual document known as a **mortgage,** creating a lien against the borrower's real property. Some loans carry a fixed rate of interest; others provide for an adjustable rate of interest based on fluctuations in the interest rate in the credit markets. In most states, a mortgage must be executed in a manner similar to execution of a deed. In fact, the typical mortgage appears much like a conveyance of property but includes a number of stipulations designed to protect the lender. The party mortgaging property is known as the **mortgagor** and the lender is known as the **mortgagee.** In some instances, particularly in sale of a residence, a seller often agrees to "take back a mortgage" as part of the purchase price. This type of legal instrument is known as a **purchase money mortgage.** To prevent subsequent purchasers of the property or a later mortgagee from gaining priority, it is essential for the mortgagee to record a mortgage in the office where deeds are recorded.

Many institutional lenders require a mortgagor to purchase private mortgage insurance (PMI) to guarantee the mortgagee against loss in the event of a foreclosure of the mortgage. In home financing often the homeowner (mortgagor) makes monthly payments of principal and interest on the mortgage loan and deposits an additional sum to pay real estate taxes, insurance, and PMI. Banks and other commercial lenders frequently sell mortgages to institutions that invest in them.

A mortgage document contains a number of covenants that bind the mortgagor. Among these are covenants to promptly make all payments required by the note secured by the mortgage, pay real estate taxes and assessments against the property, and keep any improvements on the property insured against casualty losses such as fire and windstorm. If the mortgagor transfers title to the real estate, the mortgagee's interest remains intact and the new owner of the real estate takes title subject to the lien of any recorded mortgage. In some instances a mortgage includes a **due-on-sale clause** and the mortgagor must secure approval of the new buyer by the mortgagee in order to allow the new buyer to **assume the mortgage,** otherwise the mortgagee can declare the entire loan due upon the sale.

The common law provided the mortgagee had title even though the mortgage loan was not in default. Most states today treat a mortgage as a lien that does not ripen into a title until the necessary steps to foreclose the property are completed. The mortgagee can foreclose a mortgage if the mortgagor fails to make required payments under the note secured by the mortgage or fails to comply with the other covenants contained in the mortgage. If a court enters a judgment of foreclosure, the owner of the property is generally afforded the **right of redemption.** This means that the mortgagor can pay off all sums due the mortgagee and continue to own the mortgaged property. One problem with exercising this right is the cost, including court costs, attorney's fees, and other expenses associated with the foreclosure. If the mortgagor does not exercise this right, the property is sold at a public sale and the proceeds of the sale are applied as determined by the court, usually giving a first mortgagee priority after payment of costs associated with the foreclosure. In some instances when sale of the property does not provide sufficient funds to pay the costs of foreclosure and repay the mortgagee, the court will enter a **deficiency judgment** against the mortgagor for the balance due the mortgagee.

Some states follow a different procedure, and use a **deed of trust** instead of a mortgage. The borrower deeds the property that secures the loan to a trustee. The trustee, in turn, holds title to the property. If the borrower defaults, the trustee notifies all interested parties and conducts a public sale of the property in order to pay the sums due the mortgagee. Lenders consider this arrangement preferable because it allows the lender to recover the money loaned without the formalities and delays attendant with a court proceeding.

Adverse Possession

In what today has become rare, title to land may, in some instances, be acquired by **adverse possession.** To acquire land by adverse possession, a person must comply strictly with the statutory requirements of state law. These laws vary but usually require that the adverse possessor hold the property "openly and notoriously" and continuously for a period of time usually varying from 7 to 20 years. The adverse possessor may also be required to fence, cultivate, or otherwise use the land consistent with local land-use practices for the type of property involved. Many laws require the adverse possessor to file a property tax return with local taxing authorities describing the land and to pay real estate taxes on the property.

Estates in Real Property

Estates in real property refer to how title to real estate is held, and are derived from the English common law. In addition to individual title, these estates commonly exist in the following forms: join tenancy, tenancy in common, and tenancy by the entirety.

Joint Tenancy
In a **joint tenancy,** the owners each own an undivided (usually equal) portion of the real estate. The legal instrument (deed or will) creating the joint tenancy usually provides that upon the death of one joint tenant the remaining joint tenant or tenants become(s) the owner or owners of the decedent's share. Sometimes joint tenants cannot agree on how to manage their property and they may choose to divide the property. If they cannot agree on division of the property, one party might institute a court action known as a **partition suit.** In a partition suit, the court divides the property, if feasible; and if not, it orders the property sold and the net proceeds divided according to the interests of the joint tenants.

Tenancy in Common
A **tenancy in common** is similar to a joint tenancy but does not provide for survivorship rights. A tenant in common owns an undivided interest in the real estate. Upon death of a tenant in common, who held his or her interest in his or her individual name, the decedent's heirs at law would inherit the deceased tenant's share of the property. If the decedent died with a valid will, the deceased tenant's share would be distributed according to the terms of the will. As in the case of joint tenants with right of survivorship, tenants in common can alter their interests by executing the necessary deeds or resorting to a partition suit.

Tenancy by the Entirety

A **tenancy by the entirety** is similar to a joint tenancy, but it can only exist between a husband and wife. Upon the death of one spouse, the other spouse becomes the sole owner of the property. Married couples frequently own their homeplace as tenants by the entirety. Unlike a joint tenancy, neither spouse can transfer his or her interest to anyone except the other spouse. Upon dissolution of marriage, a tenancy by the entirety usually becomes a tenancy in common unless the court awards one spouse's share to the other spouse in settlement of marital assets.

Community Property

Several states, largely in the western United States, have **community property** laws. Community property laws were unknown to the English common law. They originated from the Spanish and French laws during colonization in the western United States. Community property states have statutes defining community property rights, and while they vary somewhat, they generally provide that each spouse is deemed to own one-half of property acquired during the marriage. The community property concept does not affect ownership of property acquired by either spouse prior to their marriage or to property acquired by gift or inheritance. The concept of community property is discussed more extensively in Chapter 8.

Condominium and Cooperative Ownership

Condominium ownership is an increasingly popular form of ownership. Title may be acquired in any of the forms previously discussed. Condominium ownership may exist in business and residential properties, but the most common condominium ownership is the residential unit, where amenities vary from simple walkways and parking spaces to luxurious recreational facilities and services. Unlike the usual freestanding residence, residential condominium properties are divided into units much like apartments, either freestanding or in one or several buildings. A person who acquires a condominium unit receives a deed vesting the owner with title to a certain space in the building that includes the interior walls and space of the unit. The unit owner also acquires an interest in common in the roof and exterior walls, the common walkways, stairways, driveways, and amenities provided in the condominium complex. The condominium owner's rights and obligations are set out in a declaration of condominium (usually recorded in the office where property deeds are recorded) and in the bylaws adopted by the condominium association.

Unit owners become members of a **condominium association,** whose officers and directors usually hire professional management to assure proper exterior maintenance of the units and common facilities. In addition to real estate taxes, unit owners are required to pay fees to the condominium association to cover routine maintenance. Moreover, unit owners are subject to assessments to cover major expenses, such as reroofing and exterior painting. Often condominium associations impose regulations that may restrict unit owners as to whether pets or young children are permitted to occupy their units. Before purchasing a condominium unit, one is well advised to carefully examine all the various legal documents affecting the interest being acquired. It is wise for a purchaser of a condominium to have an attorney examine all relevant legal documents and explain the various obligations incident to condominium ownership.

In a **cooperative** form of ownership in real estate, the owner acquires shares of stock in a corporation that owns a building or complex of units. Thus, unlike the ownership of a condominium unit, the shareholder has an interest in the corporation that owns the entire complex. The corporation leases the right to occupy a unit to a shareholder who usually makes stipulated payments to the corporation to cover mortgage payments and maintenance.

Real Estate Taxes

Real estate is subject to state and local taxes assessed by a local official who is usually called a tax assessor. The assessor appraises each parcel of real estate and generally declares that appraised value (or a fraction thereof) to be the taxable value of the property. Thus real estate taxes are called *ad valorem* (at value) **taxes** and the property owner is generally billed once a year. Some states grant certain exemptions to homeowners to allow a portion of the assessed value of the home to be exempt from real estate taxes. In most states, a property owner may challenge the assessor's determination of value by appealing to a board of review usually called a **board of equalization.** Failure to pay taxes when due can result in a requirement to pay interest and penalties. Eventually, if taxes are not paid, an owner's property can be sold to allow the taxing authorities to recoup the unpaid taxes.

The transfer of real estate may require payment of certain fees and taxes including a fee for recording necessary legal documents. Of course, the sale of real estate may have income tax consequences under the Internal Revenue Code and any applicable state tax laws and regulations.

Nonpossessory Interests in Land

Besides the estates already discussed, a person may have an interest in land or a right to use land without having a right of possession. Two such interests are known as **easements** and **licenses.** An easement refers to an interest in land; a license is merely a permit that allows someone to exercise a privilege in respect to land.

In defining an easement, the Nebraska Supreme Court quoted from *Black's Law Dictionary* in stating that an easement is the "right in the owner of one parcel of land, by reason of such ownership, or use the land for a specific purpose not inconsistent with a general property of the owner."[10]

An owner of land can create an easement by executing deed or by reserving an easement when transferring property. An easement is an interest in land, but not an estate in land, because the holder of the easement gains only the right to use a part of the land for a specified purpose, but not the right to possess the land. For example, an owner might grant a utility easement to allow a power company to install power lines and poles on his or her property. The easement may be permanent or for a specified period. When given to a utility company, it is usually a permanent easement. If the owner who granted the easement transfers the title to the land, the easement would generally remain viable or as lawyers would say, "it runs with the land." Of course the interested parties may agree in writing to terminate an easement.

In some instances, a landowner acquires an **easement of necessity.** This arises where a landowner transfers title to a purchaser of a part of the owner's land without providing

THE LAW IN ACTION

Purchasing a Home

The purchase of a residence illustrates an everyday application of the law of property. Sales of homes (and other real properties such as farms and buildings) are common transactions in today's mobile society. To illustrate the process, we consider a young married couple looking to purchase a home. After selecting the area where they intend to reside, often the next step is to scan the advertisements of homes for sale, look for signs offering a home for sale by an owner, or engage the services of a real estate broker. Real estate brokers usually (but not always) receive their compensation in the form of a sales commission paid by the seller.

Once the couple find a house within their price range that meets their requirements, the next step is to sign a written offer to purchase which includes the offering price, legal description of the property, terms and conditions of purchase. Often the offer to purchase will be conditioned on the buyers being approved to assume an existing mortgage or to obtain a mortgage loan for a certain amount. The offer to purchase is generally accompanied by a good-faith cash deposit with the seller being allowed a short period of time to accept or reject the offer. When involved in the transaction, the broker retains the deposit in an escrow account. A standard form of offer to purchase and deposit receipt becomes a binding contract once accepted by the seller. This contract usually provides that if the buyers do not perform their part of the contract, then the seller may retain the good-faith deposit as liquidated damages. When a real estate broker is involved, the deposit money that is forfeited is generally divided between the seller and the broker.

An offer to purchase usually contains a number of other provisions. These include whether the purchase price is to be paid in cash or through financing, provision as to who is to furnish an abstract of title or title insurance policy, how real estate taxes and assessments are to be handled, an inventory of personal property, if any, to be included, and the closing date and place. In recent years, standard contracts for purchase of homes have included provisions to assure the buyers that there are no structural defects in the house and that electrical, plumbing, air conditioning, heating, and other systems and all appliances will be in good working order at time of closing. Depending on the locality and local customs,

other provisions may be included. Many of the items in offers to purchase are subject to negotiation. Real estate brokers often perform this function on behalf of the seller and buyer, but a couple buying a home may be well advised to secure advice from a real estate attorney before signing a document that commits them to purchase. The attorney will advise in respect to the form of the contract and factors concerning zoning, deed restrictions, easements, and others that may be important to the buyers.

In many instances the buyers will obtain a mortgage loan from a bank or other institutional lender. The buyers will complete an application for the loan. Before approving a loan, the lender will impose certain requirements. Initially, the lender obtains a credit report to find out if the purchasers are creditworthy. If so, the lender will usually have a qualified appraiser determine the market value of the house and hire a land surveyor to prepare a survey of the property and depict the location of the house on the land and show that there are no encroachments on the property being purchased. A real estate broker will assist the purchasers in handling many of the details of financing. The buyers' attorney will examine the title to the property or secure a commitment from a title insurance company to issue the new owners a title insurance policy upon their acquiring title to the property.

At the time of closing, the buyers (and their lender, if financing has been secured) will pay the balance of the contract price to the seller. The seller will execute a deed (usually a warranty deed) conveying the title to the purchasers, usually as husband and wife, and will deliver the deed to the buyers. The lender will examine the deed and submit the buyers a note and mortgage and certain disclosure statements concerning the financing of the property. The buyers then execute the note and mortgage. If the buyers are assuming an existing mortgage, approval of the present mortgage holder should be obtained along with evidence of the balance of the mortgage loan being assumed. The lender will see that the necessary documents are recorded in the land records of the city or county. An attorney who represents the buyers will examine all the relevant documents to ensure that everything is properly completed.

CASE IN POINT

DOES AN EASEMENT OF NECESSITY "RUN WITH THE LAND"?

Broadhead v. Terpening

Mississippi Supreme Court
611 So.2d 949 (Miss. 1992)

The Ratcliffs divided a tract of land and sold parcels to the defendants Broadhead and others. The Terpenings, plaintiffs, acquired a parcel of the former Ratcliff tract from someone who had purchased it from the Ratcliffs. The only established way of ingress and egress to the Terpenings' property required traversing the property now owned by Broadhead and the other defendants. The plaintiffs claimed that an easement of necessity was created in favor of those who purchased the landlocked property now owned by the Terpenings. The Mississippi Supreme Court observed that " ... the Broadheads were not the parties responsible for dividing up the Ratcliff estate in such a way that the portion now owned by the Terpenings was rendered inaccessible except by passing over the portion of the formerly unified lands." Nevertheless, the court reasoned that when the Ratcliffs parceled up their property and sold it to others, an easement of necessity was created for the person who purchased the landlocked portion of the estate now owned by the Terpenings. Such an easement of necessity, the court declared, runs with the land and passes with each conveyance to subsequent owners.

access to the land being transferred. To obtain an easement of necessity, the new owner must require an easement for necessary ingress and egress and not simply desire one for convenient access.

An easement may also be acquired by **prescription**, that is, when a person makes a continuous and uninterrupted use of property—for example, if a person has used a road right-of-way. Generally to acquire an easement by prescription the user must comply with statutory laws similar to those previously discussed concerning adverse possession of real property.

A license in real property is a right permitting someone to do some specified thing on another person's land.[11] For example, one whose land has a pond may permit a friend or neighbor to fish there. Unlike an easement, a license is not an interest in land. A license may be granted orally and in most instances it is revocable by the landowner.[12]

THE LESSOR–LESSEE RELATIONSHIP

Historically the relationship between an owner of property and the owner's tenant was referred to as **landlord/tenant law.** The term *landlord* was derived from the relationship between the lord of the English manor to whom certain obligations were due and the tenant of the land who was responsible to fulfill those obligations. As previously explained, the laws concerning real property are deeply rooted in history. Even though it is not uncommon to hear the terms *landlord* and *tenant* used today, we prefer to discuss the relationship in the modern context as between a **lessor** and a **lessee,** which most commonly occurs in either residential or commercial leasing.

Historically a lessee was required to pay rent and abide by various lease provisions but was granted only limited rights against the lessor. A lessee is often in a disadvantageous bargaining position in respect to the lessor. During the latter half of the twentieth century, courts began to look more favorably on the rights of a lessee of residential property. Legislative bodies enacted laws and ordinances to require that lessors of rental properties meet certain standards in respect to habitability, convenience, safety, and sanitation. Some laws even prescribe certain mandatory provisions that must be included in residential leases and permit a lessee to withhold rental payments when the lessor fails to comply with the requirements of the law. In some instances when a lessee would report a lessor to local authorities as not complying with the requirements to maintain safe and sanitary premises, a lessor would resort to evicting the lessee. The common law imposed no restriction on a lessor's motives in evicting a tenant if the action had a legal basis. But since the 1970s, statutes have been enacted that restrict a lessor from evicting a lessee in retaliation for reporting violations of law concerning habitability of the leased premises. Some states have enacted statutes to enable a tenant to recover damages from a lessor if the tenant suffers a **retaliatory eviction.**[13]

Residential leases, especially when the premises are furnished, often require the lessee to make a prepayment of rent and post a security deposit. Prepayment of rent affords the lessor compensation should the lessee breach the lease, and the security deposit guarantees payment to the lessor for any damages to the leased premises beyond ordinary wear and tear. A federal appeals court has described a **security deposit** as being in the nature of a trust fund.[14] Upon termination of the lease the security deposit (less any sums retained by the lessor for damages to the leased premises) must be refunded to the lessee. Courts have issued conflicting opinions as to whether the lessor is required to pay interest on the security deposit. Often this depends on statutory law.

The common law did not restrict the right of a lessee to sublet the leased premises; however, written leases commonly restrict the lessee's right to assign the lease or sublet the premises without consent of the lessor. Many written leases add that the lessor will not unreasonably withhold consent for the lessee to assign the leasehold interest. Even if the lessee is permitted to assign rights, the lessee cannot assign duties. Therefore, the lessee remains liable to the lessor for performance of the lease covenants.

Short-term rental arrangements are often handled on an oral basis where the tenancy is on a month-to-month basis and can be terminated by either party on short notice. Many of these oral rental arrangements are on a weekly or monthly basis and generally the parties are required to furnish a reasonable notice of termination. In many states the statute of frauds (see Chapter 7) requires that a lease for more than a year be in writing.

The Fair Housing Act of 1968 prohibits a lessor from refusing to sell or rent a dwelling on basis of race, color, religion, sex, national origin, familial status, or disability.[15] Some lessors have contended they have a First Amendment right based on the free exercise of religion to decline to rent to those persons whose living arrangements violate the lessor's religious convictions. By 2001, some cases were before the trial courts to determine whether a lessor's refusal to rent a dwelling to unmarried cohabitants violates the federal act or similar state statutes.

In contrast to residential leases, commercial leases are usually negotiated between more sophisticated parties and bargaining is generally on a more even basis. Professionals usually handle the negotiation and drafting of a major commercial lease and attorneys often represent the parties. Commercial leases are frequently entered into on a long-term basis and stipulate the uses of the property and include provisions for remodeling and an option for renewal. A commercial lease may include a number of other provisions including easements for vehicular parking, sometimes in common with other lessees. The forms of commercial leases are less standard than the terms of a residential lease. In a commercial lease, the rent is sometimes based on a percentage of the lessee's sales and may include an "inflation index" requiring the lessee to pay additional rent to cover annual increases in real estate taxes and property insurance. Shopping center leases and leases in mall complexes often mandate conformity with uniform business hours and include restrictions on the types of goods and services offered for sale in order to protect lessees from excessive competition.

REGULATION OF REAL PROPERTY USE

Some restrictions on use of real property are privately agreed upon by contract. Others are imposed by legislation or regulation. All levels of government impose restrictions on the use of real property. The federal government imposes certain **environmental regulations** to preserve endangered species of birds and animals, to control the discharge of industrial wastes and sewage pollutants, and so forth. State and local governmental agencies impose most regulations on the development and uses of land. Because private control of private property is a fundamental value in American culture, such restrictions are often controversial. Sometimes compliance with these regulations imposes significant economic costs on property owners. The thrust of modern American law, however, is to allow reasonable restrictions on private property that further societal interests in public health, safety, welfare, and environmental integrity.

Planning and Zoning Activities

Land-use planning is a modern method of achieving a balance of land uses within a state and a community. To ensure orderly land development, many states have initiated a comprehensive plan that requires local governmental agencies to adhere to certain standards in their planning and zoning activities. Two primary tools that local governmental agencies use to regulate the use of privately owned lands are **land-use zoning** and **building codes**.

Land-Use Zoning
Land-use zoning is a facet of the police power, and state legislatures generally grant authority to counties and municipalities to adopt comprehensive land-use plans and enact zoning regulations for lands within their jurisdiction. When a county or city initially undertakes to enact zoning ordinances and regulations, it divides the community into zones and classifies those zones as permitting residential, office, business, recreational, and industrial uses. When zoning is originally imposed and thereafter when rezoning occurs, existing uses,

which are incompatible with the zoning, are generally "**grandfathered in**" for a period of time to allow the owner of the property to recover the economic value of nonconforming improvements.

Zoning is a product of the twentieth century. It was originally undertaken on the legal premise that the police power of government is sufficient to allow it to abate nuisances and that zoning, in effect, was simply "keeping the pig out of the parlor." Disparate court decisions by state courts created considerable doubt as to the validity of zoning enactments until 1926 when the U.S. Supreme Court sustained the constitutionality of a comprehensive zoning ordinance in its seminal decision in *Village of Euclid v. Ambler Realty Co.*[16] In upholding Euclid's right to enact a comprehensive zoning ordinance, the Court rejected Ambler Realty's arguments concerning due process of law, equal protection of the laws, and contentions that the zoning resulted in unauthorized taking of property. The *Euclid* decision firmly established the right of legislatures to grant local communities the power to enact zoning controls over private lands. Courts continue to entertain constitutional challenges to zoning ordinances as they affect particular parcels of land. However, these disputes are primarily handled in state courts.

The latter half of the twentieth century witnessed considerable sophistication in the zoning process. In addition to its traditional function of establishing residential, business, and industrial districts, zoning is now used as a tool to create historical and architectural districts. It also provides for conditional uses, and to enforce certain requirements such as off-street parking for business and apartment complexes and enforce aesthetic values by regulating the size of on-premise and off-premise signs.

Local governments provide for applications for rezoning of property and for **special exceptions** based on specified criteria that must be observed in certain uses of property in a given neighborhood or area. A comprehensive zoning ordinance must provide for a **board of adjustment** authorized to grant **variances** where, because of the character or size of a parcel of land, enforcement of a zoning regulation would impose an undue hardship on the property owner. If zoning goes beyond its permitted scope it may bring into question whether a landowner's property has effectively been taken by government and subject the local government to pay the landowner just compensation.

Restrictive Covenants

A land developer who subdivides land often files a written declaration of **restrictive covenants** to bind those who purchase vacant lots or houses in the subdivision. This is to provide a certain level of quality and may limit the use of the land solely to residential purposes and prescribe that houses built are to be of a certain size within specified distances from one another. These are very common where there are no local zoning controls or in instances when the developer deems the zoning inadequate to maintain the desired quality of the neighborhood. The restrictive covenants generally provide for enforcement by the subdivider of the land or by property owners within the subdivision. Historically, restrictive covenants were sometimes used to restrain homeowners from selling their homes to people of certain races. In 1948, the Supreme Court said that judicial enforcement of racially restrictive covenants constitutes a violation of the Equal Protection Clause of the Fourteenth Amendment to the U.S. Constitution.[17]

EMINENT DOMAIN

An inherent attribute of federal and state sovereignty is the power of **eminent domain**, that is, the ability of government to take private property for public use.[18] The federal government and the governments of each state have this power, and the legislatures of the states generally grant this power to certain levels of local government, usually to counties and cities. The power to condemn property for public use is most often exercised by government to acquire lands for such public improvements as government buildings, military bases, highways, parks, and recreation areas.

The Fifth Amendment to the U.S. Constitution that stipulates "private property [shall not] be taken for public use without just compensation" is known as the Takings Clause. It means that in addition to establishing that property is being taken for public purposes, a condemning authority must pay just compensation to the owners of the property taken. Thus, the cost of acquiring property for public purposes is borne by the taxpayers.

When the condemning authority and the property owner cannot agree on what constitutes just compensation, the amount of compensation is determined by a court. The condemning authority introduces evidence that the property being taken is required for public purposes and offers real estate appraisers who offer expert opinions on the value of the property being condemned. The property owner, in turn, has the right to testify concerning the value and use of the property being taken and to present appraisers as expert witnesses to testify as to the market value of the property. In most cases a jury determines the amount of

Opinion of the Court . . .

MISSISSIPPI & RUM RIVER BOOM CO. V. PATTERSON
98 U.S. 403, 25 L.Ed. 206 (1878)

Mr. Justice Field delivered the Opinion of the Court.

. . . The right of eminent domain, that is, the right to take private property for public uses, appertains to every independent government. It requires no constitutional recognition; it is an attribute of sovereignty. The clause found in the Constitutions of the several States providing for just compensation for property taken is a mere limitation upon the exercise of the right. When the use is public, the necessity or expediency of appropriating any particular property is not a subject of judicial cognizance. The property may be appropriated by an act of the legislature, or the power of appropriating it may be delegated to private corporations, to be exercised by them in the execution of works in which the public is interested. But notwithstanding the right is one that appertains to sovereignty, when the sovereign power attaches conditions to its exercise, the inquiry whether the conditions have been observed is a proper matter for judicial cognizance. If that inquiry takes the form of a proceeding before the courts between parties—the owners of the land on the one side, and the company seeking the appropriation on the other—then there is a controversy which is subject to the ordinary incidents of a civil suit, and its determination derogates in no respect from the sovereignty of the State. . . .

compensation due the property owner. The testimony as to the amount of compensation to be awarded can become very technical when the condemning authority takes real estate that effectively abolishes or diminishes the owner's ongoing business. In such instances, accountants and economists often appear as expert witnesses on behalf of the owner.

Regulatory Takings

The drafters of the Fifth Amendment Takings Clause undoubtedly had in mind physical takings by government; however, courts have long recognized its applicability to governmental regulatory actions as well as physical takings. In some instances government regulations have greatly affected the economic value of an owner's property. For example, in 1987, the U.S. Supreme Court ruled that land-use regulation can effectively become a taking when the regulations do not substantially advance legitimate interests of the government or when such regulations deny the owners use of their land.[19] The Court has noted the Takings Clause "is designed not to limit the governmental interference with property rights per se, but rather to secure compensation in the event of otherwise proper interference amounting to a taking."[20]

The need to protect the environment has caused governmental agencies to take steps, for example, denying a permit to fill wetlands, which have greatly burdened an owner's use of private property. Some instances when courts have required the government to pay just compensation include governmental efforts to protect coastal areas from erosion.[21] In a case where the government sought to protect water quality from strip-mining activities, a federal court held that the Surface Mining Control and Reclamation Act, which permitted such governmental action, effected a compensable taking.[22]

CASE IN POINT

CAN LOCAL GOVERNMENT CONDITION THE GRANTING OF A BUILDING PERMIT ON THE PROPERTY OWNER GRANTING AN EASEMENT?

Nollan v. California Coastal Commission

United States Supreme Court
483 U.S. 825, 107 S.Ct. 3141, 97 L.Ed.2d 677 (1987)

James and Marilyn Nollan owned a beachfront lot in Ventura County, California. They wanted to tear down the small house on the lot and build a larger one. To do this they had to obtain permit from the California Coastal Commission. The Commission granted the permit on the condition that the Nollans allow the public to pass across their beach, which was situated between two public beaches. The required condition was "part of a comprehensive program to provide continuous public access along Faria Beach as the lots undergo development or re-development." The Nollans unsuccessfully challenged this requirement in the California courts, arguing that their property was effectively being taken for public use without just compensation.

The U.S. Supreme Court agreed with the Nollans. Writing for the Court, Justice Antonin Scalia said, "California is free to advance its 'comprehensive program,' if it wishes, by using its power of eminent domain for this 'public purpose' . . . but if it wants an easement across the Nollans' property, it must pay for it." In dissent, Justice William Brennan castigated the Court's "narrow view" of the case, saying that its "reasoning is hardly suited to the complex realty of natural resource protection in the 20th century."

It is not uncommon for a local government to require certain concessions from a property owner before approval of rezoning or issuance of a building permit. For example, a city may require an owner to grant an easement or dedicate land for public use. In such instances, an issue of **regulatory taking** may come into play. In 1994, the U.S. Supreme Court held that requiring the owner to deed a portion of the property to the city for use as a public greenway along an adjoining portion of the property before allowing the owner to expand her plumbing and electrical supply store and add a paved parking lot went too far and were inconsistent with the Takings Clause of the Fifth Amendment.[23]

TRUSTS

A **trust** is a legal instrument with three parties. One party, called the **grantor (settlor)** creates the trust. Another party, called the **trustee,** manages the trust for the benefit of one or more **beneficiaries.** In some instances the settlor, trustee, and beneficiary during the settlor's lifetime may be the same person. Trusts that are created during the settlor's lifetime are referred to by lawyers as **inter vivos trusts,** but more commonly laypersons refer to such trusts as **living trusts.** The transfer of assets into the trust is essential, and is usually accomplished by retitling assets into the name of the trustee.

A trust created under a will is known as a **testamentary trust** and does not become effective until death of the testator or testatrix (the legal designations for a man or woman who sign a will). In most instances one who creates a testamentary trust may revoke it simply by executing a new will. The settlor of an inter vivos or living trust can, and typically does, retain the right to revoke the trust. This is called a **revocable trust.** If a settlor does not reserve the right to revoke the trust it is known as an **irrevocable trust.**

In most states any competent adult may become a trustee. In practice, trusts are often funded with substantial assets by a settlor who is seeking competent, professional management and who chooses a trust company to serve as trustee. There are significant advantages in having professional management and corporate trustees fulfill this role, because they customarily have a staff of officers who are trained in administration and investments. A trustee is entitled to receive a fee for services. Fees are generally negotiated between the settlor and trustee. A corporate trustee who assumes its duties upon the settlor's death may ask those who bear the impact of the fee (beneficiaries) to consent to the fee.

Inter vivos trusts are often created to coordinate the management of assets with the objective of providing for the needs of beneficiaries and conserving income, gift, and estate taxes. Additionally, a settlor of an inter vivos trust may desire to avoid the publicity and costs that may be attendant to the settlor's property being administered under supervision of a probate court.

WILLS AND INTESTATE SUCCESSION

A person who has a valid will is called a **testator** or **testatrix.** A testator (testatrix) must have **testamentary capacity,** which means to be of sound mind and to understand the nature and extent of his or her property, the natural objects of his or her bounty, and the disposition being accomplished by the will being executed. To be valid, a will must be executed by a competent adult and must comply with certain formal requirements stipulated in the statutes of the state of the testator's domicile at the time the will was signed. Generally, a will must be signed by a competent person in the presence of two witnesses and declared by the signer to be his or her will. The witnesses must sign the will in the presence of the testator and each other. During his or her lifetime a competent testator may either revoke a will or may revise it by signing an amendment called a **codicil.** A codicil must be executed with the same formalities as a will. A testator who dies is said to have died testate.

Legal nomenclature designates beneficiaries of a will who receive real estate as **devisees** and beneficiaries of personal property as **legatees.** A testator has considerable freedom in determining who are to be the beneficiaries under the will. Nevertheless, most state laws provide that if a surviving spouse is dissatisfied with the share provided under the deceased spouse's will, he or she may choose to receive an **elective share** of the decedent's property. Originally this was a device to protect widows and was known as a right to elect a dower interest. In the past several decades most states have broadened the concept to equally protect widows and widowers. Usually the elective share entitlement is about 30 percent of the decedent's estate. In some states a child born after a will is executed is entitled to a share of the estate unless the testator's wills expressly excludes **after-born children.**

A will is an important legal document but it does not control the disposition of all property owned by a decedent. In many instances property is owned jointly with the right of survivorship whereby the survivor becomes the owner. Also life insurance, annuities, and retirement death benefits typically pass by contract to the named beneficiary rather than by the decedent's will or by the laws of intestate succession.

A testator's will generally appoints a **personal representative** (sometimes called an executor or executrix) to handle the administration of the estate. This may be any competent adult or a corporate trust company that is qualified to act under state law. Some states require the personal representative to be a resident of the state where the administration takes place. Upon a testator's death, the personal representative named in the decedent's will petitions the court to admit the will to probate and officially appoint the named personal representative who then administers the estate under oversight of the **probate court.**

The personal representative is responsible to inventory and protect the decedent's assets; have assets appraised; publish notice to creditors; sell assets where necessary; file necessary tax returns; and pay all taxes, administrative fees, expenses, and valid claims filed against the estate. The personal representative must collect all sums due the decedent, keep detailed records of receipts and expenditures, and file such accountings as required by the probate court. At the conclusion of administration, the personal representative must distribute the remaining assets according to the provisions of the decedent's will. The formalities and time requirements often depend on the value and character of the decedent's assets and liabilities.

Property owned by a person who dies without a will passes to the decedent's **heirs** by **intestate succession.** The law of the state of the decedent's **domicile** determines the decedent's heirs. Usually state intestate succession laws provide for inheritance by the decedent's spouse and children or descendants of deceased children. The probate court appoints someone to serve as a personal representative (sometimes called an administrator or administratrix) to handle the administration of the decedent's estate. An individual who is appointed personal representative generally must post a surety bond in an amount set by the court to guarantee faithful performance of duties. That person or corporate entity appointed must notify the decedent's heirs and in general carry out the duties as outlined for testate estates and make distribution according to law. Again, the formalities and time requirements often depend on the value and character of the decedent's assets and liabilities.

Every state has a probate court or a division of the civil court that supervises the administration of estates and the distribution of the decedent's property to the decedent's beneficiaries or heirs at law. The personal representative of an estate and the attorney who advises the personal representative are each entitled to a fee for services. In some instances, the fee is based on a percentage allowed by state law. In other instances, interested parties agree upon the fee; however, when there is disagreement the probate court is available to determine the reasonableness of fees. In some instances approval of fees by the probate court is required. When the decedent owned real estate in a state other than where the decedent was domiciled it may become necessary to have an **ancillary administration** of a decedent's estate in the state where the real property is located.

The Contest of a Will

To contest a will the contestant must have standing. An heir who has been **disinherited** or a person who was named as a beneficiary in a prior will generally has standing. Will contests usually take one of two forms. Either the contestant claims the testator did not have testamentary capacity when the will was executed, or the will was the result of **fraud, duress, or undue influence** of the testator.

Of the grounds named, undue influence is the most common. To prove undue influence the contestant generally must show the testator's mind was unduly influenced in executing the will. Disinheriting a relative does not cause a presumption of undue influence; but when a testator names as a beneficiary a person who was in a close relationship with the testator (for example, the testator's doctor, nurse, business adviser, or housekeeper) to the exclusion of close family members, a question of undue influence may arise. If such a person possessed a confidential relationship with the testator, procured the testator to execute the will, and is to receive a substantial benefit under the will, many courts raise a presumption of undue influence. Such a presumption requires the proponent of the challenged will to offer a reasonable explanation for having actively procured the testator to sign the will.

ESTATE, GIFT, AND INHERITANCE TAXES

Since the early decades of the twentieth century the U.S. government has imposed a tax on estates and gifts. Since 1977, taxes on gifts and estates have been combined. A decedent's gross estate for estate tax purposes consists of property in the decedent's sole name that is subject to probate. The gross estate also includes life insurance and annuities on the decedent's life where the decedent owned the policies, property in certain types of trusts the decedent established, business interests, the decedent's interest in jointly owned property, and certain pension and profit-sharing interests. A person may make annual exclusion gifts of certain amounts without tax consequences (currently $10,000 to each donee); however, beyond these exempt amounts the gifts made during a person's lifetime are added to the value of the decedent's estate to determine the value of the estate for **federal estate tax** purposes.

The decedent's **adjusted gross estate**—that is, the value of the decedent's estate less debts of the decedent and costs of administration—is entitled to an applicable credit amount (**unified credit**) that as of the year 2001 exempts $675,000 from the estate tax. In June 2001, President Bush signed a massive tax bill enacted by Congress exempting $1 million in 2002, rising in steps to $3.5 million by 2009, with repeal in 2010. The top rate of tax for estates exceeding the exemption was lowered to 50%.

In determining the decedent's taxable estate, the adjusted gross estate is reduced by deductions for charitable gifts, debts, and funeral expenses. In addition, the estate of a married person is entitled to a marital deduction of the value of property transferred outright or in certain other ways to a surviving spouse. Under current federal law, there is no limit on the amount of the marital deduction. There are limitations on the marital deduction when the surviving spouse is not a U.S. citizen. When the surviving spouse dies, that spouse's estate, having been increased by property received as a marital deduction, may be quite large and subject to considerable estate taxes.

Estate planning has become an important activity in present-day America. Estate planning takes into consideration a person's assets, family situation, and desires. It is designed to provide an effective method of accomplishing one's objective of distribution of assets while minimizing taxes and costs of administration. To maximize the estate that will be available to beneficiaries, a person who has an estate that may be subject to federal estate taxes should seek the advice of an attorney who practices in this field of law and other experts in the field of taxes and financial management. In this way one can be guided in making lifetime and testamentary gifts and structuring an estate plan to take advantage of available deductions.

State Estate and Inheritance Taxes

Some states impose an estate tax that is due only if there is a federal estate tax, and the laws are frequently written in such a way that the decedent's estate pays a portion of the total estate taxes to the state rather than to the federal government. Other states impose an **inheritance tax** on the value of the assets received from a decedent's estate. In these states there are generally certain levels of exemptions for assets received by close family members.

GUARDIANSHIP TO PROTECT PROPERTY RIGHTS

If, because of minority or incapacity, a person is unable to manage his or her affairs it may become necessary to secure the court appointment of a **legal guardian.** A legal guardian may become guardian of the person (called the **ward**) or of the ward's property, or both.

Often the appointment of a guardian of the property of a minor may be averted through property being given to a minor under a custodial or trust arrangement. Frequently guardianship of an incapacitated person may be avoided through proper estate planning if the person, while still competent, executes a **durable power of attorney** and an **advance directive for medical decisions.**

A **legal guardianship** of a child's property may be necessary if the child's parents are deceased or if the child receives a gift or inheritance of a value beyond a modest amount. If an adult becomes mentally or physically incapable of handling his or her affairs and has not established the means for the management of his or her finances, then a guardianship may be appropriate.

To have someone's competency determined, an interested person must petition the court. The court usually appoints a committee often composed of three individuals, including a physician, to examine the individual. After receiving reports and hearing testimony, the court makes a finding as to the individual's capacity. If the court finds that the person is incapacitated, it appoints a guardian, sometimes a relative, other times a professional guardian or trust company.

A guardian of a person who is a minor or an incapacitated person must oversee the welfare of the ward. A guardian of a ward's assets must manage and administer the ward's property, file accountings and reports, and obtain court approval if required by state law, to act on the ward's behalf to sell property owned by the ward. The guardian of an incapacitated ward may be required to have the ward examined periodically to determine if any of the ward's right should be restored.

In all guardianships, the guardian is required to file certain reports and abide by instructions from the court. The court may require the guardian to post a bond before taking charge of the ward's assets. The cost of the bond, court costs, and attorney's fees can make a guardianship an expensive alternative to proper advance planning.

CONCLUSION

One concept unmistakably emerges: Property law, long regarded as stable and unchanging, has become dynamic. History has provided a needed stability in the law of property, yet as our nation's economy has changed from agricultural to industrial, and as it now advances into the information age, new approaches to property rights have evolved. In the early history of the United States, ownership of real property represented by far the predominant wealth of individuals and businesses. By the twentieth century intangible assets represented the greatest wealth of the nation.

An individual's absolute right over the use of private property is no longer feasible. Zoning laws and building standards that were originally designed to control nuisances have become very sophisticated in their restrictions on the use of real property. In response to environmental concerns, regulations have necessarily altered the concept of free and unrestricted use of land. Where such regulations constitute a "taking" of an owner's property, the owner is entitled to receive just compensation from the government as surely as if the government effected a physical taking of the owner's property.

Modern forms of financing have enabled home ownership to become widespread and laws have been enacted to protect the interests of those whose materials and labor have created or enhanced real property. Condominium and cooperative ownership of real property is popular and growing.

The transfer of wealth from one generation to another is no longer accomplished by a simple will. With the creation of large estates in a time of unparalleled prosperity, estate planning to avoid guardianships and excessive taxes has become commonplace as have the uses of trusts in the transmission of property to new generations.

SUMMARY OF KEY CONCEPTS

In this chapter we have endeavored to present the historical background of the law of private property, which has its roots in the English common law, and to explain how these historic concepts pervade the present law, particularly the laws relating to ownership and transfer of real estate.

It is important to comprehend the different forms of personal property (tangible and intangible) and the ownership and possessory rights that arise under the doctrines of bailments, confusion, and accession.

It is important to grasp the various forms of ownership of real property and how such property is transferred and mortgaged and the nonpossesory interests in land such as licenses and easements. Although much of the law of real estate follows the English common law, the relationship between a lessor and lessee has undergone considerable changes, at least with respect to residential leases, mostly to the benefit of the lessee.

Owners of real estate sometimes impose restrictions on its use, for example, subdivision restrictions. Although the concept of private ownership of property is protected by the U.S. Constitution, government at all levels regulates the use of property, primarily through land-use zoning, building codes, and environmental regulations. Governmental units have the power of eminent domain, that is, the power to condemn private property for public use; but again the U.S. Constitution requires that the owners be fairly compensated. In some instances governmental regulations can become so restrictive that courts will hold that such regulations constitute a compensable taking.

Creation of a trust is a legal method of providing for the management and eventual transfer of property interests. Living or inter vivos trusts are created during a person's lifetime; trusts created under a will are known as testamentary trusts. By execution of a will a testator or testatrix can, subject to certain restrictions, provide for transfer of property at death and designate a personal representative to carry out the terms of the will. Otherwise, property is distributed to heirs according to the intestate succession laws of the state of the decedent's domicile. Estates must also reckon with the payment of debts and costs of administration. Larger estates are subject to federal estate taxes and in many states heirs who receive property are subject to payment of inheritance taxes. In some instances, it is necessary to secure the court appointment of a guardian of a minor or a minor's property or guardianship of a person adjudged by a court to be physically or mentally incapable of handling his or her property.

QUESTIONS FOR THOUGHT AND DISCUSSION

1. The authors state that private property is essential to American political philosophy. Is this the case? Why or why not?

2. Explain the distinction between an easement and a license as related to the law of real property.

3. You are offered a three-year lease on a residence for a monthly rental agreeable to you. What provisions would you consider to be essential in the lease? What other provisions would you look for that might affect your use and enjoyment of the property?

4. Should the law impose definite requirements on a party who leases property for residential use or should parties be free to negotiate the terms of a lease without interference from government? Justify your answer.

5. Before the city of Plainville would grant a developer a permit to construct houses in a new subdivision, the city required that the developer deed to the city a large tract of land for use for the construction of a school. Do you think this would constitute a regulatory taking in violation of the Takings Clause of the Fifth Amendment? Why or why not?

6. A person who accumulates property pays various taxes such as real estate taxes, sales taxes, federal and state income taxes, and in some instances intangible taxes. In view of the taxes exacted upon the creation of wealth, is the imposition of a federal gift and estate tax a justifiable form of taxation?

7. Why is it usually more advantageous to have a will rather than to die intestate?

8. What is meant by an "elective share" in regard to a decedent's estate?

9. Outline the functions that must be performed by a personal representative in the administration of a decedent's estate.

10. Describe a family situation in which it may be advisable for an individual with dependent children to place property in a trust rather than will it outright to the children under a will.

KEY TERMS

real property

personal property

lien

leasehold

tangible personal property

intangible personal property

chose in action

patents, copyrights, and trademarks

dominion and control

donor

donee

actual possession

constructive possession

tenants in common

joint tenants with right of survivorship (JTROS)

collateral

security agreement

security interest

lost property

abandoned property

bailment

bailor

bailee

gratuitous bailments

mutual benefit bailments

confusion

accession

bona fide purchaser

land tenure

fee simple estate

fee tail estates

life estates

estates during the life of another

will

life tenant

remainderman

grantor

warranty deed

covenants

grantee

quitclaim deed

mortgage

mortgagor

mortgagee

purchase money mortgage

due-on-sale clause

assume the mortgage

right of redemption

deficiency judgment

deed of trust

adverse possession

estates in real property

joint tenancy

partition suit

tenancy in common

tenancy by the entirety

community property

condominium

condominium association

cooperative

ad valorem taxes

board of equalization

easements

licenses

easement of necessity

prescription

landlord/tenant law

lessor

lessee

retaliatory eviction

security deposit

environmental regulations

land-use planning

land-use zoning

building codes

"grandfathered in"

special exceptions

board of adjustment

variances

restrictive covenants

eminent domain

regulatory taking

trust

grantor (settlor)

trustee

beneficiaries

inter vivos trusts

living trusts

testamentary trust

revocable trust

irrevocable trust

testator

testatrix

testamentary capacity

codicil

devisees

legatees

elective share

after-born children

personal representative

probate court

heirs

intestate succession

domicile

ancillary administration

disinherited

fraud, duress or undue influence

federal estate tax

adjusted gross estate

unified credit

inheritance tax

legal guardian

ward

durable power of attorney

advance directive for medical decisions

legal guardianship

ENDNOTES

[1] *Chicago, Burlington, & Quincy Railroad v. Chicago,* 166 U.S. 226, 17 S.Ct. 581, 41 L.Ed. 979 (1897).

[2] See *Walls v. Midland Carbon Co.,* 254 U.S. 300, 41 S.Ct. 118, 65 L.Ed. 276 (1920).

[3] U.S. Const., Art. I, § 8, cl. 8.

[4] 35 U.S.C.A. § 154(a)(3).

[5] 17 U.S.C.A. § 302 (a).

[6] *Ray v. Flower Hospital,* 439 NE 2d 942 (Ohio App. 1981).

[7] *Franklin v. Jackson,* 847 S.W. 2d 305 (Tex. App. 1992).

[8] *Weinberg v. Wayco Petroleum Co.,* 402 S.W. 2d 597 (Mo. App. 1966).

[9] See, for example, *State v. Chippewa Cable Co.,* 180 NW 2d 714 (Wis. 1970).

[10] *Frye v. Sibbitt,* 17 NW 2d 617, 621 (Neb. 1945).

[11] *Thornhill v. Caroline Hunt Trust Estate,* 594 So. 2d 1150 (Miss. 1992).

[12] *Mueller v. Keller,* 164 NE 2d 28 (Ill. 1960).

[13] See, for example, *Morford v. Lensey Corp.,* 442 N.E. 2d 933 (Ill. App. 1982).

[14] *Peterson v. Oklahoma City Housing Authority,* 545 F.2d 1270 (10th Cir. 1976).

[15] 42 U.S.C.A. § 3604.

[16] 272 U.S. 365, 47 S.Ct.114, 71 L.Ed. 303 (1926).

[17] *Shelley v. Kraemer,* 334 U.S. 1, 68 S.Ct. 836, 92 L.Ed. 1161 (1948).

[18] *Kohl v. United States,* 91 U.S 367, 23 L.Ed. 449 (1876).

[19] See *Keystone Bituminous Coal Association v. DeBenedictis,* 480 U.S. 470, 107 S.Ct. 1232, 94 L.Ed.2d 472 (1987).

[20] *First English Evangelical Lutheran Church of Glendale v. County of Los Angeles,* 482 U.S. 304, 315, 107 S.Ct. 2378, 2386, 96 L.Ed.2d 250, 264 (1987).

[21] See *Lucas v. South Carolina Coastal Council,* 505 U.S. 1003, 112 S.Ct. 2886, 120 L.Ed.2d 798 (1992).

[22] See *Whitney Benefits, Inc. v. United States,* 926 F.2d 1169 (Fed. Cir.1991).

[23] *Dolan v. City of Tigard,* 512 U.S. 374, 114 S.Ct. 2309, 129 L.Ed.2d 304 (1994).

FOR FURTHER READING

Ackerman, Bruce, *Private Property and the Constitution* (Yale University Press 1977).

Bernhardt, Roger, and Amy M. Burkhart, *Real Property in a Nutshell* (West Group 2000).

Ely, James W. Jr., ed., *Property Rights in American History* (6 vols., Garland 1997).

Epstein, Richard A., *Takings: Private Property and the Power of Eminent Domain* (Harvard University Press 1985).

Nedelsky, Jennifer, *Private Property and the Limits of American Constitutionalism: The Madisonian Framework and its Legacy* (University of Chicago Press 1990).

Seigan, Bernard H., *Economic Liberties and the Constitution* (University of Chicago Press 1980).

7

CONTRACTS AND BUSINESS LAW

Courtesy of West Group.

LEARNING OBJECTIVES

This chapter should enable the student to understand:

- the constitutional and commercial significance of the right to contract
- how contracts are classified
- the elements of a contract
- the legal meaning of *offer and acceptance, consideration, capacity to contract,* and *legality of purpose*
- the effect of the statute of frauds and parol evidence rule
- assignment and performance of contracts; legal remedies for breach of contract
- the applicability of the Uniform Commercial Code to sales, commercial paper, secured transactions, and warranties

CHAPTER OUTLINE

Introduction

Contracts

The Uniform Commercial Code

Business Associations

Consumer Protection

Bankruptcy

Conclusion

Summary of Key Concepts

Questions for Thought and Discussion

Key Terms

For Further Reading

INTRODUCTION

In this chapter we examine the basic principles of contract law and related business enterprises. The right to contract is a core value in the United States, and the freedom of individuals, organizations, and businesses to enter into contracts is basic to the free enterprise system. Article 1, Section 10 of the U.S. Constitution, which provides that "No State shall pass any . . . Law impairing the Obligation of Contracts" reveals the importance the Founders placed on contractual relations. This provision came into sharp focus in 1819 when Chief Justice John Marshall, in a landmark decision of the U.S. Supreme Court, wrote that the charter King George III granted to Dartmouth College in 1769 gave the trustees the contractual right to govern the college. Consequently, the Court ruled that the state legislature could not impair the obligation of that contract by transferring the control of the College to a new board of overseers.[1]

The basic law of contracts as developed in the English common law was accepted in the United States; however, federal and state statutes have considerably modified laws concerning contracts. As a result the freedom to contract is regulated to a considerable extent by legislative bodies and by the courts. As mentioned in Chapter 5, the American Law Institute (ALI) has developed *Restatements of the Law* in an attempt to bring uniformity in the application of legal principles. Because the law of contracts is so vital to commerce and the need for stability and uniformity in the law is so great, the *Restatement* assumes a particularly significant role in this area. The principles of contract law as restated by the ALI are frequently followed by the courts. In this chapter we make frequent references to the *Restatement of Contracts,* second edition.

Every day we enter into contracts when we buy a newspaper, buy lunch or groceries, have a vehicle repaired, buy a theatre ticket, or board a bus. These contracts seldom result in controversies and seldom do the contracting parties resort to litigation. Contracts form the backbone of modern business as individuals contract to purchase real estate, executives enter into employment contracts with corporations, and promoters raise capital from investors to start new businesses. The federal government procures material to equip the armed forces, and states contract with construction firms to build roads and bridges. The basic principles of law applicable to simple contracts apply to those involving millions of dollars.

The development of business entities has been an outgrowth of the right to contract. In this chapter we also examine the basic structure and legal aspects of sole proprietorships, partnerships, and the artificial legal beings we know as corporations. In discussing business organizations, it is helpful to understand some of the basic concepts of antitrust law, labor law, and laws relating to employment contracts and employment discrimination. We discuss these topics in Chapter 11.

CONTRACTS

A contract is basically an agreement between two or more parties that is enforceable by law. Gaining familiarity with the various classifications of contracts is a good way to start. Contracts may be oral or written. An **express contract** exists where the parties explicitly state the terms of their agreement. An **implied contract,** on the other hand, exists where the conduct of the parties evidences a contract. For example, one who orders a hamburger at a fast-food restaurant impliedly agrees to pay the price posted on the menu.

Classifications of Contracts

Another method of classifying contracts is whether they are bilateral or unilateral. A **bilateral contract** is one where parties exchange promises. Most written contracts are bilateral. In contrast, a **unilateral contract** is one where one party responds to another party's offer by performing some act. To illustrate: A homeowner offers a gardener $40 if the gardener mows the homeowner's lawn and the gardener complies. The gardener's act represents the acceptance of the homeowner's offer. This is a unilateral contract.

In contract law an **executory contract** refers to one that has not yet been fully performed, whereas an **executed contract** is one where performance has been completed. A **voidable contract,** such as a minor's contract to purchase an automobile, may be legitimately cancelled but a **void contract** is one the law does not recognize. An example would be a contract between parties to injure or kill someone.

Finally, some contracts are classified as **formal contracts** and others are called **informal contracts.** A **negotiable instrument** such as a **check** or **promissory note** requires the use of certain language and legal terms; hence it is called a formal contract. Other contracts are generally called informal contracts, for although some written contracts are very detailed and complex, the law does not specify the exact language that the contracting parties must use.

Requisites of a Contract

To have an enforceable contract there must be **mutual assent** of two or more parties who have the **capacity to contract** and there must be **consideration.** The mutual assent is generally based on one party's offer and another party's acceptance. To have the capacity to contract, a person must have attained the age of legal majority and must be mentally competent. Consideration is often thought of as being synonymous with money, but it can involve an exchange of benefits between parties, a promise, or even a forbearance by a party.

Opinion of the Court . . .

DARTMOUTH COLLEGE v. WOODWARD

4 Wheat. (17 U.S.) 518; 4 L. Ed 629 (1819)

Dartmouth College was originally chartered by King George III in 1769. Under the royal charter, the trustees of the college were "forever" granted the right to govern the institution as they saw fit. However, in 1816, the state of New Hampshire took control of the college, believing its royal charter was no longer valid. The ousted trustees sued to recover the charter, seal, and records of the college and in this way directly challenged the authority of New Hampshire to enact the legislation that transferred the college to state control. The lower court entered judgment on a special verdict adverse to the trustees. Reviewing the case on a writ of error, the Supreme Court held that a corporate charter was a contract, the terms of which could not be changed materially by the state without violating the Contract Clause (Article I, Section 10) of the Constitution.

Chief Justice John Marshall delivered the opinion of the Court, writing in part:

. . . This is plainly a contract to which the donors, the trustees, and the Crown (to whose rights and obligations New Hampshire succeeds) were the original parties. It is a contract made on a valuable consideration. It is a contract on the faith of which real and personal estate has been conveyed to the corporation. It is then a contract within the letter of the Constitution, and within its spirit also. . . .

We next proceed to the inquiry, whether its obligation has been impaired by those acts of the legislature of New Hampshire, to which the special verdict refers? . . .

A repeal of the charter at any time prior to the adoption of the present constitution of the United States, would have been an extraordinary and unprecedented act of power, but one which could have been contested only by the restrictions upon the legislature, to be found in the constitution of the State. But the constitution of the United States has imposed this additional limitation, that

the legislature of a State shall pass no act "impairing the obligation of contracts."

It has been already stated, that the act "to amend the charter, and enlarge and improve the corporation of Dartmouth College," increases the number of trustees to twenty-one, gives the appointment of the additional members to the executive of the state, and creates a board of overseers, to consist of twenty-five persons, of whom twenty-one are also appointed by the executive of New Hampshire, who have power to inspect and control the most important acts of the trustees.

. . . The founders of the college contracted, not merely for the perpetual application of the funds which they gave, to the objects for which those funds were given; they contracted, also, to secure that application by the Constitution of the corporation. They contracted for a system which should, as far as human foresight can provide, retain forever the government of the literary institution they had formed, in the hands of persons approved by themselves. This system is totally changed. The charter of 1769 exists no longer. It is reorganized; and reorganized in such a manner as to convert a literary institution, molded according to the will of its founders, and placed under the control of private literary men, into a machine entirely subservient to the will of government. This may be for the advantage of literature in general; but it is not according to the will of the donors, and is subversive of that contract on the faith of which their property was given. . . .

It results from this opinion, that the acts of the legislature of New Hampshire, which are stated in the special verdict found in this cause, are repugnant to the Constitution of the United States; and that the judgment on this special verdict ought to have been for the plaintiffs. The judgment of the State Court must therefore be reversed. . . .

Offer and Acceptance

In contract law one who makes an **offer** (**offeror**) must manifest an intention to become legally bound, while the one to whom the offer is made (**offeree**) must accept the offer on the terms proposed. Those terms must be definite and properly communicated to the offeree.

Not every proposal constitutes a legal offer to enter into a contract. For example, an offer made in jest, such as "I'll give you a million dollars for that beer," would not legally bind the offeror. Another illustration concerns advertisements. A circular arrives in the mail and advertises certain dresses for sale. A woman orders a particular dress, but it is not available. Has a contract been formed by the customer's acceptance of a legal offer? In most instances, the answer is no, because the law generally looks upon an advertisement as an invitation for someone to make an offer to purchase.[2] Certain advertisements, however, can be construed as offers. For example, Big Bargain Store places an advertisement in the newspaper stating, "The first ten people who come to our store on December 1 may purchase a particularly described pocket radio for $12." This would probably be construed as an offer rather than merely an invitation to make an offer. Why? Because it is definite as to time, place, and description of the goods, thus indicating an intention to be bound.

An offer must be accepted by the means specified in the offer, but if no means are specified then the offer may be accepted in a reasonable manner consistent with the circumstances and customs. An offer should state a time for acceptance, but in practice this frequently is not the case. If no time is stated, the offer is open for a reasonable period of time. When a court must determine what constitutes a "reasonable time," it considers the many circumstances surrounding the offer. If the offer is made during a conversation, then the law may determine that acceptance must be made by the end of the conversation. Customs play a part in a court's determination of the time of acceptance, but unless the offer specifies it is open for a set period of time an offer may be revoked prior to acceptance. If the offeree accepts it subject to conditions, the law views such a conditional acceptance as a counteroffer and in most cases is deemed a rejection.[3] But an acceptance that requests some addition to the terms of the offer does not invalidate the acceptance as long as the acceptance is not made conditional on the request.[4]

Consideration

Historically in England, the Church held that a person who took a false oath committed a serious sin. On this basis the English common law developed "oath taking" as a basis to determine if the parties to an agreement were sufficiently serious for the court to find that a contract existed. Later the common-law courts developed the concept of a seal being placed on a document as indicating a party intended to be bound. During the sixteenth and seventeenth centuries, the common-law courts decided that, in order to have an objective basis to determine whether parties to an agreement intended to be bound by their offer and acceptance, a consideration should be an essential element of a contract. The requirement was unique to the common law and was imposed to enable judges to objectively determine the parties' intent to be bound by an agreement. Consideration came to consist of some benefit to a **promisor** or some determent to a **promisee**. In this form the doctrine of consideration in the law of contracts was accepted in America as part of the common law.

By requiring consideration the law seeks to prevent attempts to enforce gratuitous premises. The most basic consideration is money; for example, a student orders a cup of coffee and pays 50 cents for it. The concept of consideration, however, goes beyond paying money for goods or services.

In addressing the requirement for consideration the *Restatement of Contracts,* second edition, § 75 states:

(1) Consideration for a promise is
  (a) an act other than a promise, or
  (b) a forbearance, or
  (c) the creation, modification or destruction of a legal relation, or
  (d) a return promise, bargained for and given in exchange for the promise.
(2) Consideration may be given to the promisor or to some other person. It may be given by the promisee or by some other person.

The following examples illustrate some forms that consideration may take:

- *An act other than a promise.* George shovels all the snow from in front of Howard's home in return for Howard's promise to pay George $50.
- *A forbearance from doing an act.* Edgar, who has the legal right to build an addition to the family home, agrees to refrain from doing so in exchange for his neighbor Frank granting Edgar the right to pipe water from Frank's well to irrigate Edgar's lawn.
- *Creation or destruction of a legal relation.* Agnes agrees to withdraw from a partnership in consideration of Cynthia becoming a partner in her place.
- *A promise for a promise.* Susan promises to pay Donald $20,000 for Blackacre and Donald promises to convey (deed) Blackacre to Cynthia for that sum. But note that a promise cannot be **illusory**—that is, it must commit the promisor to do something. For example, a promise that "I will agree to pay you sometime when I have money" is illusory for it does not really commit the promisor to anything definite.

Adequacy of Consideration

Courts do not generally look to the **adequacy of consideration**. In the United States, parties have the freedom to contract and strike the bargains they desire. Therefore, if no fraud exists, then a court will not generally set aside a contract on the ground that the consideration is inadequate. So if Alex agrees to buy a certain car from Acme Motors for $30,000, makes a deposit, and signs the agreement, but it later turns out that Alex could have bought the same car for $2,000 less from Big Town Motors, the contract would not be subject to cancellation on the grounds of inadequate consideration. Certain exceptions do apply. For example, Dana owes Baldwin $1,000 and there is no dispute as to that amount being due. Dana sends Baldwin a check for $250 and notes on the check that it is "payment in full." The $250 would not be sufficient consideration to effect payment in full. On the other hand, if there is a genuine dispute between the parties over the amount due on the account and Dana offers and Baldwin agrees to accept a lesser amount, then Dana and Baldwin have reached what the law terms an **accord and satisfaction** and the debt is extinguished.

Past Consideration and Preexisting Duties

A **past consideration** does not fulfill the requirement of consideration for formation of a contract. Therefore, the fact that a person has previously performed an act or furnished something of value does not support a contract, as a contract must be based on a present consideration. Likewise, performance of a **preexisting duty** will not be regarded as consideration to support a contract to do some act or to refrain from doing an act. To illustrate: Suppose the owner of a store promises to pay the police to answer an emergency call in the event the owner's store is burglarized. Because the police are under a duty to respond to criminal acts, the promise is not supported by a consideration.

Promissory Estoppel

In certain situations courts determine that it is unfair not to enforce an agreement not supported by consideration. Under a doctrine known as **promissory estoppel,** a court may enforce an agreement where it was foreseeable that one party in reliance on another's promise has incurred expenses. For example, Joe relied on Kenneth's promise to buy Joe's boat if he placed it in first-class condition. With Kenneth's knowledge, Joe expended a large sum of money to meet that condition. Kenneth decides not to buy the boat and Joe brings suit. A court might determine that under the doctrine of promissory estoppel Kenneth should not be permitted to deny that a contract existed on the basis that there was no consideration for the promise to buy the boat.

Many courts have employed the doctrine of promissory estoppel as a substitute for the element of consideration when a pledge to provide funds to a charitable organization is involved and the charity has relied upon that pledge. Some even take the position that a charitable pledge is enforceable regardless if supported by consideration, and even in absence of any reliance by the charity.[5] The *Restatement* takes the position that a promise to make a gift to a charitable organization is enforceable per se without the need to show consideration or any substitute therefore.[6]

In addition to the basic elements of offer, acceptance, and consideration, parties to a contract must have the legal capacity to contract. Moreover, the contract must be for a purpose that is neither illegal nor contrary to public policy.

Capacity to Contract

A minor (usually defined as a person under age 18) does not have the legal capacity to enter into contracts and thus may disaffirm a contract. In practice, we know that minors enter into contracts to purchase food, clothing, other necessary items and some things that may not be regarded as necessary. Buying lunch may be necessary, but clearly buying a new sports car is not. A minor who enters a contract for necessaries may be required to pay if those responsible for his custody do not; but a minor who enters a contract to buy a car may **disaffirm** that contract upon attaining majority. Alternatively, if not disaffirmed, the minor may ratify the contract upon attaining legal majority. Marriage removes a minor's lack of capacity to contract.

Persons under **legal guardianship,** whether as minors or for physical or mental infirmities, are legally incapable of contracting. Nevertheless, an adult placed under guardianship cannot generally avoid a contract made prior to the guardianship.

A contract made by a person who is intoxicated to the extent of impairment of normal faculties is voidable. Upon becoming sober the formerly intoxicated individual is permitted to affirm or disaffirm the contract made while in an intoxicated state. Courts generally require that action to disaffirm must be taken promptly.

Legality of Purpose

Obviously the law will not enforce a contract to do an **illegal act.** For example, a contract to injure or damage someone's person or property in exchange for a payment or an agreement to pay a bribe to a witness or public official is void. Likewise, a contract that has as its purpose to inflict fraud on a third party would be void. When a lender agrees to charge a **usurious rate of interest,** the contract may not be enforceable; however, in some instances the court will enforce the contract to the extent of the principal loaned but not the interest.

Mutual Mistake and Misrepresentations

Although not void, certain other contracts are voidable. A **mutual mistake** occurs when a contract achieves what neither party intended, and either party can avoid the contract.[7] For example, suppose a pet shop agrees to sell and a woman agrees to buy a pedigreed cat for $300. The buyer selects a Persian cat named Chelsea, but the seller thought the buyer had selected a different cat named Whitey. It turns out both parties were mistaken, so either party can usually avoid the contract on the basis of mutual mistake. On the other hand, when one party is mistaken (the law terms this a **unilateral mistake**), the law concerning mistake does not provide ground to avoid the contract. If the buyer agreed to buy a cat believing it was worth $500, but it turns out to be an ordinary cat with a minimal market value, this would be a unilateral mistake and no ground to avoid the contract.

A contract entered into based on fraud or a material misrepresentation of fact may be avoided. To illustrate: A seller of a preowned automobile represents to the prospective buyer that the car has been owned by one previous owner and has been driven only 15,000 miles, a fact disclosed by the car's odometer. It turns out that the car has had three previous owners and had been driven over 55,000 miles but the seller tampered with the odometer to cause it to be turned back to 15,000. This is the type of misrepresentation on which a plaintiff may sue to avoid a contract.

Likewise a contract is subject to being avoided on the ground of **unconscionability.** In 1977, the New York Court of Appeals defined an unconscionable bargain as one "such as no person in his or her senses and not under delusion would make on the one hand, and as one no honest and fair person would accept on the other, the inequality being so strong and manifest as to shock the conscience and confound the judgment of any person of common sense."[8] Courts have refused to enforce agreements between a debtor and creditor when the terms of the contract are oppressive or when a home improvement contract exacted a sum of money from a householder greatly disproportionate to the work performed. The **Uniform Commercial Code (UCC),** discussed later in this chapter, authorizes a court to refuse enforcement of a contract on a finding that the contract or any clause thereof was unconscionable at the time it was made.[9]

Contracts Contrary to Public Policy

The meaning of **public policy** is somewhat vague. In 1897, the U.S. Supreme Court said that in absence of constitutional or statutory provisions the courts may determine public policy which it finds in the decisions of courts and the practice of government officials.[10]

Frequently, a person who accepts employment agrees that upon termination the employee will not compete against the employer's business. Such contracts frequently involve employees who have been entrusted with trade secrets and customer lists. The law generally enforces such agreements if they are otherwise valid, if the length of the term for not competing is not too great and the geographical area in which competition is forbidden is reasonable. On the other hand, the law disfavors contracts that prevent a person from pursuing a gainful occupation and, thus, public policy plays an important role in contracts containing a **covenant not to compete.** For example, suppose a physician signs a contract with a medical group that would prohibit the physician upon leaving employment from practicing medicine in the state for 25 years. The court would undoubtedly find such a contract to be against public policy and decline to enforce it.

Courts have ruled that when a contract is made for sexual services, it will not be enforced; however, unmarried adult cohabitants are not precluded from entering into contracts regarding their earnings and property interests. This was highlighted by a famous "palimony" case decided by the California Supreme Court in 1976 (see the following case).

CASE IN POINT

CAN AN UNMARRIED COHABITANT SUE TO RECOVER DAMAGES BASED ON AN ORAL CONTRACT?

Marvin v. Marvin

California Supreme Court
557 P.2d 106 (Calif. 1976)

For seven years, plaintiff Michelle Marvin, a single woman, lived with defendant Lee Marvin, a well-known movie star. After they separated she brought suit to enforce an alleged oral agreement whereby they agreed to combine their efforts and earnings and share equally all property they accumulated. Plaintiff alleged she gave up her career as an entertainer to be the defendant's companion, housekeeper, and cook; that in return defendant agreed to provide for her for the rest of her life. The Los Angeles Superior Court granted judgment for the defendant and the plaintiff appealed.

On appeal, the California Supreme Court rejected defendant Lee Marvin's contention that enforcement of the alleged contract would be contrary to public policy because it involved an immoral relationship between the parties. The court stated, "Agreements between nonmarital partners fail only to the extent that they rest upon a consideration of meretricious sexual services. . . . The fact that a man and woman live together without marriage, and engage in a sexual relationship, does not in itself invalidate agreements between them relating to their earnings, property, or expenses." The court returned the case to the trial court with directions to determine the plaintiff's property rights.

Formal Requirements of Contracts

As discussed, a contract may be oral or written, informal or formal. But there are definite advantages that a contract, other than a simple agreement, be in writing. The English common-law judges found it perplexing to resolve disputes concerning major contracts based on conflicting and sometime fraudulent oral testimony of witnesses. This led the English Parliament in 1667 to enact a law for "the prevention of frauds and perjuries" called the Statute of Frauds, requiring that certain types of contracts to be in writing to be enforceable. Every state in the United States has a **statute of frauds** requiring certain contracts to be in writing generally adopted from the basic English statute. These statutes generally require the following types of contracts to be in writing:

- for transfer, sale, and purchase of real estate or interests in real estate, usually including a lease for a period of more than one year
- in consideration of marriage
- that cannot be performed within a year
- to pay a debt or obligation of another; for example, a contract of **suretyship** or an agreement by a personal representative of a decedent's estate to discharge a debt of the decedent from the personal representative's personal funds
- involving sale of personal property beyond a stipulated amount, usually $500

One can usually satisfy the requirement that a contract be in writing by producing evidence of informal written memoranda that sufficiently describe the parties, subject matter, and essential terms of a contract. Where real property is involved, courts often insist on a legal description of the property sufficient for a surveyor to locate the property. There is considerable litigation involving questions that arise as to whether such memoranda are sufficient. Moreover, courts often require a party who has received benefits under a contract to perform under the contract irrespective of whether the contract is evidenced by writing. A classic example is when Joe Smith, a homeowner, watches workers put in a new driveway at his home. Smith neither ordered the work done nor paid any money to the party performing the work. He has no intention of paying for the new driveway, but he fails to inform the workers that they are at the wrong address. A court would likely hold Smith liable, even though he had not formally entered into a contract.

Parol Evidence Rule

The **parol evidence rule** states that a party cannot introduce parol (oral) evidence to contradict the terms of a written agreement that is complete. The term *parol* has broader meaning than simply "oral." It prohibits the introduction of any evidence extrinsic to the written agreement that existed at or prior to the execution of the written contract. Although termed a *rule,* the parol evidence rule is more a principle of law than a rule of evidence.

Like many rules of law, the rule is subject to considerable interpretation by the courts. It does not prohibit a party from showing that a contract was entered into as a result of fraud, duress, or misrepresentation. Nor does it prohibit a showing that the contract was subsequently amended or modified by a new agreement. Construction contracts usually contain a clause that prohibits modification of the contract by oral agreements. Courts

---

CASE IN POINT

ARE ALLEGED ORAL REPRESENTATIONS MADE BY A SELLER ADMISSIBLE IN EVIDENCE TO MODIFY AN EXPRESS WARRANTY?

Foundation Software Laboratories, Inc. v. Digital Equipment Corporation

United States District Court for Maryland
807 F. Supp. 1195 (1992)

Foundation Software Laboratories (FSL) brought suit against Digital Equipment Corporation (DEC) after discovering that FSL's software would not run satisfactorily on the DEC computers it had purchased. The contract under which the purchase took place contained an express warranty that the hardware would be free from defects and that its operational software conformed to its published specifications. The contract disclaimed any implied warranties. FSL contended that representatives of DEC made oral representations about the performance of the hardware that extended the terms of the express warranty. The Court disagreed and granted summary judgment for the defendant, saying that "the parol evidence rule excludes evidence of oral assurances made before, or contemporaneous with, the execution of the [contract]."

---

have held such a provision does not prohibit the parties from entering subsequent contracts. This frequently occurs when the parties to a construction contract sign "change orders" to provide for additions or modifications to a building under construction. Courts sometimes admit parol (oral) evidence to resolve issues where there is an **ambiguity** in the legal writing and oral evidence is essential to ascertain the true intent of the parties to the contract.[11]

Assignments of Contracts

An **assignment** of a contract occurs when one party to a contract assigns rights under the contract to another who is not a party to the original contract. Contracts are generally assignable unless the contract or a statute provides to the contrary. Even then, courts may approve an assignment. Although rights under a contract may be assigned, a contracting party may not delegate the duties imposed on such person under the contract. Moreover, the nonassigning party retains all rights and defenses under the contract.

Although duties under a contract may not be assigned, in some instances, they may be delegated. In all instances, however, the original contracting party remains liable. In general, duties may be delegated where the **delagatee** is in a position to perform as effectively as the delegator. Some contracts envision a delegation. For example, a building contractor customarily delegates to a subcontractor certain specialized phases of construction. Of course, a delegatee is not liable to the **delegator** unless the delegatee is furnished consideration necessary for performance. Other duties that may be delegated include an obligation to pay money or deliver standard goods. On the other hand, professional services such as those provided by a physician, lawyer, or architect are examples of **nondelegable duties.**

Who Can Enforce a Contract?

Ordinarily it is the parties to a contract who have the right to enforce the terms of the contract; but most contracts can be assigned. For example, a buyer who agrees to purchase a certain automobile can generally assign that right to purchase to another party. The original purchaser is referred to as the **assignor** and the person to whom the right has been assigned is called the **assignee.**

The right to enforce a contract also extends to a party for whose benefit a contract is made. The party is called a **third-party donee beneficiary.** Perhaps the most common form of a third-party beneficiary contract is a life insurance policy. A parent contracts with a life insurance company that upon the parent's death the insurer will pay the face amount of the policy to the parent's child. The parent and the company are the parties to the contract; the child is the beneficiary. A parent who reserves the right to change the beneficiary may do so. A **third-party creditor beneficiary** is a party to whom a party to a contract owes some legal obligation. One of the classic cases every first-year law student studies is the 1859 decision by the New York Court of Appeals in *Lawrence v. Fox.*[12] In this case, Holly loaned Fox $300, stating at the time that he owed that sum to the plaintiff Lawrence. Fox promised Holly that he would pay that sum to Lawrence the next day. But when the plaintiff Lawrence brought suit, the defendant Fox contended that there was no proof that Holly was indebted to the plaintiff and that his agreement with Holly to pay the plaintiff was void for want of consideration. After a jury verdict, the court entered judgment against Fox and he appealed. The Court of Appeals ruled in favor of the plaintiff Lawrence and held that when a promise is made to one person for the benefit of another, "he for whose benefit it is made may bring an action for its breach." This principle, the court ruled, previously applied in cases involving trusts, should be applied in cases of third-party creditor beneficiaries. The overwhelming majority of American courts soon accepted that development in contract law.

Performance of Contracts

Fulfillment of the promises under a contract constitutes **performance.** Proper performance of all obligations under a contract discharges a contracting party. There are other means of discharge. A person may be excused from performing under a contract under the doctrine called **impossibility of performance.** For example, if Alan was hired to repair a beach cottage that was swept into the sea before his performance came due, Alan is excused from performance. If a law is enacted that makes it illegal to perform the obligations under a contract, the party obligated to perform is discharged. Written contracts frequently include provisions that the party required to perform will not be liable for delays due to strikes, adverse weather conditions, or **acts of God.** These clauses are sometimes referred to as *force majeur* **clauses.**

Remedies for Breach of Contract

Nonperformance of an obligation under a contract is known as **breach of contract.** Three judicial remedies may be available when a breach has occurred: a suit for damages, a suit for **specific performance,** and **rescission** of the contract.

Damages

The principal remedy the law affords for a breach of contract is a suit for **compensatory damages.** In law damages means "dollars" and to recover damages the plaintiff must prove with reasonable certainty that the damages claimed as a result of a breach of contract were **reasonably foreseeable** by the parties. In some instances a party must take steps to avoid damages to whatever extent possible. Failure of a party to mitigate damages can prevent recovery of such damages as could have been avoided by reasonable efforts.[13]

Damages in contract cases are usually assessed by a jury. Damages are designed to reimburse a person who has suffered losses because a contract has been breached. Damages for breach of contract follow certain general rules. Two illustrations are as follows:

- If a seller breaches a contract to sell goods or real estate to a buyer, the measure of damages would likely be the additional amount the buyer may have to pay to obtain similar goods or property.
- If a building contractor fails to complete the construction of a building but the contractor has substantially performed the contract, the damages would likely be the amount the owner would have to pay to another contractor to complete the job plus other expenses such as rent or interest on a construction loan that the owner may sustain.

One who suffers a breach but does not sustain actual damages may only recover **nominal damages.** A party who establishes a breach, but who is unable to prove having sustained any actual damages, may be awarded nominal damages of $1.

CASE IN POINT

WHEN DOES A LIQUIDATED DAMAGE PROVISION BECOME AN UNENFORCEABLE PENALTY?

Lefemine v. Baron

Supreme Court of Florida
573 So. 2d 326 (1991)

Daniel and Catherine Lefemine contacted to purchase a residence from Judith W. Baron for $385,000. They made a good-faith deposit of $38,500. When unable to obtain financing, the Lefemines sued Baron for return of their deposit. Baron counterclaimed to retain the deposit money as liquidated damages pursuant to the contract. The default provision of the contract stipulated: "If the Buyer fails to perform the Contract . . . the deposit . . . may be retained or recovered by . . . the . . . Seller as liquidated damages, as consideration for the execution of the Contract and in full settlement of any claims; . . . or Seller at his option, may proceed at law or in equity to enforce his rights under the Contract."

The trial court ruled in favor of the seller on the counterclaim, allowing Baron to retain the deposit, and the appellate court affirmed. But on further review, the Florida Supreme Court agreed that while the forfeiture provision was not unconscionable, it must fail because "the option granted to Baron either to choose liquidated damages or to sue for actual damages indicates an intent to penalize the defaulting buyer and negates the intent to liquidate damages in the event of a breach." The court remanded the case for a trial to determine the actual damages sustained by the buyers' default.

In some contracts, the parties include a provision for **liquidated damages**, which stipulates that in the event of a breach of the contract, damages shall be deemed to be in a certain amount or shall be calculated in a certain manner. Courts enforce liquidated damage provisions as long as they bear a reasonable relationship to damages that were anticipated or that occurred. But if the liquidated damages clause exacts a penalty, courts will disregard it and require actual proof of damages. Frequently, construction contracts for commercial buildings stipulate that in the event the building contractor does not complete the building by a certain date, the contractor will pay a certain sum for each day of delay beyond the agreed upon date of completion.

A court will sometimes award **punitive damages** where the party who has breached a contract has committed a willful tort involving outrageous or malicious acts. Punitive damages are much like a fine. Whereas punitive damages are not uncommon in tort suits (see Chapter 5), they are seldom awarded in contract cases.

Specific Performance

When money damages would be inadequate to compensate an injured party, a court may award specific performance of a contract. Specific performance is an equitable remedy and one that a court dispenses on a discretionary basis and only where the terms of the contract are fair and the duties to be performed are clear.

Courts often require specific performance when a contract to sell some unique item of personal property is breached, for example, when a contract involves an antique, an heirloom, or a valuable work of art and money damages would not compensate the person who contracted to buy the antique. Courts consider each parcel of real estate unique and will entertain suits for specific performance of a contract to purchase or sell real estate. Usually a court will not order a person to render personal services in a specific performance suit, for example, requiring a singer to perform on stage, as to do so may constitute involuntary servitude. However, in such an instance the court may enjoin the singer from performing elsewhere.

Rescission

Rescission of a contract is not a common remedy, but in instances when a court determines that a party was fraudulently induced to enter a contract, it may allow that party to rescind (cancel) the contract. Courts may allow rescission of a contract and require restitution (repayment of sums advanced) when a contract is void or the contracting party is unable to perform.

THE UNIFORM COMMERCIAL CODE

The Uniform Commercial Code (UCC) is a compilation of laws governing commercial transactions drafted by the National Conference of Commissioners on Uniform State Laws and submitted to the legislatures of the states. With some modifications, the UCC has been adopted in all states except Louisiana. The Louisiana legislature has enacted commercial laws that incorporate many of the provisions of the UCC. The purpose of the UCC is to make uniform laws dealing with sales of goods, commercial dealings with banks, warehouse receipts, investment securities, and secured transactions. The UCC has been a boon to interstate commerce, particularly among merchants.

The UCC is divided into articles and numbered by section. There is some variation in the statutory numbering system in different states. The model UCC consists of the following:

Article 1   General Provisions

Article 2   Sales

Article 3   Commercial Paper

Article 4   Bank Deposits and Collections

Article 5   Letters of Credit

Article 6   Bulk Transfers

Article 7   Warehouse Receipts, Bills of Lading, and Documents of Title

Article 8   Investment Securities

Article 9   Secured Transactions

Article 10   Effective Date

Much of the UCC deals with contractual matters that are commonly experienced in everyday life. For example, Articles 2 and 3 deal with sales and **commercial paper,** Article 4 deals with bank deposits and collections, and Article 9 concerns secured transactions. Articles 5, 6, 7, and 8 serve vital commercial interests but for the most part cover more sophisticated business practices or subjects of concern primarily to bankers, security dealers, and merchants.

Sales of Goods

Article 2 of the UCC applies to contracts for sales of goods. It does not cover service contracts or contracts for the sale of real estate. Article 2-204 allows a sales contract for goods to be "made in any manner sufficient to show agreement, including conduct by both parties which recognizes the existence of such a contract." Unlike the traditional common-law rule, Article 2-207 allows an acceptance of an offer in dealings between merchants even if the acceptance proposes some changes. In addition to express warranties that may accompany the sale of goods, Article 2-314 provides that, unless excluded or modified, there is an **implied warranty of merchantability** that the goods are fit for ordinary use if the seller is a merchant with respect to goods of that kind. Article 2-315 provides for an **implied warranty of fitness of goods** for the buyer's particular purpose if the seller knows any particular purpose for which the goods are required and that the buyer is relying on the seller's skill or judgment to select or furnish suitable goods. Article 2-316 allows certain warranties to be modified or disclaimed in a conspicuous manner.

Commercial Paper

Ordinarily in a contract between two persons, the law dealing with negotiation of commercial paper does not come into play, but there developed a need to have negotiable documents

CASE IN POINT

ARE THE CONTENTS OF A BOOK SUBJECT TO AN IMPLIED WARRANTY?

Cardozo v. True

District Court of Appeal of Florida, Second District
342 So. 2d 1053 (Fla. 2d DCA 1977)

Ingrid Cardozo purchased a book entitled *Trade Winds Cookery* from a local bookstore. While following a recipe for cooking a tropical plant commonly known as "elephant ears" she ate a small slice of the plant roots and suffered intense coughing, gasping, and stomach cramps that required medical attention. She sued the bookstore contending that plant roots were poisonous and the recipes had been inadequately tested. Thus, she contended the bookstore had breached its implied warranty under the UCC that the book was reasonably fit for its intended use, and that her illness occurred because of that breach.

The trial court certified the question to the appellate court, which held that the implied warranty in respect to sale of books by a merchant is limited to a warranty of the physical properties of the books and does not extend to the material communicated. While making no ruling as to the liability of an author or publisher, the court wrote "It is unthinkable that standards imposed on the quality of goods sold by a merchant would require ... a bookseller to evaluate the thought processes of the many authors and publishers of the ... thousands of books which the merchant offers for sale." On that basis, the appellate court returned the case to the trial court for proceedings consistent with its answer to the certified question.

that could be used as substitutes for money in commercial transactions where more than two persons are involved. From a legal standpoint, the essential difference between a **nonnegotiable** and a **negotiable** legal instrument is that one who takes a negotiable instrument (1) for value, (2) in good faith, (3) without knowledge that it is overdue or has been dishonored, and (4) without knowledge that there is any defense against or claim to it by any person, becomes what the law terms a **holder in due course**. A holder in due course occupies a privileged position as a transferee and (with a few exceptions) takes the instrument free of all defenses to enforcing it. Negotiable instruments are vital to commercial transactions.

The following contrasting scenarios illustrate this essential difference between a nonnegotiable and a negotiable instrument.

1. Arthur contracts to furnish certain equipment to Bill. Bill is to pay Arthur in installments. Arthur assigns the contract to Charles. Bill is dissatisfied with Charles's performance and brings suit against Charles. Contract law concerning assignments provides that Charles, as an assignee of the contract, acquired the contract subject to any defenses that Bill has against Arthur.
2. On the other hand, had Bill given Arthur a negotiable promissory note that met the requirements of negotiability under the UCC, Arthur could have transferred that note to Charles who would be a holder in due course and could have sold or otherwise transferred the note for value to a third party. Thus, negotiable instruments become a special class of commercial paper designed to be freely transferred in commerce.

As the above illustration reveals, it is important to determine whether a particular legal document is negotiable. Article 3 of the UCC deals with commercial paper and focuses on

negotiable instruments, a technical legal term dealing with checks, drafts, certificates of deposit, and promissory notes, and the specific requirements for an instrument to be negotiable. These requirements are technical but chiefly require the legal document to be an unconditional order or promise in writing payable to the bearer or "on order" (remember your check says "Pay to the order of _____"), and payable on demand or at a fixed or determinable time.

A check is a legal instrument where a bank customer (**drawer**) orders the bank (**drawee**) to pay the **payee** of the check a certain amount. A promissory note is a legal document whereby one party (the **maker**) promises to pay another party (the payee) a sum of money either on demand or at a certain time. A **draft** is a written order drawn on one party by another requesting the payment of a certain sum to a third person. Checks and drafts involve three parties whereas certificates of deposit and promissory notes usually involve only two. Historically such matters were governed by principles of law called the law merchant, which later became a part of the common law. Prior to the UCC, the Uniform Negotiable Instruments Law governed these instruments in most states. The UCC reflects much of the context of that law.

Security Agreements

Article 9 of the UCC deals with **security agreements.** A security agreement is a contract that grants a creditor a security interest in **collateral (security)** pledged by a debtor or borrower. If the debtor has rights in the collateral, a security interest attaches to the collateral as provided in Article 9. In some instances the holder of the security interest takes possession of

---

PROMISSORY NOTES	**SIDEBAR**

A promissory note is a legal document whereby one party promises to pay another party (the payee) a sum of money either on demand or at a time certain. Here is the typical form of a promissory note:

_____ [City], _____ [State], _____ [Month], _____ [Day], _____ [Year]

On _____, 200____, for value received, (I)(We) promise to pay to the order of

_____ at _____

(name of place of payment; usually a bank) the sum of _____ dollars

($_____) with interest thereon from date at the rate of _____ percent (_____%) per annum. If this note

is not paid promptly at maturity, the maker and endorsers agree to pay all costs of collection, including a reasonable attorney's fee.

_____

Signature of maker of note

the collateral. In many instances, the debtor is allowed to retain the collateral (e.g., a car), and the security interest is perfected by filing a **financing statement** with the appropriate government office. The financing statement gives public notice of the security holder's interest. If the debtor defaults, the security holder can convert the collateral into cash by conducting a sale in accordance with the provisions of Article 9.

Business Associations

The common forms of business associations in the United States are the **sole proprietorship, partnership,** and **corporation.** The selection of the form of organization is based on the size of the business undertaking, the number of investors required to capitalize the business, the need for professional management, whether the business activities will involve a risk of personal liability to the owners, tax advantages, expenses of administration, and other factors. Throughout history individuals have operated as sole proprietorships. Historians trace the development of partnerships and corporations to the Roman law, but in the United States the legal principles governing these organizations are basically derived from the English common law. Modern business law has developed from early precedents, particularly in the field of contract law, but federal and state statutes have played a key role in the last two centuries.

Sole Proprietorships

The most common form of a business organization is the sole proprietorship, a solely owned form of enterprise in which the owner has the responsibility and control, enjoys the profits, and suffers any losses. Many professionals and retail stores and services operate as sole proprietorships. Because, unlike a corporation, a sole proprietorship has no legal identity apart from the owner, it is not taxed separately for federal income taxes. A sole proprietor is personally liable for performance of contracts and for any torts resulting from the operation of the business. Often state laws or local ordinances require that sole proprietorships that operate under a name different from the owner register under **fictitious name laws.** For example, if Lilly Jones owns a women's clothing store under the name Lilly's Casuals, she may have to register the fact that she is the owner of that business. This alerts everyone to the true ownership of a business should any legal process be necessary.

Partnerships

A partnership is an association of two or more persons who combine their money, property, and skill to carry on a lawful business. A partnership can be created orally although it is preferable to have a written agreement that describes its purpose and the term for which it is to exist, stipulates the contributions and duties of the partners and how the profits and losses shall be shared or borne, and provides for dissolution and winding up the affairs of the partnership.

The advantage of a partnership is that it allows co-owners to pool their talents and capital. The major disadvantages are that each partner is liable for the debts of the partnership, and the withdrawal or death of a partner causes a termination of the partnership. Each partner is an agent for the other partners and each is individually and jointly liable for contract and tort liabilities in the scope of partnership business. Consequently, if one partner is insolvent and another partner wealthy, a creditor who obtains a judgment against the partnership may enforce the judgment against the solvent partner. Partnerships file informational federal tax returns, but, the partners report their income or losses on their personal tax returns.

The foregoing describes a general partnership, yet there is another form of partnership authorized by law in states that have enacted the Uniform Limited Partnership Act. This act authorizes formation of a **limited partnership** whereby one or more limited partners can limit their liability for the firm's debts to the amount of their investment. Organization must be accomplished as provided by the governing statute, which will include a requirement of obtaining a state certificate of partnership that usually includes the partners' written partnership agreement. A **limited partner** who actively participates in operation of a partnership business becomes liable on the same basis as a **general partner.**

In certain instances persons who are not partners cause third parties to rely in good faith on representations that they are partners in a business. The usual scenario involves apparent partners misleading a creditor who extends credit on the assumption of dealing with partners. In these instances courts may hold the apparent partners are estopped from denying that a partnership relation exists.

Corporations

Chief Justice John Marshall, in 1819, described a corporation as "an artificial being, invisible, intangible, and existing only in contemplation of the law."[14] In 1868, the Court held that a corporation is a "person" within contemplation of the Fourteenth Amendment, thereby giving a corporation a standing to sue in matters concerning due process of law.[15] Thus, as an artificial legal entity, a corporation has a legal existence independent from its stockholders who own shares of stock issued by the corporation. Corporations are chartered principally under state law. Delaware is the leading state for chartering corporations, due in part to the fact that Delaware courts have developed a large body of law concerning corporations which makes for more predictability. The **corporate charter** grants a corporation certain powers, provides for the shares of stock to be issued, and provides for the selection and duties of the officers and directors who are to govern the corporation. The shares of stock issued by a corporation represent the interests of its investors. The **common stock** carries with it the right to vote for directors and receive the net assets upon dissolution of the corporation. Holders of **preferred stock** are usually given priority to receive dividends and to receive assets upon dissolution.

Corporations may be publicly held as most large corporations are, with stockholders numbering in the thousands or millions. But corporations may be quite small where the stock is closely held, as is the case in most small-business corporations. These latter corporations are frequently referred to as closed or **closely held corporations.**

Why a Corporation?

There are several advantages to a business operating as a corporation. They may be summarized as follows:

- **Limited liability.** Unlike one who invests in establishing a sole proprietorship or partnership, those who acquire shares of stock in a corporation are not liable for its debts and are not called upon to respond to legal actions involving the corporation. A variation of the business corporation is known as a professional association (PA) in which doctors, lawyers, and other professionals may incorporate. Rules for limiting the liability of such professionals, especially in the area of professional malpractice, differ from the limited liability afforded stockholders in regular business corporations.
- **Aggregation of capital.** By selling shares of stock a corporation can aggregate the capital it requires to carry on and expand its business.
- **Perpetual existence.** Because a corporation is itself a "being" it has perpetual life or at least until dissolved according to law. Thus an incorporated business does not have to cease operations when a shareholder or director dies or becomes incompetent.
- **Transferability of ownership.** Because ownership of the corporation is represented by shares of stock, it is easy to transfer ownership. Changes in stock ownership, in general, will not affect the corporation's business.
- **Continuity of management.** A corporation's officers and board of directors can retain management to operate the business on a continuing basis.

Apart from the advantages, corporations (even closely held corporations) are burdened with considerably more administrative matters than a sole proprietorship or a partnership. Because a corporation is a separate entity it must file federal and state income tax returns. Its earnings are subject to taxes, and those earnings that are distributed to its shareholders are again subject to tax. In many cases small corporations qualify for special treatment as "S corporations" under the Internal Revenue Code. Perhaps it is not a major problem for the large corporation, but a small business operating as a corporation often finds it a financial burden to employ accountants and lawyers to comply with laws and regulations.

The Corporate Structure

Both the federal and state governments have the power to charter corporations. The federal power is exercised mainly in connection with corporations that serve some national purpose. The Tennessee Valley Authority (TVA) is an example. It was established by Congress during the Great Depression to provide electrical power to an economically deprived region that was not being served by private utilities.

In most instances a corporation for profit is chartered by an executive department of a state acting under legislative authority. Usually a group of incorporators submit their **articles of incorporation** and if the articles meet the statutory requirements, they become the **certificate of incorporation** of the new corporation. The certificate of incorporation lists the names and addresses of the incorporators and original directors and outlines the powers of the corporation, its place of business, its capital structure, rights of stockholders, and how directors and officers are to be selected. Upon organization, the corporation adopts bylaws for internal control of its operations. Corporations formed to operate banks, utilities, and insurance companies often require additional approval from other regulatory agencies.

A corporation that fully complies with the requirements of the law is known as a *de jure* **corporation.** A corporation is a **domestic corporation** in the state where incorporated. In other states it is classed as a **foreign corporation** and may have to comply with certain legal requirements to do business in a particular state.

As previously pointed out, a corporation is a separate entity apart from its stockholders. One compelling reason for organizing a corporation is that the investors' liability is generally limited to their investment. If a corporate organization is not properly completed, or the investors are using it in some fraudulent manner, courts sometimes disregard the corporate entity. Courts may find stockholders personally liable when they create a "shell corporation" without assets or employees. Lawyers who represent parties attempting to hold controlling stockholders liable may face a formidable challenge when seeking to "**pierce the corporate veil.**"

Corporate Powers

A corporation's powers are derived from its certificate of incorporation subject to the constitution and statutes of the state of incorporation. Stockholders may agree to amend the articles. The powers listed in its articles of incorporation are its **express powers.** A corporation has **implied powers** to do those things reasonably necessary to carry out its express powers.

CASE IN POINT

WAS THE OWNER OF MULTIPLE CORPORATIONS PERSONALLY LIABLE?

John Walkovsky v. William Carlton

New York Court of Appeals
223 N.E.2d 6 (N.Y. 1966)

The plaintiff was injured when struck by a taxicab owned by Seon Cab Corporation. Plaintiff alleged that Carlton is a stockholder in Seon and nine other corporations, each of which owns but two cabs. He claims these corporations are operated as a single enterprise with regard to financing, supplies, repairs, employees, and garaging. Plaintiff asserts each stockholder is personally liable for the damages caused to the plaintiff because Carlton has used the multiple corporate structures to defraud those who might be injured by the cabs. A lower appellate court ruled the grounds asserted were sufficient to allow the plaintiff to proceed against Carlton.

In reversing the lower appellate court's ruling, the Court of Appeals said: "[Carlton] is charged with having organized, managed, dominated and controlled a fragmented corporate entity but there are no allegations that he was conducting business in his individual capacity. . . . The corporate form may not be disregarded merely because the assets of the corporation, together with the mandatory insurance coverage of the vehicle which struck the plaintiff, are insufficient to assure him the recovery sought. If Carlton were to be held individually liable on those facts alone, the decision would apply equally to the thousands of cabs, which are owned by their individual drivers who conduct their businesses through corporations."

State legislatures have adopted special provisions limiting the powers of particular corporations such as banks, utilities, and insurance companies. A corporation that acts beyond its powers is said to have committed *ultra vires* **acts.** The state attorney general can bring a court action to enjoin such *ultra vires* acts and, if necessary, to dissolve the corporation. Stockholders also have a standing to challenge *ultra vires* acts in court actions.

Stockholders' Rights

The management of a corporation is vested in its directors and officers. They have a duty to the stockholders to act honestly and in good faith and to avoid conflicts of interest. Stockholders do not participate in the corporate management but they do have the right to inspect the corporation's books and records when they do so in good faith and for proper purposes. Most states require annual meetings of stockholders; however, this is usually required by the corporate bylaws. Stockholders receive notice of these annual meetings and holders of the common stock are entitled to vote for directors and for such major actions as mergers and consolidations with other corporations. Those who own corporate stock will be familiar with these annual notices that usually include a proxy form with recommendations from the corporation's board of directors. Not infrequently today, groups of stockholders make some proposal for the corporation to take some particular action, for example, to report on employment of minorities. Most of these proposals fail because stockholders making them usually own a very small percentage of stock.

Publicly Traded Corporations

Corporations whose shares are widely held by the general public are known as **publicly traded corporations.** Federal laws relate to issuance and trading in securities of such corporations. In addition, each state has its own securities laws, sometimes called **blue sky laws,** that require issuers of securities to make certain disclosures. The objective of these laws is to protect investors who purchase stock by requiring corporations to ensure that stockholders have access to relevant financial information concerning the corporation. These laws also penalize officers, directors, employees, and even controlling stockholders who have access to information that is not available to other stockholders and use such **insider information** to profit from stock transactions.

The federal government and state governments have enacted laws that impose duties on corporations to protect the public. The most prominent of these is the Securities and Exchange Act of 1934, which provides for civil and criminal penalties for conduct involving misrepresentations, omissions, insider trading, and other aspects of fraud in securities dealing.[16] The Securities and Exchange Commission (SEC) administers the act and the Commission's Rule 10(b) prohibits any person from using fraud or deception in the sale of securities.

Legal Regulation of Business

The American system of free enterprise underwent a tremendous growth in the nineteenth century. The nation's economic power became concentrated in the hands of a relatively small group of corporations. Many viewed this as injurious to the public because competition, the cornerstone of the free enterprise system, was becoming restricted and monopolies flourished. Reliance on the common law and state antitrust laws proved inadequate to control the national industrial complex. In the late nineteenth century, Congress responded to these monopolistic practices and agreements in restraint of trade that threatened the cherished American concepts of free enterprise.

With the growth of giant corporations in control of the nation's basic industrial complex, tension arose between management and labor. Again, the common law proved unworkable because it regarded attempts by employees to band together in nonviolent activities to improve working conditions and pay as criminal conspiracies. Early in the twentieth century, Congress responded by enacting legislation and by the mid-1930s the federal government had placed its stamp of approval on trade unions and their right to collectively bargain and to strike.

The population became more diverse and more women entered the workforce during and after World War II. During this time the federal government took on a more active role in the nation's economy. In enacting the Civil Rights Act of 1964, Congress prohibited discrimination in employment on account of race, color, sex, national origin, or religion. Congress followed this by passing legislation to provide for equal pay for women and prohibiting discrimination on basis of age in most occupations, providing requirements for safe workplaces, and accommodations for those who suffer from disabilities. We discuss these legislative enactments in Chapter 11.

CONSUMER PROTECTION

Historically, the English common law relegated a consumer seeking relief from unfair business transactions to a law action for fraud and deceit. The common law proscribed only fraudulent statements of fact, not opinion, and allowed a merchant the privilege of **puffing**, that is, using exaggerated sales talk. Soon the doctrine of caveat emptor (let the buyer beware) occupied a prominent place in the common law. American courts accepted the doctrine, but since the early twentieth century the legislative and judicial trend of the law has been toward rejection of caveat emptor and toward protection of the consumer. Congress and state legislatures have adopted numerous laws to protect consumers. We discuss some of the principal federal laws in the next section.

Federal Pure Food, Cosmetic and Drug Law

One of the oldest consumer protection laws is the Federal Pure Food, Drug, and Cosmetic Act. Originally enacted in 1906, the act was comprehensively amended in 1938 and has since been amended several times.[17] The act makes it unlawful to prepare or handle food, drugs, and cosmetics under unsanitary circumstances or under conditions that render them injurious to health. Included in its broad sweep are prohibitions against misbranding and adulteration of food, drugs, and cosmetics as well as requirements for truthful labeling. In 1992, Congress amended a companion statute to strengthen laws regulating poultry inspection, adding criteria concerning pesticides and food additives in respect to poultry.[18]

The Federal Trade Commission

In 1914, Congress passed the Federal Trade Commission Act, which created the Federal Trade Commission (FTC) and declared unlawful "unfair methods of competition in or affecting commerce."[19] The objective of the law was to restrain trade practices that tend toward monopoly or restraint of trade.[20]

Today many states have "Little FTC Acts" that regulate sales of motor vehicles and mobile homes, home improvement contracts, and provide relief to consumers from **unconscionable consumer contracts.** In recent years some states have adopted **lemon laws.** These laws allow a buyer of a new automobile to obtain a replacement vehicle if, after repetitive trips to the auto dealer for repairs and after the manufacturer has been given an opportunity to effect necessary repairs, the vehicle is still not functional.

State and local ordinances frequently address home solicitations and allow cancellation of subscriptions or of orders for merchandise solicited by a door-to-door salesperson. Misleading advertising is another aspect often subject to state and local control. Laws often prohibit such misleading practices as **bait and switch advertising.** This is the practice of advertising an item in short supply for a low price and then attempting to sell the customer a similar but more expensive item.

The Truth in Lending Act

As the American public became more affluent many federal approaches to consumer protection began to focus on finance and credit transactions. Many of these statutes were passed during the 1970s. One of the most important laws that protect consumers is the Consumer Credit Protection Act of 1968, better known as the Truth-in-Lending Act.[21] This act is designed to promote the informed use of credit and to protect the credit consumer. It requires disclosure of finance charges in certain real estate transactions based on the effective **annual percentage rate of interest (APR)** and provides for a three-day "cooling off" period when a consumer negotiates a loan on the security of a second mortgage on a residence. Certain provisions of the law allow a consumer the right to rescind (cancel) a contract under specified circumstances.

Garnishment is a process by which a creditor (**garnishor**) seeks to enforce payment of sums owed by a debtor by asserting a claim against a third party (**garnishee**) to obtain property of the debtor held by the garnishee. Common examples include a creditor seeking to garnish a debtor's checking account at the bank or to garnish an employer to obtain a worker's wages. The act limits garnishment of a worker's wages for any workweek to a sum not exceeding 25 percent of the worker's disposable wages for the week.[22]

Federal Consumer Credit Laws

During the 1970s Congress enacted a spate of laws designed to protect consumers in common everyday business transactions. Following are among the more important statutory enactments.

- *The 1970 Amendment to the Truth-in-Lending Act*[23] furnishes important protection for **credit cardholders.** First, a credit card may only be issued in response to an application. This does not apply to a renewal.[24] Second, it limits the cardholder's liability for loss, theft, and unauthorized use of a credit card to $50 per card.[25] The statute only limits the cardholder's liability for "unauthorized use." Therefore, a cardholder is liable for purchases by a person to whom the cardholder gave the card or otherwise authorized to use the card.

- *The Fair Credit Reporting Act of 1970*[26] gives a consumer the right to verify the accuracy of credit information on file with credit reporting agencies.
- *The Fair Credit Billing Act of 1974*[27] provides protection to consumers who challenge irregularities in accounting, goods or services that have not been delivered or accepted, and incorrect application of payments. Creditors are required to investigate claims of errors and pending investigation they are not allowed to press for payment. A debtor must pay any sums not in dispute. Subject to certain limitations, a credit cardholder may assert claims and defenses arising out of any transaction in which the credit card is used if the cardholder has first made a good-faith attempt to satisfactorily resolve any disagreement or problem.[28]
- *The Fair Debt Collection Practices Act of 1977*[29] was enacted to eliminate **abusive debt collection practices.** The act makes it illegal for debt collectors to use such tactics as falsely representing themselves as having some official status, making harassing phone calls, and making threats to notify a debtor's employer.

The Magnuson-Moss Warranty Act of 1975

The Magnuson-Moss Warranty Act was enacted in 1975 to make certain that consumers receive adequate information concerning consumer products and to encourage manufacturers to establish procedures for informal settlement of disputes.[30] The Federal Trade Commission administers the act and some of the act's provisions supersede those in Article 2 of the Uniform Commercial Code previously discussed. The act requires a written warranty to be clearly and conspicuously designated as either a **full warranty** or a **limited warranty** and to disclose in simple language the terms and conditions of the warranty and the time period for enforcing the warranty. A full warranty must meet rather strict standards and must extend to any person who purchases the product or to any person to whom the product is transferred during the warranty period. Any warranty not meeting these standards is a limited warranty. A limited warranty may not disclaim an **implied warranty.** Recall the last time you bought a hair dryer or some similar item. It probably came with a printed limited warranty that read along these lines:

> This warranty . . . excludes claims for indirect, incidental, or consequential damages. Some states do not allow the exclusion of incidental or consequential damages, so the above exclusion may not apply to you. This warranty, however, gives you specific legal rights and you may have other rights, which may vary from state to state.

The act creates a right of action for a consumer who sustains damages from breach of a written, statutory, or implied warranty, but first a consumer must resort to an informal settlement procedure. A consumer who prevails in an action is entitled to an award of a reasonable attorney's fee. Although silent on the issue of damages, it appears that state law governs as to the measure of damages that may be awarded in actions brought under the act.[31]

BANKRUPTCY

The U.S. Constitution (Art. 1, § 8) grants Congress the power to establish uniform **bankruptcy** laws. The Bankruptcy Act (Title 11 U.S.C.A.) governs bankruptcy proceedings, which take place in federal bankruptcy courts before judges appointed by the U.S. Courts of Appeals. Bankruptcy laws are designed (1) to afford debtors whose assets exceed their liabilities an opportunity to make a fresh start; and (2) to provide a fair method of distributing the bankrupt debtor's assets among creditors.

Bankruptcy proceedings are usually identified under the chapter of the bankruptcy act in which they take place. In regular bankruptcy, called a Chapter 7 proceeding, the individual or corporate debtor files a petition itemizing all debts; however, certain businesses, for example, banks and insurance companies, have to proceed under other federal laws. The filing of the petition stays civil court actions against the debtor and the debtor's property. Under some circumstances creditors can file an involuntary petition against the debtor to secure an adjudication of whether a person is bankrupt.

Creditors select a trustee who marshals the debtor's property, liquidates it, pays the expenses of the proceedings, and distributes the property among the creditors according to priorities set by law. An individual debtor has certain exemptions under state law; for example, in certain states a debtor's residence, life insurance, and personal property up to a certain value may be exempt. Alternatively under certain state laws a debtor may choose to take advantage of similar federal exemptions. An honest debtor can secure a **discharge from debts** through operation of the bankruptcy law; however, certain debts, for example, alimony and child support, are not subject to discharge.

Other forms of bankruptcy are available under federal law. Under a Chapter 11 proceeding, often used by businesses, a reorganization plan is formulated under which the debtor pays a certain portion of debts while continuing in business. A Chapter 12 proceeding allows a debtor-farmer to continue farming, and a Chapter 13 proceeding allows continuation of a business under plans formulated to pay off debts over a stated period of time while the debtor remains free from harassment of creditors.

CONCLUSION

Formation of contracts is a daily occurrence. From a nod to the street vendor to purchase a hot dog to execution of a complex hundred-page document, contracts are the lifeblood of the American economy. Like personal liberties, contracts have constitutional protection from impairment by government. Further, because contracts create a binding legal relationship enforceable in a court of law, the need for enforcement is infrequent.

The law of contracts is part of our heritage of the English common law. It has been refined by judicial decisions, mostly from state courts. Understandably, the legal precedents diverged, and as they did, businesspersons, lawyers, legislators, and legal scholars crafted a restatement of contract principles, while states adopted uniform laws to provide clarity, stability, and uniformity in business transactions. Thus, the *Restatement of Contracts* and the

Uniform Commercial Code became the outstanding accomplishments in contract law in the twentieth century.

Basic principles of contract law pervade such specialized areas as commercial paper, sales, and security transactions. And even where principles of real property law are controlling, elements of contract law are frequently present. These principles are also woven into the structure and business relationships of sole proprietorships, partnerships, and that unique business entity, the corporation.

The close relationship that existed between the producer and consumer in earlier centuries has largely given way to a less personal relationship as the nation has progressed from an economy based largely on agriculture and small businesses to today's vast financial, industrial, and information economy. With this transition the need developed for governmental regulation to assist consumers in the handling of their everyday business affairs. This role is being fulfilled by federal and state legislation and regulation. Undoubtedly as globalizations of economies continue, there will be a need for international economic regulations.

SUMMARY OF KEY CONCEPTS

In this chapter we have endeavored to impress the student with the importance of the right to enter into contracts and the constitutional proscription against laws impairing contractual obligations. The American economy and social structure is based, to a considerable degree, on private property as we discussed in the preceding chapter and the right to contract discussed in this chapter.

Contracts have their own legal nomenclature, which makes it important to understand how they are classified, and the required elements of a contract. The student should grasp the meaning of *offer and acceptance, consideration, capacity to contract,* and *legality of purpose.* It is also necessary to understand the difference between a void and avoidable contract, how the statute of frauds requires certain contracts to be in writing, and how the parol evidence rule protects the sanctity of contracts by preventing oral modification of written agreements that are unambiguous.

As we have explained, many types of contracts can be assigned but the assignor remains responsible for performance. The most common legal remedy for breach of a contract is a suit for damages; however, in some instances a contract may be rescinded. In certain contracts, for example, a contract for sale and purchase of real estate, the uniqueness of the subject of the contract may cause a court to order a party to specifically perform an obligation that has been undertaken.

The importance of commercial transactions in the American economy made it necessary for standard laws and procedures to regulate sales, commercial paper (checks, drafts, notes), secured transactions, and warranties so that commerce can flow freely. The Uniform Commercial Code (UCC), adopted in substance throughout the United States, has largely achieved that goal. It is important for the student to understand the distinction between nonnegotiable and negotiable commercial paper and the requirements that must be present for a legal instrument to be negotiable.

Business is transacted largely through structured organizations. The simplest is the sole proprietorship. Somewhat more complex are the partnership and the limited partnership. But vastly important today is the corporation that affords many advantages in management, perpetual existence, ease of transferability of ownership, and affords investors the limited liability that attracts widespread ownership in the large publicly owned business in the United States.

Finally, in this chapter we have outlined some of the most significant laws that protect consumers and have provided a brief overview of how federal bankruptcy laws operate.

QUESTIONS FOR THOUGHT AND DISCUSSION

1. What are the essential elements of a contract?
2. In a casual conversation at a party Curtis offers to sell Donald his motorcycle for $600. Donald does not accept the offer; however, the following day he calls Curtis and says "Get that motorcycle ready to go, I accept your offer." Is there a contract?
3. Alice owes Catherine $25. Catherine promises Alice that if Alice will pay her the $25 she owes plus an additional $5 that she, Catherine, will give her a certain book. Alice pays Catherine $30. Is there a consideration that will support a contract?
4. What is the purpose of a statute of frauds and to what contracts does it apply?
5. What specific areas of contract law are governed by the Uniform Commercial Code?
6. Discuss the advantages that consumers have gained from the spate of federal consumer acts passed during the 1970s.
7. If you were a state legislator assigned to a committee on consumer rights, what specific proposals would you offer?
8. What are the chief differences between a negotiable and a nonnegotiable instrument?
9. What is the extent of a credit cardholder's liability when the cardholder loses the credit card?
10. What basic rights does a stockholder possess and how are they exercised?

KEY TERMS

express contract

implied contract

bilateral contract

unilateral contract

executory contract

executed contract

voidable contract

void contract

formal contracts

informal contracts

negotiable instrument

check

promissory note

mutual assent

capacity to contract

consideration

offer

offeror

offeree

promisor

promisee

illusory

adequacy of consideration

accord and satisfaction

past consideration

preexisting duty

promissory estoppel

disaffirm

legal guardianship

illegal act

usurious rate of interest

mutual mistake

unilateral mistake

unconscionability

Uniform Commercial Code (UCC)

public policy

covenant not to compete

statute of frauds

suretyship

parol evidence rule

ambiguity

assignment

delagatee

delagator

nondelegable duties

assignor

assignee

third-party donee beneficiary

third-party creditor beneficiary

performance

impossibility of performance

acts of God

force majeur clauses

nonperformance

breach of contract

specific performance

rescission

compensatory damages

reasonably foreseeable

nominal damages

liquidated damages

punitive damages

commercial paper

implied warranty of merchantability

implied warranty of fitness of goods

non-negotiable

negotiable

holder in due course

negotiable instruments

drawer

drawee

payee

maker

draft

security agreements

collateral

security

financing statement

sole proprietorship

partnership

corporation

fictitious name laws

limited partnership

limited partner

general partner

corporate charter

common stock

preferred stock

closely held corporations

limited liability

aggregation of capital

perpetual existence

transferability of ownership

continuity of management

articles of incorporation

certificate of incorporation

de jure corporation

domestic corporation

foreign corporation

"pierce the corporate veil"

express powers

implied powers

ultra vires acts

publicly traded corporations

blue sky laws

insider information

puffing

unconscionable consumer contracts

lemon laws

bait and switch advertising

annual percentage rate of interest (APR)

garnishment

garnishor

garnishee

credit cardholders

abusive debt collection practices

full warranty

limited warranty

implied warranty

bankruptcy

discharge from debts

ENDNOTES

[1] *Dartmouth College v. Woodward,* 17 U.S. (4 Wheat.) 518, 4 L.Ed. 629 (1819).

[2] See, for example, *Ford Motor Co. v. Russell,* 519 N.W. 2d 460 (Minn. 1994).

[3] *Restatement of Contracts,* Second, § 39(1).

[4] *Restatement of Contracts,* Second, § 61.

[5] See, for example, *Jewish Federation of Central New Jersey v. Barondess,* 560 A.2d 1353 (1989).

[6] *Restatement of Contracts,* Second § 90(a).

[7] See *Twin Forks Ranch, Inc. v. Brooks,* 907 P.2d 1013 (N.M. App. 1995).

[8] *Christian v. Christian,* 365 N.E. 2d 849, 855 (N.Y. 1977).

[9]UCC § 2.30.

[10]*United States v. Trans-Missouri Freight Association,* 166 U.S. 290, 17 S.Ct. 540, 41 L.Ed. 1007 (1897).

[11]See, for example, *C&A Construction Co. v. Benning Construction Co.,* 509 S.W. 2d 302 (Ark. 1974).

[12]20 N.Y. 268 (1859).

[13]See *Apex Mining Co. v. Chicago Copper Chemical Co.,* 340 F.2d 985 (8th Cir. 1985).

[14]*Dartmouth College v. Woodward,* 17 U.S. (4 Wheat.) 518, 636, 4 L.Ed. 629, 659 (1819).

[15]*Paul v. Virginia,* 75 U.S. (8 Wall.) 168, 19 L.Ed. 357 (1868).

[16]15 U.S.C.A. § 78(a).

[17]21 U.S.C.A. §§ 301–392.

[18]21 U.S.C.A. § 453g.

[19]15 U.S.C.A. §§ 41, 45.

[20]See *Toledo Pipe-Threading Machine Co. v. Federal Trade Comm.,* 11 F.2d 337 (6th Cir. 1926).

[21]15 U.S.C.A. §§ 1601–1667.

[22]15 U.S.C.A. §§ 1671–1677.

[23]15 U.S.C.A. § 1602 (j–o); 15 U.S.C.A. §§ 1642–1644.

[24]15 U.S.C.A. § 1642.

[25]15 U.S.C.A. § 1643a.

[26]15 U.S.C.A. §§ 1681–1681t.

[27]15 U.S.C.A. 1666 e–j.

[28]15 U.S.C.A. § 1661i.

[29]15 U.S.C.A. §§ 1692–1692o.

[30]15 U.S.C.A. § 2301 et seq.

[31]*MacKenzie v. Chrysler Corp.,* 607 F.2d 1162 (5th Cir. 1979).

FOR FURTHER READING

Calamari, John D., and Joseph M. Perillo, *The Law of Contracts* (West Group 1998).

Miller, Arthur S., *The Supreme Court and American Capitalism* (Free Press 1968).

Rohwer, Claude D., and Gordon D. Schaber, *Contracts in a Nutshell* (4th ed., West Group 1997).

Siegan, Bernard H., *Economic Liberties and the Constitution* (University of Chicago Press 1980).

Wright, Benjamin F., *The Contract Clause of the Constitution* (Harvard University Press 1938).

8

FAMILY LAW

John M. Scheb II

INTRODUCTION

Family law is an area of the law that touches everyone. It is a dynamic field that is largely governed by state statutes. Many of these statutes have been based on precedent but molded to a much different society from that which produced those precedents. Family law remains essentially within the domain of the states; however, the federal government has intervened to compel support of dependents and to assist in health care and in the economic security of families.

Probably the most outstanding characteristic of the family, and hence the hallmark of family law, is change. Law generally follows societal change, and nowhere is this better illustrated than in family law. In earlier centuries the family dictated one's education, occupation, choice of marriage partners, and social status. The role of the family has changed as an economy based on agriculture and family industry has given way to vast industrial complexes and is now being melded into a technological society. With these developments came social changes with an emphasis on privacy and gender equality in areas of life formerly controlled by the traditional family and greatly influenced by organized religion. Many argue that these changes have caused a decline in "family values" while others celebrate the new emphasis on individuality, personal growth, and "free choice." Irrespective of one's perspective, the reality is that the transition of the role of the family frequently has been reflected in divorce, sexual excesses, irresponsibility in the support of dependents, and upheavals often resulting in social disorders. Family law attempts to address these problems.

In this chapter we examine the general state of family law. The reader is cautioned that statutes usually are controlling in family law and vary from state to state. Therefore, the principles we discuss should be regarded as illustrative, rather than controlling. Moreover, the application of the law can vary considerably depending on the circumstances.

MARRIAGE

Marriage is the social institution that forms the basis of the family unit. In the western world it has both secular and religious roots. In the United States, marriage is a religious rite for many, but for all it is a civil contract formed under the laws of the state where it takes place and it is governed by law. Thus, unlike contracts discussed in the preceding chapter, marriage results in a legal *status* of the parties. The state has a definite interest in regulating the institution of marriage and prescribes certain requirements for its formation and dissolution.

Historical Background of Marriage

Under the early Roman law, a man and woman who lived together and had sexual relations were considered married. Later biblical concepts resulted in the Church regarding marriage as sacramental and indissoluble. As the English common law developed, marriage remained a matter of ecclesiastical law, which recognized informal marriages where a man and woman lived together in a committed relationship. These relationships came to be called **common-law marriages**, but they were really informal marriages, not greatly influenced by the developing common law. In the latter half of the nineteenth century, the English Parliament called for **ceremonial marriages.**

The new American colonies did not insist on ceremonial marriages, but they did recognize what came to be known as common-law marriages where a man and woman cohabited in a committed relationship. This institution served a vital function in the colonies and on the frontiers during the westward expansion of the country, as often parties were unable to reach either a civil or religious official to perform a ceremonial marriage. These nonceremonial marriages became a part of the common law in the new states and the term *common-law marriage* aptly described them. Over time, judicial decisions developed various criteria as essential to the recognition of a common-law marriage, one indispensable requisite being that the parties held themselves out to the community as being husband and wife.

Although the new states coming into the Union recognized common-law marriage as practiced in the colonies and territories, they soon began to impose statutory requirements concerning age and capacity to marry. Laws prohibited marriage between persons within certain degrees of blood relationship and required a clergy person or civil official to officiate at a marriage. Almost all states have now abolished common-law marriages; however, they recognize the validity of such a marriage that occurred before their prohibitory laws became effective. The question of the validity of these unions can arise in connection with legitimacy of children, inheritance, contract rights, government benefits, and rights of action against a person who has injured or caused the wrongful death of a spouse.

Legal Requirements to Marry

Unmarried persons age 18 or over who are mentally competent to understand the consequences of their acts are free to marry. With parental consent most states permit persons age 16 to marry. A few states allow persons as young as 14 to marry with parental consent. In Georgia, there is no state-imposed age limit if the parties have consent of their parents.[1] In many states, laws give judges the discretion to approve a marriage of underage parties if they are expectant parents or parents of a living child. Most states have laws stipulating that a marriage cannot be performed when the parties are within close degrees of blood kinship.

State statutes not only prescribe the requirements to marry but also the procedures. The usual procedure is for a couple intending to be married to apply to the county clerk, magistrate, or judge for a license. Applicants are required to be male and female and to sign an affidavit that each is unmarried, not within certain degrees of kindred, and that they understand the nature of the marital contract they are about to enter. Often there is a waiting period before a license issues and the marriage is solemnized, to allow applicants to be tested for sexually transmitted diseases and, in a few instances, for HIV. States impose a modest fee to obtain a marriage license and uniformly require that a civil official, priest, minister, or rabbi perform a marriage ceremony. In some states a notary public may officiate at a marriage. Marriage ceremonies vary from brief civil proceedings in which the parties agree to be married and acknowledge the responsibilities of marriage to elaborate religious rites with extensive ceremonial trappings. Fees paid to those who officiate at marriages vary greatly according to custom and, more frequently, the generosity of the parties.

Traditionally marriage has been a covenant between a male and female. A marriage that is valid where contracted is ordinarily valid anywhere. But after the Supreme Court of Hawaii ruled that its constitution required the state to demonstrate a compelling interest in order to restrict marriage to a male and female, many states feared that if Hawaii were to license **same-sex marriages** other states would be required to recognize such unions under the Full Faith and Credit Clause of the U.S. Constitution.[2] Congress acted swiftly by adopting the Defense of Marriage Act of 1996, which seeks to relieve states of the obligation to recognize same-sex marriages. It provides:

> No State, territory, or possession of the United States, or Indian tribe, shall be required to give effect to any public act, record, or judicial proceeding of any other State, territory, possession, or tribe respecting a relationship between persons of the same sex that is treated as a marriage under the laws of such other State, territory, possession, or tribe, or a right or claim arising from such relationship.[3]

Before the Hawaii Supreme Court decreed that a same-sex marriage license be issued, the voters amended the state constitution to ban same-sex marriages. In March 2000, by a 61 percent to 39 percent margin, California voters approved a ballot proposition that recognizes only marriages between a man and a woman. Thirty states now officially recognize only opposite-sex marriages.[4]

Rights and Obligations of Marital Partners

Until the early nineteenth-century, the law in most western countries followed the **unity concept of marriage** and deemed a married couple to legally be one. Under the rationale of protecting the wife, a husband had legal control over his wife's property and laws restricted married women from entering into contracts or owning property. In 1920, the Nineteenth Amendment to the U.S. Constitution guaranteed women the right to vote, and in the early 1900s states enacted various statutes known as **emancipation acts** to allow women to own and control their own property. Although these acts allowed women a measure of control over their own property, in most instances these rights were not widely granted to women until the mid-twentieth century.

Today the law no longer looks upon a marriage in the unity concept of regarding the spouses legally as one. Married women now have the right to freely enter contracts, the right to their own wages, the right to acquire and dispose of their own property, and the right to bring lawsuits in their own names. (In Chapter 11 we discuss more fully the evolution of the rights of women in context of federal legislation.)

The contract of marriage differs from other contracts. It results in a **contractual status** that imposes mutual obligations beyond the traditional covenants of fidelity and care that parties orally assume in a marriage ceremony. The status of the relationship has changed. Historically the husband was the provider with the legal obligation to support his wife and children. Today spouses have a mutual obligation of support of one another and the off-spring of the marriage.

Laws grant certain rights to married persons. For example, federal laws permit spouses to file joint federal income tax returns, allow benefits to surviving spouses in respect to federal estate and gift taxes, provide social security benefits to eligible surviving spouses, and impose certain requirements to enable spouses to benefit from pension benefits. State laws usually allow one spouse to recover compensation for loss of **consortium,** which is the loss of the injured spouse's services and companionship when the other spouse is permanently injured (for example, in an auto accident) by another person's tort (see Chapter 5). A spouse usually has certain entitlements under workers' compensation acts when the other spouse is killed in work-related accidents. State laws provide certain benefits to spouses in respect to inheritance (see Chapter 6). Spouses have certain privileges not to testify against one another in court proceedings (see Chapter 9).

The Case for Domestic Partnerships

Because married partners receive some special benefits, certain groups advocate that same-sex couples who live together in stable homosexual relationships should be granted rights concerning health insurance, pensions, inheritance, and authority to make decisions concerning one another's health care similar to the rights conferred on married couples. Some cities have enacted ordinances to require employers to make provisions such as health insurance and pension rights for persons in bona fide **domestic partnership,** and in the past few years a number of large national corporations have voluntarily conferred these benefits on their employees. Leading religious faiths have been staging debates and usually resolving to oppose performance of religious rites that would give a blessing to a same-sex relationship. Many of the arguments pro and con are based on the cultural and religious background of individuals and institutions.

The New Vermont Civil Union Legislation

On December 20, 1999, the Vermont Supreme Court ruled that its state constitution "common benefits" clause requires the state legislature to provide same-sex couples the same benefits conferred by law on married couples.[5] The court left it up to the state legislature as to whether to allow gay and lesbian couples to marry or whether to simply allow them the benefits of marriage through some form of domestic partnership. Despite considerable opposition, but responding to its state supreme court's mandate, the Vermont legislature promptly enacted the new **civil union** legislation. On April 26, 2000, Governor Howard Dean signed the new law providing that gay couples who obtain a license and have their unions certified by a clergy person or civil official shall have the same benefits, protections, and responsibilities as married couples have under the law. Parties to civil unions are accorded such rights irrespective whether the rights are derived from statute, administrative or court rule, policy, common law, or any other source of civil law.[6]

The new Vermont law falls short of granting same-sex couples the right to marry but it grants to civil union couples all legal rights historically regarded as incident to marriage. Specifically it creates a mutual duty of support, provides for inheritance rights, and allows a civil union couple to hold title to real and personal property as tenants by the entirety (see Chapter 6) and the right to make medical decisions for each other. The law also confers on each party to a civil union the marital communications privilege and benefit of laws relating to marital immunity from compelled testimony (see Chapter 9). The new law provides that dissolution of a civil union is to follow the same procedures as in dissolution of marriage.

PRENUPTIAL AGREEMENTS

The rising incidence of divorce, the fact that multiple marriages during one's lifetime are no longer uncommon, and the right of each spouse to separately accumulate property have caused an increase in the use of **prenuptial agreements.** A prenuptial agreement is a contract entered into by persons before they marry. The typical agreement stipulates the property rights of each spouse during marriage, upon death, and in the event of divorce. These agreements are more common when the parties' assets are disproportionate. Wealthy individuals often rely on such agreements to protect their substantial assets from transfer to a spouse. Older couples marrying for a second time who have children by their pervious marriages and who desire to conserve their respective estates for their own children and grandchildren often find a prenuptial agreement an attractive option.

If a spouse attacks the validity of a prenuptial agreement, courts often inquire as to whether the parties made a full disclosure of each other's financial resources before the agreement was entered into and whether the agreement is basically fair. The issue of coercion sometimes arises. For example, coercion may be found when, just before a wedding ceremony, a wealthy male presents his bride with an agreement providing minimal rights. If, before the agreement was signed, each party made a full disclosure of assets and separate legal counsel represented each party, courts tend to look more favorably on enforcement of a prenuptial agreement.

Although not nearly as common as prenuptial contracts, **postnuptial agreements** are sometimes used when parties do not anticipate the need for a prenuptial agreement. Courts tend to scrutinize such an agreement to determine if it is fair when entered into and that it is not signed under the threat of a divorce. When a divorce follows, courts sometimes insist on determining if the agreement is fair and just as of the time of a divorce. As in the case of a prenuptial agreement, full disclosure of financial resources and independent legal counsel bolster the prospect that a court will look favorably on enforcement of a postnuptial agreement.

DIVORCE AND ANNULMENT

Divorce and **annulment** both have the same basic objective—**dissolution of a marriage contract**—but they differ in court processes and legal effects. A divorce presupposes a valid marriage and is a judicial decree dissolving the bonds of matrimony. An annulment, on the other hand, is a judicial recognition that a valid marriage did not take place. An annulment and a divorce each leave the parties free to contract a new marriage, but a divorce does not necessarily relieve a party from obligations that have grown out of the marriage.

Annulment

An annulment is a judicial decree that no valid marriage existed. It is granted only on petition of a party who was unaware of an impediment to a valid marriage. These impediments might include a situation when one of the parties was already married or because of a party's mental incapacity, physical incapacity to consummate the marriage, or when the marriage resulted from fraud or intoxication.

In earlier years it was difficult to obtain a divorce and a stigma was attached to being divorced. Annulments were sought far more frequently than they are today. Actually, annulments are infrequent today in the civil courts. They are more common in the tribunals of the Roman Catholic Church, for if the church finds that a marriage is invalid from a canonical standpoint, under certain circumstances it will grant an annulment. Although the annulment by the Church has no legal effect, **canon law** allows a person whose marriage has been annulled to remarry within the Church. Before remarrying, however, a person whose marriage a religious tribunal has annulled must still obtain a decree of divorce from a civil court.

Legal Separation

When a marriage becomes an intolerable burden, some spouses voluntarily decide to live apart from one another. This does not alter their legal responsibilities to one another or their children. In other instances a husband and wife who agree to separate opt for a more formal **legal separation** by entering into an agreement to live apart to await a resolution of problems that led to their separation or to await making a considered judgment whether to dissolve their marriage. A formal separation agreement may simply provide for an agreement to live separately without interference by each other; but in many instances the parties effectuate a settlement of their property rights and the custody of their children. Such an agreement is often a prelude to dissolving the marriage and contains a stipulation that should the marriage be dissolved, subject to the approval of the court, the agreement is to become a part of any final judgment of divorce. As in the case of prenuptial and postnuptial agreements, separation agreements that settle custody and property rights can have long-lasting effects and should only be entered into advisedly after careful review by each party's lawyer.

Separate Maintenance

Many states have provisions, sometimes known as **separate maintenance** or allowing alimony without dissolution of marriage. A wife who is living apart from her husband without her fault and who is in need of support can file a petition for separate maintenance in some states. This type of proceeding was more common when states granted divorce based on fault rather than under modern no-fault dissolution of marriage laws. Sometimes this procedure is used as a "cooling-off period" or is chosen because of religious scruples against divorce. The proceedings contemplate an award of alimony and support to a wife based on the economic circumstances of the husband and wife and may allow a custodial parent the right to the exclusive use and occupancy of the marital home. Such proceedings, however, do not ordinarily contemplate a resolution of the parties' interests in property acquired during the marriage. In some states the court will award a reasonable attorney's fee to a party awarded separate maintenance who can demonstrate a need for such assistance.

Divorce

Before 1857, the English ecclesiastical court had jurisdiction over actions relating to marriage. These courts did not grant absolute divorces, rather they could grant an annulment or a **divorce** *a mensa et thoro* (a divorce from bed and board). For a wife to obtain a divorce from bed and board she had to demonstrate that her husband was at fault and that she was entitled to live separately and receive alimony from him. This is similar to a separate maintenance proceedings discussed in the preceding paragraphs. In the United States the idea of ecclesiastical courts was unacceptable to the new settlers and jurisdiction over divorce and other domestic relations matters was vested in chancery courts.

Historically a party seeking a divorce had to file a petition in the state that was considered the **matrimonial domicile** of the parties. As a result of a series of decisions from the U.S. Supreme Court, after 1942 it was no longer necessary that a divorce be granted in the state of the last matrimonial domicile. Rather, a petitioner can establish residence "in good faith" in the state where the petitioner seeks to obtain a divorce. Under the fault concept of divorce, this became important because the grounds for divorce varied greatly among the states. New York, for example, for many years would grant a divorce only on the ground of adultery. There was an incentive for a party seeking a divorce to apply for it in a state with liberal grounds for divorce and where residency could be established in a relatively short time. This brought many petitioners to establish residence and to seek a divorce in Florida, Nevada, or in another state that had minimal residency requirements and a variety of grounds for divorce. A spouse who leaves the matrimonial domicile and obtains a divorce decree in another state may still be subject to further proceedings concerning alimony, support, and custody rights in the state where the other spouse remained. This depends on various factors, one of which is whether the respondent spouse appears in the case in person or through counsel.

The Fault Concept

In the United States, courts granted a divorce only when a spouse alleged and proved one of the statutory grounds for divorce. These grounds varied among the states but usually included adultery, habitual intemperance, extreme cruelty, ungovernable temper, abandonment, impotency, nonsupport, and insanity. A few states allowed a divorce after a spouse disappeared for a period of seven years. The respondent could contest the grounds alleged and assert such defenses as condonation (my spouse condoned the actions now complained of), recrimination (my spouse is just as guilty as I of the ground alleged for divorce), or the respondent spouse could also enter a countersuit for divorce.

If the court, after hearing the parties and their witnesses, determined that the petitioner or respondent had established grounds for divorce, it would enter a decree granting the divorce in favor of the party "not at fault." The **fault concept** was important because it had a bearing on alimony that would be awarded and often on the issue of custody of the parties' children and visitation rights of the other party. Alimony and support money were generally awarded to the wife based upon her needs and the needs of the children, if any, and the husband's ability to pay. Historically alimony was considered an obligation on the part of a husband to be paid periodically during the former wife's lifetime or until her remarriage. The obligated party (almost invariably the husband) was required to pay support money for children until each child attained majority or married.

Under the fault concept, often the object of each party was to prove the other party at fault which often led to incredible testimony. Sometimes one spouse would be willing to "pay more" or "accept less" to avoid having to disclose the details of private matters in a public judicial forum. One spouse would sometimes hire a detective to try to "get the goods" on the other spouse by proving some indiscretion. The emotional scars left by graphic court testimony often remained long after a contested divorce was final. By the 1960s it became evident to most lawmakers that the time had come to change the laws concerning dissolution of marriage and, to some extent, the criteria to determine attendant responsibilities of the parties.

No-Fault Divorce

In the 1960s, states began to move from eligibility for a divorce based on one spouse being "at fault" to the concept of **no-fault dissolution of marriage.** Today some states retain grounds for divorce under the fault concept, but all states offer some basis of dissolving a marriage when the marriage is **irretrievably broken.** By the 1980s, the transition to no-fault divorce was virtually complete.

The objective of the newer no-fault approach is to enable spouses to dissolve a marriage without becoming adversaries and by eliminating the accusations spouses formerly lodged against one another in attempting to prove a spouse to be at fault in the marriage. The no-fault approach effectively eliminates proof of a party's fault and the old defenses to divorce that we discussed in the preceding section. Although some states continue to maintain some of the traditional grounds for divorce, the reality is that marriages are now dissolved based on the no-fault concept of the marriage being irretrievably broken. Should the respondent deny that the marriage is irretrievably broken, the court may refer the parties to counseling, postpone determination for a brief period, or simply take testimony to determine whether to grant the dissolution. Contests on the issue of a petitioner's ground for dissolution are now rare. If the petitioner convinces the court that the marriage is beyond reconciliation, then this is usually sufficient. Contests in dissolution proceedings now focus on issues of alimony, property division, custody and support of children, and visitation rights of a noncustodial parent. If a spouse (usually the wife) has cause to apprehend the other spouse may react violently to a petition for dissolution, then the court may be asked to issue a temporary restraining order against any violence directed toward the apprehensive spouse.

All states require the petitioner to establish certain **residence requirements** to allow the court to take jurisdiction of the proceedings. The duration of such requirements varies from as little as 90 days to about two years. The petitioner must cause the respondent spouse to be served legal process as well as a copy of the petition reciting the statutory ground for dissolution and demands for relief in other areas such as alimony, support, custody arrangements, property division, and attorney's fees.

Today parties in dissolution of marriage proceedings often resolve their problems concerning **alimony, custody, child support,** and **child visitation rights** of the **noncustodial parent** and memorialize their resolution of these points by written agreement after consultation with their legal counsel. The parties usually request the court to incorporate their agreement into the final judgment of dissolution. Their request is usually granted if the court finds the agreement to be fair and reasonable.

As no-fault laws have progressed, the process of obtaining dissolution of marriage has become simpler. In 1983, a California appellate court pointed out that proceedings for dissolution of marriage are no longer actions by which one party seeks redress for wrongs committed by another and that the concept of a "cause of action" by one party against the other is wholly foreign to family proceedings under its Family Law Act.[7] This appears to be rather typical of the view courts now take of proceedings for dissolution of marriage. Indeed, where no children have been born of the marriage and the parties are each capable of self-support, many petitioners routinely appear in court without legal counsel. The proceedings are essentially pro forma and dissolution will likely be granted based on proof of the petitioning spouse's durational residency requirement and minimal testimony by the petitioner to show the irretrievable breakdown of the marriage.

Alimony

Alimony is the allowance to a spouse imposed by a court that grants a divorce. The concept of alimony stems from the English common-law requirement that a husband must support his wife during her lifetime or until she remarries. A wife who was guilty of marital misconduct was not awarded alimony. In making awards of alimony American courts generally required the husband to make weekly or monthly payments. Courts articulated many factors to be considered in determining the amount of alimony to be awarded. These included the ages and stations in life of the parties, their physical and mental health, the duration of the marriage, and the wife's needs and the husband's ability to pay. Often the court's judgment was affected to some extent based on which party was found to be at "fault" in the marriage. In some states the legislature provided that no alimony could be awarded to a wife who was guilty of adultery.

In the United States, legislatures and courts characteristically viewed alimony much as did the common law, that is, as an obligation of the husband and an entitlement to a wife. This view was unacceptable to the U.S. Supreme Court, which in 1979 held that alimony statutes that provide for awards only to wives violated the Equal Protection Clause of the Fourteenth Amendment to the U.S. Constitution.[8] Thereafter it was necessary for states to either amend their statutes to provide for awards to both the husband and wife or, at least, that courts apply alimony statutes on a **gender-neutral basis.** By this time, the concept of alimony had undergone considerable change and courts tended to award permanent alimony only to spouses of long-term marriages or when disabling injuries prevented a spouse from achieving self-support. Often the scenario that would justify an award of permanent alimony would be where an older wife had fulfilled the traditional role of mother and homemaker and had not enjoyed the opportunity to pursue a career on her own and thus was not capable of sustaining herself.

The Uniform Marriage and Divorce Act (UMDA) was approved by the National Conference of Commissioners on State Law in 1970 and has been adopted in nine states. Even where the UMDA has not been adopted, courts refer to the criteria it offers for determining whether to award a party *maintenance,* a term that the UMDA uses instead of alimony.[9] As amended in 1973, the UMDA, § 308 provides for consideration of the following relevant factors when a court awards maintenance to a spouse:

1. The financial resources of the party seeking maintenance, including marital property apportioned to him, his ability to meet his needs independently, and the extent to which a provision for support of a child living with the party includes a sum for the party as custodian;
2. The time necessary to acquire sufficient education or training to enable the party seeking maintenance to find appropriate employment;
3. The standard of living established during the marriage;
4. The duration of the marriage;
5. The age and physical and emotional condition of the spouse seeking maintenance; and
6. The ability of the spouse from whom maintenance is sought to meet his needs while meeting those of the spouse seeking maintenance.

The above criteria seem to be read like a mental checklist of the factors that judges traditionally consider, even absent statutory criteria.

The advent of no-fault divorce brought with it new perspectives on alimony awards. During the 1970s the concept of **rehabilitative alimony** emerged through statutory enactments. Rehabilitative alimony is designed to provide short-term alimony and is generally awarded based on the time required for a divorced spouse to be educated or trained to become self-sufficient. The trial court fixes the amount of payments and a termination date for payments based on the proposed plan of rehabilitation for the recipient. Often the court will consider a modification of the payments before the termination date, if the recipient can show a justification. Trial judges are given broad discretion in awarding rehabilitative alimony, and absent an abuse of that discretion appellate courts are very reluctant to vacate or modify such awards. Traditionally, alimony terminated upon a former spouse's remarriage, but courts differ on whether remarriage should terminate an obligated spouse's liability for rehabilitative alimony. A strong argument can be made to have the payments continue until that rehabilitation has been accomplished.

Despite the tendency to award rehabilitative alimony, there are still instances when an award of **permanent alimony** serves an important role in dissolution of marriage proceedings. Consider, for example, dissolution of a long-term marriage. The female spouse is 55 years of age and possesses no marketable skills or talents and suffers from health problems. The parties have few marital assets, but the husband is gainfully employed at a good salary. Such a spouse presents no actual and little potential capacity for self-support to enable her to live in the standard she enjoyed while married. A wife in those circumstances might present a court with a compelling case for an award of permanent alimony.

A spouse sometimes requests that the alimony be paid as a lump sum rather than in periodic installments and the lump sum may consist of assets other than cash. When a wife establishes entitlement to permanent alimony but the husband has limited resources, and the wife requires the marital home as a place to raise the parties' minor children, courts sometimes award a husband's interest in the marital home place to the wife as lump-sum alimony. In other instances the wife may be given the right of occupancy of the home place until the youngest child attains majority whereupon the home place might be sold and the proceeds distributed according to order of the court.

Attorney's Fees

In many states, statutes allow courts to award **attorney's fees** to a spouse in a marital action "to level the playing field" if the requesting spouse can show an inability to retain counsel or the other spouse has a greater ability to pay litigation expenses. Courts may sometimes award temporary attorney's fees to a spouse who requires such assistance to conduct litigation. Where the income flow of the parties is disproportionate, courts often award attorney's fees at final hearing incident to the equitable distribution of property.

Property Settlement Agreements

Often parties in divorce litigation enter into **property settlement agreements** to avoid the necessity for a judicial distribution of marital assets. Such agreements are generally executed only after counsel has had an opportunity to determine the nature and extent of the assets of the parties. This is generally accomplished through interrogatories and discovery depositions during the course of litigation.

Property settlement agreements can afford federal income tax advantages to a recipient who is generally not taxed on the assets received, whereas alimony payments are taxable to the recipient and deductible to the party paying the alimony. But there can also be disadvantages. Alimony is subject to modification based on a substantial change in the needs of the recipient and the obligated party's ability to pay. In contrast, property settlement agreements are contractual and generally not subject to modification. Courts review these agreements, and if it appears that an agreement has been entered into advisedly, the court, upon request, will generally incorporate the agreement into the final judgment of dissolution of marriage.

Court-Imposed Distributions of Property

When the parties to a dissolution proceeding do not arrive at an amicable distribution of their marital assets, it becomes the trial court's responsibility to order a fair and equitable division of assets. The common-law method was to allow each party to retain those assets titled in a party's name. This approach generally favored the husband in divorce litigation, and with the changing role of women in society it became essential for courts to look beyond legal titles in order to arrive at fair and just settlements of marital assets. Courts have developed different theories to cause a fair distribution of the marital assets.

One method of achieving a fair distribution of property, while not disregarding the concept of title to assets, has been to award a spouse a **special equity** in property. Suppose the wife had received a substantial inheritance and used her separate funds to make the down payment on a home that became titled jointly in the husband and wife. A court might award the wife a special equity beyond her ordinary marital share equal to her special contribution to the marital residence. Courts have applied the special equity doctrine to all types of personal and real property. In other instances courts have attempted to arrive at a fair distribution of property by awarding a party **lump-sum alimony** to supplement that party's distributive share of the parties' assets. Nevertheless, more effective means of arriving at a fair distribution of marital property became essential.

Arizona, California, Idaho, Louisiana, Nevada, New Mexico, Texas, and Washington are **community property states.** Statutes in these states treat all property as belonging equally to the husband and wife unless the property was acquired before the marriage or as a gift or through inheritance. When a marriage is dissolved or annulled the problem of making distribution of property is simpler because the marital assets belong equally to the husband and wife. Where **community property** is not susceptible to a division in kind, the court can order it sold and divide the proceeds equally between the husband and wife. Yet, even in community property states, courts sometimes must make adjustments in property distributions in order to arrive at a fair distribution of assets upon dissolution of marriage.

Today most states (other than community property states) have moved toward distributing marital assets on a basis called **equitable distribution.** Equitable distribution does not mandate an equal distribution, although some courts have said that is a good starting point. Unlike the common-law approach, the first step is for the court to make a determination of what assets constitute marital property and which assets are separate properties.

Many forms of real and personal property, for example, homes, vehicles, stocks and bonds, and pension rights, are subject to being divided and equitably distributed between spouses.

Section 401 of the Divorce Code of Pennsylvania sets forth factors that courts are to consider in their division of marital property as follows and provides the weight to be given to the factors in determining the equitable distribution of assets within the discretion of the trial court.[10] These factors are:

1. Length of the marriage
2. Any prior marriage of either party
3. Age, health, station, amount and sources of income, vocational skills, employability, estate, liabilities, and needs of each of the parties
4. Contribution by one party to the education, training, or increased earning power of the other party
5. Opportunity of each party for future acquisition of capital assets and income
6. Sources of income of both parties, including but not limited to medical, retirement, insurance, or other benefits
7. Contribution or dissipation of each party in the acquisition, preservation, depreciation, or appreciation of the marital property, including the contribution of a party as a homemaker
8. Value of the property set apart to each party
9. Standard of living of the parties established during the marriage
10. Economic circumstances of each party at the time the division of property is to become effective
11. Whether the party will be serving as the custodian of any dependent minor children

Some state laws either prohibit or restrict the courts from treating public pension benefits as marital property. Federal laws provide for civil service retirement benefits to be paid pursuant to a court decree of divorce, annulment, or legal separation.[11] But the Supreme Court's 1981 ruling that federal law precluded a state court from making a division of military pensions proceedings involving military retirees proved to be an obstacle to equitable distribution.[12] The problem was short lived as the following year Congress enacted the Uniformed Services Former Spouses' Protection Act.[13] The act allows a state court to order a division of military retired pay as part of a distribution of marital property in a divorce case. If the parties' marriage lasted for 10 years or more concurrent with military service, a former spouse may receive court-ordered payments directly from the government's military finance center not in excess of 50 percent of the service person's retired pay.

The New York legislature has prescribed equitable distribution of **marital property** in divorce and annulment proceedings.[14] Marital property under New York law includes all property acquired by either or both spouses during marriage and before execution of separation agreement or commencement of matrimonial action, regardless of the form in which title is held. The state's highest court held that even a college degree obtained during the marriage is to be considered as marital property.[15] Moreover, the New York courts are authorized to make orders concerning the use and occupancy of the marital home, regardless of the form of ownership. The court may make a distributive award when equitable distribution is impracticable, burdensome, or contrary to law, or to supplement distribution of marital property. Like most states, New York does not impose equitable distribution in respect to property that a spouse has acquired by will, inheritance, or gift.[16]

Because the dissolution of a marriage is absolute, courts attempt to make a distribution of property that will likewise be absolute. As the Maine Supreme Court pointed out in 1995, courts should endeavor to divide marital property in such a manner as to avoid continued financial interaction between the parties.[17]

CHILD CUSTODY, SUPPORT, AND PATERNITY

The English common-law principle of granting custody of minor children to a father yielded to an approach in the United States of courts usually granting custody of young children, particularly **children of "tender years"** (generally considered to include preteen children) to the mother. This was based on the presumption that the mother was the primary caregiver. In some instances, courts would grant custody of older boys to their father. Under the tender years doctrine it was very difficult for a father to obtain custody of young children unless he could prove the mother to be an unfit parent. In the early twentieth century, courts developed the **best interests of the child test** and attempted to award custody to the parent who could best serve the interests of the child. Again, in a time when most mothers of young children did not work outside the home, the mother was generally favored as being the parent who could serve the best interests of a child.

Changing Attitudes on Child Custody

With the increased number of mothers who now work outside the home, young children are often cared for by childcare centers and courts are prone to give more consideration to a father. Fathers today occupy a somewhat different role in the family than in previous generations. Many fathers share household duties and have developed far more parenting skills than fathers in previous generations. Court opinions in custody matters frequently make declarations to the effect that custody must be determined on a gender-neutral basis with parents given equal consideration. Yet, in most cases courts tend to find that the mother of younger children is the caregiver of choice and make custody awards accordingly.

In attempting to determine the best interests of the child, courts have articulated numerous criteria to be considered in making an award of custody. Reasons most commonly advanced by courts include the following:

- The parent who is more likely to allow the child frequent contact with the noncustodial parent
- Physical and mental health and moral fitness of the parents
- Emotional ties between the child and the parents
- Permanence of the existing or proposed custodial home
- Ability and disposition of parents to provide necessaries including medical care

Courts often consider the expressed preference of older children and such factors as the school and community affiliations and educational opportunities that will be served by the custodial parent. Historically, the religious preferences of the parents played a significant role in custody awards, but increasingly they are considered irrelevant as long as those practices do not pose a threat to a child's welfare. And while the issue of a party's misconduct has been largely removed by no-fault divorce laws with respect to most questions in dissolution of marriage cases, many courts still consider the moral conduct of the parties in deciding issue of child custody.[18] In former decades an adulterous parent was routinely denied custody of children, but the trend today is for courts to determine whether such activities pose harm to a child and to make custody decisions accordingly.

Gay and lesbian parents often experience considerable difficulty in being awarded custody; however, views on the subject are changing, as society seems to more readily accept these lifestyles. Some states have laws or court decisions stating that gays and lesbians are not to be awarded custody of children, whereas other states now have statutes or court decisions declaring that sexual orientation is irrelevant in considering custody and visitation issues.

The policy of the law has generally been to keep all the children together rather than divide their custody between the parents. The rationale is that, absent compelling reasons to split the custody of children between the parents, children should not be deprived of growing up together with some common denominator of discipline and the advantages of sharing mutual experiences within the home and family unit.

Traditionally courts have awarded the custody of children to one parent with the **right of visitation** granted to the noncustodial parent. Court decrees generally frame the right as one allowing reasonable visitation, but when the parties cannot arrive at amicable visitation schedules then courts will define visitations with reference to times and places.

Shared Custody Arrangements

During the 1980s state legislatures began to provide a new concept for child custody called **shared parental responsibility. Shared custody** (sometimes called **joint custody**) recognizes that both parents continue to have responsibility for rearing a child. Whereas in the usual custodial arrangement one parent has sole custody and the noncustodial parent is given rights of reasonable visitation with his or her child, the objective in shared parental custody is for one parent to maintain the **primary physical residence** of the child but with both parents to retain full parental rights and responsibilities and to confer on major decisions affecting the welfare of the child. Thus the concept of primary physical residence is divided from the responsibility for decisions regarding the child's education, discipline, and general upbringing.

Trial judges are vested with considerable discretion in determining whether to grant sole custody with rights of visitation or whether to grant joint custody; but the trend of judicial decisions is to grant joint or shared custody even in cases of children of tender years.

Modification of Custody Arrangements and Child Support Orders

Custody decrees are subject to modification; however, to promote stability in the parent–child relationship, courts hold that to obtain a **modification of custody** the petitioner must show that there has been a substantial change in circumstance of either the par-

CASE IN POINT

IS JOINT CUSTODY APPROPRIATE FOR CHILDREN OF TENDER YEARS?

Church v. Church

Court of Appeals of North Carolina
458 S.E.2d 732 (1995)

The North Carolina Court of Appeals reviewed a trial court decision granting joint custody where the parents separated after some four years of marriage at a time when their son was about three years old and had been cared for primarily by the mother. The trial court awarded joint custody over the mother's objection and she appealed. The appellate court cited the state statute that provides an order for custody of a minor should award custody to "such person ... that will best promote the interest and welfare of the child." Despite the mother's contention that the father had testified that other parties would also care for the child in his absence, the appellate court noted that the evidence at trial sustained the trial court's findings that both parties were of excellent character, active in church activities, and both are fit and proper persons to have custody of their child and that the best interest of the child would be promoted by awarding joint custody. The appellate court affirmed the trial court's decision.

ents or the child since the original custody decree. Likewise, a support order is subject to modification based on a substantial change in the needs of the child or the ability of a parent to pay.

What About the Grandparents?

There are an estimated 60 million grandparents in the United States. Grandparents traditionally play an important role in their relationship with grandchildren. Given the proportion of marriages with minor children that have ended in dissolution in the past 50 years, the role of grandparents has become even more significant. To ensure that grandparents have rights to visit their grandchildren, all 50 states have enacted statutes allowing **grandparents' visitation** rights. In some instances statutes allow visitation by others under varying circumstances that serve the best interests of the child.

Statutes that authorize judges to grant visitation rights to grandparents have met different reactions by courts. Some courts have ruled that such statutes violate the **parents' right of privacy**; in other instances courts have upheld such statutes. Court decisions vary greatly depending on the language of the statute involved and the circumstances of the parties.

In 1994 the legislature in the state of Washington enacted Section 26.10.160(3), which permitted "[a]ny person to petition for visitation rights at any time and authorized trial judges to grant such rights whenever visitation may serve a child's best interest." In reviewing the statute, the Washington Supreme Court held that a state may interfere with these parental rights only to prevent harm or potential harm to a child. The court then observed that the Washington statute did not require a threshold showing of harm and permitted any person to petition at any time with the only requirement being that the visitation serves the best interest of the child. Thus, it held the statute unconstitutionally infringed on the fundamental right of parents to rear their children.[19]

The U.S. Supreme Court granted review and on June 5, 2000, affirmed the judgment of the Washington Supreme Court.[20] Justice O'Connor wrote the plurality opinion of the court, noting:

> A parent's estimation of the child's best interest is accorded no deference. . . . §26.10.160(3), as applied here, exceeded the bounds of the Due Process Clause. . . . There is a presumption that fit parents act in their children's best interests, . . . there is normally no reason for the State to inject itself into the private realm of the family to further question fit parents' ability to make the best decisions regarding their children . . . Because the instant decision rests on §26.10.160(3)'s sweeping breadth . . . there is no need to consider. . . whether the Due Process Clause requires all nonparental visitation statutes to include a showing of harm or potential harm to the child as a condition precedent to granting visitation or to decide the precise scope of the parental due process right in the visitation context.[21]

Undoubtedly there will be further litigation challenging to other states' laws on the subject of grandparent visitations. Although such broad, sweeping statutes as enacted by the Washington legislature are doomed by the Supreme Court's decision, the Court's opinion does not seem to foreclose upholding grandparents' visitation rights on a case-by-case basis under more narrowly drawn statutes. A question to ponder is whether visitation statutes should make a distinction between intact families and children in custody of one parent.

The Uniform Child Custody Jurisdiction Act

As divorce has become more common and the population more mobile, the courts have been plagued with **interstate disputes concerning child custody.** Parents have shifted children from one jurisdiction to another, thereby engendering continuing controversies over child custody and visitation rights. In 1968 this led the National Conference of Commissioners on Uniform State Laws to propose the Uniform Child Custody Jurisdiction Act (UCCJA). The act received the approval of the American Bar Association and has now been adopted (sometimes with revisions) by legislatures in all states.

The basic purpose of the act is to avoid jurisdictional competition and conflict with courts of other states. It is designed to promote cooperation to the end that a custody decree is rendered in the state that is in the best position to decide the case in the best interests of the child. The act seeks to ensure that litigation concerning custody takes place in the state where the child and the family have the closest connection and to limit custody determination to one state. This requires a court to decline to exercise jurisdiction when the child and the family have a closer connection with another state. Some of the practices the act seeks to prevent are relitigation of custody disputes by a parent who loses custody in one jurisdiction and **child snatching.** To minimize the duration of the period of uncertainty and turmoil in a child's life, the UCCJA directs courts to expeditiously handle jurisdictional issues.

The Parental Kidnapping Prevention Act

Some states made revisions in their adoption of the Uniform Child Custody Jurisdiction Act that tended to weaken its application. So, despite the improvements in child custody proceedings that resulted from its adoption, Congress determined that further measures were necessary to deter **interstate abduction** of children by parents. In 1980, Congress enacted the Parental Kidnapping Prevention Act (PKPA).[22] The primary purposes of the act is to prevent jurisdictional conflicts over child custody and to reduce any incentive for parental "child snatching" in custody matters. Because it is federal law, the PKPA takes precedence over any state law, including the UCCJA.

The Support Requirement

The traditional view that the father is the parent charged with financial support of minor children has yielded to the modern view that support of children is the equal responsibility of the mother and father. A parent's responsibility for child support arises as a result of the child's birth; dissolution of marriage does not relieve a parent from that obligation. Of course, when dissolution occurs, the court may determine that the **custodial parent** and noncustodial parent have disproportionate obligations for support of their children.

The obligation for support of an adopted child is the same as for a child born of the adoptive parents' marriage. An **illegitimate child** (sometimes referred to today as a **child out of wedlock**) has the same right of support from the **putative father** as does a legitimate child. As we discuss in a later topic, courts must sometimes establish this responsibility through a judicial proceeding determining paternity. A parent's obligation to support a minor child can generally only be terminated by death of the parent or child, the child attaining majority or emancipation, by marrying, or entry into the armed forces.

Determining the Amount of Child Support

In dissolution of marriage the parties often seek agreement on the types and amounts of support for children. Sometimes these agreements are hammered out in a process of court-imposed or voluntary **mediation.** Any such agreement is subject to court approval. In absence of the parents agreeing on **child support requirements,** in making an award a court considers each parent's assets, liabilities, and sources of income. In the past decade many states have developed guidelines for support of children to cover the reasonable needs for housing, clothing, food, education, medical care, and other expenses related to child care and upbringing.

Usually a court orders child support payments to be made on a periodic basis to the custodial parent. Increasingly the practice is to require the payments to be made through a central agency such as a court clerk in order that accurate records are maintained. Court orders for child support are always subject to modification when the custodial parent experiences a substantial rise in costs of education, medical expenses, and housing. Another factor that often affects the amount of child support payments is inflation. Parents sometimes agree to adjust support payments based on the Department of Labor's Consumer Price Index. Where there is no agreement and there has been marked change in the inflation index courts may sometimes adjust support payments.

Enforcement of Child Support Orders

Failure of an obligated parent to pay child support to the custodial parent has become a major problem in the United States. Custodial parents often must resort to judicial proceedings by seeking to have the court find the defaulting parent in **contempt of court.** Other options include **garnishment** of an obligated parent's wages or even seeking criminal sanctions. These options are generally difficult for a custodial parent (most frequently the mother) to pursue and generally necessitate the employment of a lawyer or assistance from a child support office. Of course, if the court punishes a parent for being in contempt or when a parent is prosecuted it can result in that parent's inability to earn the money necessary to comply with support requirements.

If a parent who is obligated to pay child support moves to another state, an additional problem arises for the custodial parent who is seeking to collect. To aid in the collection of support payments from out-of-state parties, most states have adopted the Uniform Reciprocal Support Act of 1968, commonly referred to as URESA. The act requires each state to enforce the support obligations imposed by other states. The act itself creates no duties of family support, rather it is concerned solely with the enforcement of existing duties when the person to whom a duty is owed is in one state and the person obligated to furnish support is in another. In an effort to streamline the procedures for **reciprocal enforcement of support obligations**, the Uniform Interstate Family Support Act of 1992 superseded URESA. The 1992 act, in turn, was followed by the Uniform Interstate Family Support Act (1996),[23] which as of 2000 had been adopted by 44 states and the District of Columbia. These support acts generally have a positive effect on the ability of parents to compel support from those who otherwise might evade compliance with support requirements.

Support of Dependents: The Federal Role

Congress has taken an increased interest in the federal government taking an active role in compelling support of dependents. Federal law now provides a locator service at the disposal of the states to track down parents who default on their support obligations.[24] The revised Child Support Recovery Act (CSRA)[25] now provides that anyone who willfully fails to pay a support obligation with respect to a child, who resides in another state, and whose obligation has remained unpaid for a period longer than one year or is greater than $5,000 is guilty of a federal offense. In 1999, a U.S. Court of Appeals said that "willfully" under CSRA can mean either having the money and refusing to use it for child support, or not having the money because one has failed to avail oneself of the available means of obtaining it. The court concluded that Congress did not mean to let absentee parents evade their parental obligations by refusing to accept gainful employment or take other lawful steps to obtain necessary funds.[26]

Paternity

The presumption of legitimacy of a child is one of the strongest presumptions in law. A husband who contests **paternity** of a child born during his marriage must raise the issue promptly and not after dissolution of the marriage. In general, the following principles apply:

- A child born in wedlock is presumed legitimate. A husband who had access to his wife is presumed to be the father of her child.
- A child born during marriage is legitimate, even if conceived by the parties before marriage.

- A child born within the normal gestation period after death of a husband is presumed to be the legitimate child of the deceased husband.

Under the common law a putative father had no duty to support an illegitimate child. Today in some states, statutes affix the responsibility of support on a male who acknowledges paternity. All states have laws that provide for judicial proceedings to determine paternity of an illegitimate child and to compel the father to contribute to the child's support. Any woman who is pregnant or who has delivered a child has standing to bring suit to determine paternity of her child. The development of human leukocyte antigen (HLA) tests, and their general acceptance by the courts, has had a tremendous influence in establishing paternity. Putative fathers who contest their paternity often attack the reliability of blood tests. Other defenses commonly raised include impotency, sterility, and no access to the mother. In early years a putative father would raise the issue of promiscuity of the female plaintiff, but today attacking the mother's morals would likely fail as a defense.

The Fourteenth Amendment to the U.S. Constitution forbids states to discriminate between legitimate and illegitimate children in granting the right to parental support.[27] Court decisions generally hold that the mother of an illegitimate child cannot contract away that child's right to support from the father. In some states a governmental agency that provides support has standing to bring a paternity suit to determine a putative father's liability for support. In recent years, many legislatures have revised their statutes of limitations to cause the time for an illegitimate child to bring suit to commence when a child attains majority.

ADOPTION

From a legal standpoint, adoption is the process of substituting the **adoptive parents** for the **biological parents**. Adoption has historic roots, particularly where a childless couple wanted to perpetuate their family. Yet, as a formal legal process, adoption was unknown under the English common law. In the United States, state statutes regulate adoption and while these laws have certain commonalities, they vary considerably in eligibility of adoptive parents and rights of adoptees and in the procedures for effectuating adoption. Some states allow one adult to adopt another; however, the discussion that follows only refers to adoption of children.

Types of Child Adoptions

There are three general categories of adoption of children:

- **Stepparent adoptions.** In some instances, an unmarried woman gives birth to a child and later marries a man who is not the father and the new husband adopts the child. In other instances, a divorced parent who has custody of a child remarries, the noncustodial parent consents, and the custodial parent's new spouse adopts the child.
- **Agency adoption.** In this circumstance, a governmental or private adoption agency arranges for the adoption. Typically, the parents of the child have given their consent to adoption or their parental rights have been terminated by court action.

- **Private placement adoption.** Here intermediaries, usually a physician and lawyer, arrange for birth parents to consent to adoption. Not all states permit this category of adoption.

Who May Adopt and Who May Be Adopted

Typically state statutes that provide for adoption of children are written in general terms stating the adopting parents must be married, must jointly agree to adopt, and the adoption must be in the best interests of the child. Before a child may be adopted it is essential that the rights of the biological parents have terminated either by their consent or by judicial decree. Often statutes require a social service agency to interview the prospective adopting parents and file a written report concerning their suitability as prospective parents and eligibility of the child to be adopted. These reports usually discuss the stability of the adopting parents' relationship, and their financial and parental ability to provide the potential adoptee with a suitable home environment. Often statutes impose a waiting period before adoption takes place in order that the adoptive parents and the child to be adopted have an opportunity to bond.

Formalization of the Adoption

The legalities of adoption are formalized by a judicial hearing. At the hearing the judge examines the documentation that releases the rights of the biological parents. When such paperwork is in order, an adoption hearing is largely pro forma with the judge reviewing any social report and listening to the parents acknowledge the responsibilities they are undertaking and the legal relationship that the adoptee will have with them and their biological children, if any. This often involves a recitation of the adoptive parents' legal duty of support and the adoptee's right of inheritance.

If an adoption is contested, the hearing takes on a different complexion. Contests generally focus on the validity of the consent of the biological parent(s) or the issue of whether there has been a valid termination of the parental rights of such parent(s). The court carefully examines a consent to make certain that it conforms to the legal standards of the jurisdiction and was signed voluntarily and that no fraud, duress, or undue influence was exerted in obtaining the consent. In some states the necessity for obtaining the consent of the biological parents is waived if the evidence clearly shows the biological parent(s) to be unfit or to have abandoned or neglected the child. In other jurisdictions the court looks to whether there has been a prior termination of the parental rights of the biological parent(s). If a birth mother or father is unknown, the court must make certain that the necessary legal procedures have been undertaken to assure compliance with the standards of due process of law. In addition to the rights of a natural birth mother, in recent years an unwed father who demonstrates a full commitment as a responsible parent has rights protected under the standards of due process of law.

Some Nontraditional Adoptions

In the past social agencies have attempted to arrange adoptions based, in part, on the compatibility of the adoptive parents with the child to be adopted. They have considered a number of factors including racial and religious compatibility of the adopting parents. There have been criticisms that the criteria established by adopting agencies have been too narrow. Indeed, some of these criteria are being challenged in court. There has been an increase in the number of single parents and homosexual couples who have sought to adopt children. Approval is based on the adoption being in the best interest of the child to be adopted. Therefore court decisions do not always focus directly on the issues of homosexuality. Yet, in 1993, the New Jersey Supreme Court ruled that when a lesbian and the biological mother of a child had been in a committed relationship for approximately 10 years, the lesbian could adopt her partner's child.[28]

TERMINATION OF PARENTAL RIGHTS

As noted, a child is not subject to adoption until the rights of the natural parents have been terminated. Parents may terminate their own parental rights, for example, by consent to adoption. A common instance is when the custodial parent remarries and the noncustodial parent consents to adoption of a child by the custodial parent's new spouse.

In some instances one parent seeks to terminate the parental rights of the other, but these cases are the exception. The necessity to terminate parental rights most often begins with police action; however, police agencies generally refer cases of abused or neglected children to a state social agency. What constitutes abuse or neglect is generally defined by statute. Proceedings for **termination of parental rights** are usually initiated by a state agency. Such actions are generally based on a parent's abuse of the child or a parent's neglect to provide for a child's welfare. When a social agency discovers such parental deficiencies the child is often removed and placed in **foster care** while efforts are made to remedy the problems. A social

CASE IN POINT

TERMINATION OF PARENTAL RIGHTS

In re: Jennifer Ann Sprite and Michelle Marie Sprite, Minors

Court of Appeals of Michigan
400 N.W.2d 320 (Mich. App. 1986)

The Juvenile Division of the Probate Court entered an order terminating the parental rights of the mother and father of their two young daughters. Only the mother appealed. She contended that termination of her parental rights was not in the best interest of the children. The Court of Appeals reviewed the evidence on which the Probate Court had based its findings and order. It revealed the two children were subjected to living in an unstable home with frequent and intense parental disputes, sexual abuse by father, observation of sexual activity in home, chronic deprivation of cleanliness, lack of food in the home, and a significant lack of medical attention for the children. The evidence also included the evaluations by a psychiatrist who concluded that neither the father nor the mother are amenable to treatment and that regardless of how many parenting classes they attend or counseling they receive it is not going to make a great deal of difference in how they parent their children. The appellate court concluded that based on the mother's intentional and negligent disregard of her children's needs, her demonstrated unwillingness to correct deficiencies in her parenting abilities and her inability to protect her children, the Probate Court correctly terminated her parental rights. The Court of Appeals affirmed the judgment.

agency may offer the family a case plan with the objective of reunification of the family once the social workers find the necessary improvements are accomplished.

A natural parent has a fundamental liberty interest in the care, custody, and management of children. The level of abuse or neglect necessary to justify termination of parental rights is not always capable of precise definition. When a state agency seeks to terminate parental rights the state must establish termination of those rights by clear and convincing evidence of abuse, abandonment, or neglect. Recent decisions of the U.S. Supreme Court emphasizing the need to protect the due process rights of indigents have been persuasive in causing several jurisdictions to require appointment of counsel at public expense for indigent parents in proceedings for termination of their parental rights.

REPRODUCTIVE DECISIONS

Reproductive decisions have emerged over the years largely through decisions of the U.S. Supreme Court. These decisions concern the rights to procreate, to use contraceptives, and to obtain an abortion.

Roe v. Wade: The Supreme Court's Landmark Decision on Abortion

Any discussion today of a woman's right to choose whether to bear a child generally relates back to the Supreme Court's 1973 landmark decision in *Roe v. Wade*.[29] In writing for the majority of a divided Court, the late Justice Harry Blackmun opined that a woman's right to privacy under the U.S. Constitution is broad enough to encompass her decision whether to terminate her pregnancy. The Court went on to hold that a fetus was not a "person" within the meaning of the Fourteenth Amendment to the U.S. Constitution and therefore not entitled to the constitutional protection guaranteed persons. The Court's decision provided that during the first trimester of a woman's pregnancy that abortion was a matter between the woman and her physician without state regulation. After the first trimester, procedures for abortion could be regulated when "necessarily related to maternal health" and in the final trimester, when the fetus has become "viable" the state may prohibit abortion except "when it is necessary, in appropriate medical judgment to preserve the life or health of the mother." The Court's decision remains controversial because the issue of abortion has deep philosophical, religious, ethical, medical, and political dimensions. In 1992, the Court abandoned the trimester-by-trimester framework and declared that abortion regulations will not be allowed if they represent an "undue burden" on a woman's constitutional right.[30]

Evolution of the Right of Privacy

Although *Roe v. Wade* is the authority for women's rights to control their reproductive functions, *Roe* was preceded by a number of decisions that developed the constitutional right of privacy. Some eight years earlier the Court struck down a Connecticut law that made the sale and possession of birth control devices a misdemeanor.[31] The late Justice William O.

THE U.S. SUPREME COURT'S ABORTION DECISIONS   SIDEBAR

Since its 1973 decision ruling 7–2 that a woman's constitutional right to privacy legalized **abortion** on a nationwide basis, the Supreme Court has issued numerous abortion-related decisions. The more significant rulings are summarized below:

1976: *Planned Parenthood v. Danforth:* By a 6–3 vote, the Court ruled that states cannot allow a husband to exercise veto power over his wife's decision to abort her pregnancy. By a 5–4 vote the Court said that parents cannot be given absolute veto power of a minor decision to have an abortion.

1979: *Colautti v. Franklin:* By a 6–3 vote the Court said that states may protect a fetus that has reached viability, but determination of viability is up to doctors, not courts or legislatures.

1983: *City of Akron v. Akron Center for Reproductive Health:* Among other things, the Court by a 6–3 vote ruled that state and local governments cannot require that abortions beyond the first trimester to be performed in hospitals.

1986: *Thornburgh v. American College of Obstetricians and Gynecologists:* By a 5–4 vote the Court struck down a Pennsylvania abortion regulation that would have required doctors to inform women seeking abortions about potential risks and available medical assistance for prenatal care and childbirth.

1989: *Webster v. Reproductive Health Services:* In a series of split votes, the Court upheld the right of the state of Missouri to restrict the use of public funds, personnel, and facilities in performing abortions and requiring doctors to perform viability tests on fetuses at or beyond twenty weeks of gestation.

1992: *Planned Parenthood v. Casey:* The Court abandoned the trimester-by-trimester approach in its 1973 decision and ruled that abortion regulations will not be allowed if they impose an "undue burden" on a woman's constitutional right to obtain an abortion.

2000: *Stenberg v. Carhart:* The Court struck down a Nebraska law banning "partial birth abortion" as unduly burdensome on a woman's "right to choose." In so doing, the Court reaffirmed its basic holding in *Roe v. Wade.*

Douglas, writing for a divided Court, said that the various guarantees in the Constitution created a zone of privacy. Significantly the Court's 1965 decision which invalidated a law criminalizing the sale and possession of birth control devices began a trend for the court to base decisions concerning sexual and reproduction matters on this newly found **right of privacy.** In 1972, the Court took a further step when it invalidated a Massachusetts law that prohibited unmarried persons from buying and using contraceptives.[32] So, to many legal scholars, the 1973 decision on **abortion** in *Roe v. Wade* was simply an extension of the Supreme Court's determination to expand the right of privacy it first declared in 1965.

The Future of the Abortion Issue

Although the Supreme Court's basic pronouncement in *Roe v. Wade* appears to be entrenched, the present Court remains divided on some of the ramifications of its 1973 pronouncement. In a serious challenge in 1989, the Court split 5–4 in upholding the constitutionality of a

Opinion of the Court . . .

STENBERG V. CARHART

530 U.S. 914, 120 S.Ct. 2597, 147 L.Ed.2d 743 (2000).

Justice Breyer delivered the opinion of the Court.

"We again consider the right to an abortion. We understand the controversial nature of the problem. Millions of Americans believe that life begins at conception and consequently that an abortion is akin to causing the death of an innocent child; they recoil at the thought of a law that would permit it. Other millions fear that a law that forbids abortion would condemn many American women to lives that lack dignity, depriving them of equal liberty and leading those with least resources to undergo illegal abortions with the attendant risks of death and suffering. Taking account of these virtually irreconcilable points of view, aware that constitutional law must govern a society whose different members sincerely hold directly opposing views, and considering the matter in light of the Constitution's guarantees of fundamental individual liberty, this Court, in the course of a generation, has determined and then redetermined that the Constitution offers basic protection to the woman's right to choose. . . . "

Missouri statute that included a requirement that physicians conduct viability tests on the fetus at or beyond 20 weeks' gestation and other restrictions. But perhaps more troublesome to those who support a woman's right to choose to have an abortion was language in the preamble of the Missouri law stating "the life of each human being begins at conception."[33]

In 1992, the Court reaffirmed the essential holding of *Roe v. Wade,* but upheld some restrictions that Pennsylvania law imposed that required parental consent, waiting periods, and record-keeping and reporting provisions. The Court, however, did invalidate the requirement in the Pennsylvania law that required notification to a woman's spouse.[34] In 2000, the Court revisited the abortion issue when it struck down a Nebraska law banning a procedure commonly described as partial-birth abortion.[35] Although the vote in the decision was 5–4, the Court made clear that the Constitution protects the fundamental right to choose abortion.

SURROGATE MOTHERHOOD

Surrogate motherhood is a modern development in **reproductive technology.** Until recently, adoption was the only option available to infertile couples that desired to have a child. However, with new reproductive technologies, couples unable to have children can enter a contract with a woman to bear a child for them. In the usual procedure the woman employed to bear the child (surrogate mother) signs an agreement waiving any parental rights to the child to be born. The husband's sperm or an already fertilized egg is then implanted in the womb of the surrogate mother.

Will courts enforce a contract whereby a surrogate mother agrees to deliver the newborn child to the couple who employed her? In 1988, the New Jersey Supreme Court rendered the seminal decision on this point. The Sterns were unable to have children, so in 1985 Mr. Stern contracted with Mrs. Whitehead to bear a child for them. Mrs. Whitehead agreed to be impregnated by Mr. Stern's sperm and to bear a child that Mrs. Stern would legally adopt. Mrs. Whitehead was to receive $10,000 for her services. After the child (Baby M) was born, Mrs. Whitehead decided she wanted the child as her own and a lengthy court battle on custody ensued. The case finally went to the state supreme court which held that the surrogacy contract between Mr. Stern and Mrs. Whitehead conflicted with the New Jersey adoption laws and was invalid and unenforceable. The court said that payment of money to a surrogate mother violated a state statute that prohibited payment or acceptance of money in connection with any placement of a child for adoption. Nevertheless, the court decided that the best interests of the child would be served by placing her in the custody of her biological father and his wife, with Mrs. Whitehead to enjoy rights of visitation.[36] Since this decision in 1988, several state legislatures have enacted laws barring enforcement of surrogacy contracts.

The scenario in the case reviewed by the New Jersey Supreme Court involved the **traditional surrogacy** where a woman is impregnated with the sperm of a married man, with an understanding that the child to be born is to be legally the child of the married man and his wife. In contrast, **gestational surrogacy** involves the sperm of a married man being artificially united with the egg of his wife and the resulting **preembryo** being implanted in another woman's womb.

In 1993, the Supreme Court of California reviewed a gestational surrogacy case where a married couple, the Calverts, desired to have a child.[37] Mrs. Calvert was unable to become pregnant although her ovaries remained capable of producing eggs. In 1990, the Calverts and Anna Johnson signed a contract providing that a preembryo created by Mr. Calvert's sperm and the egg of Mrs. Calvert would be implanted in Anna Johnson, the surrogate. The agreement contemplated that the child to be born would be taken into the Calverts' home as their child. Ms. Johnson agreed she would relinquish "all parental rights" to the child in favor of the Calverts and in return, they would pay her $10,000 and provide a $200,000 life insurance policy on her life. After the **surrogate** became pregnant, relations between her and the couple deteriorated. The Calverts sued for a declaration that they were to become the legal parents of the unborn child. The surrogate then filed her own action seeking to be declared the mother. The cases were consolidated, the child was born, and a blood test excluded the surrogate as the genetic mother. The trial court ruled that the Calverts were the child's genetic, biological, and natural father and mother and that the surrogate had no parental rights to the child, and that the contract was legal and enforceable against surrogate's claims. Anna Johnson appealed from the trial court's judgment. The appellate court and the state supreme court affirmed holding that gestational surrogacy contracts do not violate public policy, adoption statutes, parental rights termination statutes, or penal statutes making it a misdemeanor to pay for adoption.

In a more recent California case, a husband and wife agreed to have a preembryo that was genetically unrelated to either of them implanted in a surrogate who would bear the child for them. After the fertilization, implantation, and pregnancy, the husband filed a petition for dissolution of marriage. He alleged that there were no children of the marriage. The wife responded, asserting that the parties were expecting a child by way of surrogate contract. The child was born six days later. The trial court declared that the parties were not the lawful parents of the child. The Court of Appeal reversed the judgment and held that both parties were

CASE IN POINT

THE CASE OF THE FROZEN EMBRYOS

Davis v. Davis

Supreme Court of Tennessee
842 S.W.2d 588 (Tenn. 1992)

Junior Davis and Mary Sue Davis married in 1980; however, the wife was unable to become pregnant. Several years later the couple signed up for an **in vitro fertilization** program at a clinic in Knoxville. There was no agreement specifying what disposition should be made of any unused embryos that might result from the cryopreservation process, and no Tennessee statute governed such disposition. In 1989, the husband sought a divorce and the wife sought custody of the frozen preembryos. The county court granted the divorce and awarded custody of the frozen preembryos to the wife. The husband appealed and the Court of Appeals reversed, finding that the husband had a constitutionally protected right not to beget a child where no pregnancy had taken place. The Court of Appeals remanded the case to the county court with directions that the parties have joint control over the embryos and equal voice in their disposition.

The Tennessee Supreme Court granted review, believing the Court of Appeals directions to the lower court were insufficient. As the litigation progressed, Mrs. Davis remarried and no longer wanted the embryos for herself, but desired the right to donate them. The court concluded that the embryos were neither persons nor property; rather they were in a category that entitled them to special respect because of their potential for human life. The court found that Mr. Davis's constitutional right to avoid procreation overrode the former wife's right to keep the embryos or donate them to others. The court directed that the clinic could proceed to dispose of them in a customary manner.

the lawful parents of the child. The court said that even though neither party was biologically related to the child, they were still the child's lawful parents given their initiating role as the intended parents in the conception and birth of the child. Further, the court stated that the same statute that makes a husband the lawful father of a child born because of his consent to **artificial insemination** applied to both intended parents. The court reasoned that just as a husband is deemed to be the lawful father of a child unrelated to him when his wife gives birth after artificial insemination, a husband and wife should be deemed to be the lawful parents of a child after a surrogate bears a biologically unrelated child on their behalf.[38]

Medical advances have outstripped the law in this area of surrogacy, which has raised a number of moral and ethical problems leading to crucial legal problems. Some would argue that a comprehensive regulatory scheme for legislating surrogacy is needed and that Congress should pass uniform legislation to regulate surrogacy.[39]

DECISIONS REGARDING MEDICAL TREATMENT

One of the serious aspects of family life is the necessity to make decisions concerning medical treatments. Competent adults have the right to make decisions concerning their own medical treatment, including the right to refuse treatment. A competent adult can also make

advance directives concerning medical care through use of a **living will, durable power of attorney,** and appointment of surrogates.

Spouses generally have the authority to make medical decisions for adults who are incompetent or unable to make decisions concerning medical treatments. Parents and guardians have the right and obligation to make health care decisions for their children or their wards. State statutes generally authorize physicians and hospitals to render needed medical treatments in an emergency when the parents or guardians are unavailable. There are controversial issues concerning the requirement of parental consent for a minor female to obtain an abortion, and there are variations in requirements to remove life-sustaining support systems of terminally ill children.

Since the 1970s considerably more attention has been given to matters concerning health care, particularly those involving the discontinuance of life-sustaining measures. There is a movement in legislative bodies and courts to shift the issue of removal of **extraordinary life-sustaining measures** from the courts and to permit the withdrawal or withholding of life-sustaining treatment for terminally ill patients at the direction of a surrogate based on competent medical advice.

Termination of Life-Support Systems

In 1975, Karen Quinlan, age 21, lay in a chronically vegetative state connected to a respirator and nourished by means of a nasogastric tube. After physicians advised her parents that she could not be restored to a sapient existence, they sought to have the respirator withdrawn. When the doctors refused, Karen's father sought approval from a local court to remove the life-sustaining equipment. That court refused and an appeal was lodged in the New Jersey Supreme Court. In a landmark decision, the New Jersey Supreme Court found that use of a mechanical respirator was an "extraordinary" medical treatment and that Karen's constitutional right of privacy included her right to decline such treatment. The court recognized the right of Karen's father to assert her right of privacy.[40]

Today courts generally accept a patient's right to order removal of **life-support systems** based on the fundamental right of privacy discussed in the case involving Karen Quinlan. In the ensuing years courts developed criteria for removal of life-support systems from children. In general they have ruled that before authorizing removal of life-sustaining procedures for a child, competent medical evidence must disclose that the child's condition is terminal, irreversible, and that life is being sustained only through extraordinary life-prolonging measures. Courts usually allow parents or other surrogates to assert a minor's right of privacy and through exercise of their **substituted judgment** to approve of discontinuance of such extraordinary measures. Most courts have not required judicial approval unless there is a lack of concurrence among the family, physicians, or hospital.[41]

All states now allow a competent adult to execute a durable power of attorney for health care and most states have enacted statutes that provide a competent adult can sign a living will to stipulate the conditions under which life-sustaining treatment may be withheld or withdrawn. A durable power of attorney for health care becomes effective if the principal lacks capacity to make health care decisions. A living will becomes operative if the signer is incompetent and terminal, or lapses into a permanently unconscious state.

As early as 1977, the Massachusetts Supreme Judicial Court permitted the guardian of an elderly, retarded man to assert the right of his ward who was suffering from leukemia to refuse chemotherapy.[42] It seems clear that a competent adult may reject extraordinary life-prolonging measures, but does that extend to the right to reject food and water? In 1986, the California Supreme Court ruled that a young woman who, although competent, was suffering from the effects of an advanced degenerative illness had the right to refuse food and water that was being administered through a nasogastric tube.[43]

By 1984, courts were issuing opinions concerning the rights of family members to approve the removal of extraordinary life-sustaining measures. In 1984, the Florida Supreme Court summarized the newer approach of the courts when it said:

> We hold that the right of a patient, who is in an irreversibly comatose and essentially vegetative state to refuse extraordinary life-sustaining measures, may be exercised either by his or her close family members or by a guardian of the person of the patient appointed by the court. If there are close family members such as the patient's spouse, adult children, or parents, who are willing to exercise this right on behalf of the patient, there is no requirement that a guardian be judicially appointed. . . . The decision to terminate artificial life supports is a decision that normally should be made in the patient–doctor–family relationship. Doctors, in consultation with close family members are in the best position to make these decisions.[44]

Legislatures and courts in states faced with the issue of whether artificial nutrition and hydration may be withdrawn or withheld have responded in various ways. Some state statutes permit the refusal or removal of some forms of life support, but exclude nutrition and hydration. Others allow the withdrawal or withholding of nutrition and hydration tubal feedings where the patient is terminally ill. Courts have arrived at different conclusions concerning the withdrawal or withholding of nutrition and hydration. As a result, physicians and hospitals recommend that patients express their preferences in these matters through an advance care directive.

Although competent adults may refuse medical treatment on religious ground, even if the refusal results in death, courts take a different view in respect to children. This sometimes poses problems when a parent chooses to rely on spiritual power to achieve healing or deny blood transfusions to a child based on Scripture. The Supreme Court in 1944 recognized that "parents may be free to become martyrs themselves. But it does not follow that they are free in identical circumstances to make martyrs of their children before they have reached the age of full legal discretion when they can make that choice for themselves."[45]

CONCLUSION

Family law touches each person's most intimate relationships. It embraces us from birth to death with decisions and relationships in between. For many of us family law regulates marriage and unfortunately, in some instances, divorce, with its attendant problems of alimony, property division, custody of children, and visitation rights. Even when we are not involved personally, laws and court decisions concerning the family shape the society in which we live. At times attitudes toward family law seem paradoxical: We insist on privacy and personal autonomy in our interpersonal relationships, yet we demand that regulatory authorities require education and support of children and protection of children and cohabitants from abuse.

Families are undergoing dramatic cultural changes, and laws must adjust to the factors bringing such changes about while retaining the core concepts of family relationships. Our mobile, technologically oriented society increasingly is characterized by diversity and pluralism and less bound by traditional mores of family ties and the constraints of institutional religion. Today the great unifying force in the United States is the law. Nowhere is this more evident than in family law.

SUMMARY OF KEY CONCEPTS

After studying this chapter a student must surely realize how family law touches everyone and the dynamic changes this area of the law has undergone since the last half of the twentieth century. Marriage has a firm secular and religious basis in the family unit. Although contractual, it results in a definite legal status of the parties. The legal obligations of the parties can be modified, to some extent, by prenuptial agreement. Today the traditional concept of marriage as being an institution of an adult male and female is being challenged, with one state allowing same-sex individuals to enter civil unions, with most of the attributes of marriage.

The process of dissolving a marriage has also undergone dramatic changes. In earlier years laws severely restricted divorce; later states allowed statutory grounds for divorce; and now the no-fault concept allows dissolution of an irretrievably broken marriage. With the educational, economic, and social advances of women, concepts of alimony, child support, custody, and visitation rights have also undergone considerable change. Except in long-term marriages, courts today tend to limit alimony to that necessary to rehabilitate a divorced spouse. The emphasis is now on a shared approach in resolving child custody, support, and visitation issues. Where divorcing parties cannot negotiate a fair and reasonable settlement of their property interests, courts today place less emphasis on permanent alimony and greater emphasis on assuring an equitable distribution of marital and nonmarital property. Child custody is now considered on a more gender-neutral basis, and there is increased enforcement of child support obligations with interstate compacts and federal government assistance.

With the increasing divorce rate, adoption can solve many social problems in families. Many adoptions are by stepparents, although agencies and private placements play a significant role. Where consent of biological parents is not secured on a voluntary and knowing basis, often the legal termination of parental rights must first be accomplished.

After evolving decisions on sexual privacy, in 1973 the Supreme Court issued its landmark abortion rights decision in *Roe v. Wade*. Its basic decision on a woman's reproductive rights appears entrenched; however, nuances continue as this controversial subject with seemly irreconcilable religious views is pitted against a woman's fundamental liberty interest in deciding whether to continue a pregnancy.

Advances in medical technology have brought more new issues of family law to the forefront. Three prominent ones are (1) surrogate motherhood and its consequences to all parties involved; (2) an individual's right to make decisions concerning his or her medical treatment; and (3) the right of surrogates to substitute their judgment, where necessary, in making judgments whether to terminate life-support systems of terminally ill patients.

QUESTIONS FOR THOUGHT AND DISCUSSION

1. Is there a justification for states to continue to recognize common-law marriages? Explain.
2. What are the different legal consequences between a divorce and an annulment of a marriage?
3. What are the most common reasons that couples enter into prenuptial agreements?
4. What are the principal criteria courts look to in determining matters concerning custody of children?
5. How did the Supreme Court's ruling in *Griswold v. Connecticut* in 1965 lay the groundwork for the Court's 1973 decision in *Roe v. Wade?*
6. Why would a court likely take a different view as to the rights of a surrogate mother in a case involving traditional surrogacy as opposed to one involving gestational surrogacy?
7. What is meant by the doctrine of "substituted judgment" in relation to the law governing the removal of life-support systems and discontinuance of artificial nourishment for a comatose patient who has not indicated a preference in regard to these matters by advance directive or living will?
8. Beyond requiring that adoptive parents be married, should statutes governing adoption of children be vague in respect to requirements for adoptive parents and the suitability of a child for adoption? Why?
9. What legal consequences affect adoptive parents as a result of a decree of adoption?
10. Do you think that a husband who has been unaccompanied by his wife while on overseas duty with the army for a period of 18 months could successfully rebut paternity of a child born to his wife 11 months after he left for overseas duty?
11. What is the rationale for a court to cause an equitable distribution of marital property? What property is ordinarily excluded from marital property?
12. Should the law provide for court-enforced rights of visitation of minor children by their grandparents? If so, what qualifications should be placed on such visitation rights?

KEY TERMS

marriage

common-law marriages

ceremonial marriages

same-sex marriages

unity concept of marriage

emancipation acts

contractual status

consortium

domestic partnership

civil union

prenuptial agreements

postnuptial agreements

divorce

annulment

dissolution of a marriage

canon law

legal separation

separate maintenance

divorce *a mensa et thoro*

matrimonial domicile

fault concept

no-fault dissolution of marriage

irretrievably broken

residence requirements

alimony

custody

child support

child visitation rights

noncustodial parent

gender-neutral basis

rehabilitative alimony

permanent alimony

attorney's fees

property settlement agreements

special equity

lump-sum alimony

community property states

community property

equitable distribution

marital property

children of "tender years"

best interests of the child test

right of visitation

shared parental responsibility

shared custody

joint custody

primary physical residence

modification of custody

grandparents' visitation

parents' right of privacy

interstate disputes concerning child custody

child snatching

interstate abduction

custodial parent

illegitimate child

child out of wedlock

putative father

mediation

child support requirements

contempt of court

garnishment

reciprocal enforcement of support obligations

paternity

adoptive parents

biological parents

stepparent adoption

agency adoption

private placement adoption

termination of parental rights

foster care

right of privacy

abortion

surrogate motherhood

reproductive technology

traditional surrogacy

gestational surrogacy

preembryo

surrogate

artificial insemination

in vitro fertilization

advance directives

living will

durable power of attorney

extraordinary life-sustaining measures

life-support systems

substituted judgment

ENDNOTES

[1] West's Ga. Code Ann. § 19-3-2.

[2] U.S. Const., Art. IV, § 1.

[3] 28 U.S.C.A. § 1738C.

[4] Mike Tharp, "A 'No' to gay marriage," *U.S. News & World Report,* March 20, 2000, p. 39.

[5] *Baker v. State,* 744 A.2d 864 (Vt. 2000).

[6] Vt. Legis. PA 91 (2000).

[7] *In re Marriage of Van Hook,* 195 Cal. Rptr. 541 (Cal. App. 1983).

[8] *Orr v. Orr,* 440 U.S. 268, 99 S.Ct. 1102, 59 L.Ed.2d 306 (1979).

[9] Uniform Marriage and Divorce Act, U.L.A. § 308 (1998).

[10] 23 Pa.S.A. § 401(d); See also *Wayda v. Wayda,* 576 A.2d 1060 (Pa. Super. 1889).

[11] 5 U.S.C.A. § 8345(j).

[12] *McCarty v. McCarty,* 453 U.S. 210. 101 F.Ct. 2728. 69 L.Ed.2d 589 (1981).

[13] 10 U.S.C.A. § 1408.

[14] D.R.L. § 236, Part B.

[15] *McGowan v. McGowan,* 535 N.Y.S.2d 990 (1988).

[16] D.R.L. § 236, Part B.

[17] *Berry v. Berry,* 658 A.2d 1097 (Me. 1995).

[18] See, for example, *In re Marriage of Dawson,* 214 N.W.2d 131 (Iowa 1974).

[19] *In re Custody of Smith,* 969 P. 2d 21 (Wash. 1998).

[20] *Troxel v. Granville,* 530 U.S. 57, 120 S.Ct. 2054, 147 L.Ed.2d 49 (2000).

[21] 120 S.C. at 2061–2064.

[22] 28 U.S.C.A. § 1738A.

[23] ULA Int. Fam. Sup.

[24] 42 U.S.C.A. § 653.

[25] 18 U.S.C.A. § 228.

[26] *U.S. v. Ballek,* 170 F.3d 871 (9th Cir. 1999).

[27] *Gomez v. Perez,* 409 U.S. 535, 93 S.Ct. 872, 35 L.Ed.2d 56 (1973).

[28] *Matter of Adoption of Child by J.M.G.*, 632 A.2d 550 (N.J. 1993).

[29] 310 U.S. 113, 93 S.Ct. 705, 35 L.Ed.2d 147 (1973).

[30] *Planned Parenthood v. Casey*, 505 U.S.833, 112 S.Ct. 2791, 120 L.Ed.2d 674 (1992).

[31] *Griswold v. Connecticut*, 381 U.S. 479, 85 S.Ct. 1678, 14 L.Ed.2d 510 (1965).

[32] *Eisenstadt v. Baird*, 405 U.S. 438, 92 S.Ct. 1029, 31 L.Ed.2d 349 (1972).

[33] *Webster v. Reproductive Health Services*, 492 U.S. 490, 109 S.Ct. 3040, 106 L.Ed. 2d 429 (1989).

[34] *Planned Parenthood v. Casey*, 505 U.S. 833, 112 S.Ct. 2791, 120 L.Ed.2d 673 (1992).

[35] *Stenberg v. Carhart*, 530 U.S. 914, 120 S.Ct. 2597, 147 L.Ed.2d 743 (2000).

[36] See *In re Baby M.*, 537 A2d 1227(1988), on remand, 542 A2d 52 (1998).

[37] *Johnson v. Calvert*, 851 P.2d 776, 1993 (Cal. 1993).

[38] *In re the Marriage of Buzzanca*, 72 Cal.Rptr.2d 280 (Cal. App. 1998).

[39] Lisa L. Behm, "Legal, Moral, & International Perspectives on Surrogate Motherhood: The Call for a Uniform Regulatory Scheme in the United States." *DePaul Journal of Health Care Law*, Spring 1999.

[40] *In re Quinlan*, 355 A.2d 647 (1976).

[41] See *In re Barry*, 445 So. 2d 364 (Fla. App. 1984); *In re L.H.R.*, 321 S.E.2d 716 (Ga. 1984).

[42] See *Superintendent of Belchertown State School v. Saikewicz*, 370 N.E.2d 417 (Mass. 1977).

[43] *Bouvia v. Superior Court*, 225 Cal.Rptr. 297 (Cal App. 1986).

[44] *John F. Kennedy Memorial Hosp. v. Bludworth*, 452 So.2d 921 926 (Fla.1984).

[45] *Prince v. Massachusetts*, 321 U.S 158, 170, 64 S.Ct. 438, 444, 88 L.Ed. 645, 655 (1944).

FOR FURTHER READING

Dolgin, Janet, *Defining the Family: Law, Technology, and Reproduction in an Uneasy Age* (New York University Press 1997).

Glick, Henry, *The Right to Die: Policy Innovation and its Consequences* (Columbia University Press 1992).

Luker, Kristin, *Abortion and the Politics of Motherhood* (University of California Press 1980).

O'Brien, David M., *Privacy, Law and Public Policy* (Praeger 1979).

O'Connor, Karen, *No Neutral Ground? Abortion Politics in an Age of Absolutes* (Westview Press 1996).

Reagan, Milton C., *Alone Together: Law and the Meanings of Marriage* (Oxford University Press 1999).

Strasser, Mark, *Legally Wed: Same-Sex Marriage and the Constitution* (Cornell University Press 1998).

Tribe, Laurence. *Abortion: The Clash of Absolutes* (Norton 1990).

PART III

THE LEGAL PROCESS

9

CIVIL PROCEDURE, EVIDENCE, AND THE APPELLATE PROCESS

Courtesy of West Group

LEARNING OBJECTIVES

This chapter should enable the student to understand:

- the jurisdiction of courts to hear civil disputes
- the parties involved in civil litigation
- court pleadings and service of process
- the social and economic role that class action suits play
- pretrial preparation and nonjury and jury trials of civil cases
- the mechanics and art of jury selection
- evidentiary phases of a trial, arguments by counsel, jury deliberations, and verdicts

CHAPTER OUTLINE

Introduction

Civil Procedure

The Rules of Evidence

Appellate Procedure

Conclusion

Summary of Key Concepts

Questions for Thought and Discussion

Key Terms

For Further Reading

INTRODUCTION

Civil lawsuits are brought in state and federal courts to redress injuries or vindicate legal rights. Civil suits stem from a variety of causes, including personal injuries, conflicts over ownership of property, contractual disputes, and various business relationships. The civil jurisdiction of state courts is often invoked to determine whether a party is incompetent, to supervise guardianships of minors and incompetent persons, and resolve issues in domestic relations cases such as dissolution of marriage and custody of children.

Courts determine outcomes in civil suits based on relevant legal principles and precedents. The rules of civil procedure and evidence are the vehicles through which courts decide these cases in a fair and orderly manner.

Civil procedure embraces the processes by which claims and defenses are presented to and adjudicated by trial courts. It includes the pretrial, trial, and posttrial phases of civil litigation.

The procedures governing civil disputes, extremely complex and protracted at common law, have been greatly simplified and streamlined through the adoption of modern statutes and rules of court procedure. In the federal courts, civil procedure is governed by rules promulgated by the U.S. Supreme Court under authority delegated by Congress. Similarly, state legislatures have authorized state courts to establish rules of civil procedure, replacing what was known as **common-law pleading** in civil cases.

The **rules of evidence** consist of principles applicable to the admission of evidence in judicial proceedings. These rules are largely of common-law origin; however, they have been modified by statutory law and court decisions. In this chapter we focus on civil procedure, the rules of evidence, and **appellate procedure** applicable to both civil and criminal disputes. Appellate procedure refers to the rules by which higher courts review lower court decisions. In Chapter 10 we amplify the rules of evidence and appellate procedure in relation to the adjudication of criminal cases.

CIVIL PROCEDURE

Those unable to resolve civil disputes informally have the right of access to the courts to attempt to obtain relief. One who files a **complaint** is known as the **plaintiff;** the party against whom the complaint is filed is known as the **defendant.** Of course, in some instances multiple plaintiffs may seek relief from more than one defendant. Plaintiffs and defendants are known as the **parties,** and their rights are determined in accordance with the principles of the substantive law, discussed in previous chapters. Civil procedure is the process that governs judicial resolution of civil disputes.

Jurisdiction: The First Step

One who seeks recourse through the judicial system must initially determine the appropriate court that has jurisdiction over the subject of the suit. **Jurisdiction** is the authority of a court to hear and determine a particular type of case and it is conferred on courts either by constitution or statute. Federal courts have jurisdiction over cases involving copyrights, patents, admiralty and maritime cases, bankruptcy proceedings, and other federal proceedings as well as over federal crimes. Congress has also vested federal courts with jurisdiction to determine cases between citizens of different states (**diversity jurisdiction**) where the party so elects and the amount in controversy exceeds $75,000.[1] Although federal procedural law is applied in diversity cases, the federal district courts apply the substantive law of the state where the court sits.[2] State courts hear most cases involving residents of the state and those affecting real property within the state.

In addition to filing suit in a court that has jurisdiction, the plaintiff must abide by the legal rules that relate to **venue,** the geographical place where a law action may be filed. Statutes generally designate the proper venue, commonly providing the place where a tort or breach of a contract occurs or where land in controversy is located. The rules become quite complex where multiple defendants are involved.

Who are Parties to Civil Suits?

Individuals, corporations, and government agencies may become parties to civil lawsuits as plaintiffs or defendants. For example, Harriet Hester who was injured in an auto accident can file a complaint against the driver and owner of a tanker truck that she claims caused the accident. The complaint might read, "Harriet Hester v. Damian Drivo and Economy Oil Company, a corporation." Individuals and entities also become parties in a representative capacity. For instance, Fidelity Trust Company, as personal representative of John Doe's estate or as trustee for John Doe might file a complaint against Unexcelled Investments, Inc., a corporation. A minor's complaint through his guardian would likely be styled "Sharon Smith, as guardian of Jonathan Smith, a minor." Or the citizen who disputes the tax assessment of her house may file a complaint styled, "Rhonda Roe, plaintiff v. James Jones, as tax assessor." In certain litigation the party who files a complaint is often known as a *petitioner* and the party against whom relief is sought is called the *respondent.* Typically a complaint for dissolution of a marriage may read, "Mary Jones, petitioner v. Paul Jones, respondent, or in some states it would be styled, "In re: Dissolution of marriage of Paul and Mary Jones."

Relief Sought by the Plaintiff

A civil suit is an attempt to obtain some form of relief through the courts. In addition to stating a **cause of action,** a lawsuit must specify the relief requested by the plaintiff. The most common form of relief sought by plaintiffs is **damages.** Damages represent monetary compensation for a party's injuries or economic losses. **General damages** are those the law implies to have accrued to the plaintiff due to a particular injury or loss. **Special damages** are those that have accrued or will accrue to the plaintiff although they did not necessarily flow from an injury or loss. To illustrate: A plaintiff who has been injured in an automobile accident suffers general damages, that is, pain and suffering; but the plaintiff may also have sustained such special damages as loss of wages and medical expenses. Finally, in some instances, when a plaintiff's rights have been violated, for example a technical trespass on the plaintiff's land, the court may award **nominal damages,** say $1.00, to recognize the plaintiff's rights have been violated but that no actual damages have accrued. Obviously, a plaintiff would not ordinarily seek to recover nominal damages.

When a defendant's actions have been fraudulent, wanton, or outrageous, the plaintiff may be allowed to recover **punitive damages.** The object of punitive damages is to punish the defendant and to deter others from like conduct. Often statutory law governs the award of punitive damages.

In some instances a plaintiff merely seeks **declaratory relief,** that is, the plaintiff requests the court to interpret the law in respect to a present factual situation when genuine controversy exists between parties, but applicability of the law is in doubt.

In other instances, a plaintiff will seek an **injunction** to prevent an injury from taking place or to terminate an ongoing injury. In unusual cases where a breach of contract cannot be remedied by recovering monetary damages, plaintiffs will ask the court to order **specific performance,** which means that the court will order the defendant to fulfill the contractual obligations that were breached. If, for example, a defendant breached a contract to sell a particular piece of artwork to the plaintiff, the plaintiff might not be content to accept monetary damages. For the billionaire who wishes to own an original Picasso, money is not the object. Such a plaintiff would likely seek to have the court force the defendant to deliver the painting.

The Initial Pleading

Recall from Chapter 1 the historic differences between the common law and equity. At common law, the **initial pleading** (request to the court) in a civil case was called a declaration; in chancery court it was referred to as a bill in equity. Today in federal and most state courts the plaintiff's complaint or the petitioner's petition is the initial pleading in a lawsuit. The purpose of the initial pleading is to demonstrate to the court that it has jurisdiction of the suit and to inform the defendant of the basis of the plaintiff's suit and the relief being sought. The plaintiff's complaint or petition must meet certain formal requirements. It must include a caption with the name of the court where the suit is filed and the names of the parties; a statement that alleges the jurisdiction of the court; the body of the complaint, which explains the basis of the suit; and a demand for a judgment. If the plaintiff is seeking to annul a contract between the parties, the demand for judgment may read, "Plaintiff seeks to rescind the contract described in this complaint." If the complaint seeks damages for injuries incurred in an auto accident, the demand for judgment might read, "Plaintiff demands judgment against the defendant for $10,000." In some cases, a plaintiff may add a demand for a jury trial.

Civil Process and How Accomplished

To notify the defendant that the plaintiff's complaint has been filed, the clerk of the court issues a formal document called a **summons** commanding the defendant to answer the plaintiff's complaint. The summons directs the defendant to respond to the plaintiff's complaint within a set period, usually 20 days, from the date the complaint and summons are served. In federal court proceedings, the process may be served throughout the United States, but in state courts the process may be served only within the state. A marshal, sheriff, or process server usually accomplishes service of the complaint and summons.

When the summons and complaint are physically delivered to the defendant, the service is referred to as **personal service.** If the law authorizes these documents to be served on someone on the defendant's behalf, the service is known as **substituted service.** For example, many states allow a plaintiff to file suit against the driver and owner of an automobile involved in an accident in the state even though these defendants are nonresidents. The rationale of such laws is that when you drive your car in another state you designate the secretary of state or some other state official to receive a summons on your behalf. That official, in turn, sends the suit papers to the defendant.

Most states also have **long arm statutes** that permit a plaintiff who is a resident of one state to sue a nonresident when the plaintiff has suffered a loss because of business the defendant has transacted in the plaintiff's state. The U.S. Supreme Court has established very definite requirements that must be met before long arm service is permitted.[3] Finally, in some legal proceedings the plaintiff can serve process on the defendant by publishing a notice in the newspaper and by mailing a copy of the complaint to the defendant's last known address. This type of service is called **constructive service** and the plaintiff is restricted as to the form of relief that can be obtained against a defendant.

If a defendant fails to timely respond to a summons, the clerk of the court enters a **default,** and in due course the court may enter a **default judgment** against the defendant. In exceptional instances a trial court may remove a default judgment and allow a defendant to proceed.

The Defendant's Response to the Plaintiff's Complaint

The common law gave a defendant the option of filing a number of motions before responding to the substance of a plaintiff's complaint. Modern rules have greatly simplified these procedures in civil disputes.[4] Nevertheless, before filing an answer, a defendant may challenge the court's jurisdiction or the validity of the service of process or seek to dismiss the complaint on ground that it does not state a legal cause of action, that is, a valid legal basis for the claim. The trial court disposes of such motions after hearing oral arguments or receiving written memoranda from the parties or their counsel. If the court determines that the plaintiff's complaint does not state a legal cause of action, then the trial judge generally allows the plaintiff to file an amended complaint to more precisely state the claim being asserted. If the plaintiff is unable to state a cause of action, the court will dismiss the case.

If the court denies the defendant's motions, or after the plaintiff alleges the basis of the complaint with more particularity, the defendant is required to file a written **answer** admitting or denying the plaintiff's allegations. The defendant's response may include specific defenses. The statute of limitations, which limits the time allowed for bringing different causes of action, and the statute of frauds, which requires certain contracts to be in writing, are examples of defenses asserted in civil cases.

A defendant may also file a **counterclaim.** For example, suppose the plaintiff sues the defendant claiming the defendant failed to pay the plaintiff the balance due for constructing the defendant's house. The defendant denies the plaintiff's claims and asserts a counterclaim alleging that the plaintiff contractor did not properly perform the contract and as a result the house has defects in construction. The counterclaim may accomplish one of three things. It may defeat the plaintiff's claim, mitigate the amount of plaintiff's damages, or even result in the plaintiff not receiving an award and the defendant recovering damages from the plaintiff.

Pleadings in a civil lawsuit often become quite complex. In some instances the defendant contends that a third party has an obligation to the defendant and brings a **cross claim** against such party. In law this is known as **third-party practice.** A cross defendant, of course, has the same options to file motions and the same requirement to file an answer as the original defendant.

Class Actions

A **class action** is a lawsuit brought against an alleged wrongdoer by a group of persons who claim to have suffered a similar wrong. Class actions are typically brought by parties who claim to represent a large group of unnamed persons who share a common interest in seeking relief. Class actions in federal and state courts have developed only since the mid-twentieth century. A class action may be maintained only where joinder of the numerous plaintiffs is impracticable. Moreover, before the court permits a class action, the plaintiffs must establish that the questions of law or fact are common to a class of parties and that one or more parties suing on behalf of the class fairly represent the class. Likewise, representatives of the class of defendants being sued may maintain a defense. Once the trial court determines that a class action may be maintained, notice is given to all interested parties. The federal rules of civil procedure provide that any member of the class must be given the option to be excluded from the class action and unless a party opts for exclusion, that party will be bound by the court's determination in the class action.[5] Rules of procedure in state courts usually impose similar requirements.

Class actions have become a major vehicle for social and economic reform. Prisoners have instituted class actions to require states to improve prison facilities. In recent years, class actions have been filed by persons claiming injuries resulting from exposure to asbestos, silicone breast implants, misrepresentations concerning insurance, and claims of antitrust violations. Such suits frequently result in court-approved compromises. In some instances the parties agree on the institution of certain reforms. In others, plaintiffs obtain monetary settlements and, after payment of attorney's fees and costs, the settlement proceeds are distributed to the class claimants.

The Purpose, Scope, and Limitations on Discovery Proceedings

Discovery is the process whereby parties in a lawsuit can inquire into matters within the knowledge of the opposing party or that party's witnesses. Discovery rules allow inquiry into matters that may lead to relevant information concerning a claim or defense. The scope of inquiry is broad, but courts limit discovery of a party's "work product" (information prepared in anticipation of litigation) or information that is "privileged" (see "The Rules of Evidence" later in this chapter).

Discovery may be accomplished by a party submitting written questions called **interrogatories** to another party and requiring answers to be given under oath. A more common method is by taking an oral **deposition** of a party or that party's witnesses. Such testimony is given under oath, often before a court reporter, and is subject to both direct and cross-examination. A party or witness can be compelled to produce documents for examination.

In recent years many jurisdictions have amended their rules of procedure to allow depositions to be videotaped. One court required that a defendant being sued for injuries resulting from a karate maneuver afford the plaintiff the right to have that maneuver demonstrated and videotaped.[6]

Discovery proceedings often lead to **out-of-court settlements.** To illustrate, a defendant being sued for damages resulting from the plaintiff's injuries will usually take the plaintiff's deposition to determine the extent of those injuries and will depose the plaintiff's physicians to learn the plaintiff's diagnosis and prognosis. Often the defendant will submit interrogatories requiring the plaintiff to itemize all claims for medical expenses, loss of income, and any other compensable items. After determining the plaintiff's injuries and economic losses, the defendant will often institute settlement negotiations.

The evidence developed by discovery processes may ordinarily be used at trial only to contradict or "impeach" the trial testimony of a party or witness. In some instances, however, if a person who has been deposed becomes unavailable for trial, courts may permit the deposition to be introduced as evidence.

Discovery proceedings are susceptible to abuse and the trial judge may step in and exercise control over the extent of the proceedings. When the discovery process becomes burdensome or seeks to obtain privileged materials, for example trade secrets, or an attorney's "work product," a judge can issue a **protective order** limiting the scope of discovery. One criticism of the discovery process is that it has become expensive and time consuming.

Additional Pretrial Procedures

Parties may take depositions to perpetuate evidence in instances when it is unlikely the witness to be deposed will be available for trial. A party may also file a written request that the opposing party admits the genuineness of a document. The trial court can assess costs and attorney's fees against a party who improperly denies the genuineness of a document.

When the mental or physical condition of a party is in controversy, the court may order a party to undergo a mental or physical examination. A report of the examination is made available to each party concerned.

Case Management and Pretrial Conferences

Trial judges often call for a **case management conference** to coordinate the progress of litigation, schedule, and limit discovery. Once a case is ready for trial, the trial judge may call for a pretrial conference with counsel for the parties. A **pretrial conference** is designed to simplify the issues to be tried, obtain admissions of undisputed facts, obtain stipulation as to the genuineness of documentary evidence, agree on the witnesses to be presented and exhibits to be introduced at trial, and set a time for presentation of evidence by each side. Additionally, a trial judge might explore the possibilities of arriving at a settlement of the case.

Will the Case Go to Trial?

Most civil suits are settled or otherwise disposed of before trial. One device available to parties in civil lawsuits is known as a Motion for Summary Final Judgment. No such device existed at common law. Rule 56 of the Federal Rules of Civil Procedure states:

> (a) For Claimant. A party seeking to recover upon a claim, counterclaim, or cross-claim or to obtain a declaratory judgment may, at any time after the expiration of 20 days from the commencement of the action or after service of a motion for summary judgment by the adverse party, move with or without supporting affidavits for a summary judgment in the party's favor upon all or any part thereof.
> (b) For Defending Party. A party against whom a claim counterclaim, or cross-claim is asserted or a declaratory judgment is sought may, at any time, move with or without supporting affidavits for a summary judgment in the party's favor as to all or any part thereof.

By the latter half of the twentieth century, state courts began to include similar provisions in their rules of civil procedure. A party who moves for a **summary judgment** generally does so based on the discovery that has been completed and affidavits submitted with the motion. The theory of the summary judgment procedure is that the right to a trial presupposes a genuine issue of material fact. Thus, the litigation should be terminated when there is no such issue as to material facts, or when, as a matter of law, the party against whom the motion is filed cannot legally recover or cannot legally defend against a claim. In determining whether to grant a summary judgment the court resolves all doubts against the moving party. Summary judgments are particularly difficult to obtain in actions involving a person's negligence and are effectively precluded where a person's intent is material. Still, thousands of lawsuits are terminated at the summary judgment stage, thereby avoiding the time and expense of a trial.

Jury or Bench Trial?

In Chapter 1 we discussed traditional common-law civil actions, where parties were entitled to a jury trial, and cases arising in equity, where the chancellor made decisions without intervention of a jury. In general, courts today follow these practices in civil suits although the boundary between law and equity has become less distinct. The Seventh Amendment to the

U.S. Constitution provides that for suits at common law the right to a **jury trial** is preserved when the value in controversy exceeds $20; however, this requirement applies only to the federal courts. In general, state constitutions preserve the right to a jury trial for common-law civil actions.

In many civil proceedings there is no provision for a jury trial either because they are historically of equity origin or have been created as statutory proceedings unknown to the common law. Among the more common proceedings that were originally cases in equity are those involving domestic relations, suits to rescind contracts, suits to foreclose liens and mortgages, and those seeking an accounting or an injunction. Judges, not juries, hear statutory proceedings to change one's name and to adopt children, most proceedings concerning administration of estates and guardianships and many disputes between lessors and lessees. A trial before a judge without a jury is known as a **bench trial.**

Opinion of the Court . . .

COLGROVE V. BATTIN

413 U.S. 149, 93 S.Ct. 2448, 37 L.Ed.2d 522 (1973)

Mr. Justice Brennan delivered the Opinion of the Court.

. . . The pertinent words of the Seventh Amendment are: "In Suits at common law . . . the right of trial by jury shall be preserved. . . ." On its face, this language is not directed to jury characteristics, such as size, but rather defines the kind of cases for which jury trial is preserved, namely, "suits at common law." And while it is true that "[w]e have almost no direct evidence concerning the intention of the Framers of the seventh amendment itself," the historical setting in which the Seventh Amendment was adopted highlighted a controversy that was generated, not by concern for preservation of jury characteristics at common law, but by fear that the civil jury itself would be abolished unless protected in express words. Almost a century and a half ago, this Court recognized that "[o]ne of the strongest objections originally taken against the constitution of the United States, was the want of an express provision securing the right of trial by jury in civil cases." . . . But the omission of a protective clause from the Constitution was not because an effort was not made to include one. On the contrary, a proposal was made to include a provision in the Constitution to guarantee the right of trial by jury in civil cases but the proposal failed because the States varied widely as to the cases in which civil jury trial was provided, and the proponents of a civil jury guarantee found too difficult the task of fashioning words appropriate to cover the different state practices. The strong pressures for a civil jury provision in the Bill of Rights encountered the same difficulty. Thus, it was agreed that, with no federal practice to draw on and since state practices varied so widely, any compromising language would necessarily have to be general. As a result, although the Seventh Amendment achieved the primary goal of jury trial adherents to incorporate an explicit constitutional protection of the right of trial by jury in civil cases, the right was limited in general words to "suits at common law." We can only conclude, therefore, that by referring to the "common law," the Framers of the Seventh Amendment were concerned with preserving the right of trial by jury in civil cases where it existed at common law, rather than the various incidents of trial by jury. In short, . . . constitutional history reveals no intention on the part of the Framers "to equate the constitutional and common-law characteristics of the jury." . . .

Jury Size

At common law, juries in both civil and criminal cases consisted of 12 persons. In *Colgrove v. Battin* (1973) (excerpted above), the Supreme Court held that federal district court rules authorizing 6-person juries in civil cases were permissible under the Seventh Amendment. The Court distinguished between the right to a jury trial in suits at common law and the incidents of the common-law jury. States have generally followed this approach and most now permit 6-person juries in civil cases.

Jury Selection

State and federal laws prescribe certain basic qualifications for jurors. Statutes commonly require that jurors be at least 18 years of age and residents in the state or district from which they are to be selected. Convicted felons whose civil rights have not been restored are usually excluded from serving on juries. Beyond this, statutes frequently carve out exemptions for expectant mothers, mothers with young children, persons over age 70, physicians, dentists, attorneys, judges, teachers, elected officials, and police, fire, and emergency personnel. The trend has been for states to restrict exemptions from jury duty so that the pool of prospective jurors reflects a cross section of the community.

The goal is to select prospective jurors at random from lists of persons representative of the community. Local officials compile a list of persons qualified to serve as jurors, generally from the rolls of registered voters, driver's license lists, or some combination thereof. From this list prospective jurors are randomly selected and summoned to court. Compensation paid to trial jurors ranges from meager to modest per diem travel and expenses.[7]

The body of persons summoned to be jurors is referred to as the **venire.** After outlining the case to be tried and reciting the names of those expected to participate, the judge may excuse those whose physical disabilities or obvious conflicts of interest based on family relationships or business connections prevent them from serving. The judge swears in the remaining members of the venire to answer questions put to them by the court and counsel. Then six or twelve of these prospective jurors are called at random to take their seats in the jury box where the judge or counsel for each side may ask further questions in a process called the *voir dire.*

The *Voir Dire*

Lawyers for the parties are permitted to challenge prospective jurors either for cause or peremptorily. A challenge is a request that a juror be excused from serving. Challenges are customarily asserted at a stage called the *voir dire* (French, meaning "to tell the truth"). The function of the *voir dire* is to enable the court and counsel to obtain the information necessary to assure selection of a fair and impartial jury. To assist in obtaining background information and thereby expedite the *voir dire* process, trial courts often prepare a series of written questions to be answered by prospective jurors in advance of their appearance in court.

In some courts the trial judge conducts the *voir dire* examination, whereas in others the lawyers perform this function. In either event, the presiding judge exercises broad discretion to keep the questioning within proper bounds. A *voir dire* examination is generally conducted before the six or twelve prospective jurors are initially selected; however, under certain circumstances some courts have allowed examination of individual jurors apart from the collective group.

Obviously, each trial lawyer wants jurors who may be sympathetic to the cause he or she advocates. Trial lawyers have their own peculiar theories on how to conduct a *voir dire* examination, but most would agree that a practical knowledge of psychology is helpful. In recent years some have even retained social scientists for advice and assistance in the jury selection process. The process of excusing prospective jurors is accomplished by counsel exercising challenges, either "for cause" or "peremptorily," that is without assigning a reason.

To determine whether to exercise a challenge, an attorney conducting a *voir dire* examination attempts to determine the attitudes, background, and personalities of prospective jurors. Trial courts limit the questions that may be asked of prospective jurors, depending on the nature of the case. Some areas of questioning are considered very delicate and usually will not be permitted. For example, in 1985 the Supreme Court of Georgia upheld a trial judge's refusal to allow a defendant to ask prospective jurors questions concerning the kinds of books and magazine they read, whether they were members of any political organization, and the kinds of bumper stickers they had on their vehicles.[8]

Challenges for Cause

A **challenge for cause** may be directed to the venire on basis of the panel having been improperly selected, for example, where a lawyer contends that the selection procedures exclude minority members. More commonly, challenges for cause are directed to a prospective juror individually concerning some fact that would disqualify that person from serving on the particular case. Among the more common reasons for disqualification of a prospective juror are having a close relationship with counsel, being significantly involved in the case as a witness, or being involved in some other capacity. The court may excuse any prospective juror who acknowledges having formed an opinion on the merits of the case and who cannot disregard it. Absent unusual circumstances concerning the parties involved in a case, a person would not be excused for cause because of religious or political affiliations.

Peremptory Challenges

Each side is allowed a limited number of **peremptory challenges** that may be exercised on *voir dire* to excuse prospective jurors without stating any reason. The number of peremptory challenges is usually provided by statute or court rules. In federal courts, each party in a civil suit is allowed three peremptory challenges.[9] States vary in the number of peremptory challenges with many following the federal practice.

Historically, lawyers were permitted to exercise peremptory challenges without advancing any reason; however, in the past two decades courts have reassessed this historic freedom. In 1986 the U.S. Supreme Court prohibited the exercise of **racially based peremptory challenges,** holding that such intentional discrimination based on race violates the Equal Protection Clause of the Fourteenth Amendment to the U.S. Constitution.[10] In 1994, the Court resolved conflict among lower federal courts and held that the Equal Protection Clause also prohibits **gender-based peremptory challenges.**[11] These decisions have required lawyers to be quite cautious in their exercise of peremptory challenges. Some commentators believe that peremptory challenges are becoming a relic in trial practice.

Empanelling of the Jury

If a challenge is successful, the prospective juror is excused or "struck" and another prospective juror is seated and questioned until all challenges are exhausted. The jury is then selected. After selection is complete, the jury is sworn in as a body by the judge or the clerk of the court. The jury is advised not to discuss the case until instructed by the court to deliberate. If the court anticipates the trial will likely be protracted, the judge may have one or more alternate jurors selected to serve should any juror become ill or have to respond to an emergency. An alternate juror sits with the jury, but unless substituted for a regular juror, the alternate is excused just before the jury retires to deliberate.

Opening Statements by Counsel

At the beginning of a trial each attorney is afforded the opportunity to make an **opening statement.** In a bench trial (a case tried before a judge without a jury), the opening statement is usually quite brief, and frequently counsel choose to waive it. On the other hand, an opening statement before a jury affords the attorneys an opportunity to "get acquainted" with the jury and outline the case to be presented, identify the participants, explain legal terms, and orient the jury as to how the case will proceed. Counsel members must be careful to inform the jury that their statements are not evidence and that the case must be decided based on the evidence produced during the trial. Experienced trial lawyers emphasize that the opening statement should not be read or given in the form of a speech or lecture, but should "tell a story" informally in narrative form.

Direct and Cross-Examination

By the time a case goes to trial the lawyers representing the parties are highly conversant with the proof required to establish their case or defense. It is the plaintiff's task to effectively establish the case by a **preponderance** (greater weight) **of the evidence.** In most instances counsel present events chronologically, but logic and strategy often dictate another order of proof. The plaintiff's lawyer conducts a **direct examination** of each witness after which the defendant's lawyer has the right of **cross-examination.** This can be followed by redirect and recross examinations.

   The purpose of cross-examination is to weaken or disprove the testimony the witness gave on direct examination. Skillful cross-examination is a hallmark of a successful trial lawyer. Although a juror is inclined to view the cross-examination as spontaneous, effective cross-examination is based on careful advance planning. Lawyers are aided greatly by the information that a witness has disclosed during the pretrial discovery phases. Unlike direct examination, the cross-examiner is permitted to ask leading questions, although the scope of inquiry is generally limited to matters brought out on the direct examination of the witness and any interest, bias, or motive of the witness. If a cross-examiner succeeds in showing that the witness's testimony is inconsistent with a prior statement, or that the witness has previously been convicted of a crime or has a bad reputation in the community for telling the truth, it impeaches the credibility of the witness.

The defendant's lawyer must seek to disprove the plaintiff's contentions and in some instances must prove a specific defense. Consider a lawsuit where the plaintiff seeks damages for personal injuries sustained in an automobile collision. In some states if the defendant proves the plaintiff's actions were a substantial contributing factor, the defendant can defeat the plaintiff's claim; in other states such proof can mitigate the award of damages to the plaintiff.

In most civil trials the witnesses' testimony comprises most of the evidence, although documents and other exhibits, referred to as documentary evidence, are frequently introduced. Medical charts, x-rays, photographs, and mortality tables showing life expectancy are often introduced in personal injury and wrongful death actions. Increasingly courts admit surveillance films or videotapes to confirm or contradict an injured party's claims. When a case involves contract rights, the parties will introduce written contracts, cancelled checks, memoranda, and business records. In a boundary dispute, counsel usually introduce deeds and land surveys.

Expert Witnesses

If scientific, technical, or other specialized knowledge will assist the court or jury in understanding the evidence presented or in determining an essential fact, a party may present expert testimony. An **expert witness** is one who by knowledge, skill, experience, training, or education is qualified to present testimony and offer opinion on a particular subject. Lawyers are given the opportunity to cross-examine witnesses offered as experts before the court rules as to whether the witness can testify as an expert. In many cases, lawyers for the parties stipulate as to the qualifications of a witness offered as an expert. Physicians are commonly called to testify in personal injury and wrongful death cases. Engineers testify in cases involving patents and controversies over claims involving mechanical defects of products. In commercial litigation and antitrust cases it is common to call accountants, economists, and statisticians. College professors are frequent expert witnesses. Whereas lay witnesses are restricted in voicing opinions, experts are permitted to give their opinions, often in response to hypothetical questions asked by lawyers.

Throughout most of the twentieth century, American courts approached questions relating to the validity of an expert's opinion by applying the "general acceptance" or *Frye* test.[12] If the principle expounded by the expert met with general acceptance in the scientific community, then the testimony was admitted. However, in 1993, the U.S. Supreme Court in *Daubert v. Merrell Dow Pharmaceuticals, Inc.*[13] rejected the *Frye* test. The Court held that admissibility of scientific evidence is controlled by the Federal Rules of Evidence and must be based on several factors, including whether the evidence can be tested and be subjected to peer review. Because the Court's ruling is not one of constitutional dimension, state courts are not required to follow it. Indeed, most state courts still adhere to the *Frye* test as a standard for admitting scientific evidence.

When the Plaintiff Rests

When the plaintiff's lawyer has completed presentation of the plaintiff's case, the lawyer "rests." At that point the defense lawyer in a jury trial will often move for a **directed verdict** for the defense. This motion, sometimes called a motion for **involuntary dismissal** in a

CASE IN POINT

ADMISSIBILITY OF SCIENTIFIC EVIDENCE IN FEDERAL COURTS

Daubert v. Merrell Dow Pharmaceuticals, Inc.

United States Supreme Court
509 U.S. 579, 113 S.Ct. 2786, 125 L.Ed.2d 469 (1993)

Jason Daubert and Eric Schuller brought suit against a major pharmaceutical company, alleging that their serious birth defects were caused by their mothers' prenatal ingestion of Bendectin, a prescription drug used to treat nausea. The federal district judge granted summary judgment for the defendant based on an expert's affidavit concluding that Bendectin had not been shown to cause birth defects. The judge rejected expert testimony introduced by the plaintiffs, determining that it did not meet the "general acceptance" test for the admission of expert testimony set forth in *Frye v. United States* (1923). The Court of Appeals affirmed. The Supreme Court re-versed, holding that the Federal Rules of Evidence, not the *Frye* decision, provide the standard for admitting expert scientific testimony in federal court. Writing for the Court, Justice Blackmun concluded that " '[g]eneral acceptance' is not a necessary precondition to the admissibility of scientific evidence under the Federal Rules of Evidence, but the Rules of Evidence . . . do assign to the trial judge the task of ensuring that an expert's testimony both rests on a reliable foundation and is relevant to the task at hand." Under this ruling federal district judges must be the arbiters of what is legitimate and what is "junk" science.

bench trial case, asks the trial judge to rule that the evidence presented by the plaintiff, taken most favorably to the plaintiff, is insufficient to support a verdict for the plaintiff. If the court rules with the defense, then the action is terminated. If, as in most cases, the motion is denied, then the defense is allowed to present its evidence and at the conclusion of the trial may again seek dismissal on the same ground.

The Case for the Defense and the Rebuttals

The defense lawyer proceeds to present the defendant's case much as previously outlined for the plaintiff's lawyer, offering witnesses and often including experts and documentary evidence. If the defense has asserted a specific defense, then it must establish that defense by the preponderance (greater weight) of the evidence.

The plaintiff is allowed to introduce evidence in **rebuttal** to the evidence offered by the defendant. In turn, the defendant is usually allowed to rebut the plaintiff's rebuttal evidence. Rebuttal evidence is much less lengthy than the parties' main cases and often consists of the testimony of one key witness.

The Court Instructs the Jury

At the close of all evidence in a jury trial, it is customary for the trial judge to confer with counsel outside the presence of the jury concerning the instructions on the law the judge will give to the jury. The trial court announces its intention to give certain standard instructions and offers to supplement them with specific instructions to be chosen from those submitted by counsel. A party is entitled to have the jury instructed on the law applicable to any legitimate issue that is supported by the evidence. **Jury instructions** are settled in advance of closing arguments by counsel so each can argue with assurance of how the judge will instruct the jury.

Closing Arguments

Because a judge is trained in evaluating evidence, counsel in bench trials frequently waive their right to make **closing arguments;** otherwise, their arguments are generally quite brief. In jury trials, however, lawyers place great importance on their closing arguments. Such arguments are designed to assist the jury in recalling and evaluating the evidence and in drawing inferences therefrom. Many lawyers begin by recapitulating the evidence in the light most favorable to their client. After that the lawyer for each side entreats the jury to rule in favor of their client. Counsel may comment on the weight of the evidence and the credibility of the witnesses, but may not state a personal belief about the merits of the case, or refer to any matters—other than those of common, everyday knowledge—that have not been introduced in evidence. Improper comments by counsel may result in a **mistrial** if the judge determines that they have improperly prejudiced the jury.

The Jury Deliberates and Returns its Verdict

When directed to deliberate, the jurors are escorted to their quarters by a court bailiff. In some cases the judge orders the jury sequestered, which means the jury must remain together until it reaches its verdict. **Sequestration of the jury,** however, is uncommon in civil cases. Once in the jury room, their first order of business is to elect a foreperson; then they are ready to commence their deliberations. Because jury deliberations are secret, we can only speculate about the reasoning processes of jurors. We do know, however, that juries usually take a preliminary vote shortly after electing a foreperson. On occasion the jury will ask the court to reconvene to answer a question before concluding deliberations; the judge, after conferring with counsel, attempts to answer such questions succinctly so that their deliberations may be completed. If the jury is unable to reach a verdict, this is known as **hung jury,** and the court declares a mistrial.

Jury verdicts in civil cases may be either general or special. An example of a **general verdict** is one the jury returns finding the defendant liable to the plaintiff and assessing the plaintiff's damages as $10,000 or a verdict simply finding the defendant not liable to the plaintiff. A **special verdict** is one where the jury specifically answers questions posed by the court on the form of verdict submitted to the jury. For example, many states have comparative negligence laws. In such states, the plaintiff's award is based on the percentage of fault the jury assigns against the defendant. A suit for damages arising out of an automobile accident is typical. The jury may find the defendant at fault, but may answer a special verdict question that the plaintiff was also at fault to the extent of say 25 percent. If the jury determined the plaintiff should receive $20,000 damages those damages would be reduced by 25 percent and the court would award the plaintiff $15,000.

Upon return of the jury's verdict the lawyers may exercise their right to poll the jury; that is, to ask each juror: "Is this your verdict?" Upon completion of this procedure the trial judge usually discharges the jury. The losing party may then ask the trial judge for a new trial based on a claim of error in the trial proceedings. Such motions are rarely granted, but they can have an important bearing on issues that the losing party can raise on appeal. In addition, the court will generally award the prevailing party the court costs and, in some instances, attorney's fees.

Judgment Notwithstanding the Verdict

Under the common law, a judge in a civil trial could not set aside a jury verdict and enter judgment for the other party based on the judge's own assessment of the evidence. If the judge erred in failing to direct a verdict for the defense prior to submitting the case to the jury, the only remedy was to order a new trial. Under the Federal Rules of Civil Procedure and most state rules, judges can, as a matter of law, enter a judgment contrary to the jury's verdict.[14] However, a judge may not do this if there is a substantial factual basis for the jury's verdict.[15]

THE RULES OF EVIDENCE

Rules of evidence govern the admissibility of factual information before a court. They are largely based on the common law and historically have been found in appellate court decisions. In the latter half of the twentieth century it became common for legislative bodies and courts to codify the rules of evidence applicable to both civil and criminal cases. In this section we discuss the general rules of evidence with emphasis on civil cases. In Chapter 10 we amplify those rules as they relate to criminal cases.

Judicial Notice

Certain matters that are beyond argument are accepted by a court without proof. Courts accept such facts, as well as laws, by taking **judicial notice.** Courts customarily take judicial notice of the calendar, names of certain public officials, the boundaries of a geographical area, and other undisputed facts well known in the jurisdiction where the court sits. Courts also take judicial notice of laws, rules of procedure, and the rules of evidence.

Evidentiary Presumptions

An **evidentiary presumption** is an assumption of fact that the law makes from the existence of another fact or facts, although unproven by evidence. These are evidentiary devices designed to aid a party who has the burden of proof. Under this type of presumption, once evidence establishes a fact, the judge and jury may infer something else is true, provided there is a rational connection between the established fact and the presumed fact. In effect this means that if a party proves certain facts, then the judge or jury accept the presumed fact as proven unless evidence rebuts the presumed fact. Most presumptions are rebuttable. For example, there is a **rebuttable presumption** that a child born during marriage is the child of the marital partners. There is a rebuttable presumption that a properly stamped, addressed, and mailed letter reached its intended recipient.[16] A party who rebuts the presumption has the burden of proving the presumption false.

Classifications of Evidence

There are several classifications of evidence. First, evidence may be real or testimonial. **Real evidence** consists of maps, blood samples, x-rays, photographs, fingerprints, knives, guns, and other tangible items. **Testimonial evidence** consists of sworn statements of witnesses. Watching a television drama might give the impression that a trial consists largely of real evidence, but the great majority of evidence presented in civil and criminal trials comes from the mouths of the witnesses, both lay and expert.

Next, evidence may be direct or indirect. **Direct evidence** is that which directly proves a fact in issue and includes **eyewitness testimony.** In contrast, **indirect evidence** only tends to establish a fact in issue and usually consists of **circumstantial evidence.** In a civil trial, a witness who actually saw an automobile accident would be giving direct evidence. In contrast, testimony by a witness who before the accident saw the defendant driving the vehicle in the accident would be giving circumstantial evidence tending to indicate that the defendant was the driver. Testimony that reveals that the defendant's fingerprints were found on a window pane of a house shortly after it was broken into is circumstantial evidence and depending on the circumstances, it may be inferred that the defendant entered the house through that window. The admissibility of circumstantial evidence is well established in American law. Contrary to popular belief, there is no real difference in the weight given circumstantial as opposed to real evidence.

Requirements of Admissibility

Before a witness testifies in a judicial proceeding, the witness takes an oath to swear or affirm to tell the truth. The common-law rule no longer bars a witness from testifying because the witness does not profess belief in a Supreme Being. Where a witness does not understand the English language, the court appoints an interpreter who must take an oath to properly interpret the questions asked and the witness's answers. Before evidence may be admitted in court, whether real or testimonial and whether direct or circumstantial, it must be relevant and must come from a competent witness or credible source.

Relevancy
To be admissible in court proceedings, evidence must be relevant. **Relevant evidence** is that which tends to prove or disprove a material fact. Consequently evidence that is relevant in one case may not necessarily be relevant in another. Trial judges have considerable discretion in determining whether evidence is relevant.

Certain relevant evidence may not be admissible in court proceedings. It may be needlessly cumulative. The following are examples where the probative value of relevant evidence is outweighed by the prejudice that would likely ensue against the party against whom the evidence is offered:

- A person's character is generally held to be inadmissible to prove that a person behaved in a certain way.
- An offer to compromise a disputed claim or statements made during settlement negotiations is inadmissible.
- The fact that the defendant carries liability insurance is generally inadmissible in a suit seeking to recover damages based on a defendant's alleged negligence.

Competency

To be admissible in court, evidence must also be **competent.** At common law, persons who had an interest in the case were not permitted to testify, and a person younger than age 14 was presumed to be incapable of testifying. Statutes and court decisions have eliminated these disqualifications in the United States. A witness, regardless of age or interest, who has the ability to understand the nature and obligation of taking an oath to tell the truth is presumed to be competent. A party who asserts to the contrary must establish that the witness is not competent to testify. Even a person adjudged incompetent might be permitted to testify if the court finds that person is lucid at the time of testifying. In the case of a very young child it is the judge's duty to determine if the child has sufficient maturity to understand, remember, and relate facts and understands the obligation of taking an oath to tell the truth. In some instances a child as young as five or six has been allowed to testify in cases of child abuse or rape of a parent. Trial judges have broad discretion to make such a determination.

Privileges

A witness may be competent to testify and may be in a position to offer relevant evidence, yet in certain instances the court may not hear the evidence. Since early common-law, courts have decided that it is in the interest of society that certain forms of communication remain confidential. Therefore, certain facts that may be relevant are not admissible in court proceedings because they are **privileged communications.** The most common privileges include:

- **Attorney-client privilege.** A communication between an attorney and client that is not intended to be disclosed to a third person is considered privileged, subject to certain exceptions. There is no privilege as to any communication by the client informing the attorney of intent to commit a crime or to perpetrate a fraud.
- **Marital privilege.** Communications between spouses intended to be confidential are privileged. The privilege emanates from the common law and is based on promoting and preserving domestic harmony and the repugnance against convicting one person through the testimony of another who shares intimate secrets of domestic life. The temptation to perjure is another consideration. The privilege not only allows a spouse not to disclose communications, but also allows one spouse to prevent the other spouse from disclosing them. Most courts hold

that neither divorce nor death invalidates the privilege. But suppose a husband confessed to his wife that he had stolen building materials from a job where he was working. The wife would be prohibited from testifying to that conversation. On the other hand, the wife could testify that her husband arrived home with some building materials. Like other privileges there are exceptions. The privilege does not apply when one spouse sues the other, when litigation arises out of child abuse, or when a spouse offers testimony on behalf of a spouse who is a defendant. A few jurisdictions have extended the privilege by making it applicable to confidential communications between a parent and minor child.

- **Clergy privilege.** Communications made by a person to a clergyperson seeking spiritual assistance are privileged. Generally priests, ministers, and rabbis are prohibited from testifying about matters related to them in confidence by a penitent.
- *Additional privileges.* States frequently have added privileges such as between an accountant and client, a physician and patient, and a psychotherapist and patient. Moreover, courts frequently allow a limited privilege not to disclose trade secrets.

Expert Witnesses

Today **forensic experts** in nearly every field make a specialty of testifying in court. To qualify as an expert, a witness must present proper credentials and be received by the trial court as an expert. After one side offers a witness as an expert, opposing counsel may cross-examine the prospective witness about the witness's qualifications. Thus, a physician who is to give evidence as to the cause of death of someone is first asked to relate his or her educational background and experience in the specialized area of medical practice in question. The trial judge has considerable discretion in determining whether a witness is to be received as an expert.

Unlike lay witnesses, expert witnesses may respond to hypothetical questions and may express opinions within the realm of their expertise. Fingerprint identification, ballistics tests, handwriting exemplars, and medical tests have been prominent among areas where expert evidence is commonly received in criminal cases. More recently evidence of speed detection devices and devices to test blood-alcohol content have become commonplace in civil and criminal trials.

An expert who has knowledge from personal observation may testify on that basis. For example, a psychiatrist who has examined the accused may offer an opinion as to the accused's sanity. If the expert is not acquainted with the person or subject from personal observation, the expert can base an opinion upon a **hypothetical question** that assumes the existence of facts the evidence tends to establish.

Testimony Generally Considered Unreliable

The majority of courts have held that hypnotically enhanced testimony is not sufficiently reliable to be admissible. In 1987, the Supreme Court held that excluding hypnotically enhanced testimony, when applied to prevent an accused from testifying as to one's own posthypnotic recall, violated the constitutional right to testify on one's own behalf.[17] Accordingly, the position of the majority of courts to exclude all hypnotically induced testimony should not prevent an accused from testifying to the accused's own posthypnotic recall.

A polygraph is a device that records the subject's physiological activities, such as blood pressure and heartbeat, as the subject is questioned by an examiner. The examiner poses certain questions and records the subject's responses. Historically, federal and state courts have declined to admit **polygraph evidence** on the ground that the reliability of polygraph testing has not been scientifically demonstrated to such a degree of certainty as to establish its reliability. However, some courts allow results of polygraph testing to be admitted in court on stipulation of counsel for both parties.

Objections

Anyone who has observed a trial, or even a television drama depicting one, is familiar with the advocates frequently addressing the court, "Your honor, I object . . . " To this, the objecting lawyer may add "on the ground that the testimony is irrelevant." This is called a **general objection.** Or, the lawyer may make a **specific objection** by adding, "because the testimony sought would be hearsay," "because the answer calls for an opinion of the witness which the witness is not qualified to give," or one or more other grounds for specific objections. We consider some of the more common grounds for objections below.

Hearsay Evidence

Hearsay evidence refers to an oral or written statement by a person, other than the one testifying in court. The general rule is often stated as: A witness may not testify as to a statement made by another if that statement is offered as proof of the matter asserted. Thus, a witness who testifies, "I know the defendant was home on the night of March 13th because my sister told me so" would be giving hearsay testimony. The hearsay rule has many exceptions. Sometimes a hearsay statement is admissible to prove something other than the truth of the statement itself. A party's out-of-court statement is generally considered an exception to the hearsay rule if it is an admission, confession, or some other statement against that party's interest. The following are among the many exceptions to the hearsay rule.

- **Spontaneous or excited utterances.** Where a statement is spontaneously made to describe or explain some event at or immediately following the event, it is deemed sufficiently trustworthy to be an exception to the hearsay rule.
- **Dying declarations.** A person's dying declaration is a statement made while the declarant believed that death was imminent. In 1961, the Maryland Supreme Court held such a statement might even be in response to a question asked by a bystander thus not requiring the usual spontaneity.[18]
- **Reputation.** Evidence of a person's reputation in the community; evidence of births, deaths, and other data contained in old family records.
- **Business and public records.** Business records kept in the ordinary course of business, hospital and medical records, and authenticated public records are exceptions to the hearsay rule.

- Statements made for medical diagnosis. Because there is a slight chance that a person who is seeking treatment will relate incorrect facts to a physician, statements made to secure medical treatment are generally held to be an exception to the hearsay rule.

The Best Evidence Rule

Ordinarily, the best evidence of a transaction must be offered in court. The **best evidence rule** applies to writings and means that an original document must be offered unless the party who offers a copy can present a plausible explanation of why the original is not available. For example, the original contract being sued upon should be produced rather than photocopies. With modern photocopying processes, lawyers often stipulate that such copies of original documents be admitted in court.

Opinion Evidence

A lay witness is supposed to testify regarding facts within the witness's personal knowledge. In addition, lay witnesses are generally permitted to testify about such matters perceived through their physical senses and matters that are within the common knowledge of most people, such as speed of a vehicle, sizes, distances, or appearance of a person. They cannot give **opinion evidence** on matters beyond the common experience and understanding of laypersons. To illustrate: A driver can give an estimate of the speed of a vehicle observed traveling on the street. But a witness must be qualified as an expert to be permitted to testify as to the speed of a car based on observation of the car's skid marks on the pavement. Such an opinion must generally be based on facts perceived by the witness and not on hearsay statements.

APPELLATE PROCEDURE

Appellate courts perform dual functions in the civil and criminal process: **error correction** and **lawmaking.** Intermediate federal or state appellate courts review most civil and criminal appeals, although in the less populous states the highest court of the state handles routine appeals. In these routine appeals, the primary function of appellate courts is to correct trial court errors. Appellate review is designed to ensure that substantive justice has been accomplished under constitutional standards of due process of law. Because of gaps in the statutory law and the inevitable need to interpret both statutory and constitutional provisions, appellate courts in effect must "make law." This lawmaking function is more characteristic of the highest courts than of intermediate appellate tribunals.

To the layperson, the jurisdictional requisites and procedures of appellate courts appear complex. Although these procedures vary in detail, they essentially follow the same basic path for both civil and criminal appeals. In some instances a party who desires an appeal must first file a motion asking the trial court to order a new trial. This is often a pro forma measure, but it affords the trial judge an opportunity to review the defendant's claim of error and award a new trial if necessary. In some appellate courts a motion for a new trial may be a prerequisite to challenging whether the evidence was sufficient to sustain the lower court's judgment.

Appellate courts possess both original and appellate jurisdiction. Most of the work of an appellate court concerns its appellate jurisdiction, that is, the power to review decisions of lower tribunals. We first discuss this phase of appellate procedure. At the conclusion of the chapter we briefly mention the original jurisdiction of appellate courts.

Filing the Appeal

Once a party has determined the correct forum for an appeal or a petition for discretionary review, a series of steps follows. First, the **notice of appeal** or petition for review must be filed in the appropriate court within a specified period of time. The courts tend to strictly enforce the time requirement because it is this notice or petition that confers jurisdiction on the appellate court to act on the case.

Rule 4 of the Federal Rules of Appellate Procedure provides that an appeal in a civil case must be filed within 30 days after the entry of the judgment. In state courts an aggrieved party usually has 30 days after entry of judgment to file an appeal. The filing of a notice of appeal must be accompanied by the payment of a required filing fee, although this fee can be waived in cases when an indigent files a motion to proceed *in forma pauperis* ("in the manner of a pauper").

Filing Petitions for Discretionary Review

A party to a civil suit or a criminal defendant is generally limited to one appeal as a matter of right; however; additional review may be available on a discretionary basis with a higher court. In the U.S. Supreme Court and most state supreme courts, discretionary review occurs through the grant of a **writ of certiorari.** Rule 13 of the Rules of the United States Supreme Court states that a "petition for a writ of certiorari . . . shall be in time when it is filed . . . within 90 days after the entry of the judgment" of the lower court. State supreme courts have similar rules but usually allow less time to seek discretionary review.

"Cert petitions," as petitions of certiorari are commonly called, are granted at the discretion of the reviewing court. In deciding whether to exercise its discretion, the U.S. Supreme Court looks to whether there is a **substantial federal question** involved. If so, the Court is then interested in whether the petitioner has exhausted all other remedies available. In deciding whether to grant certiorari, the Court follows the **rule of four,** meaning that at least four of the nine justices must vote to place a case on the docket. The highest state courts usually follow a similar procedure; that is, they require a certain number of justices to agree to grant discretionary review.

Motions

During the early stages of the appellate process, counsel use **motions** to draw the court's immediate attention to procedural matters outside the routine of the appellate process. Counsel may request additional time to meet deadlines for filing briefs or move for expedited consideration of an appeal. By appropriate motions, counsel may request to sever or consolidate multiple appeals. Upon a showing of good cause, an appellate court may stay enforcement of a lower court judgment pending resolution of the appeal.

Filing of Briefs

Filing a notice of appeal or a petition for discretionary review sets in motion a series of procedural steps governed by the rules of appellate procedure of the federal or state appellate court. It is incumbent on the appellant or petitioner to have the clerk of the trial court forward to the appellate tribunal certified copies of pertinent records and transcripts of testimony relevant to the issues to be raised on appeal. Beyond this, procedures vary somewhat depending largely on whether the appeal is one of right or whether the defendant is seeking discretionary relief.

The party taking an appeal is called the **appellant;** the responding party is known as the **appellee.** In an appeal of right, the appellant files an **initial brief** to summarize the legal posture and the factual background of the case in the lower tribunal. Briefs are the principal instruments used to persuade the appellate court to reverse, affirm, or modify the decision being appealed. The extent of background information contained in the briefs depends on the points to be presented to the appellate court. Briefs are heavily laden with citations to constitutional provisions, statutes, and court decisions that the advocates regard as persuasive. The appellee is permitted to respond by filing an **answer brief,** and the appellant may then file a **reply brief.** The whole process resembles the order of a formal debate where the affirmative presents its case, followed by the negative and a rebuttal by the affirmative.

Where a petitioner seeks discretionary review, the appellate court must first decide whether to accept or deny the request to take jurisdiction. If the court determines to proceed on the petition, it will order all affected parties (respondents) to furnish the court a written response. As in an appeal of right, often the **petitioner** is permitted to file a reply to that response. Counsel must always furnish copies of briefs and other materials to their adversaries.

Oral Argument

After the appellate court has reviewed briefs, it may schedule **oral argument** where counsel for both parties appear. Typically, appellate courts conduct oral arguments in about half the cases they decide. During oral argument, counsel for both parties may summarize their positions orally and then respond to questions from the bench. Usually each side is given 15 to 30 minutes for an oral presentation. Increasingly oral arguments are punctuated by questions from the bench. Indeed, today many oral arguments take the form of a dialogue rather than that of a structured presentation.

The Judicial Conference

Unlike a trial court, where a single judge and jury decide the case, appellate decisions are made by panels of three or more judges without a jury. Thus, appellate judges customarily confer on disposition of appeals. The **judicial conference** is regarded as an essential part of the collegial process that distinguishes the appellate role from that of the trial court. If there has been oral argument, it is common for the panel of judges who heard the case to confer shortly thereafter. At that time the panel frequently attempts to determine the disposition of the appeal but, in some instances, may find it necessary to further canvass the record or call upon counsel or the court's own staff lawyers for additional legal research. Where there has been no oral argument, the panel of judges assigned to the case usually confers after each judge has had the opportunity to review the briefs and pertinent records and the results of any research assignments given to the court's legal staff.

The Judgment of the Court

Essentially, an appellate court has three options in addressing a case before it. First, it may dismiss the appeal. This is uncommon in appeals of right, unless the appeal is untimely. Dismissal is more common in cases of discretionary review. Even after an appeal has been fully argued, the U.S. Supreme Court will sometimes dismiss a petition for certiorari as having been improvidently granted. When an appeal or cert petition is dismissed, the judgment of the lower tribunal remains undisturbed. The second option is to **affirm** the decision being reviewed, which preserves the judgment of the lower tribunal. The third option is to **reverse** the judgment of the lower tribunal. A reversal is usually accompanied by an order to **remand** the case to the lower tribunal for further proceedings consistent with the higher court's opinion. When a court of last resort remands a case to an intermediate appellate court, the latter must reconsider the case in light of the higher court's decision.

Appellate Court Opinions

After an appellate court has arrived at a decision, it remains for the court to issue an opinion announcing its decision. Some opinions simply announce the court's decision; others are quite lengthy in considering the arguments of counsel and articulating the reasons for the court's decision. An individual judge or justice generally prepares the court's opinion. If responsibility for preparation of an opinion has not been previously given to one judge, that responsibility is usually assigned at conference by the senior judge or the senior judge voting with the majority of the panel. A professional staff of law clerks and secretaries assists judges.

There are two basic types of appellate court opinions: per curiam and signed. A **per curiam opinion** represents the appellate court as a whole; it is not attributed to any individual judge or group of judges on the court. More commonly appellate courts announce their decisions by an **opinion of the court** signed by one judge and joined by other judges comprising a majority. A judge who agrees with the court's decision but wishes to address or emphasize certain arguments not addressed or emphasized in the opinion of the court may write a separate **concurring opinion**. Sometimes, a judge writes an opinion **concurring in the judgment** only, meaning the judge supports the decision of the court, but for reasons other than those articulated in the court's opinion. A judge who disagrees with the decision of the court may write a **dissenting opinion.**

Publication of Appellate Decisions

Most decisions of appellate courts in America are published in books known as **reporters.** The publication of appellate decisions plays an important role in the development of the law, because judges and lawyers regularly consult the case reporters for guidance in pending cases.

Decisions of the U.S. Supreme Court are officially published in the *United States Reports* (abbreviated U.S.). Two private organizations also report these decisions in hardcover volumes. The *Supreme Court Reporter* (abbreviated S.Ct.) is published by West, and *Lawyers Edition,* now in its second series (abbreviated L.Ed.2d), is published by the Lawyers Cooperative Publishing Company. Although the three reporters have somewhat different editorial features, the opinions of the Supreme Court are reproduced identically in all three reporters.

References to judicial decisions found in the reporters are called **citations.** United States Supreme Court decisions are often cited to all three publications: for example, *Felker v. Turpin,* 518 U.S. 1051, 116 S.Ct. 2333, 135 L.Ed.2d 827 (1996).

Since 1889, the decisions of the U.S. Courts of Appeals have been published in West's *Federal Reporter,* now in its third series (abbreviated F.3d). Decisions of federal district (trial) courts are published in West's *Federal Supplement* (abbreviated F. Supp.). A citation to a case in *Federal Reporter* will read, for example, *Newman v. United States,* 817 F.2d 635 (10th Cir. 1987). This refers to a 1987 case reported in volume 817, page 635 of the *Federal Reporter,* second series, decided by the U.S. Court of Appeals for the Tenth Circuit. A citation to *United States v. Klopfenstine,* 673 F. Supp. 356 (W.D. Mo. 1987), refers to a 1987 federal district court decision from the western district of Missouri reported in volume 673, page 356 of the *Federal Supplement.*

Additional federal reporters publish the decisions from other federal courts (e.g., bankruptcy and military appeals), but the federal reporters referred to earlier are those most frequently used in specialized legal research.

The Regional Reporters

The decisions of the highest state courts (usually but not always called supreme courts) and the decisions of other state appellate courts (usually referred to as intermediate appellate courts) are found in seven regional reporters, West's *California Reporter,* and the *New York Supplement.* Regional reporters, with their abbreviations in parentheses, include decisions from the following states:

- *Atlantic Reporter* (A. and A.2d): Maine, Vermont, New Hampshire, Connecticut, Rhode Island, Pennsylvania, New Jersey, Maryland, Delaware, and the District of Columbia
- *North Eastern Reporter* (N.E. and N.E.2d): Illinois, Indiana, Massachusetts, New York (court of last resort only), and Ohio
- *North Western Reporter* (N.W. and N.W.2d): North Dakota, South Dakota, Nebraska, Minnesota, Iowa, Michigan, and Wisconsin
- *Pacific Reporter* (P. and P.2d): Washington, Oregon, California, Montana, Idaho, Nevada, Utah, Arizona, Wyoming, Colorado, New Mexico, Kansas, Oklahoma, Alaska, and Hawaii
- *Southern Reporter* (So. and So.2d): Florida, Alabama, Mississippi, and Louisiana
- *South Eastern Reporter* (S.E. and S.E.2d): Virginia, West Virginia, North Carolina, South Carolina, and Georgia
- *South Western Reporter* (S.W. and S.W.2d): Texas, Missouri, Arkansas, Kentucky, and Tennessee

The following examples of citation forms appear in some of the regional reporters:

- *State v. Hogan,* 480 So.2d 288 (La. 1985). This refers to a 1985 decision of the Louisiana Supreme Court found in volume 480, page 288 of the *Southern Reporter,* second series.
- *Molien v. Kaiser Foundation Hospitals,* 616 P.2d 813 (Cal. 1980). This refers to a 1980 decision of the California Supreme Court found in volume 616, page 813 of the *Pacific Reporter,* second series.
- *Tinsley v. Tinsley,* 512 S.W.2d 74 (Tex. Civ. App. 1974). This refers to a 1974 decision of the Texas Civil Court of Appeals found in volume 512, page 74 of the *South Western Reporter,* second series.

Syllabi, Headnotes, and Key Numbers

The National Reporter System and the regional reporters contain not only the official text of each reported decision but also a brief summary of the decision, called the *syllabus,* and one or more topically indexed *headnotes.* These headnotes briefly describe the principles of law expounded by the court and are indexed by a series of topic *key numbers.* West assigns these key numbers to specific points of decisional law. For instance, decisions dealing with first-degree murder are classified under the topic "homicide" and assigned a key number for each particular aspect of that crime. Thus a homicide case dealing with the intent requirement in first-degree murder may be classified as: "Homicide 9—Intent and design to effect death." Using this key number system, a researcher can locate headnotes of various appellate decisions on this aspect of homicide and is, in turn, led to relevant decisional law.

Motions for Rehearing

Rules of appellate procedure uniformly permit the filing of a motion asking the appellate court to reconsider its decision in a given case. A **motion for rehearing** is designed to address some misstatement of material fact or to direct the court's attention to an overlooked or misapprehended proposition of law. In the U.S. Courts of Appeals, and in many state appellate courts, where cases are decided by panels of judges, a party may request that all judges of the court participate in an **en banc rehearing.** The likelihood of an appellate court granting a motion for en banc rehearing is greater when there are conflicting opinions between or among panels within the court. Appellate courts view many motions for rehearing as little more than attempts by dissatisfied parties to have another chance to persuade the court of their position. Accordingly, motions for rehearing are seldom granted.

Original Jurisdiction of Appellate Courts

As noted at the beginning of this chapter, appellate courts also possess original jurisdiction. This power enables appellate courts to issue writs to either mandate or prohibit certain proceedings in lower tribunals and to cause persons holding someone in custody to show cause why that person should not be released. These **original writs** include **mandamus,** a writ commanding that a lower tribunal or government official take certain nondiscretionary action; **prohibition**, a writ that orders a lower tribunal to cease exercising jurisdiction; and **habeas corpus**, a writ that requires the custodian of someone to either release the person or show cause why the court should not order the person released. Although habeas corpus is a civil writ, it is employed more frequently in a criminal law context. We discuss this writ further in Chapter 10.

CONCLUSION

Civil procedure enables courts to hear and resolve disputes in an orderly and fair manner. The rules of evidence assure litigants that courts will uniformly apply known principles to determine proof in a nonprejudical manner. Appellate procedures furnish litigants a means of correcting errors and provide an accountability mechanism in the judicial system. Because these rules are published in advance, counsel who are trained in law can assist litigants to avoid litigation by evaluating their claims and defenses. When amicable settlements cannot be arranged, counsel can enter the judicial arena with a sense of predictability.

SUMMARY OF KEY CONCEPTS

A civil lawsuit is instituted by a plaintiff filing a complaint in state or federal court. The threshold issue is determining the judicial forum that has jurisdiction. Suits involve a variety of claims, including matters relating to contracts, business, torts, property, and family matters discussed in previous chapters. A plaintiff seeks damages or other relief, but in some instances the plaintiff seeks a declaration of their rights. In other instances, the plaintiff(s) bring "class actions" on behalf of numerous plaintiffs or against a number of defendants. Class actions often play a significant role in society. After a plaintiff files suit, and once the defendant(s) are served process according to law, the defendant(s) are afforded an opportunity to challenge the claims asserted.

Most lawsuits are settled or dismissed before trial. Settlements often occur after extensive pretrial preparation involving discovery of evidence. Other cases come on for trial either before a judge in a bench trial or before a jury with a judge presiding. Jury selection is an important stage of a trial and counsel are allowed to challenge prospective jurors for causes that would disqualify a juror from sitting on a case. In addition, lawyers may exercise a limited number of peremptory challenges to remove a certain number of jurors without cause; however, such challenges cannot be based on gender or exercised in a racially discriminatory way. A lawyer is permitted to make opening and closing statements to summarize his or her case; however, judges and juries must decide cases based on applying the law to the evidence presented.

Courts adjudicate disputes based on procedures and rules of evidence known in advance to litigants. We have endeavored to give the student an overview of judicial notice and various classes of evidence, the meaning of *relevancy* and *competency*, and other basic rules of evidence. The rules of evidence are complex and have many exceptions, and there are privileges against testifying. The testimony of lay and expert witnesses, presented through direct and cross-examination, provide the bulk of evidence in a trial. Juries hear arguments of counsel, deliberate, and return verdicts, which result in courts issuing judgments.

Appellate courts correct errors of lower tribunals and "make law" where necessary to "fill in gaps" in the law. They hear certain appeals as a matter of an aggrieved litigant's right, and, in other instances, grant discretionary review. Counsel file briefs and, in many instances, orally argue their contentions. Unlike trial courts, which usually are presided over by one judge, an appellate court usually sits in panels of three judges, or in the case of the highest state courts and the U.S. Supreme Court, sit en banc. Appellate court decisions frequently include opinions on the law that are published in volumes widely used by lawyers.

QUESTIONS FOR THOUGHT AND DISCUSSION

1. How is a complaint for damages instituted in a court of law?
2. What is meant by service of process? What are the various means by which service of process is accomplished?
3. What is a pretrial conference designed to accomplish?
4. What pretrial procedures are generally available to lawyers to learn facts within the knowledge of an opposing party or witnesses?
5. Should a trial judge be allowed to offer an opinion to the jury on the quality of evidence presented at trial?
6. What is meant by (a) a peremptory challenge; (b) a challenge for cause?
7. What restrictions has the U.S. Supreme Court placed on the use of peremptory challenges to jurors?
8. Name four major exceptions to the rule that hearsay testimony is not allowed in a trial.
9. What purposes are served by opening statements and closing arguments?
10. To what extent is a layperson permitted to offer an opinion in a civil trial?
11. What are the chief functions of an appellate court?
12. What are the key steps in the progress of an appeal?

KEY TERMS

civil procedure	general damages	default
common-law pleading	special damages	default judgment
rules of evidence	nominal damages	answer
appellate procedure	punitive damages	counterclaim
complaint	declaratory relief	cross claim
plaintiff	injunction	third-party practice
defendant	specific performance	class action
parties	initial pleading	discovery
jurisdiction	summons	interrogatories
diversity jurisdiction	personal service	deposition
venue	substituted service	out-of-court settlements
cause of action	long arm statutes	protective order
damages	constructive service	case management conference

pretrial conference	real evidence	writ of certiorari
summary judgment	testimonial evidence	substantial federal question
jury trial	direct evidence	rule of four
bench trial	eyewitness testimony	motions
venire	indirect evidence	appellant
voir dire	circumstantial evidence	appellee
challenge for cause	relevant evidence	initial brief
peremptory challenges	competent	answer brief
racially based peremptory challenges	privileged communications	reply brief
gender-based peremptory challenges	attorney-client privilege	petitioner
opening statement	marital privilege	oral argument
preponderance of the evidence	clergy privilege	judicial conference
direct examination	forensic experts	affirm
cross-examination	hypothetical question	reverse
expert witness	polygraph evidence	remand
directed verdict	general objection	per curiam opinion
involuntary dismissal	specific objection	opinion of the court
rebuttal	hearsay evidence	concurring opinion
jury instructions	spontaneous or excited utterances	concurring in the judgment
closing arguments	dying declarations	dissenting opinion
mistrial	reputation	reporters
sequestration of the jury	business and public records	citations
hung jury	best evidence rule	motion for rehearing
general verdict	opinion evidence	en banc rehearing
special verdict	error correction	original writs
rules of evidence	lawmaking	mandamus
judicial notice	notice of appeal	prohibition
evidentiary presumption	*in forma pauperis*	habeas corpus
rebuttable presumption		

ENDNOTES

[1] 38 U.S.C.A. § 1332; In 1958 Congress set the amount for diversity jurisdiction at $10,000. Since then it has increased the amount presumably to take into consideration inflation and to diminish the burden that diversity jurisdiction imposes on federal courts.

[2] *Erie Railroad Co. v. Tompkins,* 304 U.S. 64, 58 S.Ct. 817, 82 L.Ed. 1188 (1938).

[3] In *Hanson v. Denckla,* 357 U.S. 235, 78 S.Ct. 1228, 2 L.Ed.2d 1283 (1958), the U.S. Supreme Court explained that nonresidents may not constitutionally be subjected to the jurisdiction of another state unless the defendant by some act purposefully avails of the privilege of conducting activities within the forum, thus invoking the benefits of its laws.

[4] Judges frequently take a more active role in the adjudication of disputes in small claims courts where, because the cost of

Endnotes

retaining counsel may exceed the amount in controversy, parties usually appear without counsel.

[5]Fed. R. Civ. P. 23.

[6]*Brown v. Bridges,* 327 So.2d 874 (Fla. App. 1976).

[7]While most states prohibit an employer from discharging an employee called for jury duty, Connecticut is one of a few states that require employers to continue to pay their employees while on jury duty. This requirement applies only to full-time employees and is limited to five days of jury service. C.G.S.A. § 51–247.

[8]*Alderman v. State,* 327 S.E.2d 168 (Ga. 1985).

[9]28 USCA § 1870.

[10]*Batson v. Kentucky,* 476 U.S. 79, 106 S.Ct. 1712, 90 L.Ed.2d 69 (1986).

[11]*J.E.B. v. Alabama ex rel. T.B.,* 511 U.S. 127, 114 S.Ct. 1419, 128 L.Ed.2d 89 (1994).

[12]*Frye v. United States,* 293 F. 1013 (D.C.Cir. 1923).

[13]509 U.S. 579, 113 S.Ct. 2786, 125 L.Ed.2d 469 (1993).

[14]Fed. R. Civ. P. 50(a).

[15]See, for example, *Slocum v. New York Life Ins. Co.,* 228 U.S. 364, 33 S.Ct. 523, 57 L.Ed. 879 (1913).

[16]*Konst v. Florida East Coast Railway Company,* 71 F.3d 850 (11th Cir. 1996).

[17]*Rock v. Arkansas,* 483 U.S. 44, 107 S.Ct. 2704, 97 L.Ed.2d 37 (1987).

[18]*Connor v. State,* 171 A.2d 699 (Md. 1961).

For Further Reading

Barclay, Scott, *An Appealing Act: Why People Appeal in Civil Cases* (Northwestern University Press 1999).

Clermont, Kevin M., *Civil Procedure* (West Group 1999).

Elligett, Raymond T., and John M. Scheb, *Florida Appellate Practice and Advocacy* (Book World Publications 1998).

Glannon, Joseph W., *Civil Procedure: Examples and Explanations* (Little Brown and Co. 1996).

Hazard, Geoffrey C., Jr., *American Civil Procedure: An Introduction* (Yale University Press 1993).

Kane, Mary Kay, *Civil Procedure in a Nutshell* (West Publishing Co. 1996).

Litan, Robert E. (ed.), *Verdict: Assessing the Civil Jury System* (Brookings Institution 1993).

10

CRIMINAL PROCEDURE

Courtesy of West Group

LEARNING OBJECTIVES

This chapter should enable the student to understand:

- Fourth Amendment rules governing searches and seizures
- the exclusionary rule designed to enforce the Fourth Amendment
- warrant and warrantless arrests and investigatory detentions
- the effect of Miranda rules on interrogation of suspects
- formal charging processes by prosecutors and through use of grand juries
- pretrial procedures, including arraignment and plea bargaining
- the role of prosecutors, defense counsel, judges, and juries throughout the stages of a criminal trial

CHAPTER OUTLINE

Introduction

Search and Seizure

Arrest and Investigatory Detention

Interrogation and Identification of Suspects

The Right to Counsel

The Pretrial Process

The Criminal Trial

Sentencing

Victims' Rights in the Criminal Process

The Appeals Process

Conclusion

Summary of Key Concepts

Questions for Thought and Discussion

INTRODUCTION

Criminal procedure consists of the processes by which crimes are investigated, prosecuted, and punished. It includes law enforcement activities such as search and seizure, arrest, interrogation, and identification of suspects. It also embraces the judicial processes that take place before, during, and after the trial of persons accused of crimes. The federal and state constitutions set the basic requirements for criminal procedure, but constitutional requisites are supplemented by federal and state statutes and by rules of criminal procedure promulgated by the courts. In recent decades the courts have expanded the constitutional rights of criminal defendants, and many rules of criminal procedure reflect constitutional requisites as interpreted by the U.S. Supreme Court and the highest state courts.

SEARCH AND SEIZURE

The Fourth Amendment to the U.S. Constitution prohibits unreasonable searches and seizures. A **search** occurs when government agents look for evidence in a manner that intrudes into a person's legally protected zone of privacy. A **seizure** takes place when agents take possession or control of property or persons. Although essential to the enforcement of the criminal law, search for and seizure of evidence often entails serious invasions of privacy and is subject to abuse. Therefore, the power of law enforcement agencies to conduct searches and seizures is limited by the federal and state constitutions, and by a number of federal and state statutes. Most important among these legal limitations is the Fourth Amendment to the U.S. Constitution, which prohibits unreasonable searches and seizures.

As a general rule, the Fourth Amendment requires law enforcement officers to obtain a **warrant** before conducting searches and seizures. Although some warrantless searches and seizures are permissible, they must all conform to a standard of reasonableness. Law enforcement officers are not permitted to conduct searches and seizures arbitrarily, or even based on their hunches about criminal activity. For a search to be reasonable under the

Fourth Amendment, police generally must have **probable cause,** which simply means that a reasonable person has reasonable grounds to believe that a search will produce evidence of crime. In certain instances police may conduct limited searches based on the lesser standard of **reasonable suspicion.** Subject to certain exceptions, evidence obtained through unreasonable searches and seizures is not admissible in criminal prosecutions.

The Fourth Amendment, like all the protections of the Bill of Rights, was originally conceived as a limitation on the powers of the newly created national government. Under the original conception of the Bill of Rights, citizens seeking legal protection against actions of state and local governments had to look to their state constitutions and state courts for relief. But in 1949, the Supreme Court held that the freedom from unreasonable searches and seizures is "implicit in 'the concept of ordered liberty' and as such enforceable against the States through the Due Process Clause [of the Fourteenth Amendment]."[1] The Fourth Amendment sets a minimal national standard; state courts are free to provide greater levels of protection under the search and seizure provisions of state constitutions. Several state courts have followed this latter approach.

When, Where and to Whom Does the Fourth Amendment Apply?

The Fourth Amendment limits search and seizure activities by law enforcement agencies at all levels of government, whether federal, state, or local. Because the Constitution limits *government* action, the Fourth Amendment protects a person's rights against the police and other government agents, but not against searches and seizures conducted by private individuals. Moreover, the amendment does not apply to searches and seizures conducted by U.S. agents outside the territory of the United States.

Travelers crossing the borders of the United States are routinely subjected to searches, even when they are not the targets of suspicion. Suspicionless **border searches** are justified by the assumption that persons crossing the national border are not entitled to the protections of the Fourth Amendment. The border search exception extends to searches conducted at established stations near the border or other functional equivalents of a border search, for example, the search of a ship when it first docks after entering the territorial waters of the United States.

Although the Fourth Amendment refers to "houses," its protections also are extended to stores, offices, and places of business. Because it mentions "effects," the Fourth Amendment applies to items of personal property as well as to real estate. The Fourth Amendment does not apply to property that has been abandoned. Therefore, police may search abandoned premises and seize abandoned property.

Most law enforcement agencies that impound automobiles for parking violations or abandonment, or pursuant to the arrest of a motorist, routinely conduct an inventory of the contents and remove any valuables for safekeeping. When conducted according to standard police procedures, an **inventory search** is generally regarded as an administrative search not subject to ordinary Fourth Amendment requirements. Inventory searches are justified by the need for protection of the owner's property while the vehicle remains in police custody, protection of the police from claims of lost property, and the need to protect the police from potential dangers that might be lurking inside closed automobiles. Of course, if a routine inventory search yields evidence of crime, it may be seized and admitted into evidence without violating the Fourth Amendment.[2]

Searches Based on Consent

The Supreme Court has refused to require law officers to inform suspects of their right to refuse to **consent to a search**.[3] More recently, the Court held that police are not required to inform motorists who are stopped for other reasons that they are "free to go" before asking them to consent to a search of their automobile.[4] For a person's consent to be valid, it must be truly voluntary and must involve more than mere acquiescence to the authority of the police.

The Scope of Privacy Protected by the Fourth Amendment

The term *seizure* refers to the taking into custody of physical evidence, property, or even a person; but what constitutes a *search* is not as clear. Originally, the protection of the Fourth Amendment was limited to physical intrusions on one's person or property, and courts looked at whether a trespass had taken place in deciding whether the Fourth Amendment was implicated. Thus surveillance without physical contact with the suspect or the suspect's property was deemed to fall outside the protections of the Fourth Amendment. Accordingly, the Fourth Amendment was not deemed applicable to **wiretapping** or **electronic eavesdropping**. In *Katz v. United States* (1967), however, the Supreme Court abandoned the trespass doctrine, ruling that the Fourth Amendment protects people, not places.[5] In *Katz,* the Court held that a suspected bookie who was using a public telephone to allegedly conduct a gambling business enjoyed a reasonable expectation of privacy, and that a police wiretap of the phone booth was a search within the meaning of the Fourth Amendment. This decision brought wiretapping and other forms of electronic eavesdropping within the limitations of the Fourth Amendment. Currently, any means of invading a person's **reasonable expectation of privacy** is considered a "search" for Fourth Amendment purposes. The critical question that courts must address in reviewing cases where police conduct surveillance or eavesdropping without probable cause or prior judicial authorization is whether such surveillance intruded on a suspect's reasonable expectation of privacy.

Diminished Expectations of Privacy

Obviously, anyone lawfully incarcerated in a prison or jail has no reasonable expectation of privacy. Jail and prison cells are routinely "swept" for weapons and other contraband and inmates are routinely subjected to searches of their persons. The Supreme Court has upheld **strip searches** of prison inmates because of the demands for institutional security.[6]

With increased concern over airplane hijacking and terrorism has come increased security at the nation's airports. Passengers attempting to board aircraft routinely pass through metal detectors; their carry-on baggage and checked luggage is routinely subjected to X-ray scans. Such searches are deemed reasonable, given their minimal intrusiveness, the gravity of the safety interests involved, and the reduced privacy expectations associated with airline travel.

Sobriety Checkpoints

One device increasingly used by law enforcement to combat the problem of intoxicated drivers is **sobriety checkpoints,** in which all drivers passing a certain point are stopped briefly and observed for signs of intoxication. To the extent that police officers at these checkpoints visually inspect the passenger compartments of stopped automobiles, these brief encounters involve searches, although in most instances these procedures entail only minor intrusion and inconvenience. Opponents of sobriety checkpoints argue that they amount to dragnet searches—during which the government searches many people in the hope of catching a few. Advocates of sobriety checkpoints argue that these measures save lives by reducing the number of drunk drivers on the streets. In 1990, the Supreme Court upheld the use of sobriety checkpoints to detect intoxicated drivers.[7] For the most part, state courts have upheld sobriety checkpoints, but have placed restrictions on how they are conducted. In November 2000, the Supreme Court did limit the use of checkpoints to detect "ordinary lawbreaking," (in this case, drug possession) as distinct from sobriety checkpoints.[8]

The Warrant Requirement

The Fourth Amendment expresses a decided preference for searches and seizures to be conducted pursuant to a warrant. The warrant requirement is designed to ensure that the impartial judgment of a judge or magistrate is interposed between the citizen and the state. With the exception of warrants permitting administrative searches, search warrants must be based on probable cause. Probable cause exists when prudent and cautious police officers have trustworthy information leading them to believe that evidence of crime may be obtained through a particular search. The Supreme Court has said that courts should view the determination of probable cause as a "commonsense, practical question" that must be decided in light of the **totality of circumstances** in a given case.[9] Some state courts have declined to follow this approach and have opted to provide their citizens more protection than allowed by the federal view.

Under normal circumstances, a police officer with probable cause to believe that evidence of a crime is located in a specific place must submit under oath an application for a search warrant to the appropriate judge or magistrate. An **affidavit** is a signed document attesting under oath to certain facts of which the **affiant** (the person submitting the affidavit) has knowledge. Generally, an affidavit by a law enforcement officer requesting issuance of a search warrant is presented to a judge or magistrate. The officer's affidavit in support of a search warrant must always contain a rather precise description of the place(s) or person(s) to be searched and the things to be seized and must attest to specific facts that establish probable cause to justify a search. The information must be sufficiently fresh to ensure that the items to be seized are probably located on the premises to be searched.

A magistrate's finding of probable cause may be based on hearsay evidence. This rule permits police to obtain search warrants based on tips from anonymous or **confidential informants.** Confidential informants (CIs) are often persons who have been involved with the police and are seeking favorable consideration in respect to their own offenses. Because their motivation may be suspect, their reliability is checked carefully. For many years the Supreme Court required magistrates to apply a rigorous test that made it very difficult for police to use **anonymous tips.** In 1983, the Supreme Court relaxed the test and permitted magistrates to consider the totality of circumstances when evaluating applications based on hearsay evidence.[10]

Exceptions to the Warrant Requirement

Courts have recognized that an absolute warrant requirement would be impractical. Consequently, they have upheld the reasonableness of **warrantless searches** under so-called **exigent circumstances.** When possible, police officers should obtain warrants, because their failure to do so may jeopardize the fruits of a successful search. The following exceptions to the warrant requirement assume that police officers have probable cause to believe that a given search is likely to produce evidence of crime.

1. Evidence in plain view: A police officer may seize evidence in **plain view** provided that (a) the officer has a legal justification to be in a constitutionally protected area when the seizure occurs; (b) the evidence seized is in the plain view of the officer who comes across it; and (c) it is apparent that the object constitutes evidence of a crime.[11]

2. Emergency searches: Police frequently must respond to emergencies involving reports of crime or injuries. Increasingly, law enforcement authorities are called upon to investigate bomb threats where explosive devices are possibly sequestered inside buildings. In these and other situations police are called upon to conduct **emergency searches.** The law recognizes that police do not have the time to obtain search warrants in such instances. Of course, police must possess probable cause to make warrantless emergency searches of dwellings. Police who make warrantless entries and searches when they reasonably believe that a person within is in need of immediate aid do not violate protections against unreasonable search and seizure. Once inside, the police may justifiably seize evidence in plain view.

3. Preservation of evidence: A frequently invoked justification for a warrantless search and seizure is the preservation of **evanescent evidence**—evidence that might be lost or destroyed. When there is a reasonable belief that loss or destruction of evidence is imminent, a warrantless entry of premises may be justified, but a mere possibility of such is insufficient.

4. Roadside searches of motor vehicles: The courts have long recognized the validity of the so-called **automobile exception,** assuming that the police officer has probable cause to believe the vehicle contains contraband or evidence of crime, on the premise that the mobile character of a motor vehicle creates a practical necessity for an immediate search.[12]

5. Search incident to a lawful arrest: It has long been recognized that a **search incident to a lawful arrest** to seize the fruits or evidence of crime is permissible, but the Supreme Court has narrowed the permissible scope of searches incident to lawful ar-

rests.[13] The rule is that police may search the body of an arrestee and the area within that person's immediate control, within the "grasp" or "lunge" of the arrestee. To conduct a more extensive search, police must generally obtain a search warrant.

6. Hot pursuit: Officers in **hot pursuit** of a fleeing suspect already have probable cause to make an arrest. The Supreme Court has long recognized that police may pursue the suspect into a protected place, such as a home, without having to abandon pursuit until a warrant can be obtained.[14]

Exceptions to the Probable Cause Requirement

Warrantless searches are often necessary and are generally deemed acceptable as long as there are exigent circumstances and police have probable cause. More controversial, however, are situations in which the courts permit limited searches based on the lesser standard of reasonable suspicion. In considering these special situations, one should keep in mind that the fundamental requirement of the Fourth Amendment is not probable cause but reasonableness.

1. Stop-and-frisk: The **stop-and-frisk** is a routine law enforcement technique whereby police officers stop, question, and sometimes search suspicious persons.[15] Concealed weapons and contraband that are discovered during the course of a legitimate frisk are admissible into evidence.[16]

2. School searches: The Supreme Court has held that the Fourth Amendment protects children in the public schools from unreasonable searches and seizures, but that such searches are to be judged by a reasonableness standard and are not subject to the requirement of probable cause, much less the warrant requirement.[17] With the recent spate of school violence, there is considerable public support for giving school officials broad latitude in the area of search and seizure.

3. Drug testing: The national "war on drugs" has resulted in the widespread implementation of **drug testing** programs for public employees. Courts have routinely upheld regulations permitting urinalysis of public safety officers based on reasonable suspicion of drug abuse. The Supreme Court has even sustained a Customs Service policy requiring drug tests for persons seeking positions as customs inspectors.[18] It has, however, invalidated a policy under which all political candidates were required to submit to drug testing as a condition of qualifying for the ballot.[19]

The Exclusionary Rule

The **exclusionary rule** prohibits use of illegally obtained evidence in a criminal prosecution of the person whose rights were violated by the police in obtaining that evidence. In 1914, the U.S. Supreme Court first held that evidence obtained through an unlawful search and seizure could not be used to convict a person of a federal crime.[20] In *Mapp v. Ohio* (1961), the Court required the state courts to follow the exclusionary rule largely on the rationale that there is no other effective means of enforcing the Fourth Amendment.[21] The *Mapp* decision was certainly one of the Warren Court's most important decisions in the criminal justice field and became emblematic of the Warren Court's efforts to enhance constitutional protections in this area.

CASE IN POINT

THE STATE COURTS MUST FOLLOW THE FOURTH AMENDMENT EXCLUSIONARY RULE

Mapp v. Ohio

United States Supreme Court
367 U.S. 643, 81 S.Ct. 1684, 6 L.Ed.2d 1081 (1961)

Cleveland, Ohio, police arrived at Dollree Mapp's home after receiving information that a bombing suspect was hiding there. They demanded access, but failing to produce a search warrant, were denied. Police returned some four hours later and forced their way into the home. Mapp, who protested the entry was forcibly detained while officers searched the home. Although police failed to locate the bombing suspect, they did find in a trunk in the basement some sexually explicit materials. Mapp was arrested, tried, and convicted under the Ohio statute proscribing possession of obscene materials. Dividing 7–2, the U.S. Supreme Court reversed her conviction, holding that the evidence had been improperly admitted against her since it had been obtained in violation of the Fourth Amendment warrant requirement. The Court overturned precedent and applied the exclusionary rule to the state courts for the first time. The Court said that this landmark decision "gives to the individual no more than that which the Constitution guarantees him, to the police officer no less than that to which honest law enforcement is entitled, and, to the courts, that judicial integrity so necessary in the true administration of justice."

During the 1960s and 1970s, the exclusionary rule came under attack from critics who argued that the social cost of allowing guilty persons to avoid prosecution outweighed the benefit of deterring police from violating the Fourth Amendment. In 1984, the Supreme Court revisited the issue and held that evidence obtained on the basis of a search warrant that is later held invalid may be admitted in evidence at trial if the police officer who conducted the search relied on the warrant in "good faith."[22] The **good-faith exception** to the exclusionary rule applies only in cases where police officers rely on warrants that are later held to be invalid; it does not apply to warrantless searches.

ARREST AND INVESTIGATORY DETENTION

A formal arrest occurs when police take an individual into custody and charge that person with the commission of a crime. As a form of *seizure,* an arrest is governed by the probable cause and warrant provisions of the Fourth Amendment. However, the formal arrest is not the only type of encounter between police and citizens that implicates the Fourth Amendment. A seizure, for Fourth Amendment purposes, occurs when a police officer uses force or the threat of force to in some way restrain a person's liberty.

Arrest Warrants

An **arrest warrant** is routine in cases where an arrest is to be made based on an indictment by a grand jury. When a prosecutor files an information, a **capias** is issued by a court directing the arrest of the defendant. In such cases suspects are often not aware that they are under investigation, and police officers have ample time to obtain an arrest warrant without fear that suspects will flee. However, most arrests are not made pursuant to secret investigations but are made by police officers who observe a criminal act, respond to a complaint filed by a crime victim, or have probable cause to arrest after completing an investigation. In such cases it is often unnecessary for police to obtain an arrest warrant, but it is always essential that they have probable cause to make the arrest.

Warrantless Arrests

At common law, police had the right to make a **warrantless arrest** if they observed someone in the commission of a felony or they had probable cause to believe that a person had committed or was committing a felony. To make a warrantless arrest for a misdemeanor, an officer had to observe someone in the commission of the act. Otherwise, to make an arrest, a warrant was required. Many states enacted statutes adopting common-law rules of arrest allowing police officers broad discretion to make warrantless arrests. As with warrantless searches and seizures, the Supreme Court has approved warrantless arrests (1) where crimes are committed in plain view of police officers; or (2) officers possess probable cause to make an arrest, but exigent circumstances prohibit them from obtaining a warrant. Absent plain view or compelling exigencies, the need to obtain an arrest warrant is unclear. As a matter of policy, it makes sense for police officers to obtain arrest warrants when possible. However, given the time it takes to obtain an arrest warrant and the fact that magistrates are not always available around the clock, it is not always feasible for police to obtain warrants prior to arrest.

Use of Force by Police Making Arrests

Because suspects frequently resist attempts to take them into custody, police officers must often use force in making arrests. Sometimes the use of force by police is challenged in civil suits for damages. Typically, in such cases, the courts have said that in making a lawful arrest, police officers may use such force as necessary to effect the arrest and prevent the escape of the suspect.

Concern over police brutality took center stage in 1991, when the nation viewed on television a videotape of what appeared to be the unnecessarily brutal beating of motorist Rodney King by Los Angeles police officers. In response to public outrage, four police officers involved in the incident were prosecuted by state authorities for assault and battery and related crimes. On the motion of the defense, the trial was moved out of Los Angeles to a suburban community. No one can forget the riot that ensued in Los Angeles in April 1992 after the jury returned its verdict of "not guilty." In response to the widespread perception that a miscarriage of justice had occurred, the U.S. Justice Department launched its own investigation of the case. In the summer of 1992, a federal grand jury indicted the four officers for violating Rodney King's Fourth Amendment rights. In April 1993, a trial jury returned verdicts of guilty against two of the officers; the other two were acquitted.

Investigatory Detention

A common form of police encounter is the stop-and-frisk or **investigatory detention.** Police are permitted to stop pedestrians or automobiles temporarily as long as they have reasonable suspicion that criminal activity is afoot. Police may then perform a limited pat-down search of the suspect's outer clothing to ascertain whether the suspect is armed. However, under the doctrine of plain view, contraband discovered during a legitimate pat-down for weapons may be admissible into evidence. For example, if during the course of a lawful frisk, a police officer feels what the officer suspects is a knife concealed in the suspect's pocket, the officer may retrieve the object. If it turns out to be a metal smoking pipe wrapped inside a plastic bag containing "crack" cocaine, the crack would most likely be admissible as evidence of crime.

Drug Courier Profiles

In recent years police have developed **drug courier profiles** based on typical characteristics and behaviors of drug smugglers. The profiles include such factors as paying cash for airline tickets, taking short trips to drug-source cities, not checking luggage, appearing nervous, and so forth. Police often use these profiles to identify and detain suspected drug couriers, a controversial practice that has resulted in disparate court decisions. In 1989, the Supreme Court upheld an investigative stop of an air passenger for which a number circumstances, including the use of the profile, furnished the police a reasonable suspicion of criminal activity. While the Court found that any one of the several factors relied on by the police may have been consistent with innocent travel, it observed that the evaluation of the validity of the stop requires a consideration of the totality of the circumstances.[23]

INTERROGATION AND IDENTIFICATION OF SUSPECTS

Interrogation of suspects is an important and often necessary component of police practice. Historically the practice of extracting confessions often entailed serious abuses of the rights of suspects, although the Supreme Court held as far back as 1897 that a coerced confession violates the Self-Incrimination Clause of the Fifth Amendment.[24] The traditional test used by the courts was whether a challenged confession could reasonably be deemed to have been voluntary. Subjective voluntariness, however, is extremely difficult to discern, even through direct observation, let alone through appellate hindsight years later. Consequently, judicial decisions in this area were often unclear and inconsistent.

The *Miranda* Decision

In its landmark decision in *Miranda v. Arizona* (1966), the Supreme Court held that before interrogating suspects who are in custody, police must warn them of their right to remain silent and their right to have counsel present during questioning.[25] Unless these warnings have been given, the Court said, no statement made by the suspect may be used in evidence.

The *Miranda* decision produced a firestorm of controversy, especially within the law enforcement community. Critics thought that the Court was "coddling the criminals" and "handcuffing the cops." Although the Court has recognized some exceptions to the Miranda requirements, it has been steadfast in maintaining the basic holding of the decision. This was clearly demonstrated in June 2000 when the Court struck down a federal statute aimed at reversing the *Miranda* decision. The statute, which had been passed in the late 1960s, made the admissibility of incriminating statements turn solely on whether they were made voluntarily.[26] The statute had been ignored for many years until 1999 when the U.S. Court of Appeals for the Fourth Circuit invoked it in a federal bank robbery case. The court concluded that, because the Miranda requirements were not themselves of constitutional origin, Congress could reverse these requirements by ordinary legislation.[27] In a 7–2 decision, the Supreme Court disagreed, holding that the *Miranda* decision announced a constitutional rule that could not be altered simply by enacting a countervailing statute.[28] Clearly, Miranda is the law of the land and will remain so for the foreseeable future.

The Fruit of the Poisonous Tree Doctrine

Under the **fruit of the poisonous tree doctrine,** evidence that is derived from inadmissible evidence is likewise inadmissible.[29] Thus, for example, if police learn of the location of a weapon used in the commission of a crime by interrogating a suspect who is in custody, that weapon is considered **derivative evidence.** If the police failed to provide the Miranda warnings, not only the suspect's responses to their questions but also the weapon discovered as the fruit of the interrogation are tainted. On the other hand, if the physical evidence was located on the basis of independently and lawfully obtained information, it may be admissible under the **independent source doctrine.**[30] Thus in our hypothetical case, if police learned of the location of the weapon from an informant, the weapon might well be admissible in court, even though the suspect's admissions are still inadmissible.

Police generally provide the Miranda warnings immediately upon arrest or as soon as is practicable, to preserve as evidence any statements that the suspect might make, as well as any other evidence that might be derived from these statements. However, in some situations the Miranda warnings are delayed because police are preoccupied with apprehending other individuals or taking actions to protect themselves or others on the scene. In 1984, the Supreme Court recognized a **public safety exception** to the Miranda exclusionary rule.[31] Police may ask suspects questions designed to locate weapons that might be used to harm the police or other persons before providing the Miranda warnings. If this interaction produces incriminating statements or physical evidence, the evidence need not be suppressed.

Identification Procedures

Law enforcement agencies employ various means to identify suspects. The principal means is through eyewitness identification; however, scientific methods have become increasingly

THE PUBLIC SAFETY EXCEPTION TO *MIRANDA*

New York v. Quarles

United States Supreme Court
467 U.S. 649, 104 S.Ct. 2626, 81 L.Ed.2d 550 (1984)

Two New York City police officers were approached by a woman who claimed she had just been raped and that her assailant had gone into a nearby grocery store. The police were informed that the assailant was carrying a gun. The officers proceeded to the store and immediately spotted Benjamin Quarles, who matched the description given by the victim. Upon seeing the police, Quarles turned and ran. One of the police officers drew his service revolver and ordered Quarles to "freeze." Quarles complied with the officer's request. The officer frisked Quarles and discovered an empty shoulder holster. Before reading Quarles the Miranda warnings, the officer asked where the gun was. Quarles nodded in the direction of some

empty boxes and said, "The gun is over there." He was then placed under arrest and "Mirandized." Later Quarles moved to have his statement suppressed from evidence since it was made prior to the Miranda warnings. He also moved for suppression of the gun under the fruit of the poisonous tree doctrine. The Supreme Court allowed both pieces of evidence to be used against Quarles, notwithstanding the delay in the Miranda warnings. Obviously, the Court believed that the officers were justified in locating a discarded weapon prior to Mirandizing Quarles. In so holding, the Court created the public safety exception to Miranda rights.

important. Such methods include comparison of blood samples, matching of clothing fibers, head and body hair comparison, identification of semen, and DNA tests. The Fifth Amendment privilege against compulsory self-incrimination does not apply to identification procedures.[32] However, the reliability and validity of particular procedures remain subject to due process–based challenges.

THE RIGHT TO COUNSEL

The Sixth Amendment to the U.S. Constitution provides: "In all criminal prosecutions, the accused shall enjoy the right . . . to have the Assistance of Counsel for his defense." The **right to counsel** is essential to preserving the fundamental fairness of all criminal procedures. The defense attorney not only represents the accused in pretrial court proceedings but also advises on strategy and often serves as the negotiator between the defendant and the prosecutor.

The Sixth Amendment has been consistently interpreted to allow defendants to employ counsel in all federal prosecutions. Similar provisions in the constitutions of the 50 states allow defendants to retain counsel in state criminal prosecutions. Irrespective of state constitutional protection, the accused is protected by the federal Constitution. In *Gideon v. Wainwright* (1963) the Supreme Court held that the Sixth Amendment right to counsel applies to prosecutions in the state courts by way of the Due Process Clause of the Fourteenth Amendment.[33]

Providing Counsel to Indigent Persons

Although criminal defendants have the right to employ attorneys to represent them, many defendants are too poor to afford private counsel. The Judiciary Act of 1790 required federal judges to assign counsel to indigent defendants in capital cases, at least when defendants requested representation. Some states emulated the act of Congress by providing for appointed counsel in capital cases, but most did not. In its 1963 *Gideon* decision, the Supreme Court decided that the Fourteenth Amendment requires states to provide counsel to indigent defendants in all felony cases, observing that "any person haled into court, who is too poor to hire a lawyer, cannot be assured a fair trial unless counsel is provided for him."[34] In 1972, the Supreme Court extended the *Gideon* decision to encompass defendants who were sentenced to jail terms for misdemeanors.[35]

The representation provided to indigent defendants might take the form of a **public defender** or an attorney appointed ad hoc by the court. Many states have established successful public defender systems that operate much like prosecutors' offices. In other states indigent defendants still depend largely on ad hoc appointment of counsel. Sometimes the public defender's office has a conflict in which codefendants want to pursue inconsistent defenses. In such instances an outside attorney should be appointed.

Federal and state laws generally leave the determination of indigency to the discretion of the courts. Courts tend to be liberal in this regard, refusing to equate indigency with destitution and are generally inclined to appoint counsel if the cost of hiring a lawyer would

Opinion of the Court . . .

GIDEON V. WAINWRIGHT

372 U.S. 335, 83 S.Ct. 792, 9 L.Ed.2d 799 (1963)

Mr. Justice Black delivered the Opinion of the Court.

. . .[I]n our adversary system of criminal justice, any person haled into court, who is too poor to hire a lawyer, cannot be assured a fair trial unless counsel is provided for him. This seems to us to be an obvious truth. Governments, both state and federal, quite properly spend vast sums of money to establish machinery to try defendants accused of crime. Lawyers to prosecute are everywhere deemed essential to protect the public's interest in an orderly society. Similarly, there are few defendants charged with crime, few indeed, who fail to hire the best lawyers they can get to prepare and present their defenses. That government hires lawyers to prosecute and defendants who have the money hire lawyers to defend are the strongest indications of the widespread belief that lawyers in criminal courts are necessities, not luxuries. The right of one charged with crime to counsel may not be deemed fundamental and essential to fair trials in some countries, but it is in ours. From the very beginning, our state and national constitutions and laws have laid great emphasis on procedural and substantive safeguards designed to assure fair trials before impartial tribunals in which every defendant stands equal before the law. This noble ideal cannot be realized if the poor man charged with crime has to face his accusers without a lawyer to assist him. . . .

prevent the defendant from making bail. More than 75 percent of felony defendants are classified as indigent. Some state statutes provide for an assessment of an attorney's fee against a defendant who is represented by the public defender's office

Self-Representation

The Supreme Court has held that there is a constitutional right to represent oneself in a criminal prosecution.[36] Moreover, the Court has said that the defendant's legal knowledge or skill has no bearing on the right to **self-representation,** but it has stressed that the defendant who waives the right to counsel and proceeds *pro se* must do so "knowingly and intelligently." Critics of this approach believe that criminal law and procedure have become too complex and technical to permit the nonlawyer defendant to engage in effective self-representation. This is why judges sometimes appoint standby counsel to assist defendants who choose self-representation.

THE PRETRIAL PROCESS

What happens during the pretrial process often determines the outcome of a criminal case, as the overwhelming majority of criminal cases never make it to trial. Some are dropped or dismissed for lack of sufficient evidence; others result in convictions pursuant to guilty pleas. Many guilty pleas result from negotiations between prosecutors and defense counsel, making trials unnecessary.

Disposition of Petty Offenses

Minor misdemeanors are often disposed through **summary justice.** In such cases, the accused is usually not placed under arrest, but is simply issued a summons to appear in court to answer the charges. In many cases, such as motor vehicle infractions, the individual who is charged may simply elect to waive a court appearance and satisfy the charge by paying a predetermined fine. If the individual appears in court to contest the charges, the entire matter is typically resolved in one proceeding. The accused enters a plea ("not guilty," "guilty," or "no contest"), evidence is taken, and the judge renders a verdict. If the defendant is found guilty, sentence is generally pronounced immediately. Although defendants clearly have a right to hire attorneys to represent them in minor misdemeanor cases, most people go it alone before the magistrate. If they lose, which is highly probable, they typically pay a fine, which tends to be substantially less expensive than hiring an attorney.

The Initial Court Appearance

In major misdemeanor and felony cases the procedure is much more complex and protracted. Typically, individuals charged with felonies are placed under arrest prior to any appearance in court. However, all persons placed under arrest must promptly be taken before a judge or magistrate. Many jurisdictions require an **initial appearance** within 24 hours after arrest. However, the Supreme Court has ruled that suspects may be detained for as long as 48 hours before being taken before a judge or magistrate.[37]

The purpose of the initial appearance is to begin the formal charging process. Essentially, the judge or magistrate must perform three important functions at the initial appearance: (1) the charges must be read so that the accused will be formally notified of the charges; (2) the accused must be informed of relevant constitutional rights, including the right to remain silent and the right to counsel; and (3) a determination must be made of whether the accused should be released pending trial or remanded to custody to await the disposition of the case.

Pretrial Release and Pretrial Detention

The most important thing to a person who has been arrested and confined to jail is to secure release as soon as possible. **Pretrial release** is commonly referred to as granting **bail** and is commonly granted by statutes or court rules. In determining whether a defendant is entitled to pretrial release, the court usually considers the accused's prior convictions (if any), character, employment history, and ties to family and the community, as well as the nature and scope of the current charges Increasingly, courts are requiring that arrested persons be drug tested. While not used as evidence, the results of the drug test helps inform the judge's decision whether to grant pretrial release and whether to impose conditions upon that release

The Issue of Excessive Bail

Recognizing the common-law practice of allowing pretrial release on bail, the Eighth Amendment to the federal constitution states that "excessive bail shall not be required." The Supreme Court has made it clear that the purpose of bail is to ensure the appearance of the accused in court, not to inflict punishment. "Bail set at a figure higher than an amount reasonably calculated to fulfill this purpose is 'excessive' under the Eighth Amendment."[38] However, the Supreme Court has never held that the Excessive Bail Clause of the Eighth Amendment is enforceable against the states via the Fourteenth Amendment, leaving the matter of **excessive bail** in state criminal cases to the state constitutions, state legislatures, and state courts.

Pretrial Detention

The constitutional prohibition of "excessive bail" is vague regarding the existence of a constitutional right to pretrial release. However, the Supreme Court has ruled that there is no right to bail under the Eighth Amendment.[39] The Federal Bail Reform Act of 1984[40] allows federal courts to hold arrestees in **pretrial detention** on the ground of dangerousness to the community, as well as the need to ensure future court appearances. In many states a defendant who is charged with a crime punishable by death or life imprisonment is ineligible for pretrial release if there is substantial evidence of guilt.

The Formal Charging Process

Prosecutors have considerable influence in the determination of criminal cases. The prosecutor decides whether to proceed with a criminal case and whether to negotiate the charges with the defense. The prosecutor causes the court to issue subpoenas to compel the attendance of witnesses to testify, to bring in documents, and to provide nontestimonial physical evidences such as handwriting specimens and voice exemplars.

State and federal prosecutors have broad discretion in deciding whether to proceed with criminal charges initiated by a complainant or the police. The prosecutor may decide to drop a case for a variety of reasons, ranging from insufficient evidence to a judgment that the criminal sanction is inappropriate in a given situation. Alternatively, the prosecutor may decide to proceed on a lesser charge.

Prosecutorial discretion facilitates the widespread yet controversial practice of **plea bargaining,** which we discuss later. Although very broad, prosecutorial discretion is not unlimited. The Equal Protection Clause of the Fourteenth Amendment imposes limitations on **selective prosecution.** This means that prosecutors may not single out defendants for prosecution on the basis of race, religion, or other impermissible classifications.[41]

In a **preliminary hearing** (not to be confused with the initial appearance), a judge or magistrate examines the state's case to determine whether there is probable cause to bind the accused over to the grand jury or (in the absence of a grand jury requirement) hold the accused for trial. The Supreme Court has said that a preliminary hearing is constitutionally required in the absence of grand jury review to determine the sufficiency of an **information,** where an arrest is made without a warrant.[42] However, preliminary hearings do not have to be full-blown adversarial proceedings. Typically in a preliminary hearing the defense has the privilege of cross-examining witnesses for the prosecution and is able to learn the details and strengths of the state's case. The preliminary hearing provides an inquiry into probable cause for arrest and detention and becomes a screening device for prosecutors, as well as an opportunity for defense counsel to discover the prosecutor's case.

The Grand Jury

In many jurisdictions, prosecutors must obtain an **indictment** or "true bill" from the **grand jury** in addition to, or instead of, the preliminary hearing. The Fifth Amendment to the U.S. Constitution states: "No person shall be held to answer for a capital, or otherwise infamous crime, unless on a presentment or indictment of a grand jury." The Supreme Court has held that states are not bound by the Fourteenth Amendment to abide by the grand jury requirement imposed on the federal courts by the Fifth Amendment. Nevertheless, about half the states have constitutional provisions or statutes requiring the use of grand juries in certain types of criminal cases. Other states use the grand jury primarily in an investigatory or supervisory capacity.

At common law, the grand jury held 23 persons, at least 12 of whom had to agree in order to hand down an indictment. Today, federal grand juries have 16 to 23 persons, but the "12 votes for indictment" rule applies in every case. States vary in regard to the size of grand juries, but in every state at least a majority of grand jurors must agree that there is probable cause for trial in order to hand down an indictment against the accused. Today grand juries seldom refuse to hand down indictments sought by prosecutors, causing some critics to question the utility of the institution as a safeguard for the rights of the accused. Perhaps it is this perception that has led a number of states to adopt the information/

preliminary hearing mechanism in lieu of the grand jury. In most midwestern and western states, the grand jury is seldom used to charge persons with crimes.

The grand jury, like the magistrate presiding over the preliminary hearing, examines the evidence and testimony the prosecution has collected against the accused. Unlike the preliminary hearing, the grand jury proceeding is normally closed: The defendant is generally not represented by counsel or even present at the proceeding. Testimony is not always transcribed, and if it is, access to transcripts is either limited or nonexistent. While controversial, grand jury secrecy encourages uninhibited testimony by witnesses and prevents the circulation of derogatory statements about persons who are ultimately not indicted. After the prosecutor has presented testimony and physical evidence, the members of the grand jury vote whether to hand down an indictment. There is some variation among jurisdictions in the rules that determine grand jury indictments, but in no case can a grand jury return a true bill unless a majority of grand jurors votes to indict.

Grand Jury Powers

Grand juries possess the authority to compel the appearance of witnesses, to **subpoena** documents, to hold individuals in contempt, and to grant **immunity** from prosecution in exchange for testimony. Immunity is of two kinds. **Transactional immunity** bars any further prosecution of the witness in regard to the specific transaction to which the witness testified. **Use immunity** is more limited, barring only the use of the witness's testimony against him or her in a subsequent prosecution. Federal grand juries are authorized to grant use immunity. Many states follow the federal practice, but some permit grand juries to grant transactional immunity.

Evidence before the Grand Jury

Many of the rules of evidence that apply to the criminal trial do not apply to the grand jury. For example, hearsay evidence is generally admissible, whereas at trial, except in certain instances, it is not admitted over the defendant's objection. Moreover, evidence excluded from trial on Fourth or Fifth Amendment grounds is also admissible before the grand jury. The theory is, of course, that the grand jury is an investigative body and that any infringement of the rights of the accused can be corrected in subsequent adversary court proceedings. Notwithstanding the fact that a grand jury may consider evidence that is inadmissible at trial, it may not violate a valid evidentiary privilege, established by the Constitution, statutes, or the common law (see discussion of evidentiary privileges in Chapter 9).

Pretrial Motions

Pretrial motions are written requests to the court on behalf of the government or the defendant. Motions commonly filed in criminal cases include a **motion for continuance** (postponement), a **motion for change of venue** (seeking to move the trial to a different location), a **motion to dismiss** the indictment or information against the defendant, a **motion to suppress** a defendant's confession or admission, a motion to require the government to identify a confidential informant (CI), and a motion to determine the accused's competency to stand trial. In some instances a motion to take a **deposition** is filed to preserve the testimony of a witness who may not be available for trial.

Arraignment

The **arraignment** is the accused's first appearance before a court of law with the authority to conduct a criminal trial. At this stage of the process, the accused must enter a plea to the charges contained in the indictment or information. The accused may enter a **plea of not guilty,** in which case the plea is noted and a trial date is set. He or she may enter a **plea of guilty,** in which case no trial is necessary, guilt is pronounced, and sentencing follows, often after a presentence investigation has been completed. In some jurisdictions, the accused has the option of pleading *nolo contendere* (no contest). The **no contest plea,** although functionally equivalent to a guilty plea in a criminal trial, provides the accused the advantage that it generally cannot be construed as an admission of guilt in a related civil suit.

Because a plea of guilty or *nolo contendere* represents a waiver of constitutional rights, it is essential that the plea be made knowingly and voluntarily. A factual basis is necessary to ensure that the accused does not admit to an offense that does not fall within the bounds of the government's accusations. Judges employ various methods to determine voluntariness of a defendant's plea and to determine whether there is a factual basis for the offense. Often these methods include interrogation of the defendant by the judge, and sometimes by the prosecutor and defense counsel.

Plea Bargaining

In most jurisdictions, more than 90 percent of felony suspects who are arraigned plead guilty or no contest. Very often the guilty plea is the result of a bargain struck between the defense and the prosecution. In a **plea bargain,** the accused agrees to plead guilty in exchange for a reduction in the number and/or severity of charges or a promise by the prosecutor not to seek the maximum penalty allowed by law. Plea negotiations are subject to the approval of the trial court. In most instances the bargain is arrived at between experienced and knowledgeable counsel on both sides and is readily approved by the court. If, however, the court is unwilling to approve the plea bargain, the defendant must choose between withdrawing the guilty plea (and thus going to trial), and accepting the plea bargain with such modifications as the judge may approve. Once the court has accepted a guilty plea pursuant to a plea bargain, the court cannot unilaterally alter it without permitting the defendant the opportunity to withdraw the plea.

In some jurisdictions, judges participate directly in plea-bargaining discussions. However, other courts disfavor the participation of a trial judge in such discussions on the basis that the power and position of the judge may improperly influence the defendant to enter a guilty plea. Plea bargaining has been sharply criticized by observers with different perspectives on the criminal process. Some critics fault plea bargaining for reducing the severity of criminal penalties. Others view plea bargaining as an unconstitutional effort to deprive defendants of their right to a fair trial. Plea bargaining has never been popular, but few critics stop to consider the tremendous costs and delays that would result if the numerous cases currently resolved through plea bargaining were to go to trial.

In addition to permitting a substantial conservation of prosecutorial and judicial resources, plea bargaining provides a means by which, through mutual concession, the parties may obtain a prompt resolution of criminal proceedings. The plea bargain, or negotiated sentence, avoids the delay and uncertainties of trial and appeal and permits swift and certain punishment of law violators with a sentence tailored to the circumstances of the case at hand. The Supreme Court has clearly upheld the practice of plea bargaining.[43]

Pretrial Discovery

The courts have long recognized a prosecutorial duty to disclose **exculpatory information** (that which tends to vindicate the accused) to the defense. This is based on the fundamental concept of our system of justice that individuals accused of crimes must be treated fairly. In *Brady v. Maryland* (1963), the Supreme Court stated that "the suppression by the prosecution of evidence favorable to the accused upon request violates due process where the evidence is material either to guilt or punishment, irrespective of the good faith or bad faith of the prosecution."[44]

The Supreme Court has held that, in addition to substantive exculpatory evidence, evidence tending to impeach the credibility of prosecution witnesses falls within *Brady*'s definition of evidence favorable to an accused. Therefore, under *Brady*, a defendant is entitled to disclosure of information that might be used to impeach government witnesses. Generally, the defense must request the disclosure of the exculpatory evidence. However, if the defense is unaware of the existence of the evidence, such a request is impossible. The Supreme Court has held that failure to request disclosure is not necessarily fatal to a later challenge based on *Brady v. Maryland,* but it may significantly affect the standard for determining materiality. In a similar vein, it has been held to be a denial of due process if a prosecutor knowingly allows perjured testimony to be used against the accused.

Most states have now adopted liberal rules pertaining to **pretrial discovery**, rules designed to avoid unfairness to the defense. Using appropriate pretrial motions, the defense and prosecution can gain access to the evidence possessed by the opposing party. Much of this is accomplished by taking depositions of prospective witnesses. Discovery in a criminal case is somewhat more limited in federal than in state courts. Under the provisions of 18 U.S.C.A. §3500, a federal criminal defendant is not entitled to inspect a statement or report prepared by a government witness "until said witness has testified on direct examination in the trial of the case." After a witness testifies, the government, upon proper request of the defense, must then produce that portion of any statement or report that relates to the subject matter as to which the witness has testified. The federal statute is commonly referred to as the *Jencks* **Act** because its effect was first recognized in *Jencks v. United States* (1957).[45]

The Right to a Speedy Trial

The Sixth Amendment to the federal Constitution guarantees the defendant the **right to a speedy trial.** The Speedy Trial Clause of the Sixth Amendment is made applicable to the states through the Fourteenth Amendment.[46] In 1972, the Supreme Court refused to mandate a specific time limit between the filing of charges and the commencement of trial. Instead, it adopted a balancing test to determine whether a defendant was denied the right to a speedy trial. Under this test, courts must consider (1) the length of the delay; (2) the reasons for the delay; (3) the defendant's assertion of the right; and (4) prejudice to the defendant.[47]

In 1974, Congress enacted the Speedy Trial Act, which provides specific time limits for pretrial and trial procedures in the federal courts.[48] For example, an indictment must be filed within 30 days of arrest; arraignment must be held within 10 days of indictment; and trial must commence within 70 days after indictment. Violations of the time limitations are remedied by dismissal of charges. However, there are a number of exceptions to the time limits, especially when defendants' motions cause delays. Most states have adopted legislation or court rules along the lines of the federal speedy trial law.

A defendant who can establish that the prosecutor intentionally delayed an indictment to gain a tactical advantage and that the defendant incurred actual prejudice as a result of the delay can assert a claim of denial of due process.

THE CRIMINAL TRIAL

A trial is the centerpiece of the criminal justice system. In criminal trials the interests of the state and the individual are in sharp contrast. In general, the procedures in a criminal trial follow the sequence of those in a civil trial as outlined in Chapter 9. However, the standard of proof required to convict a defendant is **proof beyond a reasonable doubt,** which is a more stringent standard than the preponderance of evidence standard that applies to civil trials. Moreover, in a criminal trial a number of significant constitutional guarantees come into play, and the rights of a criminal defendant must be scrupulously guarded.

The Prosecution's Case

Prosecutors are ever mindful that when a defendant pleads not guilty the government must establish the defendant's guilt beyond any reasonable doubt. In presenting the government's case, the prosecuting attorney usually calls as witnesses police officers, the victim, and any other available witnesses whose testimony can support the charge against the defendant. The government's witnesses may also include experts. For example, in a homicide prosecution the prosecutor usually calls a physician; in a drug trafficking case, a chemist; in a forgery prosecution, a handwriting expert. A technician who has conducted laboratory tests on DNA samples in homicide and sexual battery cases is often called to testify.

Significant Constitutional Rights of the Defendant

The Sixth Amendment to the U.S. Constitution is the basis of many trial rights for defendants. The Sixth Amendment is made applicable to state criminal trials by the Fourteenth

Amendment.[49] The Sixth Amendment guarantees the defendant the right to be confronted with the witnesses who offer evidence against the defendant; thus, the defendant has the right to be present at trial and to cross-examine each witness the prosecution presents. The **right of cross-examination** of an adversary's witness is absolute. The right of cross-examination is available to both the prosecutor and the defense counsel and is extremely valuable in the trial of criminal cases. The permissible scope of cross-examination, however, varies somewhat in different jurisdictions and is a matter largely within the discretion of the trial court. Courts generally agree that the right of cross-examination is limited to (1) questioning the witness about matters testified to on direct examination, and (2) asking any questions that may impeach the witness's credibility or demonstrate any bias, interest, or hostility on the part of the witness.

Although in most instances it is objectionable for a lawyer who is examining a witness to ask **leading questions** on direct examination, the rules of evidence permit a cross-examiner to ask such questions. Frequently, a cross-examiner is successful in bringing out inconsistencies and contradictions and any bias or hostility of the witness. A witness may also be subject to **impeachment,** that is, having one's credibility attacked on cross-examination. A witness's credibility may be attacked by:

- showing the witness's inability to have viewed or heard the matters the witness has testified to, or inability to recall the event testified to;
- demonstrating that the witness has made prior conflicting statements on an important point;
- showing the witness has been convicted of a crime;
- establishing that the witness bears a bad reputation for truth in the community; or
- showing bias, prejudice, motive to misrepresent the facts, or that the witness has a definite interest in the result of the trial.

The defendant's right of confrontation guaranteeing a face-to-face meeting with witnesses appearing before the judge or jury is not absolute. It must occasionally give way to considerations of public policy and necessities of the case. The constitutional **right of confrontation** came into sharp focus in 1988 when the Supreme Court held that a defendant's Sixth Amendment right to confront witnesses was violated in a sexual abuse case in which the trial judge, pursuant to an Iowa law, allowed a screen to be erected between the defendant and the two 13-year-old girls that Coy was accused of assaulting. The two children were situated so they could not see the defendant during their testimony.[50] The Court left open the question of whether a procedure that shields a child sex abuse victim may be constitutionally acceptable if there is an individualized finding that the witness is in need of such protection. Recently several states have refined their **child-shield statutes** affecting children who are victims of sexual abuse. These revised statutes have met with varying reactions from state appellate courts. To avoid the constitutional requirements of the Confrontation Clause, the prosecution must show and the trial judge must make particularized findings that a child victim of sexual abuse would suffer unreasonable and unnecessary mental or emotional harm if the child were to testify in the presence of the defendant.

Article 3, Section 2, of the U.S. Constitution provides that trial of all crimes, except in cases of impeachment, shall be by jury. Subsequently the Sixth Amendment was adopted guaranteeing that "[i]n all criminal prosecutions, the accused shall enjoy the right to a speedy and public trial, by an impartial jury." The constitutional mandate leaves unanswered questions concerning the qualifications of jurors, the method of their selection, and the requirements for a jury to convict a person accused of a crime.

An accused may waive the right to a **jury trial.** Indeed, many persons who plead not guilty to misdemeanor charges elect a **bench trial.** On the other hand, most defendants who plead not guilty to felony charges choose to be tried by jury. The Supreme Court has ruled that the constitutional right to a jury trial extends to the class of cases for which an accused was entitled to a jury trial when the Constitution was adopted. This did not include juvenile cases; hence, there is no right to a jury trial for juveniles nor is the right to a jury trial applicable to military tribunals under the federal Constitution. As now interpreted, the Sixth Amendment guarantees an accused the right to a jury trial in criminal cases where a penalty of more than six months in jail can be imposed.[51] Offenses that carry a possible penalty of no more than six months imprisonment are generally termed *petty offenses,* and a jury trial is not required under the U.S. Constitution.[52]

Size of the Trial Jury

At common law a jury consisted of 12 men. Rule 23(b), Federal Rules of Criminal Procedure, requires a 12-member jury in criminal cases in federal courts unless the defendant stipulates to fewer in writing. All states require 12-member juries in capital cases. Most require the same number for all felony prosecutions. Many, however, now use less than 12 jurors in misdemeanor cases. Six-person juries in both felony and misdemeanor cases are permissible, but states may not reduce jury size below this level.[53]

In federal courts and in the great majority of state courts, a jury verdict in a criminal trial must be unanimous. A few states, however, accept less than unanimous verdicts. The Supreme Court has approved nonunanimous verdicts rendered by 12-person juries but it has ruled that a verdict by a 6-person jury must be unanimous.[54]

Jury Selection

As discussed in Chapter 9, state and federal laws prescribe qualifications for jurors and set forth the processes by which citizens are summoned for jury duty. The body of persons summoned to be jurors is referred to as the **venire.** The jury is selected from the venire through a process known as *voir dire.* During *voir dire,* counsel will ask prospective jurors questions designed to detect biases. Counsel will challenge prospective jurors they believe to be biased against their side of the case. **Challenges for cause** require a ruling from the bench, while **peremptory challenges** do not require counsel to state a cause and are not subject to review by the court, except that peremptory challenges cannot be exercised on the basis of a prospective juror's race or gender (for more discussion, see Chapter 9).

The Supreme Court has said that **death qualification of a jury** (the exclusion of prospective jurors who will not under any circumstances vote for imposition of the death penalty) is designed to obtain a jury that can properly and impartially apply the law to the facts at both the guilt and sentencing phases of a capital trial. On this rationale, the Court upheld the removal before the guilt phase in a capital trial of prospective jurors whose opposition to the death penalty would impair or prevent performance of their duties at the sentencing phase.[55]

Free Press vs. Fair Trial

Because of First Amendment rights the Supreme Court has held that trials may not be closed without findings sufficient to overcome the presumption of openness.[56] Nevertheless, First Amendment guarantees of freedom of the press often collide with a defendant's right to a fair trial before an impartial jury, particularly when heightened public interest results in mass media coverage of a trial, with potential prejudicial effects on witnesses and jurors. When this occurs the trial court must protect the defendant's right to a fair trial by taking steps to prevent these influences from affecting the rights of a defendant. Failure to do so can result in a verdict of guilty being overturned by an appellate tribunal.

Cameras in the Courtroom

During the 1970s, many state courts began to allow radio, television, and still-camera coverage of court proceedings subject to limitations necessary to preserve the essential dignity of a trial (for example, equipment must be noiseless, and strong lights are not permitted). Also, judges may limit coverage by requiring pooling of media equipment. Nevertheless, Rule 53 of the Federal Rules of Criminal Procedure still prohibits the taking of photographs in the courtroom during the progress of judicial proceedings in federal courts. By 1993 cameras were allowed in the courtrooms in most state courts. And while there was some backlash on the televising of criminal trials following the O.J. Simpson case of 1995, still most believe that cameras in the courtroom have enhanced the public's awareness of the judicial processes.

Most state courts now permit television and photographic coverage of court proceedings, where the consent of the presiding judge is required, and judges generally have considerable discretion in control of the coverage. Coverage of jurors is either prohibited or restricted, and most states prohibit coverage of cases involving juveniles and victims of sex crimes.

"Order in the Court"

Occasionally a trial judge is confronted with a defendant or others in attendance at a trial whose disruptive behavior impedes the court from conducting a trial in a proper judicial atmosphere. This problem is more likely encountered in a so-called political trial, where there may be support for the cause the defendant claims to represent. It is not too difficult for judges to exercise control over members of the public who attend court trials. The problem that confronts judges is when a defendant becomes unruly. In most instances judges control disruption and defiance by defendants and others through exercise of the **power of contempt.** Yet in recent years some courts have had to go further. The defendant may be removed from the courtroom until he promises to conduct himself properly. The defendant may even be bound and gagged, thereby keeping the defendant in the courtroom.

The Defense Strategy in Moving for a Judgment of Acquittal

At the close of the prosecution's evidence, the defense counsel will frequently move the court to grant a **directed verdict** or, as it is called in federal courts and many state courts, a **judgment of acquittal.** The trial judge determines whether the evidence presented by the prosecution is legally sufficient to support a verdict of guilty. For the purpose of ruling on the motion, the trial judge must view the prosecution's evidence in the light most favorable to the government. Should the motion be granted, the defendant is discharged. If denied, defense counsel proceeds with the case on behalf of the defendant, and if additional evidence is offered, defense counsel may renew the motion at the close of all the evidence.

The Defense Case—Will the Defendant Take the Stand?

The defendant does not have to testify in a criminal case and often defendants choose to rely simply on cross-examination of the government's witnesses in an effort to obtain an acquittal. Or, the defendant may present witnesses in support of an alibi, to contradict the prosecution's witnesses or to establish an affirmative defense. Perhaps the major tactical decision a defendant and defense counsel must make at trial is whether the defendant will take the stand and testify on his or her behalf. The Fifth Amendment privilege against self-incrimination, which applies to the states through the Fourteenth Amendment,[57] protects the defendant from being required to testify, absent a grant of immunity. Moreover, it also forbids any direct or indirect comment by the prosecution on the accused's failure to testify. When an accused voluntarily chooses to testify in his or her own behalf, the prosecution may cross-examine the accused with the same latitude as with any other witness.

Jury Instructions

At the close of all evidence in a jury trial, it is customary for the trial judge to confer with counsel outside the presence of the jury concerning the instructions on the law the judge will give to the jury. The prosecutor and defense counsel may be asked to present proposed instructions for the court to consider. More commonly, the trial judge announces that the court will give certain standard instructions and offers to supplement them with specific instructions to be chosen from those submitted by counsel. A defendant is entitled to have the jury instructed on the law applicable to any legitimate theory of defense that is supported by the evidence presented.

Typically, at the conclusion of the closing arguments the judge either reads the indictment or information or explains the charges against the defendant to the jury. This is followed by an admonition that the defendant is presumed innocent unless and until the government proves the defendant guilty beyond a reasonable doubt of each element of the crime. The judge defines the elements of any crime charged and explains any technical legal terms. Where the jury may convict the defendant of a lesser offense, the judge must go further than merely defining the crime charged.

Jury instructions are given orally, and in some instances the jury is given a copy of the instructions. The clerk furnishes the jury forms of verdicts so they may find the defendant not guilty, guilty as charged, or guilty of some degree of the offense charged or of a lesser-included offense. In federal criminal trials and in most state courts, the judge explains the requirement for a unanimous verdict. In some states the judge is required to inform the jury of the penalties that can be imposed for the offense charged. Finally, the jury is directed to retire, select one of its members as **foreperson,** and deliberate on its verdict. Usually a jury is allowed to take with it to the jury room all exhibits received in evidence.

The Jury Deliberates and Returns its Verdict

When directed to deliberate, the jurors are escorted to their quarters by a court bailiff. In some cases the judge orders the jury sequestered, which means the jury must remain together until it reaches its verdict. **Sequestration** often requires the bailiff to escort the jurors to a hotel and to be present with them during meals to ensure that no outside influences are brought to bear on their judgment. Once in the jury room, their first order of business is to elect a foreperson. Then they are ready to commence their deliberations.

When a jury has concluded its deliberations, it returns to the courtroom and delivers its written verdict. A defendant who is acquitted by a jury is immediately discharged. If a jury finds the defendant guilty, the defendant is generally taken into custody to await sentencing. In some instances the defendant may be continued on bail, pending application for a new trial or an appeal. In cases of a **deadlocked jury,** the trial judge can either declare a mistrial or urge the jury to make further attempts to arrive at a verdict.

SENTENCING

Although every jurisdiction requires that criminal sentences for adults be imposed in open court, in many instances juvenile offenders may be sentenced *in camera*. In misdemeanor cases, sentencing usually occurs immediately upon conviction. In felony cases, where penalties are greater, sentencing may be postponed to allow the court to conduct a **presentence investigation.**

In many states as well as the federal system, the court is required to order a presentence report where the offender to be sentenced is a first offender, or under a certain age. In other state jurisdictions the sentencing judge is accorded discretion in this area. The presentence report sets forth the defendant's history of delinquency or criminality, medical history, family background, economic status, education, employment history, and other relevant factors. Additionally, most jurisdictions allow courts to order physical and/or mental examinations of defendants.

In some states, statutes, court rules, or judicial interpretations mandate that courts release a presentence report to the defendant or defendant's counsel, usually allowing some exemptions for sensitive material. In other states, courts have ruled that this is a matter within the discretion of the sentencing judge. In some instances courts will reveal factual material such as police reports, but decline to disclose statements made in confidence to investigators. The Supreme Court requires release of presentence reports to defendants who may be sentenced to death.

The Sentencing Hearing

After the presentence report is completed, the court holds a **sentencing hearing.** At this hearing, the court considers the evidence received at trial, the presentence report, any evidence offered by either party in aggravation or mitigation of sentence, and any statement the defendant wishes to make. The **pronouncement of sentence** is the stage when the trial court imposes a penalty upon a defendant for the offense of which the defendant has been adjudged guilty. Sentences are pronounced in open court, usually by the judge who presided at the defendant's trial or entry of plea. In misdemeanor cases sentencing often occurs immediately after entry of a plea or a finding of guilty by the judge or jury. In felony cases the pronouncement is often delayed until the court has received a presentence investigation report or until the prosecutor and defense counsel have had an opportunity to prepare a presentation.

Sentencing is a "critical stage" of a criminal proceeding at which the defendant is entitled to be represented by counsel. Counsel must be supplied to indigent defendants.[58] The rules of evidence are relaxed during a sentencing proceeding. The procedure at the pronouncement stage is generally outlined in the criminal procedure rules of each jurisdiction. A verbatim account is made of the entire sentencing proceeding. Traditionally a defendant has been afforded an opportunity to make a statement on his or her own behalf, a procedure often referred to as the right of **allocution.** Generally special rules govern the sentencing of a defendant who is insane, and often sentencing must be deferred for a female defendant who is pregnant.

In many instances where a defendant is convicted of a noncapital crime, courts are authorized to suspend the imposition of sentence and place the defendant on probation or under community control for some determinate period. Of course, if the defendant violates conditions set by the court, then the original sentence may be imposed. A **suspended sentence** is most often used in cases of first offenses or nonviolent offenses. A defendant who is convicted of multiple crimes must be given separate sentences for each offense. These sentences may run consecutively or concurrently, usually at the discretion of the sentencing judge.

Indeterminate, Definite, Determinate, and Indefinite Sentencing

For much of the twentieth century, legislatures commonly allowed judges to sentence criminals to imprisonment for indeterminate periods in order to assist corrections officials in the process of rehabilitating offenders. Under this system, release from prison took the form of parole. Abuses of the system, combined with the decline of popular support for rehabilitation, have led most jurisdictions to abandon the concept of **indeterminate sentencing.** Despite this trend, a number of state laws retain indeterminate sentencing for youthful offenders.

At the opposite extreme from indeterminate sentencing is **definite sentencing**, an approach designed to eliminate discretion and ensure that offenders who commit the same crimes are punished equally. The definite sentence is set by the legislature with no leeway for judges or corrections officials to individualize punishment. Under **determinate sentencing**, a variation of the definite sentence, the judge sets a fixed term of years within statutory parameters and the offender is required to serve that term without the possibility of early release. The most common approach is referred to as **indefinite sentencing**. Here there is judicial discretion to impose a sentence within a range of prescribed minimum and maximum penalties. What distinguishes indefinite from determinate sentencing is that indefinite sentencing allows for early release from prison on parole.

Mandatory Minimum Sentencing

Mandatory sentences result from legislative mandates that offenders who commit certain crimes must be sentenced to prison terms for minimum periods. Under **mandatory sentencing**, there is no option for judges to place offenders on probation. Most often, mandatory sentences are required for violent crimes, especially those involving the use of firearms. As a result of the "war on drugs" launched in the 1980s, federal law now mandates minimum prison terms for serious drug crimes. For example, a person charged with possession with the intent to distribute more than 5 kilograms of cocaine is subject to a mandatory minimum sentence of 10 years in prison.[59] Federal courts have no authority to impose lesser sentences than those mandated by Congress unless prosecutors specifically request such departures.

Penalty Enhancement Statutes

In an effort to incapacitate **habitual offenders**, the laws of many states require automatic increased penalties for persons convicted of repeated felonies. In 1980, the Supreme Court upheld a life sentence imposed under the Texas habitual offender statute mandating life terms for persons convicted of three felonies.[60] A variation on the habitual offender law is known colloquially as **"three strikes and you're out."** In 1994, California voters overwhelmingly approved a ballot initiative under which persons convicted of a third violent or "serious" felony would be incarcerated for 25 years to life. Prosecutors immediately availed themselves of this new weapon, but in many instances the new law led to controversial results. However, in 1996, a California appellate court held that trial judges had the power to strike prior felony convictions, thus making a defendant ineligible for three-strikes sentencing.[61] This interpretation of the trial courts authority attenuated somewhat the harshness of the three-strikes policy.

The 1994 Federal Crime Bill provided for mandatory life sentences for persons convicted in federal court of a "serious violent felony" after having been previously convicted, in federal or state court, of two "serious violent felonies." Currently, the federal government and more than half the states have some form of habitual offender or three-strikes statute.

Another approach to sentencing that has gained popularity in recent years is enhancing or extending penalties based on characteristics of the crime or the victim. For example, in 1993, the Supreme Court upheld a Wisconsin statute that increases the severity of punishment if a crime victim is chosen on the basis of race or other designated characteristics.[62]

In an effort to strengthen law enforcement in the war on drugs, the Violent Crime Control and Law Enforcement Act of 1994, better known as The Federal Crime Bill, included several provisions for enhanced penalties. Drug trafficking in prisons and drug-free zones, illegal drug use in or smuggling drugs into federal prisons are now subject to enhanced penalties.

Sentencing Guidelines

In the face of considerable criticism of the exercise of judicial discretion, which often resulted in great disparities in sentences, Congress and a number of state legislatures adopted **sentencing guidelines.** Some states have adopted voluntary guidelines; others have mandated that sentencing conform to guidelines absent a compelling reason for departing from them.

The federal guidelines came into being with the enactment of the Sentencing Reform Act of 1984, which applies to all crimes committed after November 1, 1987.[63] The act created the U.S. Sentencing Commission and empowered it to promulgate sentencing guidelines. The resulting guidelines drastically reduced the discretion of federal judges by establishing a narrow sentencing range with the proviso that the sentencing court may depart from the guidelines if it "finds that there exists an aggravating or mitigating circumstance of a kind, or to a degree, not adequately taken into consideration . . . in formulating the guidelines that should result in a sentence different from that described." Of course, it is impermissible to depart from the guidelines on the basis of the defendant's race, sex, national origin, religion, or socioeconomic status. Other factors not ordinarily deemed relevant in determining whether to depart include the defendant's age, education, mental and physical condition, employment history, and family and community ties.

States have experimented with sentencing guidelines with varying results. Minnesota, the first state to adopt presumptive sentencing guidelines in 1970, has a relatively simple system that has proven to be workable, although it has resulted in a higher incarceration rate. Washington's sentencing guidelines worked reasonably well until the state legislature began to mandate increased penalties overall as well as harsher minimum sentences for particular crimes. This has necessitated that the guidelines be revised. In Tennessee, the commission that established sentencing guidelines was terminated, although the guidelines themselves remain in effect.

There is still considerable uncertainty about the efficacy of sentencing guidelines. There is evidence that they have reduced unwarranted sentencing disparities, but clearly they have not eliminated this problem altogether. There is also concern that sentencing guidelines have generally promoted higher incarceration rates and have thus contributed to the problem of prison overcrowding.

Granting and Revoking Probation

With the overcrowding of prisons, courts have come to rely increasingly on probation for first-time and nonviolent offenders. Under federal law a defendant who has been found guilty of an offense may be sentenced to a term of probation unless (1) the offense is a felony where the maximum term of imprisonment authorized is 25 years or more, life imprisonment, or death; or (2) the offense is one for which probation has been expressly precluded; or (3) the defendant is sentenced at the same time to a term of imprisonment for the same or a different offense. Probation terms for a felony must not be less than one or more than five years and for a misdemeanor not more than five years.[64] Certain conditions of probation are mandatory and others are discretionary with the federal judge who imposes probation.[65] In most states, the term of probation is limited to the maximum statutory term of confinement for the particular offense. In some instances mandatory conditions are imposed by statute, but the trial court may impose additional conditions. Probation is often combined with a fine, restitution to the victim, or a short term of incarceration to give the probationer "a taste" of jail.

In every jurisdiction, the commission of a felony while on probation is grounds for revocation. In many jurisdictions, certain misdemeanors qualify as grounds for revocation. The violation of any substantive condition of probation is grounds for revocation. Typically, a probation officer is vested with broad discretion in determining when to seek revocation of probation. A probationer facing the loss of freedom is entitled to a fair hearing at which the probationer has the right to call favorable witnesses, to confront hostile witnesses, and to be represented by counsel. In 1974, the Supreme Court said that indigent probationers may have a constitutional right to have counsel appointed at revocation hearings, depending on the complexity of the issues involved, and that if counsel is not provided, the judge must state the reason.[66] In practice, counsel is usually provided. There is a statutory right to appointment of counsel for those financially unable to obtain counsel in federal probation revocation proceedings.[67]

Prison Disciplinary Hearings and Revocation of Parole

Today, disciplinary measures in prisons often consist of removal of good-time credit toward early release. If officials pursue this policy, then due process of law demands that certain procedural requirements be observed before good-time credit is removed for disciplinary purposes. Specifically, there must be written notice of the disciplinary action, and the inmate has the right to an administrative hearing with a written record. The inmate must be accorded the right to produce evidence refuting the charges of misconduct and may even call witnesses on his or her behalf. These rights have not been extended to allow an inmate to have counsel present at **prison disciplinary hearings,** however.[68]

As in the case of internal prison disciplinary actions, the revocation of **parole** is affected by due process considerations. Essentially, before parole can be revoked, the parolee has the right to a hearing within a reasonable time after being retaken into custody. The Supreme Court has said, "the process should be flexible enough to consider evidence including letters, affidavits, and other material that would not be admissible in an adversary criminal trial."[69] In addition, the Court has held that the right to counsel may apply to **parole revocation hearings,** depending on the complexity of the issues involved.[70] There is a statutory right to appointment of counsel for those financially unable to obtain counsel in federal parole revocation hearings.[71]

Sentencing in Capital Cases

In those cases where the prosecution is permitted by law to seek the death penalty, the sentencing procedure is considerably more complex. In *Furman v. Georgia* (1972), the Supreme Court imposed a moratorium on the death penalty, prompting state legislatures to rewrite their capital punishment statutes.[72] The post-*Furman* capital punishment laws require a **bifurcated trial** in cases where the prosecution seeks the death penalty. In the first stage, guilt is determined according to the usual procedures, rules of evidence, and standard of proof. If the jury finds the defendant guilty, the same jury considers the appropriateness of the death sentence in a separate proceeding where additional evidence is received in aggravation or mitigation of the punishment. To impose the death penalty, the jury must find at least one of several **aggravating factors** specified by law. The purpose of requiring aggravating factors before imposing the death penalty is to narrow the cases and persons eligible for capital punishment and make the imposition of the death penalty more predictable. In *Gregg v. Georgia* (1976), the Supreme Court upheld Georgia's revised death penalty statute by a vote of 7–2.[73] Apparently the Court was satisfied that this scheme had sufficiently addressed the evils identified in *Furman*. Thirty-nine states now have death penalty statutes modeled along the lines of the law upheld in *Gregg*.

Mitigating Factors and Victim Impact Evidence

During the sentencing phase of the capital trial, the defense usually introduces evidence of **mitigating factors**: the defendant's youth, alcoholism or drug dependency, the defendant's history of mental illness or instability, the absence of criminal record, the fact that there was some provocation by the defendant, and so forth. The jury can take anything into account by way of mitigation, assigning whatever weight it thinks appropriate. Sometimes the defense will put the mother or other close relative of the defendant on the stand to plead for the defendant's life. Prosecutors counter emotional pleas on the defendant's behalf by presenting **victim impact evidence**. This evidence takes the form of testimony addressing the impact of the murder on the victim and the victim's family, including the physical, economic, and psychological effects of the crime. For example, the victim's surviving spouse might be called to testify to the toll the homicide has taken on the family. Needless to say, such testimony is often fraught with emotion and can have a powerful impact on the jury. Nevertheless, its constitutionality has been affirmed by the Supreme Court.[74]

VICTIMS' RIGHTS IN THE CRIMINAL PROCESS

Although crime is by definition an injury against society as a whole, we must not forget that most serious crimes injure individual victims, often quite severely. The injury may transcend physical or economic injury to include emotional hardship. If during the 1960s the dominant concern of the criminal law was for the rights of the accused, since the 1990s the trend has been to recognize the rights of crime victims. A number of states—including Arizona, California, Florida, Michigan, New Jersey, Rhode Island, Texas, and Washington—have adopted constitutional amendments specifically recognizing victims' rights. Other states have adopted statutes along these lines.[75] During the 1990s, a proposal to add a victims' rights amendment to the U.S. Constitution surfaced in Congress, but the amendment was not adopted. There are now more than 9,000 organizations (mostly private) dedicated to assisting crime victims. Clearly, there is substantial public support for efforts to recognize and enhance victims' rights.

The Uniform Victims of Crime Act

The Uniform Victims of Crime Act (UVCA) is an attempt to lend uniformity to the patchwork of victims' rights laws that now exists at the state level. The UVCA was developed by the Uniform Law Commission, a voluntary association of lawyers from every state. Like the Model Penal Code developed by the American Law Institute, the UVCA has no status as law unless and until it is adopted by a state legislature.

Under the UVCA, prosecutors or court personnel must notify victims of their rights under the act, as well as the times of any court proceedings involving the person or persons who allegedly victimized them. A crime victim has a right to be present at any court proceeding that the defendant has a right to attend. If the defendant is convicted, the victim has the right to make an impact statement during the sentencing hearing and assert an opinion as to the proper sentence. Finally, the UVCA provides for victims to be compensated by the state, up to $25,000, for any physical or emotional injuries suffered as the result of the victimization. However, this amount may be denied or reduced if the victim receives compensation through insurance or restitution from the defendant.

Restitution

Restitution refers to "the return of a sum of money, an object, or the value of an object which the defendant wrongfully obtained in the course of committing the crime."[76] Although restitution was practiced under the early common law, it was eventually abandoned as a remedy in criminal cases in favor of fines payable to the Crown. In modern America, however, restitution is making a comeback in the criminal law. A number of states have enacted laws allowing trial courts to require restitution as a condition of probation, in lieu of sentencing offenders to prison.

Restitution is not practical in many criminal cases. Many offenders are not suited to probation and, even among those who are, there is no guarantee that they will be able to make payments to the victim. Recognizing this problem, a number of states have established victims' compensation commissions. For example, the Florida Crimes Compensation Act of 1977 makes victims and certain relatives eligible for compensation by a state commission when a crime results in injuries and is reported within 72 hours. Awards are limited to meeting the actual needs of victims.[77]

THE APPEALS PROCESS

Society's commitment to standards of fairness and procedural regularity is reflected in the opportunities that exist for defendants in criminal cases to seek higher judicial review of adverse court decisions. At common law there was no right to appeal from a criminal conviction prior to the eighteenth century. On rare occasions the Crown issued a "writ of error" to require a new trial, but there was no appeal in the modern sense. At early common law, *appeal* referred to an effort by a person convicted of treason to obtain a pardon from the Crown by accusing others of being accomplices to the treasonable act. Through judicial decisions and acts of Parliament, defendants eventually acquired the right to appeal their convictions to higher courts. The U.S. Constitution makes no mention of the right to appeal from a criminal conviction, although some might argue that the right to appeal is implicit in the due process clauses of the Fifth and Fourteenth Amendments. In 1894, the U.S. Supreme Court held that the federal Constitution affords no right to appeal from a criminal conviction.[78] However, Congress and the state legislatures have provided for various types of appellate review. These remedies have increased greatly in recent decades, largely through judicial interpretation of statutory provisions.

Forms of Appellate Review

Forms of review in criminal cases include **trial *de novo*, appeal of right, discretionary review,** and **postconviction relief.** Trial *de novo* occurs when a trial court of general jurisdiction reviews a conviction rendered by a court of limited jurisdiction. Appeal of right, the most common form of appeal, refers to an appellate court's review of a criminal conviction rendered by a trial court of general jurisdiction. A defendant whose conviction is affirmed on appeal may seek further review by a higher court by petitioning for discretionary review. Finally, a defendant confined to prison may seek additional review of a conviction or sentence by applying for a **writ of habeas corpus,** which allows a court of competent jurisdiction to review the legality of a prisoner's confinement. Each of these mechanisms plays an important part in the determination of cases that move beyond the trial stage of the criminal process.

The mechanics of the handling of criminal appeals insofar as relates to records, briefing, oral argument, and the court's decision-making processes are essentially as described in Chapter 9 in relation to appeals in civil cases.

What Defendants May Challenge on Appeal

In a direct appeal from a criminal conviction, a defendant may challenge any act of the trial court objected to by the defendant during the pretrial, trial, or posttrial phases of the defendant's case. Irrespective of whether an objection was made in the trial court, a defendant may challenge the trial court's jurisdiction and those trial court actions or rulings considered to be **fundamental errors.** Appellate courts take different approaches to how serious an error must be to be classified as fundamental. Courts are more liberal in reviewing errors first challenged at the appellate stage where the defendant has been convicted of a capital crime. The U.S. Supreme Court has said that when a person's life is at stake, fundamental errors not specifically challenged by the appellant should be corrected by the reviewing court.

Although appellate review is designed to correct errors that occur during or before trial, not all errors necessitate reversal. This is referred to as the **doctrine of harmless error.** To obtain reversal of a judgment, the appellant must show that some prejudice resulted from the error and that the outcome of the trial or the sentence imposed would probably have been different in the absence of the error. Where an error involves provisions of the federal Constitution, appellate courts must find beyond a reasonable doubt that the error was harmless in order to affirm the trial court.[79]

The Right to Counsel on Appeal

The Supreme Court has said that states must provide counsel to indigent persons convicted of felonies who exercise their statutory right to appeal.[80] However, the Court has also held that a state's failure to provide counsel to an indigent defendant seeking discretionary review in the state and federal supreme courts does not violate due process or equal protection.[81]

Challenging State Court Convictions in Federal Court

The Supreme Court can review only a minute proportion of the cases in which persons convicted in state courts seek to challenge their convictions on federal constitutional grounds. The writ of habeas corpus is another means of obtaining federal judicial review of state court convictions. In recent decades, **federal habeas corpus review** of state criminal convictions has become a common form of appellate procedure. It has also greatly multiplied the opportunities for persons convicted of state offenses to obtain relief. Consequently, it has become the focus of considerable controversy.

The Federal Judiciary Act of 1789 recognized the power of federal courts to issue writs of habeas corpus only in respect to federal prisoners.[82] In 1867, federal law was amended to allow federal courts to entertain habeas petitions from state prisoners who allege that their incarceration violates provisions of the U.S. Constitution or federal statutes or treaties.[83]

Prior to the twentieth century, the federal habeas corpus jurisdiction was seldom used to review state criminal convictions. Federal law had long provided that federal habeas corpus relief was available only to state prisoners who had exhausted all available remedies in the state courts. But in 1963, the Supreme Court held that a state prisoner did not have to take a direct appeal to the state supreme court in order to seek federal habeas corpus review. Nor was the prisoner barred from raising constitutional issues in federal court merely because he had not raised them on direct appeal. By the 1990s, the Supreme Court took a more conservative stance and in 1993 ruled that federal district courts may not overturn state criminal convictions unless the petitioner can show that he or she suffered "actual prejudice" from the errors cited in the petition.[84] Previously, the state carried the burden of proving beyond a reasonable doubt that any constitutional error committed during or prior to trial was "harmless," that is, not prejudicial to the defendant.

The Antiterrorism and Effective Death Penalty Act of 1996 curtailed second habeas corpus petitions by state prisoners who have already filed such petitions in federal court. Under the new statute, any second or subsequent habeas petition must meet a particularly high standard and must pass through a "gatekeeping" function exercised by the U.S. Courts of Appeals, which must grant a motion giving the inmate permission to file the petition in a district court; denial of this motion is not appealable to the Supreme Court. In 1996, an inmate awaiting execution in Georgia challenged the constitutionality of this provision, but in a unanimous decision the Supreme Court upheld the statute.[85]

Postconviction Relief in State Courts

The constitutional rights of criminal defendants were greatly expanded as a result of the Supreme Court's decisions of the 1960s thereby effectively "nationalizing" criminal procedure. During those years the states began to review the efficacy of the writ of habeas corpus as a basis for permitting challenges to judgments and sentences subsequent to conclusion of a direct appeal. As a result most states adopted statutes or court rules that permit a post-appeal challenge to an illegal conviction or sentence. These procedures, known as **collateral attack** or postconviction relief, provide a mechanism for a defendant who is incarcerated to obtain a review of judgments and sentences imposed in violation of the federal or state constitutions.

Ineffective counsel constitutes a common basis for postconviction attacks on convictions and sentences. The issue of ineffective counsel is rarely raised on direct appeal as it is not a matter that would ordinarily be challenged in the trial court. In 1984, the Supreme Court articulated a uniform constitutional standard for determining the issue of ineffective counsel.[86] First, the defendant must show that counsel's performance was deficient. This requires showing that counsel made errors so serious that counsel was not functioning as the "counsel" guaranteed the defendant by the Sixth Amendment. Second, the defendant must show that the deficient performance prejudiced the defense. This requires showing that counsel's errors were so serious as to deprive the defendant of a fair trial, a trial whose result is reliable.

CONCLUSION

The Framers of the Bill of Rights imposed constraints on law enforcement not because they were opposed to law and order, but because they were deeply distrustful of power. They feared what well-meaning but overzealous officials might do if not constrained by the rule of law. Consequently, they gave us a Bill of Rights that makes it more difficult for government to investigate, prosecute, and punish crime. During the 1960s, the Supreme Court under Chief Justice Warren interpreted these protections more broadly than courts had traditionally viewed them. In the 1980s, the pendulum swung back in the other direction as more conservative justices were appointed to the Court. In the 1990s, a more moderate Court has refrained from making major changes in this field of constitutional interpretation. Of course, the great challenge to the Supreme Court, indeed to all courts, is to strike the proper balance between society's need for crime control and our equally strong desire for individual privacy and freedom.

SUMMARY OF KEY CONCEPTS

The U.S. Constitution protects the rights of an individual accused of crime from the earliest stages of investigation to the finality of appellate review of a conviction of a crime. Central to procedural requirements are three amendments to the Constitution. The Fourth Amendment protects against unreasonable searches and seizures. Its safeguards have been fleshed out by the Supreme Court in respect to the preference for warrants and the requirements of probable cause in most instances. The Fifth Amendment and the Court's familiar 1966 Miranda requirements protect against the right against self-incrimination. The exclusionary rule, imposed against the states by the Court's 1961 *Mapp* decision, operates to restrain law enforcement from violating these rights. Finally, the Sixth Amendment guarantees a defendant the right to a speedy and public jury trial in all but cases involving minor offenses. Constitutional constraints also reach investigatory detentions, the investigatory process and the methods used by police in securing eyewitness and scientific means of identification of suspects.

In all felony and major misdemeanor processes the accusatorial processes of the law occur through grand juries returning indictments at the federal and often at the state level; however, states have the right to develop their own means of initiating prosecution and many have done so through prosecutors filing of sworn accusatorial documents known as informations. An accused in many instances is eligible for pretrial release through a variety of methods, the most common being the posting of a bail bond.

Once the federal or state government has instituted charges against a defendant, the defendant can opt to plead guilty or not guilty. A number of pretrial procedures are available to allow a defendant to learn of the strength of the prosecution's case before deciding whether to stand for trial. A defendant may be represented by counsel at all important pretrial and trial stages of a criminal prosecution and, since the Supreme Court's seminal decision in *Gideon v. Wainwright* in 1963, indigent defendants have the right to be represented by public defenders or court-appointed counsel.

A trial is the centerpiece of the criminal justice system. We have endeavored to take the student through the steps of a criminal trial, with emphasis on the requirement for proof beyond a reasonable doubt, and to explain the processes from selection of the jury to the return of the jury's verdict.

The rights of inmates have received constitutional protection; however, because victims are not the first-line players in a criminal prosecution, in the past their rights have not been accorded the attention many think victims deserve. Increasingly, legislative bodies and courts are responding to the demands of citizens to assure that the rights of victims of crime are considered by the criminal justice system.

Legislative bodies set the statutory parameters of punishment for criminal offenses; however, historically judges have been exercised discretion in imposing a sentence within those parameters. The trend has been to restrict judicial discretion in order to minimize disparities in punishment. The present approach relies heavily on sentencing guidelines that require courts to consider numerous factors when crafting a sentence within stated parameters. In jurisdictions where capital punishment is imposed, judges and juries must follow strict guidelines and consider aggravating and mitigating factors to ensure that death sentences comport with strict judicially imposed safeguards.

Finally, we have discussed the appeals process in criminal cases. The government's right to appeal is limited, essentially allowing such appeals only in respect to adverse rulings on jurisdictional matters, suppression of evidence, and the validity of charging documents. A defendant, on the other hand, has the right to appeal from a final order of conviction and sentence and to seek postconviction remedies available in federal and state courts.

QUESTIONS FOR THOUGHT AND DISCUSSION

1. In what instances and to what extent may a law enforcement officer conduct a search based on less than probable cause to believe the search will produce evidence of a crime?

2. What is the rationale for the exclusionary rule? Should the good-faith exception be extended to a situation where a police officer makes a warrantless arrest?

3. What constitutes an arrest? Is the use of arrest procedures for minor traffic offenses unnecessary? Is it better policy for a state to adopt procedures such as decriminalizing minor traffic offenses or simply give an officer discretion in handling these matters?

4. What scientific and nonscientific methods are used by the police to identify suspects?

5. What alternatives can you suggest to the traditional bail bond system to ensure the appearance of a defendant in court?

6. Should a judge participate directly in the process of plea bargaining? Why or why not?

7. Would the American system of criminal justice be more credible if the *voir dire* was conducted exclusively by the trial judge and only challenges for cause permitted?

8. In some jurisdictions trial judges now give basic instructions to the jury at the commencement of a trial. Evaluate this approach.

9. Describe and evaluate the most common forms of contemporary punishment.

10. Do you favor the use of sentencing guidelines or would giving the trial judge discretion to impose a penalty within statutory parameters be more effective?

11. What are the most common grounds urged by criminal defendants in direct appeals of right?

12. On what grounds may an incarcerated defendant seek postconviction relief?

KEY TERMS

criminal procedure

search

seizure

warrant

probable cause

reasonable suspicion

border searches

inventory search

consent to a search

wiretapping

electronic eavesdropping

reasonable expectation of privacy

strip searches

sobriety checkpoints

totality of circumstances

affidavit

affiant

confidential informants

anonymous tips

warrantless searches

exigent circumstances

plain view

emergency searches

evanescent evidence

automobile exception

search incident to a lawful arrest

hot pursuit

stop-and-frisk

drug testing

exclusionary rule

good-faith exception

arrest warrant

capias

warrantless arrest

investigatory detention

drug courier profiles

fruit of the poisonous tree doctrine

derivative evidence

independent source doctrine

public safety exception

right to counsel

public defender

self-representation

summary justice

initial appearance

pretrial release

bail

excessive bail

pretrial detention

prosecutorial discretion

plea bargaining

selective prosecution

preliminary hearing

information

indictment

grand jury

subpoena

immunity

transactional immunity

use immunity

pretrial motions

motion for continuance

motion for change of venue

motion to dismiss

motion to suppress

deposition

arraignment

plea of not guilty

plea of guilty

no contest plea

plea bargain

exculpatory information

pretrial discovery

Jencks Act

right to a speedy trial

proof beyond a reasonable doubt

right of cross-examination

leading questions

impeachment

right of confrontation

child-shield statutes

jury trial

bench trial

venire

voir dire

challenges for cause

peremptory challenges

death qualification of a jury

power of contempt

directed verdict

judgment of acquittal

jury instructions

foreperson

sequestration

deadlocked jury

presentence investigation

sentencing hearing

pronouncement of sentence

allocution

suspended sentence

indeterminate sentencing

definite sentencing

determinate sentencing

indefinite sentencing

mandatory sentencing

habitual offenders

"three strikes and you're out"

sentencing guidelines

prison disciplinary hearings

parole

parole revocation hearings

bifurcated trial

aggravating factors

mitigating factors

victim impact evidence

restitution

trial *de novo*

appeal of right

discretionary review

postconviction relief

writ of habeas corpus

fundamental errors

doctrine of harmless error

federal habeas corpus review

collateral attack

ENDNOTES

[1] *Wolf v. Colorado,* 338 U.S. 25, 27–28, 69 S.Ct. 1359, 1361, 93 L.Ed. 1782, 1785 (1949).

[2] *South Dakota v. Opperman,* 428 U.S. 364, 96 S.Ct. 3092, 49 L.Ed.2d 1000 (1976).

[3] *Schneckloth v. Bustamonte,* 412 U.S. 218, 93 S.Ct. 2041, 36 L.Ed.2d 854 (1973).

[4] *Ohio v. Robinette,* 519 U.S. 33, 117 S.Ct. 417, 136 L.Ed.2d 347 (1996).

[5] 389 U.S. 347, 88 S.Ct. 507, 19 L.Ed.2d 576.

[6] *Bell v. Wolfish,* 441 U.S. 520, 99 S.Ct. 1861, 60 L.Ed.2d 447 (1979).

[7] *Michigan Dept. of State Police v. Sitz,* 496 U.S. 444, 110 S.Ct. 2481, 110 L.Ed.2d 112 (1990).

[8] *Indianapolis v. Edmond,* 531 U.S. 32, 121 S.Ct. 447, 148 L.Ed.2d 333 (2000).

[9] *Illinois v. Gates,* 462 U.S. 213, 230, 103 S.Ct. 2317, 2328, 76 L.Ed. 2d 527, 543 (1983).

[10] *Illinois v. Gates,* 462 U.S. 213, 230, 103 S.Ct. 2317, 2328, 76 L.Ed. 2d 527, 543 (1983).

[11] *Coolidge v. New Hampshire,* 403 U.S. 443, 91 S.Ct. 2022, 29 L.Ed.2d 564 (1971).

[12] *Carroll v. United States,* 267 U.S. 132, 45 S.Ct. 280, 69 L.Ed. 543 (1925).

[13] *Chimel v. California,* 395 U.S. 752, 89 S.Ct. 2034, 23 L.Ed.2d 685 (1969).

[14] *Warden v. Hayden,* 387 U.S. 294, 87 S.Ct. 1642, 18 L.Ed.2d 782 (1967).

[15] *Terry v. Ohio,* 392 U.S. 1, 88 S.Ct. 1868, 20 L.Ed.2d 889 (1968).

[16] *Minnesota v. Dickerson,* 508 U.S. 366, 113 S.Ct. 2130, 124 L.Ed.2d 334 (1993).

[17] *New Jersey v. T.L.O.,* 469 U.S. 325, 105 S.Ct. 733, 83 L.Ed.2d 720 (1985).

[18] *National Treasury Employees Union v. Von Raab,* 489 U.S. 656, 109 S.Ct. 1384, 103 L.Ed.2d 685 (1989).

[19] *Chandler v. Miller,* 520 U.S. 305, 117 S.Ct. 1295, 137 L.Ed.2d 513 (1997).

[20] *Weeks v. United States,* 232 U.S. 383, 34 S.Ct. 341, 58 L.Ed. 652 (1914).

[21] 367 U.S. 643, 81 S.Ct. 1684, 6 L.Ed.2d 1081.

[22] *United States v. Leon,* 468 U.S. 897, 104 S.Ct. 3405, 82 L.Ed.2d 677 (1984); *Massachusetts v. Sheppard,* 468 U.S. 981, 104 S.Ct. 3424, 82 L.Ed.2d 737 (1984).

[23] *United States v. Sokolow,* 490 U.S. 1, 109 S.Ct. 1581, 104 L.Ed.2d 1 (1989).

[24] *Bram v. United States,* 168 U.S. 532, 18 S.Ct. 183, 42 L.Ed. 568 (1897).

[25] *Miranda v. Arizona,* 384 U.S. 436, 86 S.Ct. 1602, 16 L.Ed.2d 694 (1966).

[26] 18 U. S. C. A. §3501.

[27] *Dickerson v. United States,* 166 F. 3d 667 (4th Cir. 1999).

[28] *United States v. Dickerson,* 530 U.S. 428, 120 S.Ct. 2326, 147 L.Ed. 2d 405 (2000).

[29] *Wong Sun v. United States,* 371 U.S. 471, 83 S.Ct. 407, 9 L.Ed.2d 441 (1963).

[30] *Segurra v. United States,* 468 U.S. 796, 104 S.Ct. 3380, 82 L.Ed.2d 599 (1984).

[31] *New York v. Quarles,* 467 U.S. 649, 104 S.Ct. 2626, 81 L.Ed.2d 550 (1984).

[32] *Schmerber v. California,* 384 U.S. 757, 86 S.Ct. 1826, 16 L.Ed.2d 908 (1966).

[33] *Gideon v. Wainwright,* 372 U.S. 335, 83 S.Ct. 792, 9 L.Ed.2d 799 (1963).

[34] *Gideon v. Wainwright,* 372 U.S. 335, 344, 83 S.Ct. 792, 796, 9 L.Ed.2d 799, 805 (1963).

[35] *Argersinger v. Hamlin,* 407 U.S. 25, 92 S.Ct. 2006, 32 L.Ed.2d 530 (1972).

[36] *Faretta v. California,* 422 U.S. 806, 95 S.Ct. 2525, 45 L.Ed.2d 562 (1975).

[37] *County of Riverside v. McLaughlin,* 500 U.S. 44, 111 S.Ct. 1661, 114 L.Ed.2d 49 (1991).

[38] *Stack v. Boyle,* 342 U.S. 1, 5, 72 S.Ct. 1, 3, 96 L.Ed. 3, 6 (1951).

[39] *United States v. Salerno,* 481 U.S. 739, 107 S.Ct. 2095, 95 L.Ed.2d 697 (1987).

[40]18 U.S.C.A. § 3141 et seq.

[41]*Oyler v. Boles,* 368 U.S. 448, 82 S.Ct. 501, 7 L.Ed.2d 446 (1962).

[42]*Gerstein v. Pugh,* 420 U.S. 103, 95 S.Ct. 854, 43 L.Ed.2d 54 (1975).

[43]*Santobello v. New York,* 404 U.S. 257, 260, 92 S.Ct. 495, 498, 30 L.Ed.2d 427, 432 (1971).

[44]*Brady v. Maryland,* 373 U.S. 83, 87, 83 S.Ct. 1194, 1996, 10 L.Ed.2d 215, 218 (1963).

[45]353 U.S. 657, 77 S.Ct. 1007, 1 L.Ed.2d 1103.

[46]*Klopfer v. North Carolina,* 386 U.S. 213, 87 S.Ct. 988, 18 L.Ed.2d 1 (1967).

[47]*Barker v. Wingo,* 407 U.S. 514, 92 S.Ct. 2182, 33 L.Ed.2d 101 (1972).

[48]18 U.S.C.A. § 3161.

[49]*Pointer v. Texas,* 380 U.S. 400, 85 S.Ct. 1065, 13 L.Ed.2d 923 (1965).

[50]*Coy v. Iowa,* 487 U.S. 1012, 108 S.Ct. 2798, 101 L.Ed.2d 857 (1988).

[51]*Codispoti v. Pennsylvania,* 418 U.S. 506, 94 S.Ct. 2687, 41 L.Ed.2d 912 (1974).

[52]*Baldwin v. New York,* 399 U.S. 66, 90 S.Ct. 1886, 26 L.Ed.2d 437 (1970).

[53]In *Williams v. Florida,* 399 U.S. 78, 90 S.Ct. 1893, 26 L.Ed.2d 446 (1970), the Supreme Court upheld the use of six-person juries in the trial of felony offenses in Florida. Subsequently, in *Ballew v. Georgia,* 435 U.S. 223, 98 S.Ct. 1029, 55 L.Ed.2d 234 (1978), the Court held that a jury of only five persons was not acceptable under the Sixth Amendment.

[54]See *Johnson v. Louisiana,* 406 U.S. 356, 92 S.Ct. 1620, 32 L.Ed. 2d 152 (1972); *Burch v. Louisiana,* 441 U.S. 130, 99 S.Ct. 1623, 60 L.Ed.2d 96 (1979).

[55]*Lockhart v. McCree,* 476 U.S. 162, 106 S.Ct. 1758, 90 L.Ed.2d 137 (1986).

[56]*Richmond Newspapers, Inc. v. Virginia,* 448 U.S. 555, 100 S.Ct. 2814, 65 L.Ed.2d 973 (1980).

[57]*Malloy v. Hogan,* 378 U.S. 1, 84 S.Ct. 1489, 12 L.Ed.2d 653 (1964).

[58]*Mempa v. Rhay,* 389 U.S. 128, 88 S.Ct. 254, 19 L.Ed.2d 336 (1967).

[59]See 21 U.S.C.A. § 841(b)(1)(A).

[60]*Rummel v. Estelle,* 445 U.S. 263, 100 S.Ct. 1133, 63 L.Ed.2d 382 (1980).

[61]*People v. Romero,* 53 Cal. Rptr. 2d 789 (1996).

[62]*Wisconsin v. Mitchell,* 508 U.S. 476, 113 S.Ct. 2194, 124 L.Ed.2d 436 (1993).

[63]Codified at 18 U.S.C.A. §§ 3551–3586, 28 U.S.C.A. §§ 991–998.

[64]18 U.S.C.A. § 3561.

[65]18 U.S.C.A. § 3563.

[66]*Gagnon v. Scarpelli,* 411 U.S. 778, 93 S.Ct. 1756, 36 L.Ed.2d 656 (1973).

[67]18 U.S.C.A. § 3006A.

[68]*Baxter v. Palmigiano,* 425 U.S. 308, 96 S.Ct. 1551, 47 L.Ed.2d 810 (1976).

[69]*Morrissey v. Brewer,* 408 U.S. 471, 92 S.Ct. 2593, 33 L.Ed.2d 484 (1972).

[70]*Gagnon v. Scarpelli,* 411 U.S. 778, 93 S.Ct. 1756, 36 L.Ed.2d 656 (1973).

[71]18 U.S.C.A. § 3006A; *Baldwin v. Benson,* 584 F.2d 953 (10th Cir. 1978).

[72]408 U.S. 238, 92 S.Ct. 2726, 33 L.Ed.2d 346 (1972).

[73]428 U.S. 153, 96 S.Ct. 2909, 49 L.Ed.2d 859.

[74]*Payne v. Tennessee,* 501 U.S. 808, 111 S.Ct. 2597, 115 L.Ed.2d 720 (1991).

[75]See, for example, West's Annotated Cal. Penal Code § 679.02

[76]*State v. Stalheim,* 552 P.2d 829, 832 (Or. 1976).

[77]West's Fla. Stat. Ann. § 960.13.

[78]*McKane v. Durston,* 153 U.S. 684, 14 S.Ct. 913, 38 L.Ed. 867 (1894).

[79]*Chapman v. California,* 386 U.S. 18, 87 S.Ct. 824, 17 L.Ed.2d 705 (1967).

[80]*Douglas v. California,* 372 U.S. 353, 83 S.Ct. 814, 9 L.Ed.2d 811 (1963).

[81]*Ross v. Moffitt,* 417 U.S. 600, 94 S.Ct. 2437, 41 L.Ed.2d 341 (1974).

[82]1 Stat. 82 (1789).

[83]Habeas Corpus Act of 1867, 14 Stat. 385, 386 (1867).

[84]*Brecht v. Abrahamson,* 507 U.S. 619, 113 S.Ct. 1710, 123 L.Ed.2d 353 (1993).

[85]*Felker v. Turpin,* 518 U.S. 1047, 117 S.Ct. 25, 135 L.Ed2d 1119 (1996).

[86]*Strickland v. Washington,* 466 U.S. 668, 104 S.Ct. 2052, 80 L.Ed.2d 674 (1984).

FOR FURTHER READING

Amar, Akhil Reed, *The Constitution and Criminal Procedure: First Principles* (Yale University Press 1997).

Baker, Liva, *Miranda: Crime, Law and Politics* (Atheneum Press 1983).

Dershowitz, Alan M., *The Best Defense* (Random House 1982).

Heumann, Milton, *Plea Bargaining: The Experiences of Prosecutors, Judges and Defense Attorneys* (University of Chicago Press 1978).

Jacob, Herbert, *Law and Politics in the United States* (Little, Brown 1986).

Lewis, Anthony, *Gideon's Trumpet* (Vintage Books 1964).

Scheb, John M., and John M. Scheb II, *Criminal Procedure* (2d ed., West/Wadsworth 1999).

Stith, Kate, and Jose A. Carbranes, *Fear of Judging; Sentencing Guidelines in the Federal Court* (University of Chicago Press 1998).

Way, H. Frank, *Criminal Justice and the American Constitution* (Duxbury Press 1980).

Wishman, Seymour, *Anatomy of a Jury: The System on Trial* (Times Books 1986).

Zalman, Marvin, and Larry J. Siegel, *Criminal Procedure* (2d ed., West/Wadsworth 1997).

PART IV

LEGISLATIVE AND ADMINISTRATIVE DEVELOPMENTS IN THE LAW

CHAPTER 11
LEGISLATION

CHAPTER 12
ADMINISTRATIVE LAW AND PROCEDURE

11

LEGISLATION

Courtesy of West Group

LEARNING OBJECTIVES

This chapter should enable the student to understand:

- the constitutional authority of Congress and state legislatures to enact laws
- the social and economic rationale for antitrust legislation and its legislative, administrative, and judicial development
- how the Federal Reserve System and Federal Deposit Corporation have brought stability to the nation's banking system
- how federal legislation has allowed labor to collectively bargain with management
- how Social Security, Medicare, Medicaid, and unemployment laws have become the core instruments in social welfare legislation

CHAPTER OUTLINE

INTRODUCTION

During the last century the role of government at all levels changed dramatically. The industrial revolution of the nineteenth century and the technological revolution of the twentieth century gave rise to new demands on government and on the legal system. Many of these demands have resulted in the adoption by Congress and the state legislatures of new statutes regulating specific areas of economic activity and providing social benefits. As a result, the fabric of American law was altered dramatically. In this chapter, we examine some of the more prominent areas of modern legislation, including antitrust law, banking and securities law, social insurance and welfare legislation, civil rights statutes, and environmental law. Due to constraints of space, our treatment will focus entirely on federal legislation. The student should be aware, though, that in addition to their own legislative approaches, many states have adopted their own counterparts to these federal statutes.

CONSTITUTIONAL AUTHORITY TO LEGISLATE

Although state legislatures have plenary legislative authority, the U.S. Congress is limited in its exercise of legislative power to its enumerated and implied powers (see Chapter 3). Over the two centuries since the Constitution was adopted, Congress has stretched its enumerated and implied powers to legislate in many areas of social life and economic activity unimagined by the Framers. To a great extent, the confrontation between President Franklin Delano Roosevelt (FDR) and the Supreme Court over the constitutionality of the New Deal (FDR's policy response to the Great Depression) was a fundamental difference of opinion about the legislative power of Congress. Ultimately, this battle was won by FDR and Congress.

In the modern era, Congress has relied to a very great extent on its power to regulate interstate commerce enumerated in Article I, Section 8. The Commerce Clause has come to be regarded as a kind of substitute **police power** (the power to legislate comprehensively to further the public welfare). Because everything relates in some way (however remote) to

Opinion of the Court . . .

UNITED STATES V. MORRISON

529 U.S. 598, 120 S.Ct. 1740, 146 L.Ed.2d 658 (2000)

Chief Justice Rehnquist delivered the opinion of the Court.

. . . As we discussed at length in [*United States v.*] *Lopez* [1995], our interpretation of the Commerce Clause has changed as our Nation has developed. . . . We need not repeat that detailed review of the Commerce Clause's history here; it suffices to say that . . . since *NLRB v. Jones & Laughlin Steel Corp.* (1937), Congress has had considerably greater latitude in regulating conduct and transactions under the Commerce Clause than our previous case law permitted. . . .

Lopez emphasized, however, that even under our modern, expansive interpretation of the Commerce Clause, Congress' regulatory authority is not without effective bounds. "[E]ven [our] modern-era precedents which have expanded congressional power under the Commerce Clause confirm that this power is subject to outer limits. In *Jones & Laughlin Steel,* the Court warned that the scope of the interstate commerce power 'must be considered in the light of our dual system of govern-

ment and may not be extended so as to embrace effects upon interstate commerce so indirect and remote that to embrace them, in view of our complex society, would effectually obliterate the distinction between what is national and what is local and create a completely centralized government.' " . . .

As we observed in *Lopez,* modern Commerce Clause jurisprudence has "identified three broad categories of activity that Congress may regulate under its commerce power. . . . First, Congress may regulate the use of the channels of interstate commerce. . . . Second, Congress is empowered to regulate and protect the instrumentalities of interstate commerce, or persons or things in interstate commerce, even though the threat may come only from intrastate activities. . . . Finally, Congress' commerce authority includes the power to regulate those activities having a substantial relation to interstate commerce, . . . *i.e.,* those activities that substantially affect interstate commerce." . . .

interstate commerce, Congress has effectively acquired the power to legislate in furtherance of the public welfare. From the late 1930s until recently, the Court permitted Congress to legislate under the Commerce Clause without restraint. In 1995 and then in 2000, the Supreme Court began to impose limits on congressional legislative power under the Commerce Clause. In *United States v. Lopez* (1995)[1] and *United States v. Morrison* (2000),[2] the Court made clear that the Commerce Clause does not confer upon Congress plenary legislative power (see Chapter 3). Still, the legislative power of Congress is quite broad; and what it cannot mandate directly it can bring about through the use of its spending power by imposing conditions on the receipt of federal funds.

ANTITRUST LAW

One undesirable by-product of the tremendous economic expansion of the late nineteenth century was the emergence of monopolies or near monopolies in a number of major industries, most notably oil refining, mining, and manufacturing. These monopolies, or *trusts,* came about as corporations were consolidated by exchanging stock for *trust certificates*. These monopolies were able to dictate prices in the marketplace, as there was little competition to exert downward pressures on prices. When a competitor arose, the monopoly could force it out of business by selling goods at a loss. Once the competitor was vanquished, prices would return to artificially high levels. The victims of the trusts were not only the would-be competitors, but the consumers who had to pay artificially high prices for goods.

The common law had prohibited contracts that had the effect of restraining trade, but in practice American courts did little to stem the emergence of the monopolies. The doctrine of laissez-faire, which was widely adopted in the business community, held that government should refrain from interfering in the workings of the economy; but increasingly, the public demanded that the government intervene to prevent and dismantle monopolies. In 1890, Congress enacted the Sherman Antitrust Act, the cornerstone of American antitrust law.[3] The act was adopted with almost unanimous support in both houses of Congress. The Sherman Act contained two sections. Section 1 prohibited contracts, combination, or conspiracies in restraint of trade; Section 2 prohibited individuals from monopolizing or attempting to monopolize particular areas of interstate commerce. Violations of either section were punishable by fines of up to $5,000 and/or incarceration for up to a year.[4] Today penalties are much more stringent.

In 1910, in its first great antitrust decision, the Supreme Court upheld a federal district court order dissolving the Standard Oil Company into 33 separate companies.[5] Still, many believed that federal antitrust law needed to be strengthened. Congress responded by adopting the Clayton Act of 1914.[6] The Clayton Act prohibited price discrimination—charging similarly situated buyers different prices for the same goods or services. It also proscribed sales contracts that contained provisions that buyers no longer deal with the seller's competitors. Finally, the Clayton Act outlawed interlocking directorates, the practice of having the same members serve on boards of directors of competing companies. However, these practices were not prohibited per se but only to the extent that they worked "substantially to lessen competition" or "tend[ed] to create a monopoly." This language permitted the courts substantial discretion in applying the prohibitions of the statute. During the 1920s, courts were less than aggressive in enforcing the Clayton Act.[7]

In 1914, Congress also enacted the Federal Trade Commission Act, which prohibited "unfair methods of competition . . . and unfair or deceptive acts or practices in or affecting commerce."[8] Congress also established a new federal regulatory agency, the Federal Trade Commission (FTC), to enforce the act through the issuance of cease and desist orders.

The Robinson-Patman Act of 1936 amended the Clayton Act to deal specifically with price discrimination.[9] It prohibited any firm engaged in interstate commerce from selling the same commodity at different prices to different purchasers when the effect would be to lessen competition or to create a monopoly.

In the 1970s, the government brought suit against the telephone monopoly American Telephone and Telegraph Co. (AT&T).[10] The suit resulted in the breakup of the Bell System into the so-called "Baby Bells" and greatly energized the telecommunications industry.

Antitrust law is enforced three ways:

1. As noted, the FTC can issue cease and desist orders.
2. The Antitrust Division of the Department of Justice can file civil suits. States and private parties can also bring civil actions. In addition to recovering compen-

THE LAW IN ACTION

THE CASE AGAINST MICROSOFT

In July 1994, the U.S. Department of Justice filed suit under Section 2 of the Sherman Act against Microsoft, the world's largest supplier of software for personal computers. The government charged that Microsoft was unlawfully maintaining a monopoly in the market for personal computer operating systems. The suit alleged that Microsoft had engaged in anticompetitive marketing practices directed at computer manufacturers designed to perpetuate the monopoly status of the Windows operating system. The case was settled when Microsoft consented to the entry of a final judgment that prohibited the company from continuing the challenged practices. The judgment also forbade Microsoft from engaging in "other conduct that could have similar anticompetitive results."

In May 1998, the U.S. Department of Justice filed a new suit against Microsoft, charging that by integrating its own Internet browser, called Internet Explorer, into its Windows 95 operating system, Microsoft had effectively prevented its main rival Netscape from getting access to computer desktops for its own internet browser. Moreover, the Justice Department charged Microsoft with entering into noncompetition agreements with computer manufacturers that forced them to include the Internet Explorer program with each new computer shipped with the popular Windows operating system. The Justice Department argued that these practices stifled competition and innovation in the software industry.

In November 1999, after a long trial, Judge Thomas Penfield Jackson issued his findings of fact in the Microsoft case. He found that Microsoft was indeed a monopoly within the meaning of the antitrust laws and that it used its monopoly power to coerce its customers. Furthermore, the judge found that Microsoft had harmed consumers by stifling competition and innovation. The judge delayed issuing a judgment, however, allowing the government and Microsoft to attempt to settle the case. After settlement talks broke down in late March 2000, Judge Jackson ruled that "the predatory nature of the firm's conduct compels the Court to hold Microsoft liable under § 2 of the Sherman Act."[11]

Reviews of the government's suit against Microsoft were mixed: Many applauded the Justice Department's efforts to rein in a ruthless corporate giant; but others were appalled that the government seemed bent on breaking up America's most successful corporation. Others argued that the antitrust laws were written for an earlier industrial age and had little relevance to the highly dynamic world of computers and software. In the new economy, they argued, no established company, no matter its size or market share, is safe from competition. As expected, investors reacted negatively, triggering a precipitous decline in technology stocks.

On June 7, 2000, Judge Jackson issued an order that Microsoft be broken into two separate companies—one to produce and sell the Windows operating system and the other to handle Microsoft's applications software. Not surprisingly, Microsoft appealed and the U.S. Court of Appeals for the District of Columbia Circuit agreed to hear the case en banc. "An oral argument, the judges of the Court of Appeals questioned the government's lawyers rigorously, leading some observers to predict a reversal of the District Court's decision."

satory damages, plaintiffs in federal antitrust suits can collect treble punitive damages.

3. United States attorneys can initiate criminal prosecutions. Antitrust violations are felonies carrying fines of up to $10 million for corporations, and fines of up to $350,000 and prison sentences of up to three years for individuals.

Vagueness of the Antitrust Laws

Antitrust laws are somewhat vague, relying heavily on terms such as "unfair competition," "restraint of trade," "collusion," and "intent to monopolize." Regardless of how one feels about the Microsoft case or any other application of the antitrust laws, one must recognize that it is sometimes difficult for a company to know exactly what the antitrust laws permit and prohibit.

BANKING AND SECURITIES

The national government first experimented with a central bank when Congress chartered the first Bank of the United States in 1791. In 1816, five years after the charter expired, Congress established a second Bank of the United States, once again with a 20-year charter. In *McCulloch v. Maryland* (1819),[12] the Supreme Court upheld Congress's authority to establish the bank despite the fact that the Constitution did not expressly authorize this action (see Chapter 3). The Court said that establishment of a national bank was necessary and proper in light of congressional enumerated powers to coin money, regulate the value thereof, borrow, tax and spend, and regulate interstate commerce. This decision created a constitutional foundation for the Federal Reserve System, the Federal Deposit Insurance Corporation, and the elaborate federal regulation of the banking industry that would come about in the twentieth century.

The Federal Reserve Act of 1913

The Federal Reserve System, which acts as this nation's central bank, was established by Congress in 1913. The system, which is commonly known as the "Fed," consists of 12 Federal Reserve banks located in major cities throughout the country. In addition to supervising and regulating the banking industry, the Fed determines **monetary policy** by adjusting the interest rates that it charges its member banks, which in turn lend money to large commercial banks. By controlling interest rates, the Fed attempts to smooth out the business cycle, to stimulate the economy when it approaches recession and put on the brakes when it overheats.

A seven-member board of governors oversees the Federal Reserve System. Members of the board are nominated by the president subject to confirmation by the Senate. Each serves one 14-year term, although a member who completes the unexpired portion of a term may be reappointed. From the seven board members, one is appointed by the president to serve as chairperson, again with the consent of the Senate. The chairperson serves a four-year term and may be reappointed throughout the term as board member. The chair of the Fed (currently, Alan Greenspan) is one of the most powerful individuals in the country. When the chair speaks, financial markets listen and usually respond.

The Federal Deposit Insurance Corporation

The stock market crash of 1929 and subsequent Great Depression produced a crisis of confidence in America's financial institutions. Depositors rushed to withdraw their funds from banks. More than 9,000 banks closed between October 1929 and March 1933. In June 1933, Congress, at the urging of President Roosevelt, established the Federal Deposit Insurance Corporation (FDIC) to restore confidence and stability to the nation's banking system. Since the establishment of FDIC, no depositor in an FDIC-insured bank has lost money as the result of a bank failure. Today, the FDIC insures deposits up to $100,000 in nearly all this nation's banks. It also regulates state-chartered banks that are not members of the Federal Reserve System. FDIC ensures that such banks are complying with federal consumer protection and equal credit laws such as the Truth-in-Lending Act and the Community Reinvestment Act.

Securities Legislation

The stock market crash of 1929 and the Great Depression greatly undermined public confidence in the nation's capital markets. To reestablish faith in public offerings of securities and to protect investors, Congress enacted the Securities Act of 1933[13] and the Securities Exchange Act of 1934.[14]

The 1933 act is designed to ensure that investors receive truthful information concerning securities. It requires securities to be registered before being offered for sale through the mails, on securities exchanges, or any other facility of interstate commerce. It allows certain exemptions for securities offered and sold exclusively to residents of the issuer's state; however, states usually have their own laws, often called blue sky laws, that frequently parallel federal laws and regulations. The 1933 act defines "securities" to include notes, stocks, bonds, investment contracts, and so forth, but does not define *investment contract*. The U.S. Supreme Court has interpreted that term very broadly, stating that an investment contract means "a contract, transaction or scheme whereby a person invests his money in a common enterprise and is led to expect profits solely from the efforts of the promoter or a third party, it being immaterial whether the shares in the enterprise are evidenced by formal certificates. . . ."[15]

The 1934 act established the Securities and Exchange Commission (SEC) to enforce this new legislation and set standards for fair dealing and trading in securities. The SEC is headed by five commissioners who are appointed to five-year terms by the president with the consent of the Senate. The SEC enforces statutory requirements and promulgates regulations consistent with those requirements. For example, the SEC's Rule 10(b) stipulates that "insiders" who have material information about a company must refrain from dealing in the company's securities until such information is available to the general public. To enforce the securities laws, the SEC can file civil suit, invoke its own administrative processes, or refer matters to the Justice Department for criminal prosecution.

LABOR LAW

Since the late nineteenth century, labor rights activists had been trying to form unions to strengthen the bargaining position of workers in mines, mills, and factories. These efforts were steadfastly resisted by management, which regarded labor unions as a form of creeping socialism. The courts tended to side with management when strikes or boycotts threatened to disrupt production. For example, in 1911 the Supreme Court upheld an injunction against a union that had called for a boycott of the employer.[16] The Great Depression and the ensuing New Deal would forever change the legal status of organized labor.

The Wagner Act

One great accomplishment of the New Deal of the 1930s was the adoption of the National Labor Relations Act of 1935, better known as the Wagner Act.[17] The new law recognized the right of industrial workers to unionize and bargain collectively with management over wages, hours, and working conditions. The act also created the National Labor Relations Board (NLRB) to investigate charges of unfair labor practices. The Wagner Act was challenged in federal court by the Jones and Laughlin Steel Corporation, which refused to abide by an enforcement order obtained against it by the NLRB. Jones and Laughlin argued that the Wagner Act transcended Congress's power to regulate commerce and there was good reason to think the Supreme Court would agree. In 1918 the Court had struck down a federal law aimed at restricting the use of child labor in manufacturing, holding that manufacturing precedes commerce but is not a part of it.[18] Moreover, the Supreme Court was locked in battle with President Roosevelt over the constitutionality of the New Deal and had already struck down several key pieces of New Deal legislation. But in a stunning reversal, the Supreme Court upheld the statute, splitting five to four.[19] Writing for the Court, Chief Justice Hughes concluded that:

> Employees have as clear a right to organize and select their representatives for lawful purposes as the [company] has to organize its business and select its own officers and agents. Discrimination and coercion to prevent the free exercise of the right of employees to self-organization and representation is a proper subject for condemnation by competent legislative authority.[20]

The four dissenters in the case thought that Congress had clearly transcended its power to regulate interstate commerce. They argued that if Congress could regulate labor relations under the Commerce Clause, then nothing was beyond the scope of congressional legislative power. Additionally, they believed that the Wagner Act interfered with employers' freedom to enter into contracts with individuals regarding the terms and conditions of labor. Although this view had earlier prevailed in the Supreme Court,[21] by 1937 the Court was prepared to relinquish this position in favor of a more modern interpretation of the law.

The Taft-Hartley Act

As the result of the passage of the Wagner Act and its validation by the Supreme Court, labor unions and **collective bargaining** became staples of the American economy. In 1947, Congress passed a second statute of immense importance in this field. A more conservative piece of legislation, the Taft-Hartley Act imposed limits on organized labor.[22] Specifically, the act prohibited "closed shops," a policy under which one's job is contingent on belonging to the union. The act also prohibited secondary boycotts, where striking workers take action against third-party suppliers or buyers that deal with the company being struck. Finally, Taft-Hartley allowed the president to impose an 80-day cooling-off period when a strike created a national emergency. Proponents of Taft-Hartley saw it as a necessary correction to the excesses permitted by the Wagner Act. On the other hand, organized labor has always considered the Taft-Hartley Act as one of major impediment to unionization in this country, the other being the **right to work laws** enacted by 21 states. These laws forbid labor unions and companies from establishing union security agreements under which all workers who benefit from union representation are required to share the cost of maintaining the union, even if they decide to remain nonmembers.

The Landrum-Griffin Act

In 1959, Congress enacted the Labor Management Reporting and Disclosure Act, better known as the Landrum-Griffin Act.[23] Among other things, this legislation imposed financial disclosure requirements on unions and their officers, regulated union elections, and created a bill of rights for union members. This legislation was motivated by concerns over corruption in organized labor as well as ties to organized crime. Congress was particularly concerned about the corruption of the Teamster's Union, a concern that has not altogether vanished four decades later.

SOCIAL WELFARE LEGISLATION

Modern democratic governments have assumed the responsibility for the welfare of their populations. In this country, the assumption of this responsibility by the federal government began during the New Deal. Since then, Congress has enacted a wide array of **social welfare legislation.**

Social Security

Without question, the most important piece of legislation to emerge from the New Deal was the Social Security Act of 1935.[24] Never intended as a "welfare program," **Social Security** was designed as social insurance. Essentially, it works like this: Employers withhold a portion of their employees' wages, match these amounts, and transfer these sums to the government. Self-employed individuals pay into the system at a higher rate. The government places Social Security receipts in a trust fund from which benefits are paid to retirees and surviving spouses and dependents. The amount of retirement benefits one receives is a function of how much one has paid into the system.

Social Security was conceived at a time when relatively few Americans invested money for retirement. The program was designed to ensure that Americans would not have to spend their retirement years in poverty. The Supreme Court upheld the new Social Security program against a constitutional challenge in 1937.[25] Since then, what was conceived as a grand experiment has become an almost sacred institution in this country. Politicians are loath to discuss the issue, let alone consider serious reform of the system, which is facing eventual insolvency due to the impending retirement of the baby boom generation.

The Social Security Amendments of 1954 created a federal disability insurance program. This program has considerably reduced the economic insecurity of American workers, and it has also generated considerable business for lawyers. Some lawyers specialize in assisting citizens with disability claims filed with the Social Security Administration. To receive benefits under the Social Security Disability program, persons must have a physical or mental health problem that is severe enough to prevent them from working in an income-producing job for at least one year. One of the more interesting legal issues in this field is what constitutes a physical or mental disability. During President Clinton's first term, the Social Security Administration recognized alcoholism and drug abuse as disabilities, a policy that generated considerable political controversy. Critics claimed that the federal government was subsidizing alcohol and drug abuse. Under the Contract with America Advancement Act of 1996,[26] people are not eligible for disability benefits if drug or alcohol abuse is a "material factor" in their disability.

Medicare and Medicaid

Established as part of the Social Security Amendments of 1965, **Medicare** is the federal government's health insurance program for senior citizens.[27] Before they become eligible for Medicare, workers pay a tax in addition to their Social Security contributions to help support the system. When they go on Medicare, seniors pay a monthly premium. However, the bulk of Medicare costs are borne by the federal government's general fund. The Medicare program has two components: hospital insurance (part A), which helps pay for inpatient hospital services, skilled nursing facility services, home health services, and hospice care; and medical insurance (part B), which covers doctor services, outpatient hospital services, medical equipment and supplies, and other health services and supplies. Beneficiaries are subject to *deductibles* when they obtain services. Moreover, coverage is limited, so today many people have supplemental insurance obtained from a private insurer. In 2000, Congress considered a series of bills to make the Medicare system more efficient and provide coverage for prescription drugs, a major concern among the elderly.

Medicaid is a federal program that provides grants to the states to provide medical care for their indigent populations.[28] Together, Medicare and Medicaid provide benefits to more than 75 million people in this country. Both Medicare and Medicaid are administered by the Health Care Financing Administration (HCFA), located within the U.S. Department of Health and Human Services. Under the Clinton administration, HCFA allowed states greater flexibility in the administration of Medicaid. Like health services generally, Medicaid in many states has adopted a system of **managed care,** where recipients of services are required to be members of health maintenance organizations (HMOs) operated by insurance companies.

One area of legal activity surrounding Medicare and Medicaid in recent years has been the government's effort to prosecute health care providers who file fraudulent claims for reimbursement. The General Accounting Office has estimated that 10 percent of Medicare funds are spent in paying fraudulent claims. Violators include physicians, hospitals, nursing homes, clinical laboratories, and various other providers of medical services to the elderly. Medicare and Medicaid fraud includes the filing of false or inflated claims, misrepresentation of a diagnosis order to perform unnecessary medical services, and waiving patient deductibles and co-payments. Following are two prominent examples of fraud that led to substantial settlements with the government.

- In 1997, the Department of Justice launched an investigation of Columbia HCA, the nation's largest health care provider. Two former Columbia/HCA executives were found guilty of criminal fraud in 1999. In May 2000, Columbia agreed to pay $745 million to settle civil claims filed against it by the Justice Department.
- In March 2000, the Alabama Attorney General's Office reached a settlement with Providence Hospital of Mobile resulting from the state's investigation of allegations of improper Medicaid billing practices. The $500,000 settlement covered actual damages incurred by the state, administrative fines, and reimbursement for the cost of the investigation. Similar investigations by state and federal authorities have become commonplace in recent years.

Unemployment Compensation

Another important program established by the Social Security Act of 1935 was a federal program to provide temporary benefits to workers who become unemployed through no fault of their own. The program was designed to give an unemployed worker time to find a new job without suffering major financial distress. Although **unemployment compensation** programs are actually administered by state agencies (a la Medicaid), the program is funded through a combination of federal and state taxes that are levied on employers. States also determine eligibility requirements and levels of benefits, although the minimum benefits are set by federal law. The federal courts have also imposed constitutional constraints on state unemployment programs. States may not deny unemployment benefits to workers who are fired for refusing to work in a manner that violates their religious beliefs, even if they adopted those beliefs after taking their jobs.[29] Nor may states deny compensation to women fired solely because they became pregnant or chose to terminate their pregnancy.[30]

Welfare

In the decades following the Second World War, the world's advanced democracies established **welfare programs** to assist the poor. For many years the basic component of welfare in this country was Aid to Families with Dependent Children (AFDC), a program that had its genesis in the Social Security Act of 1935. AFDC provided cash benefits to families with children deprived of parental support. Like Medicaid and unemployment compensation, AFDC was based on the model of **cooperative federalism**—most of the money came from the federal government while the states actually administered the program and set eligibility requirements and benefits within parameters established by federal law.

As in the case of unemployment compensation, the federal courts have imposed constraints on state operation of welfare programs. Although the courts have never held that there is a constitutional right to welfare, benefits cannot be terminated without due process of law.[31] States also may not discriminate against new residents in providing access to benefits.[32]

Welfare has never been particularly popular, as taxpayers have always been suspicious of those who remain on welfare over the long term. In the 1980s and 1990s, conservative social critics decried the existence of a large underclass that had become permanently dependent on government for its subsistence. Critics also voiced concern about the effect of welfare entitlements on family life in that men often abandoned their parental responsibilities knowing that their children and the mothers of their children could subsist on welfare. These concerns led to demands for **welfare reform,** which was accomplished with bipartisan support in 1996.

Under the Responsibility and Work Opportunity Reconciliation Act of 1996,[33] AFDC was renamed Temporary Assistance to Needy Families (TANF). Under TANF, welfare is no longer an open-ended personal entitlement—five years is the maximum that a recipient can be paid from federal funds. During this period, recipients must demonstrate that they are making reasonable efforts to secure employment and must avail themselves of job training programs. States are free to supplement federal assistance with their own programs, which they control entirely. The implementation of welfare reform caused the nation's welfare rolls to be reduced dramatically. Of course, the economic boom of the late 1990s, characterized by historically low unemployment, facilitated the implementation of reform.

CIVIL RIGHTS LEGISLATION

The term **civil rights legislation** refers to the set of laws designed to ensure that everyone is treated fairly by society. These laws take many forms, including federal and state constitutional provisions, federal and state statutes, local ordinances, and regulations adopted by federal, state, and local government agencies. Perhaps most significant are the rulings of federal and state courts interpreting all of the foregoing. Civil rights policy is extremely complex, involving conflicts over race, gender, religion, ethnicity, disability, age, and sexual orientation in areas such as education, employment, housing, criminal justice, government contracts, and voting.

The essential purpose of civil rights laws is to prevent and/or provide remedies for unlawful forms of discrimination. The term **discrimination** refers to the denial of equal treatment to a person based on membership in some recognizable group. Thus, discrimination may be based on race, gender, ethnicity, religion, age, sexual orientation, socioeconomic status, or any number of other factors. To say that a particular action, decision, or policy is discriminatory does not necessarily mean that it is unlawful. Some forms of discrimination are entirely permissible; others are almost never so. For example, a licensing law that prohibits untrained individuals from practicing medicine discriminates against those who have not completed medical school. Yet there is little question as to the validity of the licensure requirement. On the other hand, a law that prohibited members of a particular religious sect from holding public office would unquestionably be declared invalid. The difference is that there is a rational basis for the licensure requirement, while the political restriction based on religion lacks any rational foundation.

Most contemporary questions of civil rights are not so clear cut. Lawmakers and courts struggle with difficult civil rights questions in a highly charged political environment. Valid arguments can be made on both sides of many of these issues. Consider, for instance, the issue of whether gay men and lesbians should be permitted to serve in the military. Many in the military think that permitting gays to serve therein is bad for morale, discipline, and ultimately the ability of the military to function. Others, both within and outside the military, disagree with this assessment. Gay rights activists insist that gay men and lesbians have as much of a right, indeed a duty, to serve their country as anyone else. They compare the ban on openly gay individuals in the military to the racial segregation that characterized the armed forces prior to and during World War II. Public opinion is divided on the issue, with many people looking for "middle ground." Of course, when it comes to questions of civil rights, unlike questions of economic benefits, compromise can be difficult to achieve.

Laws Prohibiting Racial Discrimination

The development of civil rights law in the United States is linked historically with the evolving status of African-Americans. The fundamental fact that defined the status of African-Americans at the time of the Constitutional Convention in 1787 was that they had been brought forcibly to this country to work as slaves. As slaves they enjoyed no rights, for they were regarded as less than fully human. Summing up the legal status of blacks prior to the Civil War, the Supreme Court in 1857 observed that African-Americans "were not intended to be included under the word 'citizens' in the Constitution."[34]

Although the Civil War and subsequent amendments to the Constitution formally abolished slavery and guaranteed the right to vote and equal protection of the law regardless of race, these rights were not readily forthcoming. African-Americans found themselves in a society in which both the power of government officials and the actions of private individuals made life incredibly unequal. Before African-Americans could begin to enjoy full participation in American society, they had to overcome a vast array of institutions, practices, and policies that were geared against them. They faced both public and private discrimination at the local, state, and national levels. This discrimination took on a multitude of forms. It would take well over a century until the battle could even be fully joined, let alone won.

The Civil War Amendments to the Constitution

Slavery was formally abolished by the ratification of the Thirteenth Amendment to the Constitution in 1865. Three years later the Fourteenth Amendment was ratified. It effectively overturned the *Dred Scott* decision by announcing: "All persons born or naturalized in the United States, and subject to the jurisdiction thereof, are citizens of the United States and of the State wherein they reside." Second, in a clause that would play a major role in many civil rights cases in the following century, the Fourteenth Amendment provided: "nor shall any State deprive any person of life, liberty, or property, without due process of law; nor deny to any person within its jurisdiction the equal protection of the laws." The Fifteenth Amendment, ratified in 1870, forbade the United States, or any state, to deny the right to vote "on account of race, color, or previous condition of servitude." Known collectively as the Civil War Amendments, the Thirteenth, Fourteenth, and Fifteenth Amendments provided a constitutional basis for the protection of civil rights. In addition to outlawing slavery, guaranteeing the right to vote, and prohibiting states from denying persons due process and **equal protection of the law**, the Civil War Amendments granted Congress the power to adopt "appropriate legislation" to foster civil rights.

Early Civil Rights Legislation

In the decade following the Civil War, Congress utilized its new authority under the Civil War Amendments by enacting a number of important civil rights laws. Two of these laws, the Civil Rights Act of 1870 and the Civil Rights Act of 1871, remain extremely important today. The 1870 statute, also known as the Ku Klux Klan Act, made it a federal crime to conspire to "injure, oppress, threaten or intimidate any citizen in the free exercise of any right or privilege secured to him by the Constitution or laws of the United States."[35] The 1871 statute permitted individuals to bring civil actions in federal court against those violating their civil rights under color of state law. Civil suits under this statute are commonly referred to as "Section 1983 actions" because the act is now codified at Title 42 U.S. Code, Section 1983. In addition to recovering compensatory damages, plaintiffs can recover treble punitive damages under Section 1983.

One of the Reconstruction Era civil rights laws, the Civil Rights Act of 1875, attempted to eradicate racial discrimination in **places of public accommodation,** including hotels, taverns, restaurants, theaters, and "public conveyances." This was an ambitious act, which, if enforced, would have represented a direct confrontation to the "southern way of life." Not surprisingly, it was challenged in federal court. In 1883, the Supreme Court struck down the key provisions of the law, ruling that the Fourteenth Amendment limited congressional action to the prohibition of official, state-sponsored discrimination, as distinct from dis-

---

CIVIL RIGHTS LAWS PASSED DURING RECONSTRUCTION — SIDEBAR

During the Reconstruction Era, Congress enacted four major civil rights acts. Most provisions of these statutes remain important components of contemporary civil rights law.

The Civil Rights Act of 1866. Provided that citizens of all races have the same rights to make and enforce contracts, to sue and give evidence in the courts, and to own, purchase, sell, rent, and inherit real and personal property. Designed to invalidate the "Black Codes" enacted in the South during the Civil War. The modern counterparts can be found at 42 U.S.C.A. §§ 1981, 1982; 18 U.S.C.A. § 242.

The Civil Rights Act of 1870. Also known as the Ku Klux Klan Act, this statute made it a federal crime to conspire to "injure, oppress, threaten or intimidate any citizen in the free exercise of any right or privilege secured to him by the Constitution or laws of the United States." The statute also criminalized any act under color of state law that subjects persons to deprivations of constitutional rights. The modern counterparts are codified at 42 U.S.C.A. § 1985 and 18 U.S.C.A. § 241.

The Civil Rights Act of 1871. This statute made individuals acting "under color of state law" personally liable for acts violating the constitutional rights of others. The Act of 1871 also permitted civil suits against those conspiring to violate the civil rights of others. Civil suits under this statute are commonly referred to as "Section 1983 actions" because the act is now codified at 42 U.S.C.A. § 1983.

The Civil Rights Act of 1875. Forbade denial of equal rights and privileges by places of public accommodation. Declared invalid by the Supreme Court as applied to privately owned public accommodations in *The Civil Rights Cases* (1883). (Access to public accommodations was ultimately achieved under Title II of the Civil Rights Act of 1964.)

crimination practiced by privately owned places of public accommodation.[36] This reading of the Constitution recognized an implicit right for private individuals to discriminate against other citizens. Moreover, this decision severely limited the meaning of the Equal Protection Clause of the Fourteenth Amendment. It would be 80 years until Congress would again attempt to pass legislation outlawing such discrimination. Meanwhile, individuals were free to discriminate. The white-dominated political culture of the South, and to some degree the rest of the country, fully supported such discrimination.

The Civil Rights Act of 1964

The Civil Rights Act of 1964 was a far-reaching, even visionary piece of legislation, and it remains the foundation of national policy on the rights of minorities. The act's most important and controversial section, Title II, prohibited racial discrimination in places of public accommodation that affected interstate commerce, including restaurants, stadiums, theaters, and motels or hotels with more than five rooms. In adopting Title II, Congress relied on its broad constitutional power to regulate interstate commerce (Art. I, § 8) as well as its enforcement powers under the Fourteenth Amendment. In upholding Title II, the Supreme Court gave its blessing to a broad extension of federal power to regulate virtually any business in the country.[37] As a result, African-Americans found restaurants, motels, and hotels throughout the South available for the first time. In addition, stores removed the "Colored" and "White" designations from their drinking fountains and rest rooms. Without question, the public accommodations section of the Civil Rights Act of 1964 had an immediate impact on people's lives, especially in the South.

The 1964 Civil Rights Act did more than ensure equal access to restaurants and hotels. Title VII prohibited **employment discrimination** on the basis of race, color, or national origin (later amended to include sex discrimination as well). Title VII made it unlawful for employers to intentionally discriminate in hiring, firing, or setting levels of compensation by adopting employment practices that are not racially neutral. It also prohibited employment

CASE IN POINT

CONGRESS OUTLAWS RACIAL DISCRIMINATION IN PLACES OF PUBLIC ACCOMMODATION

Heart of Atlanta Motel v. United States

United States Supreme Court
379 U.S. 241, 85 S.Ct. 348, 13 L.Ed.2d 258 (1964)

In order to perpetuate their policy of refusing to accommodate black customers, owners of the Heart of Atlanta Motel, located on Courtland Street in downtown Atlanta, brought suit attacking the constitutionality of Title II of the 1964 Civil Rights Act. Even though approximately 75 percent of the guests at the motel were from other states, the owners claimed that Title II could not constitutionally be applied to their establishment. In a unanimous decision, the Supreme Court ruled that the racially restrictive practices of the Heart of Atlanta Motel could impede commerce among the states and could therefore be appropriately regulated by Congress. The Court noted that in enacting Title II, "Congress was also dealing with what it considered to be a moral problem. But that fact does not detract from the overwhelming evidence of the disruptive effect that racial discrimination has had on commercial intercourse."

practices that have a **disparate impact** on minorities unless such practices are a business necessity.[38] Various sorts of preemployment tests and requirements have been challenged on the basis of disparate impact. To prevail, a plaintiff must be able to demonstrate that the challenged practice has an adverse impact on a protected class to which the plaintiff belongs. If the plaintiff makes this showing, the burden shifts to the employer to show that the challenged practice constitutes a business necessity. If that burden is carried, the plaintiff must prove that a less discriminatory business practice would be equally useful in achieving the employer's objective.

Another important component of the Civil Rights Act was the requirement that federal funding be withheld from any government or organization that practiced discrimination under the act. Practically speaking, this gave tremendous power to federal officials. Virtually every public school and university system, and almost all private colleges, depend on federal funding, even if it is the federally insured student loans that students rely upon. These institutions would later find themselves under careful scrutiny in areas they would not have anticipated at the time of the act. This is an important extension of congressional power to government agencies, which promulgate rules in order to carry out the intent of the law. These rules reach far beyond the government itself to all those who rely on federal funding. Indeed, when in 1984 the Supreme Court attempted to restrict enforcement of civil rights requirements against private colleges that received federal funds,[39] Congress re-

---

FEDERAL LAW ON EMPLOYMENT DISCRIMINATION · SIDEBAR

EXCERPT FROM 42 U.S.C.A. § 2000e-2: "UNLAWFUL EMPLOYMENT PRACTICES"

(a) Employer practices

It shall be an unlawful employment practice for an employer—(1) to fail or refuse to hire or to discharge any individual, or otherwise to discriminate against any individual with respect to his compensation, terms, conditions, or privileges of employment, because of such individual's race, color, religion, sex, or national origin; or (2) to limit, segregate, or classify his employees or applicants for employment in any way which would deprive or tend to deprive any individual of employment opportunities or otherwise adversely affect his status as an employee, because of such individual's race, color, religion, sex, or national origin.

(b) Employment agency practices

It shall be an unlawful employment practice for an employment agency to fail or refuse to refer for em-

ployment, or otherwise to discriminate against, any individual because of his race, color, religion, sex, or national origin, or to classify or refer for employment any individual on the basis of his race, color, religion, sex, or national origin.

(c) Labor organization practices

It shall be an unlawful employment practice for a labor organization—(1) to exclude or to expel from its membership, or otherwise to discriminate against, any individual because of his race, color, religion, sex, or national origin; (2) to limit, segregate, or classify its membership or applicants for membership, or to classify or fail or refuse to refer for employment any individual, in any way which would deprive or tend to deprive any individual of employment opportunities, or would limit such employment opportunities or otherwise adversely affect his status as an employee or as an applicant for employment, because of such individual's race, color, religion, sex, or national origin; or (3) to cause or attempt to cause an employer to discriminate against an individual in violation of this section.

sponded by adopting the Civil Rights Restoration Act of 1988. This act stipulated that educational institutions that receive any amount of federal funding must refrain from discrimination in all their activities and programs.

Affirmative Action

It is unlikely that Congress intended to allow for any "reverse" or "corrective" discrimination under the 1964 Civil Rights Act. However, during the late 1960s and early 1970s, the act came to be interpreted in such a way as to allow for preferential treatment members of racial minorities in order to bring minorities into the economic mainstream. African-Americans and members of certain other minority groups were accepted into colleges and professional programs on the basis of lower grades and standardized test scores. Similar preferences were established in employment both in the public and private sectors. Proponents argued that such policies were necessary to make up for past discrimination and to enhance the diversity of the educational experience and the workplace. Opponents characterized **affirmative action** as reverse discrimination, which they believed violated the principle of equal opportunity. They sought relief in the courts under the Equal Protection Clause of the Fourteenth Amendment and, where applicable, the Civil Rights Act of 1964.

Initially, the Supreme Court steered a middle course through the affirmative action controversy. It upheld affirmative action in principle, but limited the use of rigid quotas for admitting minorities to programs of public higher education.[40] In the area of employment, the Court upheld affirmative action programs that were voluntarily established by private companies.[41] However, as the Court became more conservative throughout the 1980s, it indicated in a number of decisions that it would not tolerate affirmative action programs unless they were tailored to remedy specific instances of discrimination. For example, in 1989, the Court struck down a Richmond, Virginia, policy that set aside a certain proportion of city public works contracts for "minority business enterprises." The Court based its decision largely on the fact that African-Americans constituted a majority of the city population and held a majority of seats on the city council. Moreover, there was no evidence that black-owned construction companies seeking public works contracts were being discriminated against by the city of Richmond.[42] In a key decision in 1994, the Court said that it would subject all affirmative action programs established by government agencies to the highest level of judicial scrutiny.[43] The late 1990s witnessed a rollback of affirmative action programs across the country, either as the result of lawsuits or merely in response to the threat of litigation.[44]

The Fair Housing Act

Historically, one of the biggest obstacles facing African-American families wishing to move out of inner-city ghettoes was that they faced discrimination in obtaining housing. In 1948, the Supreme Court held that **restrictive covenants,** under which homeowners agreed not to sell or rent their homes to minorities, could not be judicially enforceable under the Fourteenth Amendment.[45] Twenty years later, Congress enacted major legislation to address the problem of discrimination in housing. Under Title VIII of the Civil Rights Act of 1968 (also known as the Fair Housing Act), anyone selling or renting a house or apartment through a licensed agent became subject to penalty by refusing to sell or rent the unit on the basis of race, color, national origin, or religion. The act was later amended to include **housing discrimination** based on gender, disability, or familial status.[46]

The Voting Rights Act

After the Reconstruction Era ended, southern U.S. states systematically excluded African-Americans from the electoral process. As was the case with desegregation of the public schools, the process of opening political participation began in the courts. In 1944, the Supreme Court had struck down the infamous white primary (a primary election limited to white voters).[47] The Civil Rights Act of 1964 limited the use of literacy tests that had been employed by local officials to keep blacks from voting. In that same year, the states ratified the Twenty-Fourth Amendment, which outlawed the use of the poll tax in federal elections.[48]

In 1965, Congress saw the need to act to ensure African-Americans access to the ballot box. The Voting Rights Act[49] totally outlawed the use of literacy tests as a condition of voting in seven southern states where African-American voting had lagged far behind that of whites. In addition, the act had a triggering mechanism by which federal registrars would be sent to any county in these states in which fewer than 50 percent of those of voting age population were registered to vote in the 1964 presidential election.

The effect of the Voting Rights Act was dramatic: Black registration and voting increased dramatically. By the mid-1970s, African-Americans were voting in numbers that approached that of whites, and several thousand African-Americans had been elected to state and local office. Blacks became such a force in the politics of the southern states that very few politicians could afford to risk alienating them.

After the completion of the federal census every 10 years, state legislatures must redraw their own members' districts as well as the congressional districts in their state. Under the Supreme Court's famous reapportionment decisions of the 1960s, these districts must be drawn so as to be nearly equal in population.[50] These decisions limited **gerrymandering,** which is the intentional drawing of district borders to reach a desired political end. By the early 1990s, the Department of Justice was using its authority under the Voting Rights Act to "preclear" changes in state election systems to force states to maximize the number of minority–majority districts (those in which minority voters are in the numerical majority).[51] For example, to create a congressional district with a safe African-American majority, the legislature of North Carolina extended boundary lines of a particular district for hundreds of miles along an interstate highway to connect different concentrations of black voters. In 1996, the Supreme Court said that this sort of racial gerrymandering was unconstitutional unless the state could articulate a compelling interest.[52] In effect, the Court invalidated the Justice Department's policy of forcing states to maximize minority–majority districts. In January 2000, the Supreme Court further restricted the Justice Department's **preclearance** authority under the Voting Rights Act.[53] Nevertheless, the overall impact of the Voting Rights Act has been to enfranchise and empower African-Americans and other minorities.

Laws Addressing Gender Discrimination

At the time of the founding of the American republic, women were not accorded anything resembling legal equality. Even with the addition of the Bill of Rights and the Civil War Amendments, the U.S. Constitution contained no explicit recognition of women's rights. Indeed, even the right to vote was not guaranteed until 1920, with ratification of the Nineteenth Amendment. By the 1960s, however, a growing women's movement was demanding social, legal, and political change. The women's movement employed many of the tactics that had been successfully employed by the civil rights movement, including marches, protests, demonstrations, and boycotts. At the top of the agenda was equal pay for equal work.

The Equal Pay Act and Title VII

Congress first responded to growing demands for legal equality between the sexes by passing the Equal Pay Act of 1963, which prohibits unequal pay for equal or "substantially equal" work performed by men and women. In 1972, Congress amended Title VII of the Civil Rights Act of 1964 to add gender to the list of prohibited forms of employment discrimination. In 1981, the Supreme Court ruled that Title VII goes beyond the Equal Pay Act to proscribe discrimination not only in pay between jobs that are equal but also between jobs that are different.[54]

Traditionally, the socially prescribed role of woman as wife and mother, combined with a protectionist attitude on the part of men, served to keep women out of the workforce in significant numbers, although women were mobilized to fill jobs vacated by men during the two world wars. Today, most adult women are employed, at least part time. Indeed, roughly half of all women with children under the age of one are employed outside the home.

Despite recent gains, women on average earn only about 75 cents for every dollar earned by men. This discrepancy is partially due to the fact that women are much more likely than men to be employed in relatively low-paying service, clerical, sales, and manufacturing jobs. They are still less likely than men to be doctors, engineers, accountants, and lawyers, although the gender gap in the professions is narrowing. Finally, women have yet to gain access to the top-paying positions in corporations. Some have even complained of a "glass ceiling," an invisible barrier that keeps women out of top managerial positions.

Although women are not a minority, in that they comprise roughly 53 percent of the population, women have had to struggle as hard as minority groups to gain acceptance in the workplace. Early on, the issue was whether women should be permitted to work at all. Later the issue became which jobs, if any, were unsuitable for women. Then the issue became "equal pay for equal work." In the 1980s, women's groups attempted to define the issue as equal pay for work of "comparable worth." Women's groups argued that women should receive the same pay as men, even if their jobs were different, as long as the jobs entailed similar levels of education and experience. Critics of comparable worth argued that there was no way to implement this idea without a massive program of government regulation or numerous lawsuits, either of which would be costly and disruptive to business. In the 1990s, the momentum behind the push for comparable worth declined. Today, the highest-priority issues for working women are access to affordable day care and family leave. Although these are primarily economic issues and not exactly questions of civil rights, they are related to women's search for economic and social equality.

Title IX

Another significant enactment in the area of **gender discrimination** is Title IX of the Federal Education Act of 1972, which authorized the withholding of federal funds from educational institutions that engage in sex discrimination. The most obvious result of this statute has been the movement toward **gender equity** in collegiate athletics through which young women across the country have been afforded opportunities to participate in athletic competition that was once the sole province of men. Moreover, many young women who would not otherwise have received a college education have been able to go to college under an athletic scholarship.

Under Presidents Reagan and Bush, enforcement of Title IX was less than rigorous. The Office of Civil Rights in the Department of Education, which is primarily responsible for Title IX enforcement, was not adequately funded to aggressively pursue Title IX complaints. Consequently, in the 1990s many women with Title IX complaints bypassed the OCR and filed suit directly, often with great success. For example, in 1993, Howard University women's basketball coach Sanya Tyler sued Howard for sex discrimination under Title IX because she was paid substantially less than the men's head basketball coach. Tyler's case broke new ground in that it resulted in the first monetary award given by a jury in a Title IX case. Tyler was awarded $2.4 million in damages, although the amount was later reduced to $250,000.

Affirmative Action on Behalf of Women

Desiring to facilitate the integration of women into the social and economic mainstream, federal, state, and even some local agencies have adopted a variety of affirmative action programs to benefit women. Employers that do business with government, as well as educational institutions that receive public funds, have been encouraged to adopt their own affirmative action programs. Like the policies that grant preferred status to black applicants, affirmative action programs that benefit women have been controversial and have even been challenged in court.

In 1987, the Supreme Court handed down a landmark decision on affirmative action for women. It upheld a program under which a woman had been promoted to the position of road dispatcher in the Santa Clara, California, Transportation Agency, even though a man had scored higher on a standardized test designed to measure aptitude for the job. The man who had been passed over for the job brought a lawsuit, claiming reverse discrimination, as Alan Bakke had done some years earlier. The Supreme Court rejected the plaintiff's claim, stressing that the affirmative action program was a reasonable means of correcting the sexual imbalance in the agency's personnel, who were overwhelmingly male.[55]

An interesting hypothetical question to ponder is, Would affirmative action programs that benefit women be eliminated if women achieved economic parity with men? Although many supporters of affirmative action have characterized it as a temporary corrective measure, experience indicates that once a right or benefit is established in law, it is difficult to disestablish.

In a somewhat different form of affirmative action, some cities and states have gone so far as to require all-male social and civic clubs to admit women. The courts have generally approved such measures, even though they are sometimes challenged as violating the concept of freedom of association, which is protected by the First Amendment. In a notable 1984 decision, a unanimous Supreme Court found that the state of Minnesota's interest in eradicating sex discrimination was sufficiently compelling to justify a decision of its human rights commission requiring local chapters of the Jaycees to admit women.[56] Later decisions of the Court extended this ruling to embrace chapters of the Rotary Club, as well as private athletic clubs that served liquor and food to their members.

Sexual Harassment

In the 1980s, the issue of **sexual harassment** appeared on the public agenda as a civil rights issue. The sexual harassment issue has been particularly noticeable on college campuses, where it has entered the debate over issues related to dating, dormitory visitation, and student–teacher relationships.

The issue of sexual harassment was aired in a particularly dramatic fashion when law professor Anita Hill appeared before the Senate Committee on the Judiciary in October 1991 to make allegations of misconduct against Clarence Thomas, who had been nominated by President Bush to serve on the Supreme Court. Hill alleged that Thomas, when he was chairman of the Equal Employment Opportunity Commission, made sexual advances toward her, told off-color jokes in her presence, and generally harassed her in a sexual manner. Thomas categorically denied the charges. Because there was little supporting evidence, the Senate ultimately approved Thomas's nomination to the Supreme Court. Many women believed that the all-male Senate Judiciary Committee had been insensitive to Professor Hill and to the whole issue of sexual harassment. The Clarence Thomas–Anita Hill episode was apparently one factor that led women in record numbers to run for public office in 1992.

In 1986, the Supreme Court ruled that sexual harassment in the workplace constituted unlawful gender discrimination in violation of federal civil rights laws.[57] In November 1993, the Supreme Court adopted a legal standard that made it easier for victims of sexual harassment to sue in federal court.[58] The decision, which was joined by all nine justices (including Clarence Thomas), came in a case brought by Teresa Harris, who worked for a truck-leasing company in Nashville. Harris complained that her boss subjected her to repeated comments and suggestions of a sexual nature. The federal judge who heard the case in Nashville described the boss's behavior as vulgar and offensive, but ruled that it was not likely to have had a serious adverse psychological effect on the employee. He dismissed the case before it could go to a jury trial. The U.S. Court of Appeals for the Sixth Circuit upheld the district court's ruling. In reversing the lower courts, the Supreme Court, speaking through Justice Sandra Day O'Connor, said that it was not necessary for a plaintiff in a sexual harassment case to show "severe psychological injury." It is enough that the work environment would be perceived by a reasonable person as being "hostile or abusive." The Court's decision reinstated Teresa Harris's complaint, thus allowing the case to go before a jury in the district court. More importantly, the decision increased the likelihood that women (and men) who believe they are victims of sexual harassment in the workplace will file and win federal lawsuits. Thus, the Supreme Court effectively put employers on notice that their conduct would be subject to judicial scrutiny. To avoid litigation, employers should have policies and training programs in place and must take immediate action when complaints are filed.

Discrimination against Persons with Disabilities

Although there are few laws that overtly discriminate against them, persons with disabilities have always faced physical barriers as well as societal prejudice. For the most part it has been the Congress, not the courts, that has taken the lead in recognizing the rights of handicapped persons. With the passage of Title V of the Rehabilitation Act of 1973,[59] the Education for all Handicapped Children Act of 1975,[60] and, especially, the Americans with Disabilities Act (ADA) of 1990,[61] Congress has established a comprehensive regime of federal law protecting persons with disabilities. The ADA prohibits **discrimination against persons with disabilities** in all programs and services provided by state and local governments, private industries, and commercial establishments. Private employers that have 15 or more employees are prohibited from discriminating on the basis of disability in their employment practices. The Department of Justice enforces the ADA through civil litigation. The DOJ has established a toll-free hotline making it easy for citizens to file complaints. If DOJ prevails in litigation, the court can order compensatory damages and back pay for the complainant. They can also impose penalties of up to $50,000 for the first violation and $100,000 for any subsequent violation of the statute. The ADA authorizes various federal agencies to promulgate regulations in furtherance of the ADA's policy goals. For example, the Equal Employment Opportunity Commission has adopted extensive regulations implementing the ADA's provisions relative to employment discrimination.[62]

In essence, the ADA requires **reasonable accommodation** of persons with disabilities. An individual is considered "disabled" if that individual has a physical or mental impairment that substantially limits one or more major life activities or has a record of such an impairment. The ADA has spawned considerable litigation over such questions as the definition of *disability*, what institutions are covered by the statute, and what constitutes reasonable accommodation.

The Controversy over Gay Rights

How far should the law go in protecting the rights of people who are gay? Advocates of gay rights have called for the enactment of legislation that would protect gays against discrimination in the workplace. There is no such protection currently available under federal civil rights laws, although some states and local communities have enacted their own measures protecting gay rights. Given the moral questions involved in the practice of homosexuality, the legal issue of **gay rights** will not be easy to resolve. Civil rights claims depend for their validity on a reasonably strong societal consensus. Unless there is generally widespread agreement that society has a moral obligation to honor a given claim, it will not come to be defined as a legal right. It will be some time, if ever, before a societal consensus emerges that supports the idea of extending civil rights protections to gay men and lesbians. Clearly, this issue will be on the public agenda for some time to come.

Age Discrimination

Discrimination against the young is usually not legally problematic because persons below the age of legal majority are presumed not to enjoy the full rights of citizenship. Most questions of age discrimination involve elderly Americans who claim they have been victims of discrimination. Federal courts typically employ the rational basis test to determine the constitutionality of government policies that discriminate on the basis of age. Most age discrimination cases are not constitutional cases, however. Rather, they are based on provisions of statutes enacted by Congress and the state legislatures. In 1967, Congress enacted the Age Discrimination in Employment Act, which bars companies that deal in interstate commerce or do business with the government from discriminating against their employees on the basis of age.[63] In 1988, Congress enacted a measure that prohibits all organizations that receive federal funds from engaging in **age discrimination**.[64] Today, there is substantial litigation in the state and federal courts dealing with age discrimination by employers. These cases frequently grow out of attempts by companies to save money by dismissing people who are approaching retirement age. As our society ages, with people living and working longer, conflicts involving age discrimination will grow more numerous and more intense.

ENVIRONMENTAL LEGISLATION

One of the more important social developments of the 1960s was the emergence of the environmental movement. Within a few years, concern for the environment moved beyond the realm of a few scientists and activists and into the societal mainstream. Reflecting this new social awareness, Congress enacted a series of landmark environmental laws beginning in the late 1960s. In adopting these statutes, Congress relied on its power to regulate interstate commerce. A question to ponder is whether a strict reading of the Commerce Clause would support congressional authority in this area. Of course, states can act in this field and many have acted, either at the behest of Congress or on their initiative. Consequently, there is now a substantial body of federal and state **environmental law.**

The National Environmental Policy Act

Enacted in 1969, the National Environmental Policy Act (better known as NEPA) requires federal agencies to consider the environmental impacts of their proposed actions.[65] Because of this mandate, the **environmental impact statement (EIS)** has become a staple of American public administration. Title II of NEPA created the Council on Environmental Quality (CEQ), which oversees federal agency implementation of the act. NEPA requires the CEQ to report to the president annually on the conditions and trends in environmental quality.

The Clean Air Act

The Clean Air Act of 1970 set federal standards designed to enhance the quality of the air by deterring air polluters.[66] In 1977, Congress passed a series of amendments establishing stricter standards for air quality. As amended, the act provides criminal sanctions for violation of any provisions for which civil penalties apply, and for any person who knowingly makes any false representation in a document filed under the act. Enforcement may be delegated to the states pursuant to the State Implementation Plan (SIP), but the states are not required to enact minimum criminal provisions to receive EPA approval of their implementation plans. Nevertheless, states are increasingly toughening criminal penalties in this area.

The Clean Water Act

Better known as the Clean Water Act, the Federal Water Pollution Control Act of 1972 is designed to control water pollution by regulating industrial and other discharges.[67] Although the Clean Water Act is enforced primarily through civil means, criminal sanctions have been imposed for willful or negligent violations of certain provisions concerning permits and the making of false statements. Amendments in 1987 eliminated the "willful" requirement and imposed more stringent penalties for negligent violations and even more severe penalties for knowing violations of the act's criminal provisions.[68]

A majority of the states have programs approved by the EPA. While states vary somewhat in their approaches, many provide penalties similar to those in the federal act for either willful or negligent violations of water pollution provisions.

The Endangered Species Act

One of the best known federal environmental statutes is the Endangered Species Act of 1973.[69] This act is designed to conserve ecosystems by preserving wildlife, fish, and plants. Enforcement is largely through civil penalties; however, criminal liability is imposed against any person who knowingly violates regulations issued under the act. The act also permits federal courts to issue injunctions against projects that threaten **endangered species**. The Endangered Species Act is a powerful weapon in the arsenal of the environment movement, because enforcement of the act does not depend solely on government agencies charged with protecting the environment. Assuming they meet the requirements of standing (see Chapter 3), citizens can bring suit under the Endangered Species Act to prevent or halt projects that

---

CASE IN POINT

TVA, THE SNAIL DARTER AND THE ENDANGERED SPECIES ACT

TVA v. Hill

United States Supreme Court
437 U.S. 153, 98 S.Ct. 2279, 57 L.Ed.2d 117 (1978)

In 1973, an ichthyologist at the University of Tennessee discovered an isolated species of perch in the waters of the Little Tennessee River. Named the "snail darter," this little fish was designated as "endangered" by the secretary of the interior under the Endangered Species Act. Another federal agency, the Tennessee Valley Authority, was nearing completion of the Tellico Dam, which, when operational, would destroy the habitat of the snail darter. A group of conservationists obtained a federal court injunction to prevent the dam from becoming operational. The case became a national political issue—a confrontation between environmentalism and economic develop-ment. In 1978, the Supreme Court upheld the injunction, saying that "Congress has spoken in the plainest of words, making it abundantly clear that the balance has been struck in favor of affording endangered species the highest of priorities. . . ." Ultimately, the snail darter was discovered in another nearby river and Congress enacted legislation specifically authorizing completion of the Tellico Dam. Today, the dam is operational, much of the Little Tennessee River has become Tellico Lake, and the snail darter remains in existence, although still endangered. The Supreme Court's decision in TVA v. Hill remains an important moral victory for environmentalists.

threaten animals on the endangered species list. The building of hospitals, highways, dams, subdivisions, and office parks has been delayed, relocated, or halted as the result of civil actions brought by environmentalists under the Endangered Species Act. Without a doubt, the most famous (or infamous, depending on one's point of view) case involving the Endangered Species Act was *TVA v. Hill* (1978) (see the Case in Point above).

Hazardous Waste Legislation

One of the most serious environmental threats facing this country is the accumulation of hazardous waste. Congress has responded to this threat by enacting a series of statutes. Enacted in 1976, the Resource Conservation and Recovery Act (RCRA)[70] sought to encourage the states—through grants, technical assistance, and advice—to establish standards and provide for civil and criminal enforcement of state **hazardous waste regulations.** The EPA sets minimum standards requiring the states to enact criminal penalties against any person who knowingly stores or transports any hazardous waste to an unpermitted facility, or who treats such waste without a permit or makes false representations to secure a permit. All states have enacted statutes pursuant to the criteria specified in RCRA.

Toxic Substances Control Act

The Toxic Substances Control Act of 1976 authorizes the EPA to require testing and to prohibit the manufacture, distribution, or use of certain chemical substances that present an unreasonable risk of injury to health or the environment, and to regulate their disposal.[71] Although the act depends primarily on civil penalties, a person who knowingly or willfully fails to maintain records or submit reports as required violates the criminal provisions of the act.

The Superfund Law

In 1980, Congress enacted the Comprehensive Environmental Response, Compensation, and Liability Act (CERCLA), commonly known as the Superfund Law.[72] Its purpose is to finance cleanup and provide for civil suits by citizens. As revised in 1986, the act requires notice to federal and state agencies of any "release" of a "reportable quantity" of a listed hazardous substance. Release is broadly defined, and reportable quantity is related to each of the several hundred "hazardous substances." CERCLA also provides for EPA to promulgate regulations for the collection and disposal of solid wastes. The act imposes criminal sanctions against those who fail to report as required, or who destroy or falsify records.

CONCLUSION

This chapter has provided a thumbnail sketch of some of the more important pieces of legislation enacted by Congress. Although Congress does not possess plenary legislative power, it has ample authority to legislate in those areas that the states cannot or will not enter. Historically, Congress had to take the lead in dealing with social and economic problems through legislation. Today, however, the states are quite active in this regard. Consequently, legislation in this country is a complex and often confusing tapestry of state and federal statutes, each of which must be interpreted by courts. This is one reason why American law is so dynamic and exciting.

SUMMARY OF KEY CONCEPTS

Since the late 1800s, the federal government has achieved far-reaching social and economic reforms. This occurred through Congress exercising its delegated and implied powers, and through the Supreme Court's broad interpretation of the Constitution's "Commerce Clause." Antitrust, banking, securities, and labor legislation has brought a large measure of economic stability to the nation's financial, business, and labor forces. These policies aided the United States in becoming the world's financial and industrial giant. On occasions, the states, through exercise of their inherent police powers, have served as testing grounds for development of legislation; in other instances they have supplemented federal legislative policies. The Social Security Act and much of the social welfare legislation emerged in the 1930s as a part of the New Deal during the presidency of Franklin D. Roosevelt.

After the Civil War, Congress began to enact laws to end discrimination based on race; however, the real impetus in the struggle to end racial, gender, age, and disability discrimination awaited the social and cultural changes of the 1960s, which preceded the enactment of modern civil rights laws. Legislation that began in the latter half of the twentieth century continues today. Enactment of the Civil Rights Act of 1964 represented an epic victory in the struggle for racial equality. Since then, major legislative, administrative, and judicial accomplishments have furthered the movement to end discrimination based on race, gender, age, and disability. Guaranteeing all adults the right to vote and the right of all persons to fairness in housing have posed major legislative challenges. With the advent of large numbers of women entering the workforce, legislation has achieved modest gains in the equality of pay and prohibition of sexual harassment. Obviously, challenges remain. The struggle to end discrimination continues with legislation designed to support social and cultural changes now occurring in society.

As the nation rapidly moves into the information and technology age, the watchwords of society are to conserve and preserve. Major federal legislative enactments are still being tested in an effort to achieve a rational balance between protection of the environment and private property interests and personal liberties. The design and enforcement of environmental legislation is a major challenge today and will be in the future.

QUESTIONS FOR THOUGHT AND DISCUSSION

1. What three methods does the federal government employ to enforce the antitrust laws?
2. The authors state that "the most important piece of legislation to emerge from the New Deal was the Social Security Act of 1935." Identify three major functions that Social Security programs serve at the present time.
3. How does the Federal Reserve Board of Governors act to regulate the monetary policies of the nation?

4. What major changes in labor–management relations were accomplished by passage of the Wagner Act in 1935 and how did enactment of the Taft-Hartley Act in 1947 affect unionization practices?
5. What is meant by "cooperative federalism" and how has it been employed in respect to administration of Medicaid and unemployment compensation benefits?
6. How has Congress implemented the guarantees of the Thirteenth, Fourteenth, and Fifteenth Amendments to the U.S. Constitution?
7. What has been the impact of the Voting Rights Act enacted in 1965 with respect to city and county governments?
8. Explain the difference between the concepts of "equal pay for equal work" and equal pay for work of "comparable worth."
9. What standard of proof do federal courts require before a plaintiff can recover damages in a sexual harassment suit?
10. What, if any, new federal legislation is needed for protection of the environment?

KEY TERMS

police power

antitrust law

monetary policy

collective bargaining

right to work laws

social welfare legislation

Social Security

Medicare

Medicaid

managed care

unemployment compensation

welfare programs

cooperative federalism

welfare reform

civil rights legislation

discrimination

equal protection of the law

places of public accommodation

employment discrimination

disparate impact

affirmative action

restrictive covenants

housing discrimination

gerrymandering

preclearance

gender discrimination

gender equity

sexual harassment

discrimination against persons with disabilities

reasonable accommodation

gay rights

age discrimination

environmental law

environmental impact statement (EIS)

endangered species

hazardous waste regulations

ENDNOTES

[1] 514 U.S. 549, 115 S.Ct. 1624, 131 L.Ed.2d 626 (1995).

[2] 529 U.S. 598, 120 S.Ct. 1740, 146 L.Ed.2d 658 (2000).

[3] 15 U.S.C.A. § 1 et seq.

[4] 26 Stat. at L. 209, chap. 647, U. S. Comp. Stat. 1901, p. 3200.

[5] *Standard Oil Co. of New Jersey v. United States,* 221 U.S. 1, 31 S. Ct. 502, 55 L. Ed. 619 (1910).

[6] 15 U.S.C.A. § 12 et seq.

[7] See, for example, *United States v. United States Steel Corp.,* 251 U.S. 417, 40 S. Ct. 293, 64 L. Ed. 343 (1920).

[8] 15 U.S.C.A. §§ 41–58.

[9] 15 U.S.C.A. § 13 et seq.

[10] *United States v. American Telephone & Telegraph Co.,* 552 F. Supp. 131 (D.D.C. 1982), aff'd in *Maryland v. United States,* 460 U.S. 1001, 103 S. Ct. 1240, 75 L. Ed. 2d 472 (1983).

[11] *United States v. Microsoft,* U.S. District Court for the District of Columbia, April 3, 2000.

[12] 17 U.S. (4 Wheat.) 316, 4 L.Ed. 579 (1819).

[13] See 15 U.S.C.A. § 77a et seq.

[14]See 15 U.S.C.A. § 78a et seq.

[15]*SEC v. W. J. Howey Co.,* 323 U.S. 293, 298, 66 S.Ct. 1100, 1103, 90 L.Ed. 1244, 1248 (1946).

[16]*Gompers v. Buck's Stove & Range Co.,* 221 U.S. 418, 31 S. Ct. 492, 55 L. Ed. 797 (1911).

[17]Public Law 74–198, Codified at 29 U.S.C.A. § 151 et. seq.

[18]*Hammer v. Dagenhart,* 247 U.S. 251, 38 S.Ct. 529, 62 L.Ed. 1101 (1918).

[19]*N.L.R.B. v. Jones & Laughlin Steel Corp.,* 301 U.S. 1, 57 S.Ct. 615, 81 L.Ed. 893 (1937).

[20]301 U.S. at 33, 57 S.Ct. at 622, 81 L.Ed. at 909 (1937).

[21]See, for example, *Lochner v. New York,* 198 U.S. 45, 25 S.Ct. 539, 45 L.Ed. 937 (1905).

[22]Labor Management Relations Act of 1947, 61 Stat. 136, codified at 29 U.S.C.A. § 141 et seq.

[23]Codified at 29 U.S.C.A. § 401 et seq.

[24]Act of August 14, 1935, 49 Stat. 620.

[25]*Chas. C. Steward Mach. Co. v. Davis,* 301 U.S. 548, 57 S.Ct. 883, 81 L.Ed. 1279 (1937).

[26]P.L. 104–121

[27]See 42 U.S.C.A. §§ 1395–1395ccc.

[28]See 42 U.S.C.A. §§ 1396–1396v.

[29]*Hobbie v. Unemployment Appeals Commission,* 480 U.S. 136, 107 S.Ct. 1046, 94 L. Ed. 2d 190 (1987).

[30]*Wimberly v. Labor and Industrial Relations Commission,* 479 U.S. 511, 107 S.Ct. 821, 93 L. Ed. 2d 909 (1987).

[31]*Goldberg v. Kelly,* 397 U.S. 254, 90 S.Ct. 1011, 25 L.Ed.2d 287 (1970).

[32]*Saenz v. Roe,* 526 U.S. 489, 119 S.Ct. 1518, 143 L.Ed.2d 689 (1999).

[33]P.L. 104–193

[34] *Scott v. Sandford,* 19 Howard 393 (1857).

[35]Codified at 42 U.S.C.A. § 1985.

[36]The Civil Rights Cases, 109 U.S. 3, 3 S.Ct. 18, 27 L.Ed. 835 (1883).

[37]*Heart of Atlanta Motel v. United States,* 379 U.S. 421, 85 S.Ct. 348, 13 L.Ed.2d 258 (1964); *Katzenbach v. McClung,* 379 U.S. 294, 85 S.Ct. 377, 13 L.Ed.2d 290 (1964).

[38]*Griggs v. Duke Power Co.,* 401 U.S. 424, 91 S.Ct. 849, 28 L.Ed.2d 158 (1971). In the Civil Rights Act of 1991 Congress codified the Court's holding in *Griggs.* See 42 U.S.C.A. § 2000e-2.

[39]*Grove City College v. Bell,* 465 U.S. 555, 104 S.Ct. 1211, 79 L.Ed.2d 516 (1984).

[40]*University of California Board of Regents v. Bakke,* 438 U.S. 265, 98 S.Ct. 2733, 57 L.Ed.2d 750 (1978).

[41]*United Steelworkers of America v. Weber,* 443 U.S. 193, 99 S.Ct. 2721, 61 L.Ed.2d 480 (1979).

[42]*City of Richmond v. J.A. Croson Co.,* 488 U.S. 469, 109 S.Ct. 706, 102 L.Ed.2d 854 (1989).

[43]*Adarand Constructors, Inc. v. Pena,* 512 U.S. 1288, 115 S.Ct. 41, 129 L.Ed.2d 936 (1994).

[44]See, for example, *Hopwood v. Texas,* 78 F.3d (5th Cir. 1996).

[45]*Shelley v. Kraemer,* 334 U.S.1, 68 S.Ct. 836, 92 L.Ed. 1161 (1948).

[46]45 U.S.C.A. §§ 3604–3606.

[47]*Smith v. Allwright,* 321 U.S. 649, 64 S.Ct. 757, 88 L.Ed. 987 (1944).

[48]In 1966 the Supreme Court struck down the poll tax in state elections as a violation of the Fourteenth Amendment Equal Protection Clause. See *Harper v. Virginia State Board of Elections,* 383 U.S. 663, 86 S.Ct. 1079, 16 L.Ed.2d 169 (1966).

[49]See 42 U.S.C.A. § 1971 et. seq.

[50]*Reynolds v. Sims,* 377 U.S. 533, 84 S.Ct. 1362, 12 L.Ed.2d 506 (1964); *Wesberry v. Sanders,* 376 U.S. 1, 84 S.Ct. 526, 11 L.Ed.2d 481 (1964).

[51]Section 5 of the Voting Rights Act of 1965 requires designated states and their political subdivisions to obtain "preclearance," either from the attorney general or from the district court for the District of Columbia, before implementing changes in their election systems. See 42 U.S.C.A. § 1973c.

[52]*Shaw v. Hunt,* 517 U.S. 899, 116 S.Ct. 1894, 135 L.Ed.2d 207 (1996).

[53]*Reno v. Bossier Parish School Board,* 528 U.S. 320, 120 S.Ct. 866, 145 L.Ed.2d 845 (2000).

[54]*County of Washington v. Gunther,* 452 U.S. 161, 101 S.Ct. 2242, 68 L.Ed.2d 751 (1981).

[55]*Johnson v. Transportation Agency of Santa Clara County,* 480 U.S. 616, 107 S.Ct. 1442, 94 L.Ed.2d 615 (1987).

[56]*Roberts v. United States Jaycees,* 468 U.S. 609, 104 S.Ct. 3244, 82 L.Ed.2d 462 (1984).

[57]*Meritor Savings Bank, FBD v. Vinson,* 477 U.S. 57, 106 S.Ct. 2399, 91 L.Ed.2d 49 (1986).

[58]*Harris v. Forklift Systems, Inc.,* 507 U.S. 959, 113 S.Ct. 1382, 122 L.Ed.2d 758 (1993).

[59]Now codified at 29 U.S.C.A. § 701 et seq.

[60]Now codified at 20 U.S.C.A. § 1400 et seq.

[61]104 Stat. 337, 42 U.S.C. § 12131 et seq.

[62]29 CFR Part 1630.

[63]Now codified at 29 U.S.C.A. § 621 et seq.

[64]Now codified at 42 U.S.C.A. § 6101 et seq.

[65]42 U.S.C.A. §§ 4321–4345.

[66]42 U.S.C.A. §§ 7401–7642.

[67]33 U.S.C.A. §§ 1251–1270.

[68]33 U.S.C.A. § 1319(c).

[69]16 U.S.C.A. §§ 1531–1544.

[70]42 U.S.C.A. §§ 6901–6992.

[71]15 U.S.C.A. §§ 2601–2671.

[72]42 U.S.C.A. §§ 9601–9675.

FOR FURTHER READING

Baer, Judith, *Women in American Law: The Struggle toward Equality from the New Deal to the Present* (Holmes and Meier 1991).

Bork, Robert H., *The Antitrust Paradox* (Basic Books 1978).

Dalton, James A., and Stanford L. Levin, eds., *The Antitrust Dilemma* (Lexington Books 1974).

Davidson, Chandler, and Bernard Grofman, eds., *Quiet Revolution in the South: The Impact of the Voting Rights Act, 1965–1990* (Princeton University Press 1994).

Findley, Roger W., and Daniel A. Farber, *Environmental Law in a Nutshell* (4th ed., West 1998).

Kubasek, Nancy K., and Gary Silverman, *Environmental Law* (Prentice Hall 1996).

McCann, Michael, *Rights at Work: The Politics of Legal Mobilization* (University of Chicago Press 1994).

McKinnon, Catherine, *Sexual Harassment of Working Women* (Yale University Press 1979).

Mezey, Susan Gluck, *In Pursuit of Equality: Women, Public Policy and the Federal Courts* (St. Martin's Press 1992).

Santos, Miguel A., *Limits and Scope of Environmental Law* (Charles C. Thomas 1996).

Terry, Evan, *Americans with Disabilities Act Facilities Compliance: A Practical Guide* (John Wiley & Sons 1992).

Wagner, Travis, *The Complete Guide to Hazardous Waste Regulations: RCRA, TSCA, HTMA, EPCRA, and Superfund* (3d ed., John Wiley and Sons 1999).

12

ADMINISTRATIVE LAW AND PROCEDURE

John M. Scheb II

LEARNING OBJECTIVES

This chapter should enable the student to understand:

- how Congress and state legislatures have delegated power to administrative and regulatory agencies to carry out legislative programs
- executive, legislative, and judicial restraints on administrative rule making
- the exercise of agency investigatory authority
- available means for enforcement of agency decisions
- how administrative agencies, as quasi-judicial bodies, adjudicate disputes
- standing and exhaustion of administrative remedies as prerequisites to judicial review of agency decisions

CHAPTER OUTLINE

INTRODUCTION

Bureaucracy is the hallmark of modern government. As government has taken on increasingly more responsibility for solving social and economic problems, it has found it necessary to create agencies to administer programs and promulgate and enforce regulations. These agencies are located within the executive branches of federal, state, and local governments. While we often refer to the sum total of these agencies as the "bureaucracy," a basic distinction can be made between **administrative agencies** and **regulatory agencies.**[1]

Administrative agencies carry out government programs such as highway construction, education, or the delivery of social services. At the federal level, the Social Security Administration is a good example. Its function is not to regulate, but to administer this country's social insurance program for the elderly, widowed, and disabled. At the state and local levels, one finds agencies devoted to highway construction, education, public housing, social welfare, public health, and various other functions.

Regulatory agencies promulgate and enforce rules pursuant to authority delegated by legislatures. For example, at the federal level, the Nuclear Regulatory Commission (NRC), the Federal Aviation Administration (FAA), and the Securities and Exchange Commission (SEC) are just a few of the many agencies created by Congress to regulate particular industries (see Figure 12-1). States also have regulatory agencies that deal with everything from alcoholic beverages to the licensing of physicians. At the state level, agencies have long regulated professional and occupation licensing; adjudicated the need to issue bank charters, alcoholic beverage licenses, and insurance company licenses; and have regulated public utilities. In recent years the determination of eligibility for certificates of need for health care facilities and environmental and natural resource permits have assumed an increasing role in state administrative proceedings.

Administrative law is the branch of the law that governs the activities of administrative and regulatory agencies. It is designed to apply the rule of law to the bureaucracy to reduce arbitrariness, enhance the quality of decision making, and promote democratic values. Administrative law involves such questions as:

- Does an agency have the authority to regulate a certain product or industry? For example, in 1996, the federal Food and Drug Administration (FDA) undertook

FIGURE 12-1
Major Regulatory
Agencies of the National
Government

Agency	Date Established	Function
Interstate Commerce Commission (ICC)*	1887	Regulates railroad, trucking, and water carriers
Food and Drug Administration (FDA)	1907	Regulated safety of food, drugs, and cosmetics
Federal Reserve Board	1913	Controls money supply, attempts to stabilize the economy, sets bank reserve requirements
Federal Trade Commission (FTC)	1914	Attempts to prevent false and misleading advertising, monitors business practices
Federal Deposit Insurance Corporation (FDIC)	1933	Insures deposits in participating banks
Federal Communications Commission (FCC)	1934	Regulates interstate telephone service, cellular phones, broadcasting, and cable television
Securities and Exchange Commission (SEC)	1934	Regulates securities markets, such as the stock market
Federal Aviation Administration (FAA)	1958	Regulates airline safety
Occupational Safety and Health Administration (OSHA)	1971	Protects workers' safety and health in the workplace
Consumer Product Safety Commission (CPSP)	1972	Regulates the safety of consumer products
Environmental Protection Agency (EPA)	1972	Regulates air, water, and noise pollution
Nuclear Regulatory Commission (NCR)	1975	Licenses and regulates nuclear power plants

*Abolished in 1996

the regulation of tobacco as a drug. Cigarette makers went to court, arguing that Congress had never given FDA such authority. The Supreme Court agreed with the tobacco industry.[2] (See Case in Point later in the chapter.)

- What access do citizens have to information held by government agencies? In 1966, Congress enacted the Freedom of Information Act to give citizens such access, but the act contains a number of exemptions and continues to be the source of considerable litigation.
- What procedures must agencies follow when they deny program benefits to individuals or impose sanctions on industries they regulate? Clearly, agencies must

---

THREE ESSENTIAL PUBLICATIONS FOR THE SERIOUS STUDENT OR PRACTITIONER OF ADMINISTRATIVE LAW

SIDEBAR

- The *United States Government Manual* provides basic information on all federal government agencies, including their histories, functions, programs, and officials. It is updated annually.
- The *Federal Register* contains all executive orders, notice of agency hearings, proposed and adopted rules, and amendments to proposed or adopted rules. It is published daily.
- The *Code of Federal Regulations* (CFR) is the codification of all final rules of all federal agencies. It is updated annually.

---

afford parties **due process of law,** as required by the federal and state constitutions, but, as we shall see, the exact nature of due process depends greatly on the context.

- When can private citizens bring suits to challenge agency actions? The answer is, when they have **standing,** but a variety of legal rules govern standing in the federal and state courts.

As government in the modern era has become more pervasive, administrative law has become more important. Virtually everyone in this country has had or will have contact with an administrative or regulatory agency. The encounter may be as simple as registering to vote, paying property taxes, or obtaining a fishing license. But it may be much more complex and serious, as when a business owner is penalized for violating safety conditions in the workplace, an alien is deported by the Immigration and Naturalization Service (INS), or a taxpayer is subjected to a field audit by the Internal Revenue Service (IRS). In such situations, administrative law becomes very relevant.

DELEGATION OF LEGISLATIVE AUTHORITY

Under our constitutional system, legislatures have the primary authority to make law. However, the expansive role now played by government at all levels makes the legislative function much more difficult. The complexity of problems demanding government attention and the practical difficulties of regulation obviously limit the ability of legislatures to legislate comprehensively, much less effectively. Moreover, the slow pace of the legislative process makes it all but impossible for legislatures to respond promptly to changing conditions. Thus Congress and state legislatures have come to rely increasingly on experts for the development and the implementation of regulations. These experts are found in a host of government departments, commissions, agencies, boards, and bureaus that comprise the modern administrative state.

Through a series of broad **delegations of power,** legislatures have transferred to the bureaucracy much of the responsibility for making and enforcing the rules and regulations deemed necessary for a technological society. Frequently, the **enabling legislation** creating these agencies provides little more than vague generalities to guide agency **rule making.** For example, in 1970, Congress gave OSHA the power to make rules that are "reasonably necessary or appropriate to provide safe and healthful employment and places of employment." The rules promulgated by OSHA as "necessary" or "appropriate" take on all the force of law. A business that is found to be in violation of these rules is subject to civil penalties.

Broad delegations of legislative power are generally seen as necessary so that agencies can develop the programs required to deal with targeted problems. Others would say that broad delegations are inevitable because Congress and the state legislatures simply do not have the expertise to write detailed policies into legislation. For example, the Clean Air Act of 1990 is implemented by more than 300 particular rules adopted by the Environmental Protection Agency. Broad delegations of power may be to a great extent desirable or even inevitable, but they do raise serious constitutional questions.

Delegation is difficult to square with the principle of **separation of powers** implicit in the very structure of the U.S. Constitution. Article I vests "all legislative power" in the Congress. Thus, when Congress delegates legislative power to the executive branch, it can be viewed as violating the implicit constitutional principles of representative government and separation of powers, as well as the express language of Article I. Chief Justice William Howard Taft recognized the constitutional problem raised by legislative delegation: "[I]n carrying out that Constitutional division into three branches it is a breach of the national fundamental law if Congress gives up its legislative power and transfers it to the President, or to the judicial branch, or if by law attempts to vest itself of either executive or judicial power."[3]

Chief Justice Taft's essential point was that if the Constitution imposes meaningful limitations on government, then Congress must be very careful in transferring its own power to the other branches. In 1935, as part of an epic struggle with President Franklin Roosevelt over the New Deal, the Supreme Court struck down a major government program on the ground that Congress had delegated too much authority to the bureaucracy. In 1933, on the recommendation of President Roosevelt, Congress adopted the National Industrial Recovery Act. This statute created the National Recovery Administration (NRA), which became the centerpiece of the New Deal. NRA was empowered to create "Codes of Fair Competition" in major industries. In *Schechter Poultry Corporation v. United States* (1935), the Supreme Court held that Congress had granted "virtually unfettered" discretion to the bureaucracy to enact "laws for the government of trade and industry throughout the country."[4] Thus, the Court dealt a body blow to the New Deal and intensified a political conflict already underway—a battle that was won eventually by the president.

A Constitutional Revolution?

Because he was elected to four terms of office, President Roosevelt was able to fill eight vacancies on the Court, effectively remaking the Court to reflect his political views. As a result, the Court's orientation changed dramatically. Beginning in the 1940s, the Court manifested much more tolerance of delegation of legislative power. In effect, the Court acknowledged the legitimacy of the modern administrative state. As Cass Sunstein has noted, President Roosevelt's remaking the Court "altered the constitutional system in ways so fundamental as to suggest that a constitutional amendment had taken place."[5] Gary

Lawson has made the point more forcefully: "The post–New Deal administrative state is unconstitutional, and its validation by the legal system amounts to nothing less than a bloodless constitutional revolution."[6]

Despite numerous opportunities, not since the *Schechter* case has the Court struck down an act of Congress on delegation grounds. In the early 1980s, certain members of the Court indicated a desire to scrutinize legislative delegations more carefully. For example, in 1981, the Court sustained an OSHA "cotton dust" regulation against a challenge from the textile industry.[7] Joined by Chief Justice Warren Burger, Justice William Rehnquist asserted that in enacting the OSHA Act of 1970, Congress "simply abdicated its responsibility for the making of a fundamental and most difficult policy choice."[8] But a majority could never be mustered to rally around Rehnquist's position.

The Court's long-standing reluctance to invoke the nondelegation doctrine was reaffirmed in its 1989 ruling upholding Congress's creation of the U.S. Sentencing Commission and recognizing the constitutionality of detailed sentencing guidelines promulgated by the commission.[9] Eight members of the Court rejected the argument that Congress had impermissibly delegated its power to prescribe ranges of criminal sentences that federal judges were required to impose on persons convicted of crimes. The Court also rejected the argument that Congress had violated the separation of powers principle by placing the sentencing commission within the judicial branch and authorizing it to establish legally binding sentencing guidelines. In a lone dissent, Justice Antonin Scalia asserted that the separation

Opinion of the Court . . .

MISTRETTA V. UNITED STATES

488 U.S. 361, 109 S. Ct. 647, 102 L.Ed.2d 714 (1989)

Justice Blackmun delivered the opinion of the Court.

. . . The Constitution provides that "[a]ll legislative Powers herein granted shall be vested in a Congress of the United States," . . . and we long have insisted that "the integrity and maintenance of the system of government ordained by the Constitution" mandate that Congress generally cannot delegate its legislative power to another Branch. . . . We also recognize, however, that the separation-of-powers principle, and the nondelegation doctrine in particular, do not prevent Congress from obtaining the assistance of its coordinate Branches. . . . So long as Congress "shall lay down by legislative act an intelligible principle to which the person or body authorized to [exercise the delegated author-ity] is directed to conform, such legislative action is not a forbidden delegation of legislative power." . . . Applying this "intelligible principle" test to congressional delegations, our jurisprudence has been driven by a practical understanding that in our increasingly complex society, replete with ever changing and more technical problems, Congress simply cannot do its job absent an ability to delegate power under broad general directives. . . . "The Constitution has never been regarded as denying to the Congress the necessary resources of flexibility and practicality, which will enable it to perform its function." . . . Accordingly, this Court has deemed it "constitutionally sufficient if Congress clearly delineates the general policy, the public agency which is to apply it, and the boundaries of this delegated authority." . . .

of powers principle had been violated, concluding that the new sentencing commission amounted to a "junior varsity Congress with extensive lawmaking power."[10]

The argument over delegation of legislative power is not confined to the federal level. State courts have wrestled with this problem over the years. Like the U.S. Supreme Court, though, most state courts have come down on the side of permitting broad delegations of legislative authority to the bureaucracy. The antidelegation doctrine remains viable, however, at least in theory. It remains available as a tool to invalidate a particularly egregious instance of legislative abdication of responsibility.

Legislative Control of the Bureaucracy

Congress and the state legislatures have employed a variety of mechanisms to retain control over agency decisions. These include attaching riders to agency appropriations bills, conducting oversight hearings, reducing agency budgets, and amending statutes. Of course, if the legislature is extremely dissatisfied with the performance of a particular agency, it may rewrite the statute that created the agency in the first instance. By amending the appropriate statute, the legislature may enlarge or contract the agency's **jurisdiction,** as well as the nature and scope of its **rule-making authority.**

The Legislative Veto

A **legislative veto** is a device whereby the legislature as a whole, one house thereof, or even one legislative committee can override an agency decision that is made pursuant to delegated authority. A legislative veto provision is typically written into the original act delegating legislative power to an executive agency. In *Immigration and Naturalization Service v. Chadha* (1986), the Supreme Court held that the legislative veto is unconstitutional.[11] The essence of the Court's opinion was that all legislative vetoes are invalid because the president is not given the opportunity to veto the legislative veto of the agency's action. Obviously, the Court in *Chadha* assumed that a legislative veto is a legislative act that must conform to the requirements of Article I, an assumption that the dissenting justices and numerous commentators have found unpersuasive.

The *Chadha* decision not only invalidated the veto provision actually before the Court, but also rendered some 230 similar statutory provisions presumptively unconstitutional, making it the most sweeping exercise of judicial review in the history of the Supreme Court. As noted previously, Congress retains a number of mechanisms whereby it can control agency action of which it disapproves. Moreover, the Court's decision applied only to legislative vetoes enacted by Congress; it said nothing of similar provisions at the state level.

Many, but certainly not all, of the state legislative veto provisions have been struck down by state courts following the reasoning of the *Chadha* decision. The Idaho Supreme Court has approved the legislative veto, viewing it as a reasonable condition on the delegation of legislative power to executive agencies.[12] Many commentators on the *Chadha* decision itself have taken this position. That notwithstanding, *Chadha* remains the law of the land, and there is little likelihood that the Court will reconsider its position in the foreseeable future.

Through enactment of the Contract with America Act of 1996, Congress has created a new procedure that is functionally similar to the legislative veto. Under a section entitled

> ## CASE IN POINT
>
> ### CAN THE FDA REGULATE TOBACCO AS A DRUG?
>
> ### *Food and Drug Administration et al. v. Brown & Williamson Tobacco Corporation*
>
> United States Supreme Court
> 529 U.S. 120, 120 S. Ct. 1291, 146 L.Ed.2d 121 (2000)
>
> Under the federal Food, Drug and Cosmetic Act, the Food and Drug Administration has the authority to regulate "drugs" and "devices." In 1996, FDA adopted regulations governing the promotion and labeling of tobacco products. The regulations were concerned specifically with making these products less accessible to children and adolescents. FDA based its regulatory authority on the grounds that nicotine is a "drug" and tobacco products are "devices" that deliver nicotine to the body. Brown and Williamson, a manufacturer of tobacco products, filed suit challenging the FDA's authority in this area. The federal district court upheld the FDA's authority, but the Court of Appeals reversed, holding that Congress had not granted the FDA jurisdiction over tobacco products. Splitting 5–4, the Supreme Court also ruled against the FDA. Notwithstanding its customary deference to agency interpretations of statutes, the Court concluded that Congress clearly had not intended to give the FDA the authority to regulate tobacco products. Of course, as a matter of statutory interpretation, the Court's decision can be overturned by ordinary legislation clearly authorizing the FDA to regulate tobacco.

"Congressional Review of Agency Decisionmaking," an agency must submit a report to Congress on every new proposed rule.[13] Through simple majority vote of either house, the rule is stayed for 60 days, giving Congress ample time to prevent the adoption of the rule through the process of joint resolution. Unlike the legislative veto, the joint resolution must be presented to the President before it can become law. Thus, even though the new procedure restores some measure of control to the Congress, it cannot act autonomously to veto administrative action of which it disapproves.

RULE MAKING

When Congress and the state legislatures delegate regulatory authority to agencies, they are not authorizing agencies to make policy ad hoc. Rather, they are permitting agencies to engage in the process of rule making. Rule making is like legislation—it produces rules of general applicability. Kenneth Culp Davis, a leading authority on administrative law, observed in the late 1960s that "the chief hope for confining discretionary power does not lie in statutory enactments but in much more extensive administrative rulemaking."[14] The federal government may have heeded his words, for the 1970s initiated the "era of rulemaking" as federal agencies became much more active in this regard. Indeed, the trend toward increased rule making by federal agencies continues to the present time, despite efforts by Presidents Reagan and Bush in the 1980s and early 1990s to stem the regulatory tide (see Figure 12-2). In 1997 alone, federal agencies produced nearly 3,000 new regulations. Keeping pace with the changing regulatory environment is a daunting task for business, but is a "growth industry" for lawyers.

At the federal level, the rule-making process is basically governed by the Administrative Procedures Act (APA) of 1946, as amended.[15] Most states have similar statutes. Either they

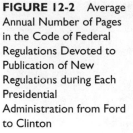

FIGURE 12-2 Average Annual Number of Pages in the Code of Federal Regulations Devoted to Publication of New Regulations during Each Presidential Administration from Ford to Clinton

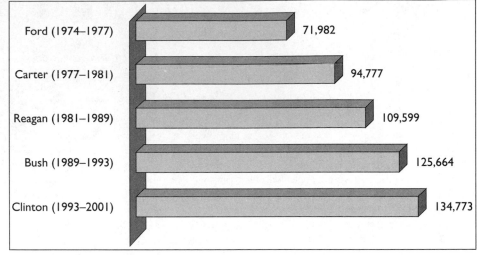

Ford (1974–1977)   71,982

Carter (1977–1981)   94,777

Reagan (1981–1989)   109,599

Bush (1989–1993)   125,664

Clinton (1993–2001)   134,773

have adopted the Model State Administrative Procedures Act of 1961, its 1981 update, or they have crafted their own legislation.

The APA requires agencies to publish a **notice of proposed rule making** (NPRM) in the *Federal Register.* Such notice must include "a statement of the time, place, and nature of public rulemaking proceedings; reference to the legal authority under which the rule is proposed; and either the terms or substance of the proposed rule or a description of the subjects and issues involved. . . ."[16] The law requires that before the rule can go into effect, interested parties must be afforded an opportunity to comment orally or in writing. Agencies are required to take comments into account before adopting a final rule. Once adopted, the final rule must be published in the *Federal Register* at least 30 days prior to its effective date. Even then, the law requires the agency to provide interested parties the right to petition for the issuance, amendment, or repeal of a rule. After a rule is finalized, it is incorporated into the Code of Federal Regulations.

The Administrative Procedures Act sets forth minimal requirements for agency rule making. Congress will often require that particular agencies go well beyond these simple, relatively informal procedures. For example, the Toxic Substances Control Act requires the Environmental Protection Agency to follow more elaborate procedures when regulating hazardous materials.[17] Another example is the extensive process the Food and Drug Administration is required to follow before approving new drugs and medical devices.[18]

Rule making is also affected by a number of general statutes. For example, the National Environmental Policy Act (NEPA) requires agencies to provide an environmental impact statement before undertaking or approving any major action affecting the environment. The Paperwork Reduction Act of 1995 requires agencies to assess the impact of proposed rules on the need for data collection and archiving. The Unfounded Mandates Act of 1995 requires agencies to assess the fiscal impact of proposed rules on state and local governments.

The Regulatory Flexibility Act, which was enacted during the Carter administration and strengthened in 1996, was adopted to ease the regulatory burden on small business.

Large companies can generally withstand economic costs associated with complying with government regulations. Small businesses are at a disadvantage in this respect. Small businesses often encounter great difficulty in trying to comprehend and comply with government regulations. Federal law now requires that before agencies adopt rules that significantly impact small business, they consider how rules can be made and enforced in such a way so as to minimize the regulatory burden on small business.[19]

Executive Control of Rule Making

Excessive government regulation of business became a political issue in the 1970s. In 1978, President Carter issued an executive order requiring federal agencies to conduct a "regulatory analysis" before adopting new rules in order to ensure that economic costs were taken into account.[20] President Reagan greatly expanded on this mandate by requiring agencies to conduct **cost-benefit analyses** and adopting only those rules that maximized net benefits to society.[21] Agencies that fail to satisfy White House **preclearance** of proposed rules are prevented from publishing NPRMs in the *Federal Register.*

White House preclearance of proposed rules is effectuated by the Office of Management and Budget (OMB), which is part of the executive office of the president. Presidents can control rule making to an extent, because agencies depend on the White House, more specifically the OMB, to submit their annual budget requests to Congress.

Adequacy of Rule-Making Procedures

In the absence of more specific congressional guidance, the Supreme Court has tended to rely on the Administrative Procedure Act as an adequate framework for agency rule-making procedures. For example, in 1978, the Supreme Court considered the adequacy of procedures used by the Atomic Energy Commission (now the Nuclear Regulatory Commission) for the licensure of nuclear power plants.[22] Of particular concern was the agency's procedure in promulgating a rule governing spent nuclear fuel. The procedure in question included the scheduling of hearings prior to adoption of the rule, as required by the APA. These hearings were somewhat informal, however, and did not include full **adjudicatory procedures,** such as discovery and cross-examination. The Court of Appeals for the District of Columbia Circuit held that the existing procedure was inadequate under the Due Process Clause of the Fifth Amendment. The Supreme Court reversed without a dissenting vote. In his opinion for the Court, Justice Rehnquist sharply criticized the Court of Appeals decision, complaining that "this sort of unwarranted judicial examination of perceived procedural shortcomings of a rulemaking proceeding can do nothing but seriously interfere with that process prescribed by Congress. . . ."[23]

AGENCY INVESTIGATIONS

Agencies have the authority to conduct investigations within the purview of their regulatory authority. For example, the EPA investigates alleged violations of the Clean Air Act,

Clean Water Act, and other federal environmental laws. In their investigations, agencies have powers to subpoena records and compel individuals to testify, as long as compelled testimony is not used as evidence in a criminal prosecution.[24] Agencies cannot enforce their own subpoenas, however, and so they often file enforcement petitions in federal district courts.[25] Courts often hold hearings on these petitions, but usually uphold agency subpoenas.

Search and Seizure

One of the most important investigative tools agencies possess is that of search and seizure. Despite the Fourth Amendment's prohibition of unreasonable searches and seizures, agencies have routinely conducted administrative inspections of the industries they regulate. In general, the courts have been more permissive toward **administrative searches** directed at business and industry than toward police searches directed at private individuals. In 1959, the Supreme Court found no violation of the Fourth Amendment when administrative searches were conducted without notice and without search warrants.[26] In the 1960s, the Court became stricter, holding that, as a general rule, warrants must be obtained to justify administrative searches.[27] The Court made an exception, however, for "closely regulated industries."[28]

A good example the stricter judicial scrutiny of administrative searches can be seen in *Marshall v. Barlow's, Inc.* (1978).[29] There the Supreme Court struck down a provision of the Occupational Health and Safety Act of 1970 that allowed OSHA to conduct warrantless searches of the workplace. However, the Court was careful to point out that to obtain **administrative search warrants,** OSHA inspectors did not have to meet the same strict standards of probable cause that govern the issuance of warrants in criminal investigations.

In the 1980s, a more conservative Supreme Court backed away from the strict scrutiny of regulatory searches manifested by the Court in the 1960s and 70s. For example, in 1981 the Court refused to invalidate a provision of the Federal Mine Safety and Health Act of 1977 that allowed the Department of Labor to conduct **warrantless inspections** of mines.[30] The Court attempted to distinguish the case from *Barlow's,* but it seems clear that a majority of the justices preferred the more permissive approach that prevailed prior to the 1960s.

In 1987, in upholding a warrantless inspection of a junkyard, the Court laid out a framework for evaluating **warrantless administrative searches.**[31] The Court said that such inspections should be upheld as long three conditions are met:

1. There must be a substantial government interest that informs the regulatory scheme pursuant to which the inspection is made,
2. The warrantless inspection must be necessary to further the regulatory scheme,
3. The inspection program must provide a constitutionally adequate substitute for a warrant.

This approach gives government agencies considerable latitude in conducting warrantless inspections of regulated industries and, accordingly, has been highly criticized. Of course, state courts can adopt stricter rules for administrative searches under their own state constitutional provisions relative to search and seizure.

CASE IN POINT

WARRANTLESS AERIAL INSPECTION OF A CHEMICAL PLANT

Dow Chemical Company v. United States

United States Supreme Court
476 U.S. 227, 106 S.Ct. 1819, 90 L.Ed.2d 226 (1986)

Acting without a warrant, EPA officials employed a commercial aerial photographer to take pictures of a chemical plant from an altitude of 1,200 feet. When the plant's owners learned of the photographic flyover, they filed suit in federal court, claiming that the EPA had violated their Fourth Amendment rights. Splitting 5–4, the Supreme Court sided with the EPA, holding that the flyover was not a "search" within the meaning of the Fourth Amendment. The Court observed:

"It may well be, as the Government concedes, that surveillance of private property by using highly sophisticated surveillance equipment not generally available to the public, such as satellite technology, might be constitutionally proscribed absent a warrant. But the photographs here are not so revealing of intimate details as to raise constitutional concerns. Although they undoubtedly give EPA more detailed information than naked-eye views, they remain limited to an outline of the facility's buildings and equipment. The mere fact that human vision is enhanced somewhat, at least to the degree here, does not give rise to constitutional problems."

Deportation and Administrative Detention

The Immigration and Naturalization Service (INS) has the responsibility for carrying out the nation's immigration laws.[32] Historically, the INS has possessed broad discretion in enforcement of immigration law and adjudication of immigration cases. More specifically, the INS conducts immigration inspections of travelers entering the United States, regulates permanent and temporary immigration (including legal permanent residence status, and nonimmigrant status), and maintains control of the nation's borders. INS identifies and removes people who do not have lawful immigration status, a process known as **deportation**. Under the Illegal Immigration and Immigrant Responsibility Act of 1996, the INS can detain illegal aliens indefinitely without bond, regardless of whether they are likely to appear for deportation proceedings and pose no danger to the community.[33] **Administrative detention** in such cases is not subject to judicial review.[34] This approach is justified on the basis that illegal aliens are not entitled to the protections of the U.S. Constitution, a theory that not everyone accepts.[35]

AGENCY ENFORCEMENT POWERS

Agencies have a variety of sanctions available, but they cannot impose sanctions without statutory authority. Agencies that issue licenses, such as the Federal Communications Commission and the Nuclear Regulatory Commission, have the authority to revoke such licenses when licensees engage in repeated violations of regulations. Agencies also have the power to impose their own administrative fines. Certain agencies, such as the National Labor Relations Board, have the power to issue **cease and desist orders**.

Civil Suits

Several federal agencies have the authority to file civil suits against violators. For example, the Civil Rights Act of 1964 authorizes the Department of Justice to file suit to vindicate citizens' civil rights.[36] It was under this provision that the Justice Department filed a highly publicized suit in 1993 against Flagstar Corporation, the operator of Denny's Restaurants. The suit alleged racial discrimination against black patrons. In a settlement, Flagstar paid $45 million in damages and established a program to prevent future discrimination at its restaurants.[37]

Often the civil rights suits filed by the Justice Department are referred to it by other federal agencies. For example, the Office of Civil Rights (OCR) in the U.S. Department of Education is responsible for enforcing a number of civil rights laws that apply to public education, including Title VI of the Civil Rights Act of 1964, Title IX of the Education Amendments of 1972, Section 504 of the Rehabilitation Act of 1973, and Title II of the Americans with Disabilities Act of 1990. The OCR investigates complaints filed by parties who believe they are the victims of unlawful discrimination, but it has no power to bring lawsuits on its own. The OCR prefers to settle discrimination complaints through negotiation with school officials, but in some instances it refers cases to the Justice Department, which then decides whether to file suit against the school district.

One agency that can bring civil suits directly against violators is the Securities and Exchange Commission. The SEC routinely files suit in federal district court against parties who are accused of securities fraud under federal law and the commission's own regulations.[38] The SEC is empowered to seek injunctions, the "disgorgement" of ill-gotten gains, and civil penalties. For example, in *SEC v. Fabri-Centers of America, Inc.,* the court entered an order requiring the defendant to pay a $25,000 civil penalty, almost $24,000 in disgorgement and nearly $21,000 in prejudgment interest.[39]

Citizen-Initiated Lawsuits

In some instances citizens can go to court directly rather than wait for a government agency to act on a violation of public policy. For example, Section 505(a) of the Clean Water Act authorizes private citizens to commence a civil action for injunctive relief and/or the imposition of civil penalties in federal district court against any person "alleged to be in violation" of the conditions of a National Pollutant Discharge Elimination System (NPDES) permit. However, Section 505(a) does not allow citizen suits for "wholly past violations."[40]

An increasingly popular form of citizen-initiated litigation is the *qui tam* action. *Qui tam* is short for the Latin phrase, "*qui tam pro domino rege quam pro sic ipso in hoc parte sequitur,*" which means "who sues for the king sues for himself as well." According to *Black's Law Dictionary,* a *qui tam* suit is "an action brought by an informer, under a statute which establishes a penalty for the commission or omission of a certain act, and provides that the same shall be recoverable in a civil action, part of the penalty to go to any person who will bring such action and the remainder to the state or some other institution." The Federal False Claims Act allows private citizens to file suit on behalf of the U.S. government charging fraud by government contractors and others who receive federal funds.[41] If the plaintiff prevails, the government can recover triple its damages in addition to civil penalties ranging from $5,000 to $10,000 per violation. The citizen (referred to as the *relator*) shares in the monetary damages collected up to a maximum of 30 percent. The False Claims Act was enacted by Congress during the Civil War in order to ferret out fraud in military procurement. Today, the law provides an incentive to whistle-blowers to reveal evidence of fraud in programs such as Medicare and Medicaid. In recent years there have been a number of $100 million settlements. Currently, about 500 *qui tam* actions are filed in federal courts each year and the number is growing rapidly.

Criminal Prosecutions

Federal agencies do not have the authority to initiate criminal prosecutions. When they obtain evidence of criminal wrongdoing, however, they can refer the matter to the Department of Justice. If the attorney general believes the matter warrants prosecution, the case is presented to a federal grand jury for indictment (see Chapter 10).

Liens, Levies, and Garnishments

Without question, the federal agency most feared by average Americans is the Internal Revenue Service. It is also among the most vital, in that it collects 95 percent of the federal government's revenues through personal and corporate income taxes; excise, gift, and estate taxes; and Social Security employment taxes. The IRS is empowered to conduct audits of taxpayers' returns, impose liens and levies on assets in order to recover unpaid taxes, and even garnish wages. However, in 1988, 1996, and 1998, Congress enacted legislation to protect taxpayers from the abuse of IRS powers. A taxpayer's principal residence is now protected from **levy** to satisfy tax liabilities of less than $5,000. The taxpayer must be provided with a levy statement at least 30 days before property is seized, during which time the taxpayer may request a hearing to challenge the levy. With respect to **garnishments,** the law now requires a 21-day hold on bank accounts garnished by the IRS, which provides more time to challenge an improper garnishment. Finally, taxpayers who are the victims of reckless or intentional disregard of proper tax collection procedures may sue the IRS in federal district court for damages up to $1 million.[42]

Forfeitures

Federal law provides for the **forfeiture** of real estate and other property used in illegal drug trafficking and other criminal activities.[43] Cars, boats, and airplanes are commonly seized under the forfeiture laws. In 1984, federal law enforcement agencies began a program called Equitable Sharing, under which federal agencies recruit state and local police to assist them in seizing property under federal statutes. Local or state police seize property and turn it over to the federal government. If the forfeiture is upheld, the state or local police agency that made the seizure shares equally in the proceeds when the forfeited assets are sold at auction.

In 1993, the Supreme Court held that a property forfeiture stemming from a drug crime is subject to limitation under the Eighth Amendment.[44] Writing for the Court, Justice Blackmun concluded that "forfeiture . . . constitutes 'payment to a sovereign as punishment for some offense,' and, as such, is subject to the limitations of the Eighth Amendment's Excessive Fines Clause."[45]

Until recently, real estate, including a residence or business, could be seized on the basis of an ex parte seizure warrant, and the property owner ousted from the property pending trial—without notice or an opportunity to be heard. The Supreme Court has held that such practices are unconstitutional when they apply to seizures of real estate.[46] Due process requires notice and the opportunity to be heard before real estate can be seized, the Court held, and that in most situations that should mean that the property owner will not be disturbed in the right of possession of the property pending trial. But the Supreme Court expressly limited the holding to real property—residential or commercial. It did not affect pretrial detention of cars, bank accounts, cash, and other personal property.

AGENCY ADJUDICATION

Agencies often must settle disputes with parties they regulate or the beneficiaries of their programs. In this respect agencies act as **quasi-judicial bodies.** Unlike judicial proceedings, however, the rules of evidence for administrative hearings are quite liberal with hearsay evidence generally admitted and only irrelevant, immaterial, or repetitive evidence excluded.

The Administrative Procedures Act

Federal agency adjudicatory procedures are governed in general by the Administrative Procedures Act (APA). Most states have their own counterpart to the APA. The APA requires the most basic elements of due process, that is, notice and hearing. Regarding notice, it provides that "[p]ersons entitled to notice of an agency hearing shall be timely informed of (1) the time, place, and nature of the hearing; (2) the legal authority and jurisdiction under which the hearing is to be held; and (3) the matters of fact and law asserted."[47] As to the hearing, the agency is required to "give all interested parties opportunity for . . . the submission and consideration of facts, arguments, offers of settlement, or proposals of adjustment when time, the nature of the proceeding, and the public interest permit. . . ."[48]

The APA's requirements for administrative hearings are minimal, allowing agencies to operate rather informally; but the APA is not the only source of procedural requirements. Depending on the agency and issue involved, other statutory requirements may come into play. The agency's enabling legislation, that is, the act of Congress that established and empowered the agency, may dictate certain additional procedural requirements. So too may the substantive statute being enforced. Contracts between agencies and private contractors may also specify additional procedural requirements respecting the termination of contracts; and some agencies develop their own internal rules of procedure that go beyond the APA and other statutory requirements. As a result, it is difficult to generalize about the procedural aspects of agency adjudication. They vary considerably along a continuum from **informal adjudication** that observes only the minimal requirements of the APA to **formal adjudication** that resembles a civil trial (see Chapter 9).

The Presiding Officer

Less formal agency adjudications are overseen by "administrative judges" or "hearing examiners." More formal proceedings are conducted by **administrative law judges (ALJs).**[49] Although ALJs are technically employees of the agencies they serve, they are supposed to function as impartial arbiters of disputes. It is essential that disputes be adjudicated by impartial decision makers.[50] Accordingly, federal law contains a number of measures designed to enhance the independence of ALJs from their agencies.[51]

Due Process Requirements

Beyond the statutory requirements regarding agency adjudication, the U.S. Constitution looms as the ultimate source of procedural protection. The Supreme Court has applied the Due Process Clauses of the Fifth and Fourteenth Amendments when it has found statutory procedures inadequate to ensure fairness or to protect the fundamental rights of individuals. During the 1970s, the Supreme Court seemed more willing to apply constitutional due process requirements in cases when agency decisions affected the economic interests of specific individuals. For example, in *Goldberg v. Kelly* (1970), the Supreme Court held that the Fourteenth Amendment Due Process Clause required a state agency to provide an evidentiary hearing before terminating a person's welfare benefits after the agency determined that

CASE IN POINT

DUE PROCESS AND TERMINATION OF SOCIAL SECURITY DISABILITY BENEFITS

Mathews v. Eldridge

United States Supreme Court
424 U.S. 319, 96 S.Ct. 893, 47 L.Ed.2d 18 (1976)

George Eldridge, who had been disabled due to "chronic anxiety and back strain," was informed by the Social Security Administration that, according to medical reports, his disability no longer existed and that benefit payments would be terminated. Although agency procedures required ample notification and an evidentiary hearing prior to final termination, the payments could be stopped initially without a hearing. Provision was also made for retroactive payments to any recipient whose disability was later determined not to have ended. Eldridge, who was concerned with the initial decision to terminate payments, relied on *Goldberg v. Kelly* in arguing that the Due Process Clause required an evidentiary hearing before any termination of benefits.

Writing for the Court, Justice Lewis Powell conceded the existence of a property interest in social secu-

rity benefits and thus the applicability of the Due Process Clause. But Powell said that "due process is flexible and calls for such procedural protections as the particular situation demands." In other words, the degree of procedural safeguards required by the Constitution depends on how much one stands to lose. In this case, the Court distinguished social security from welfare benefits and held that the "potential deprivation . . . is generally likely to be less" when social security payments are denied than when welfare benefits are terminated. In this way, the Court significantly narrowed the potential application of *Goldberg v. Kelly* without formally overruling it. In *Matthews*, the Court was willing to regard the existing agency procedures as adequate safeguards.

the individual was no longer eligible for such benefits.[52] In *Goss v. Lopez* (1975), the Court held that the 10-day suspension of a student from a public school constituted deprivation of property within the meaning of the Due Process Clause.[53] Thus, the school was required to provide basic procedural safeguards. Other Supreme Court decisions in the 1970s extended due process protections to a wide variety of claimants, including employees, automobile drivers, prisoners, and debtors.

In administrative due process cases, the Court must make two determinations. First, it must decide whether the Due Process Clause is applicable. Administrative decisions are constrained by the Due Process Clause only if they in some meaningful way deprive an individual of "life, liberty or property." Of course, today those interests are broadly defined. Second, assuming the Due Process Clause does apply, the Court must determine what "process" is due in order to ensure fundamental fairness. Here the Court has been reluctant to adopt a one-size-fits-all approach to administrative due process. In *Mathews v. Eldridge* (see the Case in Point above), the Court said that "due process is flexible and calls for such procedural protections as the particular situation demands."[54] Beyond the general requirements of fair notice and fair hearing, it is difficult to say precisely what due process requires in a specific administrative context. One guiding principle is that the greater the magnitude of the individual's life, liberty, or property interest, the greater the requirement for procedural protections.

JUDICIAL REVIEW OF AGENCY ACTIONS

One function of the federal courts is to ensure that the federal bureaucracy conforms to the rule of law. In certain instances, parties can go directly to federal district court to challenge agency actions. In most cases, however, parties must first exhaust available remedies internal to the agency. Having done so and failing to get relief, they can then file an appeal with the appropriate circuit court. For obvious reasons, the District of Columbia Circuit Court has an extensive caseload of these administrative cases. There is an elaborate body of law, both statutory and decisional, governing **judicial review of agency actions.** The fundamental distinction to be made in this area is that between threshold issues and decisions on the merits.

Access to Judicial Review

Before a federal court can reach the merits of an administrative law case, several threshold issues must be addressed. These threshold issues govern access to judicial review. By limiting access to judicial review, courts maintain manageable caseloads and, moreover, maintain comity with the executive branch. The most fundamental threshold issue is jurisdiction. The court must have jurisdiction over the parties, the subject matter, and the geographical area before it can grant review. Because the jurisdiction of the lower federal courts is wholly dependent on Congress, the legislature can preclude judicial review altogether or under certain circumstances. This is known as **statutory preclusion of judicial review.** For example, in 1994, the Supreme Court ruled that the Federal Mine Safety and Health Amendments Act of 1977 precludes a federal court from exercising subject matter jurisdiction over a preenforcement challenge to the act.[55] Similarly, in 1988, the Court held that the National Security Act of 1947 precludes judicial review of the CIA director's decisions to terminate employees regardless of cause.[56]

Standing and Exhaustion of Remedies

The Administrative Procedure Act provides "A person suffering legal wrong because of agency action, or adversely affected or aggrieved by agency action within the meaning of a relevant statute, is entitled to judicial review thereof."[57] To have standing to challenge an agency action, one must be adversely affected by that action in a way that is direct, substantial, and immediate. Parties who are direct targets of agency actions, such as beneficiaries who are denied benefits and licensees whose licenses are suspended or revoked, have virtually automatic standing to challenge adverse agency decisions in court, once they have exhausted all their administrative remedies. When a statute provides for administrative review within an agency, such review must be pursued before seeking review by the courts. Agencies are given every opportunity to correct their own errors before courts become involved. This **exhaustion of remedies** doctrine prevents judicial review that is premature or unnecessary.

Individuals and groups that are not direct parties to agency proceedings have more difficulty in establishing standing to challenge agency actions. Certainly the status of being a disgruntled taxpayer is not enough to give one standing to challenge an agency action of which one disapproves, no matter how good a legal challenge one can mount.[58] An interest group does not have standing to challenge an agency action merely because its members oppose what the agency has done.[59] If an interest group is unable to show "individualized harm" to itself or its members, it does not have standing. On the other hand, standing is not confined to those who show economic harm. If a group can show that agency action adversely affects its quality of life, it may be successful in overcoming this threshold issue.[60]

Review on the Merits

Once the barriers to access have been surmounted, a plaintiff still faces an uphill legal battle in challenging agency actions. Federal courts generally review agency actions with a fairly strong presumption of validity. In other words, the burden of proof rests with the party challenging the agency to show that the agency's action was contrary to statute or the agency's own policies. In matters of statutory interpretation, the agency's construction of a statute is presumed to be valid unless it is contradicted by unambiguous legislative intent.[61] However, when constitutional issues involving fundamental rights such as freedom of speech or the right to privacy are concerned, the burden shifts to the agency to show that its action is constitutional. Nevertheless, the Supreme Court is reluctant to invalidate agency actions on constitutional grounds.[62] With regard to factual determinations, federal courts generally do not overturn agency conclusions unless they are clearly erroneous or at least not based on **substantial evidence.**

It is fair to say that the federal courts show substantial deference to the actions of administrative agencies. A certain degree of deference is necessary to maintain the viability of the administrative state. As the recent *Brown and Williamson* case demonstrates, however, this deference is not unlimited. In extreme cases, the courts will say that agencies have operated outside the law.

CASE IN POINT

DEFERENCE TO ADMINISTRATIVE AGENCIES: THE ELIAN GONZALES CASE

Gonzales v. Reno

United States Court of Appeals, 11th Circuit
212 F. 3d 1338 (11th Cir. 2000)

In late 1999 and early 2000, the Immigration and Naturalization Service (INS) became the focus of national and international attention for its handling of the unusual case of Elian Gonzales, a six-year-old Cuban boy who was rescued at sea after his mother and nine other people drowned when their boat capsized. The INS gave temporary custody of the boy to relatives in Miami. When the boy's natural father came from Cuba to claim Elian, the Miami relatives refused to relinquish custody. After negotiations between the INS and the Miami relatives broke down, the INS used force to remove the boy from the home of the Miami relatives and reunite him with his father. While they had custody of Elian, the Miami relatives initiated a federal lawsuit to force the INS to grant Elian a political asylum hearing. The INS took the position that legally, only Elian's father could speak for him in this regard. The federal district court in Miami dismissed the case. The Miami relatives appealed to the U.S. Court of Appeals for the Eleventh Circuit in Atlanta. On June 1, 2000, the 11th Circuit ruled that the INS had acted within its legal authority in refusing to hold a political asylum hearing. The following is an excerpt from the 11th Circuit's opinion:

Edmondson, Circuit Judge:

...As policymakers, it is the duty of the Congress and of the executive branch to exercise political will. Although courts should not be unquestioning, we should respect the other branches' policymaking powers. The judicial power is a limited power. It is the duty of the judicial branch not to exercise political will, but only to render judicial judgment under the law.

When the INS was confronted with Plaintiff's purported asylum applications, the immigration law of the United States provided the INS with no clear answer. The INS accordingly developed a policy to deal with the extraordinary circumstances of asylum applications filed on behalf of a six-year-old child, by the child himself and a nonparental relative, against the express wishes of the child's parents (or sole parent). The INS then applied this new policy to the Plaintiff's purported asylum applications and rejected them as nullities.

Because the preexisting law compelled no particular policy, the INS was entitled to make a policy decision. The policy decision that the INS made was within the outside border of reasonable choices. And the INS did not abuse its discretion or act arbitrarily in applying the policy and rejecting Plaintiff's purported asylum applications. The Court neither approves nor disapproves the INS's decision to reject the asylum applications filed on Plaintiff's behalf, but the INS decision did not contradict [the law].

PUBLIC ACCESS TO AGENCY INFORMATION

In the information age, information is power. In a democratic society it is therefore essential that citizens have access to information held by government agencies. Of course, there must be exceptions to this principle in order to protect personal privacy, ensure national security, and foster effective law enforcement. At the federal level, the linchpin of this debate is the Freedom of Information Act (FOIA). Adopted in 1966, FOIA establishes a presumption that records in the possession of agencies and executive departments of the U.S.

government are accessible to the people. The statute sets standards for determining which records must be disclosed and which records can be withheld. The law provides administrative and judicial remedies for those denied access to records. Above all, the statute requires federal agencies to provide the fullest possible **disclosure of information** to the public. Together with the Privacy Act, FOIA restricts the **improper disclosure of personal information** and provides for civil remedies when an individual's rights have been violated.

The Freedom of Information Act applies to documents held by agencies in the executive branch of the federal government, including the cabinet-level departments, military departments, government corporations, independent regulatory agencies, law enforcement agencies, and other establishments in the executive branch. FOIA does not apply to elected officials of the federal government, including the president, vice president, senators, and congressmen. It does not apply to the federal courts, nor to private companies or persons who receive federal contracts or grants. FOIA does not apply to state or local governments; but note that all states and some localities have passed "open records" laws which, like the FOIA and Privacy Act, permit individuals access to records.

FOIA provides that a party making a request must ask for existing records rather than information. The law requires that each request must reasonably describe the records being sought. A request must be specific enough to permit the agency to locate the record in a reasonable period of time. Once a FOIA request is filed, an agency is required to determine within 10 days (excluding Saturdays, Sundays, and legal holidays) whether to comply. The actual disclosure of documents is required to follow promptly thereafter. FOIA permits an agency to extend the time limits up to 10 days in unusual circumstances. If a request is denied, the agency must provide reasons for the denial. FOIA contains a number of exemptions designed to protect against the disclosure of information that would jeopardize national security, privacy of individuals, proprietary interests of business, and the functioning of the government. For example, classified documents are exempt, as are records relating to internal personnel matters, internal government communications, and confidential business information. In denying a request, the agency must also indicate whether there is a mechanism internal to the agency to appeal a denial. Of course, the ultimate review lies with the federal courts. Often it is a federal court that must decide whether an agency has properly invoked one of the exemptions in denying a FOIA request.

GOVERNMENT IN THE SUNSHINE

In the contemporary era, government secrecy is considered anathema to democracy. The government in the Sunshine Act requires federal agencies headed by a collegial body composed of two or more members to hold their meetings in public.[63] There are numerous exceptions to this requirement, however. The Sunshine Act does not require agencies, for example, to hold public meetings that would reveal matters that must be kept secret for reasons of national security or those that relate solely to the internal agency personnel rules and practices. The act also exempts the disclosure of ongoing law enforcement investigations, personal information that would be an unwarranted invasion of personal privacy, and disclosures that would lead to speculation in currencies, securities, or commodities.

The federal Sunshine Act is in fact fairly narrow in its requirements of **open meetings.** State **sunshine laws** are often much broader.

Florida has one of the strictest sunshine laws, violations of which are punishable by fine.[64] Florida appellate courts have said the law must be broadly construed to effectuate its remedial and protective purpose. That purpose, one court opined, is to prevent crystallization of secret governmental decisions at nonpublic meeting to the point just short of ceremonial acceptance.[65] The Florida Sunshine Law stipulates that all meetings of any board or commission of any state, county, political subdivision, or municipality at which official acts are to be taken, are to be open to the public at all times, except as otherwise provided in the state constitution. Minutes of all such meetings must be recorded and made available for public inspection. The law does permit agencies to meet in private to discuss pending litigation, but a record must be made of such discussions and it must be made available after the litigation has been concluded. The law has been held to apply only to a meeting of two or more public officials at which decision making, as opposed to fact finding or information gathering, will occur. At the point where decisions are being made, such discussions must be conducted in public meetings after notice to the public. In an early opinion construing the law, a Florida appellate court held that a junior college president was neither a "board" or "commission" nor an alter ego of the college board of trustees. Accordingly, the court held he was outside the ambit of the sunshine law and was not required to open his meetings with representatives of career employees of the college.[66]

THE LAW OF PUBLIC EMPLOYMENT

Public officers hold positions created by federal and state constitutions or statutes. To be eligible for election or appointment to a public office, one must possess the qualifications prescribed by law. When a period of residency in a given state or locality is a prerequisite, such requirement is generally upheld by courts if it is of a reasonable duration. Likewise, prohibitions against one who has been convicted of a felony involving moral turpitude from holding a public office are usually upheld. A public officer is required to take an oath to uphold the U.S. Constitution before assuming official duties as a member of Congress, state legislature, or federal or state executive or judicial officer. States require that the oath include the obligation to uphold the constitution of the state. The U.S. Constitution also stipulates that no religious test may be required to hold office.[67]

The Civil Service

Historically, public employees at all levels of government served at the pleasure of chief executives. Under the so-called **spoils system,** mayors, governors, and presidents had virtually total discretion in hiring and firing government employees. However, beginning in 1883, the federal government enacted civil service laws and regulations to establish a merit system of employment, promotion, and discharge of public employees. Today, numerous

CASE IN POINT

THE AIR TRAFFIC CONTROLLERS GO ON STRIKE!

Professional Air Traffic Controllers Organization v. Federal Labor Relations Authority

United States Court of Appeals for the District of Columbia Circuit
685 F.2d 547 (D.C. Cir. 1982)

The Professional Air Traffic Controllers Organization (PATCO) was the recognized exclusive bargaining representative for air traffic controllers employed by the Federal Aviation Administration. Following a breakdown in negotiation for a new contract, PATCO announced a strike deadline and on August 3, 1981, over 70 percent of the nation's federally employed air traffic controllers walked off the job. The FAA revoked PATCO's status as bargaining representative and obtained a restraining order against the strike. This was followed by civil and criminal contempt citations when the restraining order was not heeded. The Federal Labor Relations Authority (FLRA) upheld the FAA's actions and eventually the case came before the U.S. Court of Appeals for the District of Columbia Circuit. In 1985, that court upheld the FLRA's actions in revoking PATCO's status as union representative for the air controllers.

federal statutes regulate federal civil service. The Office of Personnel Management is responsible for the general administration of the federal **civil service** system. The Merit Systems Protection Board is charged with adjudicating employment issues involving federal civil service employees. States and political subdivisions and in many instances municipalities have emulated the federal system. However, civil service laws at the local level often apply to limited classes of employees, for example, police, firefighters, and other public safety officers.

In 1978, Congress enacted the Civil Service Reform Act that provides a statutory basis for collective bargaining by federal government employees through their unions. Federal employees, however, have long been forbidden from striking against the federal government.[68] Many states now allow public employees to bargain collectively, but uniformly restrict them from striking. Nevertheless, in recent years some strikes have taken place.

Public officers and employees are uniformly barred from furthering their own interest through public employment. Federal employees are barred from lobbying and are limited in their participation in proceedings that affect the federal government.[69] Many states have similar laws.

Discrimination and Harassment

Title VII of the Civil Rights Act of 1964, as amended, prohibits employment discrimination on the basis of race, religion or sex. These prohibitions apply to federal, state, and local agencies as well as to the private sector.[70] Actionable issues include racial and gender discrimination in hiring and promotions, including the controversial question of affirmative action, as well as racial and sexual harassment. (For more discussion of civil rights issues in the workplace, see Chapter 11).

Constitutional Issues

Public employees cannot be dismissed merely for exercising their constitutional rights. In *Pickering v. Board of Education* (1968), a public school teacher was dismissed for sending a letter to a newspaper criticizing the board of education. On review of her dismissal, the Supreme Court held that a public employee cannot be discharged for comments in exercise of First Amendment rights.[71] In 1987, the Court reaffirmed this holding in the context of a case when a clerical worker in a Texas constable's office was fired after making an intemperate political remark.[72] When Ardith McPherson heard that John Hinckley had tried unsuccessfully to kill President Reagan, she remarked, "If they go for him again, I hope they get him." The Supreme Court held that her dismissal violated the First Amendment.

One of the more controversial constitutional questions involving public employees today is drug testing. Many local, state, and federal agencies, especially in the field of law enforcement, require their employees to submit to periodic or random drug testing as a condition of employment or promotion. The Supreme Court has recognized that drug testing by public agencies is a form of search and is therefore subject to challenge under the Fourth Amendment. At the same time, however, the Court upheld drug testing of customs inspectors, who are directly involved in drug interdiction.[73] In 1997, the Court struck down a Georgia law requiring all candidates for state office to submit to drug tests.[74] Between the two decisions lies a gray area that is now the subject of considerable litigation in state and federal courts.

Malfeasance, Misfeasance, and Nonfeasance

An employee may be discharged for **malfeasance** involving commission of illegal acts under "color of office." An employee may also be dismissed for **misfeasance**, that is, performing legal acts in an improper or illegal manner, or for **nonfeasance**, which is neglect of duties. Issues are currently in debate as to whether a public employee can be discharged for failing to take a polygraph test or refusing to take a drug test. There are conflicting court decisions, but the courts tend to uphold such requirements for law enforcement personnel.

CONCLUSION

Administrative law embraces the legal rules that govern administrative and regulatory agencies at all levels of government. Agencies bring expertise to focus on special areas of governmental concern. Indeed they have become indispensable to the functioning of modern government. In general, agencies are reasonably diligent and efficient in performing the essential functions of rule making and adjudication.

Despite its efficiency and expertise, "the bureaucracy" often suffers the wrath of the citizenry because of its insulation from the direct political control. One of the great challenges of modern democratic government is to make the bureaucracy function with regard to the traditional rule of law and constitutional protections while at the same time preserving the discretion and flexibility necessary to address constantly changing demands of society. Ultimately, this is the purpose of administrative law.

SUMMARY OF KEY CONCEPTS

Because of their pervasive influence in the social and economic life of American citizens, some commentators have termed administrative agencies, "America's fourth branch of government." Others simply refer to the federal and state administrative framework as the "bureaucracy." But an overview of the American legal system is incomplete without considering the role of administrative law, which governs such administrative agencies as the Social Security Administration and such regulatory agencies as the Securities and Exchange Commission and the Food and Drug Administration.

In this last chapter we have endeavored to depict for the student how under the American constitutional system Congress and the state legislatures make the law, yet how the nation's vast social and economic problems demand that an increasingly large degree of authority be delegated to experts in various fields. Many criticize delegation, but who would opt to have elected officials control the Nuclear Regulatory Commission? At the federal level, through legislative and executive control of budgeting and oversight over rule making, Congress and the President maintain a degree of control over administrative agencies. The Supreme Court and the lower federal courts exercise substantial control over federal agencies through judicial review of their actions.

In carrying out their functions, administrative agencies conduct investigations within the scope of their regulatory authority as they grant and revoke licenses and permits and issue orders. Where necessary, agencies impose administrative fines and bring civil suits to enforce compliance with their directives. Under certain conditions citizens can initiate enforcement. When an agency seeks to impose a criminal penalty, it must refer the matter to other governmental authorities.

Agencies adjudicate disputes through informal and formal proceedings. Interested parties must be afforded due process of law, but administrative due process is a flexible concept that depends on the magnitude of issues being resolved. In most instances, aggrieved parties who have standing and who have exhausted their administrative remedies may seek judicial reviews of final agency actions. Delegation of authority to administrative agencies has given rise to many constitutional issues as to whether delegation is warranted and whether agency rules, directives, and orders result from actions that have afforded interested parties due process of law.

To effectively participate in a democratic society a citizen must have access to information concerning the government. At the federal level, Congress adopted the Freedom of Information Act and the Government in the Sunshine Act, which requires federal agencies to hold their meetings in public. Many states have companion laws. Most federal and many state career employees are under civil service laws, which provide a merit system of employment, promotion, and discharge. The Civil Rights Act of 1964 and other legislation and regulations prohibit sexual harassment and protect public employees from discrimination because of race, religion, gender, and disability.

Although this chapter has illustrated the processes of administrative law primarily from a federal standpoint, state and local administrative agencies function parallel to many of the principles and the processes we have discussed. State and local agencies tend to focus on licensing, permitting, franchising, land-use zoning, and rate making. Due process of law in state and local administrative proceedings and judicial review in state and federal courts closely parallel those at the federal level.

QUESTIONS FOR THOUGHT AND DISCUSSION

1. Evaluate the following statement made by former Supreme Court Justice Robert Jackson: "Administrative agencies have become a veritable fourth branch of government, which has deranged our three-branch legal theories as much the concept of a fourth dimension unsettles our three-dimensional thinking."

2. Why has Congress found it necessary to delegate so much of the responsibility for public policymaking to regulatory agencies?

3. Why did the Supreme Court hold that the Food and Drug Administration lacked the authority to regulate the marketing of tobacco products?

4. What was the Supreme Court's rationale for declaring the legislative veto unconstitutional? How does Congress maintain a measure of control over administrative action of which it disapproves?

5. Explain the premise of, procedures under, and exceptions to the Freedom of Information Act.

6. What are the essential elements of administrative due process?

7. What are the general principles governing judicial review of agency actions? Be sure to discuss both access to judicial review and review of the merits.

8. Is government in the sunshine always consistent with good policymaking?

9. Under what circumstances can public employees lawfully be dismissed?

10. What is the ultimate goal of administrative law?

KEY TERMS

administrative agencies

regulatory agencies

administrative law

due process of law

standing

delegations of power

enabling legislation

rule making

separation of powers

jurisdiction

rule-making authority

legislative veto

notice of proposed rule making

cost-benefit analyses

preclearance

adjudicatory procedures

administrative searches

administrative search warrants

warrantless inspections

warrantless administrative searches

deportation

administrative detention

cease and desist orders

qui tam action

levy

garnishments

forfeiture

quasi-judicial bodies

informal adjudication

formal adjudication

administrative law judges (ALJs)

judicial review of agency actions

statutory preclusion of judicial review

exhaustion of remedies

substantial evidence

disclosure of information

improper disclosure of personal information

open meetings

sunshine laws

spoils system

civil service

malfeasance

misfeasance

nonfeasance

ENDNOTES

[1] Another important distinction is that between "independent agencies" and those that are located within the major departments of the executive branch. For example, at the federal level, the Food and Drug Administration is located within the Department of Health and Human Services, whereas the Consumer Products Safety Commission is an independent agency. Similarly, the Occupational Safety and Health Administration is located within the Department of Labor. The Environmental Protection Agency, by contrast, is an independent regulatory agency.

[2] *Food and Drug Administration et al. v. Brown & Williamson Tobacco Corp.,* 529 U.S. 120, 120 S. Ct. 1291, 146 L.Ed.2d 121 (2000).

[3] *J.W. Hampton & Company v. United States,* 276 U.S. 394, 406, 48 S.Ct. 348, 351, 72 L.Ed. 624, 629 (1928).

[4] *A.L.A. Schechter Poultry Corporation v. United States,* 295 U.S. 495, 55 S.Ct. 837, 79 L.Ed. 1570 (1935).

[5] Cass Sunstein, "Constitutionalism after the New Deal," 101 *Harvard L. Rev.* 421, 447–448 (1987).

[6] Gary Lawson, "The Rise and Rise of the Administrative State," 107 *Harvard L. Rev.* 1231, 1237 (1994).

[7] *American Textile Manufacturers Institute v. Donovan,* 452 U.S. 490, 101 S.Ct. 2478, 69 L.Ed.2d 185 (1981).

[8] 452 U.S. at 547, 101 S.Ct. at 2509, 60 L.Ed.2d at 225 (1981).

[9] *Mistretta v. United States,* 488 U.S. 361, 109 S.Ct. 647, 102 L.Ed.2d 714 (1989).

[10] 488 U.S. at 427, 109 S.Ct. at 683, 102 L.Ed.2d at 765 (1989).

[11] *Immigration and Naturalization Service v. Chadha,* 462 U.S. 919, 103 S.Ct. 2764, 77 L.Ed.2d 317 (1983).

[12] *Mead v. Arnell,* 791 P.2d 410 (Idaho 1990).

[13] See 5 U.S.C.A. §§ 801 et seq.

[14] Kenneth Culp Davis, *Discretionary Justice: A Preliminary Inquiry* 27 (1969).

[15] See 5 U.S.C.A. § 553.

[16] 5 U.S.C.A. § 533b.

[17] 15 U.S.C.A. § 2601.

[18] See 21U.S.C.A. § 355.

[19] See 5 U.S.C.A. § 600 et seq.

[20] E.O. 12044.

[21] E.O. 12291.

[22] *Vermont Yankee Nuclear Power Corporation v. Natural Resources Defense Council, Inc.,* 435 U.S. 519, 98 S.Ct. 1197, 55 L.Ed.2d 460 (1978).

[23] 435 U.S. at 548, 98 S.Ct. at 1214, 55 L.Ed.2d at 495 (1978).

[24] *Murphy v. Waterfront Commission,* 378 U.S. 52, 84 S.Ct. 1594, 12 L.Ed.2d 678 (1964).

[25] *Interstate Commerce Commission v. Brimson,* 154 U.S. 447, 14 S.Ct. 1125, 38 L.Ed. 1047 (1894).

[26] *Frank v. Maryland,* 359 U.S. 360, 79 S.Ct. 804, 3 L.Ed.2d 877 (1959).

[27] See, for example, *Camara v. Municipal Court,* 387 U.S. 523, 87 S.Ct. 1727, 18 L.Ed.2d 930 (1967). overruling *Frank v. Maryland,* 359 U.S. 360, 79 S.Ct. 804, 3 L.Ed.2d 877 (1959).

[28] *Colonnade Catering Corp. v. United States,* 397 U.S. 72, 90 S.Ct. 774, 25 L.Ed.2d 60 (1970).

[29] 436 U.S. 307, 98 S.Ct. 1816, 56 L.Ed.2d 305 (1978).

[30] *Donovan v. Dewey,* 452 U.S. 594, 101 S.Ct. 2534, 69 L.Ed.2d 262 (1981).

[31] *New York v. Burger,* 482 U.S. 691, 107 S.Ct. 2636, 96 L.Ed.2d 601 (1987).

[32] See 8 U.S.C.A. §§ 1181 et seq.

[33] 8 U.S.C.A. § 1226a.

[34] 8 U.S.C.A. § 1226e.

[35] The counter argument is that illegal aliens, as persons within the jurisdiction of the United States, should be provided due process of law much in the same way that non-citizens accused of crimes are provided due process.

[36] 42 U.S.C.A. § 2000a-5.

[37] *United States v. Flagstar Corporation,* Civ. No. 93-20208-JW (Amended Consent Decree).

[38] See Section 17(a) of the Securities Act of 1933, Section 10(b) of the Securities Exchange Act of 1934, and SEC Rule 10b-5.

[39] Case No. 5:97CV1216 (N.D. Ohio).

[40] *Gwaltney v. Chesapeake Bay Foundation,* 484 U.S. 49, 108 S.Ct. 376, 98 L.Ed.2d 306 (1987).

[41] 31 U.S.C.A. §§ 3729–33.

[42]See Internal Revenue Code, 26 U.S.C.A. §§ 1–1563.

[43]See, for example, 21 U.S.C.A. § 881.

[44]*Austin v. United States,* 509 U.S. 602, 113 S.Ct. 2801, 125 L.Ed.2d 488 (1993).

[45]509 U.S. at 622, 113 S.Ct. at 2812, 125 L.Ed.2d at 505 (1992).

[46]*United States v. James Daniel Good Real Property,* 510 U.S. 43, 114 S.Ct. 492, 126 LEd.2d 490 (1993).

[47]5 U.S.C.A. § 554b.

[48]5 U.S.C.A. § 554c.

[49]For more information on administrative judges and ALJs, see Verkuil, *Reflections Upon the Federal Administrative Judiciary,* 39 UCLA L. Rev. 1341 (1992).

[50]See M. Redish and L. Marshall, "Adjudicatory Independence and the Values of Procedural Due Process," 95 *Yale L.J.* 455 (1986).

[51]See 5 U.S.C.A. §§ 551–559; 701–706; 3105; 3344; 5372; 7521.

[52]397 U.S. 254, 90 S.Ct. 1011, 25 L.Ed.2d 287 (1970).

[53]419 U.S. 565, 95 S.Ct. 729, 42 L.Ed.2d 725 (1975).

[54]*Mathews v. Eldridge,* 424 U.S. 319, 334, 96 S.Ct. 893, 902, 47 L.Ed.2d 18, 33 (1976).

[55]*Thunder Basin Coal Co. v. Reich,* 510 U.S. 200, 114 S.Ct. 771, 127 L.Ed.2d 29 (1994).

[56]*Webster v. Doe,* 486 U.S. 592, 108 S.Ct. 2047, 100 L.Ed.2d 632 (1988).

[57]5 U.S.C.A. § 702.

[58]*Frothingham v. Mellon,* cited as *Massachusetts v. Mellon,* 262 U.S. 447, 43 S.Ct. 597, 67 L.Ed.1078 (1923), the two cases having been consolidated.

[59]*Sierra Club v. Morton,* 405 U.S. 727, 92 S.Ct. 1361, 31 L.Ed.2d 636 (1972).

[60]See, for example, *United States v. Students Challenging Regulatory Agency Procedures,* 412 U.S. 669, 93 S.Ct. 2405, 37 L.Ed.2d 254 (1973).

[61]*Chevron U.S.A. v. Natural Res. Def. Council,* 467 U.S. 837, 104 S.Ct. 2778, 81 L.Ed.2d 694 (1984).

[62]See, for example, *Bob Jones University v. United States,* 461 U.S. 574, 103 S.Ct. 2017, 76 L.Ed.2d 157 (1983), where the Court upheld a decision of the Internal Revenue Service to deny tax-exempt status to a private religious college that practiced racial discrimination.

[63]5 U.S.C.A. § 552b(b)

[64]Fla. Stat. Ch. 286.

[65]*News-Press Publishing Co. v. Carlson,* 410 So.2d 546 (Fla. App. 1982).

[66]*Bennett v. Warden,* 333 So.2d 97 (Fla. App. 1976).

[67]U.S. Const. Art. VI, § 3.

[68]5 U.S.C.A. § 7311.

[69]18 U.S.C.A. § 207.

[70]42 U.S.C.A. § 2000e.

[71]391 U.S. 563, 88 S.Ct. 1731. 20 L.Ed.2d 811 (1968).

[72]*Rankin v. McPherson,* 483 U.S. 378, 107 S.Ct. 2891, 97 L.Ed.2d 315 (1987).

[73]*National Treasury Employees Union v. Von Raab,* 489 U.S. 656, 109 S.Ct. 1384, 103 L.Ed.2d 685 (1989).

[74]*Chandler v. Miller,* 520 U.S. 305, 117 S.Ct. 1295, 137 L.Ed.2d 513(1997).

FOR FURTHER READING

Carter, Lief H., and Christine B. Harrington, *Administrative Law and Politics* (3d ed., Longman 2000).

Cooper, Philip, *Public Law and Public Administration* (4th ed., F.E. Peacock Publishers 2000).

Davis, Kenneth Culp, *Discretionary Justice* (Louisiana State University Press 1969).

Kerwin, Cornelius M., *Rulemaking: How Government Agencies Write Law and Make Public Policy* (2d ed., CQ Press 1999).

Rohr, John, *To Run a Constitution: The Legitimacy of the Administrative State* (University of Kansas Press 1986).

Shapiro, Martin, *Who Guards the Guardians? Judicial Control of Administration* (University of Georgia Press 1988).

Sunstein, Cass R., *After the Rights Revolution: Reconceiving the Regulatory State* (Harvard University Press 1990).

Warren, Kenneth F., *Administrative Law in the American Political System* (West 1982).

Appendix

THE CONSTITUTION OF THE UNITED STATES OF AMERICA

We the People of the United States, in Order to form a more perfect Union, establish Justice, insure domestic Tranquility, provide for the common defence, promote the general Welfare, and secure the Blessings of Liberty to ourselves and our Posterity, do ordain and establish this Constitution for the United States of America.

ARTICLE I

Section 1.

All legislative Powers herein granted shall be vested in a Congress of the United States, which shall consist of a Senate and House of Representatives.

Section 2.

(1) The House of Representatives shall be composed of Members chosen every second Year by the People of the several States, and the Electors in each State shall have the Qualifications requisite for Electors of the most numerous Branch of the State Legislature.

(2) No Person shall be a Representative who shall not have attained to the age of twenty-five Years, and been seven Years a Citizen of the United States, and who shall not, when elected, be an Inhabitant of that State in which he shall be chosen.

(3) Representatives and direct Taxes shall be apportioned among the several States which may be included within this Union, according to their respective Numbers, which shall be determined by adding to the whole Number of free Persons, including those bound to Service for a Term of Years, and excluding Indians not taxed, three fifths of all other Persons. The actual Enumeration shall be made within three Years after the first Meeting of the Congress of the United States, and within every subsequent Term of ten Years, in such Manner as they shall by Law direct. The Number of Representatives shall not exceed one for every thirty Thousand, but each State shall have at Least one Representative; and until such enumeration shall be made, the State of New Hampshire shall be entitled to chuse three, Massachusetts eight, Rhode Island and Providence Plantations one, Connecticut five, New York six, New Jersey four, Pennsylvania eight, Delaware one, Maryland six, Virginia ten, North Carolina five, South Carolina five, and Georgia three.

(4) When vacancies happen in the Representation from any State, the Executive Authority thereof shall issue Writs of Election to fill such Vacancies.

(5) The House of Representatives shall chuse their Speaker and other Officers; and shall have the sole Power of Impeachment.

Section 3.

(1) The Senate of the United States shall be composed of two Senators from each State, chosen by the Legislature thereof, for six Years; and each Senator shall have one Vote.

(2) Immediately after they shall be assembled in Consequence of the first Election, they shall be divided as equally as may be into three Classes. The Seats of the Senators of the first Class shall be vacated at the Expiration of the second Year, of the second Class at the Expiration of the fourth Year, and of the third Class at the Expiration of the sixth Year, so that one third may be chosen every second Year; and if Vacancies happen by Resignation, or otherwise, during the Recess of the Legislature of any State, the Executive thereof may make temporary Appointments until the next Meeting of the Legislature, which shall then fill such Vacancies.

(3) No Person shall be a Senator who shall not have attained, to the Age of thirty Years, and been nine Years a Citizen of the United States, and who shall not, when elected, be an Inhabitant of that State for which he shall be chosen.

(4) The Vice President of the United States shall be President of the Senate, but shall have no Vote, unless they be equally divided.

(5) The Senate shall chuse their other Officers, and also a President pro tempore, in the Absence of the Vice President, or when he shall exercise the Office of the President of the United States.

(6) The Senate shall have the sole Power to try all Impeachments. When sitting for that Purpose, they shall be on

Oath or Affirmation. When the President of the United States is tried, the Chief Justice shall preside: And no Person shall be convicted without the Concurrence of two thirds of the Members present.

(7) Judgment in Cases of Impeachment shall not extend further than to removal from Office, and disqualification to hold and enjoy any Office of honor, Trust or Profit under the United States: but the Party convicted shall nevertheless be liable and subject to Indictment, Trial, Judgment and Punishment, according to Law.

Section 4.

(1) The Times, Places and Manner of holding Elections for Senators and Representatives, shall be prescribed in each State by the Legislature thereof; but the Congress may at any time by Law make or alter such Regulations, except as to the Places of chusing Senators.

(2) The Congress shall assemble at least once in every Year, and such Meeting shall be on the first Monday in December, unless they shall by Law appoint a different Day.

Section 5.

(1) Each House shall be the Judge of the Elections, Returns and Qualifications of its own Members, and a Majority of each shall constitute a Quorum to do Business; but a smaller Number may adjourn from day to day, and may be authorized to compel the Attendance of absent Members, in such Manner, and under such Penalties as each House may provide.

(2) Each House may determine the Rules of its Proceedings, punish its Members for disorderly Behaviour, and, with the Concurrence of two thirds, expel a Member.

(3) Each House shall keep a Journal of its Proceedings, and from time to time publish the same, excepting such Parts as may in their Judgment require Secrecy; and the Yeas and Nays of the Members of either House on any question shall, at the Desire of one fifth of those Present, be entered on the Journal.

(4) Neither House, during the Session of Congress, shall, without the Consent of the other, adjourn for more than three days, nor to any other Place than that in which the two Houses shall be sitting.

Section 6.

(1) The Senators and Representatives shall receive a Compensation for their Services, to be ascertained by Law, and paid out of the Treasury of the United States. They shall in all Cases, except Treason, Felony and Breach of the Peace, be privileged from Arrest during their Attendance at the Session of their respective Houses, and in going to and returning from the same; and for any Speech or Debate in either House, they shall not be questioned in any other Place.

(2) No Senator or Representative shall, during the Time for which he was elected, be appointed to any civil Office under the Authority of the United States, which shall have been created, or the Emoluments whereof shall have been increased during such time; and no Person holding any Office under the United States, shall be a Member of either House during his Continuance in Office.

Section 7.

(1) All Bills for raising Revenue shall originate in the House of Representatives; but the Senate may propose or concur with Amendments as on other Bills.

(2) Every Bill which shall have passed the House of Representatives and the Senate, shall, before it become a Law, be presented to the President of the United States; If he approve he shall sign it, but if not he shall return it, with his Objections to that House in which it shall have originated, who shall enter the Objections at large on their Journal, and proceed to reconsider it. If after such Reconsideration two thirds of that House shall agree to pass the Bill, it shall be sent, together with the Objections, to the other House, by which it shall likewise be reconsidered, and if approved by two thirds of that House, it shall become a Law. But in all such Cases the Votes of both Houses shall be determined by Yeas and Nays, and the Names of the Persons voting for and against the Bill shall be entered on the Journal of each House respectively. If any Bill shall not be returned by the President within ten Days (Sunday excepted) after it shall have been presented to him, the Same shall be a Law, in like Manner as if he had signed it, unless the Congress by their Adjournment prevent its Return, in which Case it shall not be a Law.

(3) Every Order, Resolution, or Vote to which the Concurrence of the Senate and House of Representatives may be necessary (except on a question of Adjournment) shall be presented to the President of the United States; and before the Same shall take Effect, shall be approved by him, or being disapproved by him, shall be repassed by two thirds of the Senate and House of Representatives, according to the Rules and Limitations prescribed in the Case of a Bill.

Section 8.

(1) The Congress shall have Power To lay and collect Taxes, Duties, Imposts and Excises, to pay the Debts and provide for the common Defence and general Welfare of the United States; but all Duties, Imposts and Excises shall be uniform throughout the United States;

(2) To borrow Money on the credit of the United States;

(3) To regulate Commerce with foreign Nations, and among the several States, and with the Indian Tribes;

(4) To establish an uniform Rule of Naturalization, and uniform Laws on the subject of Bankruptcies throughout the United States;

(5) To coin Money, regulate the Value thereof, and of foreign Coin, and to fix the Standard of Weights and Measures;

(6) To provide for the Punishment of counterfeiting the Securities and current Coin of the United States;

(7) To establish Post Offices and post Roads;

(8) To promote the Progress of Science and useful Arts, by securing for limited Times to Authors and Inventors the exclusive Right to their respective Writings and Discoveries;

(9) To constitute Tribunals inferior to the supreme Court;

(10) To define and punish Piracies and Felonies committed on the high Seas, and Offenses against the Law of Nations;

(11) To declare War, grant Letters of Marque and Reprisal, and make Rules concerning Captures on Land and Water;

(12) To raise and support Armies, but no Appropriation of Money to that Use shall be for a longer Term than two Years;

(13) To provide and maintain a Navy;

(14) To make Rules for the Government and Regulation of the land and naval Forces;

(15) To provide for calling forth the Militia to execute the Laws of the Union, suppress Insurrections and repel Invasions;

(16) To provide for organizing, arming, and disciplining, the Militia, and for governing such Part of them as may be employed in the Service of the United States, reserving to the States respectively, the Appointment of the Officers, and the Authority of training the Militia according to the discipline prescribed by Congress;

(17) To exercise exclusive Legislation in all Cases whatsoever, over such District (not exceeding ten Miles square) as may, by Cession of particular States, and the Acceptance of Congress, become the Seat of the Government of the United States, and to exercise like Authority over all Places purchased by the Consent of the Legislature of the State in which the Same shall be, for the Erection of Forts, Magazines, Arsenals, dock-Yards, and other needful Buildings;—And

(18) To make all Laws which shall be necessary and proper for carrying into Execution the foregoing Powers, and all other Powers vested by this Constitution in the Government of the United States, or in any Department or Officer thereof.

Section 9.

(1) The Migration or Importation of such Persons as any of the States now existing shall think proper to admit, shall not be prohibited by the Congress prior to the Year one thousand eight hundred and eight, but a Tax or Duty may be imposed on such Importation, not exceeding ten dollars for each Person.

(2) The Privilege of the Writ of Habeas Corpus shall not be suspended unless when in Cases of Rebellion or Invasion the public Safety may require it.

(3) No Bill of Attainder or ex post facto Law shall be passed.

(4) No Capitation, or other direct, Tax shall be laid, unless in Proportion to the Census or Enumeration herein before directed to be taken.

(5) No Tax or Duty shall be laid on Articles exported from any State.

(6) No Preference shall be given by any Regulation of Commerce or Revenue to the Ports of one State over those of another; nor shall Vessels bound to, or from, one State, be obliged to enter, clear or pay Duties in another.

(7) No Money shall be drawn from the Treasury, but in Consequence of Appropriations made by Law; and a regular Statement and Account of the Receipts and Expenditures of all public Money shall be published from time to time.

(8) No Title of Nobility shall be granted by the United States: And no Person holding any Office of Profit or Trust under them, shall, without the Consent of the Congress, accept of any present, Emolument, Office, or Title, of any kind whatever, from any King, Prince or foreign State.

Section 10.

(1) No State shall enter into any Treaty, Alliance, or Confederation; grant Letters of Marque and Reprisal; coin Money; emit Bills of Credit; make any Thing but gold and silver Coin a Tender in Payment of Debts; pass any Bill of Attainder, ex post facto Law, or Law impairing the Obligation of Contracts, or grant any Title of Nobility.

(2) No State shall, without the Consent of Congress, lay any Imposts or Duties on Imports or Exports, except what may be absolutely necessary for executing its inspection Laws: and the net Produce of all Duties and Imposts, laid by any State on Imports or Exports, shall be for the Use of the Treasury of the United States; and all such Laws shall be subject to the Revision and Control of the Congress.

(3) No State shall, without the Consent of Congress, lay any Duty of Tonnage, keep Troops, or Ships of War in time of Peace, enter into any Agreement or Compact with another State, or with a foreign Power, or engage in War, unless actually invaded, or in such imminent Danger as will not admit of Delay.

ARTICLE II

Section 1.

(1) The executive Power shall be vested in a President of the United States of America. He shall hold his Office during the Term of four Years, and, together with the Vice President, chosen for the same Term, be elected, as follows:

(2) Each State shall appoint, in such Manner as the Legislature thereof may direct, a Number of Electors, equal to the whole Number of Senators and Representatives to which the

State may be entitled in the Congress: but no Senator or Representative, or Person holding an Office of Trust or Profit under the United States, shall be appointed an Elector.

The Electors shall meet in their respective States, and vote by Ballot for two Persons, of whom one at least shall not be an Inhabitant of the same State with themselves. And they shall make a List of all the Persons voted for, and of the Number of Votes for each; which List they shall sign and certify, and transmit sealed to the Seat of the Government of the United States, directed to the President of the Senate. The President of the Senate shall, in the presence of the Senate and House of Representatives, open all the Certificates, and the Votes shall then be counted. The Person having the greatest Number of Votes shall be the President, if such Number be a Majority of the whole Number of Electors appointed; and if there be more than one who have such Majority, and have an equal Number of Votes, then the House of Representatives shall immediately chuse by Ballot one of them for President; and if no Person have a Majority, then from the five highest on the List the said House shall in like Manner chuse the President. But in chusing the President, the Votes shall be taken by States, the Representation from each State having one Vote; a quorum for this Purpose shall consist of a Member or Members from two thirds of the States, and a Majority of all the States shall be necessary to a Choice. In every Case, after the Choice of the President, the Person having the greatest Number of Votes of the Electors shall be the Vice President. But if there should remain two or more who have equal Votes, the Senate shall chuse from them by Ballot the Vice President.

(3) The Congress may determine the Time of chusing the Electors, and the Day on which they shall give their Votes; which Day shall be the same throughout the United States.

(4) No Person except a natural born Citizen, or a Citizen of the United States, at the time of the Adoption of this Constitution, shall be eligible to the Office of President; neither shall any Person be eligible to that Office who shall not have attained to the Age of thirty five Years, and been fourteen Years a Resident within the United States.

(5) In Case of the Removal of the President from Office, or of his Death, Resignation, or Inability to discharge the Powers and Duties of the said Office, the Same shall devolve on the Vice President, and the Congress may by Law provide for the Case of Removal, Death, Resignation or Inability, both of the President and Vice President, declaring what Officer shall then act as President, and such Officer shall act accordingly, until the Disability be removed, or a President shall be elected.

(6) The President shall, at stated Times, receive for his Services, a Compensation, which shall neither be increased nor diminished during the Period for which he shall have been elected, and he shall not receive within that Period any other Emolument from the United States, or any of them.

(7) Before he enter on the Execution of his Office, he shall take the following Oath or Affirmation:—"I do solemnly swear (or affirm) that I will faithfully execute the Office of President of the United States, and will to the best of my Ability, preserve, protect and defend the Constitution of the United States."

Section 2.

(1) The President shall be Commander in Chief of the Army and Navy of the United States, and of the Militia of the several States, when called into the actual Service of the United States; he may require the Opinion, in writing, of the principal Officer in each of the executive Departments, upon any Subject relating to the Duties of their respective Offices, and he shall have Power to grant Reprieves and Pardons for Offenses against the United States, except in Cases of Impeachment.

(2) He shall have Power, by and with the Advice and Consent of the Senate, to make Treaties, provided two thirds of the Senators present concur; and he shall nominate, and by and with the Advice and Consent of the Senate, shall appoint Ambassadors, other public Ministers and Consuls, Judges of the supreme Court, and all other Officers of the United States, whose Appointments are not herein otherwise provided for, and which shall be established by Law: but the Congress may by Law vest the Appointment of such inferior Officers, as they think proper, in the President alone, in the Courts of Law, or in the Heads of Departments.

(3) The President shall have Power to fill up all Vacancies that may happen during the Recess of the Senate, by granting Commissions which shall expire at the End of their next Session.

Section 3.

He shall from time to time give to the Congress Information of the State of the Union, and recommend to their Consideration such Measures as he shall judge necessary and expedient; he may, on extraordinary Occasions, convene both Houses, or either of them, and in Case of Disagreement between them, with Respect to the Time of Adjournment, he may adjourn them to such Time as he shall think proper; he shall receive Ambassadors and other public Ministers; he shall take Care that the Laws be faithfully executed, and shall Commission all the Officers of the United States.

Section 4.

The President, Vice President and all Civil Officers of the United States, shall be removed from Office on Impeachment for, and Conviction of, Treason, Bribery, or other high Crimes and Misdemeanors.

ARTICLE III

Section 1.

The judicial Power of the United States, shall be vested in one supreme Court, and in such inferior Courts as the Congress may from time to time ordain and establish. The Judges, both of the supreme and inferior Courts, shall hold their Offices during good Behaviour, and shall, at stated Times, receive for their Services, a Compensation, which shall not be diminished during their Continuance in Office.

Section 2.

(1) The judicial Power shall extend to all Cases, in Law and Equity, arising under this Constitution, the Laws of the United States, and Treaties made, or which shall be made, under their Authority;—to all Cases affecting Ambassadors, other public Ministers and Consuls;—to all Cases of admiralty and maritime Jurisdiction;—to Controversies to which the United States shall be a party;—to Controversies between two or more States;—between a State and Citizens of another State;—between Citizens of different States;—between Citizens of the same State claiming Lands under Grants of different States, and between a State, or the Citizens thereof, and foreign States, Citizens or Subjects.

(2) In all Cases affecting Ambassadors, other public Ministers and Consuls, and those in which a State shall be Party, the supreme Court shall have original Jurisdiction. In all the other Cases before mentioned, the supreme Court shall have appellate Jurisdiction, both as to Law and Fact, with such Exceptions, and under such Regulations as the Congress shall make.

(3) The Trial of all Crimes, except in Cases of Impeachment, shall be by Jury; and such Trial shall be held in the State where the said Crimes shall have been committed; but when not committed within any State, the Trial shall be at such Place or Places as the Congress may by Law have directed.

Section 3.

(1) Treason against the United States, shall consist only in levying War against them, or in adhering to their Enemies, giving them Aid and Comfort. No Person shall be convicted of Treason unless on the Testimony of two Witnesses to the same overt Act, or on Confession in open Court.

(2) The Congress shall have Power to declare the Punishment of Treason, but no Attainder of Treason shall work Corruption of Blood, or Forfeiture except during the Life of the Person attainted.

ARTICLE IV

Section 1.

Full Faith and Credit shall be given in each State to the public Acts, Records, and judicial Proceedings of every other State. And the Congress may by general Laws prescribe the Manner in which such Acts, Records and Proceedings shall be proved, and the Effect thereof.

Section 2.

(1) The Citizens of each State shall be entitled to all privileges and Immunities of Citizens in the several States.

(2) A Person charged in any State with Treason, Felony, or other Crime, who shall flee from Justice, and be found in another State, shall on Demand of the executive Authority of the State from which he fled, be delivered up, to be removed to the State having Jurisdiction of the Crime.

(3) No Person held to Service of Labour in one State, under the Laws thereof, escaping into another, shall, in Consequence of any Law or Regulation therein, be discharged from such Service or Labour, but shall be delivered up on Claim of the Party to whom such Service or Labour may be due.

Section 3.

(1) New States may be admitted by the Congress into this Union; but no new State shall be formed or erected within the Jurisdiction of any other State; nor any State be formed by the Junction of two or more States, or Parts of States, without the Consent of the Legislatures of the States concerned as well as of the Congress.

(2) The Congress shall have power to dispose of and make all needful Rules and Regulations respecting the Territory or other Property belonging to the United States; and nothing in this Constitution shall be so construed as to Prejudice any Claims of the United States, or of any particular State.

Section 4.

The United States shall guarantee to every State in this Union a Republican Form of Government, and shall protect each of them against Invasion; and on Application of the Legislature, or of the Executive (when the Legislature cannot be convened) against domestic Violence.

ARTICLE V

The Congress, whenever two thirds of both Houses shall deem it necessary, shall propose Amendments to this Constitution, or, on the Application of the Legislatures of two thirds of the several States, shall call a Convention for proposing Amendments, which, in either Case, shall be valid to all Intents and Purposes, as Part of this Constitution, when ratified by the Legislatures of three fourths of the several States, or by Conventions in three fourths thereof, as the one or the other Mode of Ratification may be proposed by the Congress; Provided that no Amendment which may be made prior to the Year One thousand eight hundred and eight shall in any Manner affect the first and fourth Clauses in the Ninth Section of the first Article; and that no State, without its Consent, shall be deprived of its equal Suffrage in the Senate.

ARTICLE VI

(1) All Debts contracted and Engagements entered into, before the Adoption of this Constitution, shall be as valid against the United States under this Constitution, as under the Confederation.

(2) This Constitution, and the Laws of the United States which shall be made in Pursuance thereof; and all Treaties made, or which shall be made, under the Authority of the United States, shall be the supreme Law of the Land; and the Judges in every State shall be bound thereby, any Thing in the Constitution or Laws of any State to the Contrary notwithstanding.

(3) The Senators and Representatives before mentioned, and the Members of the several State Legislatures, and all executive and judicial Officers, both of the United States and of the several States, shall be bound by Oath or Affirmation, to support this Constitution; but no religious Test shall ever be required as a Qualification to any Office or public Trust under the United States.

ARTICLE VII

The Ratification of the Conventions of nine States, shall be sufficient for the Establishment of this Constitution between the States so ratifying the Same.

Articles in Addition to, and Amendment of, the Constitution of the United States of America, Proposed by Congress, and Ratified by the Several States, Pursuant to the Fifth Article of the Original Constitution

AMENDMENT I (1791)

Congress shall make no law respecting an establishment of religion, or prohibiting the free exercise thereof; or abridging the freedom of speech, or of the press; or the right of the people peaceably to assemble, and to petition the Government for a redress of grievances.

AMENDMENT II (1791)

A well regulated Militia, being necessary to the security of a free state, the right of the people to keep and bear Arms, shall not be infringed.

AMENDMENT III (1791)

No Soldier shall, in time of peace be quartered in any house, without the consent of the Owner, nor in time of war, but in a manner to be prescribed by law.

AMENDMENT IV (1791)

The right of the people to be secure in their persons, houses, papers, and effects, against unreasonable searches and seizures, shall not be violated, and no Warrants shall issue, but upon probable cause, supported by Oath or affirmation, and particularly describing the place to be searched, and the persons or things to be seized.

AMENDMENT V (1791)

No person shall be held to answer for a capital, or otherwise infamous crime, unless on a presentment or indictment of a Grand Jury, except in cases arising in the land or naval forces, or in the Militia, when in actual service in time of War or public danger; nor shall any person be subject for the same offence to be twice put in jeopardy of life or limb; nor shall be compelled in any criminal case to be a witness against himself, nor be deprived of life, liberty, or property, without due process of law; nor shall private property be taken for public use, without just compensation.

AMENDMENT VI (1791)

In all criminal prosecutions, the accused shall enjoy the right to a speedy and public trial, by an impartial jury of the State and district wherein the crime shall have been committed, which district shall have been previously ascertained by law, and to be informed of the nature and cause of the accusation; to be confronted with the witnesses against him; to have compulsory process for obtaining witnesses in his favor, and to have the Assistance of Counsel for his defence.

AMENDMENT VII (1791)

In Suits at common law, where the value in controversy shall exceed twenty dollars, the right of trial by jury shall be preserved, and no fact tried by a jury, shall be otherwise re-examined in any Court of the United States, than according to the rules of the common law.

AMENDMENT VIII (1791)

Excessive bail shall not be required, nor excessive fines imposed, nor cruel and unusual punishments inflicted.

AMENDMENT IX (1791)

The enumeration in the Constitution, of certain rights, shall not be construed to deny or disparage others retained by the people.

AMENDMENT X (1791)

The powers not delegated to the United States by the Constitution, nor prohibited by it to the States, are reserved to the States respectively, or to the people.

AMENDMENT XI (1798)

The Judicial power of the United States shall not be construed to extend to any suit in law or equity, commenced or prosecuted against one of the United States by Citizens of another State, or by Citizens or Subjects of any Foreign State.

AMENDMENT XII (1804)

The Electors shall meet in their respective states and vote by ballot for President and Vice-President, one of whom, at least, shall not be an inhabitant of the same state with themselves; they shall name in their ballots the person voted for as President, and in distinct ballots the person voted for as Vice-President, and they shall make distinct lists of all persons voted for as President, and of all persons voted for as Vice-President, and of the number of votes for each, which lists they shall sign and certify, and transmit sealed to the seat of the government of the United States, directed to the President of the Senate;—The President of the Senate shall, in the presence of the Senate and House of Representatives, open all the certificates and the votes shall then be counted;—The person having the greatest number of votes for President, shall be the President, if such number be a majority of the whole number of Electors appointed; and if no person have such majority, then from the persons having the highest numbers not exceeding three on the list of those voted for as President, the House of Representatives shall choose immediately, by ballot, the President. But in choosing the President, the votes shall be taken by states, the representation from each state having one vote; a quorum for this purpose shall consist of a member or members from two-thirds of the states, and a majority of all the states shall be necessary to a choice. And if the House of Representatives shall not choose a President whenever the right of choice shall devolve upon them, before the fourth day of March next following, then the Vice-President shall act as President, as in the case of the death or other constitutional disability of the President—The person having the greatest number of votes as Vice-President, shall be the Vice-President, if such number be a majority of the whole number of Electors appointed, and if no person have a majority, then from the two highest numbers on the list, the Senate shall choose the Vice-President; A quorum for the purpose shall consist of two-thirds of the whole number of Senators, and a majority of the whole number shall be necessary to a choice. But no person constitutionally ineligible to the office of President shall be eligible to that of Vice-President of the United States.

AMENDMENT XIII (1865)

Section 1.

Neither slavery nor involuntary servitude, except as a punishment for crime whereof the party shall have been duly convicted, shall exist within the United States, or any place subject to their jurisdiction.

Section 2.

Congress shall have power to enforce this article by appropriate legislation.

AMENDMENT XIV (1868)

Section 1.

All persons born or naturalized in the United States and subject to the jurisdiction thereof, are citizens of the United States and of the State wherein they reside. No State shall make or enforce any law which shall abridge the privileges or immunities of citizens of the United States; nor shall any State deprive any person of life, liberty, or property, without due process of law; nor deny to any person within its jurisdiction the equal protection of the laws.

Section 2.

Representatives shall be apportioned among the several States according to their respective numbers, counting the whole number of persons in each State, excluding Indians not taxed. But when the right to vote at any election for the choice of electors for President and Vice-President of the United States, Representatives in Congress, the Executive and Judicial officers of a State, or the members of the Legislature thereof, is denied to any of the male inhabitants of such State, being twenty-one years of age, and citizens of the United States, or in any way abridged, except for participation in rebellion, or other crime, the basis of representation therein shall be reduced in the proportion which the number of such male citizens shall bear to the whole number of male citizens twenty-one years of age in such State.

Section 3.

No person shall be a Senator or Representative in Congress, or elector of President and Vice-President, or hold any office, civil or military, under the United States, or under any State, who, having previously taken an oath, as a member of Congress, or as an officer of the United States, or as a member of any State legislature, or as an executive or judicial officer of any State, to support the Constitution of the United States, shall have engaged in insurrection or rebellion against the same, or given aid or comfort to the enemies thereof. But Congress may by a vote of two-thirds of each House, remove such disability.

Section 4.

The validity of the public debt of the United States, authorized by law, including debts incurred for payment of pensions and bounties for services in suppressing insurrection or rebellion, shall not be questioned. But neither the United States nor any State shall assume or pay any debt or obligation incurred in aid of insurrection or rebellion against the United States, or any claim for the loss or emancipation of any slave; but all such debts, obligations and claims shall be held illegal and void.

Section 5.

The Congress shall have power to enforce, by appropriate legislation, the provisions of this article.

AMENDMENT XV (1870)

Section 1.

The right of citizens of the United States to vote shall not be denied or abridged by the United States or by any State on account of race, color, or previous condition of servitude.

Section 2.

The Congress shall have power to enforce this article by appropriate legislation.

AMENDMENT XVI (1913)

The Congress shall have power to lay and collect taxes on incomes, from whatever source derived, without apportionment among the several States, and without regard to any census or enumeration.

AMENDMENT XVII (1913)

The Senate of the United States shall be composed of two Senators from each State, elected by the people thereof, for six years; and each Senator shall have one vote. The electors in each State shall have the qualifications requisite for electors of the most numerous branch of the State legislatures.

When vacancies happen in the representation of any State in the Senate, the executive authority of such State shall issue writs of election to fill such vacancies: Provided, That the legislature of any State may empower the executive thereof to make temporary appointments until the people fill the vacancies by election as the legislature may direct.

This amendment shall not be so construed as to affect the election or term of any Senator chosen before it becomes valid as part of the Constitution.

AMENDMENT XVIII (1919)

Section 1.

After one year from the ratification of this article the manufacture, sale, or transportation of intoxicating liquors within, the importation thereof into, or the exportation thereof from the United States and all territory subject to the jurisdiction thereof for beverage purposes is hereby prohibited.

Section 2.

The Congress and the several States shall have concurrent power to enforce this article by appropriate legislation.

Section 3.

This article shall be inoperative unless it shall have been ratified as an amendment to the Constitution by the legislatures of the several States, as provided in the Constitution, within seven years from the date of the submission hereof to the States by the Congress.

AMENDMENT XIX (1920)

The right of citizens of the United States to vote shall not be denied or abridged by the United States or by any State on account of sex.

Congress shall have power to enforce this article by appropriate legislation.

AMENDMENT XX (1933)

Section 1.

The terms of the President and Vice President shall end at noon on the 20th day of January, and the terms of Senators and Representatives at noon on the 3d day of January, of the years in which such terms would have ended if this article had not been ratified; and the terms of their successors shall then begin.

Section 2.

The Congress shall assemble at least once in every year, and such meeting shall begin at noon on the 3d day of January, unless they shall by law appoint a different day.

Section 3.

If, at the time fixed for the beginning of the term of the President, the President elect shall have died, the Vice President elect shall become President. If a President shall not have been chosen before the time fixed for the beginning of his term, or if the President elect shall have failed to qualify, then the Vice President elect shall act as President until a President shall have qualified; and the Congress may by law provide for the case wherein neither a President elect nor a Vice President elect shall have qualified, declaring who shall then act as President, or the manner in which one who is to act shall be selected, and such person shall act accordingly until a President or Vice President shall have qualified.

Section 4.

The Congress may by law provide for the case of the death of any of the persons from whom the House of Representatives may choose a President whenever the right of choice shall have devolved upon them, and for the case of the death of any of the persons from whom the Senate may choose a Vice President whenever the right of choice shall have devolved upon them.

Section 5.

Sections 1 and 2 shall take effect on the 15th day of October following the ratification of this article.

Section 6.

This article shall be inoperative unless it shall have been ratified as an amendment to the Constitution by the legislatures of three-fourths of the several States within seven years from the date of its submission.

AMENDMENT XXI (1933)

Section 1.

The eighteenth article of amendment to the Constitution of the United States is hereby repealed.

Section 2.

The transportation or importation into any State, Territory or possession of the United States for delivery or use therein of intoxicating liquors, in violation of the laws thereof, is hereby prohibited.

Section 3.

This article shall be inoperative unless it shall have been ratified as an amendment to the Constitution by conventions in the several States, as provided in the Constitution, within seven years from the date of the submission hereof to the States by the Congress.

AMENDMENT XXII (1951)

Section 1.

No person shall be elected to the office of the President more than twice, and no person who has held the office of President, or acted as President, for more than two years of a term to which some other person was elected President shall be elected to the office of the President more than once. But this Article shall not apply to any person holding the office of President when this Article was proposed by the Congress, and shall not prevent any person who may be holding the office of President, or acting as President, during the term within which this Article becomes operative from holding the office of President or acting as President during the remainder of such term.

Section 2.

This Article shall be inoperative unless it shall have been ratified as an amendment to the Constitution by the legislatures of three-fourths of the several States within seven years from the date of its submission to the States by the Congress.

AMENDMENT XXIII (1961)

Section 1.

The District constituting the seat of Government of the United States shall appoint in such manner as the Congress may direct:

A number of electors of President and Vice President equal to the whole number of Senators and Representatives in Congress to which the District would be entitled if it were a State, but in no event more than the least populous State; they shall be in addition to those appointed by the States, but they shall be considered, for the purposes of the election of President and Vice President, to be electors appointed by a State; and they shall meet in the District and perform such duties as provided by the twelfth article of amendment.

Section 2.

The Congress shall have power to enforce this article by appropriate legislation.

AMENDMENT XXIV (1964)

Section 1.

The right of citizens of the United States to vote in any primary or other election for President or Vice President, for electors for

President or Vice President, or for Senator or Representative in Congress, shall not be denied or abridged by the United States or any State by reason of failure to pay any poll tax or other tax.

Section 2.
The Congress shall have power to enforce this article by appropriate legislation.

AMENDMENT XXV (1967)

Section 1.
In case of the removal of the President from office or of his death or resignation, the Vice President shall become President.

Section 2.
Whenever there is a vacancy in the office of the Vice President, the President shall nominate a Vice President who shall take office upon confirmation by a majority vote of both Houses of Congress.

Section 3.
Whenever the President transmits to the President pro tempore of the Senate and the Speaker of the House of Representatives his written declaration that he is unable to discharge the powers and duties of his office, and until he transmits to them a written declaration to the contrary, such powers and duties shall be discharged by the Vice President as Acting President.

Section 4.
Whenever the Vice President and a majority of either the principal officers of the executive departments or of such other body as Congress may by law provide, transmit to the President pro tempore of the Senate and the Speaker of the House of Representatives their written declaration that the President is unable to discharge the powers and duties of his office, the Vice President shall immediately assume the powers and duties of the office as Acting President.

Thereafter, when the President transmits to the President pro tempore of the Senate and the Speaker of the House of Representatives his written declaration that no inability exists, he shall resume the powers and duties of his office unless the Vice President and a majority of either the principal officers of the executive department or of such other body as Congress may by law provide, transmit within four days to the President pro tempore of the Senate and the Speaker of the House of Representatives their written declaration that the President is unable to discharge the powers and duties of his office. Thereupon Congress shall decide the issue, assembling within forty-eight hours for that purpose if not in session. If the Congress, within twenty-one days after receipt of the latter written declaration, or, if Congress is not in session, within twenty-one days after Congress is required to assemble, determines by two-thirds vote of both Houses that the President is unable to discharge the powers and duties of his office, the Vice President shall continue to discharge the same as Acting President; otherwise, the President shall resume the powers and duties of his office.

AMENDMENT XXVI (1971)

Section 1.
The right of citizens of the United States, who are eighteen years of age or older, to vote shall not be denied or abridged by the United States or by any State on account of age.

Section 2.
The Congress shall have power to enforce this article by appropriate legislation.

AMENDMENT XXVII (1992)

No law, varying the compensation for the services of the Senators and Representatives, shall take effect, until an election of Representatives shall have intervened.

GLOSSARY OF KEY TERMS

abandoned property   Property that an owner or possessor has relinquished control over with no intent to regain control.

abortion   The intentional termination of a pregnancy through medical intervention.

abusive debt collection practices   Actions or threats used by debt collectors to harass a debtor.

accession   An addition or increase in property.

accessory   A person who aids in the commission of a crime.

accord and satisfaction   Payment by one party and accepted by another in full satisfaction of a disputed claim.

acts of God   Unforeseen occurrences not caused by a human being or a human agency.

actual possession   Possession of something with the possessor having immediate control.

actus reus   A "wrongful act" that, combined with other necessary elements of crime, constitutes criminal liability.

ad valorem taxes   Taxes based on the assessed value of the property taxed.

adequacy of consideration   A consideration that is reasonably proportional under the circumstances.

adjudicatory procedures   Procedures leading to adjudication in administrative or judicial proceedings.

adjusted gross estate   Value of an estate after subtracting all deductions allowed by law or regulations.

administrative agencies   Departments of federal, state, and local governments exercising regulatory authority over designated areas of services or control.

administrative detention   The privilege exercised by the Immigration and Naturalization Service (INS) of detaining illegal aliens pending proceedings to determine whether such persons are to be deported from the United States.

administrative law   The body of law dealing with the structure, authority, policies, and procedures of administrative and regulatory agencies.

administrative law judges   Officers appointed to hear and determine controversies before administrative agencies of governments.

administrative search warrants   Court orders authorizing searches to determine if there are violations of regulatory laws and ordinances.

administrative searches   Searches of premises by a government official to determine compliance with health and safety regulations.

adoptive parents   Parents who have adopted a child, as distinct from "birth parents."

advance directive for medical decisions   A written document signed by a person stating his or her desires concerning health care, often appointing a surrogate to exercise judgment as to the extent of medical procedures to be taken should the person signing the directive be incompetent or unable to give directions.

adversarial system   A system of justice involving conflicting parties where the role of the judge is to remain neutral.

adverse possession   Possession of real property without consent of owner that can result in acquiring title after a period of prescribed years upon compliance with requirements of statutes.

affiant   A person who makes an affidavit.

affidavit   A written document attesting to specific facts of which the affiant has knowledge, and sworn to or affirmed by the affiant.

affirm   To uphold, ratify, or approve.

affirmative action   A program under which women and/or persons of particular minority groups are granted special consideration in employment, government contracts, and/or admission to programs of higher education.

affirmative defenses   Defenses to a criminal charge where the defendant bears the burden of proof. Examples include automatism, intoxication, coercion, and duress.

after-born children   Children born after a testator executes a last will and testament.

age discrimination   Giving unequal considerations to persons because of their age. Especially applicable to employment situations.

agency adoption   Adoption arranged by an adoption agency, typically for a fee.

aggravated assault   An assault committed with a dangerous weapon or with intent to commit a felony.

aggravated battery   A battery committed by use of an instrument designed to inflict great bodily harm on the victim.

aggravating factors   Factors attending the commission of a crime that make the crime or its consequences worse.

aggregation of capital   Accumulation of capital assets, usually cash, from different sources. In corporations this usually occurs as a result of sale of securities to investors.

aiding and abetting   Assisting in or otherwise facilitating the commission of a crime.

alibi   Defense to a criminal charge that places the defendant at some place other than the scene of the crime at the time the crime occurred.

alimony   Regular payments of money to a former spouse as required by a court that grants a divorce.

allocution   Oral statement made by a defendant prior to sentencing.

alternative dispute resolution   A method of resolving disputes without judicial adjudication. Usual means employed are arbitration and mediation.

ambiguity   Terms or words whose meanings are unclear.

ancillary administration   An auxiliary administration of a decedent's estate in a state other than the state of decedent's domicile.

annual percentage rate of interest (APR)   The rate of interest actually paid by a borrower when the lender's fees and points are considered; the true rate of interest received from money invested when the compounding factor is included.

annulment   Judicial dissolution of marriage on the ground that a valid marriage did not take place.

anonymous tip   Information from an unknown source concerning alleged criminal activity.

answer   The defendant's response to the allegations of the plaintiff's complaint or petition.

answer brief   The appellee's written response to the appellant's law brief filed in an appellate court.

antitrust law   The body of law defining antitrust violations and providing remedies for such violations.

antitrust violations   Violations of laws designed to protect the public from price-fixing, price discrimination, and monopolistic practices in trade and commerce.

appeals of right   Appeals brought to higher courts as a matter of right under federal or state law.

appellant   A person who takes an appeal to a higher court.

appellate courts   Judicial tribunals that review decisions from lower tribunals.

appellate jurisdiction   The legal authority of a court of law to hear an appeal from or otherwise review a decision by a lower court.

appellate procedure   The rules of procedure followed by appellate courts in deciding appeals.

appellee   The party against whom a case is appealed to a higher court.

arbitration   Procedure whereby controversies are resolved by a referee or a panel of referees who make a decision on the merits of a controversy after presentations by the disputants.

arraignment   An appearance before a court of law for the purpose of pleading to a criminal charge.

arrest warrant   A document issued by a magistrate or judge directing that a named person be taken into custody for allegedly having committed an offense.

arson   The crime of intentionally burning someone else's house or building—now commonly extended to other property as well.

Articles of Confederation   The constitution under which the United States was governed between 1781 and 1789.

articles of incorporation   Document signed by organizers of a corporation setting forth the name, purpose, authorized capital stock, and other requirements.

artificial insemination   Medical procedure in which semen is injected into a woman's vagina in order to achieve pregnancy.

Ashwander **rules**   Rules of judicial self-restraint articulated by Justice Louis D. Brandeis in a concurring opinion in *Ashwander v. TVA* (1936).

assault   The attempt or threat to inflict bodily injury upon another person.

assignee   One to whom a legal right is transferred.

assignment   Transfer of legal rights.

assignor   One who assigns legal rights.

assisted suicide   An offense (in some jurisdictions) of aiding or assisting a person to take his or her own life.

assume the mortgage   Agreement to pay the balance due on note secured by a mortgage.

assumption of risk   A person's voluntary exposure to known or obvious risks.

attempt   An intent to commit a crime coupled with an act taken toward committing the offense.

attorney general   The highest legal officer of a state or of the United States.

attorney's fees   (1) Sums charged by a lawyer for representation of a client; (2) Sums awarded by a court to reimburse a litigant for fees the litigant is obligated to pay an attorney. Attorney's fees are generally only awarded only when authorized by a statute or a contract.

attorney-client privilege   The right of a person (client) not to testify about matters discussed in confidence with an attorney in the course of the attorney's representation.

attractive nuisance   A condition or machine on premises that poses a danger or special peril to children because of its attractiveness to them.

authority of law   Force of law backed by the coercive power of the state.

automatism   The condition under which a person performs a set of actions during a state of unconsciousness.

automobile exception   Exception to the Fourth Amendment warrant requirement allowing the warrantless search of a vehicle by police who have probable cause to search but because of exigent circumstances are unable to secure a warrant.

bail   The conditional release from custody of a person charged with a crime pending adjudication of the case.

bailee   Person or entity entrusted with someone's property.

bailment   Entrustment of property to someone to perform some service or repair on the property, for example, one who takes a car to a mechanic to have it repaired.

bailor   One who entrusts property to another for a specified purpose.

bait and switch advertising   Attempting to sell a customer a higher priced item after having advertised a similar item for a lower price.

bankruptcy   Legal process by which honest debtors obtain relief under laws designed to protect them from their creditors.

battered-child syndrome (BCS)   A group of symptoms typically manifested by a child who has suffered continued physical or mental abuse, often from a parent or person having custody of the child.

battered-woman syndrome (BWS)   A group of symptoms typically manifested by a woman who has suffered continued physical or mental abuse, usually from a male with whom she lives.

battery   The unlawful use of force against another person that entails some injury or offensive touching.

bench trial   A trial held before a judge without a jury present.

beneficiaries   Persons designated to receive property from another person's insurance policy, will, or trust.

best evidence rule   The requirement that the original document or best facsimile must be produced in court to prove the content of a writing.

best interests of the child test   Doctrine under which custody of a child is awarded to the parent who is better able to foster the child's best interests.

bid rigging   An illegal manipulation in submitting bids to obtain a contract, usually from a public body.

bifurcated trial   A capital trial with separate phases for determining guilt and punishment.

bilateral contract   Contract between parties based on an exchange of promises.

bill of attainder   A legislative act imposing punishment without trial upon persons deemed guilty of treason or felonies (prohibited by the U.S. Constitution).

Bill of Rights   The first 10 amendments to the U.S. Constitution, ratified in 1791, concerned primarily with individual rights and liberties.

biological parents   The male and female who are biologically responsible for conceiving a child.

Blackstone's Commentaries   A codification of principles of the English common law published in 1769 by Sir William Blackstone, an author and professor.

Blockburger **test**   A test applied by courts to determine if the charges against a defendant would constitute a violation of the constitutional prohibition against double jeopardy, that is, being tried twice for the same offense. The *Blockburger* test holds that it is not double jeopardy for a defendant to be tried for two offenses if each offense includes an element that the other offense does not.

blue sky laws   Common name for statutory laws designed to protect investors from securities frauds.

board of adjustment   A local board authorized to grant exceptions and variances from land-use zoning ordinances and regulations.

board of equalization   A local board authorized to revise the assessed values of properties subject to *ad valorem* taxation.

bona fide purchaser   One who makes a purchase in good faith, that is, withhout the attempt to defraud or deceive.

boot camps   Institutions that provide systematic discipline in a militarylike environment designed to rehabilitate an offender; employed as a sentencing alternative.

border searches   Searches of persons entering the borders of the United States.

breach of contract   The violation of a provision in a legally enforceable agreement that gives the damaged party the right to recourse in a court of law.

breach of duty   Failure to act or refrain from acting as required by law.

bribery   The crime of offering, giving, requesting, soliciting, or receiving something of value to influence a decision of a public official.

building codes   Governmental regulations specifying the requirements for the construction of buildings.

Bureau of Alcohol, Tobacco and Firearms   Federal agency located within the Department of the Treasury empowered to enforce federal statutes dealing with intoxicating beverages, tobacco products, guns, and explosives.

burglary   At common law, the crime of breaking and entering a house at night with the intent to commit a felony therein. Under modern statutes, burglary frequently consists of breaking and entering a structure or conveyance at any time with the intent to commit any offense therein.

business and public records   Records kept in the ordinary course of business and records required to be kept by governments.

"but for" test   A test to determine causation in negligence actions. The test asks "Would an injury have occurred 'but for' the defendant's actions?"

canon law   The laws of a church.

capacity to contract   Legal ability to enter into a binding agreement.

capias   A general term for various court orders requiring that some named person be taken into custody.

capital crimes   Crimes punishable by death.

carjacking   Taking a motor vehicle from someone by force and violence or by intimidation.

case management conference   A meeting between a judge and counsel to review the status of a case before the court and to plan necessary steps to conclude the case.

castle doctrine   "A man's home is his castle." At common law, the right to use whatever force is necessary to protect one's dwelling and its inhabitants from an unlawful entry or attack.

causation   An act that produces an event or an effect.

cause of action   A right to bring suit based on someone's breach of a legal duty.

caveat emptor   "Let the buyer beware." Common-law maxim requiring the consumer to judge the quality of a product before making a purchase.

cease and desist orders   An order issued by an administrative agency requiring a person to stop certain designated activities.

ceremonial marriages   A marriage celebrated in conformity with requirements of the law.

certificate of incorporation   A legal charter to conduct business as a corporation issued by a government, usually the state.

certiorari   A judicial writ by a court of superior jurisdiction directed to a lower tribunal directing that the records of that tribunal be submitted for review, usually on the ground that the lower tribunal has acted in excess of its jurisdiction or has departed from the essential requirements of the law.

challenges for cause   Objections to prospective jurors on some specified ground (e.g., a close relationship to a party to the case).

charitable immunity   Doctrine of law that relieves a charitable organization from liability for its acts; doctrine of declining importance in the United States.

check   A written document by a depositor directing the bank to pay a certain sum to the order of a named payee.

checks and balances   Refers to constitutional powers granted each branch of government to prevent one branch from dominating the others.

child-shield statutes   Laws that allow a screen to be placed between a child victim of sexual abuse and a defendant while the child testifies in court.

child snatching   A parent's removal of his or her child from jurisdiction of the court to obtain custody either by self-help or from a court in another jurisdiction.

child support   Financial obligation of a parent to support a minor child.

child support requirements   Amount required to be paid (by agreement or court order) for support of minor children.

child visitation rights   Rights of a divorced noncustodial parent to visit his or her child. Visitation rights may be established by agreement of the parents or by court order.

child out of wedlock   A child born of parents who were not married at the time the child was born and who did not subsequently marry one another.

children of tender years   Young children; sometimes preteen children are referred to as children of tender years.

chose in action   A right not reduced to possession, but recoverable by a lawsuit. Example: A right to receive wages is a chose in action.

circumstantial evidence   Indirect evidence from which the existence of certain facts may be inferred.

citation   (1) A summons to appear in court, often used in traffic violations. (2) A reference to a statute or court decision, often designating a publication where the law or decision appears.

civil action   A suit filed to enforce a private right and to seek damages or other appropriate relief.

civil contempt   Intentional disobedience of a court order.

civil disobedience   Purposeful, peaceful lawbreaking to dramatize one's opposition to the law.

civil law   (1) The law relating to rights and obligations of parties. (2) The body of law, based essentially on Roman law, that prevails in most non-English-speaking nations.

civil procedure   The rules of procedure followed by courts in adjudicating civil cases.

civil rights legislation   Statutes protecting persons against various forms of unlawful discrimination.

civil service   The system under which government employees are selected and retained based on merit, rather than political patronage.

civil suit   *See* civil action.

civil union   A legally sanctioned homosexual relationship carrying all of the rights and duties of marriage.

class action   A lawsuit brought by one or more parties on behalf of themselves and others similarly situated.

clear and present danger doctrine   The doctrine that the First Amendment protects expression up to the point that it poses a clear and present danger of bringing about some substantive evil that government has a right to prevent.

clergy privilege   The exemption of a clergy person and a penitent from disclosing of communications made in confidence by the penitent.

closely held corporations   A corporation whose stock is held by a small group of stockholders who often actively conduct the corporate business.

closing arguments   Arguments presented at trial by counsel at the conclusion of the presentation of evidence.

Code of Justinian   Code of laws compiled by the Roman Emperor Justinian c. 535 A.D.

codicil   An amendment to a last will and testament.

codification   Collection of laws usually indexed by subject matter.

coercive federalism   Refers to efforts by the federal government to use its spending power to induce the states to adopt policies they would not otherwise adopt, such as raising the legal drinking age to 21.

collateral   Cash or other asset pledged as security for repayment of a debt.

collateral attack   The attempt to defeat the outcome of a judicial proceeding by challenging it in a different proceeding or court.

collateral source rule   A rule that allows a jury, when considering an award of damages to an injured plaintiff, to consider the sums the plaintiff will receive from sources other than the defendant.

collective bargaining   Negotiations between representatives (usually union leaders) on behalf of employees and representatives of an employer.

collegial courts   A judicial tribunal consisting of more than one judge, for example, federal and state appellate courts.

commercial paper   Negotiable instruments such as checks.

common-law marriages   Marriages recognized at common law simply on the basis of cohabitation.

common stock   Class of corporate security whose holders have the right to vote to elect directors.

common-law pleading   English common-law system of filing various written documents in litigation to arrive at the issues to be resolved by the court.

community property   Property acquired by a husband and wife during their marriage, other than property acquired by gift or inheritance, in a state that has community property laws.

community property states   States (primarily in the western United States) that have community property laws.

community service   A sentence requiring that the criminal perform some specific service to the community for some specified period of time.

community-oriented policing   Style of policing in which officers attempt to form constructive and respectful relationships with the communities they serve.

comparative negligence   Doctrine of tort law that allows a plaintiff to recover damages from a defendant in a negligence action even though the plaintiff is negligent to some degree, but reduces the plaintiff's award based on the amount of the plaintiff's negligence.

compensatory damages   Amount awarded a plaintiff to compensate for injury or losses suffered.

competent   Legally qualified.

complaint   An initial document filed in court to inform the defendant of the nature and extent of the plaintiff's claim against the defendant.

compounding a crime   The acceptance of money or something else of value in exchange for an agreement not to prosecute a person for committing a crime.

compulsory process   The requirement that witnesses appear and testify in court or before a legislative committee. *See also* subpoena.

compulsory self-incrimination   The requirement that an individual give testimony leading to his or her own criminal conviction. Forbidden by the U.S. Constitution, Amendment V.

computer crimes   Crimes perpetrated through the use of computer technology.

concurrent jurisdiction   Jurisdiction that is shared by different courts of law.

concurrent powers   Powers exercised jointly by the state and federal governments.

concurring in the judgment   An opinion by a judge or justice agreeing with the judgment of an appellate court without agreeing with the court's reasoning process.

concurring opinion   An opinion by a judge or justice agreeing with the decision of the court. A concurring opinion may or may not agree with the rationale adopted by the court in reaching its decision (*See* opinion of the court).

condominium   A form of ownership in which owners have title to individual units in a multiunit structure and who have title in common with other owners to the amenities and other common elements of the property.

condominium association Organization of condominium owners that governs the maintenance and uses of the amenities and other common elements of the property.

confidential informant (CI) An informant known to the police but whose identity is held in confidence.

confusion Mixing of goods belonging to different owners.

Congress The national legislature of the United States established by Article I of the U.S. Constitution.

consent Voluntarily yielding to the will or desire of another person.

consent to a search The act of a person voluntarily permitting police to conduct a search of person or property.

consideration A benefit or detriment bargained for by parties who form a contract.

consortium The right of companionship and services that each spouse has in relation to the other spouse.

conspiracy The crime of two or more persons agreeing or planning to commit a crime. The crime of conspiracy is distinct from the crime contemplated by the conspirators (the *target crime*).

constitution A nation's fundamental law.

constructive notice Knowledge of facts imputed to someone who by proper diligence should have become aware of the facts.

constructive possession The ability to effectively control something, even if it is not actually in one's possession.

constructive service A form of service of court process other than by personal delivery to the intended recipient. Constructive service is sometimes accomplished by a notice published in the newspaper with a copy sent to the last-known address of the intended recipient.

contempt An action that embarrasses, hinders, obstructs, or is calculated to lessen the dignity of a judicial or legislative body.

contempt of court An action that embarrasses, hinders, obstructs, or is calculated to lessen the dignity of a court of law.

contingent fee A fee to be paid to an attorney only in the event the attorney prevails in court on behalf of the client.

continuity of management Pattern of uninterrupted management.

contractual status In family law, the recognition that marriage not only involves a contractual relationship, but because of the state's interest in the institution of marriage, results in a contractual status.

contributory negligence A common-law rule that provides that where a plaintiff's own negligence contributed to an injury the plaintiff is barred from recovering damages against a defendant.

conversion The unlawful assumption of the rights of ownership to someone else's property.

cooperative A form of ownership where a person buys shares of stock in a corporation in order to occupy a unit in an apartment or business building.

cooperative federalism A modern approach to American federalism in which powers and functions are shared among national, state, and local authorities.

corporal punishment Punishment that inflicts pain or injury on a person's body.

corporate charter A certificate of incorporation issued by federal or state government authorizing an organization to conduct business as a corporation.

corporation An artificial legal being created under federal or state law.

corpus delicti "The body of the crime." The material thing upon which a crime has been committed (e.g., a burned-out building in a case of arson).

cost-benefit analysis Systematic assessment of the costs and benefits that will result from a given transaction.

counterclaim A request by the defendant for relief against the plaintiff.

Court of Federal Claims Specialized federal trial court established to adjudicate tort claims brought against agencies of the U.S. government.

Court of International Trade A federal court that hears cases involving the federal government and importers of goods.

court of last resort The highest court in a judicial system, the last resort for deciding appeals.

court of limited jurisdiction   A trial court with narrow authority to hear and decide cases, typically misdemeanors and/or small claims.

Court of Veterans' Appeals   A federal court that hears appeals from denials of veterans' benefits.

court-martial   A military court.

covenant not to compete   A contract not to act in competition.

covenants   Agreements; promises.

credit card fraud   The offense of using a credit card to obtain goods or services by a person who knows that the card has been stolen, forged, or canceled.

credit cardholders   One who possesses a credit card that allows the cardholder to obtain credit in accordance with the terms of a contract between the cardholder and the issuing institution.

crime   An offense against society punishable under the criminal law.

criminal contempt   *See* contempt.

criminal intent   A necessary element of a crime—the evil design associated with the criminal act.

criminal law   The law defining crimes and punishments.

criminal procedure   The rules of law governing the procedures by which crimes are investigated, prosecuted, adjudicated, and punished.

criminal prosecution   The process by which a person is charged with a criminal offense.

critical legal studies   An academic movement spanning several disciplines but sharing a critical or radical perspective on law and the legal system.

cross claim   A claim asserted in a lawsuit by one party against a co-party.

cross-examination   The process of interrogating a witness who has testified on direct examination by asking the witness questions concerning testimony given. Cross-examination is designed to bring out any bias or inconsistencies in the witness's testimony.

cruel and unusual punishments   Punishment that shocks the moral conscience of the community, for example, torturing or physically beating a prisoner.

custodial parent   A parent who has legal custody of a minor child.

custody   The right and obligation to shelter and care for a minor child.

damages   Monetary compensation awarded by a court to a person who has suffered injuries or losses to person or property as a result of someone else's conduct.

dangerous instrumentality   An instrument that has inherent dangerous characteristics.

***de jure* corporation**   A body corporate organized and existing under law.

deadlocked jury   A jury where the jurors cannot agree on a verdict.

deadly force   The degree of force that may result in the death of the person against whom the force is applied.

death penalty   Capital punishment; a sentence to death for the commission of a crime.

death qualification of a jury   The process by which a jury is selected whose members do not entertain scruples against imposing a death sentence.

decisional law   Law declared by appellate courts in their written decisions and opinions.

Declaration of Independence   Formal document of July 4, 1776, establishing the United States of America as an independent nation.

declaratory relief   A court decision establishing rights of parties.

deed of trust   A conveyance by a borrower of legal title to real estate to a trustee who holds title as security for a lender.

defamation   A tort involving the injury to one's reputation by the malicious or reckless dissemination of a falsehood.

default   Failure to do some act required by contract or by law.

default judgment   A judgment entered by a court due to a defendant's failure to respond to legal process or to appear in court to contest the plaintiff's claim.

defendant   A person charged with a crime or against whom a civil action has been initiated.

defense of a third person   Aiding or assisting a person being attacked.

deficiency judgment   A judgment entered by a court for sums remaining due a creditor or mortgagee after the creditor repossess and sells goods or after a mortgagee foreclosed and causes the mortgaged property to be sold.

definite sentence   Criminal penalty set by law with no discretion for the judge or correctional officials to individualize punishment.

definite sentencing   Legislatively determined sentencing with no discretion given to judges or corrections officials to individualize punishment.

delagatee   One to whom a power, authority, or responsibility has been transferred.

delagator   One who transfers a power, authority, or responsibility.

delegates   Act of transferring a power, authority, or responsibility to a person or agency.

delegations of power   Transfer of legal right to act.

Department of Justice   The department of the federal government that is headed by the attorney general and staffed by U.S. attorneys.

deportation   The legal process by which an alien is expelled from a host country.

deposition   The recorded sworn testimony of a witness; not given in open court.

derivative evidence   Evidence that is derived from or obtained only as a result of other evidence.

determinate sentencing   The process of sentencing whereby the judge sets a fixed term of years within statutory parameters and the offender must serve that term without possibility of early release.

deterrence   Prevention of criminal activity by punishing criminals so that others will not engage in such activity.

devisees   Beneficiaries of real property under a last will and testament.

diplomatic immunity   A privilege to be free from arrest and prosecution granted under international law to diplomats, their staffs, and household members.

direct evidence   Evidence that applies directly to proof of a fact or proposition. For example, a witness who testifies to having seen an act done or heard a statement made is giving direct evidence.

direct examination   Interrogation by an attorney of a party or witness called to testify.

directed verdict   A verdict rendered by a jury upon direction of the presiding judge.

disaffirm   Repudiate; disavow. For example, a minor can ordinarily disaffirm a contract.

discharge from debts   The object of a debtor who files a bankruptcy proceeding. In such a proceeding, an honest debtor who complies with all requirements of the law receives a discharge, that is, a release, from most debts.

disclosure of information   To reveal or make known certain facts.

discovery   A process whereby counsel seek to obtain information from parties in a lawsuit through interrogatories and depositions.

discretionary activities   Actions taken that are not prescribed by law.

discretionary review   Form of appellate court review of lower court decisions that is not mandatory but occurs at the discretion of the appellate court. *See also* writ of certiorari.

discrimination   Treatment of persons unequally based on their race, religion, sex, or national origin.

discrimination against persons with disabilities   Treatment of persons unequally based on their disabilities.

disinherited   An heir who is deprived of receiving property from a decedent.

disorderly conduct   Illegal behavior that disturbs the public peace or order.

disparate impact   A facially neutral law or policy that has a differential impact on members of different races or genders.

dissenting opinion   A written opinion by a judge or justice setting forth reasons for disagreeing with a particular decision of the court.

dissolution of marriage   Legal termination of a marriage through divorce or annulment.

distributive articles   Articles I, II, and III of the U.S. Constitution, delineating the powers and functions of the legislative, executive, and judicial branches, respectively, of the national government.

diversity jurisdiction   The authority of federal courts to hear lawsuits in which the parties are citizens of different states and the amount in controversy exceeds $75,000.

divine law   Law ascribed to a Supreme Being.

divorce   Termination of a marriage by a court judgment.

divorce a *mensa et thoro*   A divorce from bed and board; a divorce judgment that does not legally terminate a marriage.

doctrine of harmless error   Legal principle that holds that an appellate court should not reverse a decision of a lower tribunal because of an error that does not affect the substantial rights of the parties.

doctrine of incorporation   (1) The practice of allowing one document to be made part of another by specific reference. (2) In constitutional law, the doctrine that the Fourteenth Amendment incorporates the provisions of the Bill of the Rights and thus makes them applicable to the states.

doctrine of original intent   Doctrine that holds that a court should interpret a constitution based on the intent of those who drafted it.

domestic corporation   A corporation doing business in the state of its incorporation.

domestic partnership   An agreement between two persons of the same sex to live and cohabit together.

domicile   Place of a person's permanent residence.

dominion and control   Ability to exercise the right to property and authority to direct its disposition.

donee   One who receives a gift.

donor   One who makes a gift.

double jeopardy   The condition of being tried twice for the same criminal offense.

draft   A written order drawn on one party by another and requesting that payment be made to a third party.

dram shop acts   Statutes prohibiting sales of alcoholic beverages to minors or intoxicated persons.

drawee   Party on whom a draft is drawn.

drawer   Party who draws an order on another party (drawee) requesting the drawee to make payment to a third party.

drug courier profile   A controversial law enforcement practice of identifying possible drug smugglers by

relying on a set of characteristics and patterns of behavior believed to typify persons who smuggle drugs.

drug testing   The practice of subjecting employees to urine tests to determine whether they are using illegal substances.

dual federalism   A concept of federalism in which the national and state governments exercise authority within separate, self-contained areas of public policy and public administration.

DUBAL   Driving with an unlawful blood alcohol level.

due process of law   Procedural and substantive rights of citizens against government actions that threaten the denial of life, liberty, or property.

due-on-sale clause   A provision in a mortgage that stipulates that the entire unpaid balance due on the mortgaged indebtedness will become due upon transfer of the property that is collateral for the mortgage debt.

durable power of attorney   A written document in which a person (the principal) designates another person to act as an agent for specified purposes, especially for making health care decisions. The "durable" characteristic means the power of attorney remains effective even if the principal becomes incapacitated.

duress   The use of illegal confinement or threats of harm to coerce someone to do something he or she would not do otherwise.

duty   An obligation that a person has by law or contract.

dying declaration   Statement made by a person who believes that his or her death is imminent. A dying declaration is generally considered an exception to the hearsay rule of evidence.

easement   A right of use over the property of another. This term frequently refers to a right-of-way across privately owned land.

easement of necessity   Right to use part of someone else's land as a right-of-way for purposes of ingress and egress to and from otherwise landlocked property.

elective share   Share of a deceased spouse's estate that a surviving spouse is entitled to claim in some states.

electoral college   The body of electors chosen by the voters of each state and the District of Columbia for the purpose of formally electing the president and vice president of the United States. The number of electors (538) is equivalent to the total number of representatives and senators to which each state is entitled, plus three electors from the District of Columbia.

electronic eavesdropping   Covert listening to or recording of a person's conversations by electronic means.

emancipation acts   (1) Laws that allow persons considered legally incapable of entering into legal transactions to enter contracts and other legal transactions. In past decades applied to married women. (2) Laws that remove the disability of a minor to enter contracts once the minor marries. (3) Laws that allow courts to permit mature minors to enter legal transactions.

embezzlement   The crime of using a position of trust or authority to transfer or convert the money or property of another to oneself.

emergency searches   Warrantless searches performed during an emergency, such as a fire or potential explosion.

eminent domain   The power of government, or of individuals and corporations authorized to perform public functions, to take private property for public use.

employment discrimination   Denying employment or treating employees unequally based on their disabilities, race, religion, sex, or national origin.

en banc **rehearing**   A rehearing in an appellate court in which all or a majority of the judges participate.

enabling legislation   As applied to public law, a statute authorizing the creation of a government program or agency and defining the functions and powers thereof.

endangered species   An animal species that has been officially designated as endangered by the Secretary of Interior under the Endangered Species Act.

English common law   A system of legal rules and principles recognized and developed by English judges prior to the colonization of America and accepted as a basic aspect of the American legal system.

entrapment   The act of government agents in inducing someone to commit a crime that the person otherwise would not be disposed to commit.

enumerated powers   Powers specified in the text of the federal and state constitutions.

environmental crimes   Statutes that impose punishment for violations of laws enacted to protect the environment and natural resources.

environmental impact statement   A document required by law outlining the effects that a proposed land development will likely have on the surrounding environment.

environmental law   The body of law protecting the natural environment from pollution and despoliation.

environmental regulations   Regulations adopted by administrative agencies designed to implement statutory protections of the environment.

equal protection of the laws   Constitutional requirement that the government not engage in prohibited forms of discrimination against persons under its jurisdiction.

equitable distribution   A distribution of property that is fair, just, and reasonable.

equity   Historically, a system of rules, remedies, customs, and principles developed in England to supplement the harsh common law by emphasizing the concept of fairness. In addition, because the common law served only to recompense after injury, equity was devised to prevent injuries that could not be repaired or recompensed after the fact. While American judges continue to distinguish between law and equity, these systems of rights and remedies are, for the most part, administered by the same courts.

error correction   *See* error-correction function.

error-correction function   The function of appellate courts in correcting errors committed by lower tribunals in their interpretation and application of law, evidence, and procedure.

escape   Unlawfully fleeing to avoid arrest or confinement.

estates during the life of another   An interest in real property that can be enjoyed only during the lifetime of a named person.

estates in real property   Interests in lands and property attached thereto.

evanescent evidence   Evidence that tends to disappear or be destroyed. Often police seek to justify a warrantless search on the ground that destruction of the evidence is imminent.

evidentiary presumption   Establishment of one fact allows inference of another fact or circumstance.

ex post facto law   A retroactive law that criminalizes actions that were innocent at the time they were taken or increases punishment for a criminal act after it was committed.

excessive bail   Where a court requires a defendant to post an unreasonably large amount or imposes unreasonable conditions as a prerequisite for a defendant to be released before trial. The Eighth Amendment to the U.S. Constitution prohibits courts from requiring excessive bail.

excessive fines   Fines that are deemed to be greater than is appropriate for the punishment of a particular crime.

exculpatory information   That which exonerates or tends to exonerate a person from fault or guilt.

excusable homicide   A death caused by accident or misfortune.

executed contract   A contract that has been completely performed.

executive order   An order by a president or governor directing some particular action to be taken.

executive power   The power to enforce the law and administer the government.

executive privilege   The right of the president to withhold certain information from Congress or a court of law.

executory contract   An agreement not yet performed by the parties.

exhaustion of remedies   The requirement that a party seeking review by a court first exhaust all legal options for resolution of the issue by nonjudicial authorities or lower courts.

exigent circumstances   Situations that demand unusual or immediate action.

expert witness   A witness with specialized knowledge or training called to testify in his or her field of expertise.

express contract   A contract where the terms have been expressed orally or in writing by the parties.

express powers   Powers explicitly granted by some instrument, whether a constitution, statute, or contract.

expressive conduct   Conduct undertaken to express a message.

extortion   The crime of obtaining money or property by threats of force or the inducement of fear.

extradition   The surrender of a person by one jurisdiction to another for the purpose of criminal prosecution.

extraordinary life-sustaining measures   Medical measures to prolong life beyond ordinary feeding and care. A good example is a mechanical respirator.

eyewitness testimony   Testimony given by a person based on personal observation of an event.

fair hearing   A hearing in a court of law that conforms to standards of procedural justice.

fair notice   The requirement stemming from due process that government provide adequate notice to a person before it deprives that person of life, liberty, or property.

false arrest   The tort of crime of unlawfully detaining or restraining a person.

false imprisonment   *See* false arrest.

false pretenses   The crime of obtaining money or property through misrepresentation.

fault concept   (1) In family law, the requirement that one spouse must prove the other spouse to be at fault before a court grants a divorce. (2) In tort law, the basis of imposing liability because of a person's failure to act as a reasonably prudent individual would act under given circumstances.

Federal Bureau of Investigation (FBI)   The primary federal agency charged with investigating violations of federal criminal laws.

federal bureaucracy   The collective term for the myriad departments, agencies, and bureaus of the federal government.

federal estate tax   A tax imposed by the U.S. government on the estates of decedents.

federal habeas corpus review   Review of a state criminal trial by a federal district court on a writ of habeas corpus after the defendant has been convicted, incarcerated, and has exhausted appellate remedies in the state courts.

federal magistrate judges   Judges appointed to preside over pretrial proceedings, try misdemeanor case, and with consent of parties handle civil trials in federal courts.

federal question jurisdiction   The authority of federal courts to decide issues of national law.

federalism   The constitutional distribution of government power and responsibility between the national government and the states.

fee simple estate   The highest interest the law recognizes in real property.

fee tail estates   An estate in real property conveyed to a person (grantee) and to the heirs of the grantee's body.

felony   A serious crime for which a person may be incarcerated for more than one year.

felony murder   A homicide committed during the course of committing another felony other than murder (e.g., armed robbery). The felonious act substitutes for malice aforethought ordinarily required in murder.

fictitious name laws   A law that requires persons who operate a business under a name other than their own to register that fact with a governmental office.

fighting words   Utterances that are inherently likely to provoke a violent response from the audience.

financing statement   A document filed with an appropriate government office that notifies the public that specified property is subject to existing loans.

fines   Sums of money exacted from criminal defendants as punishment for wrongdoing.

firefighter's rule   English common-law doctrine applied in many states. Treats a police officer or firefighter as a licensee thereby limiting a landowner's liability to such persons who enter premises as part of their duties.

first-degree murder   The highest degree of unlawful homicide usually defined as "an unlawful act committed with the premeditated intent to take the life of a human being."

flight to avoid prosecution   Unlawful travel to escape prosecution for a crime.

force majeur **clauses**   A contract provision excusing performance when a superior force makes performance impossible. *See* act of God.

foreign corporation   A corporation doing business or maintaining an office in a state other than its state of incorporation.

forensic evidence   Evidence usually in the form of testimony offered by a forensic expert. *See* forensic experts.

forensic experts   Persons qualified in the application of scientific knowledge to legal principles, usually applied to those who participate in discourse or who testify in court.

foreperson   The person selected by fellow jurors to chair deliberations and report the jury's verdict.

foreseeable   An event that a reasonable person would ordinarily anticipate from one's act or failure to act.

forfeiture   Sacrifice of ownership or some right (usually property) as a penalty.

forgery   The crime of making a false written instrument or materially altering a written instrument (e.g., a check, promissory note, or college transcript) with the intent to defraud.

formal adjudication   Official determination (usually by an administrative tribunal).

formal contracts   A contract that complies with specific requirements of law. Examples include a check or draft.

foster care   Placing a child in the care of a person(s) who performs the duties of a parent, usually under supervision of a social welfare agency.

Fourteenth Amendment   Amendment to the U.S. Constitution, ratified in 1868, prohibiting states from depriving persons in their jurisdiction of due process of law or denying them the equal protection of the laws.

fraud   Intentional deception or distortion in order to gain something of value.

fraud, duress, or undue influence   Intentional deception or false representations, unlawful coercion, or pressure to override a person's free will. (Terms frequently used in contests concerning execution of a last will and testament.)

freedom of association   Implicitly protected by the First Amendment, the right of people to associate freely without unwarranted interference by government.

freedom of expression   A summary term embracing freedom of speech and freedom of the press as well as symbolic speech and expressive conduct.

fruit of the poisonous tree doctrine   A doctrine based on judicial interpretation of the Fourth Amendment that holds that evidence that is illegally seized cannot be used by the prosecution.

full warranty   A written consumer product warranty that complies with the Magnuson-Moss Warranty Act.

fundamental error   An error in a judicial proceeding that adversely affects the substantial rights of the accused.

gambling   Operating or playing a game for money in the expectation of gaining more than the amount played.

garnishee   A party (usually a bank or employer) who is required to withhold payment due or to become due to someone and pay it over to the garnishor.

garnishment   Court action requiring a party (garnishee) who is indebted to a person to withhold payment and pay a sum over to a creditor (garnishor) who instituted garnishment proceedings.

garnishor   A party who institutes a garnishment proceeding.

gay rights   Summary term referring to the idea that persons should be permitted to engage in private homosexual conduct and be free from discrimination based on their sexual orientation.

gender discrimination   Treating a person in an unequal manner based on the person's sex.

gender equity   Idea that women should receive equal benefits conferred by government.

gender-based peremptory challenge   A challenge to a prospective juror's competency to serve based solely on the prospective juror's gender.

general damages   Damages that have accrued to the plaintiff due to a particular injury or loss

general intent   The state of mind to do something prohibited by law without necessarily intending to accomplish the harm that results from the illegal act.

general objection   An objection raised against a witness's testimony or introduction of evidence when the objecting party does not recite a specific ground for the objection.

general partner   A member of a partnership who shares with other partners the management and the profits and losses of the business.

general verdict   Ordinary form of jury verdict in a civil case that finds for the plaintiff or defendant in general terms; in a criminal case that finds the defendant not guilty or guilty of specified crime(s).

gerrymandering   The intentional manipulation of legislative districts for political purposes.

gestational surrogacy   A method of surrogate parenthood where the sperm of a married man is artificially united with the egg of his wife and the resulting preembryo is implanted in another woman's womb.

good-faith exception   An exception to exclusionary rule that bars use of evidence obtained by a search warrant found to be invalid. The exception allows use of the evidence if the police relied in good faith on the search warrant, even though the warrant is subsequently held to be invalid.

good-time credit   Credit toward early release from prison based on good behavior during confinement (often referred to as gain time).

grand jury   A group of 12 to 23 citizens convened to hear evidence in criminal cases to determine whether indictment is warranted.

grandfathered in   Allowed to continue. Example: If a land-use zoning ordinance changes the classification of zoning, an existing use that is permitted to continue is said to be "grandfathered in."

grandparents' visitation   The right of grandparents to visit their grandchildren.

grantee   One to whom a grant is made. Usually refers to a person or entity that acquires title to real estate.

grantor   One who makes a grant. Usually refers to a person or entity that deeds property to another person or entity.

grantor or settlor   Person who executes a document creating a trust.

gratuitous bailments   Entrustment of property for benefit of bailor to a person (bailee) who receives no compensation and has a limited responsibility.

gross negligence   Carelessness of an outrageous character.

gun control legislation   Laws restricting the manufacture, design, importation, sale, or possession of firearms.

habeas corpus   "You have the body." A judicial order issued to an official holding someone in custody, requiring the official to bring the prisoner to court for the purpose of allowing the court to determine whether that person is being held legally.

habitual offender   One who has been repeatedly convicted of crimes.

hazardous waste regulations   Government regulations affecting the shipment, storage, and disposal of toxic and radioactive waste products.

hearsay evidence   Statements made by someone other than a witness offered in evidence at a trial or hearing to prove the truth of the matter asserted.

heirs   Persons entitled to succeed to the property of a decedent who dies intestate.

holder in due course   A person who takes a negotiable instrument that is regular on its face (e.g., check, promissory note), in good faith, for value, and without knowledge of any defenses available to any party to the instrument.

hot pursuit   (1) The right of police to cross jurisdictional lines to apprehend a suspect or criminal. (2) The Fourth Amendment doctrine allowing warrantless searches and arrests where police pursue a fleeing suspect into a protected area.

house arrest   A sentencing alternative to incarceration where the offender is allowed to leave home only for employment and approved community service activities.

housing discrimination   Treatment of applicants for housing or tenants on terms unequally applied based on race, religion, sex, or national origin.

hung jury   A trial jury unable to reach a verdict.

hypothetical question   A question based on an assumed set of facts. Hypothetical questions may be asked of expert witnesses in criminal trials.

illegal act   Any act that violates a provision of law.

illegitimate child   A child born out of wedlock.

illusory   Deceptive.

imminent lawless action   Unlawful conduct that is about to take place and which is inevitable unless there is intervention by the authorities.

immunity   Exemption from civil suit or prosecution. *See also* use immunity and transactional immunity.

impeachment   (1) A legislative act bringing a charge against a public official that, if proven in a legislative

trial, will cause his or her removal from public office. (2) The act of impugning the credibility of a witness by introducing contradictory evidence or proving his or her bad character.

implied consent   An agreement or acquiescence manifested by a person's actions or inaction.

implied contract   An agreement formed based on actions or inactions of the parties.

implied powers   Powers not specifically enumerated but implied by an instrument such as a constitution, statute, or contract.

implied warranty   A warranty that is implied based on the nature of the transaction, the relationship of the parties, and circumstances and customs.

implied warranty of fitness of goods   A warranty under the Uniform Commercial Code that goods are suitable for the buyer's intended use.

implied warranty of merchantability   A warranty imposed on merchants that goods sold are such as to allow the buyer to assume they are as defined in the Uniform Commercial Code.

impossibility of performance   Where circumstances beyond the control of a contracting party make it impossible to perform under a contract.

impoundment   (1) Action by a president in refusing to allow expenditures approved by Congress. (2) In criminal law, the seizure and holding of a vehicle or other property by the police.

improper disclosure of personal information   Revealing a person's private information without that person's consent and when not required by law.

in camera   "In a chamber." In private. Refers to a judicial proceeding or conference from which the public is excluded.

in forma pauperis   "In the manner of a pauper." Waiver of filing costs and other fees associated with judicial proceedings to allow an indigent person to proceed.

in vitro fertilization   A technique whereby human ova are placed in a laboratory dish with human sperm and, after fertilization, the embryo is transferred into the uterus of a woman who is to serve as surrogate mother of the developing fetus.

incapacitation Making it impossible for someone to do something.

incarceration Imprisonment.

inchoate offense An offense preparatory to committing another crime. Inchoate offenses include attempt, conspiracy, and solicitation.

indefinite sentencing Form of criminal sentencing whereby a judge imposes a term of incarceration within statutory parameters, and corrections officials determine actual time served through parole or other means.

independent agencies Federal agencies located outside the major cabinet-level departments.

independent contractor A party to a contract who agrees to perform specified work under his or her own methods and supervision.

independent counsel A special prosecutor appointed to investigate and, if warranted, prosecute official misconduct.

independent source doctrine The doctrine that permits evidence to be admitted at trial as long as it was obtained independently from illegally obtained evidence.

indeterminate sentencing Form of criminal sentencing where criminals are sentenced to prison for indeterminate periods until corrections officials determine that rehabilitation has been accomplished.

indictment A formal document handed down by a grand jury accusing one or more persons of the commission of a crime or crimes.

indirect evidence Inferences and presumptions that tend to establish a fact or issue.

infancy The condition of being below the age of legal majority.

inflammatory remarks Remarks by counsel during a trial designed to excite the passions of the jury.

informal adjudication A form of administrative adjudication that observes only minimal procedural requirements.

informal contracts Contract for which the law does not prescribe a set form.

information A document filed by a prosecutor under oath charging one or more persons with commission of a crime.

informed consent A doctrine of consent applicable in professional malpractice cases, especially those involving surgery. For example, an informed consent to surgery is based on the physician explaining the risks before a patient consents to a procedure.

inheritance tax A tax imposed by many states on the receipt of property from a decedent.

initial appearance After arrest, the first appearance of the accused before a judge or magistrate.

initial brief Appellant's brief filed in support of issues raised in appellate court.

initial pleading Petition or complaint filed to initiate a proceeding in a judicial tribunal.

injunction A court order prohibiting someone from doing some specified act or commanding someone to undo some wrong or injury.

Inns of Court English institutions founded in the Fourteenth century where judges and experienced barristers served as teachers and mentors to those aspiring to become barristers.

insanity A degree of mental illness that negates the legal capacity or responsibility of the affected person.

insider information Information concerning financial matters and prospective actions of a corporation available only to persons within the corporation.

insider trading Transactions in securities by a person who operates "inside" a corporation and by using material nonpublic information trades to his or her advantage without first disclosing that information to the public.

intangible personal property Property with no tangible value, such as bonds, promissory notes, and stock certificates.

intentional acts Acts committed purposely.

intentional infliction of emotional distress Outrageous conduct that causes a person mental and emotional suffering. Recognized as a tort in many jurisdictions.

intentional tort committed under color of authority of law An act committed under color of state authority that deprives a person of a federal constitutional right.

intentions of the Framers The intentions of the Framers of the U.S. Constitution with respect to the meaning of its provisions.

intermediate appellate courts   Appellate courts positioned below the Supreme or highest appellate court. Their primary function is to decide routine appeals not deserving review by the Supreme Court.

interrogatories   Written questions put to a witness.

interspousal immunity   A common-law doctrine that prevented spouses from suing one another for commission of a tort.

interstate abduction   In family law, a noncustodial parent's removal of his or her child to another state usually to attempt to escape the exercise of jurisdiction by the courts of child's residence.

interstate disputes concerning child custody   Conflicting claims of jurisdiction between courts in different states concerning control and supervision of children.

intervening act   An act (either human or natural) that occurs after an original tortious act. An intervening act can excuse the original tortfeasor from liability unless the tortfeasor should have anticipated the intervening act occurring.

inter vivos trust   A trust established during the lifetime of the grantor or settlor.

intestate succession   The descent of property of a decedent who dies intestate. *See also* heirs and inheritance tax.

intoxication   A state of drunkenness resulting from the use of alcoholic beverages or drugs.

invasion of privacy   A tort involving the unreasonable or unwarranted intrusion on the privacy of an individual.

inventory search   An exception to the warrant requirement that allows police who legally impound a vehicle to conduct a routine inventory of the contents of the vehicle.

investigatory detention   Brief detention of suspects by a police officer who has reasonable suspicion that criminal activity is afoot. *See also* stop-and-frisk.

invitee   One who is expressly or impliedly invited. Generally refers to entry on another's land or into another's premises.

involuntary dismissal   Dismissal of a law action based on legal grounds.

irretrievably broken   Unable to be repaired (a term of art pertaining to divorce).

irrevocable trust   A trust that cannot be revoked.

Jencks **Act**   The common name for a federal statute that permits a defendant to review a witness's prior written or recorded statement after the witness has testified on direct examination.

joint and several liability   Usually applies where two or more wrongdoers cause an injury or where two or more makers sign a promissory note. A judgment obtained against parties who are jointly and severally liable can be enforced against any one of the parties.

joint custody   Shared responsibility of divorced parents concerning control and supervision of children.

joint ownership with right of survivorship   A method of ownership where upon death of one joint owner that owner's interest passes to the surviving owner, irrespective of the deceased owner's last will and testament.

joint tenancy   A form of holding title to property where two or more persons share in the ownership.

joint tenants with right of survivorship   A form of property ownership whereby upon death of one party, that party's interest in the property becomes the property of the surviving joint tenant(s).

judgment of acquittal   In a nonjury trial, a judge's order exonerating a defendant based on a finding that the defendant is not guilty. In a case heard by a jury finding a defendant guilty, a judge's order exonerating a defendant on the ground that the evidence was not legally sufficient to support the jury's finding of guilt.

judicial accountability   The idea that judges should answer to the public for their decisions, primarily through the ballot box.

judicial activism   Defined variously, but the underlying philosophy is that judges should exercise power vigorously.

judicial conference   A meeting of judges to deliberate on disposition of a case.

judicial decision   A decision by a court of law.

judicial disciplinary commissions   Agencies established by state legislatures to investigate complaints of judicial misconduct.

judicial independence   The idea that judges should be free from public pressure in making decisions based on the rule of law.

judicial notice   The act of a court recognizing, without proof, the existence of certain facts that are commonly known. Such facts are often brought to the court's attention through the use of a calendar or almanac.

judicial review   Generally, the review of any issue by a court of law. In American constitutional law, judicial review refers to the authority of a court to invalidate acts of government on constitutional grounds.

judicial review of agency actions   Process by which courts of law review actions or decisions of administrative and regulatory agencies.

judicial self-restraint   The idea that judges should exercise the power of judicial review cautiously and should defer to the decisions of the elective branches of government.

jurisdiction   The power of a tribunal to hear and determine subject matter involving persons within an authorized geographical area.

jury instructions   A judge's explanation of the law applicable to a case being heard by a jury.

jury trial   A judicial proceeding conducted before a body of persons sworn to render a verdict based on the law and the evidence presented.

just compensation   The constitutional requirement that a party whose property is taken by government under the power of eminent domain be justly compensated for the loss, normally at fair market value.

justifiable homicide   Killing another in self-defense or defense of others when there is serious danger of death or great bodily harm to self or others, or when authorized by law.

justifiable use of force   The necessary and reasonable use of force by a person in self-defense, defense of another, or defense of property.

kidnapping   The forcible abduction and carrying away of a person against that person's will.

knock and announce   The provision under federal and most state laws that requires a law enforcement officer to first knock and announce his or her presence and purpose before entering a person's home to serve a search or arrest warrant.

land tenure   System developed under the feudal system where an occupier or tenant held lands subordinate to a superior, usually a lord.

land-use planning   Developing criteria for present and future uses of lands. Land-use zoning is a principal tool in land-use planning.

land-use zoning   *See* zoning.

landlord/tenant law   The branch of the civil law that deals with relationships between owners and tenants.

larceny   At common law, the unlawful taking of personal property with the intent of permanently depriving the owner of same.

law enforcement agencies   Government agencies empowered to arrest and detain persons who violate the criminal law.

lawmaking   *See* lawmaking function.

lawmaking function   One of the principal functions of an appellate court, often referred to as the law development function, in which the appellate court makes law by interpreting or reinterpreting a constitutional or statutory provision.

leading questions   A question that suggests an answer. Leading questions are permitted at a trial during cross-examination of witnesses and in other limited instances.

leasehold   The legal interest in property that a tenant acquires by lease (usually written) from the owner.

legal codes   Compilations of statutory laws usually indexed according to subject matter.

legal guardianship   Court proceeding resulting in appointment of a guardian to exercise control over a ward, the ward's property, or both.

legal separation   (1) An agreement whereby married parties agree to live separate and apart from one another. (2) A court order providing for spouses to live separate and apart from one another, often making provisions for support of a spouse and children, but not dissolving the parties' marriage.

legatees   Those who receive personal property under a decedent's last will and testament.

legislative veto   A statutory provision under which a legislative body is permitted to overrule a decision of an executive agency.

legislators   Members of a legislature.

legislature   An elected lawmaking body such as the Congress of the United States or a state assembly.

lemon laws   Statutes that provide a means for a consumer who buys goods that are defective (frequently a motor vehicle) to obtain necessary repairs or replacement of the goods.

lessee   A party who leases real or personal property from a lessor (owner).

lessor   A party (sometimes called a landlord) who leases real or personal property to a lessee (tenant).

levy   (1) Imposition of a tax or assessment by a governmental agency. (2) Procedure whereby a court official takes possession of property and causes it to be sold to satisfy a judgment lien.

lex talionis   The ancient law of retaliation, commonly referred to as "an eye for an eye."

libel   The tort of defamation through published material. *See* defamation.

libertarian view of law   The idea that law should protect people from one another, but not protect the individual from his or her own vices or unfortunate choices.

licensee   A party who holds a license.

licenses   Permits to act for specified purposes.

lien   A claim of a right or interest in or charge against another's property.

life estates   An interest in property (usually real estate) that allows the life tenant to use and control the property during his or her lifetime.

life-support systems   Artificial means of sustaining life (usually refers to extraordinary means of medical treatment such as mechanical respirators).

life tenant   A holder of a life estate in property.

limited liability   A characteristic of certain forms of investment where the investor's liability is limited to his or her investment. Example: Liability of a corporate stockholder is generally limited to his or her investment.

limited partner   A partner in a limited partnership whose liability for debts of the partnership is generally limited to the partner's investment.

limited partnership   A partnership with at least one general partner and one or more limited partners organized under statutory law; a form of partnership that distinguishes between general and limited partners.

limited warranty   (1) A warranty that expressly includes certain limitations of the warrantor's liability. (2) A written consumer product warranty that does not conform to the requirements for a full warranty specified by the Magnuson-Moss Warranty Act.

liquidated damages   A fixed amount of damages that parties agree to in the event of a breach of contract.

living Constitution   The idea that the meaning of the Constitution changes to adapt to changing social and economic conditions.

living trust   A trust created by a grantor during his or her lifetime. Also known as an inter vivos trust.

living will   A document enforceable in court stating a person's wishes regarding the use of extraordinary medical treatment in the event that person becomes unable to communicate.

loitering   Standing around idly, "hanging around."

long arm statute   A state law authorizing service of process on a nonresident defendant as a basis for the court's jurisdiction. To be constitutionally applied the defendant served must have had minimal contacts within the state where the court is to acquire jurisdiction.

lost property   Property that the owner has involuntarily parted with and is without knowledge as to how or where to find it.

lump-sum alimony   Payment of alimony at one time rather than a continuing basis. *See* alimony.

M'Naghten **Rule**   Under this rule, for a defendant to be found not guilty by reason of insanity, it must be clearly proved that, at the time of committing the act, the defendant was suffering such a defect of reason, from disease of the mind, as not to know the nature and quality of the act he was doing; or, if he did know it, that he did not know what he was doing was wrong.

Magna Carta   The "Great Charter" signed by King John in 1215 guaranteeing the legal rights of English subjects. Generally considered the foundation of Anglo-American constitutionalism.

maker   One who executes a document; a term commonly applied to a person who signs a promissory note.

mala in se   "Evil in itself." Refers to crimes such as murder that are universally condemned.

mala prohibita   "Prohibited evil." Refers to crimes that are wrong primarily because the law declares them to be wrong.

malfeasance   Misconduct that adversely affects the performance of official duties.

malicious mischief   The crime of willful destruction of the personal property of another.

managed care   Medical services generally furnished through a health maintenance organization (HMO).

mandamus   "We command." A judicial order or writ commanding a public official or an organization to perform a specified nondiscretionary duty.

mandatory sentencing   Sentencing practice in which trial courts are constrained by law to impose prison terms of certain minimum duration.

manslaughter   The crime of unlawful killing of another person without malice.

marital privilege   The privilege of married persons not to be compelled to testify against one another.

marital property   Property acquired by spouses, other than by gift or inheritance, during their marriage.

marriage   A special contractual relationship formed according to law between a man and a woman that results in the social and economic status of the parties being regulated by law.

matrimonial domicile   Place where a husband and wife live during their marriage.

mayhem   At common law, the crime of injuring someone so as to render that person less able to fight.

mediation   An informal, nonadversarial process whereby a neutral third person facilitates resolution of a dispute between parties by exploring issues and settlement alternatives.

Medicaid   Federal program that provides grants to states to furnish medical care to indigent persons.

Medicare   Federal health insurance program primarily for senior citizens.

Megan's law   Law requiring convicted sex offenders released from prison to register with local law enforcement authorities.

mens rea   Guilty mind, criminal intent.

misdemeanor   A minor offense usually punishable by fine or imprisonment for less than one year.

misfeasance   Improper performance of a lawful act.

misrepresentation   An untrue statement of fact made to deceive or mislead.

Missouri Plan   Plan for merit-based selection and retention of state judges; originated in Missouri in 1940.

mistake of fact   Unconscious ignorance of a fact or belief in the existence of something that does not exist.

mistake of law   An erroneous opinion of legal principles applied to a set of facts.

mistrial   A trial that is terminated due to misconduct, procedural error, or a hung jury (one that is unable to reach a verdict).

mitigating factors   Circumstances or factors that tend to lessen culpability.

Model Penal Code (MPC)   Published by the American Law Institute (ALI), the MPC consists of general provisions concerning criminal liability, sentences, defenses, and definitions of specific crimes. The MPC is not law; rather, it is designed to serve as a model code of criminal law for all states.

modification of custody   A court judgment revising previous court-ordered arrangements for control and supervision of minor children.

monetary policy   Area of public policy affecting the supply of money in the economy.

money laundering   The offense of disguising illegal income to make it appear legitimate.

mortgage   Written contract creating a lien against specifically described real property to secure payment of a note or other undertaking. In some states, a conditional conveyance of real property to secure a debt.

mortgagee   One who takes or holds a mortgage (usually a lender).

mortgagor   One who executes a mortgage (usually a borrower) to secure payment of an obligation.

motion for change of venue   A formal request to a court to designate a different location for conduct of legal proceedings.

motion for continuance   A formal request to a court to postpone a hearing or trial.

motion for rehearing   A formal request made to a court of law to convene another hearing in a case in which the court has already ruled.

motion to dismiss   (1) A formal request to a court to dismiss a plaintiff's complaint, often on the ground the complaint fails to state a legal basis for relief sought by the plaintiff. (2) A formal request to a trial court to dismiss the criminal charges against the defendant.

motion to suppress   A request asking a court to rule that a confession or admission, pretrial identification, or fruits of a search or seizure were unlawfully obtained and cannot be used against a defendant in court.

motions   Formal applications to courts to obtain an order or grant some relief to the movant.

motive   A person's conscious reason for acting.

murder   The unlawful killing of a person by another with malice aforethought or premeditation, or through depraved indifference to human life.

mutual assent   An understanding between parties manifested by an offer and an acceptance.

mutual benefit bailments   A type of bailment where the owner of the property and the person receiving the property each receive a benefit, for example, a lease of a motor vehicle.

mutual mistake   Where each of the parties to a contract was mistaken as to a fact material to the formation of the contract.

Napoleonic Code   The codification of the civil and criminal laws of France promulgated under Napoleon Bonaparte in 1804.

natural law   Principles of human conduct believed to be ordained by God or nature, existing prior to and superseding human law.

natural rights   Rights believed to be inherent in human beings, the existence of which is not dependent on their recognition by government. In classical liberalism, natural rights are "life, liberty and property." As recognized by the Declaration of Independence, they are "life, liberty and the pursuit of happiness."

necessity   A condition that compels or requires a certain course of action.

negative defenses   Any criminal defenses not required to be specifically pled.

negligence   The failure to exercise ordinary care or caution.

negligence per se   An act or omission in violation of a duty imposed by statute or ordinance for the protection of persons or property.

negligent acts or omissions   Acts or omissions committed by a person who fails to act as a reasonably prudent individual would act under the circumstances.

negligent hiring   A tort consisting of employing a person whom the employer knew or should have known would pose a threat to the security of others.

negligent infliction of emotional distress   A tort in some states where a person in a zone of physical risk suffers demonstrable physical consequences from fright or shock as a result of outrageous acts against another person.

negotiable   Transferable by endorsement and delivery.

negotiable instrument   Commercial paper signed by the maker or drawer containing an unconditional promise or order to pay a sum certain in money, made payable on demand or at a fixed time to the order of someone or to the bearer.

negotiation   (1) As respects commercial paper, a transfer in a manner that the transferee becomes a holder in due course. (2) Method of settling a dispute between parties without a formal trial.

no contest plea   A plea to a criminal charge that, although it is not an admission of guilt, generally has the same effect as a plea of guilty.

no-fault automobile insurance laws   Statutes in some states that require automobile owners to carry insurance that reimburses the insured irrespective of who is at fault in a vehicular accident. Statutes sometimes allow an action against a party at fault in instances of major injuries or death.

no-fault dissolution of marriage   A court judgment dissolving a marriage without the necessity of one spouse proving the other spouse to be at fault in the marriage.

nominal damages   A token amount awarded to a plaintiff who proves the defendant liable but fails to prove actual damages.

noncustodial parent   A parent that does not have legal custody of one or more of that parent's children.

nondelegable duties   Duties that cannot legally be transferred to others.

nonfeasance   Failure to perform a duty.

nonnegotiable   Refers to contracts that do not comply with the requirements for negotiability under the Uniform Commercial Code. One who acquires a nonnegotiable instrument or contract takes it subject to all defenses between the original parties.

nonperformance   Failure to perform as required by a contract.

notice of appeal   Document filed notifying an appellate court of an appeal from a judgment of a lower court.

notice of proposed rule making   Notification to interested parties of an agency's intention to promulgate a rule.

nuisance   An unlawful or unreasonable use of a person's property that results in an injury to another or to the public.

obscenity   Explicit sexual material that is patently offensive, appeals to a prurient or unnatural interest in sex, and lacks serious scientific, artistic, or literary content.

obstruction of justice   The crime of impeding or preventing law enforcement or the administration of justice.

offer   Statement or conduct by a person constituting a proposal to enter a contract.

offeree   One to whom an offer has been made.

offeror   One who makes an offer.

open meetings   Meetings open to the general public.

open public trial   A trial that is held in public and is open to spectators.

opening statement   A prosecutor's or defense lawyer's initial statement to the judge or jury in a trial.

opinion   A written statement accompanying a judicial decision, authored by one or more judges, supporting or dissenting from that decision.

opinion evidence   Testimony based on a person's judgement. A witness who qualifies as an expert in a given field, e.g., a physician, is permitted to offer an opinion in the area of his or her expertise. A lay witness is only permitted to offer an opinion when he or she has firsthand knowledge through personal observation of a matter that does not require specialized knowledge, e.g., a person's appearance.

opinion of the court   The opinion expressing the views of the majority of judges participating in a judicial decision.

oral argument   Verbal presentation made to an appellate court in an attempt to persuade the court to affirm, reverse, or modify a lower court decision.

ordinance   An enactment of a local governing body such as a city council or commission.

organized crime   Syndicates involved in racketeering and other criminal activities.

original jurisdiction   The authority of a court of law to hear a case in the first instance.

original writs   Writs issued by a court in an original, as opposed to an appellate, proceeding. Original writs include mandamus, prohibition, quo warranto, and habeas corpus.

out-of-court settlements   Compromises arrived at between parties that result in dismissal of cases before formal trials occur.

oversight   Refers to the responsibility of a legislative body to monitor the activities of government agencies it created.

paralegal   A legal assistant trained to perform certain legal functions under supervision of a lawyer.

parents' right of privacy   Right of parents to deny visitation rights to grandparents and others.

parliamentary system   A democratic system of government in which authority is vested primarily in an elected legislature known as a parliament. Under this system, the chief executive or prime minister is the member of Parliament who is the leader of the party holding a majority of seats.

parol evidence rule   A rule of law providing that when a contract is complete that oral agreements made prior to or at the time of execution of the contract cannot be admitted in evidence to vary or contradict the terms of the contract absent fraud, mistake, or illegality.

parole   Conditional release from jail or prison of a person who has served part of his or her sentence.

parole board   An administrative board that determines if a prisoner should be released on parole, and if so, under what conditions.

parole revocation hearing   An administrative hearing held for the purpose of determining whether an offender's parole should be revoked.

parties   Persons involved in court actions; persons who enter contracts.

partition suit   A legal proceeding to apportion undivided interests of owners of real property. Example: A court can divide land owned as tenants in common, or if division is not practicable, it can order the land sold and the proceeds divided according to the parties' interests.

partnership   An association of two or more persons who carry on a business as co-owners and share in the profits and losses.

past consideration   Something done or given in the past that cannot serve as a consideration in the present for a contract.

patents, copyrights, and trademarks   Species of intangible property rights, often referred to today as intellectual property.

paternity   Biological fatherhood.

payee   Party to whom a negotiable instrument is payable.

penitentiary   A prison.

per curiam opinion   An opinion rendered "by the court" as distinct from one attributed to one or more judges.

peremptory challenge   An objection to the selection of a prospective juror in which the attorney making the challenge is not required to state the reason for the objection.

performance   Fulfillment of a promise under a contract.

perjury   The crime of making a material false statement under oath.

perjury by contradictory statements   Commission of the offense of perjury by a witness who makes conflicting statements under oath.

permanent alimony   Requirement to pay alimony on a permanent basis.

perpetual existence   Indefinite lifetime, a characteristic of a corporation.

personal property   All species of property other than land and things attached to the land.

personal representative   One who administers an estate, sometimes known as an executor or executrix of a testate estate or an administrator or administratrix of an intestate estate.

personal service   Service of legal process by delivery to the named person.

petitioner   A person who brings a petition before a court of law.

pierce the corporate veil   To disregard the identity of a corporation as an entity separate from its shareholders and hold the stockholders liable.

places of public accommodation   Businesses that open their doors to the general public.

plain view   Readily visible to the naked eye.

plaintiff   The party initiating legal action; the complaining party.

plea bargaining   Negotiations leading to an agreement between a defendant and a prosecutor whereby the defendant agrees to plead guilty in exchange for some concession (such as a reduction in the number of charges brought).

plea of guilty   A formal answer to a criminal charge in which the accused acknowledges guilt and waives the right to trial.

plea of not guilty   A formal answer to a criminal charge in which the accused denies guilt and thus exercises the right to a trial.

police power   The power of government to legislate to protect public health, safety, welfare, and morality.

polygraph evidence   Results of lie detector tests (generally inadmissible into evidence).

positive law The written law enforced by government.

postconviction relief Term applied to various mechanisms a defendant may use to challenge a conviction after other routes of appeal have been exhausted.

postnuptial agreements Contracts entered into by a husband and wife settling their property rights upon death of one party or in the event of divorce.

power of contempt The authority of a court of law to punish someone who insults the court or flouts its authority.

power to investigate Refers to the power of a legislative body to conduct hearings and subpoena witnesses in order to investigate an issue or area over which it has legislative authority.

precedent A judicial decision cited as authority controlling or influencing the outcome of a similar case.

preclearance Requirement under the Voting Rights Act that changes in state voting and election laws must be approved by the attorney general before they can take effect.

preconception tort A new tort based on a physician's failure to advise a prospective mother of the likelihood of conceiving a defective child.

preembryo A fertilized ovum or zygote.

preexisting duty A duty, the performance of which does not constitute a valid consideration for a contract.

preferred stock Shares of corporate stock that receive preference in payment of fixed dividends and priority in receiving assets upon dissolution of the corporation.

preliminary hearing A hearing held to determine whether there is sufficient evidence to hold an accused for trial.

preliminary injunction An injunction issued pending a trial on the merits of the case.

prenuptial agreements Contracts entered into by a man and woman before their marriage settling their property rights upon death of one party or in the event of divorce.

preponderance of evidence Evidence that has greater weight than countervailing evidence.

prescription Refers to acquiring an easement by long, continued, uninterrupted use, that is by prescription.

presentence investigation An investigation held before sentencing a convicted criminal to aid the court in determining the appropriate punishment.

presumption of constitutionality The doctrine of constitutional law holding that laws are presumed to be constitutional with the burden of proof resting on the plaintiff to demonstrate otherwise.

pretrial conference A meeting of attorneys and the trial judge in advance of a jury trial to define issues, stipulate as to evidentiary exhibits, estimate the time required for trial, and discuss other details concerning the trial.

pretrial detention The holding of a defendant in custody prior to trial.

pretrial discovery The process by which counsel for parties gain access to the evidence possessed by the opposing party prior to trial.

pretrial motions Request for certain rulings or orders before the commencement of a trial.

pretrial release The release of a defendant pending trial.

price fixing Sellers unlawfully entering into agreements as to the price of products or services.

primary physical residence In family law, the place where a child remains with a parent who has custodial responsibility for the child.

principal (1) A perpetrator of or aider and abettor in the commission of a crime (as distinguished from an accessory). (2) The amount of a debt excluding interest.

prior restraint An official act preventing publication of a particular work.

prison disciplinary hearings Informal administrative hearings required before removal of good-time credits earned by a prisoner.

prisoners' rights Refers to the set of rights that prisoners retain or attempt to assert through litigation.

private placement adoption An adoption arranged by private intermediaries, usually by a doctor and lawyer.

privilege A right extended to persons by virtue of law, for example, the right accorded a spouse in not being required to testify against the other spouse.

privileged communications Confidential communications that persons are not required to disclose in court proceedings.

pro se defense   A legal reason asserted by an individual on his or her own behalf in defense of a charged crime.

probable cause   A reasonable ground for belief in certain alleged facts.

probate court   A court that exercises jurisdiction over the probate of wills and administration of estates of decedents.

probation   Conditional release of a convicted criminal in lieu of incarceration.

procedural criminal law   The branch of the criminal law that deals with the processes by which crimes are investigated, prosecuted, and punished.

procedural due process   Set of procedures designed to ensure fairness in a judicial or administrative proceeding.

procedural legitimacy   Popular acceptance of an institution based on the perception that it operates by valid procedures.

products liability   The legal responsibility of a manufacturer, seller, or distributor of products that cause injuries to consumers.

professional responsibility   Requirement that members of the legal profession adhere to a code of professional ethics.

prohibition   A provision of law forbidding a particular form of conduct.

prohibition, writ of   A judicial order issued by a superior court directing a lower tribunal to cease acting in excess of its lawful jurisdiction.

promisee   Party to whom a contractual promise has been made.

promisor   Party who makes a contractual promise.

promissory estoppel   The doctrine of contract law under which a promise that induces action on the part of the promisee may be legally enforceable.

promissory note   A written promise to pay a certain sum to or to the order of another.

pronouncement of sentence   Formal announcement of a criminal punishment by a trial judge.

proof beyond a reasonable doubt   The standard of proof in a criminal trial or a juvenile delinquency hearing.

proper forum   The correct court or other institution in which to press a particular claim.

property rights   Refers to the bundle of rights that exist relative to private ownership and control of property.

property settlement agreement   A contract entered into by married persons providing for disposition of their assets and liabilities. In most instances the agreement becomes effective upon approval of the court, upon dissolution of the parties' marriage.

proportionality   The degree to which a particular punishment matches the seriousness of crime or matches the penalty other offenders have received for the same crime.

proprietary or operational activities   Nongovernmental activities of municipal government that may subject a municipality to tort liability.

prosecutor   A public official empowered to initiate criminal charges and conduct prosecutions.

prosecutorial discretion   The leeway afforded prosecutors in deciding whether to bring charges and to engage in plea bargaining.

prostitution   The act of selling sexual favors.

protective order   A court order protecting a person from whom discovery is sought prior to trial from annoyance, oppression, or undue expense in complying with demands of a party who is seeking discovery.

proximate cause   The cause that is nearest a given effect in a causal relationship.

public defender   An attorney responsible for defending indigent persons charged with crimes.

public figures   Persons who are in the public eye.

public officials   Persons who hold public office by virtue of election or appointment.

public policy   Guidelines (usually unwritten) by which courts make determinations whether certain acts are beneficial or harmful to society.

public safety exception   Exception to the requirement that police officers promptly inform suspects taken into custody of their rights to remain silent and have an attorney present during questioning. Under the public safety exception, police may ask suspects questions motivated by a desire to protect public safety without jeopardizing the admissibility of suspects' answers to those questions or subsequent statements.

publicly traded corporations   Corporations whose securities are traded in the public markets, for example, on a national stock exchange.

puffing   Exaggerated, but not fraudulent, claims by a seller or sales person.

punitive damages   A sum of money awarded to the plaintiff in a civil case as a means of punishing the defendant for wrongful conduct.

purchase money mortgage   A document executed by a buyer creating a lien in favor of a seller of real property for the unpaid balance of the purchase price.

putative father   A man who is regarded to be the father of a child although paternity has not been established.

qualified privilege   A defense that may be asserted against a defamation (slander, libel) action. The defense is based on a person having a justifiable basis of making a statement that may be defamatory, as long as the statement is made without malice, e.g., in reporting a crime or making a report on a former employee to a prospective employer.

quasi-judicial bodies   Public boards of administrative officers who make factual determinations as a basis for their rulings.

***qui tam* action**   Civil suit brought by a private party on behalf of the government against a party that has allegedly defrauded the government.

quitclaim deed   A legal conveyance by a grantor to a grantee of an interest, if any, the grantor has in land described in the deed.

racially based peremptory challenges   Peremptory challenges to prospective jurors that are based solely on racial animus or racial stereotypes.

rape   Common-law crime involving sexual intercourse by a male with a female, other than his wife, by force and against the will of the female. *See also* sexual battery.

rape-shield laws   Laws that protect the identity of rape victims or prevents disclosure of victims' sexual history.

rape trauma syndrome   A recurring pattern of physical and emotional symptoms experienced by rape victims.

real evidence   Refers to maps, blood samples, x-rays, photographs, stolen goods, fingerprints, knives, guns, and other tangible items introduced into evidence.

real property   Land and buildings permanently attached thereto.

reapportionment   The redrawing of legislative district lines so as to remedy malapportionment.

reasonable accommodation   Requirement under the Americans with Disabilities Act that employers take reasonable steps to accommodate employees with disabilities.

reasonable expectation of privacy   A person's reasonable expectation that his or her activities in a certain place are private; society's expectations with regard to whether activities in certain places are private.

reasonable force   The maximum degree of force that is necessary to accomplish a lawful purpose.

reasonable person   The hypothetical person referred to by courts as the objective standard for judging a person's actions.

reasonable suspicion   A person's suspicion based on objective standards that criminal activity is afoot.

reasonableness standard   Objective standard that courts employ in determining whether a person's conduct is negligent.

reasonably foreseeable   An act or event that a reasonable person would anticipate to occur as a result of a prior act or event.

rebuttable presumption   A legal presumption that may be refuted by evidence.

rebuttal   Refutation by an attorney of the opposing attorney's argument.

recidivism   Repetitive criminal activity.

reciprocal enforcement of support obligations   Statutory method whereby the states cooperate in enforcing legal obligations of support of dependants. Involves proceedings in an initiating state and responding state.

regulation   A legally binding rule or order prescribed by a controlling authority. The term is generally used with respect to the rules promulgated by administrative and regulatory agencies.

regulatory agencies   Agencies empowered by statutes to promulgate and enforce regulations within particular substantive areas.

regulatory taking   Governmental regulations that result in a substantial diminishment in the value of an owner's property.

rehabilitation   Restoring someone or something to its former status; a justification for punishment emphasizing reform rather than retribution.

rehabilitative alimony   A court-ordered sum paid by one spouse to the other to enable the recipient to become financially self-sufficient. Rehabilitative alimony is usually paid for a definite number of months or years.

relevant evidence   Evidence tending to prove or disprove an alleged fact.

remainderman   Person designated to receive an estate in real property upon expiration of the prior estate. Example: If H conveys a life estate to W with the remainder to C, C is a remainderman who succeeds to title upon W's death.

remand   To send back, as from a higher court to a lower court for the latter to take specified action in a case or to follow proceedings designated by the higher court.

reply brief   A brief submitted by an appellant in response to an appellee's answer brief.

reporters   Books containing judicial decisions and accompanying opinions.

representative government   Form of government in which officials responsible for making policy are elected by the people in periodic free elections.

reproductive technology   Modern medical devices that assist in achieving pregnancy.

reputation   Refers to a rule of evidence that provides when a person's character is in issue, proof of good character may be made by showing a person's reputation in the community.

res ipsa loquitor   "The thing speaks for itself."

rescission   Cancellation. An equitable remedy that annuls a contract.

residence requirements   Legal requirements that parties have resided in a jurisdiction for a minimum period of time before voting, running for office, or receiving certain benefits to which residents are entitled.

resisting arrest   The crime of obstructing or opposing a police officer making an arrest.

restitution   The act of compensating someone for losses suffered.

restraining orders   Court orders prohibiting named persons from taking specified actions.

restrictive covenants   Agreements among property holders restricting the use of property or prohibiting the rental or sale of it to certain parties.

retaliatory eviction   Action by a lessor to terminate a tenant's occupancy because the tenant has angered the lessor, usually by reporting a housing violation to public authorities.

retribution   Something demanded in payment for a debt; in criminal law, the demand that a criminal pay his or her debt to society.

reverse   To set aside a decision on appeal.

revocable trust   A trust that the grantor reserves the right to revoke.

RICO   Acronym for Title IX (Racketeer Influenced and Corrupt Organizations) of the Organized Crime Control Act of 1970.

right of confrontation   The right to face one's accusers in a criminal case.

right of cross-examination   Questions asked by an attorney of a witness who has testified on behalf of the opposing party.

right of privacy   Right to be let alone, that is, free from governmental interference.

right of redemption   A mortgagor's right to pay all sums due the mortgagee before a foreclosure sale and thus redeem the mortgagor's right to the property that has been foreclosed.

right of visitation   The court-ordered right of a noncustodial parent to visit with his or her child.

right to a speedy trial   Right guaranteed by the Sixth Amendment to the U.S. Constitution; however, statutes and court rules frequently specify the time periods within which a trial must be held.

right to counsel   Right to be represented by an attorney in a court, including the right of an indigent criminal defendant to have court-appointed counsel when subject to incarceration, if convicted.

right to die   Controversial right to terminate one's own life under certain circumstances.

right to keep and bear arms   Right to possess certain weapons, protected against federal infringement by the Second Amendment to the U.S. Constitution.

right to vote   The right of an individual to cast a vote in an election.

right to work laws   State statutes that provide a person cannot be required to join a union in order to obtain or hold a job.

rights of prisoners   Rights to adequate food, clothing, shelter, medical care, and sanitation as well as access to the courts; limited rights of expression and to exercise religious practices that do not disrupt prison routine.

rights of the accused   All of the rights belonging to persons accused of crimes, such as the right to counsel, the right to a fair trial, and the right to due process.

riot   A public disturbance involving acts of violence, usually by three or more persons.

robbery   The crime of taking money or property from a person against that person's will by means of force.

Roman law   Laws that prevailed among the Romans first codified in the Twelve Tables; basis of the modern civil law in most European countries.

rule of four   U.S. Supreme Court rule whereby the Court grants certiorari only on the agreement of at least four justices.

rule of law   The idea that law, not the discretion of officials, should govern public affairs.

rule making   Formal process by which regulatory agencies make rules that carry the force of law.

rule-making authority   Authority of federal and state regulatory agencies to promulgate rules of general applicability over matters within the agency's jurisdiction.

rules of evidence   Rules that govern the introduction of evidence in courts.

rules of practice   Rules regulating the practice of law before courts and administrative agencies.

rules of procedure   Rules promulgated by courts of law under constitutional or statutory authority governing procedures for trials and other judicial proceedings.

same-sex marriages   Marriages between persons of the same sex.

search   Intrusion by law officers of other government officials that affects an individual's legally protected zone of privacy.

search incident to a lawful arrest   Search of a person placed under arrest and the area within the arrestee's grasp and control.

second-degree murder   Typically refers to a killing perpetrated by any act imminently dangerous to another and evincing a depraved mind regardless of human life, although without any premeditated design to effect the death of any particular individual.

Secret Service   A federal law enforcement function located within the Treasury Department that protects the president and the president's family and enforces federal laws against forgery of government checks and bonds, and investigates credit card and computer fraud.

security   An investment in a stock or bond issued by a corporation.

security agreement   A written contract between a debtor and a creditor granting the creditor a security interest in collateral.

security deposit   A sum deposited by a tenant either with a lessor or in escrow to guarantee performance of the tenant's obligations under a lease.

security interest   An interest in collateral that a creditor acquires to assure repayment of a debt.

seizure   Action of police in taking possession or control of property or persons.

selective prosecution   Singling out defendants for prosecution on the basis of race, religion, or other impermissible classifications.

self-defense   The protection of one's person against an attack.

self-representation   *See* pro se defense.

sentencing guidelines   Legislative guidelines mandating that sentencing conform to guidelines absent a compelling reason for departing from them.

sentencing hearing   A hearing held by a trial court prior to the pronouncement of sentence.

separate maintenance   An allowance that a court orders paid to a wife who is living apart from her husband in order to provide for the wife and the parties' children.

separation of church and state   First Amendment doctrine that holds that there must be a "wall of separation" between religion and government.

separation of powers   Constitutional assignment of legislative, executive, and judicial powers to different branches of government.

sequestration   A writ directing the sheriff or other officer to take custody of property belonging to someone who is in contempt of court.

sequestration of the jury   Isolation of jurors (usually in a high-profile criminal case) from contact with the general public until a trial jury has reached a verdict.

session laws   Laws enacted at a given session of a legislature.

sex-neutral basis   Without regard to the sex of a party.

sexual battery   A modern statutory term that embraces the unlawful oral, anal or vaginal penetration by or union with the sexual organs of another person.

sexual harassment   Offensive interaction of a sexual nature in the workplace.

shared custody   The joint responsibility of divorced parents for the supervision and control of their children.

shared parental responsibility   A court-ordered relationship in which both parents retain their parental rights and responsibilities with respect to their child and are to confer with each other on major decisions affecting the child's health, education, and welfare.

sheriff   The chief law enforcement officer of the county.

slander   The tort of defaming someone's character through verbal statements.

sobriety checkpoints   Roadblocks set up for the purpose of administering field sobriety tests to motorists who appear to be intoxicated.

social host   One who furnishes alcoholic beverages to guests.

Social Security   A federal government program instituted by Congress in 1935 where employers withhold a portion of their employees' wages, match these amounts, and transfer these sums to the government. Self-employed individuals also pay into the system. From these funds the government pays benefits to disabled persons, retirees, surviving spouses, and dependents.

social welfare legislation   Laws enacted by federal and state governments to assist socially and economically disadvantaged people.

sodomy   Oral or anal sex between persons, or sex between a person and an animal, the latter commonly referred to as bestiality.

sole proprietorship   A business owned and operated by one individual.

solicitation   The crime of offering someone money or other thing of value in order to persuade that person to commit a crime; an active effort on the part of an attorney or other professional to obtain business.

sovereign immunity   A common-law doctrine under which the sovereign may be sued only with its consent.

sovereignty   The authority of an independent nation or state to govern within its territorial limits.

special damages   Compensation awarded by a court to reimburse a plaintiff for out-of-pocket losses sustained as a result of a defendant's actions. In a typical tort action, special damages include compensation for medical expenses and loss of wages.

special equity   Court-ordered interest in an asset awarded to a spouse based on his or her superior contribution to a particular marital asset.

special exceptions   Approvals by zoning boards that permit uses within a particular district conditioned upon compliance with special requirements.

special prosecutor   A prosecutor appointed specifically to investigate a particular episode and, if criminal activity is found, to prosecute those involved.

special verdict   A jury verdict with the jury answering specific questions as to its findings on issues posed by the court.

specific intent   The mental purpose to accomplish a certain prohibited act.

specific objection   Counsel's objection to a question posed to a witness by opposing trial counsel where a specific reason is given for the objection, for example, that the question calls for hearsay evidence.

specific performance   A court-imposed requirement that a party perform obligations incurred under a contract.

spoils system   A political term based on the old adage that "to the victor go the spoils." In practice, the award of contracts and jobs to supporters of a winning candidate.

spontaneous or excited utterances   Exceptions to the hearsay rule of evidence. The former is a spontaneous statement describing or explaining an event made while the declarant is perceiving the event or immediately thereafter. The latter is a statement made relating to a startling event made while the declarant was under stress caused by the event.

stalking   Following or placing a person under surveillance and threatening that person with bodily harm, sexual assault, confinement, or restraint or placing that person in reasonable fear of bodily harm, sexual assault, confinement, or restraint.

standing   The right to initiate a legal action or challenge based on the fact that one has suffered or is likely to suffer a real and substantial injury.

stare decisis   "To stand by decided matters." The principle that past decisions should stand as precedents for future decisions. This principle, which stands for the proposition that precedents are binding on later decisions, is said to be followed less rigorously in constitutional law than in other branches of the law.

state supreme court   The highest state court; however, in New York the supreme court refers to a court with trial and appellate divisions and the highest state court is the Court of Appeals.

state's attorney   A state prosecutor.

state-sponsored discrimination   Discrimination that is endorsed or permitted backed by government.

statute   A generally applicable law enacted by a legislature.

statute of frauds   A statutory law patterned after an English statute that requires certain contracts to be in writing.

statute of limitations   A law proscribing prosecutions for specific crimes after specified periods of time.

statutory construction   The official interpretation of a statute rendered by a court of law.

statutory preclusion of judicial review   Because the jurisdiction of the lower federal courts is dependent on federal legislation, Congress can enact a legislative act to preclude judicial review altogether or under certain circumstances.

stepparent adoption   Adoption of a child by the spouse of the child's natural parent, usually with consent of the child's natural parents.

stop-and-frisk   An encounter between a police officer and a suspect during which the latter is temporarily detained and subjected to a pat-down search for weapons.

strict judicial scrutiny   Judicial review of government action or policy in which the ordinary presumption of constitutionality is reversed.

strict liability   Doctrine of law whereby liability is imposed upon a party irrespective of that party's fault.

strict-liability offenses   Offenses that do not require proof of the defendant's intent.

strict necessity, doctrine of   The doctrine that a court should consider a constitutional question only when strictly necessary to resolve the case at bar.

strict neutrality   Refers to the doctrine that government must be strictly neutral on matters of religion.

strict scrutiny   The most demanding level of judicial review in cases involving alleged infringements of civil rights or liberties.

strip search   A search of a suspect's or prisoner's private parts.

structuring   Engaging in multiple smaller transactions to avoid currency reporting requirements.

subornation of perjury   The crime of procuring someone to lie under oath.

subpoena   "Under penalty." A judicial order requiring a person to appear in court in connection with a designated proceeding.

substantial capacity test   The doctrine that a person is not responsible for criminal conduct if at the time of such conduct, as a result of mental disease or defect, the person lacks substantial capacity either to appreciate the wrongfulness of his or her conduct or to conform his or her conduct to the requirements of the law.

substantial evidence   Evidence that reasonable minds accept as sufficient to support a rational conclusion.

substantial federal question A significant legal question pertaining to the U.S. Constitution, a federal statute, treaty, regulation, or judicial interpretation of any of the foregoing.

substantive criminal law That branch of the criminal law that defines criminal offenses, defenses, and specifies criminal punishments.

substantive due process Doctrine that due process clauses of the Fifth and Fourteenth Amendments to the U.S. Constitution require legislation to be fair and reasonable in content as well as application.

substantive legitimacy The belief that the government or legal system is enacting rules and policies that are fair, reasonable, and just.

substituted judgment Decisions by a relative or surrogate in respect to health care matters for an incapacitated individual. Judgment presumably is exercised on the basis of the decision maker's view as to the decision the incapacitated individual would ordinarily make.

substituted service Any form of service of process other than by personal service, such as service by mail or by publication in a newspaper.

summary judgment A decision rendered without extended argument where no material legal question is presented in a case and the moving party is entitled to a judgment as a matter of law.

summary justice Trial held by court of limited jurisdiction without benefit of a jury.

summons A court order requiring a person to appear in court to answer a criminal charge.

sunshine laws Federal and state laws requiring certain government meetings to be conducted in public.

suretyship A written contract whereby one party agrees to become liable for the debt or default of another party.

surrogate One who acts in the place of another.

surrogate motherhood A woman who relinquishes her parental rights as the biological mother of a child she has delivered as a result of having been artificially inseminated.

survival statutes Statutes that provide that tort actions survive the plaintiff and defendant.

suspect classification doctrine The doctrine that laws classifying people according to race, ethnicity, and religion are inherently suspect and subjected to strict judicial scrutiny.

suspended sentence Trial court's decision to place a defendant on probation or under community control instead of imposing an announced sentence on the condition that the original sentence may be imposed if the defendant violates the conditions of the suspended sentence.

tangible personal property Property that has physical form and substance and value in itself.

target crime A crime that is the object of a conspiracy. For example, in conspiracy to traffic in illegal drugs, the offense of trafficking in illegal drugs is the target crime.

Tax Court A federal court established by Congress in 1924 to resolve disputes between taxpayers and the Internal Revenue Service.

tax fraud False or deceptive conduct performed with the intent of violating revenue laws, especially the Internal Revenue Code.

tenancy by the entirety A form of ownership in property by a husband and wife. Upon decease of either party the survivor becomes the owner.

tenants in common A form of ownership of property with each tenant in common owning an undivided interest in property.

termination of parental rights A court judgment declaring an end of a natural parent's rights over his or her child.

testamentary capacity The legal capability to execute a last will and testament.

testamentary trust A trust created under a last will and testament.

testator A person who executes a last will and testament (male).

testatrix A person who executes a last will and testament (female).

testimonial evidence Evidence received by a court from witnesses who have testified under oath.

testimony Evidence given by a witness who has sworn to tell the truth.

third-party practice Where a defendant in a civil suit makes a third party an additional defendant in the litigation. The basis to join a third party is the defendant's allegation that such party is or may be liable to the defendant for all or part of the plaintiff's claim against the defendant.

third-party creditor beneficiary   A person designated to receive payment of an obligation as a result of a contract between other persons. Example: A party to whom money is owed who is named as a beneficiary of a life insurance policy.

third-party donee beneficiary   A person designated to receive something of value as a result of a contract between other persons. Example: A person gratuitously named as a beneficiary under a life insurance policy is a typical donee beneficiary.

three strikes and you're out   Popular term for a statute that provides for mandatory life imprisonment for a convicted felon who has been previously convicted of two or more serious felonies.

time, place, and manner regulations   Government limitations on the time, place, and manner of expressive activities.

tort   A wrong or injury other than a breach of contract for which the remedy is a civil suit for damages.

tort claims   Claims asserted for alleged torts.

tortfeasor   One who commits a tort.

totality of circumstances   The entire collection of relevant facts in a particular case.

toxic torts   Acts involving human or property exposure through absorption, contact, ingestion, inhalation, implantation, or injection of toxins.

traditional surrogacy   Impregnation of a woman with the sperm of a married man with an understanding that the child to be born is to be legally the child of the married man and his wife.

transactional immunity   A grant of immunity applying to offenses to which a witness's testimony relates.

transcript   A written record of a trial or hearing.

transferability of ownership   Ability to readily transfer ownership interests in a corporation by simply endorsing stock certificates.

treason   The crime of attempting by overt acts to overthrow the government, or of betraying the government to a foreign power.

treaty   A legally binding agreement between one or more countries. In the United States, treaties are negotiated by the president but must be ratified by the Senate.

trespass to land   An unlawful entry to another person's real property.

trespasser   One who unlawfully interferes with another person's property.

trial   A judicial proceeding held for the purpose of making factual and legal determinations.

trial by jury   A trial in which the verdict is determined not by the court but by a jury of the defendant's peers.

trial courts   Courts whose primary function is the conduct of civil and/or criminal trials.

trial *de novo*   "A new trial." Refers to trial court review of convictions for minor offenses by courts of limited jurisdiction by conducting a new trial instead of merely reviewing the record of the initial trial.

trust   A legal relationship created when a party known as the grantor or settlor transfers legal title to assets to a second party known as the trustee for the benefit of a third party known as a beneficiary.

trustee   One who holds legal title to assets transferred by a grantor or settlor to be held and administered for benefit of a third-party beneficiary.

U.S. Code   Official code of the laws of the United States.

Ultra Vines Act   Refers to acts committed by a corporation beyond the scope of its legal authority.

unconscionability   Conduct that is unfair and oppressive but not necessarily fraudulent.

unconscionable consumer contracts   Contracts that result in oppression against consumers who have no real choice as to the terms imposed.

unemployment compensation   A federal program administered by state agencies and funded through taxes on employers that provides temporary payments to unemployed workers.

unified bar   A statewide bar association that regulates the legal profession, usually under the oversight of the state's highest court, and requires lawyers to be dues-paying members of the association.

unified credit   A credit against federal estate taxes; in effect an exemption from the tax. In 2001, the credit is

$675,000 in 2002 and is $1 million. It rises in steps to $3.5 million by 2009.

Uniform Code of Military Justice (UCMJ)   A federal statute enacted by Congress in 1950. Consolidated and modified prior laws regulating the conduct of military personnel; established a revised code of military justice to apply uniformly in all the military services; and established a civilian court of appeals. The act authorizes the president to promulgate a manual for courts-martial, binding on all persons subject to the UCMJ.

uniform codes   A collection of laws designed to be uniformly adopted by the various states. The Uniform Commercial Code (UCC) is a classic example of a uniform code of laws.

unilateral contract   A contract formed by a promise being made in exchange for performance of an act.

unilateral mistake   Where one party to a contract is mistaken concerning a material aspect of the contract.

unitary system   A political system in which all power is vested in one central government.

U.S. attorneys   Attorneys appointed by the president with consent of the U.S. Senate to prosecute federal crimes in a specific geographical area of the United States.

U.S. Court of Appeals for the Armed Forces   A civilian court established by Congress consisting of five civilian judges appointed by the president for 15-year terms. Serves as a court of review for specified cases and may grant petitions for review beyond the normal channels of military review in courts-martial cases.

U.S. Courts of Appeals   The intermediate appellate courts of appeals in the federal system that sit in geographical areas of the United States and in which panels of appellate judges hear appeals in civil and criminal cases primarily from the U.S. district courts.

U.S. District Court   The principal trial courts in the federal system that sit in 94 districts where usually one judge hears proceedings and trials in civil and criminal cases.

U.S. Sentencing Commission   A federal body that proposes guideline sentences for defendants convicted of federal crimes.

U.S. Supreme Court   The highest court in the United States consisting of nine justices that has jurisdiction to review, by appeal or writ of certiorari, the decisions of lower federal courts and many decisions of the highest courts of each state.

unity concept of marriage   Common-law doctrine whereby courts treated a husband and wife as one person for legal purposes. Courts have now generally discarded the unity concept.

unlawful assembly   A group of individuals, usually five or more, assembled to commit an unlawful act or to commit a lawful act in an unlawful manner.

unreasonable searches and seizures   Searches that violate the Fourth Amendment to the Constitution.

use immunity   A grant of immunity that forbids prosecutors from using immunized testimony as evidence in criminal prosecutions.

usurious rate of interest   A rate of interest charged to a borrower that exceeds the maximum rate allowed by law.

uttering a forged instrument   The crime of passing a false or worthless instrument, such as a check, with the intent to defraud or injure the recipient.

vagrancy   Under English common law, the crime of going about without visible means of support.

vagueness doctrine   A constitutional law doctrine that holds that a statute or ordinance must be clear and understandable as to what is required or prohibited, otherwise the law is considered a violation of due process of law.

vandalism   The willful destruction of the property of another person.

variances   Deviations granted by a board of adjustment where enforcement of zoning regulations would impose an undue hardship on the property owner.

vehicular homicide   Homicide resulting from the unlawful and negligent operation of a motor vehicle.

venire   The group of citizens from whom a jury is chosen in a given case.

venue   The location of a trial or hearing.

veto   The power of a chief executive to block adoption of a law by refusing to sign the legislation.

vicarious liability	Liability of one party in place of another.

vice of vagueness	See vagueness doctrine.

victim	A person who is the object of a crime or tort.

victim impact evidence	Evidence relating to the physical, economic, and psychological impact that a crime has on the victim or victim's family.

violations of civil rights	Violations of federal and state statutes, local ordinances, and regulations designed to ensure that society treats everyone equally.

void contract	An agreement that cannot be enforced by law.

voidable contract	An agreement that a party can set aside. Example: A minor can usually set aside (avoid) a contract.

void-for-vagueness doctrine	*See* vagueness doctrine.

voir dire	"To speak the truth." The process by which prospective jurors are questioned by counsel and/or the court before being selected to serve on a jury.

ward	A minor or incapacitated individual placed under guardianship by a court.

warrant	A judicial writ or order directed to a law enforcement officer authorizing the doing of a specified act, such as arrest or search.

warrant requirement	The Fourth Amendment's "preference" that searches be based on warrants issued by judges or magistrates.

warrantless administrative searches	Reasonable searches of premises by government officials to determine compliance with health and safety regulations.

warrantless arrest	An arrest made by police who do not possess an arrest warrant.

warrantless inspection	*See* warrantless administrative searches.

warrantless searches	Searches conducted by police or other officials acting without search warrants.

warranty deed	A deed from a grantor conveying an interest in real property to the grantee with various covenants including the grantor's warranty to defend the title to the property conveyed.

welfare programs	Government-sponsored programs such as those that furnish financial assistance for dependent children, medical assistance for the poor, and unemployment compensation for persons out of work.

welfare reform	Congressional action revising the criteria for entitlements in welfare programs.

white-collar crimes	Various criminal offenses committed by persons in the upper socioeconomic strata of society, often in the course of the occupation or profession of such persons.

will	An expression (in most instances written) that expresses the intent of the signer (testator or testatrix) as to disposition of property. Also referred to as a last will and testament.

wiretapping	The use of highly sensitive electronic devices designed to intercept electronic communications.

workers' compensation acts	Statutes that require payments of monetary benefits to workers injured within the scope of their employment and to dependents of workers killed within the scope of their employment.

writ	An order issued by a court of law requiring the performance of some specific act.

writ of certiorari	*See* certiorari.

writ of habeas corpus	*See* habeas corpus.

writ of mandamus	*See* mandamus.

writ of prohibition	*See* prohibition, writ of.

wrongful act or omission	An act or omission that infringes on the rights of another person.

wrongful birth	A tort action by parents for birth of an impaired or deformed child because a physician's negligent treatment or advice deprived them of the opportunity to avoid or terminate the wife's pregnancy.

wrongful death acts	Statutory laws that allow a tort action against a person responsible for the wrongful death of an individual. The class of persons eligible to bring suit and the elements of damage recoverable vary among the states.

wrongful life	A tort action brought on behalf of a child born with birth defects whose birth would not have occurred but for negligent medical advice or treatment.

zoning	The legislative classification of lands within a county or city that specifies premitted and prohibited land uses and building regulations within each district.

INDEX

D